D1238687

Social Justice

Critical Issues in Crime and Society

RAYMOND J. MICHALOWSKI AND LUIS A. FERNANDEZ, SERIES EDITORS

Critical Issues in Crime and Society is oriented toward critical analysis of contemporary problems in crime and justice. The series is open to a broad range of topics including specific types of crime, wrongful behavior by economically or politically powerful actors, controversies over justice system practices, and issues related to the intersection of identity, crime, and justice. It is committed to offering thoughtful works that will be accessible to scholars and professional criminologists, general readers, and students.

For a list of titles in the series, see the last page of the book.

Social Justice

THEORIES, ISSUES, AND MOVEMENTS

Revised and Expanded Edition

LORETTA CAPEHEART AND
DRAGAN MILOVANOVIC

RUTGERS UNIVERSITY PRESS
New Brunswick, Camden, and Newark, New Jersey, and London

Library of Congress Cataloging-in-Publication Data

Names: Capeheart, Loretta, 1963– author. | Milovanovic, Dragan, 1948– author.
Title: Social justice: theories, issues, and movements / by Loretta Capeheart and
    Dragan Milovanovic.
Description: Revised and expanded edition. | New Brunswick: Rutgers University
    Press, 2020. | Series: Critical issues in crime and society | Includes bibliographi-
    cal references and index.
Identifiers: LCCN 2019033151 (print) | LCCN 2019033150 (ebook) |
    ISBN 9781978806863 (cloth) | 9781978806856 (paperback) |
    ISBN 9781978806870 (epub)
Subjects: LCSH: Social justice.
Classification: LCC HM671 .C384 2020 (ebook) | LCC HM671 (print) |
    DDC 303.3/72—dc23
LC record available at https://lccn.loc.gov/2019033151

A British Cataloging-in-Publication record for this book is available
from the British Library.

www.rutgersuniversitypress.org

Manufactured in the United States of America

We dedicate this work to the reader, the student, the present and past activists, and all of those seeking to know justice.

We acknowledge the many having written and acted in the interest of justice before us. Those who have had the greatest impact upon us are referenced in this text and are too many to list here. Their ideas inform our examination of justice. Their actions give us hope for the future of justice.

Knowledge must come through action; you can have no test which is not fanciful, save by trial.

—Sophocles (496 B.C.–406 B.C.)

Contents

PREFACE

CRIMINAL JUSTICE programs in the United States emerged mainly from sociology departments in the early 1960s. At that time in the United States the three major higher degree granting programs were: John Jay College of Criminal Justice in New York City, where faculty were predominantly more conservative and past or current practitioners in criminal justice; the School of Criminal Justice at the State University of New York at Albany, which established the Albany Model based on vigorous empirical and administrative analysis of criminal justice; and the criminology department at the University of California at Berkeley, which included a core group of Marxist-oriented faculty, Tony Platt, Paul Takagi, and Herman and Julia Schwendinger. The Berkeley School, as it has been referenced, had an activist, political economic focus that challenged dominant powers and advocated social change at all levels. It sponsored the critical·journal, initially entitled *Issues in Criminology* and later *Crime and Social Justice*, edited by Tony Platt and Paul Takagi. The latter PhD program was closed under Governor Reagan in the early 1970s with many faculty, students, and scholars around the world arguing that it was a case of repression directed toward the activism and leftist politics of a number of members in the department (Schwendinger and Schwendinger, 2014). In the late 1980s we began to see the establishment of more masters and doctorate granting programs as a response to the tremendous interest for more advanced education. The Albany Model continued to be adapted at larger universities. In the early 1990s students had a number of MA and PhD granting programs in criminal justice from which to choose.

Across the ocean, the critical "Brits," as they were called, remained theoretical and social justice focused from the early developments of the 1960s to present. In 1968 the National Deviancy Conference was the lightning rod for critical analysis in criminology and justice issues. Australian developments, particularly in the 1970s, were influenced by the work in Britain, Europe, and the United States. However, these developments were centered on Australia's own experience with colonialism, the plight of the indigenous and youth, environmental damage, and struggles in the development of feminism and other issues. The Department of Criminology at Melbourne University and the Department of Legal Studies at La Trobe University, Melbourne, Australia, provided critical analysis (see Carrington and Hogg, 2012). The Australian Institute of Criminology was formed in 1973. The U.S. scene remained mostly incongruous: on the one hand, more administrative forms of criminal justice emerged in the late 1960s that were not concerned with causes of crime but administration of "problem populations"; while social activism abounded, including anti-Vietnam War demonstrations, uprisings in the ghettos of large cities, the call for civil rights, feminist struggles, and peace movements amongst others.

Other influences in the development of social justice can be traced to offerings in philosophy departments in colleges and universities, more abstract in analysis, and focused on ethics, morals, rights, and justice. Notables in other fields, such as the highly cited work of John Rawls, and that of Ronald Dworkins and Friedrich Hayek were influential. And historical analysis was to impact the growing field of social justice, particularly the study of ancient philosophers Plato and Socrates; post-Renaissance writers Baruch Spinoza, St. Thomas Aquinas, John Stuart Mills, and Emmanuel Kant; and religions (Hinduism, Islam, Judaism, Christianity, and Chinese Buddhism, Taoism, Confucianism), including liberation theology developed in struggles in Central America that incorporated Marxist analysis with Christian theology. The classic sociologists Karl Marx, Emile Durkheim and Max Weber were to suggest the connection between ideologies such as conceptions of justice and political economies. And most importantly, struggles against injustices in all form from the ground up provided the very engine for the call for social change. All these influences provided scholarly contexts for taking the study of justice from abstract planes of philosophy to action—to resisting injustices, to challenging institutional inequalities, and to social change. Theory *and* action was and is central to a social justice perspective. We shall return to these in the course of the book.

To return to the evolution of social justice studies, in the mid-1990s, much unrest developed in U.S. scholarly circles interested in crime, causation, response, and prevention. Many faculty grumbled that "criminal justice" is not what they did in their colleges and universities, even as their departments were called "criminal justice departments." It was too narrow. It focused on the individual outside of context. It did not situate the field in a broader political economic field and in historical contexts. There were few texts to capture this sentiment. The notion of a new emphasis on social justice programs was often discussed in hallway meetings, at annual conferences, and in private conversations. A few universities did respond. Such was the case with the School of Justice and Social Inquiry Department at Arizona State University and the Justice Studies Program at Northeastern Illinois University. Police departments, too, were becoming more interested in police officers with broader backgrounds in their higher education.

In the Canadian context we witnessed developments culminating in the early 2000s in such programs as the Centre for Studies in Social Justice at the University of Windsor and the Justice Studies Program and Human Justice Program at the University of Regina. These programs are interdisciplinary and assume a broad view of justice. Included courses cover criminal justice as well as restorative, social, and international justice. Notions of human rights, both national and international, are addressed as well as issues concerning environmental and indigenous justice. At the University of Windsor a new, freely available, online journal was established in the fall of 2006, *Studies in Social Justice*. Consider its mission statement: [Studies in Social Justice] "will be an interdisciplinary, peer-reviewed journal that will serve as a forum to share knowledge on a wide range of social justice issues, including racism, poverty, sexuality, gender, health and class inequalities. It will also explore the legal, environmental and cultural challenges of restructuring the global economy. This electronic journal will publish high quality scholarly research that addresses ways to promote social justice and offer recommendations on policies or strategies to diminish existing injustices" (www.uwindsor.ca/socialjustice; see the *Centre for Studies in Social Justice Newsletter* 2, no. 1 [2006]).

At Northeastern Illinois University, where our department was formally called Criminal Justice, we were successful in convincing other faculty and administration that "criminal justice" was too narrowly conceived. We changed our name after many frustrating battles to the Justice Studies Program (now Department). We revised requirements for the major to better fit this orientation. Not that traditional criminal justice courses were eliminated; rather, new courses were introduced with an emphasis on social justice. The traditional criminal justice courses were now situated in a broader framework. Police officers and those aspiring to law enforcement now studied criminal justice in wider settings.

This movement coincided, in many ways, with the development of a more critical orientation toward the study of crime. The various critical perspectives aspired to expand the domain of inquiry. In the 1960s, the study of crime was situated primarily in sociology departments and the emphasis had a more sociological framework and hence contextually understood. In the early splitting of criminal justice away from sociology that occurred in the late 1960s, we witnessed a more conservative orientation, the consensus paradigm. At best, the Albany Model offered a focus on empirical and administrative analysis (statistical studies and fine-tuning the criminal justice apparatus), but little in the way of broader contextual analysis. John Jay College of Criminal Justice, in its early days, was referred to as a "cop shop" providing little beyond tweaking the criminal justice system. It was taught by former or active members of the system, infused with "war stories" of the streets—all with little attention to theory. Much of the concern was with order maintenance. John Jay has however, in the last twenty years, risen beyond to now incorporate theory and activism.

On a personal note, I (DM) recall doing my first MA degree at John Jay College, quickly finding their program at the time shallow, system maintaining, and devoid of theory. Only by taking a summer class in criminology at my former college, Queens College, discovering the work of Richard Quinney, Herman and Julia Schwendinger, and Taylor, Walton, and Young, and after doing volunteer work including teaching classes at the Queens House of Detention for Men, did the light bulb turn on. At the School of Criminal Justice, SUNY at Albany, doing my second MA and then working on my PhD, I came to realize that this was the top school (the Berkeley program had been closed down), and that it indeed offered a highly vigorous program in understanding statistical analysis, methodology, and refinement of the criminal justice system—the very best offered in the United States. But I and other more left-leaning students read considerably outside of the field, developed our own study groups, and on one occasion organized a clandestine basement visit of radical scholars (Herman and Julia Schwendinger, Paul Takagi) to see an alternative way.

Led by a key group of Marxist scholars at the School of Criminology at Berkeley as well as key ground-breaking figures such as Herman Schwendinger, Julia Schwendinger, Richard Quinney, Tony Platt, and William Chambliss, and drawing initial inspiration from Willem Bonger, a new more oppositional framework was to emerge. Initially, this movement had close ties to the works of Karl Marx, and was often referred to as Marxist criminology, or radical criminology, or even conflict criminology (see Henry and Lanier, 2014; Lanier and Henry, 2006). Feminist criminology was also developing and having a major impact on the field, including the groundbreaking work by Freda Adler, Rita Simon, Carol Smart, Jane Chapman, and Susan Brownmiller brought into more critical scope by Pat Carlen, Meda Chesney-Lind, Ngaire Naffine, Drew Humphries, Dore Klein, Nancy Wonders, Kathleen Daly, and Marjori Zatz, among others (with apologies for not including all the many in struggle). In the British scene, the National Deviance Conference established in 1968 was to become highly influential (influential figures include Paul Rock, Stan Cohen, Ian Taylor, Jock Young). Another wing, not necessarily accepting any "ruling class" model, was more concerned with "conflict criminology," following the work of Lewis Coser, Thorsten Sellin, Ralph Dahrendorf, George Vold, and Austin Turk.

A change appeared in the academy in the mid-1980s to encompass more diverse critical views. We witnessed feminist, anarchist, peacemaking, left realist, and postmodern perspectives within "critical criminology." Yet other critical perspectives began to develop: integrative criminology, gender theories, critical race theories, news-making criminology, cultural criminology, integrative criminology, constitutive criminology, postmodern/poststructuralist criminology, edgework, green criminology, etc. By the early 1990s the early form of Marxist analysis, primarily of the instrumental variety, gave way to more structuralist Marxist informed views and to a plethora of emerging perspectives. Fewer adherents now self-identified as Marxists, although they drew considerably from this body of work. Many drew inspiration from the classic critical texts by Ian Taylor, Paul Walton, and Jock Young, entitled the *New Criminology* (1973) and Richard Quinney's *The Social Reality of Crime* (1970).

Advocates of these emerging perspectives were outspoken, highly research oriented, vocal at conferences, and popular with students. Conservative fellow professors began to accept the new perspectives more openly within higher education. Students had already been receptive to their ideas, sometime irrespective of their professor's personal and often passionate ideological positions. By the middle 1990s, critical criminology did not have the same stigma it did in the late 1960s, 1970s, and mid-1980s (see the concise summary by Raymond Michalowski, 2012). In 1988, the main think tank in criminology, the American Society of Criminology, witnessed its membership elect Marxist William Chambliss as president of the organization. Susan Caringella-MacDonald and Bob Bohm were to spearhead an open panel at the 1988 Annual Meeting in Chicago at which time we established the Division on Critical Criminology of the American Society of Criminology. We also established a critical newsletter that became a key medium for discussion, the *Critical Criminologist* cofounded by Dragan Milovanovic and Bernard Headley. Brian MacLean and Walter DeKeseredy subsequently became the coeditors. The Canadian critical journal, the *Journal of Human Justice*, was also influential and became (1995) the *Journal of Critical Criminology*. Other divisions within the American Society of Criminology began to emerge such as the Division of People of Color and Crime and the Division of Women and Crime. With all of these developments a new acceptance of critical criminology emerged in the academy. The talk of moving to social justice instead of criminal justice took on greater momentum. In the early 2000s many faculty of criminal justice were considering changing the name of the discipline to one that better reflected what they were doing or wanted to do. The time had arrived for a changed orientation in dealing with crime and justice. This book arrives on the scene with this history.

Consider, for example, the recent developments in Canada at the Centre in Social Justice at the University of Windsor as well as at the Human Justice

Program at the University of Regina. Courses reflect orientations that go beyond merely studying criminal justice. For example, at the Centre in Social Justice, the introductory course reads: "Introduction to Social Justice. The course will explore diverse visions and dimensions of social justice, both past and present. It will examine the role of political economy, culture, and identity in addressing injustice in Canada and globally. It will critically assess different strategies for social change. Students will be introduced to the principles governing the production and distribution of benefits and harms, and to such concepts as distributive justice, politics of difference, civil society, empowerment, citizenship, and human rights."

Consider, too, the preamble to the Human Justice Program at the University of Regina: "Our teaching, research justice-studies and community service in the Department of Justice Studies are interdisciplinary and presume a broad conception of JUSTICE—one that encompasses criminal and legal justice, as well as social, restorative, community, and international aspects of justice. Our programs also promote a strong commitment to human rights, social equality, democratic participation, and community accountability of justice organizations." Here is a typical course description: "HJ 384AC: Restorative Justice: Concepts, Scope, and Services (systems): This course will introduce the student to the Restorative Justice paradigm. The paradigm is multi-dimensional in concepts, assumptions, scope, and services. This range will be explored, discussed, examined, and compared to existing paradigms in justice. International comparisons will be included."

At this time, a social justice focus in graduate programs has found its way to many universities, including in the United States, Australia, Great Britain, and Canada (see, for example, "20 Top Social Justice MA Programs Worldwide," https://www.humanrightscareers.com/magazine/20-great-social-justice-ma -programs/; "7 Fully-Funded PHD's in Social Justice," https://www.freedom-project.com/the-newman-report/244-more-than-100-colleges-now-offer -social-justice-programs; "College Degrees for Social Justice," https://www .affordablecollegesonline.org/college-resource-center/degrees-for-social-justice/; "Social Justice Revival," https://www.insidehighered.com/news/2012/01/31 /colleges-embrace-social-justice-curriculum). This development has not been without a conservative backlash (see for example, https://www.theblaze.com /news/2017/06/18/disturbing-number-of-colleges-offering-social-justice -degrees-crazy-socialist-courses-included; https://www.thecollegefix.com/want -credit-studying-social-justice-100-colleges-academic-programs/; "More than 100 Colleges Now Offer 'Social Justice' Programs," https://www.freedomproject .com/the-newman-report/244-more-than-100-colleges-now-offer-social -justice-programs).

Concerning possible careers—and unlike many "criminal justice departments" with their focus on careers in policing, corrections, and generally law enforcement—the preamble to the Human Justice Program at the University of Regina states: "Graduates in Human Justice are equipped with an interdisciplinary understanding of the problems and processes of justice in a global context. They have an in-depth knowledge of systems involved in the process and pursuit of justice including criminal justice, human rights, and relevant human services such as, child protection, advocacy, conflict resolution, mediation, and settlement services." (See www.uregina.ca/arts /human-justice.)

Developments in the areas of justice studies as seen in the programs described here necessitate developments in the literature to support these studies. It is also necessary to support activists in their pursuit of justice on the ground. The authors of this text are, and have long been, seriously engaged in scholarship and activism. It should be clear to the reader that our commitments to both critical scholarship and activism inform our understandings of justice and our writing of this text. This book advocates engagements. The second edition brings our further understanding of the field into focus, much of which has been aided by using the text in our classrooms and the feedback we have received from our students and other faculty.

Social Justice

CHAPTER 1

Introduction

WHEN THINKING OF JUSTICE it is not uncommon that a vision of a blindfolded woman holding a set of scales will come to mind. Or the many popular television shows such as *Law and Order* might inform one's vision of justice. Laws, courts, police, and other social control agents inform many of our conceptions of justice. But do the blindfolded woman, stories of crime and punishment, or social control agents truly represent justice or social justice? Do we need to think beyond these notions? What guidance exists for social justice principles? Does our understanding of justice impact our lives? Would an understanding of justice attained through inclusion and focused on meeting needs, equality, and deserts be more just than one focused on control? Does the accepted notion of justice privilege some and leave others in want? Does our current conception allow for diligence against injustices such as poverty, environmental degradation, or oppression? Can we find better conceptions of justice and move toward them? What would their criteria be? These are some of the questions we will address here as we take on the task of examining what justice is and how it may be attained.

Others might argue that justice is what a governing body, our elected officials, decides that it is, or that justice must be defined by the courts, or by scholars. We will offer a different vision, one that is informed by both activism and scholarship. This vision is necessarily global in scope. Social justice can be understood locally; however, given the current global realities, we have incorporated European, British, Canadian, Australian, indigenous, Middle Eastern, South African, Mexican, Central American, and South American understandings and struggles to advocate a move toward global social justice.

WHAT IS SOCIAL JUSTICE?

Social justice is necessarily broad and inclusive of historical and critical examinations. The study of social justice must attend to what justice may mean and whether this justice is available within a variety of social contexts. As human beings, we necessarily exist in social worlds. Discerning whether these worlds are just is a complex endeavor. At a first approximation, studying social justice must begin with an examination of: how dominant and nondominant conceptions of justice arise; how they are selectively institutionalized; how they are formally and informally applied; what persons and/or groups are being deprived of its formal mandates; and how, finally, to correct deviations so that justice is served.

And necessarily, we must examine the relationship of political economy to institutionalized conceptions of justice and do so within the context of growing disparities between the rich and the poor. For the latter, consider some evidence. Forty-five percent of all wealth in the world is held by only 1 percent of the global population while 84 percent of the world's wealth is held by 10 percent of the population, leaving the remaining 16 percent of global wealth to be shared by 90 percent of the global population. Those living in the United States are overrepresented among the top 1 percent of wealth holders (Inequality.org, 2019a). This is in part due to the low tax rates paid by the wealthy in the United States. In the 1950s and 1960s, the richest Americans paid income tax rates of 91 percent; now the top income tax rate is 37 percent (Inequality.org, 2019b). Furthermore, CEOs at the S&P 500 companies in the United States earn 361 times as much the average U.S. worker (Inequality.org, 2019c).

What is justice? This is our first concern. Once we accept this as an appropriate question, we must consider who provides the definition. As we will show later in this text, definitions of justice have historically been provided by and/or for the few (elites) with little attention to the needs and desires of the majority (the rest of us). There are, however, examples of justice deriving from "below" through inclusive justice traditions and/or justice struggles. These justice developments would be in line with a more genuine form of social justice.

Theorists engaged in the examination and critique of justice have developed a range of understandings that can be applied. Activists have also provided ideas and practices to the development of social justice. No single conception or practice of justice is adequate for all points in history or for all forms of society. Rather as societies develop and change through historical and political economic processes, so too does justice. The study of these developments allows for a more complete understanding of our current notions of justice and the possibilities for a more just future.

Social justice is concerned not in the narrow focus of what is just for the individual alone but what is just for the social whole. Given the current global condition, social justice must include an understanding of the interactions within and between a multitude of peoples. This is indeed a complex and inclusive pursuit. It is also an exciting and worthy pursuit. It requires the consideration of and sensitivity to all voices and all concerns, including nonhuman forms. A challenging task before us is developing a process by which historically emergent principles of justice may find arenas for their recognition, discussion, resolution, and implementation in a changing historical order, especially the new global order, with a simultaneous sensitivity to difference and commonality, and subsequent practices that carry through what has been implemented without disenfranchising persons and/or groups.

As we shall see in the following pages, justice exists both in human thought and in our deeds. If we attend to the ideas available and study the histories of justice struggles, we can advance justice. With continued movement we can achieve justice in ever-evolving society, without, at the same time, becoming committed to a static conception. We will present a broad understanding of our main conceptions of social justice through inclusive democratic discourse, meeting needs, attaining equality, and distribution of desert. Additional conceptions include: recognition, capabilities, participation, and justification. The question of "sustainabilities" is also addressed. Accordingly, at a second approximation, the study of social justice includes developing an understanding of distributive principles (fair allocation of rewards and burdens) and retributive principles (appropriate responses to harm); how they relate to political economy and historical conditions; their local and global manifestations; the struggle for their institutionalization; how human well-being and development at the social and individual levels is enhanced by their institutionalization; and developing evaluative criteria or processes by which we may measure their effects.

We want to be clear about the distinction between "distributive justice" and "retributive justice." Distributive justice concerns the various philosophies concerning the fair allocation of resources as well as of burdens. Retributive justice, drawing from *Webster's New International Dictionary*, is "recompense . . . the dispensing or receiving of reward or punishment according to the deserts of the individual . . . that given or exacted in recompense . . . ." "Recompense," in turn, is defined as: ". . . to give an equivalent for; to make up for as by atoning or requiting . . . an equivalent or return for something done, suffered . . . a repayment as by way of satisfaction, restitution, retribution, etc . . . ." Thus, retributive justice could include retribution ("an eye for an eye, a tooth for a tooth"), but also other forms of responding to harm (i.e., rehabilitation, deterrence, social defense, family model, restorative justice, transformative justice).

Away from "Criminal" Justice, and toward "Social" Justice

There are many introductory criminal justice texts. Lacking has been a textbook focusing on introducing the reader to a critically informed *social* justice. This book responds to the need for a comprehensive introduction to social justice. Criminal justice texts, often, at best, have short discussions of retributive justice (deterrence, retribution, social defense, and rehabilitation). But they seldom if ever provide, additionally, in-depth understandings of distributive justice (fair allocation of rewards and burdens). Nor do they provide how both may inform decision-making at various stages of criminal justice or other forms of justice processing. We are left to read in between the lines as to what "justice" may mean, or simply to draw from preconceived notions of justice to inform our reading and practice. Here we present a variety of understandings of justice informed by theories, histories, struggles, and movements, both local and global. This unique inquiry will expand understandings of justice and further our advances toward it.

Criminal justice, as a discipline, as we saw in the preface of this book, can be traced to developments in the 1960s. In the U.S. experience, previous to the Law Enforcement and Assistant Act (LEAA, 1967) which proclaimed a "war on crime" and provided law enforcement resources (educational and hardware) toward this end, criminal justice was studied in sociology departments in colleges and universities under courses such as criminology, penology, deviance, juvenile delinquency, and social problems. In the late 1960s, criminal justice programs and departments, aided in particular by LEAA resources, began splitting off from sociology departments. Initially, the criminal justice faculty were practitioners in the field. The discipline initially took on more conservative dimensions with a primary focus on the individual offender. In the 1970s and 1980s, this trend continued, initially at community colleges with two-year associate programs, but subsequently at four-year colleges and universities. The 1990s forward, however, has witnessed many program changes away from departments of "criminal justice" toward the initiation of new programs under some variation of "social justice."

Criminal justice has been too narrow a focus and pursuit for serious comprehensive endeavors. As we move toward the study and pursuit of social justice, we must first consider what social justice entails. Criminal justice accepts, for the most part, a politically established definition of crime (law) and focuses on process (courts) and retribution (corrections) as well as fine-tuning the machinery of criminal justice toward efficiency, speed, and finality. It has traditionally focused on these with little attention to history, political economy, culture, critique, or cross-cultural understanding of the purposes of these institutions. Social justice must consider what is just not only in reaction to "crime" but also in relation to evolving (nonstatic) society.

This book also recognizes that the study of "social justice" is intimately connected with the study of causes of harm (including officially defined crime). We recognize, equally, how unjust institutionalized principles of social justice, whether distributive or retributive, institutional arrangements, and the forms of social control that are their expression often provide the very context for harm (including crime). The two therefore must be linked. By maintaining the link between social justice and criminology, we acknowledge the institutional context of harm. Principles of distributive justice, for example, that systematically disenfranchise, discriminate, devalue, and deny self and societal development of the many, are the basis from which the motivation to resist may spring. We include in part III an orientation to students of struggles against forms of inequality and institutionalized disenfranchisement both locally and globally. We also study how dominant groups often translate resistance into legalistic categories. On the other hand, we do also see how people, subject to discriminatory forms of institutionalized conceptions of justice, may go to excesses for survival purposes or may be brutalized to the extent that their behavior will become expressive, as Marx says of the lumpen proletariat forms of crime (Tucker, 1972). This all leads to our conclusion that social justice and the generation of harm (or not) are inextricably connected.

As to retributive justice, we also link how institutionalized forms of responses to harm (including the formal workings of "criminal justice") may discriminate, disenfranchise, and deny voice to segments of the population. This is also harm. And we should study the connective links between discriminatory forms of retributive justice and the consequent harms that it may generate. Due to space limitations this book will focus on social justice, and we do not attempt to engage in all struggles for justice but offer illustrative examples. We understand full well that much more needs to be done in coming days in establishing the connection between social justice and criminology. This book is but a step toward shedding light on more comprehensive practices for human and societal well-being.

Engaging in the Process of Understanding Social Justice

This book provides readers the opportunity to look deeper into the meanings of justice, the forms of justice that have arisen or may arise across time and place, and alternative models of justice. We have organized the text in order to move naturally from the variety of theories of justice, to applying these understandings to issues, to examining attempts to gain justice through social movements. Progressing from ideas, to issues, to movements is, in our view, the appropriate direction. However, as the reader will find throughout the text, each of these areas informs the other. Ideas inform as well as emerge from issues and movements. Movements are informed by and inform ideas and influence both the understanding and progress of social issues. Therefore, each of the areas examined in the text informs social justice and the process of justice rendering.

Chapter 2 includes some classic theorists from antiquity to the present. From the classic period, we include the ideas of Plato, Homer, Socrates, Aristotle, and St. Thomas Aquinas. We include discussion of religion and philosophy of justice. Included are: Christianity, Hinduism, Islam, Judaism, as well are more activist forms, religious socialism and liberation theology. We then move to more modern expressions in social contract theory (Hobbes, Locke, Kant, Rousseau) and social justice (Mill, Rawls, Habermas, Dworkin) including feminists (Gilligan, Clement). We continue with a discussion of theorists who were more concerned with the relation of justice to socioeconomic structure (Spencer, Smith, Kropotkin, Marx, Engels). Peacemaking justice is next developed. We conclude with an introduction to postmodern forms of justice (Nietzsche). This chapter provides a background for appreciating the complexity of meanings of justice and the historical and social conflicts apparent within the varieties of interpretation.

Chapter 3 engages distributive justice, the fair distribution of rewards and burdens. It includes the classic sociologists Durkheim, Weber, and Marx. Here we find that various conceptions of justice are very much connected with evolving societies. We highlight three traditional understandings of distributive justice: equality, merit, needs. We then move to a social justice model articulated by Miller (1999). He conceptualizes three ideal forms of justice found in three types of society. He indicates the interconnection between a form of society and the logical form of justice. Next highlighted is the capabilities approach in distributive justice, which concerns actions that enhance or diminish an agent's status. We conclude this chapter with a summary of the debate between North American theorist Nancy Fraser and European theorist Axel Honneth on whether social justice should be conceptualized more in terms of "recognition" or whether it should be a question of redistribution of resources in a global order marked by increasing inequalities.

Chapter 4 centers on retributive justice (response to harm). A brief discussion of how we define crime introduces the chapter. We then summarize the traditional forms and justifications of punishment—deterrence, rehabilitation, social defense, and retribution. We again (see *Webster's* definition cited above) highlight that when we reference retributive justice, we must distinguish between general responses to harm on the one hand, and to a specific form on the other, entitled retribution theory of punishment ("an eye for an eye, a tooth for a tooth"). We next move to procedural forms of justice: crime control model, due process model (Packer), family model (Griffith), and actuarial justice (Feeley, Simon). The restorative justice model is next discussed (Ness, Strong, Braithwaite). We note its history and various forms. In many of its expressions, it is a needs-based justice.

Chapter 5 concerns the development of transformative justice. It indicates how social transformation could be part of the response to crime/harm and explains the merits of a holistic approach to justice. A brief critique of restorative justice is offered. The chapter reviews a macro/micro sociological response to harm and the social justice principles that informs it. Accordingly, we first look at the conflict transformation model. Then we turn to Black's *Behavior of Law* (1976) and his four models ("styles of social control") for insights into the furtherance of a transformative justice. The four are expanded to six where the additional two encompass micro- and macro-interconnections in the response to crime (see Henry and Milovanovic, 1996). Various other models, including a constitutive approach, are offered, which begin to look more deeply in this direction such as a transformative restorative justice model developed by Andrew Woolford.

Chapter 6 explores the challenges posed by globalism and multiculturalism. It provides various views on the ongoing changes and restructurings of our global economy and the impacts that these have upon societies and justice. Here we find that unilaterally imposed forms of justice are being tested within the economic superpower nations as well as within "postcolonial" societies. We engage Miller's distributive principles of justice for applicability for a global, multicultural social justice. We conclude with possibilities for the development of a transformative global order.

Chapter 7 explores issues in environmental, ecological, and species justice. Various viewpoints are presented, including environmental racism, ecofeminism, disparate impact, and just sustainabilities. It then applies Miller's three concepts of justice to the environment and examines grassroots struggles in overcoming the situating of toxic dumpsites in poor and disenfranchised communities. In discussion of environmental justice, we review Schlosberg's components of justice that include: distribution, recognition, participation, and capabilities. We engage the eco-justice view on the increasing interest on the rights of nature, including the development of an "Earth Jurisprudence." The chapter also highlights the extent of the problem, nationally and internationally; summarizes various community struggles in restoring justice; and suggests future strategies for distributing potential hazards, when necessary, in a less biased fashion. We conclude with the possibilities for a transformative eco-justice perspective.

Chapter 8 examines justice developed by indigenous groups, nationally and internationally, and reveals how the United Nations is dealing with the issue of safeguarding indigenous intellectual property rights. Issues of "native title" and colonial policy of "terra nullius" are reviewed. Exemplary legal cases are included from Australia, Canada, and the United States.

We also review post- and counter-colonial theory (Fanon, Spivak, Said, Bhabha).

Chapter 9 concerns postmodernist, post-postmodernist, and posthumanist perspectives in justice. It first reviews postmodern development of justice: foundations, internal versus external critique, possibilities for a positive jurisprudence, and possible developments of alternative conceptions of justice. We selectively cover Lyotard, Derrida, Rorty, and Deleuze. Each questions contemporary forms of justice that are rooted in modernist assumptions incorporated from the Enlightenment era. We summarize two key postmodern feminist writings on justice (Cornell, Butler) who build on groundbreaking treatises by Lacan and his interlocutors, Irigaray, Cixous, Moi, and Kristeva. We provide a postmodern Marxism including the influential work of Hardt and Negri, as well as dynamic systems theory ("nomadology"). We then move to post-postmodernism, which includes digi-modernism, new materialism, posthumanism, noting particularly a paradigm shift away from Newtonian ontology to a quantum ontology, and, more recently, to a quantum holographic ontology.

Chapter 10 explores legal struggles and social justice. It focuses on the legal context in the development of justice. We first visit the U.S. Supreme Court decision *Plessy v. Fergusson* (1896), which legitimized a racist order by stipulating a "separate but equal" doctrine. *Brown v. Board of Education* (1954), over a half century later, was to finally put this deplorable decision to rest. We review some central issues: essentialism versus anti-essentialism, counter narratives, reversal of hierarchies, standpoint epistemology, contingent universalities, and the multitude. We then review particular critical approaches: critical legal studies, critical feminist studies, critical race theory, critical Latinx studies, Asian American studies, gay/lesbian studies, queer theory. The chapter concludes with discussion of "intersectional" (race, gender, and class) struggles and beyond. Of particular concern throughout is the dialectics of struggle.

Chapter 11 focuses on how grassroots struggles develop alternative visions of justice, and how some were institutionalized. It goes beyond only focusing on legal struggles from chapter 10, to include broader societal struggles for justice. Of particular concern is grassroots struggles, from the bottom up. We first turn to African American struggles for justice examining the influential works, and struggles of W.E.B. Du Bois, Martin Luther King Jr., Malcolm X, and Ella Baker. We then examine Latinx, gender, sexual, LGBTQ+, and class justice. Following this is a discussion of an emerging affirmative nomadology rooted in chaos (complexity) theory, one possible derivative being the "fourth way."

Chapter 12 focuses on the emergence of justice outside of the United States. It examines how oppositional movements were stabilized, co-opted or repressed. Lessons are drawn about how emerging conceptions of more humanistic forms of justice might take on more tangible expression. The question of regime change and the development of an alternative order and justice are examined. Truth and reconciliation are examined. We also cover the notion of "transitional justice" during regime changes and consider several countries around the world as examples. The chapter includes initiatives both quantitative and qualitative in evaluating the success of transitional justice and some critiques.

This book responds to the challenge of raising awareness to emerging and often competing views on what is fair, what is just, both as a response to harm (retributive justice), and how rewards and burdens are distributed (distributive justice.). We shall see that new conceptions of justice often emerge in struggle, often from the ground up. Theory and practice are inherently interwoven. We shall also see that well-intended movements can inadvertently reconstitute forms of domination (dialectics of struggle). This book also asks the practitioner, the reformist, the activist, and the scholar to consider the variety of notions of justice that exist and encourages all to develop a fairer system of justice at the local, national, and global levels.

REVIEW QUESTIONS

Many of your views at this point will change as you read further in our book. Many of your thoughts are preliminary, more working hypotheses, subject to revisions due to engagement with what follows. Our goal is to stimulate you to critically engage with what is conventionally understood and think through possible alternatives.

1. Consider current events. Name two injustices you perceive. In each case, why are they unjust? What is the main group being negatively affected? For each, what corrective policy can you think up?
2. We have briefly identified growing income disparities between rich and poor. Can justice exist with these growing disparities? Should we leave it up to the "invisible hand" of the logic of competitive capitalism? If no, can you identify a country pursuing less income inequality and does it seem to be developing a more just society? What needs to be changed in our economy that assures less injustice?
3. Some have argued that justice can be attained by legal change (the courts), others say by activism, from the ground up. Can you formulate your preliminary thoughts on which direction may be better?
4. Ask five people (outside of the campus) the question "what is justice?" or "what does justice mean to you?" Bring back your answers for a class discussion.

5. The media provides a variety of virtual reality programing with themes ranging from police, lawyering, and judges' practices, to the functioning of the courts. Do you suppose these are accurately depicting injustices? Selectively? Not at all? Entertaining fictions? Or are they offering good guidance on understanding injustices and how to correct them?

PART ONE

Explorations in Social Justice

CHAPTER 2

Conceptions of Justice

PHILOSOPHICAL, SOCIOLOGICAL, AND CRIMINOLOGICAL

JUSTICE IS A COMPLEX notion that has been debated across the centuries and will likely continue as a contested concept beyond our time. While this chapter cannot be an exhaustive look at the infinite philosophies of justice, it does provide an understanding of some of the major theories, as well as resources for further reading. We begin with a look at the classic Greek philosophies of justice, then briefly to religious conceptions, and continue through time to include modern philosophies, sociological thought, peacemaking perspective, and postmodern ideas.

CLASSIC CONCEPTIONS IN PHILOSOPHY

Western philosophy is often drawn back to the ancient Greeks and their conceptions of justice, equality, and politics. This section of the chapter will deal with some of these ancient understandings and influences.

Plato (427–347 B.C.) and Socrates (469–399 B.C.)

In Pangle's (1980) interpretation of *The Laws of Plato* it is clear that Plato references both religious and mythical ideas of justice. In this work, an Athenian stranger inquired about the origin of laws and was told that the gods, including Zeus and Apollo, were responsible for local laws. The stranger further asked about the influence of Homer (circa 800 B.C.) upon the laws of the cities and was assured that Homer was influential.

While the physical embodiment of Homer is the source of controversy and philosophical debate, the idea of justice as vengeance is clear in the tale of the *Iliad* (Homer, 1961). The philosophical legacy of Homer was not entirely embraced by the Greeks, but was questioned and expanded upon by Plato in his documentation of Socrates' dialogues regarding questions of justice. This style of inquiry implies that ideas should not be merely handed down by gods or legends but should be debated and decided upon by a group of citizens. This exemplifies the Greek political tradition of democracy. There is no direct line from the Greek tradition to our current Western tradition of debate and decision to which we adhere (though in a different fashion) to varying degrees in a variety of circumstances. These traditions were instead appropriated after a hiatus by revolutionaries seeking to disrupt the established order. The impact of replacing the acceptance of definitions offered by gods and others with human dialogue to elucidate justice is the legacy of these philosophers.

Plato's writings illustrate competing ideas and conceptions of justice while privileging the position that justice is within the character of the individual and expressed through just behavior (Lycos, 1987). In the *Republic*, Plato (1951) recorded a dialogue between Socrates and three persons of different backgrounds attempting to answer the question: "What is justice?" An Athenian, Polemarchus, began with the Homerian understanding that it is just to harm one who has harmed you. Socrates countered that if justice is excellence, then the harming of another reduces excellence (in both parties) and cannot be just. It should not be surprising that the merchant among them, Cephalus, contended that justice is the paying of debts and returning what is owed. Again Socrates was not convinced and suggested that returning a weapon to an insane man, though he may own it, cannot be just. Thrasymacus, a teacher of rhetoric, argued that justice is whatever serves the interest of the powerful. Socrates did not appreciate this argument and in fact turned it upside down, suggesting that rulers would not seek their own advantage but seek justice for those whom they rule (Plato, 1951, 24).

Lycos (1987) asserted that Socrates and Plato (through his documentation of Socrates) were interested in placing justice within the individual informed by knowledge and reflection. The soul was described as reflecting justice within the individual through the person's "form of living" (173). It is important to note that seating justice within the soul informed through knowledge would serve the interests of philosophers such as Socrates and Plato. However, placing justice wholly outside the individual, intellect, or soul would serve the interests of others as in the examples offered in the above Socratic dialogue. Lycos (1987) suggested that these ancient ideas of justice can be seen as enabling conditions that in their best form allow individuals and communities to address not merely individual injustices but also the conditions that create injustices. This form of justice allows human beings "the power, not merely the right, to flourish and realize their potential" (174). This noble promise supports the continuing influence of the ancients upon our understandings and studies of justice.

The dialog captured by Plato illustrates a variety of definitions applied to justice. Gaus (2000) noted that the meanings we instill in terms and ideas that are inherently political such as justice are not as simple as defining a term because the conception is dependent upon a political perspective.

"What is at stake is not the meaning of a word, but a view of the world" (262). While the Greeks can be seen as progressing to a more inclusive form of politics thereby allowing a more democratic notion of justice, these writers were not democratic in our current sense of the term. Specifically excluded from citizenship, debate, and the assumption of possessing a mind or soul were women and slaves.

The understanding of justice as an excellence embodied within a just person may seem harmless or even superior to other conceptions. However, this form of justice espoused by Plato and Socrates is rife with the politics and power relations of the time. It is no accident that Plato writes of the just "man," which explicitly excludes both women and slaves. Women and slaves were held in similar states of servitude and considered equal to beasts. A conception of justice such as Plato espoused that holds that justice is embodied in the just man excludes women and slaves from the holding of justice.

Socrates also reasoned that vengeance does not serve justice; payment of debt is not required by justice if such payment may cause harm; and rulers rule for the sake of justice. These understandings of justice preclude the vengeance of the oppressed against their oppressors, slave reparation, and the questioning of authority among other possibilities. One's placement in the power structure would surely inform one's agreement or disagreement with these ideas. It is for this reason that, while we continue to study the ancients, we also continue to build upon their ideas and/or reject their ideas in preference of others.

Aristotle (384–322 B.C.)

Aristotle's ideas were, not surprisingly, similar to those of his professor, Plato. For example, their understandings of justice as a characteristic of individuals expressed through their allegiance to a just government were alike. However, according to Kagan (1965) differences in their backgrounds produced some subtle differences in their thinking. Unlike Plato, Aristotle was not born into the Athenian aristocracy. Aristotle was foreign born, middle class, and had married into the aristocracy. Gaus (2000) noted Aristotle's famous insistence on the importance of equality. While Aristotle gave more attention to the idea of equality than did his predecessors and insisted upon its necessity to justice, he was not arguing for absolute equality. Instead, he qualified equality.

Aristotle (2000) was clear that equals must be treated equally whereas unequals must be treated unequally. This idea of proportionate equality was described as just while counter-proportionate equality was described as unjust. Aristotle went to some lengths to quantify this idea of proportionality explaining that the unequal treatment of equals or the equal treatment of unequals leads to quarrels (Gaus, 2000). While this may sound very convoluted and unfair, this form of in/equality is still with us today. Aristotle (2000) offered the example of money as the measure for exchange, explaining that it would be difficult for a shoemaker and a house builder to exchange their products otherwise. How many shoes would a house be worth? With money as the measure, these two can exchange unequal amounts of money for unequal products of their labor.

Although money was used in his example, Aristotle's (2000) main concern was for political equality (equality before the state and the law) rather than economic equality. Aristotle further divides justice into distributive and rectifying with the former referencing the appropriate distribution of goods within transactions (similar to our civil law) and the latter concerned with the rectification of harms (similar to our criminal law).

There is some irony in the noble goals articulated by Plato, Socrates, and Aristotle on democratic and justice ideals at a time when a large proportion of Ancient Greece and big cities such as Athens had such a high proportion of slaves and exclusionary practices against women.

St. Thomas Aquinas (1225–1274)

Aquinas's influential writing, *Summa Theologica* (2018), included major sections on justice. He, along with St. Augustine (1964), integrated a number of biblical ideas into notions of justice. For Aquinas, the key ideas of justice were to be found in Sections 57–122 of "Secunda Secundae Partis" in the form of answers to objections. Justice was to be seen as grounded in natural law. There were objective principles that existed, naturally, and remain only to be discovered through enlightened reasoning. The source was divine will. Justice existed only where positive law (law created by legislators) was congruent with natural law. Where incongruity existed, natural law allowed disobedience.

Justice is defined as "a habit whereby a man renders to each one his due by a constant and perpetual will" (Aquinas Qu. 58, art. 7). Aquinas defined justice in two forms: "general justice," which is equated with legal justice and is based on the laws of the state, although, when faltering, ultimately it is natural law that is its base; and "particular justice," which is further divided into "commutative" and "distributive" justice (Qu. 61, art 1).

Commutative justice is focused on the relation of one person to another, whereas distributive justice is the relation of the community to the person and the proportional distribution of the common goods. Distributive justice also deals with transgressions, and requires when the law is broken that the offender be punished and that the victim be compensated. In addition, "in distributive justice a person receives all the more of the common goods, according as he holds a more prominent position in the community" (Qu. 61, art. 2). In other words, a person's rank in a community determines their dues (rewards). Unlike inequality that prevails at the distributive level, Aquinas argued that equality prevails at the commutative forms of justice most prominently found in exchange of buyer and seller.

For Aquinas, placing justice in natural law principles was grounds for questioning conceptions that are not in accordance with justice. An unjust law is simply not law. Oppressive law, then, has a basis for opposition. At the same time that it provides grounds for disobedience and struggle, however, it also opens up issues of how various parties can ground their interests in their own conceptions of natural law (Ross, 1974). Current differing views of the natural "right to life" against the death penalty and/or abortion exemplify such conflicts.

RELIGIOUS PHILOSOPHY

Christianity, Hinduism, Islam, and Judaism

We have chosen four major world religions to include alphabetically in our survey of justice ideas, although the exact figure of "major religions" differs (for concise overviews of world religions, see Boyett, 2016; Smith, 2009; for more explicit relation to social justice, see Thakur, 1996; Tillich, 1957 for liberation theology, Guttierez and Muller, 2015; Barger, 2018; for a black liberation theology, Cone, 2010). They have all, along with the gods referenced by the early Greeks, influenced notions of justice. There is no one practice or faith within these traditions. Instead, there are multiple expressions and beliefs within each. Here we attempt to distill major points of agreement within each tradition. We also include a section on religious socialism and liberation theology.

Christianity

Christians rely on the *Bible* as the word of God. It is the New Testament of the *Bible* that brings Christianity into its sharpest separation from Islam and Judaism. The teachings of Jesus Christ, believed to be the son of God, within the New Testament as recorded by various apostles are central to the Christian world view including ideas of justice. *The Religious Literacy Project: Christianity* (2018) describes the story of the Good Samaritan as the great commandment. It is through this story that Jesus commanded that Christians should love their neighbor, including people of different faiths and ethnicities caring for each other and aiding each other in times of need. Jesus continues in this way when cautioning judgement and reminding his followers that all people sin and that judgement should be left to God alone. Jesus was described as offering healing and consolation to a variety of persons, encouraging his followers to be equally open and caring to sinners and people different than themselves.

Hinduism

The Hindu faith is considered the oldest faith and is complex in its traditions and expressions. We will focus only on two major tenets here—Karma: the way of action, and Dharma: dealing with the social order (*Religious Literacy Project: Hinduism*, 2018). These are most related to social justice thought as they guide action and social structure. The notion of Karma encourages adherents to act without expectation or acceptance of any positive outcome for oneself. Virtuous action is to be done for its own good and not for self-enrichment. The Dharma includes duties and ethics as well as rituals that are performed in support of the social order from nature to inner consciousness. Dharma also instructs the duties of each caste and is different for women and men, young and old. One's duties and occupation are set within one's caste of birth. This caste system is hierarchical with the "untouchables" relegated to the bottom and performing menial tasks.

Islam

The *Quran* is the Muslim word of God. It has many similarities to the Old Testament of the Christian Bible that Christians also consider to be the word of God. For Muslims, it is the Prophet Mohammad who brought the word of God and whose teachings are followed. The *Quran* includes a variety of themes including legal matters, God's judgement, as well as instructions to moral behavior. Righteous behaviors include those that seek to assure the comfort and survival of those facing adversity. These behaviors include: looking after the poor, attending to the suffering of others, taking care of persons who are ill or orphaned, and supporting one's parents. (*Religious Literacy Project: Islam*, 2018)

Judaism

Judaism is not only a religion but a way of life of Jewish people, some of whom are not religious. The *Septuagint*, which is very similar to the Old Testament of the Christian *Bible*, is part of the Jewish tradition. The *Torah* is the guide for living for those of Jewish identity. The *Torah* is also described as a history, a constitution, and a legal document. Two major strains of Judaism inform modern expressions of Jewish life. Hasidism stresses storytelling and leadership through the example of moral authority. A more mystical tendency of Kabbalah carries a deep connection to a history of exile and meaningful personhood that offers direction. Repairing the problems found in the world is one such direction that has resulted in Jews committing to social justice movements for political and economic change (*Religious Literacy Project: Judaism*, 2018).

Religion in Justice Struggles

Here we include only Christianity, the dominant religion in the Americas. Christianity has at times been co-opted against social justice in support of white supremacy as expressed in genocide (Dunbar-Ortiz, 2014) and slavery (Kendi, 2016) and rape culture (Blyth et al., 2018). However, Protestant and Catholic traditions have also been utilized in support of social justice.

Religious Socialism (Paul Tillich 1886–1995)

Paul Tillich, particularly in *The Socialist Decision* (1983) brought protestant theology to socialism. He was responding to the question of existential meaning particularly under capitalism. His work has affinities with the Frankfurt School, which seeks to combine Marxism and Freudianism. He argues that bourgeois principles of justice obfuscate the genuine needs of the working classes, the proletariat and that we must return to socialist principles that characterize socialist movements. Christian doctrines (spiritual) as well as material critique of capitalism are necessary for developing a just society. He embraced Marxism but was critical of some of its central principles (Murphy, 1984). With Marx, he argued that human beings are reduced to mere rational calculators, reduced to objects (thingification). For Tillich, the proletariat in struggle must also develop a "prophetic attitude," which paves the way to the possible, to creativity, to going beyond the constraints of capitalism both material and ideological. He further argues that the "young Marx" was more in tune with Christian principles. Rather than principles of bourgeois egalitarian justice, Tillich (1983) argues for Eros, love and the principle of recognition as central to a more humane society (22). Thus, fundamental equality exists recognizing each person with distinct capacities, wants, and desires, but also differential results on how humans creatively deal with their environment. Justice, then, exists only when there is a recognition of an "I-thou" relationship; where the other is seen as thou, unique and offering the opportunity to I for understanding and growth. Thus, the promotion of need, much as in Marx's (2005) ideal, "from each according to his ability, to each according to his need" (180) is a central justice principle in a more liberated society. One of the key promoters in introducing the spiritual dimension particularly of Tillich's work into criminology has been Richard Quinney. In several works he has argued for the necessity of both a materialist critique as well as a spiritual embracing (religious socialism) as the direction toward a more humane society (Quinney, 1980a, 1980b, 1982), but extends this by turning to Buddhism as "a way of awareness."

Liberation Theology (Gustavo Gutierrez, 1928–)

Dominican priest Gustavo Gutierrez was one of the central developers of this area of thought in his influential text *A Theology of Liberation* (1971). These ideas were taken up by a progressive movement within Catholicism in support of a variety of struggles, particularly among colonized populations seeking liberation from colonial powers. Liberation theology (Gutierrez and Muller, 2015; Barger, 2018) received much attention in the struggles of Central America beginning in the 1950s. These ideas continue to be influential to the present though they were much condemned in the early days by the Vatican for embracing Karl Marx. This work argues that both spiritual and material struggles are necessary in progress toward social justice.

Black Liberation Theology (James Cone, 1936–2018)

Black liberation theology, born of African American struggles, has also been developed (Cone, 1969, 2010) as a response to historically based systems of oppression. Liberation theology is about understanding people's struggles in the real world and how biblical teaching can be reinterpreted in arguing for opposition rather than resignation to injustices. The Black Power Movement, Civil Rights Movements, and raising consciousness are equated with this reading. The preference is for working with the poor addressing their needs in more compatible political economic structures and engaging them in changing those structures. Responding to a history of slavery and black genocide, this movement continuously seeks to establish justice while forms of racism remain endemic, ubiquitous, and often subtle. Black liberation theology has also been developed in Africa (see Basil Moore, 1974) and Britain (see Robert Beckford, 2000). There have also been scholarly discussions on the relation of the movements to principles of distributive justice; see, for example, Michael Turner (2010) arguing for a "grace-imbued justice" based on the common good and beneficence and P. J. Naude (N.D.), engaging Rawls and liberation theology, advocates for "partisan/preferential justice" ("preferential option for the poor") and "participative justice"—both perhaps finding support in the "capability equality" principle of distributive justice (discussed in the next chapter).

MODERN INQUIRIES IN PHILOSOPHY

Depending on one's perspective, the modern age indicates different historical points. One might think of the "modern age" as any point after the invention of the wheel or as not occurring until the invention of the cell phone. Sir Francis Bacon (1561–1626) was among the first to utilize what we now think of as the scientific method in his inquiry, thus developing a new way of looking at the world. Because of this important development, it is in the time of Bacon that we place the beginnings of the modern age for our consideration of justice.

Thomas Hobbes (1588–1679)

Hobbes was a contemporary of Bacon and put forward a theory of social contract without any appeal to religious explanations. Hobbes's view of humanity was pessimistic, asserting that unless held in check through a common overseer (the sovereign) men would be in a constant warlike state. In his book, *Leviathan*, he said that "the natural condition of man . . . is war of every one against every one—in which case everyone is governed by his own reason" (Hobbes 1958, 85). Men, in short, in the state of nature were under no obligation to respect anyone. It was through the social contract of agreed upon political authority that Hobbes located justice. According to Hobbes, the sovereign was established by the people with full authority to dictate rights and judge claims to those rights (Gaus, 2000; Hobbes, 1958). Hobbes conceived of individuals as equal and rational in entering into a contract with each other to keep the peace and maintain security. The social contract expressed itself through social control by the sovereign over others. Given that responsibility, the sovereign in Hobbes's view was beyond the reproach of its subjects.

Because of his fatalistic view of humanity as naturally warlike and quarrelsome it follows that an unquestioned authoritarian government would be necessary to keep the peace. Allowing for the critique of the sovereign would allow for the emergence of conflict. Hobbes conceded the right to dissent only in the case that to obey the sovereign would threaten one's life. Hobbes saw the governing authority as protective of justice between its subjects through the resolution of disputes that arise because of the nature of humans to quarrel. Hobbes was less concerned about the potential for violations of justice by that authority (Barry, 1989).

John Locke (1632–1704)

Locke also saw the social contract as central to justice, but was not as pessimistic as was Hobbes when it came to the natural state of man. Locke had a very different understanding of the social contract. He assumed that people were morally obliged because of their belief in God.

Locke perceived the natural state of humanity as one that inherently recognized the rights of others to their lives and liberty (Locke, 1924). He did not see political authority as necessary to ward off war but as necessary to enforce violations of the recognized rights of individuals protecting the life and property of each from the other. For Locke, the war of all against all could still exist *after* the establishment of a state in so much as there still would be power differences and conflict. Locke's social contract then is extended to the political authority for the purpose of mitigating disagreements between persons that arise from the violations of individual rights, not to keep warlike people from conflict. Locke further sees political authority as constrained by the preceding natural rights of individuals. This authority then, unlike Hobbes's sovereign, should not infringe upon life or liberty. Locke's authority is held accountable by the people to respect the rights of individuals. Locke significantly influenced the classical liberal tradition.

Immanuel Kant (1724–1804)

Kant assumed human beings to be rational, having the ability to reason. "Reason proceeds by 'eternal' and 'unalterable' laws" (1965, 9). Each individual, for Kant, was unique and an end in itself, never a means to an end. Accordingly, they must be respected. The rational being was seen separable from the body and its emotionality. This notion was what is referred to as Cartesian dualism—the separation of mind from body.

Kant's classic, *Foundations of the Metaphysics of Morals* (1969), advocated morality as a categorical imperative. The categorical imperative stands for any proposition that calls forth a particular action and is seen as an absolute requirement regardless of a situation (a universal law). For example, "in order not to get wet, I need to take my umbrella," "to be good is to be respectful of others," etc. Conduct should be based on principles reasoned to be universal principles.

Kant's second principle was to "act as though the maxim of your action were by your will to become a universal law of nature" (44–45). The third was the means/ends principle sometimes referred to as the "ends formula." That is, that a human being should be seen as an end in and of itself. The fourth categorical principle was the capacity to act based on autonomy and self-governance. The fifth, which was to also locate him in the social contract tradition, is that we should act according to terms that could universally be derived from rational thought. This principle, called a "kingdom of ends," is explained as "the systematic union of different rational beings through common laws" (58). Each person pursuing their interests acknowledges other rational beings pursuing theirs, all being bound by rationally developed laws. The social contract would be but one example.

For Kant, the just state can only be realized by the collective will of the people. It should be in the form of a republic (1983, 112). The republic is but the call for freedom and reason. For Kant, a hypothetical "original contract," derived from reason, could be examined in terms of the justness of laws passed by the Republic. "[I]t [original contract] obligates every legislator to formulate his laws in such a way that they could have sprung from the unified will of an entire people" (77).

Rousseau (1712–1778)

Rousseau was more similar to Locke than Hobbes in his understanding of the social contract. Like Locke, Rousseau (1973) envisioned a more cooperative than combative human nature and extended this view to an understanding of property as shared. It was not until private property was taken and recognized that the social contract became necessary. He found a certain conflict between civil society and the state of nature of Hobbes. For Rousseau, the state of nature was not one of a war of all against all but rather, by nature, peaceful, and the war of all against all was only to come about with the onset of the development of society. With the desire for self-improvement people entered cooperative relations that, in turn, lead to greater desires for products, possession, and subsequently inequalities. This leads ultimately to conflict, establishment of civil society, and law. It is this point in history that Rousseau finds destructive to the natural state requiring the social contract to deal with the inequalities that arise.

The social contract binds people (whom Rousseau insisted were not merely a collection of individuals but an aggregate) into a common good to which each submits to avoid the dependence on the will of any individual (Gaus, 2000). Whereas in society prior to the contract, people were moral because of compassion, in contractual forms of society, it is reason that determines morality. It is the general will incorporated in the social contract that expresses this consensus, and thus individuals are bound by its terms.

Modernist Sociological Thought

More recent investigations into social justice have developed within the Sociological tradition. These considered the social contract and offered feminist ethics of care. Further development is offered by those who focused on social structure and the impact of those structures on justice.

Sociological Developments of the Social Contract

John Stuart Mill (1806–1873)

Mill's approach to justice was inductive. One reasons from facts and observations to arrive at principles. His primary principle of utility (justice) cannot be grounded foundationally, and hence must be developed indirectly and inductively by recourse to our senses and "internal consciousness." In an essay on utilitarianism he states his primary principle of utility as: "Actions are right in proportion as they tend to promote happiness; wrong as they tend to produce the reverse of happiness" (Mill 1961, 198). He also states that "happiness is desirable, and the only thing desirable, as an end; all other things being only desirable a means to that end" (220). All other principles, which are also much more common, are secondary to this prime one. We should, he tells us, be guided by an action's consequences rather than any particular personality traits of the person doing the action. Where secondary principles come into conflict, it is ultimately to the primary principle that we must look for resolution.

Society is supposed to promote social utility. As long as we seek, through our actions, happiness, without cost to anyone else, those actions should be protected by the terms of the social contract. Ultimately, when conflict exists, the resolution should be by an appeal to the utility principle. "Just" means respecting other's actions toward happiness including rights belonging to them by law; thus "unjust" means anything that deprives the other of such things as their personal property or liberty. As he says; "it is just to respect, unjust to violate" (228). His desert-based justice principle proposes that: "it is universally considered just that each person should obtain that . . . which he *deserves*; and unjust that he should obtain a good, or be made to undergo an evil, which he does not deserve" (228).

Mill included within his five aspects of justice the idea of just deserts but did not leave justice in the hands of the free market (228–231). Instead, Mill included other essential elements of justice that indicated the inclusion of social institutions beyond the market. A related aspect of justice according to Mill is the right to liberty, property, and other belongings. This position is tempered with his second notion, which is that if someone is in possession of a thing or right by law that does not serve justice, then no injustice is committed by the taking of that thing or right. An example of the competing positions here might be the legal right to slave ownership, which would not preclude the emancipation of slaves in service to justice. With these seemingly competing ideas, Mill distinguished between legal and moral justice. The remaining aspects of justice addressed the necessity of keeping agreements and impartiality. Mill's concepts require the engagement of civil and criminal legal structures in the keeping of justice.

John Rawls (1921–2002)

Rather than counter-posing the social contract with the demise of the state of nature, Rawls located the entrance into the social contract through a hypothetical "original position" (Rawls, 1971). He approached this position inductively. This original position allows for the just construction of the social contract through the devising of the terms of that contract in ignorance ("veil of ignorance") of one's position within the social structure. This position of being unaware of one's social class, social position, and other characteristics would presumably allow for the construction of a just contract. This contract would neither privilege nor oppress any position because to do so would not be in the interest of the creator of the contract who is unaware of their position within the structure.

In this original position, Rawls (1963) tells us two principles of justice would be agreed upon. His first principle dealt with the right to equality and the second with the conditions for any inequality that might be included within or created by the social structure. His first principle of equality stipulated freedom to speech, assembly, private property, and freedom from arbitrary forms of arrest and seizure. His second principle determined that inequality is just only if it serves the common good. For Rawls, it is the first principle that would have priority over the second. One's liberty, for example, should not be restricted except for the purposes of protecting overall liberty or increasing it, not for increasing economic and social benefits, nor for the increasing benefit of the worst off (see also Reiman, 1990, 261). Further, he asserted that in order to be just, the better positions within an unequal system must be equally accessible to all members of that system. The distribution of wealth in society, for Rawls, must be to all's advantage. He assumed hierarchical organizations, equally open to all, but that the distribution of income, status, and power do not have to be equal ("difference principle").

The "difference principle" states: "social and economic inequalities are to be arranged so that they are . . . to the greatest benefit of the least advantaged . . ." (302). Allowing unequal distributions of wealth and income so long as it maximizes the benefits of the worst off in a society. In other words, whatever distributive scheme a society has in place, particularly where it allows inequalities, it should be such that it should benefit the worst off maximally.

Jurgen Habermas (1929–)

Habermas has some affinities with Rawls. He argued for the possible materialization of an "ideal speech situation" where each party in discussion or conflict may freely dialogue and reach consensus. Supposedly, out of this situation, much like Rawls's original position of a "veil of ignorance," rational people will arrive at just and fair principles and use those when resolving differences. In this view, legitimate authority is rationally justifiable by developments within ideal speech situations.

For Habermas, human beings enter discursive moments with differing truth claims, or what he calls validity claims to truth, correctness, veracity, and comprehensibility (1976, 161). Where background assumptions of each speaker are more in agreement, these are not questioned; in other words, a background consensus exists. Where it dissipates, however, conflict exists and consensus must be re-established. Genuine consensus can only be re-established in the ideal speech situation where each speaker, as a rational speaker, is equally able to contribute to the discussion. Habermas's formulation addresses how a practical consensus can be achieved. He is in apparent agreement with Rawls, "there exists no independent criterion of justice. What is just is defined by the outcome of a consensus under certain specified conditions" (Phillips 1986, 82). A moral or just principle "is valid only to the extent that it would be mutually acknowledged under certain ideal conditions—freedom, rationality, equality, knowledge—by all agents to whom it applies" (83). Habermas acknowledged that this is only an ideal, rarely if ever attainable in practice, but something toward which we should strive. For Habermas, one does not need to incorporate a particular vision of a just society in order to have his consensus theory work, although implications are abundant.

Ronald Dworkin (1931–2013)

Dworkin (1978) developed a "liberal theory" of justice. In his view, justice and law are connected. His justice in action view defers considerably to enlightened judges. He named his ideal judge "Hercules" and referenced this judge in his justice examples.

Dworkin made a distinction between a rule and a principle. A rule is applied in "an all-or-nothing fashion" (24), whereas a principle refers to a criteria that is external to rules (22). A principle is a standard that should be applied because it reflects justice and fairness. Judges, then, in difficult cases (the "hard cases") often refer to principles when no rule seems operative or binding. But principles, too, are embedded in law, be they more general orientations. In these cases, the judge, Hercules, must decide by looking at intentions of a particular law and its embedded principle. This too becomes the basis of future reasoning and decision-making by judges (*stare decisis*). In doing so, the judge is searching for fair and just principles that are assumed embedded in the intentions of legislators or founding fathers. So for Dworkin, the Herculean judge must integrate a particular rule, principles, and notions of justice in decision-making.

He then developed his idea of rights in reference to the United States (U.S.) Constitution stating that "certain moral rights are made into legal right by the Constitution" (190). These rights, therefore, have a moral status that stands outside the law. These rights are further divided in terms of abstract and concrete. Abstract rights, such as freedom of expression and assembly, have "a general political aim the statement of which does not indicate how that general aim is to be weighed or compromised in particular circumstances against other political aims" (93). Concrete rights are those that consider the various conflicts of interests and how to in fact operationalize their meaning in a particular setting. Thus freedom of assembly and expression can be restricted in time, place, and manner. Judges focus ultimately on concrete rights. Justice and fairness are seen in these contexts. And ultimately, the credibility of the theory of which the judge makes use, is based on "the greatest degree of moral acceptability in terms of a broader moral and political theory" (Phillips, 1986, 292). This in turn is based on society's existing "conventional morality" (Dworkin, 1978, 40). The judge must look to their own conception of what this societal wide morality is at a given time in justly deciding the hard cases.

FEMINIST ETHICS OF CARE

Feminist analyses such as those by Carol Gilligan and Grace Clement argue that a distinct difference exists between male and female notions of what constitutes justice. Formal equality before the law overlooks the factor that the male notion' of justice is incorporated in discussions of what is just, and female notions are relegated to subordinate positions or are devalued. Care, however, should be praised as a virtue especially in consideration of differential vulnerabilities in society that often preclude uniform reception of care. Advocated is that a responsibility for care should be nourished by both men and women. They indicate aspects of justice that differ by gender. Tronto (2005) has identified four components of the ethics of care: attentiveness (requiring recognition of the other), responsibility (considers obligation as a component), competence (ability to provide care), and responsiveness (from the care receiver). Butler (2015) problematizes these analyses by problematizing gender. We are witnessing a considerable interest in this area and are witnessing many variations (e.g., liberal, radical, Marxist, socialist, postcolonial, global, ecological, postmodern, psychoanalytic, existential, see Tong and Williams, 2009; see also application to care for animals, Manning, 1996). Early writing on the subject includes the works by Mary Wollstonecraft of the late 1700s (1988) and those by John Stuart Mill of the 1880s (1970). Due to space constraints, we will limit ourselves to the presentation of three key authors: Carol Gilligan, Grace Clement, and Judith Butler. There has also been lively debate and critique of ethics of care (for a brief overview, see Sander-Staudt, 2018).

Carol Gilligan (1936–)

Gilligan (1982) is arguably the most prominent developer of a feminist ethics of care as a response to male forms of justice (see also Nodding, 1984; Held, 1995; Tong, 1993; Ruddick, 1989; Kittay, 1999). Her ethics of care was developed as an alternative to an ethics of responsibility. The ethics of responsibility, most notably constituting contractarian forms of justice and embedded in formal law, focuses on notions of equality; whereas the ethics of justice focus on attachment, need, and care. Thus, two distinct forms of justice exist, with the latter, in contemporary society, being subordinate to the former. Gilligan's position has been identified as "essentialist," in so much as she is arguing the objective nature of the differences between the two. Her work was based on a gender binary. In her book, *In a Different Voice*, Gilligan, criticized Kohlberg's studies on moral development as biased due to his focus only on males' responses to various hypothetical moral situations. Her underlying theoretical framework, however, was derived from Piaget (1965) and Kohlberg (1969) on the moral development of the child. She found distinct differences from which she concluded that girls and boys have different conceptions of justice from which they draw. And further, one may then distinguish an ethic of care as a feminine ethic, and an ethic of justice as a masculine ethic. She posed the following specific short situation to her subjects to elicit their forms of moral reasoning:

> In Europe, a woman was near death from cancer. One drug might save her, a rare form of radium that a druggist in the same town had discovered. The druggist was charging $2000, ten times what the drug cost him to make. The sick woman's husband, Heinz, went to everyone he knew to borrow the money, but he could only get together about half of what it cost. He told the druggist that his wife was dying and asked him to sell it cheaper or let him pay later. But the druggist said, "No." The husband got desperate and broke into the man's store to steal the drug for his wife. Should the husband have done that? Why? (Kohlberg, 1969, 379).

From the answers received, Gilligan (1982) formulated specific forms of moral reasoning. One polarity tended toward abstract reasoning; the other, tended to concrete reasoning. Gilligan concluded that the ethics of justice demands reasoning from some abstract set of principles culminating into finding the rule necessary for an answer. This was more likely connected to boys' responses. Ethics of care, on the other hand, is exhibited by subjects trying to discern the specific concrete and unique factors of the situation. This was connected with the girls' responses. Gilligan further reasoned where moral judgements are based more on notions of equality we have the ethics of justice; where the moral judgement was based on attachment and needs factors, the ethics of care prevailed. The conclusion by Gilligan was that two distinct ethics, one more male oriented, one more female oriented due to socialization, were operative in moral development.

Grace Clement (1963–)

Feminist analyses by Clement (1998) have examined the two ethics underlying Gilligan's work to see if in fact they are two separate ethics of justice or if they are interdependent. Stating at the outset that either ethic does not necessarily attach to either boys or girls, she nevertheless accepted the ethics of justice as attached to a masculine ethic and the ethics of care to a feminine ethic (3). She concluded that the two are complementary, that neither is subordinate to the other, that each informs the other, and that the two must remain in this oscillating state for more genuine justice to take place.

Clement (1998) argued that the ethics of justice assumes much of the baggage of contractarian theorists: individualism, rationalism, autonomy, choice, importance of abstract thought, formal equality, reliance on rules, and human separateness. This is most often found in formal law and bureaucracies. The ethics of care, however, assumes relational factors—that is, attachment, connectedness, relations, context—as most important; in other words, the interactional dynamics of specific human beings in contextualized settings are prioritized. This is most often found in family and friendship settings. The assumption in the ethics of care model is that the self is socially constituted in its ongoing relationships with various others.

Clement then examined whether there is or should be a privileging of one ethic over the other. Her answer is in the negative. As she informs us, "each ethic provides a check against the exaggerated, ideal form of the other ethic . . . used alone, either ethic tends to result in forms of moral reasoning which are both distorted and oppressive to women" (113). It is around this conclusion that much feminist analysis polarizes, some more essentialist, some more nonessentialist. The essentialist pole holds that there is a feminine ethic (care) and a masculine ethic (justice), per Gilligan, while the nonessentialist pole contends that these ethics are interrelated and not essential to either gender identity.

Judith Butler (1956–)

Butler has long informed our understanding of essentialism, queer identities, and gender. Her understanding of gender as a performance rather than a static reality allowed for a more fluid and therefore inclusive understanding of both gender and justice (1988). Whereas Gilligan and Clement recognized the socialization of gendered norms and understandings, Butler asks that we "undo" gender (2015). Her work has become more salient as people's open gender expressions have expanded beyond a binary (see literature on LGBTQ+ and queer theory). We revisit these notions in later chapters. At this point we note that there is significant and longstanding work dealing with gender and justice that does not impose a gender binary and in fact, aims to problematize that binary.

JUSTICE AND SOCIAL STRUCTURE

Social structure was implicit in the ancients' understandings of justice and explicit in the social contract theories. However, the following sets of

ideas regarding justice include as a substantial part of their frameworks concrete social structures beyond the abstract and sometime esoteric notions of
the social contract explored above. These social structures are analyzed not
as the outcome of a social contract or as necessarily the seat of justice but as
impacting upon our ideas regarding justice and the ways we think about
what society is and what we may owe each other within a social contract.
Some theorists here deal explicitly with social change and/or the need for
social change in the pursuit of justice.

Herbert Spencer (1820–1903)

Spencer based his ideas of justice on economic assumptions of humanity
that would define justice as the receiving of appropriate rewards (or punishments) in exchange for behaviors (Spencer, 1897, 1969, 1978; see also Carneiro, 1967; Miller,1976, 180–208). In his words, "each individual ought to
receive the benefits and the evils of his own nature and consequent conduct"
(1978, 17). His conception of justice was based on desert (Miller, 1976, 186).
There should be a proportional relation between act and result; benefit
should be proportional to input. Those in a superior position, too, are rightful beneficiaries of this status, whereas those in inferior positions in life are
so as a result of their deficiencies.

His notion of justice was to emerge from the evolutionary dynamics of
a market society. Contrary to much conventional wisdom, it was he, rather
than Darwin, who proclaimed the slogan "survival of the fittest." According to Spencer, human beings are competitive, independent, utilitarian
driven, and egotistical. Rewards gained in the competitive marketplace, then,
are just according to the contribution egotistically driven individuals make to
society as a whole. Justice, thus, is naturally related to desert; the drive for
profit in the marketplace by all will assure the progression of society to its
perfection. The state should enforce contracts that were freely made.

Adam Smith (1723–1790)

Smith placed the free market at the center of justice, contending that
when engaged in the free market each person would work toward their own
best interest and that through this pursuit, others would benefit (Smith
1976, 2003). This was his notion of the "invisible hand" in *Wealth of Nations*
(1776). Individuals following their self-interest with minimal constraint—
bounded only by law and justice—competing with others of similar mind,
would assure and benefit a collective development. Smith wrote during a
period of rapid industrialization and newly accumulating wealth. Smith's
analysis places attention on those profiting during this time that suggests
that those who are industrious, entrepreneurial, and engaged in the market

could not only make a personal fortune but provide employment and income to others.

In his book *The Theory of Moral Sentiments*, Smith explained his merit-based system of justice: "That whatever appears to be the proper object of gratitude, appears to deserve reward; and that, in the same manner, whatever appears to be the proper object of resentment, appears to deserve punishment" (2000, 136). Accordingly in the economic sphere, those who excel in gaining gratitude should be rewarded while those who induce resentment deserve punishment.

Peter Kropotkin (1842–1921)

Kropotkin has been identified as of the most prominent promulgators of an anarchist philosophy (1902; 1924; 1926; see also Miller 1976, 209–244). His approach was positivistic and antitheological. It was both inductive (making observations and working toward generalizations and theories) and deductive (making predictions based on a theory or principle that were subject to further verification). He was also inspired by Darwin's and Spencer's notions of the competition of species and the outcomes of such competition. However, in *Mutual Aid* (1902) Kropotkin outlined a history of humanity in terms of cooperation centering on mutual support and aid. It was in modern times that many of these institutions faltered or disappeared all together. Thus, for Kropotkin, cooperation, not competition, was the key motor to evolution.

By "mutual aid" Kropotkin meant a naturally (instinctively) based disposition to be concerned with the other, particularly to others' needs. Supportive activity toward the other is not based on potential rewards but instinctive feelings for solidarity. There is no further coherent foundational principle. Justice, according to Kropotkin, would arise from the foundational principle of mutual aid. Once principles, such as treating others as you would have them treat you, are instituted, we have mutual aid institutions. This principle is based on the generalized idea that one's aid will find reciprocation on future occasions.

Kropotkin also wrote about self-sacrifice as a form of higher morality. There are times where one gives beyond expectations, and beyond expectations of return. Self-sacrifice draws from notions of mutual aid, justice principles, and the drive toward social solidarity, but goes beyond these notions to include human drive to excel, to create, to express. These are "the sources of progress and invention in human society" (Miller, 1976, 218).

Kropotkin questioned whether law is necessarily a source of justice. Law, he informed, is imposed by powerful groups and thus a model for exploitation. Since collective ownership assumes that not one person has an unequal contribution or share it would be illusory to try and determine with precision each individual's contribution, the very basis of merit or desert-based systems of justice. Merit or desert-based systems also predispose class distinctions and hierarchies. According to Kropotkin, cooperation and mutual aid would assure distribution. The key is the satisfaction of each person's needs and the assurance of voluntary organization, not imposed from above. Thus, Kropotkin argues that mutual aid institutions would continue to flourish in these environments. His goal was the creation of a society devoid of states, laws, criminal justice systems, and penal systems—all coercive institutions—and the development of self-regulating communities.

More recent applications of a needs-based system of justice have been promulgated by Dennis Sullivan and Larry Tifft (1980, 2001). They criticize desert-based justice as inherently hierarchical and divisive. Their needs-based justice is focused on more genuine responses to the unique needs of each human being. In encouraging alternative responses to law breaking they suggest that all voices need to be addressed. This idea is particularly embraced in recently developed restorative justice-type programs where mediation and conflict resolution is the working principle of coming to terms with transgression (Van Ness and Strong, 2014). Sullivan and Tifft argue for mutual aid institutions where a "true self" (self-actualizing and engaged in mutual aid) might emerge rather than the "power-based self," which is the product of hierarchies, formal law, and social control institutions. Going beyond restorative justice, they argue that we need a transformative justice where social structural arrangements are critically examined and targets of transformation while still adequately responding to those who do harm to another.

PEACEMAKING CRIMINOLOGY
Harold Pepinsky (1945–) and Richard Quinney (1934–)
Larry Tifft (1941–) and Dennis Sullivan (1941–)

Pepinsky and Quinney collected a set of essays that were published under the title *Criminology as Peacemaking* (1991), which can mark the formal introduction of the perspective. Larry Tifft and Dennis Sullivan, in *Restorative Justice: Healing the Foundations of Our Everyday Lives* (1981), had earlier developed some of the beginning components of what eventually was to be called peacemaking criminology. Operating independently, Pepinsky and Quinney also developed some of its key components. Peacemaking criminology has since developed into a subfield of criminology focusing on social structure as the producer of crime and offering solutions to crime that require the restructuring of society. Its popularity can be attested to by a Google search. On a recent day (11/14/18), we googled "peacemaking criminology" and found over 145,000 hits. Pepinsky (2013) offers a retrospective of peacemaking criminology from his retirement. He notes that to get beyond merely containing violence on a temporary basis, "peacemaking is the only way to transform" our society to nonviolence (337). Peacemaking criminology has informed how we understand transformation. It has been utilized in relation to crime, international conflict, and understanding the relationship of gender to peacemaking during a national uprising.

Its main themes, developed by John Wozniak (2000), are: It offers a global critique of the entire criminal justice system and its warlike history; it shows how everything is interconnected; it turns the premises of traditional criminology upside down; it seeks to preserve the dignity of the individual; it focuses on what actually works to create a safe community of goodwill and respect for all human beings; it concentrates on building rather than severing social ties; it is a criminology of compassion for and of empathy with all who suffer; it defines the role of police as peace officer rather than as a crime fighter; it is interested in avoiding structural conditions that exclude people from having their needs met and defines such unresponsiveness as a form of structural violence; and it attempts to negate power relations in all its forms and seeks way to structurally and interpersonally minimize violence, harm, and the negation of democracy (272).

Dalsheim (2013) is concerned with peacemaking within the Israeli/Palestinian conflict. Her analysis of ongoing struggles "suggests there are important alternatives that might be woven together in a form that decenters the linear narration of the nation and might not result in the 'cunning of recognition'" (74). As with Hippchen (1981), she is suggesting new structures within which to seek peace and justice. Ahmad and Rae (2015) look to the restructuring of gender within Islam in support of peacemaking.

Peacemaking criminology offers critiques and solutions to our most pressing and violent social problems. This introduction is meant to aid in the understanding of alternative forms of justice that will be addressed in upcoming chapters.

Postmodern Conceptions of Social Justice

Postmodern perspectives on social justice have been influenced by French scholars predominantly from the late 1960s to the 1980s (see Arrigo et al., 2005). Much of this work has witnessed incorporation and integration by other nonpostmodernists.

Postmodernists question the core assumptions embedded in modernist and premodernist thought. The Enlightenment period (circa the1700s), it is argued, brought with it core assumptions that remain embedded in thinking about social justice. Core assumptions of modernists include the privileging of the rational, logical subject; free will; and potential liberation by way of enlightened reasoning, formal liberties, and economic progress.

These were all questioned by postmodernist thinkers who attempted to develop conceptions of justice from an alternative framework. Such thinkers as Nietzsche, Derrida, Lyotard, Foucault, and Rorty were to advocate a re-orientation in thinking about justice. Feminist postmodernists were to bring many of its key components into sharper relief. Recognized were the decentered notion of the subject (the person is more determined than determining); nonlinear rather than linear historical developments (genealogy); the manipulative effects of media, monopolies, governmental agencies; restrictive assumptions embedded in the dominant ideology; and the imprisoning effects of dominant discourse. To provide some idea as to the impact of postmodernism-oriented theory, doing a recent Google search using "postmodern criminology" witnessed over 616,000 hits.

For the postmodernists, social justice needs to be rethought around these new ontological premises. In this view, social justice must be examined in terms of the indeterminacies embedded in social structure, the dynamic notions of language and how consciousness is but its reflection, the multiplicity of languages, and how principles of social justice must be rethought to include these logics.

Perhaps one of the most cited thinkers in postmodern thought, Friedrich Nietzsche (1844–1990) rejected natural law and conceptions of justice that logically arose with it. As he informed us, "law of nature [is] a superstition," and principles of justice are ideas created by differences in power and their interests (1974, 356; 1986, 216). Nature has been interpreted to justify given power inequalities. The individual, in terms of a unitary, self-directing, determining subject is a fiction; there is no "being behind doing, affecting, becoming; the 'doer' is merely a fiction added to the deed" (1967, 45). Thus the notion of the juridical subject, the so-called reasonable man in law, would be seen as a legal fiction, serving interests that do not necessarily enhance human development and well-being.

For Nietzsche, the development of justice principles underwent two historical phases. In the first stage, justice reflected competing powerful groups—those who were able to dictate contracts to the weaker and punish noncompliers—who established a standoff amongst themselves. "Justice (fairness) originates between parties of approximately equal power . . . Justice naturally derives from prudent concern with self-preservation" (Nietzsche, 1986, 49). The second stage arrived with Christianity and its emphasis on pity, equality, fairness, and needs of the weaker. The weaker were to organize themselves against the stronger in the development of conceptions of justice. The weaker ("slave morality") now saw themselves as good, the stronger ("master morality") were seen as bad and evil. Thereafter history is about the conflict between the two and who could attain supremacy (hegemony) at any particular moment.

Nietzsche's suggestion is that we should recognize a will to power by which human beings attempt to maximize forces for life preservation, affirmation, self-overcoming, and growth. Thus, justice principles must respect the open and amorphous character of this ontology. Justice and law must be continually experimental and allow for the maximal possibilities of self-exploration, self-mastery, and self-overcoming. In this schema, the will to power knows nothing short of continuous transcendence. Conceptions of justice, therefore, cannot ever be rooted in some natural law or natural justice, or foundational principles. These can be best exemplified in the U.S. *Declaration of Independence*, which references the laws of nature to ground its proclamation. These, for Nietzsche, are merely metaphysical baggage that hinders, not promotes, human development. All too often we create fictions that attempt to explain our indeterminate nature and cosmos. These fictions must be continuously confronted.

We will return to a fuller discussion of postmodernism and its impact on social justice in a later chapter, and also suggest developments since the early 2000s are leading to a post-postmodernism that sometimes is referred to as sociomateriality, post-humanist, or digimodernism. Included here are some initial forays into introducing quantum mechanics and its impact on social justice, much of which is built on the vital work of Karan Barad, *Meeting the Universe Halfway* (2007). This calls for a rethinking of objects, cause, responsibility, and thus, concepts of social justice must build on new foundations.

This chapter has provided some introductions to select areas of social justice. It is not meant to be exhaustive. We will, however, return to some in later chapters for further inquiry.

REVIEW QUESTIONS

1. Look back at the classical section of the chapter. Among the ideas presented there, are there any that have fallen out of favor, or that you personally find problematic in our current world? Describe at least one of these ideas and why it is no longer viable.

2. Select two of the traditions presented in the section on religious philosophy. Compare these ideas as presented. Then compare other ideas related to the two religious traditions that you chose. These ideas may come from your own faith, your general understanding from other study, or your general understanding from mainstream media and/or culture.

3. Choose two thinkers from different sections of the chapter that occur after religious philosophy. Explain how the conceptions of each of these people are still relevant to our current notions of justice. Be sure to provide the name of the thinkers, the concepts that you chose, and how they are still relevant to our idea of justice.

4. How do the sociological conceptions of justice differ from the philosophical conceptions? Did you notice any changes as you moved through those readings? Do you find either approach more useful? Write a few sentences answering these questions and share them with at least one other person in the class. Read the answers shared with you by another person in the class and think about similarities and differences in your responses.

5. Prepare a short, one- or two-paragraph summary of one of the conceptions and/or thinkers in the chapter that you find compelling. Be prepared to present this summary to the class.

6. Social justice is sought in many ways in our current society. One way is through social movements. Find a news article from any source that describes the demands of a current social movement in enough detail that you can relate those demands to an idea of social justice presented in this chapter. Bring the news article to class and be prepared to discuss the movement's demands and which ideas from the chapter are reflected in those demands.

7. We have seen that several approaches exist in a feminist ethics of care. How could this approach be incorporated in a peacemaking approach? How could the approach be actually employed in everyday social engagements? Could peacemaking and care be nourished as a central value? Could it be done in capitalism? Is change to a more socialist society necessary?

CHAPTER 3

Distributive Justice

DISTRIBUTIVE JUSTICE has to do with notions of fairness in the distribution of benefits and burdens in a society. It is distinguished from retributive justice, the subject of the next chapter, which focuses on responses to harm. In developing distributive principles, central questions include: what precisely are the benefits and burdens (economic, education, jobs, health—resources and opportunities)?; what factors should be considered (formal equality, unique differences, luck, cost benefit, utilitarianism)?; to whom and to what do they apply (humans, social relations/relationships, citizens, animals, environment)?; what is assumed by agency (free will, individual responsibility, determinism, dialectic, constitutive, intra-action)?; and how and by whom will they be distributed (the state, nongovernmental organizations, communities, United Nations, international organizations)? Three dominant approaches in the literature are equality, desert, and need, but others have provided lively differences and are in various stages of development. The capability ("capability equality") approach in particular will be reviewed.

Distributive justice provides "moral guidance" in everyday choices at every level of social organization (Lamont and Favor, 2017). Our approach will favor both sociological analysis of historically based social-political-economic systems and their internally generated logics (i.e., more comparative, the work of Weber, Marx and Durkheim), one of which being notions of social justice (see Herzog, 2018, 112; Sen 2006), as well as political science approaches often generating abstract ideals (i.e., the distinction between "nonideal" and "ideal," Rawls, 1999; Simmons, 2010). Each informs the other.

TRADITIONAL POLITICAL PHILOSOPHICAL
VIEWS OF DISTRIBUTIVE JUSTICE
Equality

An idea traced to Aristotle, among others, and receiving much attention in liberal orientations, argues that each person is fundamentally equal and should therefore be treated equally. Formal equality is but one expression found in state documents such as the "equal protection clause" of the Fourteenth Amendment to the U.S. Constitution. Rawls, particularly with his theorizing a "difference principle"—whereby inequalities are allowed as long as the levels of the less off are raised—has been its key developer and has demanded much attention in the literature (summarized in chapter 1). Two important questions arise in the equality literature (Lamont and Favor, 2017, 4): development of an index beyond merely money-based measures (i.e., opportunities, health care, jobs) that could appropriately assess fair distribution of goods and services; and the time frame that should exist for its exercise. For example, a "starting-gate" approach specifies that equality at some initial starting point should prevail but thereafter practice could produce unequal results (5). A subset of an equality emphasis is "luck egalitarianism" (Lamont and Favor, 2017, 7–8; Dworkin, 2000), and is also noted in desert principles (Miller, 1999, 143–146), which highlights the idea that in some circumstances, opportunities arise not because of the actor's efforts, responsibility, and actions but because of favorable but uncontrollable, unpredictable factors or natural talents in which they can gain advantage. Race, gender, ethnicity, class, and/or their often intersectional nature can be factors for the differential opportunities that often follow. Thus, being born into a racialized gender role, with accessibility, and/or medical needs could place actors in disadvantaged opportunity possibilities (patterned discrimination). How much, then, should be offered to compensate for luck?

Some problematics with the approach cited in the literature include: a disregard, noted by Marxist Robert Wolff (1977), of an understanding of capitalist relations themselves as well as the emphasis on private property hence a deference to things as they are; a denial of the uniqueness of each human being and their unique drives, desires and motivation (Sandal, 1982); an insensitivity to hierarchies embedded in family relations (Okin, 1989); an inadequate theorizing of the "original positions" (Arrow, 1984; Harsanyi, 1975); and downplaying the role of differences in how effective agents are in using goods and services to attain their goals, especially in the notion of differentials in capabilities (Sen, 1992). There has also been substantial engagement by significant others (Dworkin, 1973; Nagel, 1973; Nozick, 1974; MacIntyre, 1984; Sandel, 1982; Walzer, 1983; Okin, 1989; Miller, 1999).

Need

A key developer of this approach is Karl Marx with his needs principle, "from each according to his [her/their] ability, to each according to his [her/their] needs" (Marx, 2005, 180; Pashukanis, 1980, 324). This had also been expressed by the anarchist Peter Kropotkin, in his emphasis on "mutual aid," particularly in assuring mutual benefits, and by feminists' notions of an "ethics of care." Karl Marx's life-long friend, Friedrich Engel, in "Against Arm-Chair Justice" (cited in Solomon and Murphy, 2000) admonished philosophers who theorize justice principles for their limited value in dealing with actual people's struggles and suffering, and that the goal was to change the world toward a more substantively just one. Needed was not just another bourgeois self-serving, system-sustaining theory, but a discourse emanating from the repressed expressing *their* needs. Most compelling is Amarty Sen's introduction of the notion of capabilities (to be covered in more detail in a final section of the chapter). Here opportunities, capacity, and functionality are critical components. As Miller (1999, 201) sums up, "need is judged in terms of capacity to function in a variety of ways, not in terms of an individual's choice about whether to exercise a particular capacity . . . needs could be identified as those conditions that allowed people to lead a minimally decent life in their society." The problematic here is to identify what functionings we see as most basic. Various lists have been offered including such things as ability to read and write, being able to have good health, nutrition, shelter. The issue, however, of luck re-emerges as it was the case for equality advocates. Miller (1999, 143–44) clarifies two forms: "integral luck" simply is where pure chance produces an advantageous position; and "circumstantial luck" is where some luck opportunity exists but it is then the person's actions that thereafter produce positive results. Miller's solution: "integral luck nullifies desert . . . and circumstantial luck may lead us to qualify our judgement about the deserts of those who are its beneficiaries" (146).

Some problematics/issues include: what constitutes need?; who defines it?; how to precisely operationalize and implement it?; the "index problem"; how does one understand different needs by diverse persons in society?; how does the principle of need play out in multiple contexts and times?; can societal agreement be established on the criteria constituting need?; how will different demands be dealt with in a society of scarce resources?; how will intensity of desire be factored in?; in situations of conflict, how will they be resolved?; how will cultural and subcultural variations in defining need be handled?; how will demands for different principles of distributive justice in the same situation be weighed and resolved?; is suffering and need always directly correlated? (see Miller 1999, chapter 10).

Desert

Deserts as a distributive principle of social justice suggests that each person should receive for their efforts their dues (Lamont and Favor, 2017; Celello, 2018, Miller, 1999, Lamont, 1994). Plato was an earlier developer of the approach, later advocated by John Locke, although Aristotle too advocated "virtue" as the bases of distribution. This is just deserts: a person's actions (efforts, intentions, and performance) are said to call forth appropriate deserts. A person's efforts can produce greater deserts; less effort, fewer deserts. Assumed are freely motivated, intentional, and responsible individuals pursuing ends that produce "social productive work"—increasing living standards (Lamont and Favor, 2017, 13; Celello, 2018, 4–5). Desert is primarily "backward-looking" in so much as the past and present effort and performance are constitutive elements for determining social productive action and accompanying desert. The question of nonhumans and desert poses some difficulties for desert theory; if, for example, one assumes some degree of self-awareness by nonhuman animals, then desert theory, it would seem, is appropriate for further consideration. Desert has been distinguished from merit. Celello's (9) reading of David Miller's distinction is "merit would be based on persons' abilities and talents, whereas a system based on desert would focus on persons' efforts and performances for which they are responsible" (9). Merit, on the other hand, does not necessitate responsibility as it does for desert principles. It is also distinguishable from welfare for the latter, effort and performance are not dominant factors. Welfare often downplays human beings as determining beings. And it is distinguishable from "entitlement," which is more focused on claims that can be made in particular organizations or invocation of legitimate rights (Celello, 2018, 9; Lamont and Favor, 2017, 13). The question of luck as was the case for "luck egalitarianism" reappears in desert discussion.

Questions and issue arise (see especially, Miller, 1999, chapter 7; Lamont and Favor, 2017; Celello, 2018; Lamont, 1994), which include: how do we determine the criteria for desert?; what factors should be considered to establish a desert basis?; are we able to accurately attain an understanding of all relevant elements constituting effort and performance?; what should be considered in determining contribution to the social good?; do we actually have some control of factors that contribute to some performance?; what is the relation between desert and luck? (We are often faced with unpredictable events that shape our actions); if effort and performance are key ingredients in judging desert, how do we weigh the contributions of each (Celello, 2018, 4)?; what of variations in opportunities to engaged in some activities in the first instance?; what about diversity in one's capacities or endowment (Miller, 1999, 146)?; do plants and objects have some rudimentary endowments of self-awareness, and if so, how is just deserts applied?; does responsibility necessarily apply in judging desert?; should contextual factors be considered in just deserts?; is traditional desert analysis restricted to the discursive practices engendered by particular political economies (capitalism, socialism, communism)?

Critiques levied for each approach are meant to encourage further questions and dialogs. Perhaps what could be included are: the question of context and the play of particular principles in time and space. Miller's conclusion after his extensive analysis is that for a society to be just "it must comply first with principles of need, second with principles of desert, and third with principles of equality" (1999, 247). Again, these key issues are suggestive rather than dismissive in furtherance of refinement of the need principle and its institutionalization toward a just society.

CLASSIC SOCIAL THEORISTS ON JUSTICE

Our starting point for a distributive social justice principle is sociological research that has investigated how the structure of political economy, and its embedded ideology transmitted by stabilized discursive practices, itself shapes logics, particularly principles of justice. For Emile Durkheim, we shall see, it was the division of labor and the late organic form that shaped a desert or substantive equality principle of social justice; for Max Weber, it was the emergence of rationalization in capitalism that engendered formal rationality and a formal equality principle; for Karl Marx, it was commodity fetishism, a capital logic, that called forth formal equality principles but disguised inherent differences (legal fetishism). Only in the higher forms of communism, according to Marx, would a needs principle resonate.

Emile Durkheim (1858–1917)

Durkheim provides valuable analyses of the development of modern society, which is said to be held together, the bond, by "organic solidarity." This is generated by differentiation in the division of labor. Distributive principles of justice are illuminated in his discussion of the just contract and the idea of social value that suggest both a form of "luck egalitarianism" (uniqueness of each person's aptitude/talents) and desert principle of distributive justice. Durkheim's influential writings, accordingly, focused on the nature of social solidarity. He found that the existing form of law was an index to the kind of solidarity in existence. He identified two forms of solidarity. These two forms of solidarity—"mechanical" (based on similarity) and "organic" (based on differences)—were situated in historical developments. He theorized that society tended to develop toward ever more differentiation. The key factor for social differentiation (e.g., division of labor in society) was moral/social density. A society without any disturbance from external factors (political, economic, etc.) was to naturally progress from the less differentiated form (e.g., less division of labor), with a consequent premium on mechanical bonds of solidarity, to a greater differentiation and organic bonds of solidarity. This was the course of the spontaneous division of labor.

The collective conscience (a commonly internalized notion of morality) of the less developed form was to assure stability. With the greater division of labor this was undermined considerably. Within a mechanically bonded society, there are few interrelated, complex tasks. Most can master these to one degree or another. There is, therefore, little dependence on others for carrying out one's own duty. In such circumstances, ideas of morality and justice are shared as the functions of each within the group are common and undifferentiated. When a society differentiates and individuals take on specific tasks, we become more dependent on each other. Consider, for example, movement from the pen as the instrument for writing toward computer software. In the university of old, if one were to break or lose a pen, they could merely pick up another and continue writing. However, given the current technical complexities, should one's software program break down, become infected with a virus, or suffer some other mysterious injury leaving it unworkable, the writer would most likely depend upon a technical worker within the university to repair/replace the software. In this environment, the writer must become adept at communicating with the technical person. It is unlikely that the writer will share many ideas of the primacy of technology in the writing process that the technical person will hold true. However, because of the writer's dependence upon the technical person, they will no doubt come to understand and accept many ideas about the importance of backing up data, updating virus protection software, and other computer-related tasks that serve the interests of both the writer and the technical person. These computer protection ideas are part of our current collective conscience.

Whether this acceptance of the protection of software is a moral stance is an interesting idea to consider given Durkheim's (1984) writings on morality. "We may say that what is moral is everything that is a source of solidarity, everything that forces man to account of other people, to regulate his actions by something other than the promptings of his own egoism, and the more numerous and strong these ties are, the more solid is the morality" (331). One could argue then that the acceptance of the need to protect one's computer software in the service of the greater good of the university (to protect the systems of others, reduce the demand on technical staff, etc.) is a moral choice. This choice is made when the consciousness of the writer has shifted to include the ideas of the technical staff. This is a form of organic solidarity as it is not necessary in the mechanical sense. The writer could give up software and go back to the pen, thereby eliminating the concerns of the technical staff. This would not only reduce the productive capacity of the writer but would also remove them from organic solidarity with others in the university.

The move from less to more division of labor is an artifact of social development requiring the specialization of labor. This development is not an individual or a moral choice; it is a social force to which we adapt for the purpose of continued social progress. This shift develops in response to the adaptive needs of individuals and groups within a given society. Moving from one form of solidarity to another requires a shift in consciousness from individual concerns to one that includes the concerns of other workers within a structure. This shift in consciousness occurs in response to the new social realities that require more social interaction and is not necessarily an individual choice, though Durkheim would argue that it is moral if it serves social cohesion.

Along with these developments in social structure there emerged certain conceptions of justice, law, and notions of contract. "Repressive law" was characterized by some loss inflicted on the offender, some pain and suffering. This included some loss such as to life, liberty, fortune, property, and honor. It is akin to present-day criminal law. It was most often found in societies with less division of labor. "Restitutive laws," on the other hand, focused on "the re-establishment of troubled relations to their normal state" (Durkheim, 1964b, 69). These are more in the form of civil, constitutional, administrative, and commercial laws. Their emphasis has a nonpunitive focus. These laws became more abundant with the greater division of labor in society. If we consider the complexities inherent in the ever-increasing specialization of labor and the expansion of our collective conscience to include new ideas, it follows that more complex notions of justice must also develop.

For Durkheim, it was the contract that was "par excellence, the juridical expression of co-operation . . . the contract is the symbol of exchange" (1964b, 123, 125). And hence, justice was to be understood in the context of the type of contract in existence, which in turn was based on the form of society, reflecting the general degree of the division of labor in a society. In the less developed form it was the blood covenant that assured justice. Each exchanger would duplicate the blood ties of family by exchanging drops of blood, for example. One could also share common food or drink. The real contract was where each exchanger simply exchanged without ceremony. The solemn contract included a declaration in words and an oath summoning up some divine being for enforcement (i.e., "so help me God"). The consensual contract, or contract by mutual consent, was a more recent invention. It separated the invocation of some divine from verbalized promises. It came about due to the new pace of the developing commercial order. It invoked the will. Each exchanger was assumed to be free to make an exchange. But, for this contract, Durkheim recognized that even though two people might "freely" enter an exchange relation, one may have greater abilities to impose their will on the exchange than the other. For example, the common worker has little to say about the terms of the work contract in which they enter. "Take it or leave it" is the employer's stipulation.

JUST CONTRACT, SOCIAL VALUE, AND DISTRIBUTIVE PRINCIPLE OF SOCIAL JUS-
TICE. Durkheim's ideal contract is the contract of equity, or the just contract. Justice, for Durkheim, should not only revolve around consent. He
sees it connected with "social value." Social value (Durkheim, 1964b, 382)
has three components: "[1] the sum of efforts necessary to produce the
object; [2] the intensity of the needs which it satisfies; and [3] the extent of
the satisfaction it brings." The first one deals with production, the next two,
consumption (Herzog, 2018, 115; Sirianni, 1984). Thus, justice exists where
"the services exchanged have an equivalent social value . . . each receives in
effect the thing he desires and delivers what he gives in return so that each
has a values for the other" (Durkheim, 1964b, 383). In other words, the
three components can be weighed to generate a sum that can be theoretically
compared between and among individuals. Just exchange is only where
"inherent" inequalities (i.e., differences in muscular dexterity, temperament,
dispositions, talents—"individual aptitudes," "natural inequalities") with
external conditions being equal (similar opportunities for developing these
talents) are reflected in the exchange. Hence subsequently developed
inequalities are allowable if equality of opportunity exists and social values
are established at the starting point. Here a form of "luck egalitarianism" is
implicated; so, too a desert-based principle of social justice. If external conditions (inheritance, rigid class and caste difference) grossly impact this
exchange where one has a distinct advantage over another it is no longer a
fair exchange. "If one class of society is obliged, in order to live, to take any
price for its services, while another can abstain from such action thanks to
resources at its disposal which, however, are not necessarily due to any
social superiority, the second has an unjust advantage over the first in law"
(Durkheim, 1964b, 384).

Unfortunately, women have been neglected in Durkheim's discussion,
and often relegated to subservient roles (Lehmann, 1994; Lamanna, 2002).
There has also been some discussion as to the nature of talent: is it natural
or based on socialization, or both?; is it fixed or ever-changing? (see Lukes,
1985, 177; Sirianni, 1984, 454–455).

ABNORMAL FORMS OF THE DIVISION OF LABOR. Durkheim went on to say
that the greatest disparity in justice exists with the "abnormal forms" of the
division of labor, even though, ironically, consensual contracts might be the
most respected in law. Abnormal forms are occasions where "external conditions" (i.e., advantage of inheritance, class and caste differences) offset the
natural accommodative relations developing in the ever-growing division
of labor. One form, "anomic," is where a great incongruence exists between
these adjustments. Here there are too few norms that are adequately assuring equilibrium (homeostasis) in a society. A second form is where the rules

and laws themselves constrain workers into roles that are not "fitting" to them. Here, too many rules abound that constrain individual development. A third form is where workers are deprived of fulfilling activity. In the abnormal forms, there may indeed be justice based on mutual consent; however, the just contract, the contract of equity will be subordinate to it.

Under anomic conditions, labor is divided to such an extent that little solidarity remains between and among workers. Durkheim (1984, 291–308) explains that this results in both the reduced power of workers to revolt for better wages and a reduction in the ability of producers to gauge the need for goods on the market. "Forced" divisions of labor also undermine solidarity. This occurs when social forces (unequal distribution of access) prevent workers from choosing labor, but instead forces some into work for which they are not fit. Labor is not divided by natural aptitude and talent, but instead is divided by predetermined statuses (such as inherited wealth or social class). Under these conditions, social contracts do not establish equivalent "social value," nor fulfill just deserts. This weakens the collective conscience and produces "subversive tendencies" (315). Similarly, the deprivation of fulfilling work (through overspecialization—becoming a "cog in the wheel") weakens solidarity and the moral order. Thus, Durkheim connects production with distribution. One can readily recognize these abnormal forms in our current social structure. The engaged reader should reflect for a moment to consider these three abnormal forms, their manifestations and effects, and to identify occurrence within their own life or community.

Max Weber (1864–1921)

The writings of Max Weber have been among the greatest influences on a large variety of topics in the social sciences. In a two-volume work published after his death, *Economy and Society*, his key thoughts on law were developed as they related to contractual justice. It was here that Weber developed his notion of the forms of law and legal thought and sense of justice that inhere within each. Ultimately, Weber focused on the tendency toward rationalization and systematization in capitalism. In this scenario, formal rationality leads to formal equality as a distributive principle of social justice. He was also quick to point out substantive inequalities are disguised in ideological structures of capitalism.

Weber was concerned with the various institutions that developed with the rise of capitalism. He dismissed mono-causal explanations, particularly exclusively economic explanations; rather, he always advocated a multi-causal approach. Be that as it may, once capitalism was to emerge, the central force for further development was "rationalization." He used this term in different ways. At times he saw it to mean the systematic codification of laws. At other times he saw it to mean increasing differentiation and coordination toward greater efficiency or productivity. This development was due to a coincidence of historical forces, he would argue: "two forces operating side by side . . . on the one hand, capitalism interested in strictly formal law and legal procedure . . . on the other hand, the rationalism of officialdom in absolutist states led to the interest in codified systems and in homogeneous law . . ." (Hunt, 1978, 109).

Market forces have an interest in formal law because these structures assure calculability, predictably, accountably, and manageability. Consider the legal specialties that have developed around these formalities (the variety of financial regulations alone abound). The state on the other hand has interest not only in market forces but also in broader social forces and must attempt to balance those with rationality and consistency. The state can claim equality before the law only if laws are consistent and based on rational reasoning. The common interests of the market and the state produce formal rational legal systems. The logic of rationalization whereby all undergoes a continuous splitting into component parts ever brought under some form of coordination and hierarchy of control was typified by the bureaucracy. This, too, led to further systematization of principles of law and justice (legal formalism). In the extreme, this led to the "iron cage," a loss of freedom and meaning as all things became increasingly objectified, quantified, categorized, and systematized without concern for all that constitutes the human being.

CONTRACTS AND SOCIAL JUSTICE. Alongside this development there was also a historical transformation in the forms of contract. In earlier times, in those societies organized more on the basis of clans, kinships, and household communities, it was the fraternal contract that was of a premium. Any exchange with another meant a dramatic change in relations with the other. The other would now become "somebody's child, father, wife, brother, master, slave, kin, comrade-in-arms, protector, client, follower, vassal, subject, friend, or, quite generally, comrade" (Weber, 1978, 672). Here, too, there existed collective responsibility; accordingly, individual liability was not the dominant outlook. All kinship members were responsible for the contract made by members. It was the community that would assure the fulfillment of contracts.

In later societies, those marked particularly by the capitalist mode of production, the notion of collective responsibility was to dissipate and notions of individual liability became dominant. This was especially so with the emergence of the market economy, commerce, and the competitive marketplace. Weber (1958) expertly describes the impact of Puritanism on individualism. His text draws out the relationship between religion and economic development, documenting the importance of both on social life and social understandings. The religious traditions that privileged the individual and individual responsibility were especially important to the development of capitalism, which also privileges individual responsibility and action over the collective. It seems consistent that if one is to stand alone before God for judgement in the afterlife that one should be held accountable individually for judgement before the court or in contractual relations.

Within the capitalist economy the purposive contract was to dominate. These were momentary interactions that had very specific transactions. Stability and predictability in previous societies was assured by collective responsibility. The new economy demanded a plethora of momentary exchanges. The purposive contract was to be discovered. And the abstract bearer of rights, the juridical subject in law, the assumed rational, logical, and self-directing subject, we recognize as the "reasonable man in law." So, connected with the forces of rationalization, the rise of capitalism, central states and their need for coordinating administration, and the demands of the competitive marketplace, was a new notion of the subject and new notions of responsibility. Now individual responsibility was elevated to a central place in law and in principles of contractual justice.

DISTRIBUTIVE PRINCIPLE OF SOCIAL JUSTICE, FORMAL AND INFORMAL. Weber's forces of rationalization would lead to the stress on formal equality as a principle of distributive justice. However, Weber was skeptical about justice in the forms of contractual justice that may exist, particularly substantive equality. "The result of contractual freedom, then, is in the first place the opening of the opportunity to use, by the clever utilization of property ownership in the market, these resources without legal restraints as a means for the achievement of power over others. The parties interested in the power in the market thus are also interested in such a legal order" (Weber, 1978, 73).

The increase of contractual justice does not necessarily bring greater freedom or fairness (substantive principle of social justice). Contracts clearly formalize and articulate expectations within the agreement. However, this does not guarantee that the expectations or the agreement are just. Neither do contracts guarantee that the conditions under which the agreement was made are just. Formal qualities of law are not the basis of understanding justice. After all is said and done, it is the given property distribution in a society that will determine overall freedom, level of coercion, and justice. It is the supporting role of ideology in the form of legitimizing principles by which subjects are pacified into accepting the form of contract in existence. As Weber (953) tells us, "every highly privileged group develops the myth of its natural . . . superiority." Most of the time, for Weber, the "negatively privileged group" accepts the given order because of the existence of legitimation principles that abound in societal-wide ideology.

Contractual justice, then, is reflected in the type of legal order and form of legal thought that is dominant. "Formal rationality," or the formal legal system most prevalent in capitalist forms of society, privileges the juridical subject, and forms of legal thought identified as syllogistic reasoning and deductive logic. Given core axioms, such as "constitutional rights," then, decisions and justice can be arrived at by a mechanical, linear, and logical analysis to a conclusion in law. Said in another way, we start with a major premise, apply it to the minor premise or "facts" of a case, and deductively in a step-by-step fashion arrive at a conclusion in law. In other words, the right to equal access to education, for example, is protected through a linear legal process that considers whether equal access is being denied, concludes that it is being denied, and finds that this denial is unjust (i.e., denial of equal protection under the law, protected by the 14th Amendment to the U.S. Constitution). Thus, the equality principle of distributive justice is valued in capitalism. However, other forms of justice may compete.

"Substantive rationality" is where some "outside" principles, criteria, ethics, and notions are employed. By outside we mean outside the formally recognized (dominant) principles in law. Thus, affirmative action is based on substantive rationality. So too is "comparable worth," drawing from United Nation's notion of human rights, demands of justice based on the notion of contract of equity, etc. Here, doing justice entails drawing from principles that are not necessarily recognized in the official body of laws. In the free equal access example above, substantive rationality may allow for the unequal access of some groups to educational facilities if it is found that principles or ethics outside of the law are being violated. This is to "level the playing field," contributing to more genuine equal access to opportunities. For example, the Reserve Officers' Training Corps (ROTC) was banned from several college campuses during the Vietnam War era when students protested that the exclusion of homosexuals from the military violated their stated campus principles of inclusion. This reliance on principles of inclusion as outlined in the campuses' equity statements was used to exclude the ROTC based on the military's exclusionary practices. The campus equity statements were outside the formal law yet utilized as a basis to invoke justice. Here, a form of "luck egalitarianism"—consideration of substantive factors—is more dominantly considered than pure application of the equality principle of distributive justice either privileging or de-privileging "external factors."

Another form of law and justice is "substantive irrationality." Here, some outside principle is invoked, and little in the form of long-term rationalization is sought in law. Irrationality is used here not as a judgement of appropriateness, but as a descriptor to distinguish this form of law and justice from that which requires rationalization. A jury decision-making process is a case in point. Here, the jurors, at the end of the trial phase are instructed by the judge as to the charge and criteria with which to employ in determining guilt or innocence. This is formal rationality. However, once the jurors return to the jury room for deliberation, it is more often a mixture of formal rationality and substantive irrationality, with the latter playing a more dominant role. In other words, it is the unique worldviews and assumptions of various people and ethnic and cultural groups that may play a greater role in the determination as to what is just. This notion finds itself also at play in many societies that make use of "khadi justice," where some religious figure is the sole determiner of each infraction and its resolution. Therefore, no rationalization or formal code is available. Here an outsider knows neither the principle being invoked nor its particular application in a concrete situation. A benevolent dictator, for example, would claim a nuanced understanding of their subject's desires and would distribute resources accordingly (needs principle of distributive social justice). This also invokes "luck egalitarianism" as a form of distributive social justice principle.

The fourth form of justice, according to Weber, is "formal irrationality." Here some formal principles of justice might be invoked, but only the authority knows how to interpret these principles. This appears in decision-making that relies on the oracle, magic, or revelation. Here, justice is concretely determined by the decision-making authority, but is applied differently to even similarly situated persons. Perhaps the needs principle of distributive social justice is paramount. Although it might be argued that the formal part invoked suggests where two people somehow are judged as having equivalent talents or aptitude, the desert principle is implicated. Nevertheless, only the authority knows how this weighing took place, even though it may conceivably be internally consistent; hence, in Weber's schema, a display of "irrationality."

Contractual justice entails the interplay of principles of rationalization and principles of formality. Rationalization applies some criterion to all like cases; formality makes use of criteria that are internal to the legal system (using external criteria would make it low in formality or substantive). A decision is seen as fair where societal members generally accept the form of law, legal thought, and the sense of justice embedded within it. Considered legitimate it is an order worthy of orientating behavior. Nevertheless, for Weber, distributive social justice is ultimately determined in capitalism by the unequal distribution of property in a society of differential access to opportunities. The dominant perception and enforcement are, however, the equality principle of distributive social justice.

Karl Marx (1818–1883)

Along with Durkheim and Weber, Marx stands out as one of the most influential thinkers in the social sciences. He never was interested, directly, in the form of law. But issues of justice were central to his writings. Marx advocated the needs principle of distributive justice, but its dominance would only take place in the "higher forms" of societal development, communism. Socialism, as a stage between capitalism and communism, would advocate more genuine formal equality and more genuine allocation of the deserts principle of distributive social justice. Developed principles of distributive justice in capitalism, however, would be ideological representations that derive from and sustain capital logic. Unlike political science approaches that advocate abstract principles such as Rawls's starting point, the "original position" in a "veil of ignorance," in determining what principles of justice would emerge Marx examined real historical, political, and economic factors in explaining how emerging principles of distributive justice were connected to them. Rawls did not challenge class structure, but stressed equality of opportunities, and in this sense, has sometimes been accused as an apologist for the political and economic inequalities in capitalism (see for example: Wolff, 1977; Kanatli, 2015; Wei, 2008; Wei, 2015; Christie, 1988).

All phenomena, including law, ideology, and conceptions of justice, were ultimately connected with a particular mode of production in existence. For example, he tells us (cited in Cain and Hunt, 1979, 138), a contract "is just whenever it corresponds, is appropriate, to the mode of production. It is unjust whenever it contradicts that mode. Slavery on the basis of capitalist production is unjust; likewise, fraud in the quality of commodities."

Marx's guiding principle in historical and political economic investigations was the mode of production.

> In the social production of their existence, people inevitably enter into definite relations, which are independent of their will, namely relations of production appropriate to a given stage in the development of their material forces of production. The totality of these relations of production constitutes the economic structure of society, the real foundations, on which arises a legal and political superstructure and to which correspond definite forms of social consciousness. The mode of production of material life conditions the general process of social, political and intellectual life. It is not the consciousness of people that determines their existence, but their social existence that determines their consciousness. (1967, 20–21)

In this view, the base is the economic system, the superstructure is the totality of belief, consciousness, law, ideology, ethic, principles of justice, etc. The base is said to "determine" the superstructure. Thus, four pure forms of the modes of production were explained by Marx: slavery, feudalism, capitalism, and communism. Socialism was an in-between category, between capitalism and communism. Within the base two elements existed: the forces of production (sometimes referred to as "means of production," which includes technology, natural resources, skills and knowledge, etc.) and relations of production, or socio-economic relations (how people actually interact in a patterned way). It is said that the forces of production shape the relations of production. Given an assembly line, for example, specific relations develop. Given the internal combustion engine, particular relations of production develop. When these two, forces and relations of production, are in relative accord, we have an equilibrium, or stasis. When forces of production change too rapidly, there is a gap, a contradiction between these and the relations of production, called an anti-thesis.

Within this contradiction change will emerge, either peacefully, or where the contradictions are the most extreme, by outright revolution. This is the notion of the dialectical materialism: thesis → anti-thesis → thesis → anti-thesis. It is the motor of historical change. Marx also tells us that when these contradictions are extreme, the mode of production itself changes into new forms. These are objective conditions. These contradictions in the mode of production such as overproduction and/or economic crises are the concrete conditions for revolution. However, Marx was also adamant regarding the subjective conditions for revolution. These conditions are related to class consciousness or the knowledge held by the revolutionary class (working class under capitalism) that something can be done to change the social conditions and that they/we are the class to produce that change. In other words, we need recognition of not only a "class in itself" but for a "class for itself." Hallas (2003) recounts Trotsky's description of the development of a revolutionary consciousness within the working class. This consciousness requires experience in class struggle. Lenin (1989) suggested that work within labor unions and general political work with and for the interests of the working class are ways to experience that struggle. Marx informed our understanding of the objective and subjective conditions for revolutionary change. Later chapters in this book will deal with examples of social change and the structures and actions that served and/or impeded justice.

PRINCIPLES OF DISTRIBUTIVE SOCIAL JUSTICE. Notions of justice must be seen in terms of the mode of production in existence. What is seen as fair is specific to a particular mode of production. People are offered "definite

relations" that are "independent of their wills." Consciousness, then, follows one's existence, according to Marx. A "just" contract or dealing with
the other is whenever "it corresponds, is appropriate, to the mode of production. It is unjust whenever it contradicts that mode" (Marx cited in Cain
and Hunt, 1979, 138). In feudalism, for example, the serf or peasant in this
hierarchical form of society finds themselves subordinate to the lord. In this
society, one's rights, privileges, and notions of justness follow one's position
in the hierarchy, and do not necessarily follow as one moves to another village or town. Resources, opportunities, benefits, and burdens all follow
class location.

The issue of what constitutes justice can be interpreted in at least four
ways in Marxist analysis: instrumental Marxist, structural Marxist, structural interpellationist, and constitutive Marxist. Instrumental Marxist
analysis would have it that those with economic power also have political
power. In fact, in the more rigid form of instrumental Marxist analysis, it is
this group that is a capitalist ruling class that is homogeneous in its interests
to maximize profit and is conspiratorial in its functioning to do so (see
Quinney, 1974). The state, law, criminal justice system, and notions of justice are then organized to promote the interest of the ruling class by way of
ideological state apparatuses (i.e., school, family, media). Justice, in short, is
what the ruling class defines from its self-interested position to maximize
profit (surplus value). In times of increasing contradiction or social crises,
this maximization of profit can also be interpreted as maximization of
exploitation (declining wages/increasing work hours). Depending on the
level of class consciousness, this may be interpreted as unjust and be followed by social change. However, under stable conditions, the maximization of profit will be seen as just within a capitalist structure.

Structural Marxists see things differently. Notions of law and justice
emerge from commodity exchange (Pashukanis, 1980). Marx, in the first
100 pages of *Capital*, explained the notion of commodity fetishism: the concreteness of things exchanged, their use values, are transformed into abstractions, exchange values. Pashukanis, who appeared after the 1917 Russian
revolution, was to rise to preeminence in the new dictatorship of the proletariat directing the socialist state. It was he who developed, from Marx's
commodity exchange logic, the notion of legal fetishism. Briefly, to develop
the commodity exchange perspective, we start with two commodity owners
entering a competitive marketplace. Through the constant exchange of their
commodities something mysterious happens, with profound effects. Initially, a commodity has use value—it corresponds to two differences that
inhere within it: differences in the amount of labor needed in its production; differences in the concrete needs to which it corresponds. However,
with the constant exchange of commodities new appearances (phenomenal

forms) emerge. That is, the two commodities are brought within an equation of equivalence: two pounds of butter = 4 gallons of milk, two of this equal four of that. This is a mathematical ratio. It is money that becomes the universal equivalent standing for value. Henceforth, the use value recedes from consciousness, replaced with its ratio of exchange. We now have exchange value. The concreteness of things, the uniqueness of things is now transformed into a quantitative relation. Differences disappear. So, too, Pashukanis tells us, does the unique, concrete person in capitalism. This hidden process is sometimes also referred to as commodification.

With the constant exchange of commodities certain appearances take form to which lawyers give idealized expression (verbal form): first, the appearance of free will as each exchanger assumes it of the other; second, the appearance of equality as each at the instant of transfer assumes it of the other; and third, proprietorship interests, as each assumes the other is the owner of the commodity being exchanged. Thus, the formal notions of freedom, equality, and proprietorship interests emerge in this instance. The principle of distributive justice that follows is equality. The subject is now transformed, much like the commodity into an exchange value, the juridical subject, a legal subject in law with formal rights. This is the notion of legal fetishism, which is similar in development to commodity fetishism. In both cases differences and concrete existence (qualitative differences) are replaced by abstract quantitative terms. Thereafter, justice is measured in terms of applying an equal measure (criteria) to unique persons. In other words, an equal measure is applied to differences. For Marxists, an equal standard applied to differences is inherently unequal and unjust. Thus, the formal equality principle of distributive justice disguises the substantive equality that exists.

In the structural version of Marxism, then, notions of justice emerge from these commodification processes. Fairness in contract dealings is only an outcome where reasonable people prevail as juridical subjects in law. This is in line with Max Weber's model of formal rationality and in line with Durkheim's consensual contract. The person becomes an abstraction, which can be simply plugged into various principles of law to see to what degree they are in conformity with the reasonable person in law. A person becomes a mathematical average.

A third Marxist model exists. It could be referred to as the structural interpellationist perspective. In late capitalism, that is, in advanced monopoly capitalism that was said to emerge in the early to the mid-1900s, the state had to become more actively involved in overcoming the internal contradictions that threatened it. It must also deliberately develop legitimation principles that support decision-making. Thus, in law, the principle of interest balancing now prevailed. The courts weigh the government's interests against a particular person's or group's interests and determine the appropriate balance. The notion of the formal, abstract subject is now being replaced with the notion of interpellated rights: various groups in society are now relegated to positions (status) with particular rights respected in law. Consider how the notion of "persons" found in the due process of clause of the Fourteenth Amendment has found continuously new definitions by the higher courts. Status now determines rights respected in law. Justice in this model becomes much more contentious. It is mobilization of interests and struggle that accounts for particular rights and stabilized expectations of justice. In this context, the equality principle of distributive justice derived from capital logic and the fetishism of commodities, law, and justice is retained but finds tension with emerging demands for a substantive needs and deserts principle.

In a Marxist analysis, mobilization of interests is based on class interests and may be an expression of capitalist interests or working-class interests. When corporations seek protection from one set of laws as individuals and exceptions from other laws as corporations, they are seeking a particular status in keeping with their interests. This is an example of a mobilization by the capitalist class in their own interest. When a labor union seeks recognition in a workplace it is seeking a particular status in its interest. If the union is democratic and representative of its members, this would be an example of a mobilization in the interest of the working class.

A fourth and more recent Marxist inspired model is the constitutive model. In this view, base effects superstructure, but superstructure effects base. Each is constitutive of the other, and the two elements of the mode of production can no longer be easily separated, each inheres in the other. Legal consciousness and what constitutes justness is an ongoing process. In Ewick and Silbey's (1998) study of struggles within legal structure, they tell us that "as individuals express . . . their consciousness, they draw from and contribute to legality . . . [P]eople relied on culturally available narratives of law to interpret their lives and relationships" (247). Thus, in this perspective, justice undergoes an active and ongoing constitutive construction in everyday storytelling. When faced with conflict, subjects resort to cultural recipes in combination with what is understood as law and fair distributive principles of social justice. There is coproduction of the meaning of justice that is enacted or performed, that is, played out in every-day actions. It is the historically determined configurations of forces (political, economic, juridical, ideological) that are embedded in social structure that becomes the context for these constitutive constructions of principles of distributive justice. Equality principles of distributive justice have efficacy and a dominant role due to their repetitive practice sustaining them. The incorporation of the idea of conflict into a Marxist analysis is important given Marx's writings concerning the centrality of conflict in social arrangements and the necessity of struggle for social change and for disruptions of conventional, system-serving ideologies.

Marx's understanding of justice as based on the mode of production was also informed by the class structure. As he and Engels (1973b) wrote in the *Manifesto of the Communist Party*, "The history of all hitherto existing society is the history of class struggles" (108). It is through this struggle that Marx places the impetus for revolution in the mode of production and the evolution of human consciousness. Marx explained the interplay between struggle, change, and consciousness. As Marx saw it, class struggle develops the consciousness of those involved in struggle, therefore leading to increased possibilities for social change through revolutionary processes (Hallas, 2003). These processes further develop the consciousness of those involved. These ideas clearly inform Ewick and Silbey's (1998) conception of justice as a coproduction. However, because consciousness reflects social conditions, collective understandings of justice will be rooted in the social conditions of the time.

Marx has also explained how an overall principle of justice would emerge in given modes of production. "Right can never be higher than the economic structure of society and its cultural development conditioned thereby" (Marx, 1967, 19). He had predicted that with the increasing contradictions in advanced capitalist modes of production there would be a transformation to socialism, which, in turn, with its own contradictions, would transform into communism. In capitalism, principles of justice would center on notions of formal equality. In other words, an equal measure (formal equality) would be applied to unique (different) people. The uniqueness of people is subordinated under a common measure. In socialism, "the narrow horizons of bourgeois thought" would still prevail, but the principles of justice would be more genuinely applied, but with two qualifications: 'he who does not work, neither shall he eat', and 'an equal amount of products for an equal amount of labour'" (Lenin, 1975, 150). Here the residues of the equality principle would still exist.

In the higher forms, the communist mode of production, where private property and the state would disappear, where no stratification into fixed classes exists, and where each person's contribution would see a more complete return (just distribution) doing away with the creation of surplus value that the bourgeois appropriate, principles of justice would transform to: "from each according to his abilities, to each according to his needs" (Marx, 2005, 180; Lenin, 1949, 152–163; Pashukanis, 1980, 324). This is referred to as a "needs principle," but perhaps more correctly, with the inclusion of two key components, the "needs-abilities principle." Differentials in needs and abilities work against a formal equality principle. Thus, principles of distributive social justice would revolve around acknowledging differences: differences in abilities, differences in needs. So, rather than the language of reward, we shift to needs; and in abilities we shift to methods of production. Both are integral in articulating a principle of distributive social justice.

TOWARD A SOCIAL JUSTICE MODEL OF DISTRIBUTIVE JUSTICE

There are more recent attempts at developing distributive social justice principles. Here we will focus on three erudite analyses that are suggestive for further study: David Miller, Amartya Sen, and the "recognition and distribution" debate (Alex Honneth, Nancy Fraser).

David Miller: Mode of Human Relationship and Principle of Distributive Justice

One notably clear analysis is provided by David Miller in *Principles of Social Justice* (1999). According to Miller (ix), to develop a social justice understanding "is to discover the underlying principles that people use when they judge some aspect of their society to be just or unjust." To this end, he begins his specification of three ideal types of modes of human relationships (solidaristic community, instrumental association, and citizenship) to which he shows particular forms of justice are connected, respectively, to need, desert, and equality. By looking at a particular mode of human relationship we can then see what demands of justice people often make on one another. By modes he follows Max Weber's notion of ideal types. These are abstractions, developed more for illumination than for literally explicating specific moments (28).

Miller wants to further a more explicit connection between political economic social organization and principles of justice. He also wants to indicate how tensions and conflicts exist when people find themselves in more than one mode of human relationship. He does not dispute the three previous classic theorists; in fact, one can see that he derives a considerable amount of substance from them.

His first mode is that of a solidaristic community. Here there is a sharing of a common ethos and identity in a relatively stable group (Miller 1999, 26). It entails much direct interaction with the other and the consequent generation of mutual understanding and trust. Thus, people find themselves in solidarity due to a shared culture, kinship, or acquaintanceship. In premodern society it was found in the village community. In modern society it is more prevalently found in the family. This form of solidarity is less so in various other forms of association, e.g., work organizations. Within solidaristic communities justice is defined in terms of need (27). "Each member is expected to contribute to relieving the needs of others in proportion to ability, the extent of liability depending upon how close the ties of community are in each case . . ." (27). This understanding is reminiscent of Marx's expectations for justice within a communistic society (from each according to his ability, to each according to his need).

The second mode of relationship is the instrumental association. Central here is utilitarianism: people relate to each other in terms of various goals, aims, and purposes, which can be ideally realized in working together with others (Miller, 1999, 27). Economic relations are exemplary. Commodity owners exchanging at the capitalist marketplace is an example where each attempts to maximize their profit. It is also found where people work for various organizations and engage in instrumental action for advancement, pay, or goal realization. The principle of justice that emerges is that of desert. "Each person comes to the association as a free agent with a set of skills and talents that he deploys to advance its goals. Justice is done when he receives back by way of reward an equivalent to the contribution he makes" (28). A person's desert is related to the goals of the particular association. The criterion of desert, then, can be operationalized as how much one contributes to the goals and how much one is rewarded. Implicit is the notion of proportionality: greater contributions should receive greater rewards. This mode is consistent with Weber's formal rationality outlined earlier in this section.

The third mode of human relationships is citizenship. Human beings not only relate with others in terms of solidarity and/or instrumental activity but also as bearers of abstract rights (e.g., expectations and obligations defined in law) that identify their status as citizens (Miller, 1999, 30). Here the principle of justice would be [formal] equality. "Each person enjoys the same set of liberties and rights, rights to personal protection, political participation, and the various services that the political community provides for its members" (30). Thus, citizenship is a status. It encompasses, for example, the notion of the reasonable person in law. This mode would be consistent with Weber's notion of formal rationality.

Each of the three ideal types, in actuality, often finds degrees of overlap as people find themselves in more than one form of association at a particular point in time or within particular relationships. These overlapping relations produce tensions and cries of unjust as an unexpected standard(s) of justice is being assumed and practiced. In other words, given the more fluid nature of associations—solidaristic, instrumental, equality—a given situation may suggest one principle of justice being the more operative than another.

Consider the solidaristic form of justice that many of us experience within our families. We rely upon each other and support each other because of our kinship bond reflecting Miller's first mode. However, the genesis of a family in modern Western societies is typically a marital contract that formalizes the relational expectations. This contract is entered by two free agents with the common goal of mutual benefit. This contract reflects Miller's second mode of human relationships. Remaining within the familial context we can see the overlap with the third mode when we consider the rights and benefits provided by the community for married couples (in the United States this is reflected in access to health care and retirement benefits among other things) because of their status.

Herein lies the dilemma: with two people in conflict drawing from different modes of relations, which criterion to choose as relevant and operative? From our example above, we can see that conflict between marital partners could allow for competing criteria for resolution depending on the matter at hand and/or the perspectives of the individuals involved in the conflict. Miller's suggestion is that we need to develop a "pluralistic theory of justice" that would be contextually sensitive, where the three criteria would be "held in consistent balance with one another" (41). This is increasingly apparent with issues of globalism and multiculturalism where a particular criterion might clash with another (246). We will continue to consider these ideas of multiple modes of justice in later chapters.

Capability Approach: Amartya Sen

Having some traces to Aristotle, Marx, and Adam Smith, the capabilities distributive justice principle (sometimes called capabilities equality) begins not with abstract principles generated by some primordial position (Rawls's "original position") but rather with well-being (decent life) and opportunities (capabilities) to achieve it as a fundamental floor (Sen, 1992, 2011; Nussbaum 2011; Robeyns, 2016). Nussbaum (2011, 18), developing it further in her "human development" approach, defines it as "as a comparative quality-of-life assessment and to theorizing about basic social justice." "What are people actually able to do and to be? What real opportunities are available to them?" (x). For Sen, these are established by consulting a particular society/community to see what its members deem a normal state of well-being. And what they are able to do (doings), and what they are able to be (beings), together constituting functionings (Nussbaum, 2011, 23–33; Robeyns, 2016). Functionings, in other words, are the actualization of capabilities. These are fundamental freedoms. Genuine opportunities must exist for their realization.

Whereas Sen resists offering a definitive list, Nussbaum (2011, 13) does not shy away from offering a ten-item list of basic capabilities, which includes: being able to have good health, being able to live a normal life, being able to enjoy recreational activities, being able to move from one location to another, being able to develop one's emotions, etc. Any just social political system must offer some threshold level for their realization. Capabilities, then, are opportunities or genuine freedom to attain functionings for realizing human dignity. Judging a particular society in terms of distributive justice can consider three components (Robeyns, 2016, 2): "(1) the assessment of individual well-being; (2) the evaluation and assessment of social arrangement; and (3) the design of policies and proposal about social change in society." This approach looks at opportunities (capabilities) to actualize doings and beings. Resource distribution is critical. Along with this, a conversion factor—how readily resource can be converted into a functioning—considers both internal abilities (personal) and opportunities (social and environmental) (Robeyns, 2016, 6). Thus, indexes can be constructed for each component and societies can be compared. Rather than using the gross national product for judging society's economy and health, for example, alternative indexes should be referenced and new ones constructed such as the Human Development Index and the Inequality-adjusted Human Development Index.

For Miller (1999, 210) this approach falls within a needs principle of distributive justice—"needs is judged in terms of capacity in functions in a variety of ways." It provides the basis of evaluating social policies. Do they enhance, promote, support or do they restrict, hinder, or deny basic capabilities? Others argue that it is more compatible with an equality principle, particularly luck egalitarianism. Here, individual differences in talents and natural aptitudes could, after threshold values of fulfilling basic capabilities are met, be the basis of variations in outcomes. Robeyns (2016, 11–12) argues that the capability approach is only one component of a more complete distributive principle of social justice. So, the question remains for a fuller theory: what distributive principle is required when the thresholds are attained? What about responsibility with which little has been said in the capabilities literature? Who or what agency will be endowed with expanding basic capabilities? On the other hand, Sen (2011; cited in Robeyns, 13) questions whether we need some utopian model of a distributive principle of justice, and rather the capability approach could be an evaluative mechanism for comparing and evaluating injustices in various societies sensitizing us to the imperative of social change. Can, ultimately, a capabilities approach be developed into a fuller theory of distributive justice without considering hierarchical institutional and class structures such as in capitalism (i.e., inherent in capital logic)? Many instructive critical discussions have taken place, for example, Okin's (2003) critique arguing that Nussbaum's approach does not respond sufficiently to poor women, and Nussbaum's (2004) response (see also Wells, 2018; Alkire, 2005; Stewart, 1995). For differences between Sen and Nussbaum's approach see Well's concise summary (2018, 22). Some have integrated capability equality with Marx's notion of needs (DeMartino, 2003).

Alexander (2012) and Hoberman (2012) have offered substantial evidence for the need of including policy analyses and social structure within the study of distributive justice. These writers look specifically at the U.S. criminal justice system and medical inequalities, respectively. Race is central to these analyses and should be well considered by students of justice. We will return to these findings later in the text.

Alex Honneth and Nancy Fraser: Distribution and Recognition

Social movements since the 1990s have witnessed considerable attention to recognition (more cultural dimension), at some times, usurping discussion of redistributive/distributive principles of justice. This has been particularly punctuated by identity politics in its various forms. Recognition, sometimes equated with acknowledgement, is often traced to Hegel's (1977) classic statement in *Phenomenology of Spirit*. Here intersubjectivity is key: the idea that reciprocal relations, self and other, whereby each sees the other as equal, thus mutual recognition. Whereas distribution has to do with resource distribution, particularly economic.

A provocative book illustrative of the tension between the two is *Redistribution or Recognition?* (2003). It concerns a debate by two theorists (Nancy Fraser, Alex Honneth) over the appropriate relation of recognition to redistribution in developing a distributive justice framework. Honneth advocates a recognition approach, rooted in Hegelian philosophy (the struggle for recognition), where distribution is seen as being derived from it. Fraser, on the other hand, sees the two as cofundamental and mutually irreducible dimensions of justice. In other words, neither category is privileged, but work together.

Honneth, having affinities with Charles Taylor (1994) argues that identity politics—the struggle across the globe for recognition of unique ways of being, of unique cultures—provides a suitable starting point in understanding a bona fide conceptualization of justice. In short, some conception of the good life must be incorporated in principles of distributive justice prior to understanding adequate notion of distribution or redistribution of resources. For Honneth, a recognition-based justice must incorporate some founding principles. He identifies three elements of recognition—love, law, and achievement—love as an intersubjective quality expressed in family and personal relationships, law concerns recognition in the legal sense, and achievement more in the economic and public sphere. Care and love, if not provided early in a child's upbringing, will produce dysfunctional forms of recognition of the other. Recognition and respect for the autonomy of the other in the form of the equality principle must be assured in law in terms of specific rights. And persons must be able to attain social esteem through individual achievement. He also entertains the possibility of a fourth founding principle, which recognizes individuals as members of cultural communities, but after some analysis, restates his position that it is love, legal equality, and merit/achievement that should be the elements of justice based on recognition. These would ultimately contribute to individualization and to social inclusion. People would not only undergo continuous self-actualization/realization but they would also be respected in a society with their unique differences. In short, one recognizes the other, while also being recognized by the other as explained also by Hegel (1977). It is only when each of us recognizes the other that self-realization may be enhanced.

Nancy Fraser sees things differently. She wants to simultaneously focus on the distribution of resources as well as claims to recognition, especially those oriented around race, sex, ethnicity, and gender differences. She states from the outset that recognition does not need to go into specifying the constitutive elements, but rather can be seen as a matter of justice in itself. Thus if a person is denied status as an equal in society because of institutionalized forms of denial, then that is unjust in itself. There must be parity of participation and institutional changes that foster it. The recognition element of justice is based on justice itself, not on self-realization, Fraser tells us. But this is only one element of justice.

The other element deals with redistribution of resources. In her words, "a theory of justice must reach beyond cultural value patterns to examine the structure of capitalism. It must ask whether economic mechanisms that are relatively decoupled from structures of prestige and that operate in a relatively autonomous way impede parity of participation in social life" (35). The two principles, one based on recognition, the other based on distribution, are connected. She traces these principles as already implicit in folk paradigms of justice, our everyday intuitive understandings.

Fraser's project is rooted in pragmatism and discourse ethics, pragmatics because she privileges contexts and discourse ethics because she does not found her principles on foundational principles (a form of essentialism) but rather by providing parity in participation where justice would emerge out of the process as each recognizes in ongoing discourse the other as equal. This has some affinities with Habermas's call for an ideal speech situation and the potential to establish consensus. In other words, specific components of justice would emerge out of this state of affairs and one does not in advance have to describe what they in fact are as in Honneth's essential notions of care/love, legal equality, and merit/achievement.

Fraser also tells us that globalism has intensified differences and inequalities, and hence the salience of a two-dimensional notion of justice is necessary. Her approach does not need an ethical dimension of justice, the good life that Honneth sees as an essential component; rather, participants in parity will decide what the good life is in pragmatic encounters, in discourse in social institutions respecting parity of participation. Honneth's response would be that yes, Habermas's initiative toward linguistically mediated interaction (discourse ethics) is important, but that it is unclear from where the eventual insights will come, whether from discourse itself, or from language's formal properties as a language (247). Honneth further argues that not all is linguistic, not all gets directly communicated in formal language; some forms of recognition simply exist in physical gestures, the nonverbal domain. In his view, any participatory parity includes implicit ethical principles of the good; parity does not exist in a vacuum. Fraser, again, argues that we need not state at the outset foundational elements of justice, but to let them emerge in context, pragmatically, in discourse where each person in the encounter has institutional assurances of parity.

Others have offered critical engagement, perhaps the most poignant being critical race and postcolonial theorists. Thus prior to Honneth's struggle for recognition, the question arises, for example, of racial impediments brought about by racial ordering (Bannerji, 2000; Oliver, 2001; Puwar, 2004; Swanson, 2005; Almeida, 2013; Bonilla-Silva 2017). Here, recognizing the other, the colonial or white master, but only being recognized back as an inferior, the slave, is hardly recognition. "What does the intersubjective component of Honneth's recognition look like if, in accordance with Hegel's master-slave relationship, the white subject's existence as white depends on the non-white, non-subject who, through being conferred recognition to become a full autonomous individual subject possesses a potential threat to and can limit the white subject's freedom?" (Almeida, 2013, 85). Franz Fanon (1967) explained how in colonial society the oppressed often began to identify with the colonizer (master) to gain recognition. As to Honneth's offering of the legal component for recognition, here arguing for legal equality, critical race theory has demonstrated the obfuscations under the banner of formal equality in law pointing out class and race justice. Honneth's third component, achievement, has been criticized for once again establishing the standards of value and achievement from white and colonizer's cultural reference points (Almeida, 2013, 88; Schaap, 2004). Postmodernists Jacques Derrida and Jean-Francois Lyotard have pointed out that the "différand," the left out, is embedded in everyday linguistic practices (we shall return to the postmodernist in a later chapter).

Nancy Fraser's position has also been the basis of much discussion (see useful highlights by Swanson, 2005; Thompson, 2005; see also Young, 2000; and discussion between Fraser, 1997 and Butler, 1997b). The notion of social structure, reminiscent of our early discussion on various forms of Marxist perspectives, returns as a basis of discussion, particularly the relation of culture to economics (capitalism), and hence a fuller understanding of distribution *and* recognition attained through resistance and struggle. For Swanson (2005, 100) the task is to encourage or cultivate a movement by which those in struggle for recognition and redistribution identify with "new, emancipatory social formations" that emerge in historical development. We will have occasion in later chapters to revisit this call, including Michael Hardt and Antonio Negri on the "multitude" and the "commonwealth."

REVIEW QUESTIONS

1. Durkheim, Weber, and Marx express differences on the development of the contract and the embedded distributive principle of justice. But there are also some commonalities. Can you articulate the commonalities? Consider possible commonalities with Durkheim's "social value."

2. There is a difference between formal equality and substantive equality. Work with one or two other people in the class to develop an explanation of the difference. Then offer at least two examples of how these different equalities function in our current society.

3. Compare each of Miller's three scenarios to each of the three classic sociologists. Where are agreements? Where are disagreements?

4. The capability and needs approaches have some compatibility and some differences. Can you explain them?

5. Marx's principle of distributive justice in political economies argues that both abilities (production) and needs (distributive principle) are intimately connected. How so? Discuss these connections with at least one other person in class and work together to explain these connections, offering at least one example from our current society.

6. Rawls grounds his principles on a hypothetical "original position" and a "veil of ignorance." What is the value of grounding this approach in this way? What are some criticisms?

7. The U.S. Supreme Court, in *Plessy v. Ferguson* (1896) concluded with a distributive principle "separate but equal." Engage, in turn, need, equality (include capabilities equality), and desert, and explain,

from the perspective of each, the problem with this conclusion by the high court.

8. Affirmative action in higher education brings out the tension between formal equality, desert, needs. Consult *Fisher v. University of Texas*, 2016. Identify which principle was more dominant. Sometimes it remains more hidden and you will have to read in between the lines. Compare the majority's with the minority's decision.

CHAPTER 4

Retributive Justice

DISTRIBUTIVE JUSTICE has to do with how resources in a society are fairly distributed. Retributive justice, however, starts with a violation committed and then attempts to devise the just response. Retributive justice can be used in two senses: it can refer to an eye for an eye, a tooth for a tooth type of punishment, or a response to harm that includes, but is not limited to, retribution. Here, we are concerned with the second sense.

DEFINING CRIME

In discussing retributive justice, a key question at the outset has to do with how one is defining crime. Is it merely the definition of crime that the state identifies in law? Or is this too narrow a consideration of the variety of harm that exists?

The definition of crime that is most often assumed in the discussions of retributive justice is the legalistic (see Tappan, 1947, in Lanier et al., 2015, 15). This is the dominant conceptualization employed by our criminal justice system. It reads: "Crime is an intentional act in violation of the criminal law (statutory and case law), committed without defense or excuse, and penalized by the state as a felony or misdemeanor." For a crime to be so legally, one must show: that both *mens rea* (state of mind; criminal intent) and *actus reas* (the act) existed, that a particular law was violated, that there was no defense or excuse (duress, insanity, necessity), and that there is a formal penalty attached (a misdemeanor is anything punishable up to a year and the time spent is in jail; a felony is punishable by more than a year and time spent is in prison). Many critical scholars, however, have noted that merely using this definition overlooks other forms of harm; some, indeed, have argued that by using the state definition of crime we are extending class justice whereby crimes of the powerful receive less harsh response than crimes of the powerless.

Several alternative definitions emerged due to the perceived narrowness of the legalistic definition (Lanier et al., 2015). Schwendinger and Schwendinger (2001) have provided the following: "any person, social system, or social relationship that denied or abrogated basic rights to anyone are criminal" (88). Thus persons, social systems, or social relationships that deny in some way these basic rights to others are criminal. Another approach is the crime prism (Lanier et al., 2015); it indicates how crime is commonly perceived and the conventionally understood acceptable responses. It indicates the differential response to and understanding of crimes of the powerful as opposed to crimes of the powerless.

Another definition of harm is the constitutive definition: "the expression of some agency's energy to make a difference to others and it is the exclusion of those others who in the instant are rendered powerless to maintain or express their humanity" (Milovanovic and Henry, 2018). By "agency" is meant "those who invest energy [excessive investors] in denying others through harms of reduction or repression." Agents might include human beings, social systems, groups, agents of social control (i.e., police), the state, etc. Two forms of crime are specified: crimes of reduction (reducing a person from a status s/he once had) and crimes of repression (denying the person the ability to self-actualize). The issue here concerns the justness, the fairness of a response to a human being's actions. To answer this appeal, some justification for punishment or particular interventions must be provided.

Given our acceptance of a definition of crime we move to the second-order question of what constitutes punishment? The definition of punishment itself is often vague and illusive. Antony Flew (1979) has provided a useful beginning in specifying five elements. First, "it must be an evil, an unpleasantness, to the victim" (32). The victim referenced here is the victim of the punishment and supposed perpetrator of the crime. Second, it must be defined as an offence in the sense that the punishment would be offensive to the recipient. Third, it must be directed to an offender. Fourth, it focuses on human agency in inflicting penalties. Many penalties (negative consequences) for conduct exist, but it is only where a state or some institutional body inflicts the pain and suffering that there is punishment. In other words, in our everyday activity we can blame circumstances, accidents, and God for our misfortunes, but it is only where human agency (i.e., the will of a state through its representatives) inflicts pain and suffering that we have punishment. And fifth, some designated authority, some legitimately conceived body and its constituted laws are necessary for its infliction.

TRADITIONAL PHILOSOPHIES OF PUNISHMENT

In arguing for a justification for punishment, one is providing a reason for a particular form of intervention (Flew, 1979, 35). The reason offered is connected with the definition of crime employed and supporting assumptions of what is defined to be just.

Deterrence

This philosophy of punishment assumes individual free will, responsibility for actions, hedonism, and utilitarianism. Individuals have choices available and rationally decide to act one way as opposed to another. Many of these assumptions were developed and stabilized during the Enlightenment period. Cesare Beccaria (1986) best expressed many of these voices in his book *On Crimes and Punishment*, originally published in 1764. The classic school of criminology, which was derived from it, embraced many of these core assumptions (circa 1700s to early 1800s). In this model individuals are constantly engaging in rational calculations to maximize benefits and to avoid pain. Accordingly, deterrence theory assumes that if this is so, then all the sovereign needs to do is to make it clear that for certain contemplated activities certain negative consequences will be forthcoming. Since people weigh benefits versus pain, they will move toward pleasure maximization. In this model, we punish to threaten. It is thus future oriented. Punishing someone (ironically, acknowledgement of the failure of this logic) is a means to deter others (e.g., general deterrence) and to deter that person from committing future crimes (e.g., individual deterrence). In this model justice is captured by the notion "let the punishment fit the crime." For deterrence theorists, punishment is not a good in and of itself, it is an evil; but it is good to the extent that it deters future harms and it is a "moral educator" (Hawkins, 1979, 120).

Retribution

In retribution, society punishes a person because they broke the law, are culpable, and deserve punishment. It is backward-looking to the extent that the lawbreaker's degree of culpability is assessed. It is not forward-looking in terms of primarily justifying punishment in terms of the future good. This justification assumes individual responsibility, free will, hedonism, and a rational calculator (utilitarianism). As was the case with deterrence theory, many of the core assumptions of human nature were developed and stabilized during the Enlightenment period. In this justification a law breaker deserves punishment in proportion to the crime committed. It calls for: let the punishment fit the crime. Justice demands equal suffering. In this model the language is one that includes culpability, deserts, blameworthiness, atonement, and expiation. From *Webster's Dictionary*, expiation is the "act of making satisfaction or atonement for a crime or fault; the extinguishment of guilt by suffering or penalty." "Atonement" means "the state of, or act of bringing into concord, restoration of friendly relations." In its most raw statement, retribution is *lex talionis*, an eye for an eye and a tooth for a tooth. The question is always, given the person's degree of culpability in committing a crime, what is the appropriate desert?

Rehabilitation

This response assumes that a person is formed by forces beyond their control. These forces can be internal (biological), external (social factors), or both. Free will does not exist. Hence, *mens rea* should wither away; it does not make sense in this model. Since people and their behavior are determined by forces beyond their control, the natural consequence should not be punishment, but rehabilitation, since they did not will their crime. This approach is forward-looking in so much as the concern is to reform the person for the future good. In this model the call is: let the punishment fit the criminal. This acknowledges individual variation. Note the substitution of criminal for crime.

The positive school in criminology embraced this model during the mid-1800s up to the early 1970s. The development of the sciences and the scientific method in the mid to the latter part of the 1800s led to the belief that for all phenomena, including crime, there must be some antecedent cause(s). The ideal was to discover the laws that govern human interaction. Crime is a symptom in this model; the assumption is that there is some underlying disease. This is the medical model. Thus, experts (psychiatrists, psychologists, social workers, etc.) are more involved in the criminal justice system's concern with what to do with the offender. There is a wide exercise of excuses, justifications, and defenses such as duress and insanity. The entrapment defense, for example, acknowledges the potential overbearing and determinate nature of particular police-created environments (i.e., sting operations). Similarly, police station house interrogations have been acknowledged by the courts in possibly creating excessive forces for incriminating oneself. The insanity defense also has a wide appeal in this approach.

In this view, varied sentences allow the prison system needed time to work and rehabilitate the offender. The time necessary for rehabilitation would vary depending primarily on the offender and their psychological makeup. Hence, indeterminate sentencing (open sentencing) is a derivative of this logic. A person would be sentenced to, say, five to fifteen, two to twelve, ten to twenty. The rationale was to give correctional authorities time to work with the individual. Decision for release then moves to a parole board. The overall response, in this model, is ostensibly therapeutic, not punitive.

Social Defense (Incapacitation)

The final model justifies intervention or response in terms of protecting society. The offender is seen as a danger to the society as a whole. The concern is with the dangerous tendencies and/or violent tendencies of the

person. Various laws try and focus on sexual psychopath, defective delin-
quents, the criminally insane, sexually dangerous/violent persons (see, for
example, 18 U.S. Code 4248). Instruments are valued that can predict dan-
gerousness. In this model, the response is less concerned with why one has
committed a crime and more with how to protect society from similar acts.
The language employed by the sovereign, then, is quasi-medical. One asks:
what is the appropriate measure, consequence, or provision that is compatible with this offender so that society can be spared victimization?

In *Crime, Responsibility, and Prevention*, Barbara Wooton (1979) argues
against looking at the motivation of the offender in the determination of
how to respond to the offender. "If the object of the criminal law is to prevent the occurrence of socially damaging actions, it would be absurd to
turn a blind eye to those which were due to carelessness, negligence or even
accident. The question of motivation is *in the first instance* irrelevant" (Gerber and McAnany, 1979, 168). Wooton argues that the person who has been
found totally irresponsible or "wholly incapable of controlling his action,"
is still a danger to society. It is the future risk that is the concern of society.
The verdict guilty but insane is exemplary.

Wooton (1979) therefore advocates a two-step model. The first trial
would concentrate only on the question of whether the suspect did the
crime or not. This is a case of strict liability. The second stage would determine the appropriate response or measure. For some, it may be rehabilitation; for others, it might be punishment; yet for others, some combination
of measures. According to Wooton, in this model there would be a blur
between prison and hospital. It therefore is a quasi-medical model. There is
a shift from legal responsibility to a social responsibility (see Newman, 2017).

Perhaps the clearest use of social defense in contemporary society is
with the release of convicted sexual offenders. Given their high recidivism
rates, many states now place their whereabouts, their pictures, and some
details on a public website. Indefinite civil commitment proceedings against
convicted sexual offenders approaching the expiration of criminal sentences
are a related contemporary practice (see *Kansas v. Hendricks*, 1997; *Kansas v.
Crane*, 2002; and White, 2004). In these cases a convicted offender com-
pletes a criminal sentence only to find that at the end, that civil commitment proceedings result in indefinite incarceration until such time that it is
proven that they no longer present a danger (see also *People v. McDougle*,
1999; *People v. Burns*, 2004).

PROCEDURAL JUSTICE: THE BATTLE MODEL

We often make distinctions between procedural and substantive justice.
Procedural justice is the process involved in responding to harm, whereas
substantive justice includes factors that lie outside formal equality or formal

rationality (i.e., equal protection clause of the U.S. Constitution). Substantive justice, for example, on the one hand might invoke differential needs or necessity of remedying past historical injustices (i.e., racism); on the other hand, it may focus on plea bargaining ("let's make a deal") under the name of efficiency, finality, and crime control.

Criminal justice in common practice witnesses competing models in justice rendering. Two models developed in a widely influential book by Packer (1998) described the values supportive of each. The first model that we will address here is the "crime control model," which looks very much like substantive rationality, or even the substantive irrationality model (see Max Weber, chapter 3). The second model, termed the "due process model," looks very much like what Weber described as formal rationality. Packer argues that these are two extremes along a continuum. At the substantive rationality end of the spectrum, the underlying understanding of justice is concerned with controlling crime through swift response to infractions. Policies and procedures are almost a nuisance to getting to justice. At the formal rationality end of the spectrum, the focus is on policy and procedure to prevent or correct mistakes that are assumed possible. As ideal types these models are useful in understanding the dynamics of justice rendering in criminal justice systems. Packer cautions us that various actors in the criminal justice system—police, lawyers, judges, prosecutors, lawmakers—often, in their daily activities, do not consciously reflect and articulate the values intrinsic to each; nor should they be seen as incorporating all values at a particular time.

Crime Control Model

This model places the highest value in repressing criminal conduct. It is concerned with ferreting out crime as quickly and as trouble free as possible (Packer, 1998, 12–16). Not enforcing laws will lead to disrespect, promoting plentiful transgressions. In this situation, overall liberty will be in jeopardy. Thus the criminal justice system must valorize efficiency: to identify suspects, to screen those who are probably guilty, to procure guilt, and to process the offender as quickly and definitively as possible.

To succeed, this model must maximize efficiency rates (i.e., clearance rates) in apprehension, convictions, and dispositions. Speed and finality, according to Packer, are what provide high conviction rates. "Speed, in turn, depends on informality and on uniformity; finality depends on minimizing the occasions for challenge. The process must not be cluttered up with ceremonious rituals that do not advance the progress of a case" (13). Informality in police interrogations and in further processing is said to move the assembly line best. And uniformity assures efficiency: "Routine, stereotyped procedures are essential if large numbers are being handled" (13).

What best fits this model is an assembly line: "The image that comes to mind is an assembly line conveyor belt down which moves an endless stream of cases, never stopping, carrying the cases to workers who stand at fixed stations and who perform on each case as it comes by the same small but essential operation that brings it one step closer to being a finished product, or, to exchange the metaphor for the reality, a closed file" (13). Thus decision-making by the various officials who process the case must operate routinely. The assembly line must not be stopped, nor slowed down, otherwise efficiency will be jeopardized.

The working presumption throughout this process is one of guilt, contrary to the value of presumption of innocence until proven guilty. Each operative who makes a decision to move the case along does so by determining the probability of guilt or innocence. The underlying presumption is that the everyday practices of police and prosecutors are reliable indicators of probable guilt. There is a valorization in confiding with police and prosecutors in their informal determinations of guilt.

Plea bargaining is one example of processing those presumed guilty in an efficient and informal manner. In large city courts 90 percent or more of the cases have guilty pleas and most are because of plea bargaining. It is an informal process in which the prosecutor and defense counselor attempt to come up with a deal in which the defendant pleads guilty in exchange for a more lenient sentence. To move the assembly line during court backlogs, the prosecutor can make better offers for the defendant to plead guilty, even adding additional charges for incentive to accept. The defendant, on the other hand, will hold out for a better deal. Here the courts (prosecutors, district attorneys) will attempt to reduce the case load (and increase their batting average and the appearance of crimes being solved) by making a deal by which they will alleviate the court of further processing.

Due Process Model

This model has very different notions of justice. According to Packer, "If the Crime Control Model resembles an assembly line, the Due Process Model looks very much like an obstacle course" (1998, 16). In this model, formality, not informality is of the highest value. Justice demands higher principles than efficiency. There is constant vigilance concerning the possibility of human error, in reportage, in witness recollection, in interpreting physical evidence. "The Due Process Model insists on the prevention and elimination of mistakes to the extent possible" (17). Since formal fact-finding proceedings are always open to appeal and reconsideration, the demands for finality in this model are low. Rather than conducting informal processing, the value is on adversarial fact-finding procedures where opposing parties, the prosecutor and the defense counselor, battle it out for the truth at every critical stage of the proceedings.

The due process model's underlying working presumption is innocent until proven guilty. Thus, there is a valorization of the high standard, proof beyond a reasonable doubt. In much contemporary discussion on capital punishment, there is a call for an even higher standard when the death penalty can be inflicted: guilt without doubt. This model operates to protect the factually innocent and convict the factually guilty. Packer's metaphor is one of quality control exercised in factories: "The Due Process Model resembles a factory that has to devote a substantial part of its input to quality control. This necessarily cuts down on quantitative output" (17).

The due process model is wary of governmental power. It recognizes that the stigma of being convicted of crime and the collateral damage that follows (restrictions on employment, voting, holding office, certain business transactions, etc.) can be substantial and lifelong. Efficiency can lead to abuse: "maximal efficiency means maximal tyranny" (18). Thus, efficiency is sacrificed to a degree to assure that maximal liberties are maintained.

The due process model places a priority on formal equality. Financial differences should not be the basis of justice rendering. Thus legal access should be available to all; in cases of the indigent, government resources need to be drawn upon. Thus, before entering a plea, the defendant should have legal representation. Nevertheless, Packer (1998) states some pessimism about the relation of representation and financial means and to justice rendering: "It [his equality norm] has made its appearance on the scene comparatively late, and has therefore encountered a system in which the relative financial inability of most persons accused of crime results in treatment very different from that accorded the small minority of the financially capable" (21).

There is skepticism in this model about justice rendering. Cries of injustice must therefore remain an ongoing concern and a basis of continuous scrutiny of decision-making processes as a check on power.

Differences in Process, Not in Substance

While these models have their differences, they are both reactive in nature and retribution focused. They seek to locate and punish offenders, though through different processes. Because of the focus on battle in these two models they are often exemplified in popular drama (for a good summary, see Ranker, N.D.). Think of the introduction to the long-running TV franchise *Law and Order*. "In the criminal justice system, the people are represented by two separate but equally important groups: The police, who investigate crime, and the district attorneys, who prosecute the offenders" (Wikiquote, 2018). The police often exemplify crime control working to quickly catch the criminal often cutting corners and breaking rules. The district attorneys are characterized as following the law and fixing earlier mistakes by the police to put forward a strong prosecution. Dramas such as these rarely look beyond two parts of the system or question which people this system represents or whether the system is working toward justice. Substantive justice looks beyond guilt or innocence and queries alternatives in locating justice. We will see the development of that sort of focus later in the chapter.

PROCEDURAL JUSTICE: ACTUARIAL JUSTICE

Actuarial justice has recently emerged as a focal point in criminal justice. It places a premium on prediction in criminal justice processing. It has affinities with the crime control model. In this model, the criminal justice system focuses on maximizing efficiency in processing. Externally, it is focused on minimizing risks and maximizing safety. It argues for security and prevention and has ushered in risk management. Rather than a focus on such conceptions of justice as equity or individualized justice, the focus is on statistical analysis and probability theory (Kraska, 2004, 280, 303).

The central figure in this model is the actuary. This is a specialist in assessing risk by statistical examination, particularly looking at people in the aggregate. The term "actuary" is borrowed from insurance industry usage. Adherents argue we already do this in traditional criminal justice processing in such standards as probable cause, beyond a reasonable doubt, preponderance of evidence, clear and convincing. A number of theorists have noted actuarial development (Ericson and Haggerty, 1997; Feeley and Simon, 1994, 2004; Haggerty and Ericson, 2006; O'Malley, 1992, 1996, 1999, 2004; Kraska, 2004; Zinger, 2004). Some have built on insights concerning the "risk society" (Beck, 1992) in late modernity. Some focus on the development of statistics that could study aggregate figures such as populations and discern patterns that exist. Yet others have traced the developed of actuarial justice to developments in capitalism (Rigakos and Hadden, 2001). With 9/11, and the passage of the Patriot's Act, the United States has increased its importance in decision-making, surveillance, profiling, selective/preventive detention, and prosecution.

There has been a flurry of empirical studies in criminology. Those who Jock Young (2011) in *The Criminological Imagination* refers to as "datasaurs" are the flagbearers of predictive models (see the continuous work of Berk, 2012), others providing key overviews (Ridgeway, 2013), yet others, quite critical (Hamilton, 2012, 2019; Starr, 2014; Ferguson, 2017a, 2017b; Rieland, 2018), particularly pointing out ethical, race, and ethnic biases. With police and the courts embracing prediction instruments, it has aptly been called a "black box justice" (Popp, 2017).

Actuarial justice has been exemplified in developments in tort law (Feeley and Simon, 2004, 303). Prior emphasis on individual responsibility (i.e., focus on fault and negligence) has given way to no-fault and strict liability. Actuarial discourse is concerned with management of risks and social utility. Police focus on hot spots and high-risk career and long-term offenders through the accumulation and use of law enforcement data. This actuarial discourse is being played out at every level. A new penology has emerged, which categorizes, segregates, and watches more intensely and ubiquitously. The new managers are versed in operations research, systems theory, and statistics (Feeley and Simon, 2004, 303, 313). Their concern is less with individuals than aggregates. Actuarial justice has been brought to bear on preventive detention (see also *United States v. Salerno*, 1987), drug courier profiles, drug testing, recidivism, probation and parole (Feeley and Simon, 1994). Actuarial risk assessment tools include base expectancy scores, level of supervision inventory, salient factor score, and statistical information on recidivism scale (see Dolan and Doyle, 2000, 304). It has also been applied to managing sex offenders, particularly sexually violent persons and sexually dangerous persons (Logan, 2000; see also *Kansas v. Hendricks*, 1997; *Kansas v. Crane* 2002; and White, 2004). A sexually violent person is someone who has "been convicted of a sexually violent offense and who suffers from a mental abnormality or personality disorder that makes the person likely to engage in predatory sexually violent offense." (see U.S.C. 14071(a) (3)(C); see also Logan, 2000). More recently, actuarial tools have been applied to fighting cybercrime (Van 2005). Van has noted that software is being developed to detect credit and Medicare fraud and hackers by the using a statistical package for the social sciences.

A number of critiques of actuarial justice have appeared in the literature, many of which concern the notion of the false positive. A false positive is a person who has been predicted to be dangerous in some way, but turns out not to be so. These studies have been rather extensive in the clinical area (see the reviews by Dolan and Doyle, 2000; see also earlier cases: *Baxstrom v. Herald*, 1966; Steadman and Cocozza, 1974; Monahan, 1984; Steadman and Cocozza 1974). The general results are an alarmingly high occurrence of false positives. Consider, for example, the classic study by Steadman and Cocozza (1974) that noted a false positive rate of 80 percent (i.e., only 20 percent had been reconvicted after a four-year follow-up study, with most for nonviolent types of harms). Dolan and Doyle (2000) summarizing Hart (1988a, 1988b) have noted deficiencies in actuarial instruments: downplaying individual variations, ignoring professional expertise, using static variables, failing to specify important variables, and their relative importance.

Further, a data problem is present. Actuaries base their models on historical data in attempts to predict the future. This is a highly scientific and complex mathematical undertaking. The assumption that the data on which these calculations are made are without bias is incorrect in most instances. These data were gathered through human judgement and actions within racist structures in the United States and other countries. Alexander (2012) documents this history in the criminal justice system and Kendi (2016) does so more broadly. Postcolonial and counter-colonial theorists (see Gabbidon, 2015; Wacquant, 2001, 2015) have explained how patterns of crime and a pool of suspects are constituted in historical, political economic practices and a legacy of slavery generating ghettos in large cities providing both a ready supply of menial workers, as well as a target population for higher surveillance and a pool of potential suspects. Over the years the ghetto has become indistinguishable from prison (Wacquant, 2001) where a cycle is established in moving from one to the other. Londono (2013) offers an analysis of racial bias in capital punishment that illustrates the underlying compounding nature of racial bias that infuses the U.S. criminal justice system at each level, resulting in extreme bias in capital cases. Utilizing data that are infused with bias similarly compounds that bias within predictive analytics. Williams (2017) warns that the history of slavery in the United States encodes whiteness with safety and black bodies as dangerous. These codes then follow throughout every calculation, no matter how scientific on their face to magnify bias while at the same time justifying continuing structural racism. Actuarial risk assessment instruments are on their face accepted by Thomas and Reingold (2017) as adding reliability to parole decisions. However, these instruments have added a layer of decision-making that should then be subject to judicial review. Parole decisions have moved from a subjective decision to an actuarial decision with no concurrent shift in review to assure just application. The reader should consider the full ramifications of the application of actuarial judgement within a criminal justice system that has consistently been found biased, particularly against people of color. Key unexamined questions remain as to how underlying and unexamined race and class factor into mathematical calculations of problem populations.

In sum, actuarial justice has as its motto: "Walk softly and carry a big . . . calculator" (Rigakos and Hadden, 2001, 75). In this procedural form of justice, individual factors are eclipsed by aggregate analyses relying on historical data.

PROCEDURAL AND SUBSTANTIVE JUSTICE: THE FAMILY MODEL

In 1970, John Griffiths wrote a provocative challenge to Packer's central assumptions. He found the crime control model and due process model to be limited approaches that incorporated the idea of a battle metaphor, hence they could be termed battle models. He suggested a family model as a third model, although he did not see this alternative being attainable in its pure form. Nevertheless, it was a suggestion offered as a way of breaking out of the limited thinking about how justice could be otherwise served—more humanely, more conciliatory, more just. Here we begin to explore substantive justice. The family model is a move away from battle and into a way of rendering justice that is concerned with the whole human being rather than only the criminal behavior exhibited.

Griffiths (1970) began his examination of Packer's battle models by addressing underlying unexamined assumptions. First, Packer is steeped deep in retribution theory as a philosophy of punishment. "The function of the criminal sanction," Packer wrote "is to help prevent or reduce socially undesirable conduct through the detection, apprehension, prosecution, and punishment of offenders" (1998, 293).

Second, Packer's model rests on an understanding of the relationship of the individual to the state in terms of irreconcilable differences of interests, of struggle, of battle. Much of this derives from Hobbes (Griffiths, 1970, 416). For the crime control model, the threats to social order and welfare are generated by self-interested human beings pursuing their self-interests. The crime control model ostensibly is primarily protecting society by favoring it in the rules of battle. In the due process model, on the other hand, the threat comes from the use of state power. Thus, rules are more favorable for the accused. In either model—the former being an assembly line form of justice, the latter, posing an obstacle course—the battle metaphor along with constitutive linguistic terminology is celebrated in conventional understanding, discussion, and policy making. In short, Packer assumes, "disharmony, fundamentally irreconcilable interests, a state of war" (371). A family model would need a new vocabulary, a new language.

Griffiths's beginning point of analysis in the practice of justice rendering is to assume "reconcilable—even mutually supportive—interests, a state of love." Griffiths looks at dynamics in the family. He notes that punishment does indeed exist. Offenses are "normal, expected occurrences." But "punishment is not something a child receives in isolation from the rest of his relationships to the family; nor is it something which presupposes or carries with it a change of status from 'child' to 'criminal child'" (376).

Similarly, drawing from sociological evidence, Griffiths (1970) argues that "crime" and the "offender" are categories, statuses, created and stabilized in society. In his review of the literature, "criminals are just people who are deemed to have offended—that we are all of us both actual and potential criminals—that 'criminals' are not a special kind and class of people with a unique relation to the state" (374). In a family model, these formal and abstract categories should wither away.

The battle model outcome is to separate, categorize, compartmentalize, and often stabilize identities. In the family model, on the other hand, when a child is punished by a parent, each knows afterward that they will continue to live as before. In the battle model there exists an exile function: the person is categorized and, through a series of status degradation ceremonies, is diminished in being (stigma) and vanquished from the community. "[O]ur attitude, after his conviction stamps him with his special status, is one of indifference" (Griffiths, 1970, 371). Moss (2013) establishes the lack of justification for incarceration within retributive models of justice supporting Griffiths's critique. In the family model there would be no exile function, no strict confinement in a particular criminal status. Instead, the substance of what is just for the larger society and the offender are considered in this model.

But to do all this, several attitudes need changing. First, a basic faith must exist with public officials to act in good faith. Second, new roles for the defense counselor should include attitudes that are cooperative, constructive, and conciliatory. "Together with the representative of the state, defense counsel would direct his energies toward assisting the tribunal to come to that decision which best incorporates and reconciles the interests of all concerned" (Griffiths, 1970, 383). Third, an attitude of respect for rights, dignity, and individuality should exist. "An offender would be perceived first and fundamentally as a *person*, rather than as a member of the special category of 'criminal'" (384). Lloyd and Whitehead (2018) offer historical insight juxtaposing the slave trade and its imposition of slave identity with current penal practices and the imposition of inmate identity. Their analysis calls for the rethinking of penal structures to recognize individual humanity in support of justice.

Conflict is indeed inevitable in a complex society with various interests clashing. And it is apparent in punitive proceedings. But we must, says Griffiths, separate ourselves from the fiction that consensus, harmony, and identity of interests can be established. Even so, we can still work for reconciling interests within a framework that does not give significance to a battle. For the transgressors whom are punished, we can still make it clear that their well-being is our concern, that we will not separate ourselves from them, and that they will be reintegrated back into the community.

Griffiths concludes by acknowledging his proposed family model is only an ideal toward which we may work. However, he does support active rethinking of how we render justice beyond battle logic. This rethinking is central to substantive justice.

RESTORATIVE JUSTICE

Restorative justice has a long history. It has gained momentum since the early 1990s and now is a much discussed topic worldwide, with various implementations of its theoretical underpinnings. In one of its early framings restorative justice stood for not only acknowledging harms committed by persons but also for the desirability for the active participation of victims and offenders in attempts to resolve the conflict (Eglash, 1977). Substantive justice is further developed in restorative justice to include both victim and offender in the process of justice rendering (Ness and Strong, 2014; Johnston, 2013).

The use of restorative justice can be traced back to the ancients. In those early years of civilization (prior to state societies), the majority of harms were not considered harms against the state or the collective. Instead, harm was understood as specifically inflicted on a victim and/or their family. The offender had to make amends with the victim and their family (Van Ness, 1990). In contemporary society, many indigenous groups still cling to this mechanism (see Van Ness and Strong, 2014). A change in ancient thinking is largely attributable to the Norman invasion of Britain. The king was to replace local and church methods of repair. In the twelfth century, the notion of the "king's peace" was established and harms done were now seen conducted against the king and his peace (Berman, 1983; Van Ness and Strong, 2014). In this scenario, the victim was to become secondary in the process of making amends. It was the state that was offended and must now be appeased. The focus switched from making the victim whole to deterring future offenses. Thus rituals of public torture, fines, and the death penalty now became the state's response.

In the eighteenth century, the idea of rehabilitation was discovered, which was to remain as an ideal in Western countries, including the United States, until perhaps the early 1970s. Foucault (1977) explained that the early forms of public torture and corporal punishment were generally replaced during the latter part of the 1700s. Inflicting pain on the body gave way to attempts at understanding the soul of the lawbreaker. However, the rehabilitation model fell in disfavor in the early 1970s. The movement returned to the classical school of thought with the emphasis on responsibility, free will, deterrence, and retribution theory. But the 1970s and 1980s saw large increases in crime and imprisonment. Recidivism rates soared. It was out of this climate that alternatives were sought. Restorative justice began to develop an appeal particularly in the early 1990s and continues to grow strong to the present.

Several movements in particular led to the establishment of restorative justice, including experiments in informal justice programs, restitution programs, victim's movements, mediation and conferencing programs, and social justice programs advocated by the Quakers (Van Ness and Strong, 2014). According to Zehr in his book *Changing Lenses* (1990) we either see things by way of a retributive justice lens or a restorative justice lens. "Crime is a violation of people and relationships. It creates obligations to make things right. Justice involves the victim, the offender, and the community in a search for solutions which promote repair, reconciliation, and reassurance" (181). Here we are witnessing a broadening of formal rationality (Weber, 1958, 1978; see chapter 3) to include substantive principles (substantive rationality, Weber) as well as a beginning call for a needs-based distributive justice. In this definition of justice, we can see the limitations of the crime control model that seeks only to locate and punish offenders where speed and finality eclipses formal rational principles found in the due process model. The crime control model, in other words, is a form of substantive rationality that has substituted its own values (speed, minimal adherence to legal formalities, finality) outside of those integral to a due process model. Restorative justice, as an alternative to the battle model, incorporates substantive justice, which is holistic, inclusive, and healing.

Armstrong (2014) laments the inability to properly define restorative justice within a retributive frame. Given the incorporation of substantive justice, retributive and restorative justice may become less compatible. Daly (2016) suggests that restorative justice can and should be defined to assure proper use and support. She is concerned for current inconsistencies in definition and practice and the problems posed in the full assessment of restorative justice. She suggests that restorative justice be conceived as a contemporary justice mechanism rather than narrowly defined. We accept these insights and offer ideas for progress herein.

There are currently several forms of restorative justice. Among the most prominent are victim–offender mediation programs where the victim and the offender meet with trained mediators to seek resolution. Family group conferencing is another important form and was legislated in New Zealand in 1989. It is now used in Australia, the United States, and in Europe. With family group conferencing, there is a facilitator, not mediator, who coordinates discussion between the offender and victim as well as family members, other groups, and police. With victim–offender panels, victims face a group of offenders who have committed a similar crime to those that the victims have suffered, such as drunken drivers (Van Ness and Strong, 2014).

There are five general elements to a restorative justice encounter: *meeting* (the offender and victim meet face-to-face); *narrative* (each presents their particular story); *emotion* (each expresses anger, fear, sorrow); *understanding* (each begins to empathize with the other); and *agreement* (some kind of resolution is attained). There are four elements to a successful resolution, or amends: apology, behavioral change, restitution, and generosity. A central focus is reintegration, meaning a return to the whole of community as a person beneficial to the community. Reintegrating communities (support groups) are especially important. Another central value is the inclusion of the victim in various stages of criminal justice processing (Van Ness and Strong, 2014).

Various objections (conceptual and practical) to restorative justice are discussed by Van Ness and Strong in the second edition of 2002, but in the most recent edition, the fifth, chapter 8 ("Conceptual Objections to Restorative Justice") and chapter 9 ("Practical Objections to Restorative Justice") have been replaced by, respectively, "Making Restorative Justice Happen" and "Toward a Restorative System." In the earlier version of the book, Van Ness and Strong provide engaged answers to questions raised about the approach. Preliminary studies have indicated substantial success rates (in terms of happiness with results, recidivism rates, and feeling of involvement, among others) that far exceed those attained by traditional criminal justice programs and its battle model (Braithwaite, 2002, chap. 3).

JUSTICE IN RESTORATIVE JUSTICE

Defining what constitutes justice in restorative justice programs has taken several forms, from a zero tolerance for punishment (violence still exists whether committed by an offender or in the name of correcting an offender), to a decentralized form, which includes punishment (sanctions), to seeing it as a necessary element in shaming the offender.

Restorative Justice: Needs-based Justice

In *Restorative Justice* Dennis Sullivan and Larry Tifft (2005) provided a model of justice that is heavily derived from a Kropotkin-based anarchist perspective. Any form of violence, whether committed by a lawbreaker, or committed in the name of responding to a lawbreaker for deterrence or retributivist purposes, is illegitimate. The latter are power-based methods of corrections. According to Sullivan and Tifft, "the best way to respond to violence and other forms of harm—whether defined by the state as harmful or not—is to respond to harm-situations primarily in personal terms, in terms of the suffering and misery they have created for those affected by the violence (viii)." Thus, healing by way of apology, forgiveness, and reconciliation can take place in forums where those harmed can share their stories of loss to one another. Ostensibly the methods would rely on those "that are standard practice in the world of mediation and conflict resolution" (viii). Underlying the model is the supreme value of voluntary participation. We are left, however, without further operationalization concerning the specifics of this process and the nature of the forums.

As with Pepinsky and Quinney's (1991) peacemaking criminology, needs-based justice in restorative justice depends on restructuring current social institutions and relations from a focus of containing violence to one of supporting peace. Included in the support of peace would be the respect and recognition of the humanity of all individuals. Gill and Harrison (2013), while supporting the need for better handling of rape cases in India, note the importance of "identifying Indian society's patriarchal frameworks as the foundation upon which crimes against women occur" and further suggest reflecting "on the extent to which social attitudes and norms contribute to the climate of misogyny that feeds the commodification of women and, ultimately, violence against women" (177). The United States and other countries could benefit from the same to begin the sort of restructuring that would focus on peace and safety rather than only responding to violence.

Restorative Justice: Restorative Proportionality

Van Ness and Strong's (2002) version does include some sanctions or punishment, but it would not be unilaterally inflicted by state authority; it would be decentralized and creatively developed at the community and interpersonal level by those directly impacted by the harm. In this section we will focus on Van Ness and Strong's *Restoring Justice* since the included chapters 8 and 9 address critiques directly. This version incorporates components of Sullivan and Tifft's proposal and attempts to operationalize the process and type of necessary programs.

The first issue in the determination of justice concerns multiple parties (victims, offenders, communities, and government) pursuing multiple goals (redress, fairness, healing, and rehabilitation) (Van Ness and Strong, 2002, 159–163). This issue, too, faces conventional criminal justice practices and poses substantial challenges. But it is precisely because restorative justice is holistic in orientation that it ostensibly can deal with multiple parties and goals. And, ultimately, justice is defined in terms of fairness: "the community process of responding to crime focuses equally but distinctly on the needs of the victim and the offender for healing and rehabilitation" (162).

This leads to the second issue of potential disparities in sanctions. "Will similar offenders receive dissimilar sanctions for the same act? . . . [and] will similar victims receive dissimilar reparation even though they suffered from the same criminal act?" (176). These authors seem to have situated the dilemma in the classic insoluble conflict posed by Weber, that is, the conflict between formal rationality and substantive rationality. This issue revolves around proportionality. Van Ness and Strong argue that restorative justice programs are similar to retributivist's philosophy in so much as it is backward-looking (retrospective)—focusing on the degree of culpability of the offender. For the retributive model the call is for the punishment to *fit* the crime, which implies proportionality. Van Ness and Strong's focus, however, is on a restorative proportionality (the term was devised by Walgrave and Geudens, 1996, 375–376). Van Ness and Strong argue that the focus would be less on traditional retribution theory (retributive proportionality) and more with the "link between the severity of the material, relational and social harm caused by the offense and the degree of restorative effort required by the offender" (Van Ness and Strong, 2002, 177). Justice, here, demands that victims, offenders, and immediate community are best situated to do this justice rendering in encounter sessions.

But what of guidelines, they ask? Inspiration can be drawn from two sources: first, current tort law, based on common law, has established a body of information whereby harms have been translated into monetary terms while considering liability factors as well as mitigating and aggravating issues (178). The second inspiration is from deserts theory. This draws particularly from the work of Von Hirsch (1993). He explains how paying off one's debt can be translated into various commodities; in other words, penalties can be brought within some equivalent measure and hence substituted for each other while still retaining the notion of proportionality (desert) in the response to harm. Thus deserts "could be established by determining the seriousness of both crime and punishment based on how each impedes the standard of living of the typical person" (Van Ness and Strong, 2002, 178). Van Ness and Strong are quick to point out that Von Hirsch focuses on typical harm inflicted by typical persons, whereas restorative justice individualizes within a holistic perspective.

These two sources of guidance would be introduced by the mediator/coordinator/facilitator, allowing the disputants to adjust their understandings or claim that a variance is necessary due to the uniqueness of the situation. These sources of guidance can also come into play during overall evaluation of the particular restorative justice program to asses to what degree agreements developed correspond with some proportionate schema, and how they compare to traditional practices in the formal criminal justice system.

Equity rather than equality is needed within restorative justice. Equality means that everyone gets a pair of shoes. Equity assures that everyone gets a pair that fits their feet. This is easier done with shoes than justice. However, differences would surely need to be considered. Johnston (2013) advises consideration for offenders' vulnerabilities within penal institutions when anticipated for those with mental illness. Within a restorative process, also, considerations for mental capacities and other differences in individual offenders would seem prudent to just outcomes.

Where differences in economics exist (i.e., differences in how much a person earns), perhaps a version of the "day-fine" used in a number of

European countries could be implemented (Wright, 1982). Given two offenders and similar harms, one making $500 a day, the other making $25 per day, a day-fine, which reflects the seriousness of the offense, might be, say, five days. Thus the first offender pays $2,500, the second $125 for the same offense. Van Ness and Strong's extension of this logic would be that, given differences in income, where the offender cannot pay the designated fine because of economics, an established compensation fund will make up the difference; and where another offender pays more than the expected, the balance would be placed in the compensation fund (179).

In short, justice in this model would certainly see some remnants of what Weber calls the insoluble conflict between justice principles stemming from formal rationality and those from substantive rationality (or irrationality). Restorative justice proponents seem to want to build in some rational measures, standards, and criteria in response to formal rationality ideology, while at the same time seeing "justice" as more unique, situational, and self-enclosed (substantive rationality/irrationality).

Restorative Justice: Reintegrating Shaming

Braithwaite, in *Crime, Shame and Reintegration* (1989), and in *Restorative Justice and Responsive Regulation* (2002), sees punishment as integral to his model of restorative justice. This is in marked contrast to a needs-based justice as developed by Sullivan and Tifft. For Braithwaite, shaming is an essential ingredient in the response to the lawbreaker. His model has a component of retribution; it is backward-looking, and shaming is in proportion to the culpability and violation. The model's second component is reintegration, hence the combined term "reintegrative shaming." For Braithwaite tolerating crime is not a solution, and shaming is necessary to show the community's displeasure for the act; at the same time, restorative justice does not want to be drawn into dynamics that sustain the status of an offender. Thus, shame and respect should work together.

Shaming can take on two forms. One form, "stigmatizing shaming," casts a more permanent status on the offender with life-long consequences, argue labeling theorists. In other words, status degradation ceremonies attached to processing, convicting, and sentencing do not have a decertification process whereby the human being returns, is restored to a full-fledged community member. "Reintegrative shaming" form of response can even be quite harshly inflicted on the offending person. But after paying their dues, after suffering the shame, they are reintegrated into the community without the status of offender. Braithwaite's theory predicts low crime rates where reintegrative shaming is the norm, and high crime rates where stigmatizing shaming exists. The latter exists because the person is more likely to find opportunities for self-expression in deviant subcultures or in illegitimate opportunity structures. He tells us his theory can work with both harms committed by the powerful (i.e., corporate offenders) as well as by the powerless. Braithwaite's thesis has been subject to extensive empirical studies indicating support for "reintegrative shaming" (for example, see tax offenders, Murphy and Harris, 2007; juvenile offenders, Kim and Gerber, 2011; drunk drivers, Dansie, 2011; cross-national homicide, Schaible and Hughes, 2011).

Braithwaite's second book builds on his first, although departing somewhat from the shaming framework. In developing guidelines for justice in practice, based on a "republican normative theory," Braithwaite tells us, "because equality for victims and equality for offenders are utterly irreconcilable, the more practical justice agenda is to guarantee victims a minimum level of care and to guarantee offenders against punishment beyond a maximum limit" (2002, 12, 126; Braithwaite and Pettit, 1990). Thus the underlying conception of justice in his republican theory and restorative justice program is that of maximizing freedom while minimizing domination. For Braithwaite, deserts theory is not a guideline and should not be part of the program (Braithwaite 2002, 126–127). "Rather, restorative justice should settle for the procedural requirement that the parties talk until they feel that peace has been restored on the basis of a discussion of all the injustices they see as relevant to the case" (126). In comparison, beginning our response with the question of: what is the correct punishment? leads back into traditional criminal justice ideology where differences and voice are obliterated.

Braithwaite also rejects notions of proportionality in punishment, even rejects the reliance on notions of abstract attributions of individual responsibility (129). He makes a distinction between passive and active responsibility. Passive responsibility is where one person holds another person responsible for certain activity. Being held responsible rather than taking responsibility is an act of domination. Having been pronounced guilty provides an opportunity to proclaim innocence and an excuse for not taking responsibility in making things right. Active responsibility, on the other hand, is the virtue of taking responsibility for putting things right. In this schema, active responsibility is encouraged. The offenders can see the consequences of the harm inflicted. "A wrongdoer taking responsibility is a morally superior outcome than being made to be responsible by an imposed sanction" (129).

Restorative justice creates a space within which active responsibility can take place and wrongs can be righted. According to Braithwaite, this space should not be restricted in terms of many of the traditional ideologies of our formal criminal justice system if genuine dialogue is to flourish. In this direction, Braithwaite argues the challenge is to develop institutions that are less dependent on lawyers, less reflective of the rich, and less occupied with anger (245). In traditional practices the victim and offender suffer additional hurts and escalation in anger, whereas evidence presented in restorative justice programs indicate emotional healing takes place both with the offender as well as with the victim.

Braithwaite closes with a call for careful and critical examination of the direction restorative justice programs are currently moving. Indeed, globalization, he tells us, is having a major effect on the further development of restorative justice. But there remain impediments. For example, feminist critiques indicate domesticating stories of violence where mediation efforts may become methods of domination (Cobb, 1997; Coker, 1999). The mediation makes private what should be public, resituating conflict from public awareness to the realm of the private, and hence the invisible, and that this reinforces gender hierarchies, where men control important resources and women do not (Astor, 1994). A counterpart to the feminist critique appears within critical race theory. Major structural changes in paving the way for restorative justice need to be addressed, and Astor advocates social movement to embrace the call (263).

Review Questions

1. What are the strengths and weaknesses of the traditional philosophies of punishment reviewed in this chapter? Are some of these philosophies better suited to particular crimes/criminals? Explain how each would best be applied and to what/whom.

2. If you were to develop a TV drama to represent justice outside the battle model, what people, institutions, etc. might you include? What kinds of crime would be your general focus? Who would the criminals be? How would victims be portrayed? Feel free to work on this project on your own or with one or two other people for class.

3. Actuarial justice relies on data mainly collected by policing and other law enforcement agencies. Find this article online: https://www.eastbayexpress.com/oakland/racial-profiling-via-nextdoor com/Content?oid=4526919. How do the experiences described in this article relate to actuarial justice? How might "false positives" be amplified by interactions described in the article? Is it safe to assume that police data do not include data related to interactions such as those described in the article? Who in the article would be most likely labeled "suspicious" by police if a call were made to them?

4. Actuarial justice, many have argued, is already being employed in the criminal justice system (i.e., decision-making standards such as probable cause, proof beyond a reasonable doubt, mere suspicion,

etc.), and hence the introduction of mathematical predictions is but a rational extension of decision-making dynamics already in existence. Those, however, engaging the negative effects in criminal justice of factors such as gender, race, ethnicity, class, and sexual preference would hesitate in accepting decision-making practices merely based on actuarial justice whether more or less formal. Explain.

5. The family model may seem familiar to you if you've been raised in a family and/or are raising children yourself. Do you find that this model would be effective for adult offenders? Explain why you feel that it would or would not work for adults.

6. As an example of needs-based justice an article was referenced dealing with the need to respond to violence against women by including steps to develop a society free of misogyny. Who else could benefit from a peace-centered world? Who would not benefit from a peace-centered world?

7. Reintegrative shaming is considered important by some who espouse restorative justice. Do a Google search and find at least one example of current or historical use of this method. Make sure that the information includes a description of the reintegrative shaming technique. Summarize the technique and then critique it based on your current knowledge of restorative justice. Does it seem to fit within the restorative model? Do you think that it will be effective? Would you add or remove anything from the technique as it is described?

CHAPTER 5

Toward Transformative Justice

RESTORATIVE JUSTICE: Restore to what? For those theorists attempting to develop an alternative to our criminal justice system and social justice understandings, restorative justice has provided an alternative. And, as currently constituted, it has raised a number of criticisms, especially from those advocating a transformative justice. The latter theorists seek to not only respond to the immediacy of the conflict or harm but also situate it in a broader framework addressing structural issues. Because restorative justice does not deal with structural issues, it has been accused of being system supporting. The glaring question is: restore to what? If structures and a particular form of community organizations reduce or repress the search for self-development and actualization, then, the transformative theorists argue, simply to "restore" relations to this previous state is by itself contributing to the sustaining of reductive or repressive practices.

An example of restoration to repression versus transformation to justice may be contained in the response to Hurricane Katrina, which devastated New Orleans and much of the southern United States in September 2005. Whereas the hurricane itself was destructive, the flooding that followed the failure of the levee system in New Orleans was perhaps the most injurious force. Also, glaringly harmful and more globally damaging was the abandonment of the city's and region's poor to fend for themselves in the face of these natural and human made disasters. A similar disaster and lack of proper response occurred in Puerto Rico when two Category 5 hurricanes devastated the island within weeks of each other. On September 7, 2017, the eye of Hurricane Irma passed just north of the island, and then on September 20, Hurricane Maria, directly hit and crossed the island. Environmental Justice in Chapter 7 will in part address the conditions that lead to extreme storms such as Katrina, Irma, and Maria. For now, we will deal briefly with the aftermath of these storms.

The island of Puerto Rico is an unincorporated territory of the United States with even lesser access to supports than residents of New Orleans in the state of Louisiana; the trajectory of recovery, however, appears similar.

Sovacool, Tan-Mullins, and Abrahamse (2018) compared recoveries follow-ing four global disasters, including Katrina, concluding that four processes are consistent within each. While they did not look at Puerto Rico post Irma/Maria, the same four processes are already in place. These are enclo-sure, exclusion, encroachment, and entrenchment. Enclosure refers to the taking of profit by private entities from public operations. Exclusion includes the nonsupport of residents in need who are often forced to leave their homes in search of basic necessities. Encroachment is the relaxing of envi-ronmental standards to allow for repairs and other building as part of the recovery effort. And, entrenchment is the abandonment of poor and minor-ity communities while at the same time supporting private developers.

At this writing, the recovery in Puerto Rico is ongoing; a recent article in the *Chicago Tribune* announced "'Better than Before' Puerto Rico's Recovery is Nearly Complete" (Sachs, 2018), surprising one of the authors here (LC) who has been living on the island for several months experienc-ing the lack of progress toward recovery firsthand. The article reads much like the local hype from politicians and wealthy developers. It focuses on a grand old hotel in San Juan that is frequented by the rich and famous while briefly allowing that "[m]uch work remains, especially in residential areas, but Puerto Rico has made great strides in all categories of travel." While things are better in most places than the days immediately following the hurricanes, it has become normal for households to buy individual water and power backup systems, if those can be afforded. Those who cannot afford these systems often do without power and water during the frequent breakdowns of each system. This reality privatizes to individual responsibil-ity what once was in Puerto Rico and is in most of the United States a gov-ernmental responsibility. If Puerto Rico follows the patterns seen in other post disaster communities, privatization of formerly social responsibilities will intensify in the coming months and years at great expense to the people and to the great profit of private entities (Sovacool, Tan-Mullins, and Abra-hamse, 2018).

Restoration following a hurricane typically is done at the individual level with the replacement of lost goods and housing by insurance, govern-mental assistance, and/or other individual/group efforts. The restoration of individuals was confounded in the wake of Katrina given the neglect of the levee system and necessity of restoring it to a far better condition in order to assure future reliance. In Puerto Rico, the continuing colonial status of the island along with the debt burden that this relationship has imposed has cre-ated multiple barriers to recovery. Transformative justice will require inde-pendence and self-determination for the island and either a forgiving of the debt or a placing of that debt burden on the bondholders who created it (Walsh, 2015). Puerto Ricans living on the island have no vote in U.S.

presidential elections and had no say in the board that is currently empowered to oversee debt repayment. Yet, they are made to endure the insults of a president throwing paper towels at them, refusal to recognize immense loss of life, and tweets against a popular mayor by a president who they did not have the opportunity to vote for or against, as well as the increased taxes, threats against pensions, and school closings imposed in service to debt payments to wealthy bondholders. The restoration of trust in New Orleans and Puerto Rico will require a transformation of the system that neglected infrastructure at the great expense of people (especially the poor among which women, African Americans, and other nonwhites are overrepresented) to a system that places human need and safety at the center of decisions. This transformation will require the rejection of all colonial and racist notions infused in the current structure.

In both New Orleans and Puerto Rico we can plainly see that restoration to the previous condition is far from adequate for justice. We invite the reader to consider the progress made toward justice in New Orleans and Puerto Rico. Has there been a restoration? To what extent has restoration occurred? Has a transformation occurred? Have these restorations and/or transformations brought justice? If not, what is necessary? Consider these questions again following your completion of this chapter to see if your ideas have changed in response to the ideas offered here. Films focusing on the aftermath of the storms in New Orleans and Puerto Rico have been produced by Spike Lee (2006) and Naomi Klein (2018), respectively, and may be of interest.

SELECTED FORMAL CRITIQUES
OF RESTORATIVE JUSTICE

Let us review some of the more outstanding critiques levied against restorative justice (RJ). We do this only to set up a possible framework for what transformative justice might look like. Assuredly, for the transformative justice theorists, particular components for RJ may, with some modification, also be elements of a transformative justice. Apart from detailed responses by advocates of RJ to raised concerns (see, for example, Van Ness and Strong's eight conceptual and five "practical objections, 2014, 156–183, 185–203).

A first group of critiques has been raised by Ruth Morris (2000, 1–19; see also Harris, 2006, 557–558), who earlier had embraced RJ. She argues: it needs to go further in its suggestions; it begs the question, "restorative to what?" (do we seriously want to "restore offenders to the marginalized, enraged, disempowered condition most were in just before the offense?"); that RJ implies we had justice at some point in the past and we can return to it overlooking that many people processed by the criminal justice system have been "victims of distributive injustice" (i.e., gender, class, race, and intersectional biases); that central concepts of RJ have been coopted by the criminal justice system by reinstating punitive dimensions; that mediation efforts in RJ introduces mediation after the fact and does not sufficiently examine conditions toward changing them; that structural sources, in short, as the basis of injustices are not examined for possibilities of change, and the focus is on individuals and their harm; and that RJ restricts itself to state-defined harms without seeking broader and more inclusive dimensions.

A second group of critiques is feminist based. Three particular critiques are raised (Harris, 1989; Cobb, 1997; Coker, 1999; Braithwaite, 1989, 251–254; Daly, 2003a, 2003b; Hudson, 2002; Presser and Gaarder, 2000; Sherman, 2000; Stubbs, 2002; Gaarder and Presser, 2006). See also in the Canadian context of aboriginal justice and women (Cameron, 2006; see also 2004, 2005; Turner, 2004; MacDonald, 2001). The first concerns the "domestication" of harm. Harms are reconceptualized as "conflict," and victim rights are reconceptualized as victim's needs. Thus, diminished is the very nature and extent of the harm inflicted. The second concerns the further institutionalization of power inequalities; it highlights the concern that male domination is further reinforced, since they have greater resources at their disposal. And the third critique concerns making "private" what should be public. In other words, harms done to women are denied public awareness by being channeled into more informal processing. Harms are seen as private affairs; the harms inflicted are denied public awareness, discussion, and potential change. Thus, some feminist critiques would see RJ as maintaining continued repression of women, but in the name of an alternative to the formal criminal justice system.

The third line of critiques comes from more sociological-oriented theorists in the tradition of "conflict resolution" who oppose alternative dispute resolution (ADR). ADR arguably is not indistinguishable from restorative justice. For Scimecca (1991), ADR is inherently about social control. He summarizes six specific criticisms. First, it lacks a consistent underlying theoretical framework explaining the nature of conflict. As he tells us, "ADR emphasizes the *how* to deal with conflict, and in most instances without any real theoretical justification for *when* and *why* to use conflict intervention techniques" (274; emphasis in the original). Second, ADR is focused on the notion of the individual and individual responsibility without looking at structural inequalities and its contribution to the conflict. The individual is seen as inherently rational and able to rationally resolve conflicts. If no resolution is reached, then it must be based on irrational individuals. Third, ADR often is more concerned about "misunderstandings" rather than inequalities and power differentials in structural arrangements. This narrow focus leaves power differentials and inequalities unexamined, unattended, and unchallenged. Fourth, ADR centers on the neutrality of the mediator/facilitator in proceedings. They are concerned with compromise; the ideology is inherently supportive of the status quo. Support of the status quo is problematic to those concerned with structural injustices and inequalities. Fifth, ADR is more concerned with opening up opportunities for professionals and well-paid jobs. Sixth, ADR has been usurped by professionals; few direct connections materialize between community grassroots organizations. Scimecca does, however, qualify this criticism in advocating more expansive use of professionals that have training in collaborative problem-solving skills in conflict resolution programs. This is so because of the necessary long practice and experience needed to gain necessary skills, especially in sensitively and skillfully dealing with structural issues (Scimecca, 1991, 264–265).

Those advocating conflict resolution rather than alternative dispute resolutions have a different emphasis. For example, Burton (1979; see also Scimecca, 1991) sees conflict resolution making use of "collaborative problem-solving." A neutral third party facilitates two disputants in mediation efforts where the goal is to get to the root of the problem (Scimecca, 1991, 264–265; Burton, 1989, 1990). In other words, the disputants are not only interested in resolving the immediate conflict but want to understand the source of the problems and the possibility of preventing it from happening in the future.

A fourth group of critics come from the postmodern tradition (we will have more to say about the postmodernists and justice in chapter 9). Pavlich (1996, 2005; see also Woolford, 2010), for example, applying Foucault's (1977) idea of "disciplinary mechanisms" whereby subjects are pacified and normalized (e.g., trained to accept system directives, rules, and roles), argues that victim-offender mediation programs are ultimately system supporting (see also Schehr, 2000; Arrigo, Milovanovic, and Schehr, 2005, chapter 7). Mediators help encourage agreements that are consistent with dominant interests, values, norms, and other ideologies, celebrating work, merit, property, and authority (Schehr, 2000). Arrigo and Schehr (1998) have argued that victim-offender mediation programs rely extensively on a master discourse within which system-sustaining frames of reference are rehearsed, thus assuring predictability and stability in the programs. In other words, victims are encouraged to verbalize their hurts in the language of mediation (reconciliation, healing, restitution, responsibility, etc.). This language is already ideological and points to certain outlooks (see also Acorn, 2004; Pavlich, 2005; Woolford, 2010).

Cameron (2006), applying Foucault's notion of "disciplinary mechanisms," has shown how Western restorative justice programs (unlike aboriginally derived) function more as a "discipline of silence." In her examination of a number of Canadian court cases that have made use of "sentencing circles"—a variation of restorative justice in which the judge, victim, offender, and others participate—she finds that the female victim of violence in the family finds little verbalization in the judge's narratives of the case. The underlying assumptions with which the justices make use are often reflective of traditional opposite-sex, two-parent families. Further, the female victim is often held responsible for restoring the offender and for the prevention of further harm to herself.

A fifth basis of critique questions the notion of a "needs-based" justice. This perspective on justice was summarized in our previous chapter. A needs-based conception of justice has been given most articulate expression by Sullivan and Tifft (2005). Drawing from Kropotkin (1924), needs are defined in terms of maximizing the "expression of the voice of each [person]" (113). As they theorized: "the well-being of everyone involved in a given social situation is taken into account: that is, everyone involved is listened to, interacted with, or responded to on the basis of her or his present needs." Each person has unique needs and justice is done when they are reflected in social interactions and structural arrangements.

Other "needs" such as those developed by Maslow (1954) in his classic "hierarchy of needs" exist. Each person is born unique with certain potentialities and is not necessarily driven by greed and hedonistic factors (recall Hobbes). Thereafter they seek to actualize these potentialities. Lower-level needs (i.e., physiological and safety needs) have to be fulfilled before higher-level needs (i.e., belongingness and esteem needs) are activated. When a person is at the pinnacle of this hierarchy of needs, they self-actualize, experienced as a natural good feeling (e.g., "peak experience"). When lower-level needs are blocked, repressed, or denied by situational, community, and/or structural arrangements, the person engages in reactive behavior. Yet another version of "needs" appears in some of the literature on conflict resolution. Burton (1990), for example, has developed nine "universal" human needs. The theory is that a set of universal needs exists, and when they are thwarted, conflict arises.

The notion of "needs," however, has been critiqued by Miller (1999; see also chapter 3). He raises two general issues. First, how would a needs principle operate in a society of relative scarcity, by which is meant a society in which given individual demands, resources are not adequate (204). He refers to Marx's (1977) notion, "from each according to his ability, to each according to his need," and indicates that some theorists read this justice principle as being operative in a society of abundance, not scarcity. As Miller informs us, "my interest is in the use of the principle to establish claims of justice in circumstances where needs have to compete with other demands, and where there is no guarantee that all needs can be met." A needs principle, then, must be able to "deal with conflicts among different people's claims of need" (205).

The second reservation by Miller (1999) concerns a person's understanding of what "needs" may mean. Can people collectively in society, or in some segment of society, agree on the definition of needs? These two questions lead to several others. Which claims, in the first instance, count as needs (229)? Which needs invoke the necessity of justice? How are priorities established, given various qualifying claims? Doesn't the invocation of needs suggest some "interpersonal criteria for deciding what counts as a need" (205)? Thus, for Miller, the slogan "to each according to his needs" is problematic. Not that it is fatal, but it must address these issues. Certainly, Miller's is a call for response.

Finally, a sixth group of critiques appears under the rubric of "paradoxes of restorative justice" (Pavlich, 2005). Pavlich has argued that restorative justice is a "simultaneous attempt to offer a substitute for criminal justice while predicating . . . [itself] on (and so imitating) existing criminal justice arrangements" (14–15). He calls this the "imitor paradox." His specific examples include: that the very definition of harm that restorative justice makes use of is predicated, in the final analysis, on traditional criminal justice ideas, even in a more expansive format than offering a new way of defining harm (35); that its central thrust is often an appeal to a medical model and thus the focus is on technical issues, not ethical (35, 41); that restorative justice's concern with narratives of restoration "obliges" it to construct victim identities in a particular way to which a particular discourse will be seen as appropriate (49; see also Acorn, 2004)—in other words, victims and offenders must be "prepared" for playing a subsequent appropriate role in mediation efforts (54, 57); that "empowering" the victim does not include challenging social conditions and injustices but indirect victimhood itself and how to deal with it (60); that restorative justice attempts to convince the offender of their individual responsibilities, to accept it, which is a predicate for further "restoration" and reintegration (69, 81–82), which is precisely what the traditional criminal justice system attempts to do; that restorative justice programs, with their emphasis on the individual, are hard pressed in dealing also with the realities of certain communities with complex forms of gang violence and other social problems and hence restoring communities is hardly a pursued goal (100); and that restorative justice's notion of community assumes a consensual model and becomes potentially a model advocating the superiority of one over another form of community (102). In short, restorative justice, although seemingly offering many benefits—restoration, healing, empowering, "changing lenses," etc.—ultimately, and paradoxically, reproduces many key assumptions of traditional criminal justice.

TRANSITIONS

Instructive commentary on comparing criminal justice (retributive justice) and restorative justice in relation to a possible transformative justice was offered by two key figures in the literature (Howard Zehr and Kay Harris). Howard Zehr, author of *Changing Lenses* (1995), an icon in the restorative justice literature, has reflected on the differences in a "tweet" (2011). He tells us that he was considering the use of transformative justice in the 1980s and dismissed it for the possible contributions to practitioners as "too ephemeral" for their acceptance. He also questions the restorative justice model as "too backward-looking," and, like criminal justice, is a Band-Aid approach. But he is highly receptive to Kay Harris's work (2006). Instructive are her four different viewpoints that appear in the debates on RJ compared to TJ (summarized by Zehr, 2011; Harris, 2006, 556):

1. Restorative justice and transformative justice are distinct and should be so treated.
2. Restorative processes transform conflicts, participants, and communities, hence restorative justice can "create spaces" for transformative justice.
3. Restorative justice lies between traditional criminal justice and transformative justice.
4. Restorative justice and transformative justice are two names for the same thing, and properly understood, the terms should be considered interchangeable.

Zehr would like to believe in the fourth, but disagrees arguing they are very different. He advocates the second and third. To flesh out the differences, he, along with colleagues, have devised useful pedagogical class exercises (see Review Question 1 at the end of this chapter). It remains to be seen which of the four will dominate in the literature. It would seem that a reasonable conclusion is that transformative justice draws from some of the more useful concepts of restorative justice while resituating the field of study in a more, be it emerging, holistic perspective.

CONFLICT TRANSFORMATION

Compelling literature contends that the term conflict transformation situates the broader, umbrella perspective under which transformative justice is best understood (see, for example, McDonald and Moore, 2001). Harris (2006, 560–561) argues that some of this literature gravitates back to central concepts of restorative justice and often to individual change, perhaps at best, opening up spaces toward the development of a possible transformative justice (see second point above). For example, the favorable offering of a transformative mediation (Folger and Bush, 2014, 2015) by the editors of *Berghof Glossary on Conflict Transformation* (Austin, 2012, 49), an approach focusing on mediation that has empowerment and recognition as central components apparently going beyond problem-solving mediation, although important components, has not only undergone much internal critique, but does not address the larger issues that conflict transformation itself identifies. Nor do many of the offerings sufficiently introduce how understandings of structural sources of harm can be part of the mediation process, a "conscientization" (Paulo Freire), with outstanding exceptions in the integrate work by David Dyck (2000, 2006) to which we will return below. Folger and Bush (2014, 22) have acknowledged their hesitancy in using this term for its considerable implications. At best, it would comport with Harris's (2006) second point concerning creating spaces for social transformation. Other approaches such as conflict management and conflict resolution according to Bush and Folger are too restrictive.

One of the developers of conflict transformation, John Paul Lederach (2003) has offered a definition of the field (emphasis in the original): "conflict transformation to *envision* and *respond* to the ebb and flow of social conflict as *life-giving opportunities* for creating *constructive change processes* that reduce *violence*, increase *justice* in *direct interaction* and *social structures*, and respond to real-life problems in *human relationships*" (14). Other definitions have been offered: see *Berghof Glossary on Conflict Transformation* (Austin, 2012); the Institute for Conflict Transformation and Peacebuilding (Wikipedia.org, 2019a); TransConflict ("Principles of Conflict Transformation") (ND); and a succinct summary by Miall (2006).

Key developers of conflict transformation can be traced back to the peace and conflict studies of the late 1960s through the 1990s. But perhaps two of the most exhaustive statements are by John Paul Lederach (1995, 1997, 2003) who advocates development of a peace system as a counter to an often practiced war system (e.g., consider the battle model in criminal justice summarized in the last chapter), and Diana Francis (2010) who provides a global perspective. Recognized, too, are constructive and destructive forms of social change (Dudouet, 2006) as well as identifying agents of violent change and agents of peaceful change and their dialectical manifestations. Many central ideas appear on the continuously updated, online publication, *Berghof Handbook of Conflict Transformation*, and in *Berghof Glossary of Conflict Transformation* (Austin, 2012). The central idea is that conflict and violence are ubiquitous; that causes are multilevel, contextual, and nested in multiple levels; that culture, institutions, structures, and ideologies are necessary focuses of analysis; and that only a holistic approach engaging causes and social change will be efficacious in developing a more just society.

Important strategies for change, to which we will return, have been offered by Doudouet (2006), Lederach (2003), and Miall (2006). See generally *Berghof Handbook of Conflict Transformation*. Neglected, however, is an active engagement with the classical sociologists we have previously encountered (Durkheim, Weber, Marx), and their historical analysis of developing societies—their political economies (Feudal? Capitalism? Socialist? Communist? Commonwealth?), forms of domination, ideology, legitimation principles, internal logic (i.e., Marx's commodity fetishism and the development of formal equality as well as the abstraction, the juridical subject with distinct rights). Further, although conflict transformation theorists argue for the necessity of structural analysis of conflicts and harm, more distributive justice and retributive justice principles are less developed, often looking very much like those offered in restorative justice. On the other hand, those prioritizing mediation and problem-solving responses to harm (retributive justice) can benefit by consulting the work of conflict transformation that generally provides a more general picture of conflict at all levels from personal to global. The need to integrate the two more thoroughly stands out.

Returning to restorative justice, Sullivan and Tifft (2005, 112) make use of the needs-based notion of distributive justice, but in their view with an eye toward structural change (116–117). This is also in accord with conflict transformation's concern with basic needs (Miall, 2004, 5). However, a transformative justice would also make use of the capabilities approach to distributive justice along with a retributive model that has participatory, inclusive components of restorative justice. After all, it is not just about needs, but also about conflicts and harms that arise be they inadvertently, and perhaps a component of the complexities, contradictions, and problems in living, ubiquitous in late capitalism. Needs-based orientations and conflict-based responses are connected. In this case, some immediate action needs to take place (retributive justice) and the question becomes, what form should it take? Clearly, on this level, restorative justice has much to offer. Critical awareness is needed that a particular conflict is often rooted in larger questions of structure and various forms of harms of reduction and repression such as racism, sexism, ageism, classism, homophobia, transphobia, etc. and their intersectional forms of expression. For example, some authors (Harris, 2006; 563–564; Dyck, 2000, 2006) have argued that surface-like conflicts are nested in various levels extending from the micro, meso, and macro. Each subsystem, in this view, is related to the other, and all must be understood in a comprehensive, holistic theory. Here, again, conflict transformation literature is critical, but needs the integration of a more precisely defined notion of transformative justice offering *both* distributive principles (for example, needs-based in combination with capabilities approach) *and* retributive principles (for example, restorative justice reliance on mediation efforts). Miall (2004), as a key advocate of conflict transformation, argues, "it seeks to engage with conflict at the pre-violence and post-violence phases, and with the causes and consequences of violent conflict . . . it aims to develop capacity and to support structural change, rather than to facilitate outcomes or deliver settlements" (2). Miall's point implies both distributive and retributive dimensions of justice (see also Lederach, 2003, 48–60).

TRANSFORMATIVE JUSTICE

The notion of transformative justice has had a less-developed history than that of restorative justice and remains with contrasting definitions. Ruth Morris (1994, 2000) was one of the first to popularize the term. More recently, Van Ness and Strong (2014) provide a chapter (10) in their highly influential book that looks beyond restorative justice, "restorative justice must be ongoing transformation," (174, 180) to include transformation of persons, perspective, and structure, although many could argue that it is not a fully developed view. Sullivan and Tifft (2006) have often been better connected with advocating transformative justice, even though they also advocate a form of restorative justice based on needs. Let us briefly examine each for their contributions. In the literature, when the word *transformative* is used in connection with justice, it is often related to how individuals and communities undergo change through healing processes. The question of structure providing the framework within which we exist remains unexamined, sometimes more implicit.

Ruth Morris (1994, 2000), a Quaker who has investigated the Canadian system of justice, advocates looking at the nature of and response to crime in terms of its potential in providing insights about causes of crime and hence steps needed to prevent it. In responding to crime we also can learn about its etiology; in the response, people are transformed. The key distinguishing factor from restorative justice, for Morris, is that transformative justice focuses on the causes of harms requiring healing. She (1999, 2000) argues that traditional restorative justice approaches fall short in the response needed. She (1996) also considers structural forms of injustices such as racism. Her transformative component (2000) has been expressed as follows: "transformative justice includes victims, offenders, their families, and their communities, and invites them to use the past to dream and create a better future" (1). In this sense, hers has a future-directed component that also connects with the past and the present of the harm and its response.

Ness and Strong's (2014, 239–249) brief foray into a transformative component of restorative justice focuses on transformation of persons, perspectives, and community. Transformation of persons means that the parties involved in mediation efforts undergo change. They begin to feel healed and empowered. Transformation of perspectives means creativity in resolving harms. It incorporates risk; but through risk-taking and creative response, older patterns of responding to harm are changed into ones that heal and transform. Transformations of structures receive two pages of examination. It recognizes imbalances of power and of poverty. These inequalities can be political, economic, and social. In their words, "just as individuals must accept responsibility for their acts, so societies must assume some responsibility for the inequalities that plague them . . . to discern imbalances, inequities, or disparities that result in less justice for some, and to seek remediation and even transformation of those structures" through "healing, reconciliation, negotiation, vindication and transformation" (246). However, their version of restorative justice is primarily operative at the personal and community levels.

Perhaps the clearest expression and ongoing development of a transformative justice approach is developed in Sullivan and Tifft's (2005) work. Noting that the notion of restorative justice on its face is too restrictive, they argue for extending the focus "to take into account the 'transformative,' economic, and structural dimensions of justice: that is, the social-structural conditions that constrain our lives and affect the extent to which any one of us can live restorative lives" (34). They argue for a more holistic approach to include personal, community, and structural components in our dealing with harm. Justice exists, both distributively and retributively, when structures are responsive to our needs (95). Hence, their call is for a needs-based justice. Both rights-based justice and desert-based justice, they argue, simply accept given social hierarchical structural arrangements. Thus their emphasis is on a transformative justice that is still "restorative," but "seeks to affect social-structural, institutional arrangements, while simultaneously helping those whose lives have been affected by interpersonal conflict" (x). They are concerned with both healing and transforming social institutions (i.e., the school, family, community, and workplace—in short, a needs-based economy).

VISTAS: TOWARD HOLISTIC MODELS

In this final section we want to extend the notion of transformative justice, building on Zher's and Sullivan and Tifft's inspired work to consider, more holistically, the focus on persons, community, structure, perspective, and discourse. We should add that there is little in the way of a comprehensive view on this topic, and that what we develop below is merely suggestive as a contribution to further dialogue in this area. A fuller model of transformative justice must include both response to distributive injustices as well as the injustices of victimization (Morris, 2000).

Current use of transformative in the context of restorative justice all too often privileges the change the person is seen to undergo, at times extending this change to the community. However, a more complete meaning of transformative entails changes at the structural and discursive levels. There are two areas here that need to be addressed in a social justice approach to transformative justice: the immediate need of a response to harm (retributive justice); and, offering viable principles of distributive justice. For the latter, transformative justice would seem to have as an imperative a needs-based and/or a capabilities distributive principle. After all, unfulfilled needs and blocked opportunities for fuller development are often generators of conflict, harm, and violence. Accordingly, we will first look at the level of structural responses to harm (retributive justice). We will highlight two models of justice rendering—Black's classic models (1976) of social control and Henry and Milovanovic's (1996) addition of two structurally focused components—to see how responses to harm and justice may be connected at the various levels (persons, community, structure). We then move to Roberto Unger's work with which a reformist remedial style is accommodative. We conclude with perhaps the most ambitious and illuminating work by Andrew Woolford (2010) that provides distinct proposals in the direction of a full-fledged transformative justice.

Black's Four Styles of Social Control (Retributive Justice)

Donald Black (1976) has briefly outlined four possible responses to harms (see Table 5-1). These models operate at the individual level, and arguably at the community level. The penal style (criminal law/justice) and compensatory styles (civil law) are more connected to a battle model (Packer's crime control and due process models). The therapeutic style (rehabilitation), although a form of retributive justice, introduces a needs-based distributive justice. The conciliatory style (mediation) is more in line with restorative justice and one possible form of retributive justice. Arguably, it is connected to a needs-based distributive justice principle. Drawing from Max Weber (see chapter 3), the first two are within the domain of formal rationality, the second two, more substantive rationality.

The penal style and compensatory are collectively seen as the "accusatory styles." Here there is a zero-sum game (all or nothing) as to responsibility and punishment/payment; both have a winner or loser. This is more connected to Packer's two models, the crime control and the due process model (see chapter 3). The therapeutic and conciliatory models are collectively seen as remedial styles. They are "methods of social repair and maintenance, assistance for people in trouble" (Black 1976, 4). It is not a question of a winner and loser, but "what is necessary to ameliorate a bad situation" (4). Rather than zero-sum, it advocates variable-sum activity where responsibility

Table 5-1
Four Styles of Societal Responses

	Penal (criminal law)	Compensatory (civil law)	Therapeutic (rehabilitation)	Conciliatory (mediation)
Standard:	prohibition	obligation	normality	harmony
Problem:	guilt	debt	need	conflict
Initiation of case:	group	victim	deviant	disputants
Identity of deviant:	offender	debtor	victim	disputant
Solution:	punishment (accusatory style)	payment	help (remedial style)	resolution

Source: Adopted from Black (1976, 5)

for action is variable. The conciliatory style implicates restorative justice discussions.

Black also indicates how these various styles of social control behave in predictable ways: response is patterned. He provides propositions as to how they behave (for a student's guide, see Taylor, 2008). Thus, given a problematic event (harm, violence), a particular style could be operative that varies according to the time of day, week, month, year, and even historically. Consider, for example, how spouse battery was responded to by a conciliatory style a couple of decades past (domestic disputes), and now is handled by way of a penal style (intimate disputes/violence). Note, too, public outcries of unjust when one becomes aware of disparate treatment often invoking arguments of denial of equal protection, discrimination, prejudicial behavior, while referencing assumptions of free will, responsibility, formal equality, and just deserts.

Briefly, when we consider stratification (e.g., the differences in wealth arranged hierarchically, or socio-economic status) we see that penal law is more likely to operate in a downward direction (e.g., when we consider victim-offender differences, law applied against the lower income person) and the compensatory and therapeutic model in an upward direction (e.g., law applied against a higher income offender). Conciliatory law "varies inversely with stratification" (Black 1976, 30); the greater a society is stratified, the less likely is a conciliatory style employed and the more likely the penal, compensatory, and therapeutic model employed. Examples of differential imposition in the highly stratified U.S. society are easily recalled. The penal response to illegal drug use by the poor as opposed to the therapeutic responses to illegal drug use by the middle class and/or wealthy is one such example. While the poor are more likely to be sentenced to prison terms than treatment programs if/when caught using illicit drugs, the middle class and the wealthy are more likely to receive sentencing to treatment programs (if any sentence is imposed) than to be sentenced to prison. Consider other examples of differential imposition.

When we look at the degree of intimacy and integration, what Black calls "relational distance," he predicts that the greater the relational distance, the more likely the use of the penal, compensatory, and therapeutic styles; whereas, the less the relational distance (e.g., friends, intimates), the more likely the conciliatory style will be employed. And his "behavior of law" predicts that those on the margins of society are more likely to have the accusatory style imposed on them, whereas those more integrated will have a conciliatory style employed.

Response to Harm (Retributive Justice):
Radical Accusatory, Reformist Remedial

Close scrutiny of these models indicates that they operate at the individual but also begin to implicate the community level. Henry and Milovanovic (1996, 189) have extended the response to crime to include structural dimensions. We apply a version of theirs (see Table 5-2).

Incorporating Black's four models we can extend the responses to harms include structure thereby producing six types of response. The radical accusatory model would implicate the whole of society for harms done by individuals. Thus, what is necessitated is a radical transformation of society itself. Perhaps the Marxist model we encountered in chapter 3 is exemplary. There it was said that with the change from the socialist to the communist mode of production, a new principle of justice would arise: "from each according to his [their] abilities, to each according to his [their] needs." What would be of a high premium is sensitivity to differential abilities and needs. Justice would be very much in accord with Weber's notion of substantive rationality, or even substantive irrationality in so much as abilities and needs are unique and hence could not be brought under any equivalent measure. In other words, each person is their own standard. Impositions of criteria or standard that are universal would be repressive.

The reformist remedial style still attributes societal pathology to structural sources, but there is optimism that they can be re-engineered by various adjustments of the core institutions resulting in less harm. In other words, some version of capitalism might still be accepted, but resources, benefits, and rewards would be redistributed in a more equitable manner. Exemplary here is the work of Roberto Unger and his classic *False Necessity* (1987; see also 1996). It draws more from a Weberian approach. It is instructive as to possible alternative structures in which new principles of justice would

TABLE 5-2

Types of Responses to Harm

	Level of Intervention		
	Agent (the person)	Social-relational (community)	Structural (society)
Accusatory	Punitive accusatory	Compensatory accusatory	Radical accusatory
Remedial	Therapeutic remedial	Conciliatory remedial	Reformist remedial

SOURCE: Adopted from Henry and Milovanovic (1996, 189)

emerge and not necessarily changing the mode of production itself as in the radical accusatory style. He terms his model "superliberalism" and an "empowered democracy." His (1987) model incorporates economic and legal change as well as structural changes at the workplace. Components include:

Economic change: Establish "rotating capital fund" available for teams of works with low interest rates to be used for administration and encouraging "socially responsive investment" (34);

Workplace change: "Role jumbling" and "role defiance" (564)— rotating jobs for job enrichment, and allowing for experimentation (564);

Deviationist doctrine: Structures/bureaucracies tend toward ossification and closure resisting criticism. "Destabilization rights" would protect those who offer critique (much like "whistle blower" laws) (137);

Core Rights: These would include: immunity rights providing zones of privacy and protection, destabilizing rights protecting those who challenge the given organization, market rights that provide funds for teams of workers to engage in innovative programs, and solidarity rights established ongoing as various conflicts are resolved (520–539).

This model suggests inductive processes, e.g., ground up specifications of what constitutes justice rather than deductive logic (formal rationality). It is more pragmatically oriented. Perhaps Unger is also thinking in terms of abduction; here, such thinkers as Peirce (1931; see also Schum on abduction in "discovery" in law, 1994) argue that actual processes entail both.

Unger's model argues for increased imaginary play, creativity, challenge, and assurances of nondomination; but at the same time, this would increase the occasion for conflict. But conflict, in his model, would be an occasion not of despair, but an opportunity to understand more genuinely the other as well as self through the other. They will gain in the "ability to entertain fantasies about possible self-expression or association and to live them out. Its goal is the strenuous enlargement of enacted possibility" (579). For Unger, "the citizen of the empowered democracy is the empowered individual. He is able to accept an expanded range of conflict and revision without feeling that it threatens intolerably his most vital material and spiritual interests" (580).

Unger (1987) also suggests that the impact would be a revised notion of community. There will be a shift away from the sense of community that is based on "the sharing of values and opinions and the exclusion of conflict" (562), to an acceptance of "heightened notions of vulnerability, within which people gain a chance to resolve more fully the conflict between . . . their needs for attachment and for participation in group life and their fear of the subjugation and depersonalization with which such engagement may threat them" (562). Thus, conflict is both a threat and also something with productive possibilities. Conflict under the conditions offered by Unger, the empowerment of individuals within a community, would necessarily take on a different character than do current conflicts that take place in a highly stratified and often disjointed social structure.

Unger does not tell us how precisely these conflicts will be handled, but a transformative justice view, based on a reformist remedial model, seems quite compatible with his thoughts. In other words, he predicts greater occurrences of conflict, but assumes their resolution without specifying the appropriate mechanism. He does suggest that alternative forms of justice would arise from an alternative "empowered democracy."

To this end (conflict handling), two examples can be provided in which space is provided for the possible emergence of transformative justice, one employing a more Freirian critical pedagogy approach, the other a transformative mediation approach. These approaches would be compatible with Harris's second model in the restorative or transformative relationship reviewed above. Schehr's (2000; see also Arrigo, Milovanovic, and Schehr, 2005, 112–113) examination of juvenile's victim offender mediation program provides an additional component: critical literacy (see also Woolford, 2010, 157). In other words, using the insights of critical pedagogy (Freire 1972, 1985), Schehr (2000) and Arrigo, Milovanovic, and Schehr (2005) advocate that mediators not remain neutral, but should attempt to provide the dynamics to both empower the clients as well as to create a milieu where marginality and disenfranchisement are relevant components of discussion. Thus, a space is created within which mediation both deconstructs and reconstructs understandings of harm in the context of political, economic, and cultural institutions. Paulo Freire (1972, 1985) had called this process "conscientization," a process by which the disempowered would develop a more critical consciousness that is more sensitive to micro-macro connections and the discourses which are their expressions. "[B]y exposing youth to critical literacy as a component of restitution, the seeds of a transformative transpraxis could be planted" (Arrigo, Milovanovic, and Schehr, 2005, 112). David Dyck (2000, 2006) attempts to combine key notions from conflict transformation and Freirean forms of mediation. He highlights the importance of mediation efforts that center sources of conflict generated in class, gender, race, ethnicity systemic contexts. Normal mediation practices, he tells us, tend toward resolving the immediate conflict, restoring the prior condition. Conflict resolution not addressing deeper sources of conflict is a Band-Aid preserving the system/structure while focusing on individual pathology or issues. As Dyck (2006) tells us, "there is a tendency to define problems in shallow, simplistic, linear, cause-and-effect terms" (530) rather than seeing them in nested patterns that span the micro, meso, and macro levels (see also Dugan, 1996). Thus, Dyck integrates analysis of power differentials (Lederach, 2003) and useful mediation practices to engender conscientization. Facilitators would develop knowledge and skills of intervention and mediation practices that make visible nested structures generating conflict and bringing this knowledge into the mediation efforts. The ideal would be to promote and cultivate a "consciousness-raising, education, advocacy, and negotiation/conciliation/mediation (i.e., dialogue)" (120) that develops a structural consciousness.

The notion of transformative mediation (Bush and Folger, 2004; Folger and Bush, 2014) has also been offered for creating spaces at the relational level, but focusing on empowerment and mutual recognition, a position favorably mentioned by some advocates of conflict transformation but falling short of the Freirian approach in developing a more critical consciousness toward systems and structural change. Conflict transformation argues for a more pragmatic problem-solving format whereby the immediacy of the conflict demands that something be done (Saunders, 2003).

An example of a potential transformative justice program, one consistent with the reformist remedial style, that incorporates a middle level of intervention (meso level)—one between community and structure—, is developed by Christine Parker (1999). Her proposal connects with Unger's view of an empowered democracy and superliberalism. Although her emphasis is more traditional restorative justice, it has implications in developing a transformative justice from the ground up. Let us see how. Her definition of justice is: "those arrangements by which people can (successfully) make claims against individuals and institutions in order to advance shared ideals of social and political life" (49). Her principle is more means-oriented than ends-oriented; it deals with access and opportunity to make a claim and to be listened to in a meaningful way. She argues that in late modernity (post mid-1980s), legal disputes are increasingly centered in organizational contexts where power inequalities are ubiquitous, i.e., in schools, workplaces, families, governmental organizations, as well as community organizations (174). Parker's criterion of justice revolves around maximizing freedom as nondomination (49; see also Braithwaite, 1989, 127; Braithwaite and Petit, 1990).

Parker's specific proposal is for developing access to justice plans that should be incorporated in all large organizations. These would require an organization to: first, in consultation with those most likely to be affected, come up with a common list of possible injustices; second, establish restorative justice programs to focus on these injustices; and third, set up machinery that assures access to these forums. She also advocates external monitoring to assess improvements or a lack thereof. Increase in nondomination and increase in justice are indicative of improvement. The model encourages the development of a multiplicity of decentralized restorative justice sites, with the state being an outside monitor rather than the forum for the initial discussion of harm. As Braithwaite (1999) explains, "access to justice becomes less something the state provides, more something the state regulates others to provide" (255). Where a particular organization is not making progress, where it continuously experiences cases of similar nature, or where citizens continuously seek civil and criminal remedies, the organization will undergo closer scrutiny and penalties may be established.

Those from a transformative justice perspective would see how the emphasis on decreasing domination through access to justice plans could conceivably produce dramatic changes at various levels: persons, community, perspective, discourse, and structure. It is a suggestion that promotes a more transformative than restorative justice. The ground-up approach provides the possibility of rethinking justice, moving away from unqualified desert-based and rights-based forms of justice, and decreasing overall harms, including those committed by the state in the name of reducing harm. A new discourse would emerge and, in all likelihood, attain a degree of stability that reflects the various practices of justice rendering in multiple sites. A sense of empowerment would emerge as people harmed, regardless of rank, see that they have an ability to make a claim, have it meaningfully engaged, and have more genuine resolutions (i.e., responding to distributive justice principles of recognition, needs, capabilities, and participation). At the structural level, momentum could be built whereby we begin to deconstruct hierarchical work environments, begin to construct more fulfilling and less-dominating forms, and become more willing to engage people's unique needs.

In sum, the two more structural models, radical accusatory and reformist remedial, view the human being situated within the context of community forces, which in turn exist in the context of structural forces

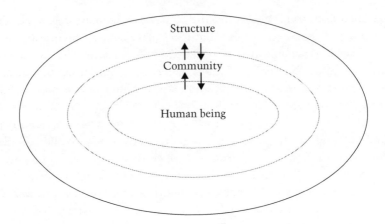

5-1. Holistic Model of Human Becoming, Community, Structure

(see Figure 5-1). Justice, in a transformative model, must acknowledge the interplay of all three levels and particularly their nested character in both distributive and retributive forms. For example, when a person commits a harm, not only is the response directed to them but also to the community and structural arrangements. A harm inflicted, then, could be conceived of as a litmus test for dysfunctional social arrangements. In responding to harm, we ask how we may sensitively consider the totality of circumstances within which it is committed. In comparison, when traditional criminal justice processing focuses entirely on the individual doing the harm, it is also saying they alone are the responsible agent. Here, structural arrangements behind poverty, discrimination, inequality, etc., remain beyond incrimination.

Constitutive Justice: Justice in Practice

In doing transformative justice, we must recognize that these nested levels (Fig. 5.1) are not separate spheres but interconnected, coproduced, and enacted in practice, as constitutive theory advocates (Milovanovic and Henry, 2018). That is, models of justice appear in everyday communicative practices. They are instantiated, or enacted, in their use. Take Black's propositions of the behavior of law as an example. When law "behaves" in a predictable direction it constitutes criminals (or not): both the person's identity who is engaged in problematic behavior and operatives' identities in the criminal justice system result from the process of law behaving where each coproduces the reality that emerges, being both contributor and end result; thus, agents coproduce a discourse that enacts the reality of how law behaves. Consider how the invocation of the penal style (criminal justice) constitutes criminal identities: the civil model, the debtor; the rehabilitation model, victim; and the conciliatory model, disputant. These identities arise from co-constitutive practices where an invocation of one style of social control produces a different identity than the enactment of another. Said in another way, a particular discourse enacted structures a particular response to harm. Reality is constituted in the process. Once certified criminal, identities are transformed, others reinforced (the police, lawyers, judge; the good guy, the bad guy). The telling of the story, invoking relevant contextual discourse, in short, is equivalent to "doing things with words" (see, for example, Gubrium and Holstein, 1997, 45–52; Wierder, 1988; and Milovanovic review of the relationship of "gangster rap music" to street codes and onset of violence, 2014, 141–44; similarly, economics does not just observe the economy but constitutes it [Callon, 1998]; journalism constitutes that which it purports to report; the criminal justice system constitutes the very deviant identities that it seeks to understand, explain, punish, and correct—in each, the agent is not passive but a coproducer). In developing a transformative justice, then, interventions must be sensitive to the interconnection and coproduction taking places in nested contexts, be they micro, meso, or macro. And be vigilant to the emergence and enactment of forces of violence as well as forces of peace.

For an understanding of how justice principles exist in practice and are interconnected at three levels, let us briefly look at an early work by Ewick and Silbey, *The Common Place of Law* (1998). They argue that legality (and we argue, justice) is not a phenomenon that simply takes place in top-down fashion, where recipients merely act out its mandates. Rather, "legality is constituted through everyday actions and practices" (43). In other words, people in various everyday practices continually construct conceptions of legality and what is just, in various contexts. Constructing reality is based not only on societal-wide mandates in law and formal principles of justice but also their nuanced understandings and iterations in contexts. Structure must be defined in terms of cultural schemas and resources that together produce patterns in social interactions. Consciousness is not an effect of structure but a constitutive part of it. That is, it is both produced by structure and coproduces structure. Legal consciousness is played out in storytelling. In their study, "people relied on culturally available narratives of law to interpret their lives and relationships . . . [t]hey combined elements of different schemas with scraps of their own biographies to forge distinctive accounts of events and relationships" (247).

A similar logic exists with the development of notions of justice. David Matza, in *Delinquency and Drift* (1964), shows how the very techniques of neutralization that juveniles use in excusing or justifying their crimes, or providing legitimate reasons for committing crimes, can be traced back to legal conceptions that have trickled down to their particular subcultures.

In their eyes, justice is not being violated in their infractions. In some cases, they are doing justice in their very infraction (e.g., rightful retaliation). Similarly, Schwendinger and Schwendinger (1985, 13) have shown that youths often incorporate an "instrumental rhetoric" (discourse), which is a form of moral rhetoric (a sense of rightness/correctness/fairness), but highly stripped of standards of fairness. This rhetoric is further traced to a survival rationalization that is embedded within capitalist economy. Between the competitiveness of capitalism at the macro level, and the decision-making at the micro level, lies this discourse, along with various others, within which everyday activity is structured.

Thus, justice in practice, much like law in practice, is a coproduced phenomenon. In its everyday production, it too reinforces dominant conceptions. Conceptions of justice move fluidly among the three levels (human being, community, and structure) and draw elements of its definition from the iterative everyday practices within each.

We could conceptualize three forms of constitutive transformative justice (TJ): conservative-conservative TJ—here parts and wholes are mutually constituted through repetition, iterative practices that reproduce the same (i.e., system/structure continue to produce conflict tendencies and maintains things as they are, even being the producer of crime itself, even sustaining a certain amount of crime for system's needs); liberal-conservative TJ—where components of intervention strategies are introduced to counter iterative practices between parts and wholes producing the same, but ultimately focusing on individual change and isolated events, strategies devoid of critical and structural consciousness; and critical-constitutive TJ—whereby the time for change is in the now, where even seemingly minor disruptions can produce disproportional effects as dynamic systems theory (chaos theory) tells us, where mediation efforts would disrupt underlying system-generating assumptions and talk, where more dissipative structures would emerge and continuously morph into the new. Dissipative structures, borrowing from chaos theory, are emergent, providing a degree of order, but sensitive to even the smallest input that can produce dissipation and transformation into a new dissipative structural form.

Comparing the reformist remedial to the radical accusatory model, it is doubtful that the reformist remedial can provide genuine justice since, often recognized in the more critical literature is that the mode of production itself generates key logics. Recall Emile Durkheim's critique of the consensual contract driven by forces of differentiation, and its expression particularly in the abnormal forms of the division of labor; Max Weber's admonishment of formal rationality driven by the forces or rationalization and systemization; and Karl Marx's point that under the capitalist mode of production driven by capital logic, insatiable accumulation of surplus value, hierarchy, and class division appear, where principles of law and justice serve the interests of the ruling class, elites, or hegemonic group. Consider, for example, the Marxian notion of fetishism of commodities, which explains the source of notions of formal equality, notwithstanding a form of late capitalism that has emerged, transformation of use-values (uniqueness) takes place to exchange-values (commonalities), and to universal equivalents (universalities). Forms of universal equivalents include the juridical subject (the legal subject, the "reasonable man in law") and formal equality. And all is given idealized expression by lawyers whether wittingly or unwittingly. Some have argued that distributive justice principles of equality and/or merit are logically connected with the capitalist mode of production and needs-based as well as capabilities-based are antithetical to this internal logic. Can a reformist remedial style pave the way for substantive changes? Thus, the open question: can genuine distributive principles of justice become centralized without a concomitant transformation of the mode of production itself (radical accusatory)? How does a transformative justice perspective come to terms with this dilemma?

Andrew Woolford: Transformative Restorative Justice

Andrew Woolford (2010) offers a compelling multilevel approach in his "transformative restorative justice" perspective that remains crucial for a more fully developed transformative justice. His work can be situated between grand theorizing on the one hand, to implementation on the other, a continuum. This encompasses conceptualization and specification of grand theories. Of course, implementation requires its own address. Woolford first critiques traditional restorative justice programs drawing much from engaging the work of George Pavlich and Michel Foucault. He moves from these constructive critiques toward a new way bringing clarity, reasoned, and highly useful directions for more genuine responses to harm. He also recognizes the necessity of developing distributive principles of justice highlighted in his review of Nancy Fraser's work on recognition, distribution, and representation. The latter remains more rudimentary, and in need further of development.

Woolford dismisses the concept of "social justice" (too static, assumes an attainable end state) and prefers transformative justice due to ongoing, process-orientation with undefined final solution; nor does he advocate developing blueprints (too rigid), arguing instead for guidelines or signposts (2010, 147–148). He builds on the work of George Pavlich calling for a re-imagining of justice (145). He first proposes a reformulation of key identities (victim, offender, facilitator, community). One needs to remember,

Woolford insists, that identities are social constructions established and re-established in everyday discourse. Second, with Nancy Fraser (2000), he proposes assessment instruments for successful transformations, and third, political strategies.

REFORMULATING IDENTITIES. The identity of victim, traditionally understood, is produced by harmful acts. Instead, victims should also be understood as situated in the context of processes: social, legal, political, i.e., definitions of harm, recognition of victimization, acceptable explanatory stories, differential labeling, and resource distribution (98). In short, a new language needs to develop about what it means to be a victim. Quick replacements like "client" come with the baggage of an economic model of choice whereby the client is a consumer of justice services and hence this ideology merely reinforces utilitarian decision-making in the marketplace (97).

The identity of offender often overlooks the underlying labeling process at work, reinforces an ideology focusing exclusively on identifiable agents, does not engage the rationalization/neutralization processes embedded in discursive practice that denies offense, and ultimately creates specific target populations as representative of harmful acts and thus brings them within the purview of disciplinary forces of law enforcement, and further reinforces the identity that an offender should take. Rather, a broader view/context should be entertained inclusive of the multilevel forces that intersect at a particular time and place producing the offender, including better understanding a person's ability to resist negative forces.

The identity of community, often a centerpiece of discussion in restorative justice, with the assumption of an in-out group and distinct boundaries, often reinforces separation. Alternative notions need to be established such as "becoming communities" (Agambam, 1993; Fraser cited in Woolford, 2010, 107) whereby community is more open, flexible, and dynamic, in continuous process of change, a becoming defying fixity and closure in structure. Drawing from Pavlich (2001), Woolford advocates the incorporation of the language of hospitality and the good host (144), whereby the other is welcomed for their unique differences and in interactions each gets to know the other, and each understands more fully oneself through understanding the other including the person who has committed harm.

Facilitators in restorative justice increasingly have undergone professionalization with its tendency toward rationalization, categorization, and technical practices reserved for professionals, not laypersons. We must, Woolford argues, seek those who bring perceptive but informal skills such as local understandings and sensitivities in empowering participants, which could better lead the way toward mutually acceptable outcomes. Formal credentials alone should not be the standard for seeking facilitators.

ASSESSMENT. Developing transformative guidelines rather than strict blueprints also needs assessments. Accordingly, Woolford turns to Nancy Fraser (2000). Three central terms concerning injustices are identified (149–153): recognition, an acknowledgment rather than misrecognizing or rendering invisible; redistribution of economic resources responding to gross inequalities; and, representation, providing voice and meaningful input, responding to exclusionary practices. Each can be examined in terms of whether it is merely affirmative in its approach, or alternatively, whether it is transformative. Thus, affirmative recognition remains superficial without addressing underlying causative patterns, whereas transformative recognition delves deeper for understanding embedded cultural and symbolic patterns of injustice; affirmative redistribution is piecemeal with only superficial distribution of payments for wrongs, whereas transformative redistribution would seek roots in historically and political economic sources that are crystallized in relations of production themselves; and finally, affirmative representation is where affected groups are provided only a token voice in decision-making bodies, whereas transformative representation seeks to correct exclusive practices of representatives and to provide meaningful input for those affected. Each of these could be seen as guideposts for the further development of transformative justice. Thus, any response to a particular instance of injustice can be assessed. Transformative approaches provide visibility to deeper structural roots and thus can become targets for social change policy. Woolford, with Fraser (1997), additionally highlights that the three injustices often intersect with various results, some, unintended, some contradictory. Consider, for example, a corporation paying a hefty sum for damages (environmental, gender/race discrimination) only to redistribute the costs to consumers in increased prices to the consumer for its product. Pursuing a more affirmative strategy in one approach and a more transformative in another might witness a cancelling out of productive results, whereas aligning all three in the transformative direction would produce greater positive effects.

STRATEGIES. Finally, Woolford (2010) offers some strategies toward the goal of making transformative justice a reality. Raising critical consciousness is one element, but also pragmatic social change must take place. Accordingly he suggests: "play to restorative strengths"—seek opportunities in social movements to engage and continuously evaluate central concepts of transformative restorative justice (TRJ); "ideas are not enough"—seek to implicate ways of incorporating central concepts of TRJ in various forums including everyday life events to build alternative methods in responding to harm; "there are opponents"—be prepared to be inclusive and incorporate vested and entrenched interests that insist on conventional responses to harm (they are part of the conversation!); "seek popular rather than professional legitimacy"—professionalization often reduces persons to pure categories for smooth systems processing and the task is to also embrace the experiential expertise of sensitive nonprofessionals and to resist incorporation and cooptation to merely formal rational logic; "link up and network"—activists must link up the central ideals of TRJ with the ongoing concerns of other activist groups and indicate commonalities and a broader understanding of common causes via, for example, the Web; "keep going"—there is no final ideal state of justice, it is ongoing and must continuously be invigorated with awareness of changing historical, economic, political, and cultural forces and with their intersectional nature; and, "commit to reflexivity"—reflexive engagement must be a continuous reflection on one's own often taken for granted thoughts, and one must be willing to rethink them toward developing higher forms of social justice (self-transformation) (157–162).

A useful dialogue is also needed with the literature on conflict transformation, which expands regional conflict analysis to the global arena. We must resist discipline or perspective closures. For a useful summary of central components for conflict transformation in practice we can consult the work of Hugh Miall (2004; see also Lederach, 1997, 2003; Dudouet, 2006). Key components include identifying phases and factors for increasing or decreasing conflict. For example, at the escalation phase, identifying escalators and de-escalators and causes and preventers of conflict at different levels: global, regional, state/society, international. At the global level, identifying causes attributed to post colonialism, whereas preventers can be organized into global minority groups. Triggers and transformers at different levels, from micro, to meso, to macro need to be identified. It is also important to identify kinds of transformations (context, structure, actor, issue, personal/elite). Changes in structure could include power structure changes in the economy, society, and/or the state. Each transformation can then be usefully related to: phases and factors that increase or decrease conflict; the various levels of the causes of conflict; and triggers of conflict and transformers at different levels. Any intervention practice is unique to each peace process. It is a recognition that both constructive conflict and destructive conflict exist and must be identified as so. We must also recognize key players, or actors in conflict transformation: "states and inter-governmental organizations; development and humanitarian organizations; international NGOs concerned with conflict prevention and transformation; and parties to the conflict and other relevant groups within the affected society" (12).

Finally, we must develop constructive assessment instruments to gauge progress as well as to be mindful of the necessity of transformations of the transformers themselves, both by way of self-reflection and spiritual engagement (16; see also Lederach, 2003).

Whereas conflict transformation has provided sensitivity to structural and systemic sources of harm and conflict while not providing a more fully and convincingly developed model incorporating transformative justice in mediation practices, transformative justice has often not sufficiently addressed the insights of conflict transformation as to the multilevel and nuanced nature of conflict and harm. David Dyck (2006) offers clear guidelines to the integration and possible synthesis of the two, particularly drawing from the work of Lederach, on the one hand, and Freire on the other. Moreover, retributive principles of justice responding to unjust practices need to be rethought to develop a more holistic transformative justice that reconciles itself with distributive principles and responds to distributive injustice (Harris, 2006, 558). This holistic model would counter the criminal justice model (battle model) that generates disempowerment, stigmatization, nonrecognition, distancing, diminishment, and separation. Transformative justice seeks to integrate retributive principles responding to all forms of harm and conflict, while acknowledging the immediacy of harms, need for redress, resolution, empowerment, recognition, and a necessity for a structural consciousness, and distributive principles that are redistributive in form, addressing needs and capabilities sensitive to diverse participants in conflict situations.

REVIEW QUESTIONS

1. Instructor will provide a case study of harm (consult illustrations by Zehr, 2011; Dyck, 2006). Then, the class will be divided into three groups. Each group will discuss the case using: (a) retributive approach, answering the questions: What rule has been broken? Who is to blame? What punishment do they deserve?; (b) restorative approach Who has been hurt and what are their needs? Who is obligated to address these needs? Who has a "stake" in this situation and what is the process to involve them in making things right and preventing future occurrences?; and (c) transformative justice— What social circumstances promoted the harmful behavior? What structural similarities exist between this incident and others like it? What measures could prevent future occurrences? How to respond to the immediacy of the harm?

2. Consider a contemporary social issue or problem where the recognition, redistribution, and/or representation principles were being invoked. Explain whether they were of the affirmative or transformative forms

(review Fraser). If affirmative, what actions would need to take place to make them more transformative?

3. Some in restorative justice would advocate a focus on problem-solving in mediation efforts, others from a transformative tradition would argue for a critical transformative mediation inspired by Paulo Freire's idea of conscientization. Contrast the two approaches. What are the strengths and possible limitations of each?

4. How would you get those from the transformative justice perspective and those from the conflict transformation perspective to actively engage with each other's work? To what extent do you think it becomes the question of maintaining distinctions and preserving turf, protecting one's own perspective?

5. We saw that some in the transformative literature do not advocate the development of blueprints but, rather, guidelines. What are the advantages and disadvantages of this strategy?

6. The reformist remedial style of responding to harm has been questioned regarding its ability to *adequately* consider the necessity of change in fundamental structures that exist in a particular mode of production (political economy). Why so?

7. Group exercise. Instructor presents a contemporary conflict or social problem in society. Divide the class into two groups, one applying the restorative justice approach, the other, the transformative approach in mediation techniques to address the conflict/social problem. Have each group summarize and present their findings for class discussion.

PART TWO

Issues in Social Justice

CHAPTER 6

Multiculturalism and Globalism

CHALLENGES AND OPPORTUNITIES FOR DEVELOPING FORMS OF JUSTICE

MULTICULTURALISM AND GLOBALISM are realities of our current society. Whether one is actively engaged in these processes or not they affect our social world and therefore our understandings of justice and social justice. Multiculturalism can be understood as the coming together of a variety of cultures within a space and time. Distinctions in culture can be expressed through language, religion, cuisine, family structure, life styles, and attire. While multiple cultures have existed throughout history, the overlapping of cultures was previously less common. The development of mass transportation, transnational industries, the Internet, and increased immigration have allowed for an unprecedented convergence of cultures.

Like many new experiences, multiculturalism has created new challenges and opportunities within societies. Abu El-Haj (2002) warns of the usages of "culture" to re-assert old racist notions in new ways. Her work specifically challenges our understanding of Muslim and Arab communities, but can be applied to many uses of the term *culture*. At this point it is important to know that while understandings of law and justice may be seated within cultural contexts, placing the blame for specific injustices upon a "culture" is problematic. As we will find through our examination of the literature, injustices are often imposed by social structures regardless of the language, religion, cuisine, or family structure of those inhabiting the structure.

Globalism expresses itself in our understanding of our place on the planet. While as individuals we may identify our citizenship within national boundaries, few corporations are fully bound within national borders. Even nations themselves are more likely to express themselves globally through organizations such as the United Nations, the World Bank, the International Monetary Fund, World Trade Organization, the G7, and other organizations. The global character of capital (money invested for the purpose of profit) is especially important to the understanding of globalism (see the anthology by Aronowitz and Gautney, 2003; Appelbaum and Robinson, 2005). Global capital and capitalism will be important to our considerations of the challenges to developing forms and ideas of social justice.

Global capitalism is particularly challenging for people without a voice in decisions regarding their economic development. While we will address colonialism, post-colonialism, and anti-colonialism more completely in a later chapter, here we introduce the problems inherent in the control of one nation by another. Puerto Rico is officially labeled an unincorporated territory of the United States. Colón Morera (2016) describes Puerto Rico as able to resist U.S. policy and legislative control. However, with the imposition of the Puerto Rico Oversight, Management, and Economic Stability Act (PROMESA) in July 2016, the United States imposed a Fiscal Control Board locally referred to as the *junta* to oversee all decisions down to the municipal level (Molina, 2016; Reyes, 2017; Klein, 2018). Important political and economic policies of the nation are controlled by the United States, leaving Puerto Ricans with little to no voice over the policies that greatly impact their daily lives. The current economic and debt crises on the island were created through policies not directed by Puerto Ricans, but through the "subordination of local industrial policy to US industrial and fiscal incentives, creating a modality of dependent industrialization" (Caraballo-Cueto and Lara, 2017, 3). When the United States found that its prior imposed industrial policies might interfere with its own interests, the tax incentives for businesses to locate in Puerto Rico were removed, leaving the island to suffer rapid de-industrialization and creating the current economic crisis that necessitated the current debt while former industrial jobs on the island fled to even cheaper labor markets, not the United States (Caraballo-Cueto and Lara, 2017). Global capitalism creates economic challenges for many nations. Nations typically are allowed to set policy within their own government. This is not the case in Puerto Rico where the United States sets policy as granular as school closings, pension payments, and public employee benefits. This colonial arrangement will be revisited and is addressed here as it is a space within globalism and multiculturalism with no solid national boundaries.

NEOLIBERALISM

Neoliberalism is the economic policy that has dominated the U.S. and global economies for decades. While there are competing ideas within the neoliberal schools of thought, there is agreement within neoliberal thought for the most part that absolute freedom for capital and markets are essential to economic progress. Regulations or other interventions by governmental bodies are considered problematic and dangerous to the workings of the market (Britannica.com). Neoliberal economists also encourage the moving of formerly governmental responsibilities into the private market. Private prisons, increased use of contractors doing the work of governmental agencies, and charter schools have dramatically increased under this reasoning.

Skousen (2005) finds that the Austrian and Chicago schools of thought are equally committed to capitalist economies with little governmental interference. One of the main neoliberal economists, Austrian Joseph Schumpeter, is, however, not convinced that capitalism can survive the inevitable market swings and finds that socialism can survive (Skousen, 2005). Frederich Hayek, on the other hand, believes that capitalism can survive market swings through coordinated banking and credit markets (Arena, 2015). Alternatively, the reader is reminded of Karl Marx's model stipulating increasing contradictions within a mode of production that will reach a tipping point at which time a major change to a different mode of production results (see chapter 3). How an economy can survive the instabilities that are known to occur within capitalism are among the most prominent disagreements in the neoliberal economics schools as relate to social justice. Foley (2010) writes that while Hayek believed that governmental intervention to correct or smooth these instabilities is a threat to freedom, Schumpeter believed that the instabilities would ultimately lead to people instituting a form of rational socialism. Skousen's (2005) description of this disagreement between these two economists warns of totalitarianism as a necessary companion of socialism. Yet, socialism does not require totalitarianism as capitalism does not require democracy. However, these political and economic systems are often paired in discussion as if they necessarily correspond.

Thomas Piketty (2014) offered an analysis of inequality within our current era of capitalism that caught the attention of many. Economic inequality has intensified since the 1970s within the United States and globally. De Haan (2016) found Piketty's idea for addressing these inequalities, a global capital tax, worthy of consideration. A capital tax on wealth above one million euros at the global level was suggested. The collected tax would be redistributed to equalize global social goods such as education. This tax might also ease the current practice of sheltering taxes in offshore accounts. No nation would have the incentive to offer such shelters if each nation would instead benefit from the taxing of these funds. While Piketty (2014) himself characterizes many of his ideas as utopian, this description, similar to the pairing of totalitarianism and socialism and capitalism and democracy, may be more indicative of our acculturation into capitalism and neoliberalism than the actual possibilities of new economic arrangements.

IMMIGRATION

One of the most important outcomes of globalization is one of the producers of multiculturalism, immigration. Uneven trade policies, war, and a surge in extreme weather events have increased global insecurity and concentrated work opportunities into fewer countries, mainly in the Global North (Lewis et al., 2015). At the same time, austerity measures taken within the nations of the Global North result in insecurities and economic deprivation in the local populations. This noncausal correlation can result in anti-immigrant sentiment and lead to unexpected outcomes. Brexit, the decision by voters in Britain to leave the European Union, was the result of such sentiment and insecurities (Powell, 2017). In the United States, the criminalizing of immigrants also carries a political value that averts attention from the inequities built into the neoliberal political economy that creates the crises that lead to immigration (Montana, 2016). Buschman (2016) recognizing these pressures, suggests a dynamic solution, democratic global citizenship. This form of citizenship would both unsettle our identities as well as force a reconsideration of our ideas of justice as they relate to national boundaries. Within these considerations, justice would require that we also consider the 350 to 600 million indigenous persons whose human rights have been intensely violated not by immigrants, but by colonial settlers wishing to divest those populations of their places on the planet (Conway-Long, 2016).

MULTICULTURALISM AND GLOBALISM

Miller (2001) defines multiculturalism as "the process whereby a variety of groups within existing states—religious groups, ethnic groups, groups defined by gender or sexual orientation, and so on—increasingly assert their separate cultural identities and demand that those identities be given political recognition" (246, 252). Thus multiculturalism concerns the growing recognition of diverse societies and cultures and diverse principles of justice.

Multiculturalism is often mistaken for the mere representation of diversity within a group or organization. When the United States elected its first black president much was made of the post-racial era. However, Obama was a very particular black man (MacArthur, 2008) who presided over a time when the realities of people of color did not improve. True political recognition was not had, though the face in the White House had changed. Similarly, a popular musical, *Hamilton*, which was created by a man of color, a Puerto Rican, Lin Manuel Miranda, and stars mainly people of color, has been heralded as the best musical ever written. "*Hamilton* knits the past up with the present not only through its cast, multi-racial as now we are, and its language but with delightful anachronisms" (Treanor, 2018). Yet, few have taken a close look at the show and the incongruity of presenting people of color as slave-holding founding fathers of the United States. A more critical review was less effusive about the show, looking instead at the historical realities that are distorted on the stage. "It is a brilliant ahistorical monument to Orwellian, fake-progressive bourgeois identity politics in service to the very predominantly Caucasian financial elite and ruling class hegemony" (Street, 2016). We present these counter narratives to indicate that what is often considered multicultural may in fact be hegemony in a new shade. The multiculturalism we write of here must actually empower the voices and experiences of various identities and include those in all processes.

Globalism has been defined in a variety of ways in the literature. Miller (2001) defines globalization as "the process by which national political boundaries are eroded in such a way that people's life chances everywhere increasingly depend on the workings of a global market over which states have little control" (246). Burbach (2001) describes how the "global economy exercises a transcendental importance in our lives and societies" (21). Beck (2000) sees globalization taking place when "borders become markedly less relevant to everyday behaviour in the various dimensions of economic, information, ecology, technology, cross-cultural conflict, and civil society" (20). His key dimensions include the economic, work organization, culture, civil society, ecology, and communications technology. And for Barlow (2002), "globalism is the spread of a very wide range of ideas and practices, principally economic ones, beyond the boundaries of individual nations into the world arena" (2).

Globalism has also been explained in terms of a historical movement. For example, Burback (2001) identifies four "epochs." The first epoch (about 1492–1789) is marked by the appearance of capitalism and its spread from Europe. This is about the time of Columbus's voyages to the Americas. The second epoch (about 1789–1900) is connected with the rise of the bourgeoisie and the development of nations states. This was the period of the French Revolution. The third epoch (1900–early 1970s) was a time of monopoly capitalism. Contemporary society, according to Burback, marks the arrival of the fourth epoch. It is the epoch of globalization.

Beck (1999) provides another periodization. "First modernity" is "based on nation-state societies where social relations, networks and communities are essentially understood in a territorial sense" (1–2). During this period, in other words, people orient themselves with national states. The "second modernity" arrives perhaps in the 1980s, and the previous notions of self-enclosed states became unglued (Beck, 2000). Competition, conflict, and power differences necessitate new relations. Borders become porous. The world is now a stage.

Two additional aspects of globalization are important for further consideration: the Internet, and a global risk society. Sometimes referred to as a "global information economy," sometimes the "information age," the epoch of globalization is also characterized by the spread of the Internet and consequently of values, practices, ways of being, attitudes, and understandings (Barlow, 2002; Burbach, 2001; Castells, 2001; Arononwitz, 2003). The economy and the Internet in fact now form a feedback loop, the two symbiotically feed off each other (Barlow, 2002; Burbach, 2001). Some of the new economic elite have been referred to as the new high-tech robber barons (Burbach, 2001; see also Hardt and Negri, 2000, 2004). The early twentieth century robber barons in steel, automobile, oil, and chemical industries are increasingly supplanted by those in telecommunications, computers, online selling, and software. Struggles, by those opposing various global conditions, whether by Al Qaeda, White Nationalists, or Zapatistas, also have access to the advances provided through new technologies.

The second aspect of globalization is the nature of risks (Beck, 1992, 1999, 2000). Increasingly, hazards are having international affects. The nature of risk is such that it is becoming more and more incalculable; we cannot completely account for the possible hazardous effects of products we produce and their byproducts (1992, 22). These could be ecological, nuclear wastes and catastrophes, pollutants, or environmental damage.

As we can see, many argue that there are major problems with globalization. There are some, however, who argue for the benefits of globalization (Sen, 2002, Barlow, 2002). Supported components include the following: that it has been a vehicle for the dissemination of science, technology, and knowledge generally; that it encourages democratic practices worldwide; that yearnings of freedom have been provided a strong support; that discussions of what constitutes justice have taken on a global arena and hence sensitivity to multiculturalism has become more keen; that jobs have been created in otherwise poor countries, notwithstanding the often exploitive practices of some industries; that poverty has been somewhat abated because of the influx of foreign investments; that even anti-globalists are becoming global in their organization and denouncements. Alan Greenspan (2001), former chairman of the U.S. Federal Reserve Board, said: "Globalization has been a powerful force acting to raise standards of living. More open economies have recorded the best growth performances; in contrast, countries with inward-oriented policies have done less well." Certainly the anti-globalists would have a few words of difference.

Others (Hardt and Negri, 2000, 2004) indicate that globalization is two-faced: on the one hand, new hierarchies, divisions, and mechanisms of control are being produced; on the other, new opportunities for cross-national contacts, discussions, and sharings of diverse peoples have developed. This potentially produces both an appreciation of difference and a new sense of a global community.

Principles of Distributive Social Justice in a Global Context

Miller (2001) offers a comprehensive analysis of the three principles of social justice (need, desert, and equality) while contemplating the possibilities of these principles within current multicultural and global societies. He contends that globalization and multiculturalism require that we reexamine the principles of social justice and the means by which social justice might be achieved.

According to Miller (2001) social justice requires that everyone's basic needs be met according to a common standard of need. In a multicultural global society coming to a common agreement about what each needs and developing the institutions to meet those needs are complex tasks. The prospects for needs provision and desert distribution are problematic according to Miller because of individual notions of needs and deserts that may not agree with the common notion and the resulting pressure upon those individuals to seek their own needs and deserts. Miller describes current liberal democracies as balancing the social justice conflicts with state provisions for some needs, such as state-funded medical care while also allowing the purchase of medical services through the private market. While attending to the compromise for those at the upper end of needs and desert attainment in his discussion, little is provided in the way of critique of this arrangement, which may infringe upon the needs of all in service to the deserts of the few.

The medical market is a good example of such infringement in our current society as those in need of basic medical service and resources are often left wanting because of understaffed public hospitals particularly hitting the poor the hardest. At the same time, those able to pay for private medical care have little trouble locating multiple specialists to attend to their need (necessary medical attention) and/or desert (elective medical services).

Social justice also requires just deserts for individual effort. Assuring desert would require equal opportunity to the conditions necessary for success (quality education, for example) and nondiscriminatory practices. Miller also argues that competition must remain so that those able to best supply others' demands would be rewarded for such. He further argues that the effects of luck would need to be minimized to prevent the accumulation of benefits not based on effort or talent. While he admits that desert would lead to inequality, he suggests that these inequalities would be just and less severe than currently existing inequalities.

Along with suggesting the justness of less extreme inequalities, Miller (2001) is pessimistic about the possibilities for equality within the global market. He argues that the declining nation state and new primacy of international markets make policy-oriented corrections to inequalities unlikely and further argues that interference in market-driven inequalities may infringe upon efficiencies (260).

Miller (2001) includes equality before the law or equality as citizens as required for social justice. Within a multicultural global society this principle is necessary to ensure that citizens recognize their membership in an inclusive community with a common goal of achieving social justice principles. He provides a critique of the notion that differences in culture lead to differences in values regarding justice. He finds that few such differences exist within multicultural societies (see Boekmann, Smith, and Huo 1997). While new immigrants may express some disparities in ideas, these are quickly assimilated as persons take on the ideas of their new existences. Miller also provides evidence that while there is agreement between men and women, rich and poor regarding ideas of distribution according to merit, those on the lower end of the current stratification model (women and the poor) are less likely to see the current meritocracy as just or fair. This suggests that while ideas are shared between diverse groups, the realities of each do not match the other, thereby creating incongruence between ideas of justice and the realities experienced by those at the lower end of the stratification structure.

Miller does propose that since commitment to a particular group plays such a large role in how the group defines justice for itself, and since it is less likely to see outsiders as privileged to also having access to this standard, the real challenge would be in developing new identities of citizenships that are inclusive rather than exclusive. Some have argued in the same direction and advocated a "global civic culture" (Barlow, 2002, 16) and others offer the idea of a "global citizenship" (Holland, 2011). The Internet has been offered as one of its promoters (Barlow, 2002, 4, 6).

Young (2007) argues that we are doing the opposite of what is necessary to build a global civic culture. Instead, he finds that with the intensification of globalization has come a rejection of multiculturalism and suspicion of others. This in turn has resulted in increased intolerance, anger, and aggression. In overcoming othering, Young states that we must hybridize identities rather than remain static and tradition bound (see also Young, 2011).

Miller concludes that defending the ideals set out in the principles of social justice should not fly in the face of the real social changes that encompass globalization and multiculturalism. Instead, he argues that we should reconsider our ideas of social justice and whether they are compatible with the new global realities.

Distributive and Retributive Justice in a Global Order

The development of the notion of justice in a multicultural global order poses many challenges. We want to look at two specific approaches, the first focusing on distributive justice, the second on retributive justice. David Miller (2001) has offered us some of the key issues in terms of the possibilities of just principles developed from a needs, desert, and equality perspective. John Braithwaite (2002) has offered the idea of a global restorative justice program.

David Miller: Desert, Need, and Equality in a Multicultural Global Society

Miller's (2001) conceptions of desert, need, and equality as principles of social justice are grounded in the understandings of people. Much of the literature deals with issues of need and equality. The issue of desert, however, is not often explicitly considered in the global order. While it is clear that desert is a concept needing attention in our understanding of justice, the current levels of poverty and inequality throughout the world may be pushing this notion aside. Perhaps desert (like dessert) must be left for after the main concerns of need and inequality (the broccoli, if you will) are settled. It is not a lack of respect for the needs of desert to justice that this issue is set aside for the moment. We will, however, put our attention to need and equality in this summary.

Need, as Miller (2001) points out is a contested notion that changes from person to person or place to place. This does not however prevent a common definition or understanding. Poverty is commonly understood as an economic condition that does not allow one (or a family) to maintain basic human needs (food, clothing, health care, housing). Even within highly diverse multicultural settings, these things can be agreed upon. While the actual dollar amount below which a person (or family) must drop to be considered impoverished varies, the understanding is common and can be applied across place and time with varying numbers of dollars (or other currency). Meeting needs in service to social justice then would require that all persons/families have access to all goods necessary to human existence. A minimalist would argue that this revolves around basic service, health, education, and physiological needs. A maximalist would extend this to include quality-of-life issues. Consider, for example, to what extent can quality of life be enhanced with a U.S. Federal definition being $25,100 in 2018 for a family of four (Lee [Amanda], 2019). The Federal definition of "poverty" includes 40 million Americans. Perhaps these figures might be rosy to some people in countries with higher poverty rates; considering cost of living in determining quality of life, this figure is disgraceful.

The current form of globalism as it is expressed in the globalization of capital, as much of the literature indicates, has reduced the ability of many in the world to meet their basic needs. As Gledhill (2001), Aiyer (2001), and others have shown, this is not due to global laziness or inability, but is due to the downward pressure on wages (among those lucky enough to find work) and the disappearance of work for many. While global capitalism can be easily seen as counter to justice, escaping this reality is not nearly so easy. Let us for the moment separate the notions of globalism and capitalism (though one is the impetus for the other in our current system). Globalism in and of itself is not necessarily problematic. When we consider the exciting developments possible through global exchange, the notion of moving into nationalist isolation is unsettling if not impractical. The transportation systems made possible by and for the needs of global capital have also served to shrink our planet to a travelable and understandable size. The development and great expansion of the Internet has also made the world much smaller in time and space. The exchange of ideas, goods, scientific discoveries, and health remedies among other positive global attainments make globalism itself progressive and perhaps necessary for social justice.

Globalization for the purpose of moving capital in the interest of profit, however, is quite different. It is this form of globalism that appears problematic and counter to social justice. It is not the provision of factory jobs to people in Mexico that is in and of itself problematic. It is the provision of those jobs with the understanding that profits must always rise (meaning that wages must fall) that sets injustice into place. Jobs in service to profit rather than in service to human need is the problem with global capitalism.

Inequalities within and between nations have grown substantially in the past twenty years (Aiyer, 2001). Globalism and multiculturalism do not in themselves necessarily produce these inequalities. Market-oriented policies meant to ease the movement of capital and lessen state spending and intervention are, however, directly related to these growing inequalities. As the state reduces spending on social supports, those with the greatest need go with less and those previously depending on the jobs serving the interests of the public become unemployed or take lower paying jobs. Similarly, goods and services once provided by the state (free quality education, for example) must now be purchased in the market, decreasing the living standards of those at the bottom further. At the same time, those who do not depend on wages but instead invest capital, gain significant profits as both wages and taxes fall (Aiyer, 2001). Equality as a principle of social justice is then endangered by global capitalism, but not necessarily by globalism or multiculturalism.

Miller (2001) suggested that the state has a place in supporting the attainment of needs but also suggested that strategies for gaining social justice should not fly in the face of current globalization. However, current neoliberal policies call for reductions in state spending, and the institutions that oversee structural adjustment programs often require austerity measures that prevent assurances of meeting needs. His suggestions for attaining more equality (though not absolute equality) depend upon competition within the market to assure that those who perform best will receive their just deserts. He further contends that mitigating the impact of luck would assist in lessening current levels of inequality.

Others have different ideas about meeting needs and supporting equality. Watson (2002) argued that capitalism is the enemy of equality and justice and must therefore be overcome as did Lenin (1975). Martin (2003) is optimistic about the alignments between divergent groups that seek to battle capitalism in service to justice. Ferrara (2003) and Charlesworth (2000) both contend that political understandings of justice, injustice, and cultural norms are required to find justice. Cahill (2003) and Benatar (2001) look to structural change as the means for attaining international justice. Rao (1999) and Noël and Thérien (2002) have shown that national and international equality and justice are connected and must both be addressed. Gledhill (2001) asserted that attention to wages and working conditions is primary to addressing human need, equality, and justice. Korzeniewicz and Smith (2000) call for unity between nongovernmental organizations (NGOs), labor unions, and others interested in social justice to sway the current agenda toward meeting human need and lessening inequalities. Aiyer (2001) suggests a reassessment of democracy in the Americas, calling for more attention to the abusive tendencies of militarization and criminalization that develop out of neoliberal policies. Maskovsky (2001) calls for modes of empowerment for the poor so that they may free themselves and demand their own needs, whereas Lake (2002) suggests a return to state intervention. Marcuse (2002) calls for more attention to those in need and less attention to corporate interests. Chase (2003) suggests a new activist agenda for academics and their students.

There are many ways forward. Social justice, however, requires that we move beyond our current state of global poverty and inequality.

John Braithwaite: Globalization and Restorative Justice

In a previous chapter we developed Braithwaite's vision of restorative justice, which was bottom-up; that is, following Parker (1999), it suggested that we decentralize justice practices. The government's role would be a watchdog that assures decentralized programs are moving toward more empowerment, less domination, more justice, especially for otherwise disenfranchised people. In *Restorative Justice and Responsive Regulation* (2002) Braithwaite also addresses global justice by using the same principles of restorative justice, with the inclusion that there should be a top-down component—preventive diplomacy and mechanisms for curtailing conflicts.

Braithwaite (2002) recognizes the potentials for the recently developed International Criminal Court of the United Nations, but questions its efficacy, since, it is in the same direction of our traditional criminal justice system, which relies predominantly on a system of abstract rights emphasizing punitive responses and potentially is replete with all the problems associated with it (recall Weber's concern with the "insoluble conflict"—the difference between formal and substantive outcomes). He is concerned with the scope of conflicts both international as well as national that claims hundreds of thousands of lives, hardly deserving of the label "low intensity conflict."

He does provide evidence for the usefulness of mediation in international conflicts. For example: Touval and Zartman (1985, 1989) cited eight cases in particular where mediation efforts led to agreements and peace; Nelson Mandela's and Desmond Tutu's (1999) restorative justice work in South Africa, which restored peace between black and white and truth and reconciliation committees in South Africa, El Salvador, and Chile and other countries is well in line with restorative justice principles. But many international mediation efforts have not produced acceptable results. It is to these that Braithwaite's work on global justice sheds light.

Calling his global restorative justice "responsive international peace-making," Braithwaite suggests a pyramid that could be a guide. He refers to it as "A Responsive Regulatory Pyramid of International Diplomacy" (Braithwaite, 2002, 195). The first priority in dealing with conflicts, located at the base of his pyramid, is some form of restorative justice. If that fails, we move up the pyramid by employing international powers and the United Nations to persuade the disputants to engage in peacemaking. If that fails, then a resolution by the Security Council of the United Nations is in order. If that fails, then sanctions are imposed. Shaming, as was the case with Braithwaite's original model, is also part of this package. If that fails, then military action by the United Nations is in order to persuade the disputants to return to the tables and negotiate.

Braithwaite has indicated that because of the United Nation's unwillingness to follow through on these steps, we continue to have long, drawn out conflicts with hundreds of thousands of people, even millions over the course of time, being injured, disabled, killed, faced with health crises, and starved. We cannot stay idle while neighboring states slaughter hundreds of thousands of people. Without any movement by the disputants, it is the global community that must immediately and decisively intervene.

Braithwaite (2002) develops his bottom-up approach to restorative justice in the global order. He argues for a more pragmatic form of justice. The international community, the growing global order, must be quick to insist warring factions attempt genuine restorative justice toward peacemaking. Rather than necessarily seeking scapegoats for prosecution, the international community can push versions of the truth and reconciliation committees. Here, much like restorative justice programs that were envisioned for more garden-variety crimes, Braithwaite sees a healing process that is essential to global peacemaking. Forgiveness is an essential part of this package (203).

Of course, the issue of a growing world risk-society as envisioned by Beck (1992, 1999, 2000) sees other forms of international harms—including ecological, environmental, pollution—that also need to be addressed. According to Beck, the long-range nature of many of these developing risks is noncalculable. When damage does occur, we enter inevitable conflict as to who is at fault. Restorative justice provides a forum for these discussions and some resolutions.

Braithwaite does acknowledge that critical components of his initially conceived restorative justice program, interdependence and community, are also at the center of developing global restorative justice. With globalism more interdependence is taking place as countries increasingly find themselves in essential relations with others, similarly, with the idea of community. Increasingly, we are developing into an international community. Braithwaite, therefore, is optimistic, for these are two key elements that come into play when some shaming must be directed at unacceptable behaviors of some states or warring states. Thus emerging, in his view, is a global civil society and thus an inevitably receptive one for the use of restorative justice as well as shaming. But where shaming is initially inflicted, states must also follow with reintegration into the global civil community. The occasion for resolution could also be time for rejoicing the solidified bonds of solidarity that are the outcomes.

In short, Braithwaite's suggestion for global justice is to create a space, be it at a more local level, or at an international level, in which alternatives can be engaged. Justice, in a multicultural global order, can revolve around discussion, reaching mutually acceptable agreements, forgiveness, and healing. Using primarily force only escalates its call and use. Restorative justice, for Braithwaite, is a pragmatic answer to growing, and inevitable, conflicts in a global order.

New Global Realities and the Principles of Distributive Social Justice

Much literature exists regarding the process of globalization and its impact on social justice. Less literature directly examines multiculturalism and justice. However, the globalization literature often subsumes or assumes multiculturalism within its examination. While the following is not an exhaustive review of the literature in these areas, it is a representative review that offers an introductory understanding of the challenges inherent in our current global existence and ideas about creating social justice in this complex world.

Watson (2002) described global capitalism as immiserating the working class on a global scale through profit seeking sped up by new technologies no longer requiring place in the same way. Governmental and nongovernmental agencies have been effectively used by profit seekers to support the capitalist enterprise. This usage has been successful given neoliberal claims that there is no alternative to global capitalism and neoconservative claims that this aggressive form is progressive. Watson notes that neoliberal claims are false because labor can exist without capital but capital cannot exist without labor (38). The falsity of neoconservative claims of progress through globalization is apparent for the majority who have lost ground economically, but less apparent to the minority at the top of the economic structure who have profited greatly and retained political power. Ravallion (2003) offers an analysis of a variety of data that substantiates growing inequalities through globalization and explains the contradictory reports of both decreases in poverty rates in some areas while many remain in abject poverty. Further he shows how those rising above impoverishment are not gaining as much as they might in a more planned economy.

Watson (2002) warns that post-Marxist ideas of localized capitalism are doomed to failure because equal power is not possible under capitalist hegemony. He claims instead that "capitalism is still the issue" (41). Globalization from below is offered as a way forward toward more just economic distribution, greater equality, and assurance of meeting basic human needs. This project, according to Watson, will require workers' struggles to overcome capitalism in order to plan and organize society in the interests of the majority.

Lenin (1975) used the term *imperialism* to describe the sort of globalization present at the turn of the last century. While the terms differ, the injustices are quite similar. Lenin described the movement of capital across national borders as necessary to the continuing growth of profit. As Lenin pointed out over one hundred years ago, the export of capital is not undertaken with the intent or outcome of raising the living standards of the people in either the exporting or importing countries, but exclusively for the purpose of increasing profits for the investing capitalists. Similar to Watson (2002), Lenin (1975) indicated that what he described as imperialism was in fact capitalism, though in its declining phase. Justice will require the replacement of capitalism with an economic system organized in the interest of people (socialism) rather than profit. This, according to Lenin, would be the cure for the economic injustices created by imperialism/capitalism.

Martin (2003) examined the overlapping ideas of justice held by Marxists and liberation theologists. These overlapping ideas include a recognition of global capitalism as the driving force of oppression and economic decline of the many and wealth accumulation among the few. Also overlapping are ideas that justice must include the meeting of basic human need and the prevention of destructive development. Martin also shows that Marxists and liberation theologists both include revolutionary action within the range of options for overcoming the violence and oppression imposed by capitalism. While neither group of thinkers/activists glorifies violence, each finds it an appropriate tool for overcoming the ravages of capitalism (Hardt and Negri, 2000). Of specific concern to Martin is the need to respond to the impact of globalization on the peoples and lands of Latin America. His article not only compares Marxism and liberation theology but shows how these traditions can come to work together across their divergent views regarding religion. Religion is often aligned with culture and can impact upon the development of society. Martin's work indicates that the forces of globalization have actually aligned those who sharply critique religion and those who find it a transformative force onto the same side of the anti-capitalist battle.

Ferrara (2003) offered an approach to human rights that he argues is not subject to the variety of complications inherent in globalization and the multicultural reality. He finds that in order to escape the unexamined objective connection (essentialization) of justice to moral precepts that may be appropriate for some populations/circumstances, but not others, political understandings must be included. These political understandings must be encoded in law to assure equal rights. His approach further suggests that justice should not be managed by those serving the status quo, but, rather, is protective of human rights and articulates the international order required by justice.

Charlesworth (2000) considered the questions of culture and national sovereignty and found that neither needs be a barrier to feminist internationalism. As she points out, the oppression of women (and others) has been/is often defended as local or cultural practice not to be violated by outsiders. She, like Ferrara (2003), calls for a political analysis of oppressive practices in order to uncover the interests involved in defending oppression. This analysis can lead to not only the recognition that oppression is often defended in order to protect economic or political benefits but also to the uncovering of the realities of tradition and culture that are often masked by oppression and may inspire respect and trust within and between groups.

The history of the United States and the values of those within its boundaries are instructive here. Is the United States a slave culture? Are those within its boundaries committed to the injustices of slavery? These questions may seem out of place currently; however, consider their place in our history (see Wacquant, 2001, 2009). Did slavery serve the citizenry of the United States? Or, was it a practice defended on national/state sovereignty grounds to protect the interests of a few southern plantation owners? Wacquant (2001) explains the convergence of ghettos and prisons resulting from the legacy of slavery in the United States. Is our ongoing imprisonment binge a continued interest in maintaining control over black bodies?

Charlesworth (2000) particularly pointed out the need to understand the barriers to justice for women created by states and their legal positions. It is also important to consider these barriers and the possibilities of their deconstruction/replacement for general social justice. In other words, globalization and multiculturalism bring both challenges and possibilities for social justice. If we find a way to replace oppressive regimes with just international constructs, we may serve social justice in our struggles to deal with these challenges. Consider the struggles against slavery in the United States and the service to social justice inherent in both those struggles and their ultimate outcomes.

Cahill (2003) examined globalization as it impacts our understanding of ethics and biotechnology. She wrote that given the global implications of disease and health, we must move beyond individualistic understandings of the world and accept justice as the ethical norm. As she explained, justice "requires equality, solidarity, and attention to the basic material and social needs of all peoples" (42). Cahill further asserted that the attainment of justice would require change to the current social and economic structures. Benatar (2001) offered a similar analysis of international economic apartheid. He suggested that a discussion of global justice has begun, but must continue and must address the economic inequalities created and sustained by the current market system.

Rao (1999) argued that justice cannot be achieved without equality. Within a global economy that intensifies inequalities within and between nations, he further argues, equality must become a cooperative and international project. As Rao noted, support for economic equality must be understood as not only self-interested but as a social good that serves all. Through collective action, people become aware of this good and support the outcomes of justice and equality. According to Rao, we have not yet come to the time when international cooperation for justice and equality is eminent, but he also warns that we are beyond the time when inequality and injustice can be treated as national (rather than international) issues.

Noël and Thérien's (2002) research illustrated the link between local and global justice. In their analysis of European attitudes and policies they found that where poverty and inequality were low (such as Denmark) attitudes and policies toward international redistribution were positive and strong. At the same time, nations (such as France) where poverty and inequality were higher (though not as problematic as in the United States which was not included in the study) support for international redistribution was weaker. These authors conclude that first achieving justice at home can achieve support for global justice most effectively. Meeting needs and supporting equality must be realized within nations first and then, second, internationalized.

Gledhill (2001) examined the third way ideas for addressing the injustices of increasing inequalities and poverty that have accompanied increasing globalization. While he is not supportive of either the neoliberal or neoconservative agendas, he is also critical of the third way. As he explains, this way is overly demanding of those experiencing declines in wages and standards of living expecting that the least privileged give up any counter market or illegal strategies for survival and instead commit more fully to the capitalist enterprise. At the same time, this way calls upon those gaining economic ground to become more concerned with the plights of those at the bottom and increase their civic responsibility. In other words, the structural programs associated with a global economy should be addressed through the individual acceptance by those at the bottom of the economic strata and increased charity by those at the top of the economic strata. Gledhill does not accept the third way as the way forward or even a true alternative to neoliberalism. As he explains, this way fails to address the issues at the heart of the global economy, declining wages. He illustrates the decline in wages both in the United States, even in the high-technology industry, and in Mexico, even in the industrial sector, and suggests that there is a way forward and it must address declining wages and working conditions.

Korzeniewicz and Smith (2000) offer an optimistic view for the possibilities of social justice in Latin America. While these authors admit the problematic nature of reconciling global capitalism with social supports, they argue that NGOs working within communities for progress maintain enough independence from supranational organizations (SNOs), which work outside of communities typically in service to global capitalism (the World Bank, for example). And they have developed appropriate relationships with political activists within labor unions and other organizations to push for increased attention to issues of poverty and inequality. Unlike Watson (2002) who rejects the assumption that capitalist markets are necessary to economic development, Korzeniewicz and Smith accept the neoliberal ideology of TINA (there is no alternative) suggesting that market-driven development can co-exist with social development if those markets are held accountable by NGOs and activists concerned with educational opportunities, medical services, and other basic human needs. These authors suggest that there is a new understanding by SNOs that continually increasing impoverishment and inequalities threaten market economies and that these organizations could be influenced by NGOs, labor unions, and others to work toward social justice.

Aiyer (2001) offers an analysis of neoliberalism in the Americas that includes consideration of militarization and criminalization as tools of democratization. In his article, he outlines the impact of neoliberal policies throughout the Americas highlighting the increases in inequalities and poverty throughout the continent. These increases in social injustice are, according to Aiyer, side effects of the increasing global nature of capitalism in the form of imperialism and are directly maintained by policy decisions within the United States that sway policy elsewhere.

The privatization of formerly state institutions decreases employment, wages, and access to basic human needs such as land, education, and health care. While the use of private prisons and mercenary armies has increased, the command of criminal justice and military functions remains firmly in the hands of the state. Aiyer argues that these functions are essential to the program of neoliberalism in service to imperialism. As he asserts, swaying attention toward issues of law and order, especially around the war on drugs, allows for increasingly strong responses from the state, which result in the criminalization of inner city youth and rebel groups alike. As the United States increases its prison population to almost 2.3 million people (Wagner and Sawyer, 2018), it isolates especially young minority men from political engagement and social interaction. U.S. policies also pressure trade nations to similarly ramp up their drug wars and imprison their own populations. The United States further utilizes its military force in the war on drugs and to stabilize low intensity conflicts.

Low-intensity conflicts allow for the continuing presence of the U.S. military and the ongoing funding of the military apparatus that is highly profitable for military contractors. Yet U.S. interventions into these conflicts are unsuccessful in their expressed goals of reducing the drug trade and/or democratizing a region. Intervention into the conflicts of other nations also disallows local solutions to these conflicts.

These operations negatively impact the poor in the regions of occupation through land losses and decreased funding and access to public sector jobs and social support programs and criminalization/imprisonment and in the United States through decreased funding and access to public sector jobs and social support programs and criminalization/imprisonment. Criminalization occurs through widening the net—that is illegalizing more behaviors and increasing punishments for illegal behaviors—and isolating poor and working-class communities from work and opportunities once supplied by the withering state (see also Wacquant, 2001; 2009).

Chase (2003) proposes serious consideration among academics regarding the role of scholarship and teaching in the pursuit of social justice. He suggests that engagement in scholarship focusing on the needs of activists and communities is necessary. Beyond teaching critical thinking or teaching in a critical manner, he also advocates the training of students as activists and organizers. This, he argues, will serve the needs of social justice. Given the attacks on public space for protests following September 11 (Marcuse 2002), the recent attacks on academic freedoms and the vilification of activist scholars, Chase's suggestions are both necessary and challenging.

Toward Transformative Global Justice

Transforming the world in service to global justice is indeed a utopian idea. Often within the scholarly literature as well as within mainstream political discussions, social justice is met with skepticism and hostility viewed as beyond our human capacity. History tells a different story. There were better times. When the current authors were starting out, there were injustices, no doubt, however, there was hope, progress, and dare we write, optimism. We likely saw utopian ideas as a good thing. As time has progressed, it seems hopes for true social justice with the absence of racism, not color blindness, the end to poverty, not a war on the poor, and world peace, not endless war, have dimmed. Transformative global justice requires an audacity beyond hope.

As the learned theorists reviewed above have rightly shown, differences throughout the globe related to need, equality, distribution, and retribution abound. These differences, however, are surmountable, with time and adequate attention. As we indicated in the section on multiculturalism and globalization, true inclusion must not only be about representation but about recognition and voice. The World Justice Project (WJP) is attempting this with their index for justice. The WJP intends to "advance the rule of law worldwide" (https://worldjusticeproject.org/). While this project is fairly new, and does adhere to the idea of law as justice, it is a step forward for global justice in that the project seeks to assure consistency within the laws of a nation, not as imposed from outside that nation. The WJP also seeks to "measure government openness based on the general public's experiences and perceptions worldwide." These are lofty goals and are informed by the people within the nations studied. Such attempts at measuring justice may provide multidirectional information sharing to further inform strategies for increased global justice. Of course, the WJP needs also to engage and incorporate social justice principles that are not necessarily derived from given principles of law, such as formal rationality (see, for example, Max Weber, chapter 3).

Niță (2018) contends that the morality of law in our current era of globalization requires that laws are written to benefit all. As Niță points out, much of current law is written for contractual obligations within highly unequal relationships. These social constructions will need rebuilding with the inclusion of those who are to be bound in these laws to assure that interests beyond the powerful are attended in the new social constructions of law.

Michael Hardt and Antonio Negri's *Empire* (2000) and its sequel, *Multitude* (2004), draw from revisionist Marxism, postmodernist analysis, informatization (dominance of services and information), and post-colonial theory, amongst others (see the critiques in Passavant and Dean, 2003). These authors indicate two faces of globalization: one face is about the global spread of divisions, hierarchies, and new methods of control; the other, reflects new potentials created for cooperation, collaboration, diverse encounters, and dialogue. In short "it provides the possibility that, while remaining different, we discover the commonality that enables us to communicate and act together" (Hardt and Negri, 2004, xiii).

The new global order is about empire, a sovereignty that has no boundaries, that has succeeded the notion of a nation-state. Empire is akin to the previous forms of monarchical and aristocratic powers, perhaps best represented in the Roman Empire (Hardt and Negri, 2004, 109). Though nation-states continue to maintain a certain degree of control and regulation in economic, migration, legal, and cultural values, the ultimate authority is becoming ever more externally driven (110). The notion of a social contract, contractual justice, is mythology. Echoing Derrida, its foundations are based on a violent act (114). How, then, will justice emerge?

Hardt and Negri offer the notion of the "multitude," a term that can be differentiated from other ideas of the human being such as the "masses," "people," and the "working class." The multitude, "is composed of innumerable internal differences that can never be reduced to a unity or a single identity—different cultures, races, ethnicities, genders, and sexual orientations; different forms of labor; different ways of living; different views of the world; and different desires" (xiv). And herein is the challenge: "for a social multiplicity to manage to communicate and act in common while remaining internally different" (xiv). Here, too, lies the possibility of new forms of justice. The multitude is about continuous invention, of experimentation, new forms of life, and hence offers the possibilities of the people yet to come. According to Hardt and Negri, change, for them, comes by way of active resistance, direct confrontation, revolution. "In Empire, ethics, morality, and justice are cast into new dimensions" (Hardt and Negri 2000, 20). Conceptions of justice will be based on immeasurable factors rather than trying to bring everything under an equal measure such as in formal equality. "Values will be determined only by humanity's own continuous innovation and creation" (356). The courts of Empire will gradually move away from adjudication and sentencing to an organ that will "dictate and sanction the interrelation among the moral order, the exercise of police action, and the mechanism legitimating imperial sovereignty" (38). It is this, too, that will be the object of the multitude's struggles.

Similar ideas have been offered beyond the courts. Taylor (2016) in a review of the demise of the American dream argues that in order to avoid collapse, our social economy must be informed and directed to address social values rather than narrow economic interests. Attending to these values within the United States would allow for increased concern for global equality. In the global arena, citing the World Social Forums as seats of transformative justice. Smith (2017) finds that social movements in support of global justice are also necessary to combat the rise of the far right. The success of many far right candidates and movements around the globe are in part due to the scapegoating of immigrants and the exploitation of the very real damages inflicted upon local populations by austerity measures. The only relationship between increased immigration and economic suffering of local populations, however, is that both are imposed by neoliberal policies developed in service to global capitalism. Organizing locally and globally to counter messages that obscure the realities of these causes serves to protect those scapegoated and to highlight economic disparities and injustices. Regardless the label given to the politics that rise from movements for justice, Murakami Wood (2017) argues that "our politics must be defined by a rediscovery of collective desires, the bringing together of multiple fractured movements to recast a planetary future for humanity based on equality and ecology" (369).

Intensifications of inequality and poverty on a global scale have at once resulted in a retreat from social justice with the rise of nationalistic politics and at the same time have informed and energized movements toward social justice to consider new and global ideas (Smith, 2017). As Kumar (2017) suggests, we must "bring together intersectional analysis with a structural critique of neoliberal imperialism and the inequities it perpetuates both domestically and globally" (2071). These analyses enhance and may contribute to a movement toward transformative global justice.

Compelling issues for a global, or for others, transnational justice, or for critical scholars, transformative global justice, have become more apparent with the European refugee crises that reached a crescendo in 2015. Due to historical instabilities engendered from multiple sources, not the least of which was colonialism, geopolitics, expansionist policies, questionable intervention practices, global capitalism's need to find ever new resources and markets to exploit, religious assertions, etc., we witnessed over 1.8 million refugees from Syria, Iraq, Afghanistan, and from North Africa (Nigeria, Somalia, Eritrea) entering by boat or by a Balkan route. Germany, France, and Italy received the majority, though per capita, Sweden, Hungary, and

Austria led the way (United Nations High Commissioner for Refugees, 2017). There has been an alarming death rate for refugees attempting to escape their conditions (see International Organization for Migration). It has also been estimated that there are almost 60 million forcibly displaced people across the globe (United Nations High Commissioner for Refugees Global Focus 2017). And we also are witnessing refugees flowing from Central America attempting to enter the "land of opportunity" of the United States along its southwestern border in late 2018. This is indeed a monumental crisis. European countries have replied; some have been granted refugee status and are being integrated into the countries of entrance, some have been resettled in other countries, and many have been denied refugee status (i.e., Germany in 2016 had denied nearly half of 700,000 requests for asylum) and thus are subject to deportation. And the injustices against refugee and asylum seekers are extensive. In the United Kingdom, they "are subject to detention, inhuman living conditions, mis-framing, unequal living and working conditions, low levels of support, restricted access to health care, poor welfare outcomes, racism and discrimination" (Phillimore, 2018). Clearly, policy changes must take place to materially accommodate refugees. But what underlying philosophy of distributive justice exists that is a key ingredient in policy making? Even pragmatists must admit that their action is based on some notion of fair distribution.

We also find discussions by activists and scholars concerning the nature of distributive justice in a global order reaching more poignant and insightful levels. A transformative global justice could build on Nancy Fraser's (2007) "Re-Framing Justice in a Globalizing World." Fraser argues that framing the problem is essential. This is the question of how we conceptualize and create territorial (state) boundaries, insiders and outsiders, principles of justice due its members, internal impediments to their realization, and the nature of discourses ("grammars") generated within bounded territories. Drawing from earlier work on affirmative and transformative evaluations for justice in practice, here, in a global order, Fraser connects "affirmative" forms of framing to a "Westphalian grammar" of frame setting that is more focused on border issues and what constitutes justice within its boundaries. The term "Westphalian grammar" has become more popular in global discussions, traced to the Treatise of Westphalia (1648) where after a thirty-year war spheres of influence (boundaries) were created. Thus, territorial integrity is the focus of analysis in affirmative framing.

"Transformative global justice," on the other hand, would go further questioning how, historically, borders were, and often are, constructed but also how an alternative discourse (grammar) must engage the interterritorial nature of the global order—cross-national issues, problems, crises that affect more than one territory. Here advocated by Fraser is that issues should be framed for "all affected" in decision-making regardless of borders: "all those affected by a given social structure of institution have moral standing as subjects of justice in relation to it . . . [is not a question of] geographical proximity, but their co-imbrication in a common structure of institutional framework, which sets the ground rules that govern their social interaction, thereby shaping their respective life possibilities, in patterns of advantage and disadvantage" (25). In other words, affirmative framing in globalism apart from dealing with the immediate problem at hand does not include the transnational nature of problems such as environmental degradation, the very causes of the problem itself, and the generation of new grammars that are not restricted to purely territorial claims.

Transformative global justice framing seeks to situate issues within geo-politics, imperialism, colonial policies, transnational corporations, insatiable thirst of capital logic and profit so that these realities are included in the analysis. Consider for example, historical decisions such as Britain and France's initiatives (1916) to divide Syria, Iraq, Israel/Palestine, Jordan, and Lebanon into "spheres of influence" (Renton, 2017) through imposed borders (see the "1916 Sykes-Picot Agreement"; Baerwaldt, 2018). And consider the war in Iraq with the justification given to neutralize "weapons of mass destruction" (none were found), costing in some estimates a half million dead and millions displaced (Baerwaldt, 2018; Hagopian et al. 2013). Consider the long history of European countries' colonizing practices and the legacy of genocide, slavery, racism, and cultural imposition. There has also been a long history of U.S. intervention in foreign governments installing and/or shaping the installation of "friendly" governments, extending from Central America to the Middle East, Balkans, and Southeast Asia (Blum, 2004). All these undermine stability and often produce millions of displaced persons. So, the sources of "crises" must enter the frame of discussion. Thus, "grammar of argument has altered . . . disputes that used to focus exclusively on the question of *what* is owed as a matter of justice to community members now turn quickly into disputes about *who* should count as a member and *which* is the relevant community" (Fraser, 2007, 19; italics in the original).

Global justice, argues Fraser (2007), calls for an additional dimension to her otherwise two-dimension model (distribution, more economic; recognition, more cultural) to include "representation" (more political). This cuts across separate state territories around the globe. Representation, she continues, "is a matter of social belonging; what is at issue here is inclusion in, or exclusion from, the community of those entitled to make justice claims on one another" (21). It includes the procedures and processes by which issues are contested. Her call for a transformative justice is to "democratize the process of frame-setting" (24) by including "all affected" in decision-making processes by assuming equal moral worth and "participation-parity."

Affirmative frame setting accepts the idea that boundaries are subject to interrogation and accepts that a territorial state is still the appropriate goal, remaining within a Westphalian grammar. Shared membership within boundaries is still acknowledged as an ideal. In a global order transformative justice attends to the cross-boundaries nature of many injustices. The very grammar (language, discourse, narrative) must change to reflect a global order and injustices that cross borders. Fraser's first principle focuses on consideration of "all affected"—"all those affected by a given social structure or institution have moral standing as subjects of justice in relation to it" (25). Consider, for example, people living in a particular state who are being adversely affected by pollution and exploitive transnational corporations that cut across state boundaries. We are, for example, more and more cognizant that the Amazon rain forest is a major supplier of oxygen producing over 20 percent over the globe. With deforestation, the world community is being affected.

Also relevant to transformative global justice is: changing views of "othering" whereby dichotomies are established, "we" pitted again a "them," we the civilized, they the uncivilized (Dhaliwal and Forgert, 2015; see also Young, 2011, on three forms of "othering"); "spectacles of migrant" transgressions [media dramatization] whereby negative images and discourses are constructed from select image portrayal of "them" (De Genova, 2013; Brouwer, van der Woude, and van der Leun, 2017); and metaphor usage such as "people are represented as entering in streams, flows, floods, tsunamis, swarms and plagues . . . in this context, radical action is called for to curtail an invasion third-world-looking outsiders" (Baerwaldt, 2018). All, in transformative global justice, must be deconstructed, tracing the causes to where they primordially begin (i.e., framing in time and space). Baerwaldt offers a critical approach to understanding crises. It must include deconstructing: "(1) the ways in which a crisis is represented, (2) the premises underlying dominant crisis representations, (3) what the actors involved in representing a crisis set to gain and lose from specific representations, (4) the silences traversing representations, (5) the solutions proposed, their histories and their anticipated effects, and (6) the ways in which harmful representations can be subverted." And along with deconstruction is reconstruction. Identity reconstruction, for example, being mindful of Woolford's call (2010) for new identities (victim, offenders, community, mediators) in transformative restorative justice practices resonates with a transformative global justice in the call for alternative forms of "othering." For example, Young (2011) provides three forms of othering (the way we see the other) engendered by late modernity: the conservative and liberal forms of othering still distance and diminish the other; the third form, "ethnographic othering," is accommodation to difference, and engenders mutual growth in interactions, new understandings, more "I-other" relations. Here, multiculturalism and globalization can be reconciled in enhancing human well-being, perhaps Hardt and Negri's work (2004) on the "multitude" and the "commonwealth" provides useful directions. And of course, redistribution is a necessary component in this reconstruction along with distributive principles that enhance human well-being as well as nonhuman forms (see chapter 7).

Principles of distributive justice must engage these sources if they are to be genuinely useful. Several approaches have emerged. Fraser's contribution (2007), we have seen, is particularly relevant with the refugee crisis in Europe and argues that beyond recognition and distribution a third dimension, representation, that is participation equality (participation parity) is necessary in conceptualizing global justice. All must have equal access to democratic decision-making. All should be provided equal access to influencing others.

Others have expanded distributive justice to include a "right to justification" (Forst, 2007; 2014). Forst is arguing for "first things first," which for him is justification. Here argued is that "equal dignity" demands freedom or the capacity to demand justification of action both addressing cause and a moral justification. "And if you cannot justify this act or choice to me, then take it back, repair it, compensate me for the damage you have done" (Van den Brink, 2008, 57). All should be able to demand that a decision or policy be justified. Thus, for Forst, this is the question of power and its unequal distribution. And not only unequal distribution of power is a concern hindering the realization of a basic right to justification but also people who have become "subjectified"—those like Fanon's colonized subjects who unquestionably assume identities, norms, morals, and institutions of power groups or oppressors.

Distribution, in other words, particularly highlighted by global crises, has been increasingly conceptualized as having more dimensions than needs, equality, merit, and narrow notions of economically based redistribution. In chapter 7, for example, we shall visit Schlosberg's (2007) expansion to: recognition, capabilities, and participation. Indeed, Fraser (2007) argues that "globalization is changing the way we argue about justice" (17). Framing social justice has now found itself center stage in globalization and is playing itself out during the European refugee crises as well as the U.S. myopic policies with Central American refugees. Problematic is precisely what ordering do these emerging principles of justice follow? That is, needs, equality, merit, recognition, participation, representation, justification? And how does this relate to distribution? We will return to Schlosberg's extension to participation and capabilities, in following chapters. And what more inclusive grammars can arise centering on global citizenship? How do we reconcile multiculturalism with globalization in relation to identity politics? Each must be studied within historical and changing material social conditions (i.e., relations and forces of production) and cross-national realities, further informed by activist struggles, and the dialectics of struggle.

REVIEW QUESTIONS

1. What is the difference between globalization and multiculturalism? How are these concepts related?

2. The United States and many other Western nations are considered multicultural societies. Think about the definition of multiculturalism offered in this chapter and do a bit of searching online for information on a country that considers itself multicultural. Does the country truly live up to the ideals of multiculturalism suggested in the chapter?

3. *Vanity Fair* reported that Amazon was set to become one of the largest military contractors in the United States (https://www.vanityfair .com/news/2018/08/has-bezos-become-more-powerful-in-dc-than -trump). How does this development relate to neoliberalism and globalization? Read the *Vanity Fair* article and consider the impact of this contract on the privatization of governmental responsibilities.

4. With one or two other students in your class, agree to do a bit of online research on a country other than the one in which you currently live or have lived. Locate information on economic equality, political power, and one other measure of social justice that you believe is important. Prepare a short presentation for the class to include: the current state of social justice within that nation and how much agreement you believe that there is between your own ideas of social justice and those that are espoused by the nation that you chose. Do not worry if you are giving a complete picture of the nation, this exercise is meant to be a start in thinking about global justice.

5. On your own, do a bit of online research regarding globalization. Select a corporation that you believe to be international in size. Look at the website for that corporation and count the number of countries in which the corporation is currently active. Prepare a short description of the activities of your chosen corporation and the numbers and locations of countries in which it is active (is it an employer in these locations, provider of goods/services, or any other activities found).

6. Do a bit more research on the company that you located for question five. See if you can find any reports of lobbying or other governmental activities of this corporation within nations beyond its

nation of origin. In other words, if you chose a corporation head-quartered in China, see if you can find any reports of company officials or lobbyists working on behalf of that corporation attempting to impact governmental, regulatory, or legal decisions in a country other than China.

7. In developing a transformative global justice we increase discussions concerning "causes" of global crises and particularly the interventionist practices of states. Why is this important?

8. How would you prioritize the various principles of distributive justice in a global arena? Would need, for example, be more important than merit? Equality? Recognition? Representation? Participation? Justification?

CHAPTER 7

Environmental, Ecological,
and Species Justice

INCREASINGLY IT IS BEING recognized that harms done to
the environment are leading toward a global catastrophe. Responding to
this concern, particularly in the last two decades, has been a tremendous
increase in research, writing, policy reformulations, and a variety of environmental agencies. We have seen the development of new journals that
focus in this area such as *Journal of Environmental Law, Journal of Environmental
Studies and Science,* and *Journal of Environmental Management*; handbooks such
as *Routledge International Handbook of Green Criminology* and *The Oxford
Handbook of Environmental Political Theory*; textbooks such as Lynch et al,
Green Criminology; and organizations such as *International Center for the Right
of Nature* and the *Community Environmental Legal Defense Fund* (CELDF). We
are witnessing a plethora of emerging themes in this literature.

Environmental and ecological concerns are separate yet closely related
justice themes. Low and Gleeson (1998) describe these related themes as
"two aspects of the same relationship" and suggest that these aspects are
"the justice of the distribution of environments among peoples, and the
justice of the relationship between humans and the rest of the natural world"
(2). Taylor (2000) has even envisioned an "environmental justice paradigm"
that would "link environment and race, class, gender and social justice concerns" (42). Some have been even more explicit about making the connections. Middleton and O'Keefe (2001, 16, 100), for example, argue that we
must not only deal with symptoms (uneven impact of environmental
hazards) but with the causes, that is, with social injustice (see also Haughton, 1999; Agyeman, Bullard, and Evans 2003). Because the relationship
between people and the natural world is defined and affected by the distribution of environments among them, and the distribution of environments
between people is defined and affected by the relationship between people
and the planet, this is in fact the same relationship.

Environmental justice struggles are inevitably multicultural, highly diverse,
and increasingly global in their methods, interests, and goals (Mihaylov and

Perkins, 2015). Those involved in these struggles often have pressure toward accepting unity in spite of differences. As Schlosberg (2004) found, movements for environmental justice develop and implement theories of justice from within rather than accepting notions of justice established from without the movements. While struggles are ongoing and include important global youth movements (Hertsgaard, 2019), here we will focus on the development of ways of understanding justice and how these understandings are or can be applied to the environment, ecology, and species.

GREEN CRIMINOLOGY

The formal beginning of Green Criminology is often traced to Michael Lynch's (1990) seminal essay "The Greening of Criminology." Initially, the term has provided an umbrella conceptualization of several perspectives still in their infancy. Perhaps the clearest expression of various perspectives has been articulated by David Schlosberg (2007) and Robert White and Diane Heckenberg (2014). First, they note that not only does a green criminology dealing with environment harm exist, but we can conceptualize brown environmental harms related to the disposal of waste, and white environmental harm caused by genetically altered products and results of laboratory processes (White and Heckenberg, 2014, 14–15). When studying causes of environmental harm, we are witnessing the emergence of a variety of approaches that focus on some aspect of environmental harm: radical green criminology is a broad approach including not only ecological, environmental but species justice, along with a focus on capitalism itself; eco-global criminology dealing with transnational corporations; conservation criminology (natural resources); environmental criminology (contexts/situations); constructivist criminology (labels, categories, language, media constructions); and speciesist criminology (harms against animals) (18–20). The source of harm is often traced to: humans, technology, populations, capitalism, and corporations (21–22). Even though there are certain emphases in each of the above, more often the interested researcher crosses boundaries. When relating crime and justice, particularly in light of transnational harms, White (2011; White and Heckenberg 2014, 29) offers three ways of conceptualizing harm: legal conceptions (those established in law—i.e., illegal logging, fishing, dumping, transportation of hazardous products); ecological conceptions (more holistic, particularly concerned with various species and their relationship to the environment and their mutual sustainability—i.e., climate change, pollution/waste, diminishing biodiversity); and justice conceptions (more egalitarian concerned and more specifically including humans, animal rights, and ecological aspects).

Green criminology has also witnessed several attempts to bring environmental crime within the purview of traditional criminological theory

(Brisman, 2014; South, 2014). For example, Agnew (2012) has explained climate change by the use of strain theory; Du Rees (2001) has applied Sykes and Matza's theory of "techniques of neutralization"; Stretesky (2006) has applied "rational choice" and deterrence theory as to the possible responses by regulatory agencies (see also Brisman, 2014; Stretesky, Long, and Lynch, 2013; South (2014) has suggested postmodern theory with its emphasis on "diversity, plurality, and availability of the experiential" (11); and Hall (2017) has applied a cultural criminology perspective. This literature responds to "how and why environmental crimes occur, but also the meaning of such crime and harms" (Brisman, 2014, 21). It remains to be seen to what extent we can break out of more mainstream criminological thought to generate more specific holistic explanations of particular forms of environmental crime. Perhaps White's call for an eco-global criminology begins this discussion.

Literature often returns to discussion about global capitalism and transnational corporations (Lynch, 2015; Stretesky, Long, and Lynch, 2013; Lynch and Stretesky, 2010; White and Heckenberg, 2014, 31–36). The capitalist mode of production, as we read in chapter 3, is built on production of commodities that have undergone a change from use value to exchange value, an objectification that allows exploitation of commodities and their producers. In other words, commodification (commodity fetishism) is the process by which uniqueness and differences (use values) are replaced by sameness (standardized), an abstraction/objectification that allows an easier exchange and profit maximization in the marketplace. Similar capital logic pertains to what is now referred to as the commodification of nature and "market environmentalism" (Prudham, 2016; Kosoy and Corbera, 2010). For example, government often sets the cap for pollution levels, and those companies that have a remainder can save, exchange, or profit from them (called "cap and trade" or "emissions trading"). Or consider the highly profitable fresh water bottling companies generating billions of dollars in revenue. Thus, air and water have become commodified. Consider, too, how this drives the form of distributive justice we see (formal equality), itself a product of fetishism of commodities (commodification of the legal form, e.g., the equal protection clause of the Fourteenth Amendment of the United States Constitution; see also chapter 3).

Capitalist logic has also become globalized with exploitive transnational corporations in search of ever more exploitable resources with often minimal concerns for humans, animals, and the ecosystem. Colonialism, too, has left a legacy of a culture of exploitation and harms against humans, animals, and ecosystems. The unrestrained search for profit maximization has undercut sustainable practices, the latter often minimized by corporations in their cost-benefit analysis of exploitable marketplaces. This has led to "resource depletion, disposal problems, corporate colonization of nature, and species decline" (White and Heckenberg, 2014, 34–35). Attempts to ameliorate damage to the environment must actively deal with capital logic, hence, the call for an eco-global criminology.

Eco-Justice Perspective

Evolving from the numerous approaches to environmental justice are frameworks or perspectives that provide guidance to various aspects of harm and justice. Often in the literature, authors cross boundaries. This provides both the good (conceptualization and focus) and the bad (mixing very different aspects). We return to the work of White (2013c) and White and Heckenberg (2014). This eco-justice perspective distinguishes three approaches (2014): environmental justice that is centered on human well-being including future development, seen as an extension of human rights to a viable environment; ecological justice finding humans are but one part of a more holistic ecosystems vision, environmental rights; and species justice including nonhuman forms such as animal rights against suffering (46). Each also conceptualizes particular forms of harms—humans, ecosystems, and nonhuman forms. This vision responds to the more conservative anthropocentric approach that sees humans as the centers of importance and that nature instrumently serves humans, an approach referred to as speciesism (47; see also Beirne, 2009; Sollund, 2008).

This also suggests that particular discourses exist and are emerging on eco-justice. Anthropocentric discourse, or species-specific discourses focused on human well-being, are beginning to be tempered by new narratives (see Brisman, 2017). New forms of story-telling, including everyday dialogues that are increasingly incorporating environmental concerns, can shape new visions of global well-being. Hence, drawing from the narrative criminology approach in traditional criminology could shed light on the development of a new discourse/narrative.

EARLY DEVELOPMENTS

We can learn much from a historical survey of early struggles in defining the contours of a field. Halsey (2004) offers an instructive critique of the criminological discourse concerning environmental and ecological justice. The general oversight of this area of study by criminologists is among his concerns; however, he attends mainly to the conceptualization of environmental justice within criminology. Of particular concern to Halsey (2004) is the binary nature of much of the debate, which places two opposing forces at odds with each other without consideration for other more complex sets of interests. For example, much of the literature contrasts the interests of capitalism and humanity, or capitalism and nature. While this understanding offers a direct sense of how to categorize and judge interests, it may actually limit our understanding of environmental justice.

Halsey (2004) argues for a need to de-categorize our perspectives and the discourse around our understandings of environmental justice. The very questions of the meaning of the terms and notions of nature and human nature are in need of serious and multiple considerations. Halsey suggests the path offered by Henry and Milovanovic (1996, 2019) in their conception of harm (harms of reduction, harms of repression), which does not rely upon ideas of human nature or a universal subject. This conception of harm instead allows for a fluid understanding of harm as it shifts across time and place and is understood as an expression of power. Expressions of power that induce or inhibit can be understood as harmful. This conception opens our understanding of harm to include the silencing of those wishing to express their own desires. Allowing these expressions may in fact promote justice for the expresser and/or others.

Seis (2001) offers an instructive example of both the usefulness and limitations of the sort of binary analysis that Halsey (2004) critiques. Seis (2001) illustrates the conflict inherent between capitalism and the environment and underscores the importance of movements against environmental degradation across the globe. Certainly he is correct in asserting that questions of environmental justice are political and in dire need of redress. Conclusions that social movements are appropriate in addressing environmental justice concerns in a political manner are also on target. Left unexamined, however, are some of the deeper questions regarding nature, harm, and humanity.

This sort of critique may seem overly academic; however, consider the work of Najam and Robins (2001), which exemplifies the dangers of leaving these questions unexamined. They set out to explain the dual crises of the 1999 World Trade Organization (WTO) meeting in Seattle, which was met with mass protests outside the meeting and refusals by poorer nations of the South to accept the limits offered by the wealthier nations of the North. The article is useful in its assertions regarding the abilities of nations of the North to not only attempt to impose environmental agendas in their own interests upon the nations of the South, but in failing this, succeed in vilifying the Southern nations as anti-environmental. The authors provide an example of either-or thinking.

It was in the interests and within the rights of the Southern nations to resist the imposition of environmental standards by other nations. It does not, however, follow that such resistance suggests an anti-environmental stance. Najam and Robins (2001) are clear on this. However, these authors are less clear concerning the limits imposed in their recommendations to the South. The authors illustrate a perception (not their own) of the South as opting out of the environmental movement through resistance to the

WTO. The move forward suggested by the authors is to opt back in through a balance of sustainable development and sustainable trade. While the analysis of options is not entirely false, it is limiting to and accepting of market-driven notions of environmental justice. A broader understanding of the harms done to the South both environmentally and economically through the impositions of the powers of the market and those who espouse its centrality would offer a more complete understanding of environmental justice for both the South and the North.

Agyeman and Evans (2004) offer a glimpse at the possibilities for future discourse that could open our analyses and our options for environmental justice. They argue that in Britain and less so in the United States, linkages between social justice and environmental justice have informed and elevated the discourse of these movements in such a way that progress on both is possible. These authors are also concerned with the ability of the movements to frame understandings, ideas, and values appropriately for such progress (163). These links and discourses hold hope for the inclusion of those silenced by the binary nature of the current discourse, which is most often limited to a few voices speaking for market interests and a few voices speaking for the interests of "others" who often have no voice in developing these interest claims. To this end, some have offered a focus on narratives, how stories are told, including those addressing harms against the environment (Brisman, 2017, who builds on the work of Presser and Sandberg, 2015). In this view value exists in changing the kinds of stories we tell about harms that better reflect the depth and scope of the problem. Inclusion of, for example, environmental racism where burdens of toxic pollution are unequally distributed (Dicochea, 2012), as well as inclusion of a more holistic view of environmental harms recognizing the balance between the interests of human, eco-system, and nonhuman forms (White and Heckenberg, 2014).

Buckingham (2004) explicitly offers hope through the "radical edge" of the ecofeminist movement (153; see also Mies and Shiva, 1993; Kheel, 1995; Warren and Erkal, 1997). As she explains, it is through this edge of the movement that women, minorities, and other excluded groups are able to influence not only the movements themselves but larger politics in general. Because the poor, women, and other minorities are excluded from the mainstream political discourse, it is through social movements that their voices are heard. When the harm of silence to these voices is overcome, then movement toward more just environmental policies necessarily informed by the newly empowered is possible.

Also finding hope for a nonbinary and inclusive discourse around issues of environmental justice is Schlosberg (2004). He points to activists engaged in what he terms critical pluralism as showing the way for inclusion of varieties of identities, interests, and voices. This inclusion is necessary to not only do justice for those involved but to ensure that the debate includes the multitude of interests. We know from the devastation of rain forests that silencing the voices that best understand the importance of these ecosystems was an injustice to these voices and to the planet. The calls to include disempowered voices is not merely a gesture of inclusion of these individuals (although this is reason enough to listen), but on a larger scale allows for the inclusion of valuable information not available from other sources.

DISTRIBUTIVE AND RETRIBUTIVE SOCIAL JUSTICE PRINCIPLES

Just Sustainabilities

A considerable amount of literature is beginning to emerge concerning sustainable development (for an especially insightful anthology, see Agyeman, Bullard, and Evans, 2003). Increasingly it has become clear that to talk of environmental justice is also to talk about social justice; that is, issues of fairness and quality of life are interconnected. Middleton and O'Keefe (2001) have said "sustainability can mean nothing unless development is socially just" (100). Perhaps the clearest definition of a just sustainable development has been Agyeman, Bullard, and Evans (2003): "to ensure a better quality of life for all, now, and into the future, in a just and equitable manner, while living within the limits of supporting ecosystems" (2). In this direction, there has been some movement in advocating environmental rights (Adeola, 2000; McLaren 2003; Agyeman, Bullard, and Evans 2003, 10–11). We will return to the rights question later in this chapter. The just sustainabilities paradigm is especially concerned with the disproportional impact on the poor. They are at greater risk to experiencing environmental "bads." Thus, for example, we have outright environmental racism, or eco-apartheid (Rees and Westra, 2003, 100; see also Cole and Foster, 2001; Burger and Gochfeld, 2011; Dicochea, 2012).

There are, however, authors who have argued that connecting environmental justice with social justice has to be carefully thought through. For Dobson (2003), one set of vital questions to answer is: "What is to be sustained? Critical natural capital? Biodiversity? The value of objects that naturally appear?" (87–89). He adds another set of questions: "What should the principle of distribution be? Need? Desert? Entitlement?" (89–90). In other words, is distribution according to, respectively, need, desert, and entitlement compatible with environmental sustainability? If we take the first set of three questions and multiply them by the second set of three questions, we can devise nine specific questions that we need to address in specifying more precisely what we may mean by "just sustainability" (90, 94–95).

Distributive Justice: Miller's Principles and Environmental/Ecological Justice

Hobson (2004) argues that environmental justice cannot be separated from social justice. The environment is where the social exists and is the provider of the raw materials necessary to human (and other) life. Social justice would then seem to depend upon environmental justice. This is a question of distributive justice; namely, the issue of unequal distribution of environmental toxic substances and their effects (see Bullard, 1997; Cole and Foster, 2001). A social justice would attend to disparate outcomes as they are related to gender, race, ethnicity, class, sexual preference, and intersections.

Miller's principles of social justice, recall, include need, desert, and equality. Applying these principles to the environment/ecology offers clarity for the purpose of sharing an understanding, but also brings challenges. The following principles are among many important ideas and concepts currently contested.

ENVIRONMENTAL/ECOLOGICAL NEED. What an individual and a society needs in the form of environment/ecology may differ from place to place, time to time, and group/individual to group/individual. As with economic need (the poverty line), however, we are often able to agree upon definitions of need that can be applied across a group within a given time. Agreements made, however, are always contestable with new scientific evidence, party politics, and emerging oppositional groups. Environmental/ecological needs might include such basics as clean water and air. The definition of "clean" would no doubt be contested with interest groups on each side vying for lesser and stricter standards. While those profiting from polluting industries have an interest in greater tolerance of pollutants others have an interest in lesser tolerance. What is clear is that somewhere between pristinely clean air and water and intolerable toxicity is the accepted standard. Setting that standard comes down to not only the environmental sciences but also to the political influences at play.

While the scientific standards for clean air and water can be agreed upon within the scientific communities, information regarding these standards and the criterion by which they are set must be available to the public. The mystification of standards allows for political manipulation from either side of the spectrum and leaves most citizens with little ability to judge proposed standards within a political or community setting. The history of tobacco is instructive to this argument. It was common in the 1950s to find tobacco advertisements in all forms of media extolling the virtues of cigarette smoking. Decades of public health campaigns and increased regulations have affected the public's perception of cigarette smoking, but have certainly not ended the use of this carcinogenic product. Some would argue that continued smoking by older persons and starting smoking by younger persons is an individual choice made with a fully informed understanding of the health consequences. Others find that advertising campaigns and continued denial by corporate interests of liability for cancer cases serve profits for these corporations even within the informing process.

Defining the needs of environmental/ecological justice is necessarily a complex procedure. The scientific process may be fairly straightforward and simple; however, the social/political process is neither. The scientific community must be allowed to independently set healthy standards based on scientific evidence alone without the influence of powerful granting bodies or other interests. Guaranteeing the independence of this process could prove a challenge in itself. Assuming this challenge is met, once the scientific community establishes appropriate health standards, the public must be informed in an unbiased fashion of what these standards are and how they were decided. Once the public is informed of the standards, any variance from healthy standards may then be judged and, hence, responses developed.

Need is also related to environmental/ecological justice beyond air, water, and other basic needs. Foreman (1998) suggests that communities must understand the costs of environmental regulations as well as the benefits. His text proposes that trade-offs must be balanced in making decisions regarding regulations and other legal restrictions on environmental usage. These notions of trade-offs have in fact been institutionalized in policies that allow one industry/nation to purchase pollution quotas from other less-polluting industries/nations. This notion of balance and trading is currently utilized by industries that purposefully decide upon nonenvironmentally friendly and/or illegal production with the understanding that any fines/liabilities imposed will be less costly than the potential losses in profits. If, however, a community, nation, or industry were in desperate need of the item being traded, would a fair agreement regarding trade-offs for environmental/ecological damage become possible? Can persons, nations, or institutions with unmet needs of other necessities of existence be responsible to make a fair trade for their environment/ecology? If not, then the meeting of all other needs must preclude any attempts to trade or balance environmental/ecological standards.

Once individuals, communities, groups, nations, etc. are fully informed and educated about the standards and criteria for healthy environments and ecological systems and these persons/groups are without need of basic necessities of life, a discourse regarding appropriate standards can begin. Prior to these conditions, any such discourse is bound to be fraught with misunderstandings and manipulations.

ENVIRONMENTAL/ECOLOGICAL DESERTS. The desert of environmental/eco-logical justice is closely bound with need. Because all humans (as well as animals and the planet itself) need a healthy and sustained environment and ecology, we all also deserve such. Do some deserve more health than others? Cigarette smoking may prove instructive here as well. If individuals with clear and understandable evidence of the carcinogenic properties of ciga-rettes choose to smoke despite this risk, are they deserving of clean air while smoking, in light of its consequences? Is it possible to ingest ciga-rette smoke and clean air at the same time? What about the cohabitants of the smoker? Do they deserve clean air? An adult cohabitant might have the choice of finding other housing, but what about the children of a smoker? Are the children of smokers more or less deserving of clean air than those of nonsmokers?

Individual and familial trades against clean air are difficult. Social and institutional trades are even more complex. Polluting industries have his-torically hidden their polluting behaviors and the impact of these behaviors on the surrounding communities, workers, and the planet. If, however, complete information regarding the pollution and its impact upon commu-nities, workers, and the planet were fully disclosed, how might agreement come about regarding the need for that pollution and who would deserve the pollution? Would the workers who need their jobs to maintain a stan-dard of living deserve the effects of the pollution? Would the surrounding community that might include workers from the industry and others deserve pollution of their environment because they accommodate the industry in their neighborhood? Would the stockholders and/or company owners deserve pollution in proportion to their profit? How do we measure the deserts of the earth, water, plants, animals, and air?

Preston (2004) offers some insight into this line of questioning. Although he is mainly concerned with reasonability and the limits of reason on environmental rights, he examines some extremes to make his point. He chose to examine radical vegetarian concerns for the health of animals. Do animals deserve protection in an environmentally just world? If, as some vegetarians claim, meat is murder, then perhaps they do. But, as Preston (2004) points out, claims to justice must be reasonable and judged so by the citizenry. Following our discussion of environmental need then, critical is an informed citizenry in democratic decision-making practices that should decide whether animals should be protected from inhumane factory farm conditions and/or slaughter, subject to representation for the species affected such as legal guardians and advocates. We will return to these ideas later.

If we consider smokers and vegetarians, we can see that choices on each end of the health spectrum are left to individuals when it comes to individual consumption. However, decisions about the impact of individual choices on the social condition have created new protections for nonsmokers such as nonsmoking businesses and workplaces. Given enough time and evidence of the desert of justice for animals, consuming meat may eventually become a focus of redefinition, and perhaps, for some, attribution of murder by a reasonable public. The current understanding of the relationship between cattle and humans, however, leaves us in a meat-is-dinner state of affairs. Desert, then, like need, must be decided upon by an informed public in a democratic and reasonable fashion. These decisions must necessarily follow and not preclude the discourse and decisions regarding environmental need.

ENVIRONMENTAL/ECOLOGICAL EQUALITY. Equal access to a healthy environment is sorely lacking. Therefore, developing ideas about what this sort of equality would entail are important for moving beyond the current state of inequality and injustice. Equal treatment of the environment/ecology brings difficult questions regarding the human relationship to our natural environment. How do we assess equal treatment of plants, animals, air, earth, and water?

If we are to abide by the justice principles outlined by Miller (1999), we must give serious consideration to the notion of equal environmental justice. Preceding equality, some authors argue, would, however, necessarily be assessments of need and desert. We must know and be fully informed of the environmental standards needed for healthy human life and agree upon the deserts of persons and institutions before setting about to assure equal access.

Once the needs and deserts have been established, policies and monitoring programs would be required to assure that environmental goods and burdens are equally distributed. Torres's (2005) account of the movement to demilitarize Vieques, an island east of Puerto Rico, is instructive here. Some areas were used as bombing ranges by the U.S. military, and many hazards were left behind. As she notes, the movement against the environmental degradation of Vieques was strengthened with the call for access to a healthy environment. The unequal burden carried by the people of Vieques was evidenced by increased health risks. Educating concerned persons about these risks assisted in forcing the military out of Vieques. As Torres (2005) notes, however, to assure that these or other burdens are not again inflicted upon Vieques, there must be assurances that the government will not discriminate against the island in its decisions regarding military and other polluting activities, and an international monitoring body must remain vigilant in protecting this area.

Commitments to nondiscrimination and vigilant oversight would be necessary in assuring equal treatment of people and places. Because of historical inequalities, discrimination, and a lack of oversight, attaining equality will be required before establishing equal environmental protection.

Distributive Environmental Justice: Schlosberg's Four Components

Schlosberg (2007) offers four components of justice: distribution, recognition, participation, and capabilities. White and Heckenbert (2014) apply them to three components of an eco-justice perspective: environmental justice, ecological justice, and species justice (48–49). Integrating Miller's three components of distributive justice is more in line with environmental justice, and like Rawls, is more concerned with fair distribution of goods and burdens. The focus was more anthropocentric (humans' well-being). Principles privileged by Miller, we have seen, include needs, equality, and desert. That is, "how, and to what end, should a just society distribute the various benefits (resources, opportunities, and freedoms) and the burdens (costs, risks, and unfreedoms) required to maintain it" (Brighouse cited in White and Heckenberg, 2014, 12). Schlosberg (2007) builds on these notions of distributive justice to include recognition, participation, and capacities (capabilities). Each of these aspects or dimensions is integral for a composite approach, a social justice approach.

Schlosberg provides two forms of what more generally is called environmental justice: environmental justice and ecological justice. White and Heckenberg separate the latter into two, ecological justice, species justice producing three particular approaches in eco-justice: environmental justice concerned with rights to healthy environment for human well-being, ecological justice regarding both human and eco-systems, and species justice calling for the rights of animals not to suffer and for their care and respectful treatment.

Schlosberg draws from the Fraser and Honneth debate (recognition v. distribution, see chapter 3) to show that even dichotomized, each is essential. *Recognition*, or acknowledgement, is necessary for diverse voices to be heard. Diminishing the other reduces the person in their nuanced abilities. Axel Honneth has well made the case. *Distribution* must be fair because without fair distribution, humans' well-being is adversely affected. John Rawls and others such as David Miller attend to this. Both are integral components as can be seen in the Fraser v. Honneth debate. Both recognize the importance of redistribution as well as recognition. The polarization in the discussion was more for clarification of central components, not for dismissal of the other, argues Schlosberg.

However, two additional components are integral. *Participation*, or what Schlosberg calls, somewhat misleadingly, "procedural justice," are necessary as well as *capacities* or capabilities. Participation refers to participatory democratic decision-making. Without meaningful input by diverse agents, justice cannot be genuine (see also Young, 2000). Capacities, or capabilities, we have previously seen, drawing from Armatya Sen and Martha Nussbaum, concern how distributions may or may not enhance humans' well-being, particularly their "functionings" and specifically their "doings" and "beings." A doing, such as eating, is connected with being, such as being well nourished. Thus, the concern is for opportunities to transform distributed resources to enhance doings and beings toward well-being.

Social justice for Schlosberg concerns how all four components are articulated. It is a multifaceted perspective. Fraser, recall, argued that to correct maldistribution, there must be a restructuring of political economies—both the redistribution of resources as well as cultural patterns. Only in this way are we on the road to a genuine social justice. Schlosberg has extended this to tease out what sometimes is implicit in the literature and extends on the importance of capabilities. His is a response to the mostly distributive emphasis in much of environmental justice literature (nature equitably serving human interests) including the inequitable burdens faced such as toxics and heightened risks by the poor, people of color, and disenfranchised groups.

Applying his multifaceted approach to the nonhuman world (ecological justice, species justice), distribution (need, desert, equality) can encompass humans as well as nonhumans (White and Heckenberg, 2014, 50). Thus, Miller's application of three distributive principles of justice can be extended to eco-systems (ecological justice) and diverse species (species justice), but further augmented by the notions of recognition, participation, and capabilities.

Recognition can be extended to the nonhuman world to acknowledge the interests of diverse eco-systems (ecological justice) and to diverse species (species-justice). These are more often reduced to givens for human needs (anthropocentrism, human benefits). Nature, in this view, has too often been seen as exclusively serving humans, nature is a slave to humans. Nature is voiceless in this view. One of the few early studies that included recognition in discussion of environmental justice is the work of Figueroa (2003; Schlosberg 2007, 59). For environmental justice activists, misrecognition still remains structurally embedded, as, for example, legalistically, "intent" to discriminate may be difficult to prove in a court of law (Schlosberg 2007, 59; Cole and Foster, 2001). This exists where polluting industries often make the argument that the poor and minorities willingly move to higher-risk areas, overlooking (misrecognition) the fact that these areas may be some of the few where lower-priced housing exists. Thus, environmental risks and misrecognition are connected. Environmental activist groups, too, are often devalued, disrespected, dismissed, or ignored (Schlosberg 2007, 61). Recognition can also be applied to diverse eco-systems and species, especially in the recent interest of rights of nature. Recognition in the eco-justice perspective would entail providing guardians, representative, and advocates to address the many issues concerning eco-system's character, dynamics, and well-being. Similarly, and more recently, a growing call exists for the rights of animals, that is, recognition for what they intrinsically are, not what they may instrumentally mean, for human beings.

Capabilities can be extended to the nonhuman world: here "capability means that each thing should be able to flourish as the thing it is" (Schlosberg 2007, 61). Environmental justice advocates can, in addition to the traditional understanding of distributive justice (needs, deserts, equality), also include the call for safe, productive, fulfilling environments for well-being as well as for future generations' well-being, for greater and equitable opportunities for developing their capabilities (functionings, doings, and beings). For ecological justice, capabilities, Schlosberg (2007, 144) argues that Nussbaum's work (2006a, 2006b) is suggestive, even offering a capabilities list for animals, an examination of mistreatment of animals, a call for equal dignity for animals, an engagement with traditional theorists of distributive justice, and a critique of capabilities defined as enhancing only human well-being. But this is incomplete, often resigned to the examination of only sentient possibilities of animals and not with broader eco-systems and retains an individualistic emphasis (Schlosberg 2007, 145–146). Thus, Schlosberg (2007) says that we must also include habitats and ecological systems that support species life. It is this larger position of intertwined capabilities that form systems that must be the focal point, the functioning, the doings, and beings of human and nonhuman forms. The new discourse includes dignity, respect, integrity, flourishing, enhancement, and sensitivity and respect for different notions of agency in relation to specific habitats/systems.

Participation can be extended to the nonhuman world by providing representatives for their interests who can speak on behalf of the eco-system and animals (Schlosberg, 2007, 51). The environmental justice movement, too, has shown how impacted human groups are often denied meaningful participatory democratic channels for expression. And this is often along class, gender, race, and intersectional dimensions. Thus, equity demands for participation are essential in the call for social justice. This can be extended to eco-justice and species justice. The question is how diminished capabilities and recognition can now be addressed. Since Schlosberg's writing (2007), a number of developments in law, constitutional change, and policy-making have taken place that are increasingly acknowledging some notion of the rights of nature and animals. Participation in these developments is being considered through legal guardians and advocate representatives of nature and animals who will provide for their interests in participatory democratic decision-making. This will be taken up more fully in a following section. Important here is to recognize Schlosberg (2007, 157–158), inspired by Nussbaum (2006a), connecting recognition, capabilities, and distribution with the notion of participation or what he terms procedural justice.

Greater clarity on each of these extensions to the nonhuman is needed. In practice these four principles of justice have to be balanced, particularly tempered by sustainability issues. And this balance must also consider future generations, learning from the past, and being attentive to the present and emerging harms. Contemporary literature is tackling this question and the contours are yet to be clearly delineated. Distributive justice principles, in this thrust, must go beyond the traditional discussions of needs, desert, and equality to include recognition, participation, and capabilities. Often, in activist struggles, all four components of Schlosberg's model are implicit, but not necessarily fully articulated. A multifaceted discourse that encompasses all four components is the call for better understanding of distributive justice, whether more directed toward environmental justice, ecological justice, or species justice.

ISSUES IN ECO-JUSTICE

Disparate Impact: Social Justice, Disparate Impact, and Two Fallacies

Studies that show disparate impact—certain groups are more likely to be adversely affected—have often been answered by two main ideologies (Cole and Foster, 2001, 58). The first ideology is that the very lifestyle choices of racial minorities are such that they choose to live near waste sites. But this does not explain why they do, only that they are likely do so. It does not answer why poor African Americans or Latinos are segregated in cities and become recipients of various pollutants, why farm workers are often poor and Latino. This ideology merely blames the victim and naturalizes disparate impacts; it leaves structural issues removed from discussion.

The second related ideology is market dynamics (Cole and Foster, 2001, 60). The argument goes: people are choosing to live in neighborhoods with toxic dump sites because they are rational economic calculators. Thus, they knew in advance the problems they would incur. However, this once again downplays structural choices available and elevates capitalist market ethos to a self-explanatory ideology. It hides racial discriminatory practices under the name of choice. It says nothing about how choice is narrowed for certain segments of the population. It says nothing of housing discrimination, red-lining mortgage practices, and rental discrimination. It says, in short, nothing about the very legitimacy of market forces, whether they are just or not. And it allows a form of distributive justice that is seemingly self-explanatory and legitimate.

Social Justice, Disparate Impact, and Intent

A second narrative that sustains disparate impact, embedded in law, can be traced to the notion of intent. Since the U.S. Supreme Court case *Washington v. Davis* (1976), in order to construe "race discrimination," one needs to show individual intent. The focus is on the bad apple. In a 1991 federal court case, *R.I.S.E., Inc. v. Kay* (placing a landfill in a dominantly African American community), the justices stated "the Equal Protection Clause does not impose an affirmative duty to equalize the impact of official decisions on different racial groups". This clause, it was argued, "merely prohibits government officials from intentionally discriminating on the basis of race" (Cole and Foster, 2001, 64, 126–129).

According to Cole and Foster (2001), to begin to develop a social justice view on environmental issues we need an approach that "(1) retains a structural view of economic and social forces as they influence discriminatory outcomes, (2) isolates the dynamics within environmental decision-making processes that further contribute to such outcomes, and (3) normatively evaluates social forces and environmental decision-making processes which contribute to disparities in environmental hazards distribution" (65).

Political Biases in Environmental Justice Debates

Most, Sengupta, and Burgener (2004) examine the complexities and outcome differences associated with methodological choices. As they show, new complex technologies and software utilized by environmental researchers concerned with disparate impacts on minority populations lend "an aura of authority" (584) that can veil poor research design. Beyond research design, conflicts in scientific agendas are also of concern. Fuller (2004) reflects upon the controversy surrounding a best-selling text by Bjørn Lomborg (2001), which contends that environmental problems are regularly overstated by environmental scientists. While Fuller does not dispute Lomborg's claims, he is concerned with the process by which scientific claims are reviewed for ethical rigor. Because of the competing groups aligned on each side of the environmental debate, ethics within environmental science appear particularly consequential.

Claims made within the environmental literature often extend beyond the scientific to include not only the political but also the moral judgements of the author. Political biases are inherent in justice debates as we all come to an issue with our underlying philosophies of right and wrong justice and injustice (whether we realize it or not) and our writing (including our subject and method of choice) is informed by these philosophies. Moral biases, however, are often less clear and not supported by a philosophical base. Donohoe (2003), for example, writes of an impending Malthusian disaster. He argues that our current tenuous state was created by several conditions including overpopulation and over consumption. He attends briefly to overpopulation as especially problematic within Africa, Asia, and Latin America. He also notes that the maldistribution of wealth is problematic and that it is the wealthy in the United States, and not the U.S. population in general, that are responsible for overconsumption.

Donohoe (2003) is at once political and moralistic concerning our environmental condition. His concerns for overpopulation are left unexamined while other concerns are clearly supported by data and a transparent philosophy of equality and justice. Population growth in Africa, Asia, and Latin America are not necessarily problematic unless one has taken a moral stance against all population growth. A political argument for or against population growth necessitates a philosophical base informed with data to support the argument. To merely claim that increasing populations on some parts of the globe, especially when the areas identified as problematic are nonwhite, is neither useful nor appropriate in a scholarly debate. Even the more complex arguments relying on the interactions of population growth, affluence, and technology are problematic. While increased consumption is more taxing on the environment, it is not necessarily so, but is so because of the current modes of producing, distributing, and marketing consumables. Further, all persons located in "high consumption" areas are not necessarily overconsuming and in fact are at times impoverished.

Fuller (2004) notes that the debate regarding sustainability and population growth is contentious. This debate does not necessarily require a far-left and far-right political divide. One may be on the left and find that it is necessary to allow persons throughout the globe to decide their own reproductive futures, even if this means population growth. This finding would be informed with a philosophical base accepting that meeting human need is primary for environmental justice. One may also be on the left and find that restricting birth rates is necessary to protect the environment. This finding is informed by a philosophical base that accepts the environment as primary and human need as secondary.

When examining the environmental literature, as with any other literature, the reader must attend to the claims made and the data offered to support those claims. Further, the reader must be aware of her/his own philosophical foundation (reflexivity) and those underlying the consumed literature (ideology). Otherwise, the literature can appear quite contradictory and confusing. Once a reader is aware of the methods, politics, and moral stances that inform the literature, however, one is able to disentangle the contradictions and take from the literature the knowledge that is sought. This knowledge is then useful in informing one's own philosophy toward environmental issues and can assist us in incorporating an understanding of environmental justice with other social justice issues and ideas.

FINDINGS OF ENVIRONMENTAL/ ECOLOGICAL (IN)JUSTICE

Evans and Marcynyszyn (2004) found that low-income children in upstate New York were susceptible to bad health outcomes because of their exposure to poor environments (see also Burger and Gochfeld, 2011; Gochfeld and Burger, 2011). Indicators for environmental risks for these researchers included crowding, poor housing quality, and noise. For many of us, this finding would suggest a social condition in need of address. Foreman (1998), on the other hand, would seemingly reject these concerns as nonsocial. He argues that such housing conditions are not a social concern, but a private familial/individual concern not rising to the level of a social or environmental justice issue.

Hill (2001) is also concerned with the quality of housing and environmental justice. When it was discovered that home sites in Ciudad Juarez, Mexico, were polluted and unsafe for habitation, the landowners were given incomplete and contradictory information regarding the safety of their lands. As no reparations were forthcoming and the landowners could not afford to leave their homes, they chose to not only stay, but to guard the remaining lands around them. With insecurities in housing, the investments already made in the area by these mostly poor citizens, and the manipulations by local politicians, those who had been sold plots of land in the landfill carefully guarded these plots rather than organizing to demand reparations and relocation. This took the pressure off the local government, which instead of correcting this problem successfully used an environmental catastrophe to their own advantage, placing the responsibility for the polluted land back on the owners (e.g., blaming the victim).

Housing is a basic human need that would surely be included in any social justice scheme of need. Finding and keeping safe affordable housing is often problematic for those isolated in poor inner-city communities and those isolated in poor rural communities. Evans and Marcynyszyn (2004) and Hill (2001) note the economic status of the subjects of their studies of housing as increasing their chances for suffering negative environmental impact. However, as Mills (2001) notes, race is the primary indicator of the placement of toxic waste sites (see also Cole and Foster, 2001, 54–58; Been, 1995; Dicochea, 2012; Burger and Gochfeld, 2011; Gochfeld and Burger, 2011) and has continued even though recognized (i.e., much publicized cases such as The Dakota Access Pipeline; Flint, Michigan, and toxic wastes; Chester, Pennsylvania, and toxic wastes). Black communities are more likely than any other to be burdened with the wastes of others. Housing and environmental justice then are linked to both economic and racial inequalities. These injustices regarding equal access to safe housing are typically located within the borders of a nation. However, many environmental justice issues are borderless.

Gbadegesin (2001) examines the impact of global waste dumping and the exploration activities of global corporations on the Niger Delta region. He reports that the dumping of toxic (including nuclear) wastes on the African continent by non-African nations is not at all uncommon and results in what he terms "toxic terrorism" for its impact on the health and well-being of the African populations. Non-African oil corporations also utilize the African continent for exploration purposes and fail to abide by environmental standards, leaving local populations to deal with the pollution without even the economic benefits (jobs, for example) that might come from exploration by locally owned companies.

While racism and economic injustices within nations can lead to great local injustices, these injustices exported on a global scale create global injustices. Not only are environmental and health damages created, also endangered are local control, governmental protections, and democratic discourse.

The North American Free Trade Agreement (NAFTA) greatly affected the global economy and has with its legislation already and will continue to impact our understanding of environmental justice. Chapter 11 is a provision within the NAFTA agreement that frees corporate interests residing in the included nations from the environmental legislation of other included nations (Public Citizen and Friends of the Earth, 2001). The basic premise of this portion of the NAFTA agreement is that nations should not be allowed to impede the profits of nonresident corporations through environmental regulations. Nations are allowed to make and impose regulations, but at a cost. If the local nation finds that these costs are too high, environmental regulations, and with them, the needs of local citizens, may be sacrificed. These sorts of decisions occur within and without the NAFTA signing nations.

Renteria (2003) explains that while globalization has an impact upon the relationship between the state and its citizens, that relationship is complex and often leaves citizens unprotected in unexpected ways. "Glocalization" is the term she uses to express the impact of globalization on local legal structures. The state of India is used as an example, but any nation is susceptible to the same pressures. When international pressures build upon a nation-state, that state often makes decisions not in the interests of the local citizens or in accordance with local law but instead in the interests of global markets, investors, and institutions. The nation-state is not entirely irrelevant, but in fact as in the case of the Narmada dam project in India, may choose to continue projects even after local uprisings have forced abandonment by the World Bank or other powerful institutions. The nation-state, as in the case of India, may then seek other investors for these damaging projects regardless of citizen needs.

Issues of globalized environmental harms infringe upon the natural environment and upon the created social structures such as local law. Within and without these local legal structures are indigenous communities. In the United States, American Indians have been spatially separated and legally separated from other citizens. This separation has created multiple injustices that we will not address here. What is of concern here are the appeals of indigenous peoples for not only environmental justice but to their own identities and futures.

Sylvain (2002) offers an analysis of our often-contradictory understanding and usages of indigenism, which both promote protection of and violate the environmental needs of the groups thus identified. Of particular concern to the work is the San identity of indigenous people of southern Africa. While this identity imposes particular ethnic and cultural understandings, it also implies the necessity for protecting the land and water used by this group. At the same time indigenous identities (as imposed and/or claimed) have the effect of ignoring the complex history of this and other indigenous groups. As those labeled as keepers of indigenous culture seek social and economic justice, they must walk a fine line of remaining "indigenous" to maintain some protections while seeking their own paths to the future. As Sylvain (2002) explains, we must remain ever vigilant to understanding the imposed and generated identities of indigenous people while allowing these groups to make their own way without either unnecessary intrusion or paternalistic protections.

Distributive and Retributive Eco-Justice Principles in Action

Environmental Protection Agencies: United States, United Nations

With environmental hazards or potential hazards crossing boundaries—acid rain, greenhouse effects, global warming, contamination of fresh water supplies, deforestation, unestablished consequences of genetically modified foods, etc.—the search for social justice is taking on a global significance. We already witness organizations developing: the United Nations Environment Program; the Earth Observation Summit (2002); The Global Earth Observation System of Systems' (GEOSS) ten-year plan; the U.S. Environmental Protection Agency (EPA) agency's "global warming" initiative; the Kyoto Protocol; and the Paris Climate Agreement, 2015, among many others, attest to the new concerns for global environmental justice. Along with these initiatives are concerns with how best to deal with issues of retributive justice particularly when dealing with transnational corporations (see Kalas, 2001).

Emerging are innovative ideas as to how to respond to national and international polluters. For example, the so-called internationally based Kyoto Protocol was established in 1997 as a method for dealing with greenhouse gases. Here the mechanism for diminishing adverse gases revolves around market-based policies concerning credits that can be traded as commodities (see Evans, 2004). Here, an industry is provided a certain limit on emissions, but can develop credits if it falls under the limit, which can be traded, sold, or saved. This is referred to as emissions trading. This approach has been used since the early 1980s in the United States with arguably some success in reducing pollution. The EPA has also advocated conflict regulation (alternative dispute settlements) in responding to transgressors of environmental laws.

Many authors beginning from the early 1990s, however, question whether transnational corporations can adequately meet the challenge without a new vista. The call is for the establishment of environmental rights (Kalas, 2001, 15) or to some international right to a healthy environment (Lee, 2000). As Lee (2000) wrote, "the recognition of the right to a healthy environment is the first step toward providing environmental justice to many individuals harmed by the tortuous and sometimes criminal conduct of large multinational corporations" (16). He suggested the establishment of an International Environmental Court toward this end. This would, amongst other things, create criteria for the assessment of risks, how to manage risk, and a scientific body to deal with technical points.

Given an acceptance to move ahead with the notion of an internationally recognized right to a healthy environment, many issues of justice must be resolved. Should the right be connected to individual claims? Group claims? Both? (Lee, 2000, 4). Western concepts are strongly connected with individual rights; but African and Islamic rights are more directed to the group. It would seem, therefore, that a Western notion must be integrated with a group notion of rights and justice. Lee (2000) has provided hints about the possibilities when we look at the notion of class action suits practiced in the U.S. court system, particularly in tort actions.

Consider Miller's three conceptions of distributive justice (needs, desert, equality) in a global environmental context. Lee (2000) would argue for a universal standard of justice—a universal right to a healthy environment, a principle of justice resting on the equality principle. However, acknowledged are economic realities that undermine the establishment of principles of justice based on equality. For example, in the Universal Declaration of Human Rights established in 1948, universal standards are specified, whereas in the North American Agreement on Environmental Cooperation (established in 1993), binding the United States, Canada, and Mexico, standards are allowed to vary by country, and hence, by economic conditions (Lee, 2000, 2). Accordingly, we have a functional equivalent of a regional principle of justice based on desert.

Key to the establishment of a universal principle (equality) for environmental justice, according to Lee (2000), would be linking the nature of the environment to the right of development (12).The Rio Conference on Environment and Development (1992) establishes this linkage between a healthy environment and the right to sustainable development. Consider some of the principles Lee reported (2000, 31, n. 194):

Principle 1: Human beings are at the centre of concerns for sustainable development. They are entitled to a healthy and productive life in harmony with nature.

Principle 4: In order to achieve sustainable development, environmental protection shall constitute an integral part of the development process and cannot be considered in isolation from it.

Principle 12: States should cooperate to promote a supportive and open international economic system that would lead to economic growth and sustainable development in all countries, to better address the problems of environmental degradation.

Principle 25: Peace, development and environmental protection are interdependent and indivisible.

The European Union, in a Resolution on Industrial Restructuring and Relocation in the European Union (November 13, 1996), "sees an urgent need to shift the basis of the framework for international action on trade and investment from a relatively narrow focus on growth and preservation of free trade and investment, to the more complex goal of sustainable development, which means integrating economic efficiency, macroeconomic stability, social justice and environmental sustainability" (reported in Lee 2000, 32, n. 206; see also Agyeman, Bullard, and Evans, 2003).

When we examine retributive principles of justice at the global level, we find that responses to violations vary by economics, politics, corruption, and ideology. Thus, we once again have an undermining of principles of equality. Lee's (2000) suggestion is to focus on the notion of "degradation" of an environment that is shown to produce serious health problems for a definable group of people, or a "'disruption' of a people's way of life" (15). Both commissions and omissions would be constitutive of injury (16). As to unintentional omissions, because uncertainty sometimes exists in long-range consequences, the precautionary principle should be applicable (see Kamminga, 1996): no current violation has taken place, but there is a strong possibility of future harm stemming from the current activity. A precautionary principle could be developed that is anticipatory in nature that focuses on "state omissions that risk imminent and serious violation of [a] . . . well-defined standard" (Lee, 2000, 16). As a consequence, state responsibilities would be implicated.

More recently, proposals in the United States and around the globe are calling for a "Green New Deal," modeled after the U.S. response to the Great Depression called the "New Deal" in the 1930s. Many have said the latter economic intervention as saving capitalism, for it seems we were at the bifurcation point of transforming into a new mode of production. There has also been established a "Global Green Economy Index" (see Dual Citizen), which compares countries on their progress toward correcting eco-system damage. There has been some resistance to commodification of nature and market-based mechanisms ("emissions trading," "carbon dumping," "enslavement of nature"; see White and Heckenberg, 2014, 12, 31–35). Other critiques are grouped as green imperialism (impositions of standards by powerful countries). Alternative proposals have also been suggested (People's Summit at Rio+20 for Social and Environmental Justice, 2012; we will return to the latter in chapter 11).

In sum, the notion of a human right to a healthy environment has been repeated in a number of ways in various U.N. conferences. Lee (2000) cites, most importantly, Principle 1 of the Rio Declaration: "Human beings are . . . entitled to a healthy and productive life in harmony with nature" (17). Principles of social and environmental justice will surely become increasingly globally defined.

Eco-Justice and the Rights of Nature: Legal Change? or Legislative Change?

Indigenous communities have different relationships and ethics regarding the natural world than do current overriding cultural norms (Callicot 1997). Beyond indigenous communities, the question of whether trees, rivers, glaciers, animals, and even plants can have legal rights may challenge sensibilities, but increasingly courts and legislators are acknowledging this idea. Iconic was Christopher Stone's "Should Trees Have Standing?" (1972). Legal decisions protecting whole rivers (Ganga, Yamuna) and animals in India and habitats (Amazon) in Colombia have been won. We are witnessing legislative enactments protecting a lake in the United States, a river in New Zealand, and constitutional changes in Ecuador and Bolivia (see also Hillebrecht and Berds, 2017). Just as the movement of human rights over time has witnessed changes such as the abolishment of slavery, expanded women's rights, juvenile rights, rights of persons with disabilities, and rights to sexual preference and gender expression, there is an increasing acknowledgement of the rights of nature.

Sigal (2019) reported on the people of Ohio's vote regarding the rights of Lake Erie. In a special election, voters were asked whether Lake Erie should be "granted legal rights normally reserved for a person." The measure passed, giving citizens the right to sue on behalf of the lake whenever they feel its rights are being violated. As the article points out, and as we do here, other nations have also allowed for legal status to rivers, lakes, rain forests, and plant species.

Instructive to complexities is a high court decision in India, *Mohd Salim v. State of Uttarakhand and Others* (March, 2017), in which the court stipulated that the Ganga and Yamuna rivers were living entities, legal persons or entities, "with all corresponding rights, duties and liabilities of a living person . . . they are also accorded the rights akin to fundamental rights/legal rights." The decision included that these eco-systems can be given voice by guardians, a concept of *in loco parentis* (assignment of legal representatives for others) under the general umbrella of *parens patriae* (acting on behalf of agents who cannot speak for themselves, i.e., children, mentally disabled). The Indian court assigned specific persons to be representatives of the respective rivers.

The decision was, however, overturned by the Indian Supreme Court, through narrow reasoning concerned that the two rivers in question pass through other states and hence the lower court could not rule on implementation. There were also questions about who would be responsible if the river floods and who would be the guardians? And questions concerning the protection of particular religious views. Perhaps another higher court could have provided creative logic that could have been a jump in thinking, a break from the past, such as in the U.S. Supreme Court's *Brown v. Board of Education* overruling a half century of "separate but equal" logic and recognizing a history of injustices directed toward African Americans and hence providing the grounds for affirmative action, and in *Griswold v. Connecticut* protecting privacy.

This court case is illustrative of the movement toward an eco-jurisprudence. One of the key questions for activists concerns whether more lasting change is better via the courts *or* through legislative acts (O'Donnell, 2018; Pecharroman, 2018; Sanders, 2018). A central concern is in constructing legal entities, legal personalities the answer to which begins with common legal practices that create legal fictions out of nonhuman entities: corporations, municipalities, businesses, not-for-profit organizations, religious organizations, etc. This legal logic is beginning to be applied to nature. In specifying how nature can speak, the logic of *parens patriae* along with *in loco parentis* has been central. Together, these provide standing (recognition, participation) in court for litigation.

Fruitful discussion concerning pursuing rights of nature by way of the courts or by legislation has been provided by Erin O'Donnell and Julia Talbot-Jones (2018; see also Pecharroman, 2018; O'Donnell 2017; Sanders 2017). They write that legal rights for nature can take on a two-pronged approach that makes use of legal as well as legislative avenues. They specify issues which rely exclusively with either legalist or legislative change. First, legislative acts likely engage multiple audiences, and hence when passed, have multiple bases of support. Legal decisions by lower courts are more unstable, subject to being overruled, and ultimately rest on the highest courts' findings. Second, legal decisions can often leave the implementation of their decisions unfunded or underfunded. Third, legal decisions that appoint legal guardians may not reflect all interested parties, and often surfacing are questions of sufficiency of independence from state governments. Fourth, legal cases may conflate and prioritize human interests (environmental harms that reduce humans' well-being) with harms against nature itself and hence undermine the integrity of nature. Fifth, the sheer expense and difficulties in having a case heard in court, including establishing legal standing are compelling impediments. Sixth, courts often make use of balancing and this often can downplay the interests of nature itself.

On the other hand, first, creating legal rights for nature by way of legislation includes questions of sufficiency of depth, scope, prioritizing, appropriate definitions, force and effect; notwithstanding, we add, legislators' personal biases, concerns with lobbyists, re-election, and internal pressures within political parties, and the dominance of an institutional structure that privileges certain segments over others for their respective inputs in decision-making processes. Second, contemporary legislators' commonsense thinking, when pressed, can fall back to an exclusively environmental justice perspective privileging human well-being, reinforcing the notion that nature is the slave of the state, and, we add, downplaying sensitivity to ecological justice and species justice in their cost-effectiveness balancing. Third, legislation often creates such market logic as "water markets" and pollution markets where allocations are made and companies may sell or trade their allocated ceiling amounts. This certainly reflects and reinforces capital logic: use values of products are transformed into commodities for commodity exchange; intrinsic values of the product are reduced to exchange value in the marketplace. Intrinsic values are obfuscated and replaced with market recognized objects for exploitation.

Notwithstanding many legal and legislative hurdles that await, providing legal rights for nature, argue O'Donnell and Talbot-Jones (2018), first "can be created within a range of legal and institutional settings to address a number of complex socio-environmental and economic problems" (13); second, is the possibility of creating rights for nature in both legal and legislative channels; and third, that the establishment of rights for nature are no longer summarily dismissed, even though providing sufficient force and effect of laws of nature is still in its infancy of development.

As to species justice, legislation and legal decisions are beginning to grapple with the idea of the rights of species. The High Court of the state of Uttarakhand, India, we have seen, on July 4, 2018, in *Narayan Dutt Bhatt v. Union of India and Others*, ruled that "the entire animal kingdom including avian and aquatic" are granted legal personhood and that all citizens within the state are henceforth persons *in loco parentis*. Each entity has "a distinct persona with corresponding rights, duties and liabilities of a living person." We are beginning to see this line of thought in occasional media highlighting animal rights such as with the fast-food chain, McDonald's, and their requirements for raising of chickens by their suppliers (cage-free egg policy, increasing space, restricting debeaking, providing better habitats); the appropriate way of killing lobsters (away from boiling to death to considerations of other methods such as the use of a knife, or freezing first); and such heavily publicized cases as the football star Michael Vick's sponsoring dog fights. We already have implemented rights regarding cruelty against animals and for preserving endangered species, thus suggesting some rights to well-being of animals. Much of this literature implicitly is arguing for legal rights for animals (see Beirne, 2009). The India court has taken the lead in making rights of animals and other species more explicit.

Schlosberg applies each of his principles of justice (distribution, recognition, capabilities, participation) to species well-being. Distribution in recognizing needs and in parity or equality in terms of letting each (humans, eco-systems, *and* species) to flourish, to "maximize general functioning, the 'to be' and 'to do' of life" (White and Heckenberg, 2014, 185), to give equal opportunity for each to flourish and fulfill its potential (183). This would also include redistribution policies. Recognition pertains to acknowledging the uniqueness of each species. Status injury is suggested for harms against distinct ways of life of species, a mis- or a mal-recognition (138–139). The notion of ecocide has also been introduced. Capabilities require being sensitive to flourishing of the species, and preservation of dignity and respect for the uniqueness of species' well-being. "No sentient animal should be cut off from a chance for nourishing life, a life with the type of dignity relevant to that species, and . . . all sentient animals should enjoy certain positive opportunities to flourish" (Nussbaum cited in Schlosberg, 145; see also Nussbaum, 2006a, 2006b). Unlike Nussbaum's more individualistic approach, even positing a capabilities list for animals that parallels a human list, Schlosberg insists that we need to better recognize the relation of species to their particular natural habitat, to eco-systems, and that a better way is, as demanding as it may be, developing a species-specific capabilities list ("species norms") related to that environment. As to the fourth component of justice, participation, Schlosberg suggests his term could mean "recognition of the consideration of the natural world in human decision-making" (158) while assuming parity (moral worth, political status).

In short, we are witnessing a growing "Earth Jurisprudence" recognizing the rights of eco-systems and diverse species. A certain critical mass is in the process of development whereby the decision of the High Court of Uttarakhand, as well as Christopher Stone's 1972 article on "should trees have standing?" are becoming more receptive to the public (recognition) and for serious engagement. To this end, a growing body of literature is suggesting the establishment of national and cross-national "environmental courts" (see Wright and Heckenberg, 2014, 256–275).

Restorative Justice, Problem-Solving, and Environmental Courts

Given recognition of victimization, be it of humans, specific environments/eco-systems, or species (animals and plants), then how do we proceed in a more holistic fashion in correcting its occurrence, accepting responsibilities, restoring status injuries to more natural states of beings and doings (functioning), considering and respecting diverse stakeholders, restoring harmony or balance among the various parties impacted, compensating for harms, and protecting future generations? One significant approach advocated is applying restorative justice and a participatory problem-solving emphasis rather than exclusively punitive retributive responses (Preston, 2011). Another approach is specific environmental courts that are separate from criminal and civil courts (Pring and Pring, 2016). It is argued that environmental courts are more in tune with the complexities of environmental issues.

Restorative justice, it is argued, can best accommodate various components of eco-justice (distribution, recognition, capabilities, participation) in arriving at a viable, long-lasting holistic decision: distributing benefits and burdens according to relevant principle of justice (needs, equality, deserts); recognizing and respecting each stakeholder; providing voice in participation; maximizing the capabilities (maximum functioning of "doing" and "beings"); and redistributing resources in more balanced, equitable, and harmonious ways—all tempered by sensitivity to sustainability. This problem-solving method can better serve injustice faced by eco-systems and species as compared to the accusatory style that only relies on winners and losers in a zero-sum game.

TRANSFORMATIVE ECO-JUSTICE PERSPECTIVE?

We have been developing various perspectives in eco-justice that arguably, in most cases, can be situated within a reformist remedial style (chapter 4) such as environmental restorative justice. The radical accusatory style would question the limits of this reform (see also Stretesky, Long, and Lynch 2013; also acknowledged by a key exponent of eco-justice, White and Heckenberg 2014, 31–35, although ultimately arguing optimistically for reform potentials). Those from a radical accusatory style would point out that a mode of production such as capitalism has inherent limitations to change before it undergoes a qualitative change to a different form. Within capital logic and the discourses that are generated within its terms, we witness class divisions; gross inequalities (growing disparities between rich and poor); excessive competitiveness; the commodification of all (the conversion of use values into abstraction, exchange values); objectifications such as formal equality and the juridical subject, creating competitive market values on exchange values, even on air and water), reduction of the species being to mere cogs in machines with narrow range of duties; legacy of colonialism remaining in continuous racial inequities; and dominance of class privilege. Given the crucial call by eco-justice adherents for more inclusive sensitivities to a world community of humans and nonhumans, how will the internal limits of capital logic be negotiated? What are the limits of redistribution, recognition, capabilities, and participation? Are harms of reduction (diminishment) and repression built in? Will sustainability calculations follow capital logic? Would the same class and race institutionalized structures and practices find their way into the actual implementation of eco-justice principles, defining nonhumans, for example, in terms of privileged groups? Some would argue that the increasing framing of everyday and political narratives in terms of eco-justice could reach a critical mass for a new understanding of a world community. And a growing "earth jurisprudence" is assuring the institutionalization of legal foundations for eco-justice. In this view, the reformist remedial style is optimistically said to generate what radical accusatory adherents desire, but in the long run.

We have already visited Woolford's critique of restorative justice toward the development of a "transformative restorative justice," particularly his focus on calling for new identities (victim, offender, community, facilitator) that go beyond traditional criminal justice sensibilities producing more encompassing components of each. Victims' identities, within an eco-justice perspective, could be extended to nonhumans; offenders' identities can more widely incorporate harms to eco-systems and nonhuman species; community can be expanded to include the voices of the disenfranchise nonhumans; and facilitator's proceedings could be infused with a "conscientization" component. We also note Preston's (2011) much-cited work advocating an environmental restorative justice, remaining in a reformist remedial style, where he revisits conceptions (identities) of victim, offender, community, environment, and the justice system. He makes use of "transformative" to indicate that we are beginning to develop new narrative frameworks that break from purely punitive retributive models toward holistic ones, the latter focusing not only on final results, but on causes, reparation, rehabilitation, restoration, and sustainable outcomes. Transformative eco-justice, however, needs to go further.

We could begin to critically and constructively engage various suggested dimensions in the eco-justice movement. We could, for example, argue for capabilities, not only including functionings concerning "beings" and "doings" toward well-being but also needed is a transformative component, "becomings." Humans and nonhumans are ever developing: do we want to constrain them to some form of return to things as they were? To restoration and reparations that seek to return stability and previous states? To rehabilitate to restore to previous ways of being and doing? "Becomings" are functionings that are moving autopoetically forward toward new tentative equilibriums and not necessarily understood futures. Key are experimentation, emergents, new states and relations of beings, doings, *and* becomings. This is visionary work that makes leaps beyond present compelling global issues and conceptualizations in eco-justice. In this view, we need not only pragmatic solutions to the eco crises before us but visions short of blueprints toward truly transformative models of the possible.

A transformative eco-justice would also critically engage the much accepted and unquestioned sustainabilities thesis. Discourses revolving on this signifier have been appropriated by various audiences and are often used as a quick but superficial answer to more complex questions, even a fad in popular conceptions. Unfortunately, the groundbreaking work in eco-justice by White and Nussbaum does not critically engage the term. Substantively, in sustainability discourse, often employed is some form of cost-benefit analysis, often reduced to monetary values (exchange values) where response to scarcity and needs is weighed. However, the deeper underlying causes for scarcity, needs, and their more induced states are unexamined. Sustainability discourse that does not engage the cause of scarcity such as the capitalist mode of production and its global forms sustains the status quo, which is reflective of its internal logic. Class divisions, privilege of power, legacy of postcolonial and slavery policies, magnification of racial hierarchies, commodification, creation of growing disparities between the rich and poor, "ideological apparatuses" that spin out system supportive ideologies and narratives (i.e., "it's up to the individual" discourse), degradation of environment as normal practices—all, in much of conventional sustainability discourse, are not prominent issues or not sufficiently engaged. Often, too, "greenwashing," a co-optation, has been employed by corporations to dress up their language in sustainability discourse, obfuscating key information for consumers.

In the direction of a transformative eco-justice are the emerging "critical sustainability studies" (Ferreira, 2017; Cock, 2011; Bluhdorn, 2016; Cachelin and Rose, 2018). Advocated is cultivating the development of a critical consciousness along the lines suggested by Paulo Freire (1972) with his notion of conscientization. We have already examined how this strategy may be employed in a critical mediation infusing traditional restorative justice programs with opportunities to examine further questions of causes traced to system-induced inequities. Naming injustices is critical, and it is through a dialogical pedagogy, not just problem-solving, that new signifiers and signifieds (that to which signifiers refer) can be established in the participation of diverse stakeholders.

DiChiro (2018) critically examines everyday storytelling that is constituted by an anthropocentric narrative that inadequately considers the relations between humans and nonhumans; nor does it provide stories about colonization and enslavement in terms of power inequalities (see also Anantharaman, 2018); nor how "growth" within capital logic leads to ever more exploitation of natural resources, degradation of the environment, and social inequalities (Clark, Auerbach, and Longo, 2018). Alternative storytelling, infused with the spirit of eco-justice, however, can disrupt everyday institutionalized power structures; can move us to more transformative storytelling/narratives based on more relational, system-focused framing with de-emphasis on privileging commodification processes; that engages holistic visions that value ecological integrity and well-being (Cachelin and Rose, 2018).

A "critical sustainabilities" approach must also look toward social movement literature for further guidance for a transformative eco-justice. It is not by words alone that change is fostered. Part three of this book provides us some directions for social change.

Transformative eco-justice is concerned with re-establishing an interspecies and inter-eco-systems holistic integration connected to justice principles. Just as Christopher Stone's seemingly outlandish question raised in 1972, "Should Trees Have Standing?", has in recent days led to much serious discussion in the wake of global environmental crises, others are beginning to give serious thought to Eduardo Kohn's (2013) provocative thesis "How Forests Think." Shocking to contemporary sensibilities as it may be, it attests to the hold speciesism and anthropocentrism has on us. Unlike those who advocate establishing law guardianships for those who apparently cannot speak for themselves (acting *in loco parentis*), Kohn and others have argued this form of participation is inherently short of doing justice (recognition, representation, participation) to the uniqueness that diverse species and eco-systems retain. For Kohn, we must get closer to allowing the latter to speak for themselves. Kohn's thesis resonates with the call by post-postmodernists ("posthumanist") view, decentering the human and re-establishing the interconnections of all (we will return to in chapter 9).

His was a four-year ethnography study living with the people of the Runa village in Avila, located in the upper Amazon reaches of Ecuador interested in the interconnections between the Runa and the rain forest.

Critically drawing from and refining the work of Bruno Latour and Jane Bennett, Kohn, according to Conty (2018) has it that: "forests, rivers and all other ecosystems are alive because they think and represent using semiotic signs . . . they can represent themselves, and do not need human delegates to 'speak' for them in a representational democracy" (86). They don't, in other words, need to be thingified or objectified in order to be represented. And Conty adds, in order to hear these agents, the human animal must be reinstated into the material world. For the Runa, "communicating directly with the ghost jaguars, the trees, the flying ants and the spirits of the dead" (86). This is similar to humans participating in Internet technologies, in virtual worlds, but also with others, and "real" worlds. Where "material world" can be understood for Kohn as a dynamic loci of humans, forests, trees, and animals being mutually constituted in semiotic production coproducing form and identities, whereby producers and product are both causes and effects interconnected in dynamic, evolving, contingent states of beings and becomings. Material is a loci of these dynamic states constituting boundaries and identities. Humans, trees, forests, and animals can only be understood in this holistic framework. In this context, employing principles of recognition, representation, and participation here mean gaining better understanding of forests, rivers, diverse species, and eco-systems as living entities, and being in tune with their unique contributions toward an integrated, holistic global well-being.

Challenging, of course, is how to precisely "hear" forests, rivers, diverse species, and eco-systems? (but see, for listening to trees, Haskell, 2018; interview of Haskell, Toomey, 2017; for rainforests, Hausheer, 2015; and note various studies of communication by dolphins, whales, and sharks). In an interview of Haskell (Toomey, 2017) on his book *The Sounds of Trees* (2018), he states: "an ultrasonic detector applied to a tree, particularly in the summertime, reveals how as the morning passes into afternoon, the tree goes from a state of full hydration to a place of distress, where there are all sorts of little ultrasonic clicks and fizzles emerging from the inside of the tree as water columns break, as the tree becomes more dried out. By applying an ultrasonic sensor, the tree suddenly has its inner life revealed."

One direction offered to enhance recognition, and possibly communication, is, with reservations noted below, to create a typology of statuses for each species (Fraser, 2000; Schlosberg, 2007: 138–142), a normative pattern or even a listing (capabilities), following Nussbaum (2006). Perhaps, for example, by employing bioacoustics (Haskell, 2018; Toomey, 2017) whereby some variations from the normative pattern (of forests, trees, species) could be seen as the particular agent communicating ill-health, much like studies with humans on heart rate variability whereby distinct patterns register for emotionality and health; see chapter 9). This could allow a direct voice rather than representation by way of law guardians (*in loco parentis*) whereby voice can be usurped and/or obfuscated. Of course, the danger here is the reification of formal equality as an evolving logic that has a parallel with commodifying nature (Marx, capital logic). Here, inherent uniqueness (use values) is converted into commonalities, abstractions/objectification (exchange value) subject to the imposition of sameness and ripe for the logic of the capitalist marketplace ("commodification of nature," "market environmentalism"; see Prudham, 2016; Kosoy and Corbera, 2010). For those from the transformative eco-justice perspective, we must proceed cautiously in taking this direction, creatively reinstating use value as primal and articulating distributive justice principles to include recognition, participation, and capabilities that are its derivative.

Kohn brings this to center stage as a challenge, as audacious as it might appear. We must break from the shackles of present-day sensibilities to engage the imaginary and the possible practical implications. A transformative eco-justice can engage this provocative thesis toward a more holistic vision of global well-being. Nancy Fraser's call for participatory parity can be extended to all life-forms.

In sum, a fundamental challenge before us in a global economy is to develop some principle of a universal right to a healthy environment in connection with a critically informed sustainable development. Distributive and retributive principles of global justice need further development. That task is indeed demanding. We are, however, already witnessing numerous movements in the international community in this direction.

REVIEW QUESTIONS

1. Corporations often respond to members of disproportionally impacted impoverished communities that their opposition to toxic wastes and to air pollution is their own fault. They had a choice to move into the neighborhood where the corporation was already operating. How would you respond to this question of "free will," choice?

2. Reformist remedial styles in eco-justice such as restorative justice are said to have their limits. What do those from a radical accusatory approach say about these limits?

3. Why should trees, rivers, glaciers, rain forests, and animals have rights? Provide arguments for and against.

4. A critical sustainabilities approach provides one direction toward transformative eco-justice. List and explain the impediments to its realization.

5. Some have argued that change is better realized through the courts, others through legislation, yet others through the street. List the positives and negatives for each approach to social change relating to eco-justice.

6. Some argue that prosecution (retributive justice) of environmental harms should be primarily through the courts (via a "battle model"—crime control model, due process model), others through an environmental restorative justice approach. What are the positives and negatives of each?

7. Select a recent picture (image) popularized in the media concerning pollution, or deforestation, or harms against an animal. Now point out to your audience how, in this picture, principles of justice come into play (distributive—needs, equality, merit; recognition, participation, distribution, capabilities; see Schlosberg). Show how your new narrative (storytelling) about the image raises consciousness about eco-justice (hint, consult Paulo Freire and his concept of "conscientization").

8. Select a recent article reported in a newspaper on an environmental issue. Now, critically examine the article in terms of inclusion or exclusion of the following components of distributive justice: three traditional notions of distributive justice (need, equality, merit), but also recognition, distribution, participation, and capabilities. Point out to your audience your main points.

CHAPTER 8

Indigenous, Post-Colonial and Counter-Colonial Forms of Justice

ONE ASPECT of globalism and multiculturalism is the question of indigenous forms of justice. Indigenous peoples have long struggled for land, recognition, sovereignty, resources, intellectual property rights, and self-determination. Here we selectively focus on the plight of indigenous populations in Australia, New Zealand (Aotearoa), Canada, and the United States. With globalism, assuredly the question of indigenous peoples will begin to become much more visible and audible. Ours is not an exhaustive list, but an introduction to some of the more glaring issues dealing with globalism, indigenous populations, colonialism, post-colonialism, counter-colonialism and social justice.

INDIGENOUS JUSTICE

The definition of "indigenous" in indigenous cultures precedes any discussion of historical, political, juridical, and economic issues. The very definition of the term, "indigenous," is itself controversial. Existing definitions often lead to the imposition of standards of human rights that might be undermining of indigenous people's unique way of being (Niezen, 2003, 18).

The United Nations Working Group on Indigenous Populations defines indigenous peoples in terms of: "priority in time; voluntary perpetuation of their cultural distinctiveness; self identification as indigenous; experience of subjugation, marginalization, dispossession, exclusion, and discrimination by the dominant society" (Havermann, 1999, 21). In Australia they are often referenced as First People; in Canada, First Nations; in New Zealand, Maori; in the United States, native peoples, and sometimes as American Indians (Havermann, 1999; Wilkins, 1997).

Perhaps one of the most enlightening discussions on definitions comes from Niezen (2003). He sees three ways of conceptualizing the term: (1) in legal or analytical terms—attempts are made to identify distinguishing factors of original inhabitants and to develop these into distinct categories;

(2) in practical terms the U.N. Working Group on Indigenous Populations maintains an open-door policy for any who want to participate under the name of indigenous; and (3) in collective terms, although there is a clear difference between them and the particular state within which they find themselves, there is more often identification with some regional group, and beyond this the actual definition remains rather unverbalized yet distinctively understood by members. The danger of the first is in the possible omissions; the danger of the second, is that unexpected and questionable indigenous groups or individuals may profess their indigenousness as a mask for some other issue; the third definition suffers from the potential that some power groups will impose a definition. Thus, any discussion of indigenous peoples begins with controversy (see Fleras, 1999).

Indigenous peoples do have indigenous ways of knowing and ways of justice rendering. Much of this is communicated orally, without written records. Consider the Aboriginals from Australia and their communication about their culture through the dreamtime. Before being colonized, the Maori already had a form of restorative justice that did not rely on written law. In their response to harms, key elements were shaming (*whakama*), healing, and embracing—factors that are key to the development of contemporary restorative justice programs (Braithwaite, 1989). Indigenous peoples in Australia, Canada, United States, and New Zealand rely on elders who are perceived as having heightened abilities, special talents infused with spirituality, referred to as "mana" by the Maori (53). The Maori also have tribal councils (*runanga*) and committees (*komiti*) to manage their affairs.

Dual Courts and Justice

Melton's (2005) analysis of the dual courts that exist for some native peoples in the United States offers a comparison of legal systems of the United States and the tribes. These tribes have been able to establish distinct systems. Her descriptions indicate both the need for distinct courts and the points of incompatibility with the European-style courts that dominate the U.S. legal system. Dual systems that do not include a system by and for the indigenous communities can result in injustices. The Associated Press (2014) found that a dual court system in the West Bank resulted in unequal justice. Palestinian minors were more likely to be arrested, convicted, and given harsher sentences than were Israeli minors. In this case, neither court was set up or controlled by Palestinians. Both courts in the dual system are controlled by the state of Israel.

Malaysian courts have established a dual justice system to include civil and Syariah courts. After gaining independence from Britain in 1957, Malaysia developed a legal system more fitting for its own population, but still highly infused with and influenced by its former colonial masters. This legal system is still fairly young and underwent a constitutional crisis in 1988. That crisis resulted in the equalizing of the dual system, removing the civil court from the position of higher court, allowing equal standing to the Syariah court (Tew, 2011).

Spitzer (2018) in a review of Canadian case law finds a need to rethink democracy in legal processes. The insistence on the centrality of individual rights is found limiting and a basis of conflict. Instead, Spitzer suggests that democracy move to universalism in application of law and in political representation.

Returning to Max Weber's four ideal types of legal thought and its relation to justice (see chapter 3), notwithstanding the postmodern critique that law and justice are separate entities (see chapter 9), we can envision much of indigenous forms of legal thought and retributive justice in terms of substantive rationality or substantive irrationality. In other words, the elders do in fact have some sense of the overall ways of being and notions of law and justice, but decisions in restorative justice formats were based on concrete situations and thus not systematized in a formal law. Of course, with colonization, it was to formal rationality that the colonizers looked to substantiate their ways of being, values, ideology, and notions of justice over those of indigenous peoples (e.g., "repressive formalism").

Terra Nullius and Sovereignty

A leading article on the Middle East crisis in the *Chicago Tribune* read, "Settlers in West Bank Fight Eviction" (June, 20, 2003, 1). One cannot cease being impressed as to the ideological underpinnings. Settlers? In the United States, it brings images of the West being settled. Conveniently forgotten is how indigenous peoples were dispossessed of their lands in the name of the sovereign and law.

The international arena has seen the rise of principles that justify the taking of indigenous people's lands. After all, an otherwise rational international community of sovereign states could not steal the land. They would need to come up with some legitimizing principle for claims of ownership. One was invented. One of the most common legitimization principles is the principle of discovery. The conquerors claim title to the land based on the assumption that either the land is: (1) not being occupied, is without an owner, is deserted; or (2) occupied, but by an uncivilized people (de Vitoria, 1934; Vattel, 1971; Green, 1998; Fitzpatrick, 2001). We see this played out in the United States, Australia, and New Zealand (see Pockock, 1992).

Johnson v. McIntosh (1823) was the first crucial U.S. Supreme Court case applying the doctrine of discovery. It dealt with issues of sovereignty and native title. Justice Marshall's opinion was to set the stage for further ideological spin on the legal subordination of indigenous peoples (Williams,

1990; Wilkins, 1997). His much quoted decision speaks for itself: the American Indians "were fierce savages . . . whose subsistence was drawn chiefly from the forest . . . to leave them in possession of their country, was to leave the country a wilderness" (*Johnson v. McIntosh*, 1823). The privileging of sedentary versus nomadic is traced to Enlightenment-era thought and consequent modernist assumptions (Pockock, 1992). Marshall's opinion fell short of a fully blown principle of *terra nullius*, but nevertheless provided the legal justification for the dispossession of indigenous people. The "actual condition" of the indigenous people was such that "it was impossible to mix, and who could not be governed as a distinct entity" (*Johnson v. McIntosh*, 1823). The denial of indigenous people's native title was not conquest according to Marshall, but discovery (Fitzpatrick, 2001). And even with words of sympathy, Marshall ultimately deferred to the rule of law: "this is not the tribunal which can redress the past or prevent the future" (*Johnson v. McIntosh*, 1823).

In effect, tribal claims were henceforth reduced to a landlord-tenant relationship (Wilkins, 1997). The sovereign state now stands as the landlord governing its tenants by the rule of law. Thus interiority—the bringing of ever more phenomena within the gravitational pull of normalizing forces under predominantly formal rational principles in law—now allows the further regulation, control, and exploitation of the colonized peoples through the rule of law.

A related question is one concerning the notion of sovereignty, that is, how a state legitimizes its boundaries. Wilkins's (1997) study of fifteen key U.S. Supreme Court decisions dealing with the American Indian argued that they have been engaged in producing masks covering or obfuscating violations of indigenous people's claims. Some earlier cases, however, did acknowledge the sovereignty of indigenous peoples; see, for example, *Worcester v. Georgia* (1832) affirming the legitimacy of Indian treaties; *In the Kansas Indians* (1867) "the conduct of Indians is not be measured by the same standard which we apply to the conduct of other people"; *In Ex parte Crow Dog* (1883) the Court recognized sovereignty by the tribes and said federal courts lacked jurisdiction in dealing with offenses committed by one indigenous member on another; *Talton v. Mayes* (1896) "as the powers of local self-government enjoyed by the Cherokee nation existed prior to the Constitution, they are not operated upon by the Fifth Amendment"; *United States v. Winans* (1905) "the treaty was not a grant of rights to the Indians, but a grant of rights from them—a reservation of those not granted"; and in *Merrion v. Ficarilla Apache Tribe* (1982) "held that the tribe had the inherent power to impose a severance tax on petitioners' mining activities as part of its power to govern and to pay for the costs of self-government" (Wilkins, 1997, 308). In the New Zealand context the State has increasingly recognized the unique forms of dispute resolution by the Maori supported by the elders, *kaumatua* [male] and *kuia* [female] (see Pratt, 1999). But apart from these aberrations, according to Wilkins, the courts in the United States have continued to undermine and mask the sovereign status of indigenous peoples, and at best have extended the tentacles of formal rationality into the everyday life of indigenous peoples in every manner.

Onuf (1991) has suggested sovereignty has three components: unchallenged domination over a given territory; majesty, meaning legitimation principles that show the omnipotence of the state, or in Deleuze and Guattari's words, magical capture; and agency, meaning legislators and jurists who construct legal myths supporting the rule of law. Thus, with the notion of juridical capture one can see how Marshall's opinion first subordinated the indigenous peoples to the rule of law of the sovereign, and second made them subject to the force of law. In short, it is tantamount to lawful state violence (see Patton, 2001; Derrida, 1986, 1989).

Native Title

The notion of *terra nullius* is coming to an end. Several higher court decisions around the globe have undermined its very logic and have ushered in a new imaginary and symbolic framework within which alternative discussion has, and will continue, to unfold (Patton, 2000). In the Australian experience, the High Court decision, *Mabo v. Queensland* (1992), rejected the principle of *terra nullius* and granted "native title" (see Hendrix, 2012; see also the Aurora Project, "The Rights of Indigenous Peoples"). Native title stands for the recognition of traditional rights and interests of indigenous people. The following comparable treaties/cases exist: in New Zealand, the Treaty of Waitangi (1840) and the Treaty of Waitangi Act (1975); in Canada, *Calder et al. v. British Columbia (Attorney General)* (1973) (see the discussion by Asch [1999]); see also the Supreme Court of Canada's decision *Delgamuukw v. British Columbia* (1997) (see discussion by Lefebvre [2008, 206–238]). These have been defining moments (Fleras, 1999).

There is, however, retrenchment by the legislative branch (Myers and Raine, 2001), not unlike the U.S. experience after the Supreme Court decision of *Brown v. Board of Education* (1954). This landmark Supreme Court decision defining equal access to education is an instructive example for two reasons. First, as in the case of defining indigenous rights through the cases cited above, this definition is essential to placing our understanding of justice within the formal realm. Second, although the right to equal education has been defined and codified, it has also been violated through lack of action or support through other justice arenas. Kozol (2005) documents the continuing segregation in U.S. schools and the impact of this departure from the *Brown v. Board of Education* (1954) decision.

Indigenous rights thought to be protected within existing law are also continually violated. For example, Lyon (2016) reported on violations of Native land rights, human rights, and cultural rights regarding the now infamous Keystone XL oil pipeline that is planned to run through the North Dakota Sioux reservation. The Sioux did not agree to the pipeline construction on their sovereign land, the pipeline will put their drinking water (and that of others) at great risk, it also threatens natural habitat and wildlife, and the pipeline will disturb sacred burial grounds. Resistance to this violation rose and pulled native communities and others concerned for justice to the reservation in attempts to protect the land and the peoples and other beings living on that land. As of yet, the pipeline is progressing. In a later chapter we will look more closely at this resistance and the potential for achieving justice for this land and its inhabitants.

In pursuit of indigenous justice, what has been recognized is native title, and this in itself is important although not sufficient in the guaranteeing that such title will be recognized. Land claims by indigenous peoples have been rethought in light of an understanding that they were never relinquished, but forcefully taken by colonizers. As Fleras states, indigenous peoples cannot be compared with multicultural minorities, those who immigrated or were descendants of immigrants. Rather, ". . . indigenous peoples represent *peoples*. They are descendants of the original occupants of the land, whose inherent and collective rights to self-determination over the jurisdiction of land, identity, and political voice have never been extinguished by conquest, occupation, or treaty, but only need to be reactivated as a basis for redefining their relationship with the State. Indigenous peoples' claims go beyond the demand for equality and removal of discriminatory barriers." (Fleras, 1999, 219)

INDIGENOUS INTELLECTUAL PROPERTY RIGHTS

Pervading U.S., Australian, and United Nation's law on indigenous intellectual property rights is a tension between an individualistic and a communal notion of authorship. The notion of the individual author and its celebration as a central value in Western thought was developed during the Renaissance period. It is one of the core assumptions that has stabilized in modernist thought. In copyright law, we only have to look to the middle of the eighteenth century to see this assumption's incorporation into the notion of the modern author (sometimes referred to as the "romantic author," see Riley, 2000; Woodmansee, 1992). In contrast, the pre-Romantic author was seen as the "master of a craft, master of a body of rules, or techniques, preserved and handed down in rhetoric and poetics, for the transmission of ideas handed down by tradition" (Woodmansee, 1992, 280; see also Hendrix, 2012).

From the early 1700s to the early 1800s there was a gradual transition from seeing the author as a craftsman who worked with other previous and contemporary artisans in jointly producing a product to a view of an individualistic and imaginative inventor that alone was responsible for the product (Woodmansee, 1992; Riley, 2000). Much codification of intellectual copyright law followed this development. In the U.S. experience, consider the U.S. Supreme Court decision, *Burrow-Giles Lithographic Co. v. Sarony* (1884), in which "author" is defined as "he to whom anything owes its origin; originator, maker" (53, 58).

The modernist notion of the individual author was challenged by Michel Foucault in an important work, "What is an Author" (see 1977b). He specified that an "author" has historical specificities. Riley (2000) also indicated a contemporary tension in copyright law founded on the Romantic author. Indeed, Woodmansee (1992) suggested a connection between indigenous community's notions of authorship with emerging postmodern renditions. In short, the romantic assumptions are being fundamentally challenged by postmodern thought, perhaps Foucault's treatise on the death of the author being one of the most important. Nevertheless, the Romantic author remains the core assumption of contemporary intellectual property law.

The conflict between the two notions of author has been central in indigenous copyright law. Along with colonization and subsuming the native population to the axiomatics (e.g., core principles, often defined by the higher courts as compelling state interests), indigenous populations were denied their worldviews by the constraints of the law under the guise of sovereignty. After all, *terra nullius* assumed an uninhabited land, or, where it was inhabited, inhabited by uncivilized beings. Discovery assured that the indigenous population would be denied their culture and its protection in law. In indigenous cultures, it is the *group* that is responsible for the production of its cultural artifacts. Much of the techniques remain communicated orally. Attributing authorship to a lone person is an alien way to think. But modernist analysis in law has it differently. Even where Western law acknowledges joint work, it is still an assumption of several individual authors at work (Riley, 2000). Thus it is virtually impossible to attribute *individual* authorship to the Aboriginal who chants about the "dreamtime." Consider Riley's point: "Cultural property is the very soul of Indian tribes. These creative works—whether creation stories, ceremonial songs, or medicine pouches—provide a window through which the Native world can be viewed. In a holistic society, an object's meaning is defined by the context in which it is used. The world is not divided up into distinct pieces, but is interdependent, organic, and cyclical. Native people imagine the world—natural and supernatural, mundane and magical—as balanced, alive, and ever changing" (Riley. 2000, 196). In short, a communal view of property rights (and of knowledge, nature) assume an interconnected, dynamic, fluid, balanced, interdependent, cyclical, and holistic state of affairs.

The Australian response to the U.N. Draft Declaration and the Berne Convention on indigenous intellectual property rights was to amend the draft resolution to force indigenous peoples into structuring and framing their differences into the existing dominant legal system (Ransley and Marchetti. 2001; Grad, 2003). In short, this has everything to do with juridical capture, subjugating all conflicts within capitalistic legal axiomatics. Underlying *Mabo* is also a call for ultimately framing differences within the dominant legal system. In short, in both the U.S. and Australian responses, "white rule" is ultimately asserted (Moreton-Robinson 2001).

Joint Work / Joint Authors

A prima facie case seems attainable for arguing that joint work, protected by copyright law in the United States, could be extended to include community authorship (Farley, 1997; Jordan, 2001). U.S. federal copyright law (17 U.S.C. para. 201, 1994) provides that a property right "vests initially in the author *or authors* of the work"; (emphasis added). Paragraph 101 defines "joint work as prepared by two or more authors with the intention that their contributions be merged into inseparable or interdependent parts of unity whole." As Jordan (2001) points out, "the collective work exception to authorship is applied by statute to 'a work, such as a periodical issue, anthology, or encyclopedia, in which a number of contributions, constituting separate and independent work in themselves, are assembled into a collective whole'" (97). Although seemingly adaptable to indigenous community rights, applications have been difficult as exceptions to individual notions of authorship. Inherent in copyright law is the notion of original author.

Tribal creations, however, have roots in groups from generations past. In any present manifestations they reflect some slight variance. This remains in a community context. As Turner (1997) explains, when coming to terms with human rights, we need not only grapple with the notions of rights but also with the meanings of human. Current Western ideas of humanness rely upon an understanding of an individual separate and apart for a social group. This understanding is neither relevant nor appropriate for other traditions: the human subject is not identified out of this context. Thus, no "original author" can be clearly identified (Jordan, 2001, 98). Jordan cites the example of the Hopi's production of kachina dolls. The knowledge for its production goes back centuries and has no clearly identified historical author.

Jordan entertains the possibility of arguing that a tribe could be conceived as an "author," and thus could apply for copyright protection. If this could be an acceptable legal extension, indigenous intellectual property could be protected. However, in traditional legal understanding (formal rationality), after a certain specified time, the right disappears as it becomes part of the public domain, hence undermining once again the tribal notion of continuity with the past, present, and future.

Jordan also reviews the U.S. law passed in 1990, the Native American Graves Protection and Repatriation Act. This legislation was meant to protect burial sites. It does, however, provide an extension to tribal artifacts but not to symbols. It does open a space to consider tribal claims to objects but not property rights. In this legislation there is acknowledgement of communal property by the concept of cultural patrimony. The act defines this as: "objects having ongoing historical, traditional, or cultural importance central to the Native American group or culture itself, rather than property owned by an individual Native American, and which, therefore, cannot be alienated, appropriated, or conveyed by an individual regardless of whether or not the individual is a member of the Indian tribe . . . and such objects shall have been considered inalienable by such Native American group at the time the object was separated from the group."

In this sense, according to Jordan, cultural property could be constructed as cultural patrimony. Grad (2003), however, questions whether the act is sufficient to provide a remedy for enforcing these rights. Settlements for reclamations of objects are usually private affairs. Little legal precedent is set and thus theft issues remain delegated to more hidden negotiations. The doctrine of joint work still assumes a group of individual authors (Riley, 2000).

Moral Rights

The United Nations has provided, by far, the most creative protections for indigenous peoples in the production and use of their cultural artifacts. The Berne Convention for the Protection of Literary and Artistic Work (1990) is a case in point. It creates a moral right in intellectual property. In 1989, the United States accepted this notion and subsequently incorporated this concept in the Visual Artist's Right Act of 1990, which specifically deals with paintings, drawings, prints, and sculptures. It incorporates rights of attribution, with claim of authorship or not, and integrity, the right to prevent "intentional distortion, mutilation or other modification of work which would be prejudicial to his or her honor or reputation" (Jordan, 2001, 102).

The most important initiative in the United Nations dealing with moral rights is the United Nations (U.N.) Draft Declaration on the Rights of Indigenous Peoples, which was approved within the U.N. subcommittee in

1994. The draft was specifically developed by indigenous peoples world-wide. The U.N. Declaration on the Rights of Indigenous Peoples was finally adopted by the General Assembly in September of 2007. Four countries, the United States, New Zealand, Canada, and Australia, voted against the Declaration. By 2016 all four of these countries had reversed their positions to support the Declaration. The Draft (now Declaration) specifies moral rights for indigenous intellectual property (see Dietz. 1993). Its heritage traces back to the common law of several European states—France and Germany, in particular. Dietz (1993) notes that these rights are "perpetual, intellectual and imperscriptible" and protect the "personal, intellectual, and spiritual interests of authors" (199).

Four specific rights, as a "bundle of rights," fall under this schema (Jordan, 2001; Dietz, 1993): (1) the right to paternity, or attribution, which deals with authorship and assuming "a family-like tie to its creator" (Grad 2003, 212); (2) the right of integrity, which deals with response to any distortions that compromise honor or reputation; (3) the right of divulgation, which deals with the right to make public what the author had previously made private; and (4) the right to repent, which deals with the right to take the product out of public circulation. These rights are distinguished from property rights due to the "intensely personal nature of its creation" (Ledwon, 1996, 69). "The created work comes from within the author and is a part of its creator" (Grad, 2003, 212). There has been some question about mechanisms for correcting violations. Some U.S. states have passed legislation for two moral rights in the visual arts: attribution and integrity. The Australian Copyright Amendment Act of 2000 also includes these moral rights.

Limitations with moral rights exist, a primary one being it does not protect folklore, including songs, customs, myths, and stories, which are mostly communally based and oral. The right of integrity is mostly limited to the lifetime of the person who created the product, with a usual time span attached. Thereafter it falls within the public domain. Accordingly, the generational aspect of the communal production is lost. The phrasing of moral rights remains individualistic (Grad, 2003; Jaszi, 1991). Although Australian and U.S. legislation and court decisions seem to be rectifying some of the injustices done to indigenous people's intellectual property, it is unclear whether an eventual acceptance of the communal nature of indigenous people's creative endeavors will take place. Indigenous people's ways often fly directly against the very foundations of Renaissance-generated core assumptions incorporated into law. Perhaps, however, indigenous forces within an advancing technological society may be the producers of new understandings that, full circle, reproduce the preclassical joint-author (Woodmansee, 1992; Riley, 2000).

Beyond the Profit Paradigm

There is a link between technological changes and the potential for a receptiveness of communal intellectual property rights. Woodmansee's work is seminal. In many ways, it suggests the death of the modern author, the sole creator, as we know it. The emerging notion of authorship is one situated at dissolving boundaries of law. Technological advances, by way of the Internet and email, for example, have provided the milieu for new forms of collaborative, interactive thought. "Modern [more precisely, postmodern] writing is about cooperation and the integration of ideas, fueled by the ease with which intellectual musings and textual discourse can be bounced from innovator to innovator through advanced technology" (Riley, 2000, 195). Electronic technology is reviving the pre-Romantic author. In short, there are but few additional steps needed before reaching the notion of protected group rights. Resistance, no doubt, will be forthcoming. "By relying on traditional models of originary, clearly individuated authorship and creation, we may distort or stifle undreamed-of creative possibilities and block new directions in which innovative technologies and their applications may lead us" (Riley, 2000, 196).

Liebesman (2015) laments the inability of the courts to write clear and concise decisions regarding technology and copyrights. As she describes, the court often uses comparisons to current technologies to make decisions that will be applied to future technology and uses of that technology. Because courts are typically backward-looking in their orientation, they may be incapable of producing forward-looking laws. Further, because legislators cannot predict future technologies or applications, they may be equally limited. Phillips (2009) argued that amending Australia's Copyright Act would be appropriate to assure rights of communal interest and folklore. The 2000 Moral Rights amendment, while an improvement, has failed to adequately protect Aboriginal artists. An amendment as suggested by Phillips has yet to occur. The Aboriginal and Torres Strait Islander Heritage Protection Act of 1984 has also proven inadequate with the Copyright Act still regarded as the primary Act within the law. This has left Aboriginal art to be appropriated, reproduced, and misused by those seeking to profit from it (Phillips, 2009).

Kerr (2010) addressed the problems of profiteers seeking knowledge from Aboriginal Australians and Amazonian South Americans without properly informing those populations of the reasons for their interests, without including those populations in decisions made about that knowledge once shared, and without attribution or inclusion of these populations in the transformation of their knowledge into profitable products. He refers to this practice as bio-piracy. This form of piracy occurs when pharmaceutical interests seek Aboriginal and Amazonian knowledge regarding the uses of plants and other biological materials in the treatment of ailments. This piracy threatens biodiversity, sacred knowledge, and the peoples who hold that knowledge (Kerr, 2010).

Ismail and Azmi (2015) argue that because harms occur when traditional cultural expressions are appropriated, these appropriations should be criminalized utilizing current legislation and/or developing legislation that corresponds to these needs. Such criminalization would offer a space for redress of appropriations and may prevent appropriations of traditional cultural expressions. Collins (2006) cautions that overreaching applications of copyright laws intended to protect music produced within Ghana actually resulted in the taxing of Ghanaians who distributed their own indigenous folklore. The overextension of law meant to protect national interests can in fact infringe upon the people of that nation wishing to express their folklore through production.

Native peoples often use copyright laws to defend their arts, culture, and sacred traditions from appropriation and exploitation. In China, copyright laws on printed materials existed for a short time between 1911 and 1949 and did not resurface again until 1991 (Mun, 2010). As Mun explains, it was the imposition of capitalism and markets onto printed communications that necessitated these laws in the country where the printing press was invented. Prior to a profit motive within communications, printing and distribution of materials was done in small facilities to meet the needs of the people rather than to enrich the owners of vast communications industries as occurred earlier in other areas of the world.

China has only recently joined the capitalist economic sphere and has rapidly industrialized, displacing millions of people from agrarian lives into metropolitan lives, not before seen on our planet. Chowdhury (2018) reminds us of Rosa Luxembourg's contribution to understanding imperialism. Her attention to the movement of peasants into cities to perform the labor necessary to advance capitalism is important to the understanding of China. While neither the indigenous person nor the Chinese peasant-turned-worker can completely escape the pressures of imperialism, their relationships with it are unique and related. The Chinese worker increases the profits of the powerful in China, and those with power invoke copyright to protect profits. At the same time, less powerful indigenous peoples are forced into the language of copyright to defend their human rights.

China's rise within the capitalist global economy unsettles prior global alignments and priorities. These forces occupy the elite in their pursuits of profit and power. At the same time, indigenous people around the world remind us of the fragility of the environment and increasingly convince us that we must attend to the survival of our species and others. As of this writing, China has nineteen cities with populations larger than New York City, the largest U.S. city (worldatlas.com). Chinese laborers in these cities as well as indigenous persons around the globe are concerned with water, air, dignity, and other human rights. There exists a common struggle to maintain identities, cultures, and humanity within capitalism, imperialism, and colonialism. Meeting these and other human needs may not be compatible with any of these "isms."

The call is for the development "of a more inclusive copyright paradigm" (Riley, 2000, 196). In this view, then, recovering indigenous notions of communal work is in line with the evolving developments in the technological sphere and its call for a new paradigm of copyright law. Because the profit paradigm requires the imposition of legal logic in the form of copyrights that fail to recognize indigenous ideas and other more communal production, the new technological sphere must expand beyond capitalism. Whether this is a return to the pre-copyright era of production for need, or some mode that we do not yet know, this paradigm must allow for the retention of indigenous cultures, the open exchange of ideas, and a more flexible authorship free of the legal trappings and logic of capital.

WEBER AND THE "INSOLUBLE CONFLICT": HUMAN RIGHTS VERSUS CULTURAL RELATIVISM?

Weber, as we discussed (see chapter 3), described four ideal types of legal thought: formal rationality, formal irrationality, substantive rationality, and substantive irrationality. He also explained three forms of domination, defined not as subjugation, but an orientation to some order guided by some principles (e.g., maxims). When we look at the plight of indigenous peoples, we can see how the tension between formal rationality and legal domination, and substantive rationality and traditional domination, plays itself out in some complex ways. Niezen (2003), for example, poses the issue in terms of relativism on the one hand, and a growing global concern for human rights, on the other. The former has been equated with anti-essentialism in philosophical discussions, the latter, essentialism.

Niezen argues that much of the formal rational and legal form of domination that comes with such U.N. declarations as the Universal Declaration of Human Rights, the International Covenants, and the International Bill of Human Rights, originates from societies well versed with bureaucracy, the rule of law, and rationalism. Indigenous peoples, however, more often communicate through an oral tradition, through elders, through myth (e.g., the dreamtime of the Aboriginals in Australia), and everyday artifacts. The latter is more situated in traditional domination and substantive rationality/irrationality. And herein resides the dilemma. Should for, example, indigenous peoples, in seeking redress to grievances, express themselves in the written form of dominant groups, and thus subject themselves to a transformation of their way of life? Consider the effects: undermining elders, privileging the written form over the oral form, establishing alien time frames, and separating phenomena into abstractions rather than assuming interconnectedness.

What about excesses inflicted by indigenous peoples themselves? Consider, in the extreme, such practice as female genital mutilation, a practice within thirty countries of the world, affecting millions of girls per year, in which typically a three- to ten-year-old girl has her clitoris partially removed. In the extreme case, the clitoris is totally removed along with her labia minora, and parts of the labia majora. The procedure is usually performed by a midwife, not a doctor (UNICEF, 2016; Annas, 1999). Should outsiders impose an ethical principle that this is plainly wrong? Charlesworth (2000) and Ferrara (2003) remind us to examine the underlying political reasons for these practices. While some assume that female genital mutilation is a religious practice, it in fact crosses many religious lines. It is instead a way to control female sexuality (Annas, 1999). This understanding frees concerns for imposing upon religion and culture and instead allows a way forward in addressing the universal rights of women and girls.

Brosius (1999) warns against neutrality, which, in the face of ongoing injustice, is complicity. However, as he continues, much care and consideration must be given when interpreting and otherwise judging activities outside one's own understanding. These judgements may be (and have in the past been) used to the detriment of those under judgement and others. Fraser's (2007) call for frame setting and inclusion of all affected parties may alleviate pressures toward neutrality and complicity while guarding against outsider judgement.

Turner (1997) offers a useful interpretation of culture and cultural practices that is instructive in such cases. As he notes, cultural practices themselves are not essentialist; however, the development of cultural practices are inherently human. It is the processes and structures through which culture and cultural practices are developed that are to be examined and understood. For example, in Mexico some individuals recognize the term "machismo" as including the oppression of women in positions of servitude and at times in abusive relationships. These sexist expressions, however, are not inherently Mexican nor are they cultural. Sexism exists around the planet and has no essentially national character. It is, however, supported through social processes and structures. These forces of social production must be examined rather than the culture within which sexism/machismo is expressed. These examinations alleviate the need to judge the other, and allow for a more holistic understanding of cultural practices as social productions rather than inherent expressions. Understanding social practices in this way also allows for the natural process of conflict arising from difference. The debate and discourse surrounding this conflict may then address the social structures and processes that produce the practice in question rather than attaching itself to the identities and humanities of those involved.

In *The Origins of Indigenism*, Niezen (2003) examines the insoluble conflict between relativism and human rights. He reviews theorists such as Talal Asad (1997) who argues for more critical discussion on the unexamined assumptions behind the "meaning" of such clauses as "cruel, inhuman and degrading treatment" built into such documents as the U.N.'s Universal Declaration. Consider, for example, religious flagellation, which brings to the fore the voluntary nature of such self "punishment." Niezen rejects both applied anthropology, which inherently advocates relativism, and postmodernist analysis. In being opposed to notions of universal human rights, Niezen argues, certain harmful practices of indigenous peoples themselves are allowed to continue.

People for the Ethical Treatment of Animals (PETA) celebrated the extension of the U.S. ban on cockfighting to all five U.S. territories, including Puerto Rico in 2019 (PETA, N.D.). Cockfighting is a blood sport and any person concerned for animal welfare would not support this practice. As Puerto Ricans make clear, this is not a cultural practice but is a long-standing tradition that often supports rural families and larger economic interests. What feels like yet another imposition by the imperial powers of the United States has not been well received, even though more Puerto Ricans support a cockfighting ban, 43 percent than oppose it, 21 percent (Martinez, 2019). An approach including the voices and concerns of the people directly impacted by this ban as well as those who have been seeking protection from other forms of violence on the island, particularly violence against women (Martinez, 2019), would have been more just and may have proven more productive for the roosters and the people of Puerto Rico.

Niezen (2003) also provides other examples whereby indigenous peoples engage in harms against their own; see, for example, Nancy Scheper-Hughes's (1992) criticism of the exploitation and cruelty inflicted on Brazilian women in a shantytown she studied. In her words, should we "suspend the ethical"? These are dilemmas that need to be addressed. Hence, for Niezen, the question becomes: "How can indigenous peoples be given the justice they deserve when there is confusion, both in general and in specific cases, over their place as victims, responsible actors, and violators of the human rights of their own people or others?" Said in another way: "The indigenous encounter with modernity is thus oversimplified, stripped of agency and the immediacy of suffering" (Niezen, 2003, 110). Niezen's careful analysis of the potential usefulness of human rights as universals would be tempered by including considerations such as contingencies, social nuances, and local perceptions.

Niezen, privileging a modernist's position, which we found in an earlier chapter to be rooted in the Enlightenment, would thus celebrate liberalism's focus on equality and individualism, yet be tempered with the notion of group rights. He also recognizes that the meaning of a people is still problematic. Cultural pluralism, Nietzen argues, drawing inspiration from Taylor (1994), has already undergone a profound global change away from privileging honor attached to hierarchies, to notions of justice more connected with notions of equal dignity reflecting social recognition and affirmation of equal worth. Postmodernist Jacques Derrida (see chapter 9) suggests a notion of justice that was centered on a duty to the other, which seems compatible with the emerging notions of recognition and affirmation of the other.

This in turn leads to the issue of recognizing the right to self-determination (Kymlicka, 1995), which creates the dilemma of how to be both sensitive to and supportive of self-determination while being prepared for excesses where they are used as justifications for reducing the other within or external to the group. The Weberian dilemma in terms of justice rendering seems insoluble. "There is no way to defend traditional societies without in some way transforming them—without, above all, taking on some of the trappings of bureaucracy and written law" (Niezen, 2003, 142). In other words, the tools employed in protecting indigenous peoples and multiculturalism are the very tools that will change them in a particular direction, such as toward embracing formal rationality and core ideological assumptions generated from the Enlightenment, or by outright capture by the disciplinary mechanisms (Foucault, 1977a). Human rights are about universals, about consensus, about formal standards; on their face, therefore, they are antithetical to the notion of relativism. In short, formal rationality encourages the written over the oral; the lawyer over the elder; the formal rationale over myth and dreamtimes; the individual, over the group; the abstract over the concrete.

In reviewing the work of Michael Blake (2000), Niezen also brings up the notion of social change. Cultures do change, some indeed disappear. If so, "does not an enlightened and compassionate society have a moral duty to ease the inevitable transition, to bring the benefits of superior knowledge, faith, technology, and bureaucratic method?" (Niezen, 2003, 129). This raises the issue of privileging the intervention by an all-knowing other, who often may be well-versed in formal rational principles and highly receptive to legal domination. This is what Roberto Unger rejects in *What*

Should Legal Analysis Become? (1996). Rather, he—like the Realists of the early part of the twentieth century and postmodernists Lyotard and Rorty—would insist on experimentalism, discovery, the emergence of the in-between, of boundary crossing, of the play of chance, irony, contingency, and of inductive over deductive legal reasoning.

Farmer (2006) examined the cultural influences on responses to HIV/AIDS in Haiti. He found that the history that marks the first black nation to overthrow its colonizers is far more important in understanding both internal and external responses to Haitian HIV/AIDS patients than are Haitian traditions. Haitian culture is forever marked by slavery, colonialism, and anti-immigrant racism. As Farmer (2013) advises, when looking at culture, we must first make sure that it is the culture of the subject of our concern that is actually at play in the injustices that we find and not instead a more powerful culture or, hegemony, that is causal. When seeking to understand culture, the history of colonialism and other forces are important to consider.

COLONIALISM

In order to provide a context for post-colonial theory, we need to first provide a brief review of colonialism, neocolonialism, and counter-colonialism. Colonialism is thought by many to be a historical artifact of the past through which European nations divided the world and utilized resources (humans included) in distant lands for the economic and military benefit of the colonizing nation. Notably colonized were the entire continents of Africa, North and South America, much of Asia, and Australia. The British, Spanish, Dutch, and French were leaders among the colonizing nations who through these colonies became empires. We focus on these areas not because this is a complete history, but because it is useful in understanding post-colonial theory as much writing and theorizing comes from Africa, the Americas, Palestine, India, and Australia.

A useful starting definition of colonialism has been provided by Blauner (1969): "Colonialism traditionally refers to the establishment of domination over a geographically external political unit, most of them inhabited by people of a different race and culture, where this domination is political and economic, and the colony exists subordinated and dependent on the mother country. Typically the colonizers exploit the land, the raw materials, the labor, and other resources of the colonized nation; in addition a formal recognition is given to the difference in power, autonomy, and political status, and various agencies are set up to maintain this subordination" (395).

Becky Tatum's (1994; see also Gabbidon's useful review 2015, 178–181) pioneering work, drawing from Franz Fanon, has provided clarity to the stages existing in colonization. In the first phase, an "outsider" group forcibly enters a country mostly motivated to exploit economic resources. In the second phase, an outsider's culture is imposed on the population. The colonized are depicted increasingly as lesser than the "civilized" colonizers. History and culture of the colonized are downplayed, increasingly replaced by the colonizer's world views. I (DM), remember attending grammar school in Adelaide, Australia, where our classroom had a very large and prominent picture of colorful British soldiers landing by boat on shore with their flag, with the caption reading "Captain Cook Discovers Australia." "Discovers?" What of the indigenous population? In the third phase, governmental structures and institutions, including the legal apparatus, reflecting the colonizer's values, begin to prevail, and a split is established between the colonizers and colonized in all sectors of society. The criminal justice system becomes but an agent of the colonizer's rule. Definitions of crime, selective processing, disparities in enforcement and sentencing, etc. follow, even as "the rule of law" (formal rationality, Weber) is announced (Killingray, 1986; Greenberg and Agozino, 2012; Gabbidon, 2015, 179). Even the study of criminology is tainted with the colonizer's values (Igbinovia, 1989), as well as practices (see Saleh-Hanna, 2008 and her notion of "penal colonization" whereby practices in Nigeria follow those found in the prison systems of the West). In the fourth stage, a racist caste system is systematized having cross societal effects. Tatum (1994; see also Gabbidon, 2015, 181) also argues that an "internal colonialism," quite apparent with African Americans, follows similar dynamics "when foreign control of a state or territory is eliminated and the control and exploitation of subordinate groups passes to the dominant group within the newly created society" (41).

Failing to recognize the legacy of colonialism impacts our lives in many ways. Rothbaum (2016) reported on the opening of a restaurant in Portland, Oregon, celebrating the food and culture of colonial Britain. When neighbors in the quickly gentrifying historically African American neighborhood protested the restaurant as racist, the white owner was defensive. Among the owner's claims were that there was a good side to colonialism and that most people liked Winston Churchill and would like to have food similar to that which he ate. That there was a good side to colonialism requires a particularly narrow and elitist view of the world. And, though the owner may be correct in assuming that most of their clientele like Winston Churchill, they may do so not knowing the depths of his racism and murderous actions against the people of India and others. One might see this as a lapse in judgement by a less-than-informed restaurant owner, but it was quickly followed by the publication of a highly controversial article in which the learned author extolled the virtues of colonialism suggesting that nations that had gained independence should bring back colonial rule in order to progress (Gilley, 2017). It is a startlingly imperialist article, but not terribly surprising given the current state of neoliberalism that promotes market and imperial forces. Both the restaurant owner and Gilley (2017) chose a particular lens through which to approach their work. That is a colonial lens, which privileges power over justice and the powerful over those whom they colonize. We take as a starting point the very real damage that colonialism now and in the past has wreaked on the majority of people and places on the planet in service to a few elite within the colonizing nations.

Agozino (2014) contends that because criminology is dominated by those from the colonizing populations, attention must be paid to the colonized in finding alternatives to colonialism, a counter-colonial criminology. He advocates a decolonization of criminology. As he wrote (2003; see also Gabbidon, 2015, 186–193) "criminology is a social science that served colonialism" (1; in the Australian context, see also Cunneen and Tauri, 2016; in the U.S., New Zealand, Australian, and particularly Canadian context, see, Kitossa, 2012). Criminology is infused with colonizers' theories with the omission of indigenous ways and detrimental impact of colonial interventions. Applying labeling theory, Agozino shows how the criminal label is selectively applied, most glaring in imposing "terrorist" labels to those who subsequently became leaders and heroes of social change. He particularly suggests that white supremacy, which is infused throughout the colonial enterprise and imposed upon the colonized, cannot be overcome without a rejection of colonialism and a turning to the colonized for ideas and practices to move toward a post-colonial understanding that progresses toward justice. Continuing to use the colonizer's lens will only leave us within a colonized idea of justice that overlooks the majority of the world in service to the interests of a few. This is not to argue that all whites from European backgrounds are white supremacist or racist, but those populations, the institutions and systems that they built, and the populations that they have dominated are infused with white supremacy. It is difficult to recognize that reality. As we cannot see the air that we breathe, we often cannot see the white supremacy, racism, and colonialism that our worldview contains. It will take active attention to counter those worldviews and change the structures and systems built around those views. The colonized are in a position to offer necessary counter narratives. We must be wary, however, of the impact of existing dominant discourses that frame constructions of reality. Can the "subaltern" break from the very categories of given language itself? Paulo Freire's work (1972) is here implicated as well as visions of transformative justice (see chapter 5).

Two specific suggestions are offered by Agozino (2004). One is for reparative justice, reparation in the aftermath and legacy of slavery and subsequent inequalities, particularly noting that punishment is more directed to the poor. The other is establishing criminology programs that better reflect historical understanding of colonialism, harms inflicted, and mechanisms of social control, while being well versed in colonizer's form of criminology (see also comments by Gabbidon, 2015, 190–191).

The U.N. definition of a colony requires that there be a physical distance between the colonizing nation and the people who have been colonized (Byrd, 2011). However, this erases the experience of peoples and lands colonized in place by colonial settlers (Dunbar-Ortiz, 2015). Native Americans including Native Hawaiians, and Canadians, Alaskans, Palestinians, Aboriginals in Australia, and other peoples and lands have been colonized by those commonly referred to as "settlers" who built their nations and even empires upon the colonized. We recognize that colonialism goes beyond the definition allowed by the United Nations. Native Hawaiians are colonized even if their land has been made part of the colonizing power. Native Americans on the mainland are colonized, internally colonized (Byrd, 2011), Puerto Ricans continually appeal to the United Nations (United Nations General Assembly, 2017) for recognition of their colonial status (that status will not change if they are made a state within their colonizers nation), and Palestinians are actively resisting settlers on their land in opposition to colonialism and genocide (Amnesty International, 2018). Other colonial experiences include the expulsion of the colonizing power when national independence is gained. In either case, the colonial experience remains and continues to impose itself on the peoples and lands in ways that require a thorough re-imagining or reclaiming of history, identity, and justice.

Both slavery and colonialism require racism. Three successive forms of racism described by Alexander (1987) are racism of slavery, racism of empire (tied to colonialism), and anti-immigrant racism (6). Some Africans were enslaved to older (British) and burgeoning (U.S.) colonial powers. This resulted in the internal colonization of Africans within those empires (Pinderhughes, 2008) as their lands of origin were also colonized along with the peoples who remained. U.S. colonial history marks various peoples within the three forms of racism. Some of those colonized by Spain became citizens of the United States when borders moved across them and their lands. The identities of these peoples as they see themselves may include Indigenous, Mexican, and/or American and other identities. The anti-immigrant racism expressed by the call for a wall along the southern U.S. border has resulted in indigenous peoples joining in the struggle to maintain the integrity of the land and the peoples of the region on either side of the border (Bova, 2019). We will address these struggles in a later chapter. At this point, we want to illustrate the complexity of imposed and organic identities of the colonized.

Some refer to neocolonialism in contrast to colonialism to describe more recent impositions of imperial powers that often utilize individuals within the colonized population to serve as representatives for the interests of the colonizer. Puerto Rico could be considered as in a state of colonialism or neocolonialism. It is best for those directly dealing with the current situation to parse out their exact experience. Here we offer some conditions that echo neocolonialism as examples, not to impose a diagnosis. Puerto Rico's Governor Rosselló failed to hold FEMA and President Trump accountable for the deadly inadequate response and the severe minimization of the number of lost Puerto Rican lives following Hurricane Maria (Wilkie, 2018). This provided cover to the U.S. president rather than representation for the people of Puerto Rico. Governor Rosselló and the local legislature also approved a deal with wealthy bondholders (mainly from the United States) to alleviate part of the island's debt "without the participation of the people, without public hearings" (Minelli Perez, 2019). This agreement was approved on February 5, 2019, by a judge in Boston who lamented the likely ultimate default on payments and the impact of the deal on public services in Puerto Rico (democracynow.org, 2019a). Puerto Ricans expressed trepidations about this deal well in advance of the judge. Minelli Perez (2019) reported on the concerns of economist Martín Guzmán who concluded that the deal would result in Puerto Rico becoming "a country for a few people, with an elite that will live well and a middle class who will have to follow their dreams in other places or accept that those dreams of personal and family growth cannot be fulfilled here." This representation of the interests of mainly U.S. vulture capitalists (democracynow.org, 2019a) at the expense of the people of Puerto Rico is another example of neocolonialism. Similarly, as Ayala (2018) documents, the removal of profit from the island at levels double that of Ireland indicates a colonial/neocolonial economic arrangement with the United States. Ayala (2018) found that fully 33 percent of Puerto Rico's gross domestic product (GDP) leaves the island. By comparison, the United States retains 100 percent of its GDP. The elite in the United States utilize a few of the colonized in positions of power, as well as U.S. courts, to maintain the colonial/neocolonial arrangements benefiting U.S. investors at the expense of Puerto Ricans.

Counter-colonialism refers to a range of resistance to and struggles against colonialism and neocolonialism. In the following section, we provide a review of post-colonial theory from which much resistance and struggles are informed. In a later chapter, we look at such struggles on the ground. Post-colonialism as we use the term does not propose that the colonial period is over, but positions itself as counter-colonial, in opposition to the injustices of the colonial enterprise and the lasting impact of the imposition of powerful nations upon the peoples and lands colonized.

POST-COLONIAL THEORY/
COUNTER-COLONIAL THEORY

Post-colonial theory can be formally traced to the 1960s and the writings of Franz Fanon. Key thinkers include Gayatri Spivak, Edward Said, and Homi Bhabha. "Post" in post-colonial, however, is controversial: one meaning is that we have gone beyond colonialism; the other, only that a new phase has taken place. The second is better connected to counter-colonialism. Even though the concept has a multiplicity of meaning, the concept includes two key foci: first, resistance to colonization, and second, attempts to break away from the strong influence of colonial thought after independence and liberation. In this approach, principles of social justice are seen as being imposed by colonizers. The question then becomes one of re-articulating what had been, or developing conceptions of justice of the people yet to come (Smith, 1999).

The emphasis of post-colonial theorists is on a critical examination of history, literature, film, dominant discourse (master narratives), and culture. European texts imposed and projected their own desires and anxieties onto colonized peoples, while masquerading as truth and the embodiment of rationality, logic, and objectivity. Post-colonial theory draws not only from the pioneering work on Franz Fanon and his many proponents but also significantly from discourse analysis and some key postmodern thinkers, Foucault, Lacan, and Derrida in particular. Marxist and revisionist Marxist ideas are also applied. More recently, we have witnessed a feminist post-colonial approach (Lewis and Mills, 2003; Switala, 1999). Let us review key thinkers.

Franz Fanon (1925–1961) was born to descendants of slavery on the Caribbean island of Martinique. His training included medicine, psychiatry, and philosophy. His book, *Black Skins, White Masks* (1986), was a direct outgrowth of his experience as a black person in colonized Martinique (by the French at the time). He also wrote *The Wretched of the Earth* (1967) after he developed leukemia. He had a major influence on third-world revolutionary movements in the 1950s and 1960s, particularly revolutionaries Che Guevara and Steve Biko, as well as anti-colonial film directors and writers such as Sembe Ousmane, Tsitsi Dangarembga, and Ngugi Wa Thiongo. The Palestinian and Black Panther movements were also heavily influenced by his work. He drew from Marxist analysis but did not accept Lenin's notion that the revolutionary party (i.e., the communist party) should lead the struggle. Rather, one should look within the ranks of those directly participating in the struggle, in their daily activities of opposition; *they* would formulate its principles.

Fanon argued that white colonizers imposed an image on the black victims that was degrading, subordinating, and alienating. It was this image to which the black person had to adjust. And we must be wary, Fanon tells us, to simply replace white colonizers with European trained black bourgeoisie; for, surely the legacy of colonial ideology will continue. Conceptions of social justice would thus arise from grassroots struggles to overcome the shackles of colonization. It cannot be developed top down, but must follow the logic of historical struggles—first, to overthrow the colonizers, and second, to replace the embedded influence of colonization and its ideological elements.

Gayatri Chakravorty Spivak (1942–) was born in Calcutta, West Bengal, to a middle-class family and completed her formal education at Cornell University. Her first recognition was with her English translation of Derrida's *Of Grammatology*. Her theoretical work draws from Marxism, feminism, and Derrida's deconstruction. There are also connections with Jacques Lacan, Michel Foucault, and Gilles Deleuze, although critical. She herself has often self-identified as a "Marxist-feminist-deconstructionist." Her indebtedness to Derrida and his notion of deconstruction is quite apparent not only in her earlier translation of *Of Grammatology* but in her book *A Critique of Postcolonial Reason* (1999) where she includes an extensive appendix to explain his main points. She is particularly interested in how marginalized peoples may enter dominant positions and subvert that which has been privileged.

Spivak's key points were justice and responsibility, the subaltern, and strategic essentialism. Her notion of justice and responsibility follow Derrida's classic views (see chapter 9). In other words, justice has everything to do with orientation to the other, a duty to the other, in making room for the other to speak and be heard. She refers to this as an "ethical singularity" (1999, 384; Landry and MacLean, 1996). In other words, each person tries to reveal all to the other, but knows that we always are not doing so. Justice, then, is built on this duty to the other, to reveal oneself to the other while at the same time being open to the other. "Ethical singularity is approached when responses flow from both sides" (1999, 384). Justice, then, follows the logic of the gift, explained by Derrida. It cannot be completely reflected in law, even while attempts are made to capture it in law.

The second key point for Spivak, "can the subaltern speak?" has aroused much discussion. Drawing somewhat from Gramsci's early writings (1971), the subaltern represents the dispossessed, the disenfranchised, the marginalized, the voiceless; it is the Other. Those colonized are subaltern: They have been denied their voice. Spivak asks how they can speak in their own voice. There seems an impossibility to speak otherwise. The colonized must make use of dominant discourse to express themselves, hence finding themselves imprisoned within its logic. For example, to argue race, class, and gender discrimination one gives legitimacy to these terms as if they have some real objective existence. But to not to do so, how is one to argue discrimination exists? As soon as the subaltern attempt to gain a voice, they must make use of dominant discourse and thus, ironically, they vacate themselves from their subaltern speaking position. What can be done?

This leads us to a third major idea, that of strategic essentialism. Spivak, committed to the deconstructionist method that questions essentialism, some objective truth, suggests that the conceptualization of the subaltern may, nevertheless, be the basis of developing agendas for social change and for defining social justice. The strategy is to assume dominant positions within various hierarchies and discourses for strategic purposes, yet maintain a critical distance from these assumed positions (see also Rorty's "ironist," chapter 9). By doing so, they may undermine hegemonic discourse from inside out. Thus, in this strategy, some agendas and organizations may develop to challenge dominant power. The danger, of course, is being seduced by the positions assumed.

Other ways to come to terms with essentialism have been expressed. Paulo Freire (1972), in his "pedagogy of the oppressed," develops a dialogical pedagogy whereby the cultural revolutionary and the *campesino* together deconstruct and reconstruct codifications of reality. Jacques Lacan's discourse of the analyst argues for the cultural revolutionaries working with the hysteric (or read as persons in opposition rather than a clinical description) to encourage them to both distance themselves from dominant master signifiers that subordinate and to replace these with new master signifiers that better embody their desire (Bracher, 1993). Michel Foucault (1977b) has argued that the role of the intellectual is to try and create the conditions for the subaltern to speak for themselves. Judith Butler (1990) has argued for "contingent universalities," by which she means the subaltern can develop agendas reflecting historical subordination (universalities), but these are always contingent, subject to change—refinement, qualification, deletion, substitution. Agozino (2003) addressed criminology directly in his text arguing for a counter-colonial rather than post-colonial reasoning. In short, struggles for social justice are connected with narrative constructions and how alternative ones may develop in which we owe a duty to others, to listen, to understand, to be responsive.

Edward Said (1935–2003) was born in Jerusalem, Palestine. He attended schools in Jerusalem, Cairo, and Massachusetts. He received his PhD at Harvard University. Said was a committed activist campaigning for the rights of the Palestinians. He came under continuous attacks by conservative Jewish and Christian Zionists. His groundbreaking book, *Orientalism* (1978), is seen as one of the key treatises of post-colonial theorists. He also wrote the influential treatises *Culture and Imperialism* (1993) and *Representations of the Intellectual* (1994). Said draws inspiration from Muslim academics such as Anwar Abdel Malek and other writers from the 1960s Parisian scene who were inspired by Freudian, revisionist Freudian, and Marxian theory. He was also inspired considerably by the works of Michel Foucault and his connection between knowledge and power as well as his analysis of discourse, particularly how all representations are coded in language. He has, however, retained a critical stance toward Foucault, particularly on the exclusive importance placed on power, knowledge, and discourse to the exclusion of "the role of classes, the role of economics, the role of insurgency and rebellion" (1983, 243).

Orientalism concerned the conflict between the Orient and the Occident—loosely, the East (actually, more the Middle East) versus the West (mostly Britain, France, and the United States). It was Said's point that the Western colonizers have imposed a perspective on those from the Orient that is more in conformity with the West's attitude of superiority. Part of this, Said explained, was because cultures (and identities) tend to want to explain themselves in comparison with other cultures (and identities). The East was seen as static and backward; the West, as dynamic, creative, growing, developing. This was represented in what Foucault called discursive formations, where power is played out. Orientalism, in short, is a discursive formation in which realities are constructed in a very constricted fashion.

Even though the Orient is the cradle of civilization, the very basis of the West itself, the West places it in an inferior position. However, the two, Said tells us, are not separate, but have distinct historical continuities. Much of this neglect, suppression, and revisionism may in fact be unconscious; nevertheless, literature, scholarship, and cultural images of the Other are constructed in a subordinate manner. Thus it was more the desire of the colonizers that constructed a picture of the world of the Orient, the world of the Other.

Orientalism, thus, is a way of looking at the East. The binary, East versus West, allows the West to maintain a sense of superiority by way of its imposed imaginary and discursive construction of this Other. In fact, it allows for easier colonization since the Other needs to be "civilized." The Other is seen as an inferior Arab, with an inferior religion (Islam) and way of life. This stereotype has been reinforced since September 11, 2001 (9–11). Many Middle Easterners have been selected for governmental surveillance, deportation, and profiling programs. Social justice will only emerge when we unlearn this method of domination and articulate the Other on their own terms. This is the decolonization of knowledge. Said (2004) specified the role of the intellectual to counter orientalism and to provide insights for a more just order: "the intellectual's role is dialectically, oppositionally to uncover and elucidate . . . to challenge and defeat both an imposed silence and the normalized quiet of unseen power wherever and whenever possible"

(135). He concludes with the task at hand: "the intellectual's provisional home is the domain of an exigent, resistant, intransigent art into which, alas, one can neither retreat nor search for solutions. But only in that precarious exilic realm can one first truly grasp the difficulty of what cannot be grasped and then go forth to try anyway" (144).

Homi K. Bhabha (1949–) was born into a middle-class family in Bombay, India. He completed his bachelor's and master's degrees at Bombay University and his doctorate in philosophy at Oxford University. He has been influenced by postmodernist theorists Jacques Derrida, Michel Foucault, and Jacques Lacan. In his book *Nation and Narration* (1990), he shows how narrative constructions have tended to imprison the colonized within narrow identities. In *The Location of Culture* (1994), he outlined how ambivalence always exists whenever colonial powers attempt to dominate. There is, in short, no unilateral imposition since ambivalence provides the space within which an otherwise can be articulated. It is in these spaces, sometimes referred to as "interstitial spaces" sometimes "liminal spaces," that cultural emergents appear—that is, alternative articulations of such things as identities, notions of the other, and the meaning of justice (see also the accessible summary by Graves, 1998a).

Some readers and writers of post-colonial treatises critique the abstract theorizing that is at work in such writers as Bhabha. For many activists, theory is downplayed and those who use it often are seen as elitists. For him, however, "there is a damaging and self-defeating assumption that theory is necessarily the elite language of the socially and culturally privileged" (1994, 28). Indeed, between theory and practice is the liminal space, and what may be produced, hybridity. Culture, then, does not merely get iterated, but alternated within the dynamic flux of this region (see also Lippens, 2000). Ambivalence within these liminal spaces is a positive force for rethinking domination, contesting unilateral dictates, and the crucible for novel articulations (see also Graves, 1998b). These are the very spaces for resistance (Graves 1998c). It is where the clash of subaltern yearnings and dominant impositions can attain various novel articulations.

An additional concept of which Bhabha makes use is mimicry (1994). This has indebtedness to Jacques Lacan's writings. Any time we connect a signifier to a signified (e.g., the word "tree" connected to the image of a tree), we also implicate one of the two semiotic axes of production (the other being metaphor, see Lacan, 1977). In other words, metonymy, a slippage of meaning, exists in narrative constructions. With this slippage of meaning, new meanings can assert themselves. There is always an excess. With a slight emphasis on a different part of the statement (narrative), a different meaning emerges. For example, in the statement, "support our troops in (. . . name a country)," are we saying support our troops, regardless of where they may happen to be? Or are we saying, support them specifically in the country mentioned? For Bhabha, in the liminal spaces, a third space, with its attendant ambivalence, ever-new meanings are being constructed. Thus, even as dominant semiotic production (i.e., colonial discourse) attempts to impose a truth, mimicry allows for the constant redefining of its meaning. This allows the subaltern to develop their own meanings even as a unilateral imposition is taking place. In short, desire is allowed an alternative expression. The third space allows for hybridity. It is at this level that intervention is transformative. For Bhabha, then, social change and the struggle for social justice is a continuous process. Embedded within modernist and colonizer discourse are unsettling interstices that provide ambivalence, mimicry, and the possibility of new identities, signifiers, and narrative constructions.

To sum up, post-colonial/counter-colonial writers have focused on two facets of colonial subjection: (1) explaining how the subalterns are created and suggesting methods of subversion, and (2) addressing the vestiges of colonial discourse after liberation. Principles of social justice emerge from struggle. Post-colonial theorists do not see formal equality as the only ideal, although in the short run, perhaps that can be so, nor are the principles of merit and need as defined by colonial powers helpful for guidance. Rather, post-colonial theorists seek emergents, from the ground up. Social justice is connected with the "people yet to come" and a "justice yet to come."

REVIEW QUESTIONS

1. How are indigenous forms of justice unique from the national justice system under which others near you live? Are there ways that indigenous forms might improve upon the national forms?

2. What forces lead to a need for individual ownership of socially produced good? Is justice best served by continuing to enforce this need for individual ownership? How might justice be improved by removing individual ownership of socially produced goods?

3. Find an example of a violation of a native title that was not addressed in the text. Bring that example to class to discuss how the violation occurred, against whom it occurred, and how it might be corrected.

4. In 2007, the United States, New Zealand, Canada, and Australia voted against the U.N. Declaration of Human Rights. Locate an article (any source is fine) that explains why at least one of these countries voted against the Declaration. Bring the article to class and be prepared to discuss the reasons for the no vote as well as what you believe may have occurred to result in eventual backing of the Declaration.

5. In a group with other classmates agree upon a "cultural practice" that you all find problematic. Discuss the probable underlying generator of this practice. Then devise a way to address that practice with the hope of eliminating it.

6. Identify at least three colonial ideas that you see still at play in our lives. How do these ideas benefit the colonizer? How do these ideas harm the colonized? Do these ideas harm those who are not colonized? If so, how?

7. Counter-colonial theory offers various strategies that include both theory and practice, together. Name and explain three strategies mentioned in the text that are in your view the best for social change and the development of more responsive principles of social justice. Be prepared to articulate and support your views in class.

CHAPTER 9

Postmodern, Post-Postmodern, and Posthumanist Forms of Justice

POSTMODERN THOUGHT begins with a rejection of many of the core assumptions and ideologies developed during the Enlightenment period (see the edited volume by Arrigo and Milovanovic, 2010). It questions the privileging of grand narratives, the celebration of the individual, a dominant and universal Truth, linear logic and reasoning, possibilities of universal and stable foundations, and the neutrality of language. It suggests maintaining a skeptical eye toward the possibility of developing conceptions of justice that are grounded in self-evident truth claims founded in prevailing and dominant ideologies. The possibilities of a bonafide conception of postmodern justice, however, are only recently emerging. There have also been two variants: a negative postmodernism that focuses on criticism and deconstruction without many suggestions for an alternative; and the positive (affirmative) form of postmodernism that does indeed make suggestions for change. In the early 2000s we witnessed a new emergence, a post-postmodernism, some of which is referred to as posthumanism, new materialism, digimodernism, and more challenging, quantum holographic. Some see it as a clean break from postmodern thinkers, others not so.

ISSUES IN DEVELOPING A POSTMODERN JUSTICE

Several key issues have emerged for those who are attempting to develop a postmodern rather than a modernist form of justice. First, postmodern theorizing in justice studies is skeptical of any possibility of establishing foundations. That is, attempts to ground any reasoning, rationale, or logic on some objective measure are dubious. For example, the reliance on a natural state or natural rights pre-given by God, some original positions, or on reason itself, is question begging.

Second, postmodernists tend to conduct external critiques. Internal critiques include those that take a practitioner's point of view (e.g., officials—judges, lawyers) in criminal justice (Litowitz, 1997, 20–34). Dworkin's contributions to the literature, for example, are from an internal perspective.

Postmodernists do not privilege the views of practitioners of the legal system; they stand outside the system in critiquing it.

Third, postmodernists would oppose positive jurisprudence; this opposition would extend to conceptions of justice. Positive refers to practice for legislators and practitioners in articulating a particular normative framework that will then be the basis of decision-making by judges. A normative framework defines what falls within the normal and what is abnormal or deviant.

Finally, modernists are more likely to rely on passive notions of justice, whereas postmodernists incorporate an active conception of justice. A passive justice takes place where human beings are seen as not owing affirmative duties (i.e., care) to the other, outside of civil rights issue. Active justice suggests that we do indeed owe duties to the other. The notion of responsibility, in short, has a more holistic sense in the latter.

In arguing against foundations and normative frameworks, postmodernists need to then situate their conceptions of justice in more contingent frameworks. According to Litowitz (1997, 41), "The solution is to adopt fallible, provisional foundations strong enough to support normative claims but not rooted in problematic modernist claims about human nature, reason, and truth." This is precisely what some postmodernists are currently attempting. Litowitz also asserts that a progressive theory need not necessarily be evaluated only on practical possibilities, but can be measured by the degree to which it generates insights (40). Nevertheless, there will still be demands for translating external critiques into practical internal applications.

Postmodern Theorists and Justice

Jean-Francois Lyotard

The development of principles of justice is articulated in three books by Lyotard: *The Postmodern Condition* (1984), *Just Gaming* (1999), and *The Differend* (1988). Lyotard (1984, 66) states his direction quite clearly: "consensus has become an outmoded and suspect value . . . we must . . . arrive at an idea and practice of justice that is not linked to that of consensus." It is in *The Postmodern Condition* that Lyotard launches an attack on "grand narratives"— that is, dominant discourses within which reason and justice is defined and practiced. Legal language is an example (see Tiersma, 2000, for an analysis of its development). He advocates, instead, a proliferation of smaller, localized ("petite") narratives.

Modern society was characterized by the grand narrative born from the Enlightenment period. Postmodern society, on the other hand, is marked by a plethora of micro narratives. Each person lives within several of these petite narratives. Lyotard borrows from Wittgenstein (1953) in refereeing to them at times as language games. One is a product of the various language games one frequents. Each has its own notion of justice based on the particular rules found in them. Justice cannot be a universal, but resides in the many locations one frequents. There is, then, a multiplicity of justices that are played out (Lyotard, 1988, 100). Consider, for example, the workplace, school, leisure, various friendship circles, family, clubs, various business associations; each provides a milieu within which justice may be defined in a nuanced manner. Consider a street corner setting where juveniles often resort to playing odds or evens for decision-making in determining distribution of resources or burdens. Consider, too, Whorf's (1964) comparison of the Hopi Indian language with English. Whereas the grammar of the English language situates a subject (I), a verb, and an object, as if the "I" was the sole author of the act, for the Hopi, some verb describes the whole act, indicating that it is illogical to abstract an "I" as the sole causal entity. Consider what this may mean as to establishing responsibility in law.

The desire for consensus spelled out in Jurgen Habermas's ideal speech situation is therefore illusory, unattainable. "Consensus does violence to the heterogeneity of language-games" (Lyotard, 1984, xxv). It is terror. The practice and idea of justice, therefore, should not be connected with consensus. "Let us wage a war on totality . . . . [E]very one of us belongs to several minorities, and what is important, none of these prevail. It is only then that we can say that the society is just" (1988, 82, 95). In other words, Lyotard believes that we should maintain differences and the uniqueness of language games; to do otherwise is to repress indigenous ways of knowing and doing justice that are more sensitive and reflective of their interpersonal relations and being.

In *Just Gaming*, Lyotard (1999) extends on this theme. There cannot be a "just society" (24). Justice can only exist within the petite narratives, within each language game. To assure justice we must keep the language games autonomous from each other. This multiplicity of justices assures that diverse segments of the population remain with voice, with justice (see also Lyotard, 1984).

In *The Differend*, Lyotard introduces the notion of the différand. It is the person who experiences versions of justice from at least two different petite narratives, where the person finds themselves in a subordinate role. Inevitable conflict will arise. A person judged from a different language region may find that they are left without voice, without the ability to speak and express their desires. This is the différand. Lyotard's examples include the Jews of World War II, wage workers, and indigenous peoples (see Litowitz 1997, 120). Feminists and critical race theorists would argue that women and African Americans are examples of the différand.

So, what then can Lyotard offer toward developing a more tangible justice? He offers several thoughts. First, "one must maximize as much as possible the multiplication of small narratives" (1999, 59, 87). Second, only "temporary contracts" should be invoked and narrowly exercised in time and place (1984, 66). Third, consensus (defining the rules of the game and appropriate moves within it) is desirable only within petit narratives; that is, they must be at a local level, must be agreed to by the local players, and must be eventually rescinded. This is, according to Whyte's (1991, 136) interpretation, "the least objectionable alternative . . . a politics of 'lesser evils'." Fourth, "justice" is not just about observing the rules of a particular narrative, "it consists in working at the limits of what the rules permit, in order to invent new moves, perhaps new rules and therefore new games" (Lyotard, 1999, 100). In other words, the boundaries remain always questioned and reformulated anew. Fifth, Whyte finds implicit in Lyotard the desire to move away from a justice that is situated on the act and toward an orientation to otherness, a responsibility that is not act oriented, but other oriented. Here, justice would revolve around "fostering otherness, born of a deeper understanding of finitude and the delight in difference emerging therefrom" (Whyte, 1991, 137). This principle would also reduce the movement to dominate since in limiting the other, one limits oneself in so much as diminishing the heterogeneous possibilities that may follow. Thus a premium is placed by Lyotard on listening to the other (1999, 72; Whyte, 1991, 110, 118); this is the "recognition" component of justice argued in earlier chapters. Rather than predominantly privileging authoring in a dialogue, Lyotard tells us that justice demands opening oneself to the other ("recognition" principle of justice). In other words, the author's tendency to situate the other in their own interpretive framework should be countered by allowing the narrative of the other to remain in suspension as it plays itself out between the respective interpretive frameworks of self and the other. In the process, mutually responsive understandings emerge, boundaries are often approached, challenged, and crossed, and new frameworks are established. It is within this space that justice emerges.

Jacques Derrida

Derrida's work is demanding reading. Nevertheless, he has been extremely influential in many fields, including law and justice. Two particular articles focus, at some length, on justice: "Declarations of Independence" (1986) and "Force of Law" (1989). *The Gift of Death* (1995) offers further insights on justice. Each has been the basis of a tremendous amount of commentary (see especially Litowitz, 1997; Caputa, 1997, 125–55).

In "Declarations of Independence," Derrida sets out to deconstruct the grounding for constitutions. Consider, for example, the preamble to the U.S. Declaration of Independence, which makes reference to the grounding in "Laws of Nature, "Nature's God." The "principles" section states that "all men are endowed by their Creator with certain unalienable Rights, that among these are Life, Liberty and the pursuit of Happiness." These are assertions, but long forgotten in subsequent history. Founding principles are always a fictional creation ("mystical foundations"); constitutions are enacted by an act of force. At the foundation of a legal system there is a primordial act of violence. As Derrida (1989, 14) informs us: "Since the origin of authority, the foundation or ground, the position of the law can't by definition rest on anything but themselves, they are themselves a violence without ground. Not to say that they are in themselves unjust in the sense of 'illegal.' They are neither legal nor illegal in their founding moment."

Founding principles, once established, along with subsequent logical constructions based on it (consider Weber's notion of formal rationality and deductive logic), thus become part of a feedback loop in which original intent is traced to the founding principles, which in turn become the basis of decision-making in law (Derrida 1992, 191–192; Litowitz, 1996, 94). This circularity tends to hide any discussion of founding principles. It may be true that foundations are often articulated in reference to reason, logic, God, natural law; but each can be deconstructed to show that the grounding is illusory. Consider, for example, the gender and class of the founding fathers of the U.S. Constitution. At best, we can only make reference to custom and practice in rooting law (Derrida, 1989, 12).

Derrida makes a distinction between law and justice. Whereas law can always be deconstructed, for it is based on a fiction, an illusion, justice cannot be so critiqued. Derrida, much like Lyotard, derives inspiration from the work of Emmanuel Levinas (1969, 1987) on his notion of the duty to the other. Justice is something experienced and cannot be adequately deconstructed. Law and justice, therefore, stand in separate realms. Litowitz (1997, 94–95), summarizing Derrida, says that justice "cannot be fully coded in the legal discourse of specific rights, duties, and obligations without losing its irreducible character. One is called to do justice toward the other, yet this justice is excessive, incalculable, unreachable" (95). There can never be a point where one can say justice has been attained, that some decision-making was just (Caputo, 1997). Law, on the other hand, requires that justice be translated into specific rules and procedures, which it can never do (Litowitz, 1996). In this attempt, it is doomed to failure. Justice is like a gift; it is given without thought of return. Justice is beyond calculation; it is a duty one owes to the other.

Three years after his presentation of "The Force of Law," Derrida wrote *The Gift of Death* (1995; for an accessible commentary, see Caputo 1997, 140–55). In it he shows that the structure of justice follows the structure of the gift. A true gift is an act of the impossible. If one feels that one must reciprocate, which is most often the case, then the gift is no longer. As

Derrida (1997b, 18) says, "a gift is something that you cannot be thankful for. As soon as I say 'thank you' for a gift, I start canceling the gift, I start destroying the gift, by proposing an equivalence." And similarly with justice: "A justice that could appear as such, that could be calculated, a calculation of what is just and what is not just, saying what has to be given in order to be just—that is not justice. That is social security, economics. Justice and gift should go beyond calculation" (19). In other words, a gift, like justice, must not be situated in economics—a field of calculation, exchange, utilitarianism, laws, and equity. There remains, therefore, a perpetual divide between law and justice.

Law, however, finds itself bound to the economic—"a calculated balance of payments, of crime and punishment, of offense and retribution, a closed circle of paying off and paying back" (150). We always experience ourselves between the gift and economy, between justice and law, "always trying to interrupt the authoritative voice of the law with the soft sighs of justice, to relieve the harsh strictures of the law with the gentleness of a gift" (151). This is an inevitable task that we all must undertake in our everyday activities. Between law and the gift lie our resolutions.

Thus, for Derrida, justice is a duty we have to the other without payment; it is a duty to recognize the other. The giver can never be repaid, for the debt is incalculable. Justice is both ongoing, but never attainable: "justice is an experience of the impossible" (Derrida 1989, 16). For Derrida, then, justice can never be completely articulated, can never find itself embodied in law; it is a relationship a person has with another. It is a duty owed to the other, without requirement of repayment. "Justice . . . [is] an impossible demand, an incalculable duty to speak to the other in the other's language, to give to the other without expectation of return" (Litowitz, 1997, 107). In short, justice is never attainable; it is always situated in a specific relation to the other.

Richard Rorty

The pragmatic wing of postmodern analysis of justice is represented by Richard Rorty. Pragmatists (for example, William James, John Dewey) focus on everyday real-world behavior and seek to develop understanding inductively, from the ground up. Rather than beginning with well-established laws and theories and applying them deductively, downwardly, in a linear fashion toward some conclusion, Rorty's pragmatism begins with everyday, real-world activities and struggles and how principles are discovered through practice (inductive). Perhaps Rorty's book *Contingency, Irony, and Solidarity* (1989) is the clearest expression of his pragmatic approach to justice.

Like most postmodernists, Rorty dismisses universal claims to justice. Principles of justice are contingent; they vary cross-culturally, and even within cultures. According to Rorty, we should give up a search for objective standards. A search of the past also will not do. "We must start from where we are" (198). His view is both antifoundationalist and pragmatic. Those who do try to find foundations on justice will engage in circular reasoning: "we judge our practices by our preferences, and our preferences have been shaped by our practices" (Litowitz, 1997, 139). Rorty rejects much of our inherited vocabulary established during the Enlightenment; although perhaps necessary at a certain stage of development, it is now "an impediment to the preservation and progress of democratic societies" (Rorty, 1989, 44).

Rorty's vision of a just political economy revolves around balancing competitive capitalism with left-wing reform; he is very much in a reformist remedial mode. According to him, "The most hopeful alternative seems to be governmentally controlled capitalism plus welfare-statism (Holland, Sweden, Ireland). There is nothing sacred about either the free market or about central planning; the proper balance between the two is a matter of experimental tinkering" (Litowitz, 1997, 140).

The notion of contingency runs through Rorty's pragmatism. When we talk about a sense of self, community, or discourse we must acknowledge its contingent nature. That is, they vary in time, space, and form of expression. It is chance, accident, and experimentation that define them (Rorty, 1989; Litowitz, 1997). There is no essential or objective nature of any of these concepts. They are human creations. As Rorty states, "the suggestion that truth, as well as the world, is out there is a legacy of an age in which the word was seen as the creation of a being who had a language of his own" (1989, 5). Rorty's utopian citizens would be liberal ironists. They would acknowledge the contingent nature of their conscience and of the nature of the community. Ironists have questions about the universality and objectivity of the discourse of which they make use—using it as necessary in everyday behaviors, but acknowledging its contingent nature. Consider, for example, critical race theorists who use law as a weapon for social change, but simultaneously acknowledge its inherent bias that privileges the powerful, and that by using law, it is legitimized. Rorty's cultural hero would be the "'strong poet' rather than the warrior, the priest, the sage, or the truth-seeking 'logical,' 'objective' scientist" (53). The strong poet would not privilege Enlightenment discourse or foundations but would situate the present form or society in comparison with other possible historical forms.

Rorty's notion of justice draws inspiration from the legal realists and pragmatist philosophers. The focus is on experimentalism. Judges, in determining what is just, should be seen as visionaries, whose decisions are often leaps in the dark. "The visionary leap is a 'romantic' move that tries to forge new legal paradigms through a creative, 'poetic' act of imagination"

(Litowitz, 1997, 146). Consider, for example, some truly exceptional legal decisions that often went well beyond *stare decisis* (decision-making based on precedents): *Brown v. Board of Education* (1954), *Roe v. Wade* (1973); in the Australian context, *Mabo v. Queensland* (1992). Judges should have some latitude in applying the law so that justice reflects perceived aspirations and shared outlooks of human beings engaged in everyday practices. Judges are problem solvers; they can be the good prophet. Good prophets are result oriented and make no pretenses that their vision is necessarily rooted in "reason, autonomy, human nature, and so on" (Litowitz, 1997, 147). Consider how far this is from the selection criteria employed for the determination of U.S. Supreme Court justices, criteria for which often is restricted to "strict constructionist," a person who can trace decision-making to "original intent," linear logic, deductive logic, *stare decisis*, formal rationality.

Social justice comes by way of experimenting, tinkering, and doing. Ultimately, we must have faith that "a judge will be compassionate and sensitive enough to know how to decide cases in an appropriate manner consistent with the tradition of great judges in America" (148). The legal realists of the earlier part of the twentieth century (Wendell Holmes, Benjamin Cardozo, Roscoe Pound, Jerome Frank, Karl Llewellyn) saw the hard cases as decided by both existing law as well as personal sensitivity to and understandings of real world happenings. Not abstract thought, but a pragmatic orientation itself would lead to leaps in the dark from which justice would proceed. "A good judge will not act in 'bad faith' by mechanically applying precedents, nor can he or she acts as a freewheeling philosopher-king enforcing a private moral vision" (Litowitz, 1997, 150).

Anxiety around deciding the hard cases should not translate into acts of bad faith. See, for example, Duncan Kennedy (1997) who shows that many justices decide cases based on bad faith and denial. Rather than being true to the facts of the case and what they may imply, Kennedy tells us that justices often rule to maintain an image of themselves as having complied strictly to the rule-of-law requirements (formal rationality). Unger, in *What Should Legal Analysis Become?* (1996), similar to Rorty, has provided more thoughts in the direction of experimentalism, pragmatism, and creative decision-making. Like Rorty, he questions the institutionalization of formal rationality.

Rorty also acknowledges leaps in the dark that are repressive: for example, decisions like *Dred Scott v. Sanford* (1857), *Plessy v. Ferguson* (1896), and *Korematsu v. U.S.* (1944) are always possible. Rorty is hard pressed to provide a mechanism to counter these possibilities (see also Litowitz, 1997, 148–49); at best, Rorty argues for justices to not act in bad faith.

Gilles Deleuze and Felix Guattari

A fourth representative theorist of a postmodern perspective on justice is Gilles Deleuze (1983, 1986, 1988, 1990, 1994; for accessible introductions, see Colebrook, 2002; Patton, 2001; Hardt, 1993; Holland, 2013). Deleuze often co-authored with Felix Guattari (more below). From Deleuze we could derive statements on the possibility of retributive and distributive principles of justice, although extant work has run more in the direction of ethics.

An abstract retributive principle of justice is illusory in the Deleuzian schema (1994). Following Nietzsche, Enlightenment thought provided the illusion of the individual that is exclusively determinative of their conduct. Accordingly, in this view, an absolute accountability standard can be established. Each person therefore can receive a similar standard for similar conduct. Deleuze, along with Nietzsche, opposes this. To fix responsibility is to know all conditions of the past leading to the present act, which is impossible. Therefore, justice can never be served. "Judgement is unjust because it lacks measure" (Goodchild, 1996, 35). Justice is always infinite, whereas some judgment is finite—it applies an equal measure to inherently unequal persons (Deleuze 1993, 1994). A debt owed for some deviant act implies "an infinite knowledge of space, time, and experience" to generate an appropriate response, which is illusory (206). Groundings are, therefore, impossible. Ultimately, justice grounds itself in its own circular reasoning. It is to a particular political economic-based social structure that we must look to see how a particular system of axioms are created and diffused through society.

This reasoning also accounts for why Deleuze was against "human rights," as outlandish and contradictory as that position may initially seem. An emphasis on safeguarding rights maintains a static notion in an otherwise evolving society even as it offers protection against injustices. A more pragmatic approach assumes a dynamic society in flux, and hence resolving conflicts that emerge necessarily demand more creative and responsive invention of rights (Lefebvre, 2008, 54–59, 82–87; Deleuze, 1996). According to Lefebvre, "declarations of right are seldom made in conjunction with those whom they concern [i.e., non-recognition]; these declarations, in other words, fail to connect to a milieu and hence fail to be determined by the situation [i.e., differential needs, capabilities, etc.] they are designed to improve [recognition, capabilities, and participation]" (brackets added) (85). This is reminiscent of those (Roscoe Pound, Jerome Frank, and Kurt Llewellyn) from the legal realist perspective in the early 1900s who advocated pragmatism focused on problem-solving that was fair in specific conflicts, that is in specific concrete encounters. Deleuze referred to his ideal as "jurisprudence" more in line with case law that resolves the singularities of conflict situations. Thus, rather than applying some equal measure (formal equality) to all situations, confined by some institutionalized principle specifying a human right, his was more in the direction of substantive rationality (see Max Weber, chapter 3).

Toward alternative notions of rights, Lefebvre's (2018) provocative thesis is that we can integrate Michel Foucault's (1986) late work on "the care
of the self" with "human rights education" literature for a transformative
way, reformulating, for example, the work by Baxi (2012) and Print and
Ugarte (2008) on human rights education to engender human rights as a
way of life: thus building on Baxi, it is "a continual collective search for the
plenitude of life, for meaning that confirms individual and collective dignity, and for the resources of human coexistence" (Baxi 2012, 15). We add,
social justice education, whether distributive (redistribution, recognition,
participation, capabilities) or retributive in form, could, within a Deleuzian
frame, include and expand the functionings of "doings" and "beings" in
considering capabilities, but also adding becomings in transforming "persons who do not just claim these rights [and so too principles of social justice] for their individual existence but who also affirm, and practice,
humanity as a vibrant community of rights" (Lefebvre, 2018, 182–183,
building on Baxi, 2012).

Let us return to a possible distributive principle of justice that may be
extrapolated from Deleuze. At the outset, Deleuze would extend on Nussbaum's notion of capabilities that includes functionings of "doings" and
"beings" to include "becomings." Humans and nonhumans are not only in
states of being but always in the process of developing, transforming, and
transcending.

Deleuze (1983) would advocate justice principles that would emerge
from liberating active forces, the will to power (e.g., desire), and "lines of
flight," a nonlinear movement that produces constant mutation and change
that in turn further enhances these forces. His notion of justice cannot be a
rigid construction, but more attributed to the extent to which the overall
quantity and quality of active forces (increasing capabilities) dominate over
reactive forces (restrictions to capabilities). Thus justice is not something
that can be placed in rigid categories. But it can be determined by the overall development of active forces in a society versus their antithesis, reactive
forces that know only nihilism, ressentiment, and fetishisms. Let's briefly
explore these notions.

Deleuze (1983), following Nietzsche sees the cosmos as composed of
dynamic forces—that is, forces that are constantly combining, recombining, settling, attaining stasis, undoing, etc. Chance plays a good part in how
these combine. Some forces are active forces; these lead to growth, self-
actualization, transformation, desire, becoming—Eros, or the life preserving force. Some are reactive forces; these lead to merely being (stasis), as

well as to nihilism, bad conscience, worship of ascetic ideals (fetishism), resentment—Thanatos, or the death wish. A human being is a composite of forces of overcoming as well as self-destruction at work. It is the will to power that is behind the organization of forces; will to power, not to mean domination, but the activation and direction of forces. Desire, in the Deleuzian framework, is not based on lack as is the case for Jacques Lacan (1977). For Lacan, desire is mobilized on each occasion in which one feels a sense of incompleteness. This originates, according to Lacan, from the early inauguration of the child into society, to the Symbolic Order. Desire is a reaction to lack. Desire, for Lacan, is a reactionary force that mobilizes the psychic apparatus. For Deleuze, however, desire is a will to power that knows only becoming, transforming, mutation, overcoming. It is an active and productive force.

Deleuze defines various models of societies as they emerge in historical conditions. In current capitalist state societies, there is a predominance of a "machine of capture"; that is, all phenomena are coded and axiomatized by some powers, by state apparatuses. Said in yet another way, all phenomena, including law, justice, the legal subject (reasonable man in law) are codified in abstract categories and systematized in a closed self-referencing system. They are further brought within the purview of rationality and linear deductive logic. Once axiomatized—that is, once a major premise has been created, backed by the force of the state—then, through syllogistic reasoning, certain results follow and not others. Weber's notion of "formal rationality" would be compatible. Foucault (1997), for example, shows how a new method of surveillance and control (panopticism) has come to dominate in society; more and more we are being observed, categorized, labeled, and subjected to some examination and potential intervention.

Deleuze has argued that the forces that put axioms (its logic) in motion are abstract machines. Thus principles of formal equality, the work of panopticism (Foucault), the forces of rationalization (Weber), division of labor (Durkheim), dialectical materialism (Marx), and Absolute Spirit (Hegel), to name a few, are equated with an abstract machine that produces particular results. For example, with principles of justice employed in a society valuing formal rationality, the juridical subject and formal equality, an illusory perception of fairness results; with panopticism, a regulated, normalized, and obedient subject is created in law that willingly accepts the notions of justice from which they are being constituted.

Consider, for example, the notion of a rights-based justice, particularly the notion of formal equality that is incorporated in the Fourteenth Amendment of the U.S. Constitution. The incorporated equal protection clause basically stipulates "equally situated should be equally treated." Pashukanis (1980) links the development of this equivalence principle as well as the notion of the legal subject to competitive market forces (legal fetishism). Once established, the formal equality principle becomes an axiom that is the basis of conceiving justice. Legal reasoning provides the mechanism in its emphasis on deductive logic and syllogistic reasoning. This linear form of logic takes us from a major premise, applies it to the minor premise, and arrives at a conclusion in law. It is this that is taught in law school and worshiped as the appropriate form of reasoning in law. Judges who stray are often chastised for not following this rigid, linear form of logic.

The state then cultivates reactive forces; by doing so, it impinges on human development. For Deleuze, the possibility of justice only emerges when these are challenged. His "war machine" is an orientation whereby fixed orders are challenged; they are, to use his language, "deterritorialized," in order to release the potentials that have been blocked (Deleuze and Guattari, 1987). Thus, the goal of the war machine is to undo the axioms that dominate us. It is to release active forces so that they may play out their effects in the world (he calls these "lines of flight"). It is also to take advantage of the acute tendency of capitalism, more than previous modes of production, to continuously decode ("deterritorialization") and recode ("reterritorialization"). These offer opportunities for alternative conceptualizations.

Thus, Deleuze's notion of justice is connected with political economies and whether they tend to release lines of flight, or whether they tend to capture them, turn them into system-supporting axioms, reduce the person to being, rather than to cultivating an ethic of becoming. His notion of justice would revolve around maximizing the opportunities to becoming other—to explore alternative forms of being, to experience new intensities, to engage in transformations. Patton (2001) put it succinctly: rather than embracing only "negative liberty" or positive freedom, Deleuze's notion of justice equates with a critical freedom. Critical freedom means transgressing, transcending, overcoming the very limits within which one has lived. They are turning points, critical points in which a qualitative change has taken place. Rendering justice, in short, must be connected with institutions and social structures that maximize critical freedoms (see Milovanovic, 2011). Turning points are what Rorty would call leaps in the dark. In court decisions we occasionally see these take place in which precedents and formal rationality are not followed, or are at best strained. The energy released (lines of flight) and the active forces that emerged dramatically changed the imaginary and symbolic order, and our system of justice.

Thus, a desire-based justice would evaluate a society in terms of the extent to which it limits or enhances critical freedom. Deleuze also cautions us. A desire-based form of justice may have both good and bad consequences. By moving away from categorized and systematized notions of justice and law, we also move away from given evaluative standards; the danger is that processes of mutation, change, and transformation may have unintentional negative consequences (Patton, 2000). We must always be vigilant as to these possibilities.

Michel Foucault

Foucault's development can often be conceptualized in terms of three phases: an early phase on discursive practices—how discourses arise in historical conditions and what they readily allow or not; the middle phase of surveillance and disciplinary mechanisms—modes of observing, categorizing, normalizing, correcting; and the late phase on sexuality, care of the self, biopower, and governmentality—the latter phase was particularly the focus from 1981 to his death in 1984. His late work on "governmentality" traces how the state has become decoupled from any central monarchical powers. Governmentality is a method in which all important functionings in the socius are subject to surveillance, coding, normalizing, and, where deviations exist, correcting. The formal rational contract enforced by the state paved the way. Durkheim and his spontaneous division of labor, Weber and his thesis on bureaucratization and rationalization, and Marx with his analysis of commodification—all can be seen as suggesting the way. For Foucault, governmentality also extended to encouraging or coercing human beings to take greater control of their biopowers, a self-disciplining, self-regulation ("care of the self"). "Technologies of the self" were abundant for their reinforcement. As Lefebvre (2018) noted, "the self is not seen as a fixed substance or pregiven essences. It is a material to be crafted in light of an end or telos" (15). We see this at play in Woolford's (2010, 85–87) insightful critique of restorative justice in showing how participants' identities are shaped by an underlying logic that coerces all to make use of the language of restorative justice rather than retributive justice, "disciplined to norms of effective listening and interest-based negotiation," and to proceed with harmony as the goal, playing down any legitimate claims to their conflict; a model, in short, employing a soft coercion. This is both pacification and disciplining.

We note online sources instructing the appropriate presentations in small claims courts, some even suggesting the litigant consult reality TV shows, prior to their day in court, on the etiquette of small claims proceedings. Industry has also profited from these ideas with the insistence on "self-care" as a panacea for work-related stress, racism, sexism, mental health, and other concerns (McCrea, 2018). This is the notion of "responsibilisation." The exercise of power now extends to the "capillaries." Thus, the human being is coerced and manipulated to accept modes of care of the self, a self-regulation in service of the rational logical principles of governmentality. West Virginia teachers, for example, went on strike in part to refuse a requirement that they wear Fitbits in order to receive affordable health care (McAlevey, 2018). Capabilities have now been extended to technologies of self-governance. Truths and reality are, therefore, constructed, but now by willing (or not) subjects. Principles of justice take form employing the logic of governmentality, extended downward to everyday people.

The logic of governmentality is also extending to nonhumans with "green governmentality," or "eco-governmentality," (see Rutherford, 2007, 2017; Luke, 1999). Eco-justice, too, will be subject to greater purview by central government categorizations creating and shaping (typologies), principles of justice, logic, rationality, enforcement. For example, we have already seen this in the commodification of nature. Governmentality, with a little help from its friends ("care of the self," "technologies of the self") will thus not only be the basis of control but also constitute identities (see also Litowitz, 1997, 79; Lefebvre, 2018). Rutherford (2017), for example, explains the creation of new subject positions (identities), "green citizens" (in tune with environmental issues) and even "climate accountants" (who assume the logic of accounting practices in assessing and changing climate issues and corrective practices).

Foucault does offer a possibility for transformative justice, practices of resistance, be it undeveloped in the notion of the aesthetic practices, an "ethics of self-mastery," moments of which appear in the cracks in the exercise of power (Litowitz, 1997, 84). Consider, for example, Foucault's study of Bentham's panopticon, a roundhouse model of prisons, still found in some countries (i.e., Stateville Prison, Illinois). Although he saw surveillance as a one-way (asymmetric) exercise of power—the guards in the central tower observing all inmates in the outside rows of cells without in turn being observed—he overlooked the resistance by which an inmate could simply stay outside of their cell at the call to return, making the full prison population their audience and thus re-establishing a symmetry in power for the moment (observed by DM in his John Howard Association prison visits). But Foucault, too, could not complete his answer to the call of Spivak, "from where can the subaltern speak," since dominant discourse itself didn't provide a space from which to speak. Illuminating remarks about resistance in the Foucauldian scheme have been presented by Lefebvre (2018). For Lefebvre, an ethical duty in caring for the self is an ethics based on resistance, a cultivation of the soul and nurturing love and joy in human relations. Litowitz (1997, 83) cites Foucault: "we have to create ourselves as a work of art." Juridical concepts (responsibility, blame, guilt, innocence, utility, calculation) must give way to the aesthetic, the relational nature of self to others, others to self, an I-thou in which, consistent with Derrida and Levinas, justice is better seen as a gift, an infinite duty of care for the other, which in action constitutes the caring and receiving subjects.

POSTMODERN FEMINISTS AND JUSTICE

Postmodern feminists have challenged male-centered standards of justice. They draw particularly keen inspiration, even though critically based, from the works of Jacques Lacan, Jacques Derrida, Gilles Deleuze, and Felix Guattari. First-wave postmodern feminists such as Luce Irigaray, Helene Cixous, Toril Moi, and Julia Kristeva have brought much of this discussion into sharp relief (see Arrigo et al., 2005). Second-wave theorists include Judith Butler, Drucilla Cornell, Elizabeth Grosz, and Rosi Braidotti. Some, however, have more recently moved beyond a postmodern approach. We want to focus on one representative theory, that of Drucilla Cornell. Third-wave theorists have built on the insights of the first two waves, developing nuanced perspectives, such as Queer Theory. Cornell is arguably the leading second-wave theorist in postmodern feminism as it relates to law and justice. Three early key books, amongst others, lay out the basic position of an "ethical feminism": *Beyond Accommodation* (1999), *At the Heart of Freedom* (1998), and *Transformations* (1993). A fourth book co-authored with Stephen Seely, *The Spirit of Revolution* (2016), defending much of postmodern theory's focus on a need to explain human agency, also engages the emerging post-postmodern (posthumanist) perspective. We focus on the first three books and then briefly turn to the fourth.

Cornell argues against standards of justice based on formal equality, in particular where women's struggles are coached in language of equality with men. She finds one of the main culprits within feminist circles of this in Catherine MacKinnon (1987, 1989). Not only does Cornell critique her for her reliance on legal standards such as formal equality but she also argues that MacKinnon's call is more for a revenge politics in that empowerment comes by way of a "reversal of hierarchies" (1999, 132). In a reversal of hierarchies, previously subordinated groups attempt to gain the dominant position in hierarchical arrangements and then dispose of the dominant group in the same way as they had previously been. This maintains repressive practices, even while changing the relation of who is dominated.

Cornell's suggestions are inspired by the work of Jacques Lacan and Jacques Derrida. Lacan has indicated how gender roles are stabilized in the dominant order, particular in culture and language, on one level, and in the unconscious, at another. Lacan, a revisionist Freudian, who integrated linguistics in the understanding of the unconscious and the workings of the psychic apparatus, indicated that the law of the father is the organizing principle within the unconscious and hence all is tainted with the male voice. Women remain subordinated. Women, according to Lacan, are left out ("pas toute") in the male-centered symbolic order. Cornell (1999), using Lyotard's conception, says they are the "différand" and proposes an ethical feminism. She sees society as "'peopled' by individuals, 'sexed' differently . . . a different way of being human" (191).

Rather than a "proceduralist conception of justice," Cornell advocates an "equivalent evaluation." Proceduralist views of justice center discussion of justice on formal equality, best characterized by the Fourteenth Amendment to the U.S. Constitution in the equal protection clause. Syllogistic reasoning applied to situations of racist or sexist practices attempts to correct these practices as standards of formal equality are applied. We must, however, argues Cornell, create an alternative space from which to think sexual differences and justice. As "sexuate beings," each of us orients ourselves differently in the world. To develop maximum possibilities for this orientation, she defends protecting the imaginary domain, an alternative space, and the many possibilities generated by thinking otherwise than conventional.

There are two aspects to Cornell's standard of equivalent evaluation: first, "is a demand for women's inclusion in the moral community of persons" (e.g., establishing free and equal standing); and second, "a demand for fair, and thus, equitable treatment whenever our sexual difference needs to be taken into account" (1998, 11). She does not oppose addressing gender discrimination, but argues, "if we are not equivalently evaluated as free persons as an initial matter, we will be unable to *fairly* correct that definitional inequality; our life chances and prospects will be limited by the very definition of our inequality" (20). She provides an example of a woman being defined as disadvantaged and a program initiated to correct for this disadvantage. This often appears in patronizing forms. This is different from recognizing the woman as a free person and that women "be given the chance to live out their lives to the fullest and be provided with the full scope of rights, resources, capabilities, or primary good that a theory of distributive justice defends" (20). Her principle of equivalent evaluation would assure that a person's right to self-representation as a sexuate being be protected. The standard of comparison should not be the male, but human beings as sexuate beings. The standard of equality imposes a similar measure, whereas sexuate beings are inherently dissimilar; nevertheless, each should be treated in respect to their differences (substantive justice, substantive rationality), but not in denying resources, benefits, and rights that are available to all.

Cornell suggests, then, a principle of justice that must recognize human beings as sexuate beings providing them with a maximum amount of liberty, and provide principles that go beyond distributive principles of justice advocated by formal equality in well-being. This new principle would have to address the "question of what scope of rights, opportunities, and social goods would be needed to maintain freedom and equality" (20). This has some similarities to the capabilities justice principle.

Cornell provides one example of a change to recognize the nature of sexuate beings in revised law of adoption and those pertaining to the family. Consistent with her equivalent evaluation principles, she argues that "we must demand that we are entitled to rights, not because we are mothers, but because we are persons" (104). In other words, it is not some notion of an abstract legal subject that commands. It is the imaginary domain of the sexuate being that is being protected. Thus, her reconstituted family would: protect lovers who choose a domestic relationship; allow for the notion of custodial responsibility whereby one of two partners may relinquish their responsibility for being a caregiver and allow for another to share in the responsibility, even while keeping the partnership intact, but with the protection of governmental resources; and provide for adequate health care and minimum income for families. In this way the imaginary domain of sexuate beings would be protected. It would also assure stability for the upbringing of children while at the same time acknowledge the different possibilities of living as sexuate beings.

In 2016 Drucilla Cornell, along with co-author Stephen Seely, wrote *The Spirit of Revolution*, more in the spirit of what we identified as the "radical accusatory" style (chapter 5). Here, given recent movements (early 2000s) toward a posthumanist perspective, they insist that human agency must not be jettisoned, or alternatively, be jettisoned prematurely for a true revolution to take place. They insist that revolution must engage two simultaneous dimensions: horizontal, transforming economic and political arrangements under capitalism; and vertical, transforming the spiritual, a political spirituality. Drawing from Fanon, Foucault, Derrida, Irigaray, Marx, Spinoza, and Lacan, among others, they insist capitalism must go to allow for new relationships based on caring, loving encounters, an openness to the other, a call for new collective practices, and this should extend to nonhuman forms. This cannot happen, they insist, under capital logic. The vertical dimension can be aided by Foucault's late work on "care of the self" for transformative ways of being. "Transformation, demands . . . new forms of conducting ourselves individually and with others through new ways of relating to who we imagine ourselves to be" (Cornell and Seely, 2016, 79). And this is particularly highlighted by the legacy of colonization and the traumas wrought. In their view, we cannot know in advance the contours of the socius to come. Social justice principles, in short, can be studied in the context of the current vertical and horizontal structures, and transformative social justice principles emerge in the struggles themselves; no blueprint will lead to a particular end state, "a thoroughly decolonized democratic socialist common world" (146).

POSTMODERN MARXISTS AND
CONTEMPORARY INTEGRATIONS

A number of potential integrations of postmodern theory as it applies to justice studies are beginning to take place. Some have been especially keen on integrating Marxist analysis (a neo-Marxism, or post-Marxism) into a postmodern Marxism. They are the subject of much debate. Let us briefly review several to give an indication of their direction.

Roger Burbach

Burbach (2001) developed a postmodern Marxist framework and applied it to the phenomena of globalization. He argued that traditional Marxist principles need to be revised given the nature of current global society. Integration with postmodern thought, he theorizes, would revive it. Conceptions of justice must confront the growing globalization movement and its potential for domination. Thus the current information age, the Internet, new modes of communication, and post-Fordism have led to new socio-economic relations that have to be re-theorized as to articulate possible principles of justice in a global order. A neo-Marxist view would be postmodern in "that it believes a multiplicity of social groups and fragmented classes exist in the era of globalization that have little or no relationship to the universalized proletariat enunciated by Marx and Engels" (Whyte, 1991, 88). The issue becomes more of temporary alliances, fragmented goals, means of communication, and new methods of organization in a global order. Needed is the development of new conceptions of justice relevant to a global order.

Nick Dyer-Witheford

In a similar direction, Nick Dyer-Witheford, in *Cyber-Marx* (1999), suggested an integration of Marxism with postmodern analysis. He identifies the Italian autonomist Marxists as amiable to this challenge, particularly the works of Negri and postmodernists Guattari and Deleuze. Rather than the mode of production, the notion of mode of information would capture an emergent postmodern force necessary for integration in the contemporary era (Poster, 1984). He describes "concepts of social identity as decentered, transitory, and heterogeneous" (167). Notions of somehow accurately grasping totality are given up as illusory. Identities are unstable, finding reference in electronic media, commercial production, and emerging architectural spaces (169). Such theorists as Negri would argue that since capitalists in a global order now have to better communicate and organize, so too those in struggle. Those in struggle now have a new source for organization. It is the era of the postmodern proletariat (Dyer-Witheford, 1999, 177). Immaterial labor—"labor that produces immaterial products, such as information, knowledges, ideas, images, relationships, and affects" (Hardt and Negri, 2004, 65)—will be key factors in postmodern society and its emergent institutions, structures, law, identities, and forms of justice.

Felix Guattari

In writings with his longtime co-author Deleuze, Guattari has spoken against postmodernists such as Lyotard and Baudrillard. However, the notion of postmodern Marxist takes a new significance in his co-authored book with Negri, *Communists Like Us* (1990), and his single-authored book, *Molecular Revolution* (1984). The key for Negri, Guattari, and Deleuze is called the "rhizomatic" organization, which is "decentered, divergent, transverse, nonhierarchical, lateral, or transverse modes of organization" (Dyer-Witheford 1999, 182). In other words, social movement theory needs to recognize the newly emergent forms of global organization of those in struggle that are nonhierarchical often multiple issues in focus, defy specific leadership roles, and reach out to various other groups in struggle. Notwithstanding the always possible fascist forms emerging, these authors are pushing ahead in arguing that new forms of organization and new principles of justice will emerge, more bottom up, inductively. No singular form of society is privileged; rather, these postmodern Marxists argue that new spaces are developing within which diverse life forms can co-exist.

Hardt and Negri

Negri (neo-Marxist) and Hardt (postmodern) have co-authored three influential books, inspired by Deleuzian concepts, *Empire* (2000), *Multitude* (2004), and *Commonwealth* (2009), which stand, in many theorists' eyes, as the present-day counterpart to Marx's *Communist Manifesto*. In their view, justice cannot be refined in law, but must ultimately find its expression in the social (Hardt and Negri, 1994). Bringing a Marxist and a postmodern view to their critique of Rawls's distributive justice principle, they review criticism that Rawls's principles of justice neglect the sphere of production and prioritize the sphere of distribution and circulation (226; see also Sandel's insightful critique of Rawls, 1982). In Rawls, the sources of justice are mystified. Hardt and Negri's more recent writings hold much promise for the new global proletariat, the "multitude," which will articulate new insights on justice based on global struggles. A multitude is composed of diverse people, each in their nuanced ways of being and becoming, which can never be reduced to an abstraction such as the juridical subject or the people, or the working class. It is only within the multitude that a common position can emerge, that society can be formed. Foundational principles of justice can only be found in the processes inherent in the movement of the multitude. Common positions are not fixed but dynamic, more like dissipative structures (chaos theory, dynamic systems theory; see below), and people may align themselves differently on different issues.

In the third book of their trilogy, *Commonwealth* (2009), Hardt and Negri turn to critique and reconstruction. Neither capitalism, nor socialism, is the desired goal, but a return to the "commons" where all share the wealth and resources. They are driven by the virtue of love and the teachings from poverty to reconsider Foucault's biopower toward a metamorphosis [transformation] end. It will be enhanced by a stance of refusal of power domination and the energy transformed into resistance and positive change, and cultivation, drawing from Spinoza, of joyful relations in "a quest for the common" (53). "What the private is to capitalism and what the public is to socialism, the common is to communism" (273). They call their approach centered on an "altermodernity" rather than a strict postmodernism. Their critique, it should be noted, is somewhat belied due to their focus on negative, reactive forms of postmodernism (merely deconstruction, negation, reaction) rather than the affirmative postmodern perspective (deconstruction *and* reconstruction, overcoming, becoming, transformation).

They turn to Ludwig Wittgenstein and the nature of language to show how truths are multiple depending on the language games unique to each, rather than an overall dominating language. Identities, too, are localized in particular languages and thus can find an alternative basis in pursuing the common. Seizing the moment of ruptures in capital logic provides opportunities for not only political organization but an activation of focused biopower (151). The notion of the nuclear family, structures of corporations, and of the nation must all be challenged. Love and recognition are central ingredients in the new discourse of the common, a "reterritorialization" drawing from Deleuze and Guattari, a transformation of conflict to joyful and productive relations. For Hardt and Negri, "the common is the locus of freedom and innovation—free access, free use, free expression, free interaction—that stands against private control, that is the control exerted by private property, its legal structures, and its market forces" (282). Specific proposals include minimum guaranteed income and assuring basic means for existence [needs principle of social justice], participation equality—"free and equal use of resources and wealth" (381)—, and construction of participatory democratic institutions at every level of government whereby social cooperation as well as self-rule will be cultivated (310). Identity politics such as Axel Honneth's seeking recognition rely too much, for Hardt and Negri, in separation politics rather than a search for the common, identities that both reflect nuanced beings of becoming as well as becoming commonalities in dynamic social organization.

Stuart Henry and Dragan Milovanovic

Henry and Milovanovic (1996, 2019) have developed a constitutive perspective in law and justice studies (for an application to penology, see Arrigo and Milovanovic, 2009). In this view all is a coproduced, dynamic event: we are both the creators and the created in mutual constitutive practices. When our difference-making possibilities are denied, repressed, or reduced, we are rendered less than human. Crime is "the power to deny others their ability to make a difference" (Henry and Milovanovic, 2019). Justice principles can be derived from a reconceptualization. That is, if we reject the legalist definition of crime, and substitute the notions of harms of repression and reduction, we can also look at its reverse to discover principles of justice based on concern for the other and specify an active role in enhancing the other's well-being; rather than repression and reduction, we have enhancement, cultivating fuller possible expressions, and care for the other. By defining, cultivating, and practicing justice in terms of concern for otherness, as in Derrida and Lyotard, and the ethics of care in feminist studies, overall justice is enhanced. Along with the call for a necessary redistribution, constitutive theory would support a distributive social justice principle that puts a premium on needs, recognition, capabilities, participation, and justification among others. In countering harms of reduction and repression, minimal needs must be met; recognition of the other acknowledged; denied capabilities countered and new ones cultivated expressing greater range of human capabilities; justification for action explained; and inclusive and meaningful decision-making established. Substantive equality and yet-to-be imagined standards of merit must also be rethought away from elitist views incorporated in law and conventional understandings of justice.

Dynamics Systems Theory: Nomadology

Several approaches have recently employed dynamic systems theory (chaos theory) to developing notions of justice (Holland, 2011; see also Schehr, 1997, 1999a, 1999b; Arrigo and Milovanovic, 2009; Pycroft and Bartollas, 2014; Fieguth, 2016). Principles of justice will emerge from far-from-equilibrium conditions (dynamic conditions; nonhomeostatic) in the form of "dissipative structures," which are open ended and highly sensitive to individual input. Robert Schehr (1996a, 1996b) integrates chaos theory in the development of a nonlinear perspective on social movement theory and justice. Milovanovic (2004) has reconceptualized lawyer-client relations in terms of Paulo Freire's dialogical pedagogy, Lacan's four discourses, and chaos theory, to indicate how new conceptions of justice may emerge in practice. Chris Williams and Bruce Arrigo (2001) have integrated chaos theory with anarchist theory in indicating how a better understanding of justice may emerge.

Eugene Holland (2004, 2006, 2011) has brought dynamic systems theory into political economy by advocating a social practice referred to as "nomadology" toward the constitution of "nomad citizenship" in a free-market communism. This is in sharp contrast to current U.S. citizenship, which Kumar (2017) describes as an imperial citizenship relying on an assimilation to rigidity and national security. Nomadology is a practice valuing: nonlinear developments (small inputs can produce disproportional effects, via iteration); spontaneous generating dissipative structures (organizations that both provide temporary order but are always subject to change with the very smallest of inputs, self-organization); singularities (moments of disruptions where novelty and creativity can be born); and emergents (becomings).

The image of jazz improvisation captures the idea, so too the games of soccer and of "Go"; as opposed to classical music, an orchestra, U.S. football, or chess (20–24). Consider the organizational structure of each. He applies this model in investigating possible new social forms. This includes "nomad markets" whereby commodification is freed (from abstract exchange values) and thus use values are re-established as the basis of exchange (i.e., review Durkheim's notion of "social value" in chapter 3); free-market communism whereby slave wage labor (fate of the proletariat) gives way to free circulation of use values rather than monetary valuations tied to standards, all left to more genuine "free-market mechanisms" (137), which are free from reliance on universal standards of value and without central command authorities dictating terms; and nomad citizenship with emergent relational identities in social collectivities that continuously form dissipative structures, all in an endless process of becoming. He asks: "What if . . . market agents routinely took into account not just personal desires and price information but information regarding products' circumstances of production, conditions of distribution, environmental impact, and so on? The result of the aggregate mechanism of the market would then be more than mere efficiency: It would be an aggregated version of the Common Good" (109). This is the emergence of new identities beyond those found in capitalist market places, nomad market agents. Examples they provide of nomadological organizations include: the Orpheus Chamber Orchestra (leaderless); the Internet, especially with viewers' contributions to a body of knowledge such as Wikipedia and Internet encyclopedias such as *Encyclopedia Britannica Online*; the free open-source software movement. For example, Richard Stallman, the inventor of the GNU-Linux operating system, a free software, has argued that the operating system can "create community and social justice" (Wikipedia.org, 2019h). The Linux system allows users to access the codes of the software, modify them, and publish their new versions for access for others to use and develop without cost. Consider, also, the Zapatista form of organization as well as that of Occupy Wall Street, which we address in later chapters.

Holland concludes his book calling for a slow-motion general strike whereby experimentation, emergents, self-organization, dissipative structures, nonlinearity and the development of the nomad citizen gradually undo the capitalist mode of production toward a more general free-market communism (for one study on comparing effectiveness of Hardt and Negri's with Holland's model, see Kieresy, 2014; for Holland's engagement with Hardt and Negri, 2011, 151–156). This transformative justice does not entail violence, but social change through an "engaged withdrawal" from capital logic toward self-organization, dissipative structures, and nomad market identities.

Post-Postmodernism: Posthumanism

NEW MATERIALISM, QUANTUM HOLOGRAPHY. The first decade of 2000 witnessed increased critical response to postmodern thought, although including some of the key points, but rejecting others. Perhaps coming under the umbrella term, post-postmodernism, it includes "new materialism" (Cole and Foster, 2001), posthumanism (Haraway, 2018), digimodernism (Kirby, 2009), hypermodernism, postanthropocentrism. Whereas modernism emerging from the Enlightenment period privileged a centered subject, a self-conscious, self-directing individual, and whereas postmodernism rejected these claims arguing instead how language shapes identities and how subjects must be decentered, for post-postmodernists, instead, identified are material forces (persevering, enduring, repetitive structures, not necessarily physical), the decentered agent, the constituted nature of reality, holism, and the rejection of the Anthropocene. Acknowledged is the plurality of agencies, not just human, while recognizing structural impediments.

Many continue to acknowledge the continuity with some postmodern thinkers such as Deleuze and Guattari, Foucault, Derrida, and Butler (Barad, 2007; Braidotti, 2013; Law, 2007; Latour 2007, 2014); others advocate a separation, and proclaim a death of postmodernism (Rudrum and Stavris, 2015; Kirby 2009). There has also been some movement away from the Newtonian ontology (ontology, meaning what we are willing to accept as reality) as core assumptions of Classical as well as some of the postmodern perspectives. Classical thought privileges: objects as distinct entities in space and time; human individuals as privileged causal agents; linear notions of causality; time flowing from past, to present to future; locality—meaningful causative forces located in immediate environment; proportional relation between cause and effect—particular increases in input values produce an equivalent proportional increase in output values; order, and predictability (a "clockwork universe"). Post-postmodernists from a quantum perspective offer counters to each of these core assumptions necessitating a rethinking of core assumptions, including those that generate justice principles. Albert Einstein rejected quantum theory. In his continuous debates with quantum theorists, especially Niels Bohr, he had quipped, "God does not play dice," whereas the quantum side responded, "Don't tell God what to think."

Turning to the new materialist view, rejected is the claim of the separation of the social and the material, now replaced with the unhyphenated "sociomateriality" recognizing the mutual constitutive, relational, contextual nature of reality acknowledging the multiplicity of agents. Latour's (2007) "actor-network" theory is prominent along with the work of physicist-turned-philosopher Karan Barad (2007). Deleuze and Guattari's Spinozian notion of the differential capacities to affect and be affected is prominent in consideration of the nature of agency and in ethical reformulations (Milovanovic, 2011). Agency is now extended to nonhuman and even to the inanimate (i.e., technology, buildings, etc.), now redefined, by some, as "actants." Some make a distinction (Kohn, 2013) between life forms (humans, animals, plants, rain forests) and the inanimate (grains of sand, chemicals, desks, etc.); others subsume both animate and inanimate as equivalent agents ("actants," Latour, 2005; for a useful discussion, see Conty (2018). Events are now replaced with "eventing," continuous processes of coming-to-be, privileging emergents. Justice in action must be studied as emergents, enacted and performed events in particular contexts. New materialism and its sociomaterial thrust has found adherents in sociology (Fox and Alldred, 2018), psychology (Taguchi, 2012), philosophy (Braidotti, 2013; Barad, 2007), as well as the informational sciences and organizational studies (Orlikowski, 2007). Little has transpired, however, for theorists and practitioners in criminology, law, and eco-justice (for a recent exception, see the application in criminology by Campbell, 2019, on the nature of responsibility in riot conditions). But it promises to usher in radically new analysis of responsibility, causation, rationality, time, locality, and agency in developing a sociomaterially informed notion of social justice principles.

NEW MATERIALISM, QUANTUM MECHANICS, AND KARAN BARAD. Barad (2007) stands out as the central player in sociomaterial studies, even as many argue for the prominence of Bruno Latour. Most of the literature in sociomateriality that employs her concepts has embraced her notion of "intra-action," "agential cuts," and the role of apparatuses. Apparatuses are specific, historic, contextual "physical arrangements," specific material reconfigurations of the world" (142), for example: research contexts (lab?, field?) and tools (cameras, interviews, questionnaires) for studying phenomena; or consider school settings; contexts for police surveillance cameras (e.g., street corner cameras); or hospitals, courthouses, prisons, jails, mental institutions, etc. (Many equate apparatus with Deleuze and Guattari's notion of assemblages [Fox and Alfred, 2018], whereas others make a distinction [Barad, 2007], not to be considered further here.) Consider the courthouse—necessarily implicated is the architecture, court decorum, roles and offices, body of laws and proce-dures, use of deductive logic, and legal discourse—the latter allowing only restricted language for constructing "reality." Each apparatus provides a con-text for agents of observation and their "objects." Consider: police and those observed, lawyers and those bringing an issue to them, researchers using questionnaires and search for truth, participant observers and those studied. Identities (objects, with distinct boundaries and properties), i.e., suspect, liti-gant, defendant, felon, and ex-offender are created by way of intra-action. The neologism intra-action suggests we do not have identities prior to some performance or enactment that induces a "cut" in the ongoing, dynamic worldly activities. Interaction, on the other hand, assumes separate identities (objects) prior to any engagements. Consider the change of objectified iden-tities from suspect, litigant, defendant, felon, and ex-offender.

Barad, inspired by Niels Bohr, a founding figure in quantum mechan-ics, argues that in natural states all is quantumly entangled (intraconnected) phenomena (Quantum Entanglement, 2019) without specific boundaries, properties, and identities. It is only in material discursive practices, that is, in performances or enactments between some object (phenomena) and an agency of observation that specific boundaries, properties, and identities are formed that now assume an objective status. Think, for example, how a natural scientist sets up a laboratory; each object is in itself the product of intra-action culminating in the precise instruments of measurement being employed. Consider, too, questionnaires. A quantum mechanics view is that answers are *created* in the context of the question being asked; truth is not already there waiting to be summoned as is the assumption in tradi-tional research. Consider a juror at the point where they have to make a decision. Prior to the decision, "truth" has not yet been solidified (e.g., yes, guilty; no, not guilty; Busemeyer and Bruza, 2014). Consider the various changing identities in relation to the criminal justice system (apparatus) and the ongoing intra-actions between humans and those with whom they engage: citizen with rights, person of interest, accused, defendant, con-victed, ex-felon. Each's identity takes form in intra-action with the crimi-nal justice system (apparatus) and its various agents operating within the limits of material discursive practices that define their duties (judges, pros-ecutors, specialists, witness, accused, secretaries, police, etc.; roles, or better discursive subject positions) and with the prevailing architectural arrange-ments (courtroom, holding pen, interrogation rooms, etc.), law practices, and rules for engagement, etc. With citizen identities we have a plurality of possible instantiations of identity (quantum superposition), but with the criminal justice involvement some identities are more likely, with a tendency, following labeling theories in criminology, for the development of "secondary deviance"; meaning, the probability state of everyday manifestation can become a more permanent ex-felon identity to be now negotiated with normal citizens (Milovanovic, 2014b).

Barad's insight stems from the classical "double-slit experiment" (for a brief YouTube tutorial, see "Double-Slit Experiment," 2019). Initially a thought experiment, but in the last 10–15 years, continuously confirmed by experimental results, it shows how all, in its natural state is a waveform (phenomena)—vibrational entities with distinct frequencies, moving through time and space. Each waveform is represented by the Schrödinger equation, devised by Erwin Schrödinger in 1926, which provides only the probability of a particular state appearing in context; otherwise all is an evolving, dynamic "cloud of possibilities." In other words, at any instance there are multiple possible states (superposition) of instantiation with each state a probability event. It is in the measurement or observation that the wave function collapses so that what appears is an object form in the instance with distinct boundaries, properties, and identities. This is the "agential cut." These ideas represent the concept of wave-particle duality. This version is also known as the Copenhagen Interpretation, one of several in quantum mechanics. Consciousness, it is said, collapses the wave function.

We witness a scant few applications to law, and where appearing, more metaphor: see, for example, Kuttner (2011), who's work on alternative negotiation principles has identified two forms, "wave-like dynamics" where privileged are more open states, mutual development toward solutions, emergents, as opposed to "particle-like dynamics," whereby fixity of positions and interests guide compromise solution. Justice for the former acknowledges recognition, participation, needs, substantive equality, capabilities, etc.; for the latter, it acknowledges formal equality with some exceptions noted in law (i.e., duress, reduced responsibility, mental insanity, entrapment, etc.). See also Kelsey (2013, 94–101) who reviews Newtonian versus Quantum influences in justice practices, noting a law-equity duality. Doing justice entails either a particle approach (law, more Newtonian) focused on deductive logic, formal equality, reliance on written law, original intent by framers, uniform application, and court's prior reasoning; or it entails a wave approach (equity approach, more quantum) with more engaging exceptionalities and particularities (i.e., needs, substantive equality). The two often work together in particular justice practices. The two, according to Kelsey, rest on similar dualities encountered with trying to reconcile quantum and general relativity theory. Which one prevails is indeterminate. Justice in practice is guided by "two competing strong towers of justice: the generally applicable law with its virtue of objective uniformity, and the specifically applicable equity with its virtues of particularity and tailored mercy" (101).

Barad also reviews one variant of the double-slit experiment, again, with much current support, called "quantum eraser" or "delayed choice" (for an introduction, see YouTube videos: "Delayed Choice," 2019; "How the Quantum Eraser Rewrites the Past," 2019). The upshot is that what has transpired (a beam of electrons or photons passing through a grid on their way to recording on a screen) can be changed when an observation is made immediately *after* the electrons have already passed the grid (retro-active causality). Rather than a wave pattern recorded on the screen, we now see a particle pattern. Remove the observation and the waveform appears. The past, then, is not fixed, but always subject to being revisited; but, for Barad, contrary to some physicist, everything is not erased in these revisitations, but rather traces remain that are the subject of the revisitations. Consider, for example, witness recollections; consider, too, what labeling theorists call retrospective interpretation (biographical reconstructions). We are permanently quantumly entangled with our memories and with all with whom/what we intra-actively engage.

Barad (2010, 2015) has made applications to social justice, particularly drawing from the work of Derrida on the ethics of othering, responsibility, and justice-to-come. Derrida (cited in Barad 2010, 261) stated, "no justice . . . seems possible or thinkable without the principle of some responsibility." According to Barad, we always already remain in constitutive relations of "responsibility to the entangled other" (265), a "response-ability" of obligations and indebtedness to the other, where each quantum entanglement leaves a trace in both the other and self. As Barad says, "living compassionately requires recognizing and facing our responsibility to the infinitude of the other, welcoming the stranger whose very existence is the possibility of touching and being touched, who gifts us with both the ability to respond and the longing for justice-to-come" (2015, 162; Milovanovic, 2018). Justice-to-come represents not only the emergent quality of justice but also how in contexts justice is enacted, performed, and played out. Critical researchers could note that further principles of justice could be implicated in the use of the concept response-ability beyond the implicit recognition principles advocated by Barad, to include capabilities, needs, participation; each of the latter are integrally entangled with Barad's concept, to further recognizing the need for redistribution away from harms of reduction and repression.

We can see how revisiting postmodern thinkers can provide a new directionality in researching social justice. For example, from Derrida, the call for the infinite duty of care to/for the other recalls the needs principle, recognition, and participation; from Deleuze and Guattari, their Spinozean ethics of continuous expansion of the ability to affect and to be affected by the other, recalls the capability perspective in social justice—not only "doing" and "beings" as with Naussbaum, but also "becomings"; from Henry and Milovanovic's constitutive theory, the antedote to harms of reduction and repression is in the cultivation of recognition, substantive equality, need, justification, and material redistribution; and, all drawing from an engagement with Barad are enriched by a quantum entangled notion of responsibility (response-ability), the ongoing contributions of each agent leaving traces in the social fabric, the inherently and irreducible intraconnected nature of reality, a becoming of identities and their contingent emergence, and the idea that justice is not just a being and doing, but an ever becoming.

Posthumanists, too, would argue that human beings are not the only actants that are important (Anthropocene), but all animals have (a degree of) consciousness, cognitive capacities, memory, intelligence, calculating powers, and ability to communicate; many argue for a plant neurobiology and plant intelligence to the chagrin of traditional plant physiologists (Garcon, 2007; Marder, 2012; see also the journal, *Plant Signaling and Behavior*). Plants, too, even though not possessing neurons, can exhibit and respond to electric waves, an electrochemical form of plant signaling (see also plant electrophysiology; bioacoustics; Lautner, 2007; see also quantum effects and quantum memories of plants by Karpinski and Szechynska-Hebda, 2012). Counter to commonsense, this demonstrates the embeddedness and resistance of the Anthropocene. Definitions of intelligence, consciousness, memory, calculating skills, etc. need to be revised. Thus, problematized here are possible justice principles that are not human being specific. Thus, capabilities, needs, participation, and recognition will need to be reformulated for a viable eco-justice.

QUANTUM HOLOGRAPHIC TURN. A turn to quantum holography (QH) has begun, initiated by Dennis Gabor, a recipient of a Nobel Prize in 1971, with applications to neuropsychology by Karl Pribram and to black holes by leading theorists Leonard Susskind, Gerard 't Hooft, Juan Maldacena, and Jocob Bekenstein. Initial application of QH to sociology has been by Raymond Bradley (2006, 2016) and in criminology, law, and justice by Milovanovic (2015, 2018); for useful introduction to QH, see the YouTube, "The Holographic Universe, Part 1 and 2"; Staretz and Mitchell, 2011). A hologram is created by interference patterns between two waves that intersect. Take two ships at sea and their wakes intersecting, or throw two stones in a pond and witness the ripples overlapping. The intersections (interference patterns) represent moments where information is stored in the form of a hologram, now recorded on some surface. Information about the size, shape, trajectory, and the speed of the stones or ships are encoded at these intersection points. Similarly, ongoing interference patterns are being created within various contexts. Holography indicates that if we shine a beam of light ("reference beam") with the appropriate frequency anywhere on the recording surface, the encoded three-dimensional image will reappear. Information is nonlocally stored. All entities emit, or are waves, with distinct frequency patterns ("phenomena"). They constantly intersect producing holograms. Karl Pribram showed how information is recorded holographically within the brain; Irvin Laszlo (2007) notes that information, including long-term memories as interference patterns, are stored "out there" in the "in-formation" field, the quantum vacuum, or more recently, perhaps the Higgs Field; leading cosmologists have noted that information within any bounded space is recorded on its boundaries, much like in the dynamics of black holes with its "event horizon." For the latter, consider from criminologists, a street corner setting (bounded space) where juveniles access "techniques of neutralization" rationalizing/justifying deviant activity. Information, including techniques of neutralization, is encoded and embedded on the boundary. Those within the boundary region have access to this information in constructing everyday reality. In some extreme models, we live in a hologram not knowing it, much like experiencing dreams and the appearance of the real. The mechanism for accessing and decoding this information is Pcar—phase conjugate adaptive resonance (Staretz and Mitchell, 2011). It has been pointed out that nonhuman entities already access information this way (i.e., dolphins, bats, whales).

Applying this to a critically informed QH justice, it highlights the importance of, on the one hand, understanding human agency as well as the agency of other nonhuman, animate forms, and on the other, more enduring historically constituted structural-like forms ("affordances," more dissipative structures, or dynamic holograms that encode superposition probability states) that appear in social space. New Materialists often neglect both ends (see "critical realist's" Elder-Vass, 2008; Regret, 2018). Milovanovic's (2014a) contribution here is Schema QD (for elaboration and diagram, see Milovanovic, 2011; Batiz and Milovanovic, 2017). It portrays an inter- and intrasubjectively constituted moral and ethical subject, constituted by multiple possible states of expression (superposition), more "phenomena" awaiting particular instantiations by way of intra-action and Pcar. Redeveloped from Jacques Lacan's Schema R, it includes four key components (ego, ego-ideal, Other, generalized community Other) arranged for depiction as corners of a rectangle that is given a twist and glued at the edge, producing a continuous surface (Möbius band). Each component finds itself in an intra-active relation to each of the other, particularly exhibited when Möbius bands can be cut, following a figure eight from a four-dimensional topological figure called the "cross cap." Here, all four components are connected at the point where the twisted rectangle was glued, and at the edge, producing a continuous surface. The "line of intersection" represents not only the moment where all four components are connected but also the loci for the momentary appearances of an "I" that can take a position in a particular discursive subject position (role) from which it can speak, tempered further by the forces stemming from a more abstract generalized Other (e.g., normative standards that are societal wide). Each occasion for an encounter finds these four key components, normally in superposed states, realigning in terms of the constituted value of each through constitutive intra-action. We have different matrixes than can take form. A matrix is the source for a distinct wave pattern generated, and emitted "out there." Non-human animals may also be mapped with their own distinct intra-acting components producing distinct matrixes and signature waves (yet to be fully developed). It is this signature wave (reference beam) that holographically encodes all information about the particular matrix. The mechanism of Pcar provides ways of accessing information "out there," decoding it, and sending it back to the source where the collapse of the dynamic quantum hologram produces a distinct "particle-like" appearing "reality" with distinct boundaries, properties, and identities (Staretz and Mitchell, 2011). Dynamic holograms retain superposition states and are subject to revision, much like in Barad's examination of quantum erasure and the nature of the "trace." Social justice is not something that predates its development; it must be enacted, performed in intra-active, contextual engagements (apparatus, assemblage). More enduring "structures," "affordances" (Gibson, 2014), not static but more dissipative affordances (dynamic quantum holograms), remain with higher probability states in the collapse of the wave function.

Repetition of affordance (Barad's iterative intra-action) reinforces the dominant form. Doing social justice, a war machine to use Deleuze and Guattari's language, disrupts regularities, undoes repetition, and releases other possible superposed probability states leaving a trace of the outcome, a dynamic hologram. Lyotard's otherwise denied subjects, the "différand," re-emerge. And, following Barad, humans have a response-ability, a duty to the Other in the spirit of Derrida, following Levinas, offering hospitality, in reconstructing intra-actively emerging dissipative structures toward a transformative justice. Here, becomings are a premium, aided by an ethical principle that cultivates the development of greater capabilities, the ability to affect and be affected, according to Deleuze and Guattari. QH, in short, can be applied to rethinking information storage, accessing, and decoding particularly how certain principles of social justice are repetitively and performatively re-enacted, denying other superposed probability states, or how emerging possibilities can take form. In this quest, both historically specific emerging structures (whether rigid or dissipative in form, be they iteratively reconstituted by way of intra-active practices) as well as human and nonhuman agents must be considered in theorizing and implementing social justice principles.

REVIEW QUESTIONS

1. Jacques Derrida explains the difference between law and justice. What is the difference according to him?

2. Lyotard argues for a multiplicity of justices due to various petit narratives. Explain. Applying Lyotard, describe a situation in which conflict occurred between yourself and another based on different narratives employed, particularly how in each justice was defined differently.

3. Transformative justice, it is said, can embrace dynamic systems theory. Holland has offered one derivative in the notion of "nomadology." Does one benefit to think in this direction in developing social justice? Why or why not? Explain.

4. One of Derrida's contributions to justice is the notion of "hospitality," derived from a long history of those advocating an infinite duty of care toward the other (Levinas). He also notes some dilemmas with his notion. Explain what these dilemmas entail.

5. Deleuze wants to extend Marx's principle to acknowledge "becoming" beyond just "doings" and "beings" suggested in Nussbaum's capabilities notion of justice. How does Deleuze and Guattari's notion improve on understanding social justice?

6. Search the news and find a report on environmental justice that seems to implicate Foucault's notion of "governmentality." Explain how Foucault's notion is implicated.

7. Recall a recent issue you may have had with some bureaucratic organization where you felt you were dealt with unfairly. Now revisit it in terms of quantum mechanics and wave-particle duality (Hint: review the work of Kuttner, "wave-like dynamics" v. "particle-like dynamics" and/or Kelsey's notion of "law-equity duality.") Would a fairer, more just, outcome have resulted by using "wave-like dynamics" and/or "equity" dynamics? (This can be either a written assignment or a short presentation to the class.)

8. Review the model offered for the quantum hologram (QH) toward the end of the chapter. Create a representation of interactions (intra-actions) that you have with at least one social group (family,

school, work, friends, etc.) that in context enacts justice principles. Be creative and do not worry about your artistic abilities. Feel free to draw freehand, use a computer, or any other form that you prefer. If you want to go for an advanced presentation, include Schema QD; and if you are totally into this project, go ahead and include a Möbius band with or without a cut. Bring your creation to class for discussion of how interactions (intra-actions) can be presented within QH theory.

PART THREE

Struggles for Social Justice

CHAPTER 10

Legal Struggles and Social Justice

ATTAINING SOCIAL JUSTICE by way of legal struggles is problematic. Weber's notion of the conflict between formal rationality and substantive rationality is key. On the one hand, law provides the tools for challenge in a court of law—an opportunity to be heard, to be able to name an injury in words recognized in law, to introduce evidence, to cross-examine, and to have an enforceable decision applied to injustices. On the other hand, it often undermines grassroots mobilization by denying genuine expression of those in struggle, allowing legal constructions to represent otherwise complex issues. It often relegates the final word to specialists (lawyers) denying indigenous understandings, and redirects oppositional energy into legal channels that may take many years to resolve, thus often cooling out dissent. And, lest we need reminding, laws are established in a political context where dominant groups have an excess of power. This is not to say some court decisions have not changed the course of history such as the U.S. Supreme court decisions *Roe v. Wade* and *Brown v. Board of Education*, and in the Australian context, *Mabo v. Queensland*, as well as in the Canadian context, *Delgamuukw v. British Columbia*. But we are continuously reminded of *Korematsu v. United States*, *Plessey v. Ferguson*, and *McCleskey v. Kemp*.

AMBIVALENCE IN LEGAL STRUGGLES FOR SOCIAL JUSTICE

Under such doctrines as *terra nullius*, supported in law, indigenous peoples were being repressed in law. In the so-called Indian cases in the United States in the early to mid-1880s, higher justices provided further legal grounds for the repression of indigenous peoples. In addition, the Dred Scott decision legitimized a second-class status to African Americans. In *Plessy v. Ferguson* (1896), with its "separate but equal" standard established by the Supreme Court, repression of peoples continued. This doctrine was overturned in *Brown v. Board of Education* (1954), which decided that "separate but equal is inherently unequal." This radical departure by the Supreme Court later led to a movement away from focusing on *conditions* that fostered racism (i.e., employment, educational, medical, etc.) and statistical disparities to focusing on *perpetrators* and requirements of proving *individual* intent. Some (Bell, 1980) argued that *Brown v. Board of Education* was not based on enlightened thought but on concern with what the alternative might bring. More recently, gays, lesbians, and queer theorists have seen both U.S. Supreme Court decisions restricting their aspirations as well as qualifiedly supporting them.

Perhaps one of the main confrontations the law has had with social science is the finding that racism is implicated in the use of the death penalty. In 1987 the U.S. Supreme Court delivered *McCleskey v. Kemp*. McCleskey, an African American, was convicted of homicide and sentenced to death for killing a white police officer. In his appeal, his lawyers presented the most sophisticated and credible study in the literature on who receives the death penalty, the so-called Baldus study (1994). This study covered over two thousand convicted murderers in Georgia. In every instance, blacks convicted of homicide were statistically more likely to be sentenced to death than whites. Those charged with killing whites were eleven times more likely to receive a death sentence than those charged with killing a black victim. Even when the data were refined, defendants charged with killing whites still had over four times the likelihood of the death sentence than in a case where the defendant was charged with killing an African American. The U.S. Supreme Court dismissed these statistics (by a one vote margin) and said McCleskey had to prove discrimination only in *his* case. The court effectively made moot any statistical analysis of even the most blatant disparity (see also other implications of this decision on the criminal justice system and justice rendering by Cole, 1999). One can only wonder if the high Court ruled otherwise what impact it may have had for social justice.

Feingold and Carter (2018) illustrate that the use of statistics by the U.S. Supreme Court in *Grutter v. Bollinger*, while seemingly contradicting the *McCleskey* decision, was actually consistent. The consistency is not with the statistics, but with the ideology of racial hierarchy. Justice Rehnquist, who served in both *McCleskey* and *Grutter*, wrote the dissenting opinion in *Grutter*, arguing that the statistics presented showed that white students were being discriminated against. The majority in *Grutter* confirmed judicial and social biases regarding minority students—that they have come to higher education with deficits of their own making rather than as a result of a highly racialized context of demonstrable biases that have limited opportunities. According to the court, consideration of race is to be done under strict scrutiny to assure that white students have no disadvantage. *Fisher v. University of Texas at Austin* similarly relied on statistical evidence and upheld the University's rights to racially balance admissions, if white students do not suffer any disadvantage. What these decisions do not consider is the wider social context in which minority students are greatly disadvantaged because of race throughout their lives prior to college applications. In California, the top 9 percent of each high school is given initial admission to state colleges/universities. This is one strategy for equitizing students graduating from disparately funded high schools.

Allen et al. (2018) establish the clear struggle of African Americans attempting to obtain access to higher education over the forty-year period from *Bakke* to *Fisher*. As Laidler (2013) wrote about the U.S. Supreme Court, those with the power to decide the meaning of the Constitution have "the power to decide about the final meaning of the legal, social, economic, and political relations" (271). In this way, the court has finalized the relations of minority students to racist institutions finding that it is white students that need protection from disadvantage.

As Dudas (2005) illustrates, the politics of resentment have also entered into the courts with expressed intent of overturning treaties with Native American tribes and otherwise limit any "special" rights gained by oppressed groups. These legal struggles endanger the progress that decisions such as *Brown v. Board* had implied.

Several issues and strategies for social change have emerged in various legal struggles: essentialism versus anti-essentialism; counter-narratives/counter-storytelling; reversal of hierarchies; standpoint epistemologies; contingent universalities; and the multitude. To each we turn.

Essentialism versus Anti-essentialism

In order to have standing in law, one must show some particular form of being (i.e., status, category, etc.) and discrimination disallowed by law. Categories created can be helpful in redressing a grievance, but can also be a hindrance to open social interaction, self-actualization, and social solidarity. Many critical theorists have argued that categories such as race, class, and gender are social constructions; they do not have any real or objective meaning (Butler, 1990, 1993; Delgado and Stefancic, 2017). They are created categories. Queer theory, for example, sets out to deconstruct these categories. Much current debate has to do with whether these categories are real (essentialism) or are only labels (anti-essentialism).

This has become a continuous debate in present-day literature in defining people and forms of life. We will not attempt to resolve the dispute here. We do, however, note that there exists a dialectical dynamic in the usage of these categories by those seeking justice in law. At times, defining injustices necessitates creating self-labels, and acting as if they are real in order to mobilize, to set political agendas, and to obtain redress in courts of law; at other times, these very categories can become a hindrance in understanding the other in their complexity. Matsuda (1996), for example, notes two forms of anti-essentialism. In regressive essentialism, the courts see all women or all African Americans as not being alike and thus cannot claim some right. Progressive anti-essentialism argues for diversity within created categories, but only as a basis for a more nuanced understanding and sensitivity to the range of possible differences.

It may well be that both are true, in practice. The difference between race and ethnicity has often been blurred. Some argue that race is better connected with a person's physical characteristics such as color of skin, genetics, and biology; ethnicity, then, is more represented in the literature as connected with cultural and social factors, such as language, lineage, and identifications. Many others take issue with biological difference (Gannon, 2016; Onwuachi-Willig, 2013) and argue instead for its social construct nature, a position advocated in the present text. While there is no biological reality to race and the traits that we ascribe to gender may appear biological, on closer examination, they are in fact socially constructed as is race, and U.S. legal history has made such categories real in practice. Davis (1983) offered a history of race, class, and gender that indicates the realities of these categories as they were imposed upon persons of particular characteristics. Bonilla-Silva (2017) also documents the legal and social constructions of race through U.S. history and the lasting impact of that construction well beyond individual attitudes. Kendi (2016) documents racist ideas used against African Americans from the beginning of United States history. Dunbar-Ortiz (2015) and Byrd (2011) offer histories of the racialization of Native Americans. Cole (2009) offers an analysis of the racialization of people of color and people not of color, linking that process to the needs of capitalism.

Wills (2016) writes of an essentialist paradox in analyzing narratives of Asian persons who have been adopted by non-Asians. She describes essentialism as separate from biology and instead tied to the need for a connection to one's history. If we think of essentialism in this way, it becomes less reductive and more expansive. Native Americans, for example, have been subjected to genocidal programs that have left many groups (often called tribes) with limited membership because of the way that the U.S. government has constructed tribal membership utilizing "blood" quantity measures long used in essentialist racialization schemes. Indigenous peoples construct their own ties. Instead of requiring that a person have a particular parentage, for example, they accept a person of lesser "blood" who lives within the traditions and identifies with the culture and members of the group. Doing this, they maintain what is important to their traditional understanding of tribal membership while rejecting the "blood" requirements of the United States. At the same time, these groups reject persons with no social or cultural connection to them claiming membership (Cherokee.org).

Counter-narratives

Counter-storytelling, or counter-narratives, sometimes referred to as legal storytelling, attempts to give voice to disenfranchised people. Often borrowing from such notions as "différand" (Lyotard) or *pas-toute* (Lacan), this approach argues that dominant groups are not capable of understanding the plight of the disenfranchised and that only the latter are in a position to speak for themselves. At best, liberals attempt to speak for disenfranchised peoples, whereas critical race theory argues that disenfranchised peoples must be able to speak for themselves. "Critical writers," argue Delgado and Stefancic (2017, 49), "use counterstories to challenge, displace, or mock . . . pernicious narratives and beliefs." Further, "many victims of racial discrimination suffer in silence or blame themselves for their predicament. Stories can give them voice and reveal that others have similar experiences. Stories can name a type of discrimination; once named, it can be combated" (49). This approach seems to lean toward essentialism and produces some internal tension for those who advocate it. Advocates of this position have been confronted with some sharp criticism (see Farber and Sherry, 1997; Kennedy, 1989; Posner, 1997) which has led to some illuminating discussion (see Delgado and Stefancic, 2017; Yosso, 2005).

Reversal of Hierarchies

Early feminist literature was often concerned with reversal of hierarchies. Men were seen as dominant, women as subordinate in a hierarchical relation (MacKinnon, 1987). The strategy was to reverse the power holders, where women would now be in a more influential position. This, without qualification, has undergone much criticism. On its own, this strategy simply produces a new dominant and dominated group. One set of critique has been levied by Drucilla Cornell (1998). She has gone as far as saying this too quickly becomes a form of hate or revenge politics.

Standpoint Epistemology

In the early 1990s standpoint epistemology was developed in feminist and African American literature. In this approach, one should take the position of the disenfranchised and be sensitive to their constructions of reality (Harding, 2004, 2009; Crasnow, 2009; Kourany, 2009). Critics (see Rouse, 2009) were soon to argue that, first, even these constructions are subject to the sterilizing effects of dominant discourses (i.e., legal discourse) and that the repressed ("subaltern") often must use dominant discourse to express themselves, hence having their distinctive issues obfuscated; this relativism begs the question about ethical and moral standpoints. How does one evaluate a particular "standpoint"?

Contingent Universalities

In the early to mid-1990s contingent universalities emerged (Butler, 1990, 1997a). Faced with the compelling issue of what constitutes bona fide social change and the need for establishing some political programs and agendas for change (universalities), this position argues for the contingent nature of political agendas; that is, given historical conditions and diverse peoples, at best, we can only establish tentative platforms that can be the bases of focused attempts at social change. But these agendas are always subject to reflection, critique, change, deletion, augmentation, and substitution. This position attempts to make accommodations to both essentialist and anti-essentialist positions in providing the grounds for agenda building, a sensitivity to changing forms of life, emerging principles of social justice, and for positive social change. Critics, however, have often demanded the specification of an ethic that may be articulated with this position (see, for example, who argues from a postmodern perspective, Thomassen, 2010).

Multitude

A more recent conceptualization has emerged focused on global struggles that advocate the notion of the multitude (Hardt and Negri, 2000, 2004, 2009; Hardt, interview, 2018; see also the dedicated journal, in French, *Multitudes*). Here the inherent Marxian antagonism between two classes—the bourgeoisie and the proletariat—are dismissed and replaced by a new antagonism, empire versus the multitude. In this strategy, diversity is assumed—"a continuing plurality of its elements" (Hardt and Negri, 2004, 82–83)—which evolves into network struggles often connected to the Internet, whereby "there is no center, only an irreducible plurality of nodes in communication with each other" (83). A multitude, much like a "rainbow coalition," seeks to cut across various identity categories, in search of temporary commonalities for struggle, cultivating convergence among a variety of struggles, acknowledging difference on other issues, and is a leaderless organization in form. Network struggles create new ways of being, new subjectivities, and new forms of life. One celebrates the emergence of self-organization into cooperatives, be they temporary units. This is consistent with Deleuze's call for a people yet to come. Hardt and Negri have added to their trilogy with the publication of *Assembly* (2017; see also review by Fuchs, 2017). Turning to contemporary social movements they ask the question: "Why have the movements, which address the needs and desires of so many, not been able to achieve lasting change and create a new, more democratic and justice society?" They offer a variety of reasons and return to the notion of the assemblage; a "digital assemblage" form as a new force for social change, while recognizing the potential for liberation and transformation as well as domination (dialectics). Hardt and Negri's notion of multitude has seen much discussion, critique, but also integration in emerging perspectives in social struggles (see Brown and Szeman, 2006; Harvey, Hardt, and Negri 2009; Tampio, 2009; Fuchs, 2017).

In sum, these various strategies often are not expressed in pure form, nor are they totally conscious. Nevertheless, they act as conflicting background assumptions for those in struggle. Each strategy has been subjected to critique, response, and counter critique in the literature. In some cases, activists commit themselves to one strategy against various others. At other times, the held assumptions remain in a tentatively contradictory form guiding struggle. When these strategies interface with legal change, however, they are brought within the logic of formal rationality with its linear logic (i.e., deductive logic; top-down reasoning), reliance on precedents (*stare decisis*), focus on formal equality, assumption of legally defined signifiers, assumption of an individual self-consciously directing conduct, and on continuous transformations of real events into the language of law. Some groups have argued that the legal arena does indeed provide them with at least some tools or weapons for social change; outside of that, they argue, philosophical discussion does not provide the necessary concrete tools for social change. Thus, the use of the legal arena brings contradictory results: on the one hand, grievances may lead to legal standing and possible redress instituting concrete changes in the amelioration of discriminatory practices; on the other hand, issues and activists are redefined in the language of law, reinforcing the ideology and legitimacy of the law, and thus, the law itself is often part of the problem. This notion of contradictory results with unintended consequences, the dialectics of struggle (Balbus, 1977), remains center stage.

LEGAL STRUGGLES

We have selected seven areas plus the question of "intersections" and beyond for explication. This is not to say there are no others, or that others will not emerge, or that we are attempting to be exhaustive of the complex issues. We are more content in showing how some struggles for social justice have emerged in the legal arena and to explicate some of their respective elements. In the following chapter we will continue with more broadly defined struggles for social justice, but much of which is outside of the legal arena.

Critical Legal Studies ("Crits")

The crits formally arrived with their first national conference in Madison, Wisconsin, in 1977, as a response to the rigidities of legal formalism (formal rationality). They were a small but very vocal and influential group of lawyers, often with positions at some of the most notable law schools in the country. They questioned the neutrality of law, the worship of deductive logic as the way decision-making takes place, the very ideology embedded in law. Their early focus was on trashing. The legal decision-making process and its institutions were critically examined in order to understand their basic ideological and political components. They even saw law school itself as a preparation for hierarchy. That is, the very subordination and worship of forms of legal reasoning as well as to obedience to law professors, they argued, assures a cheerful robot for the needs of capitalist economy. To the crits, law was politics and ideology. They launched strong polemics against contract law, tort law, antidiscrimination law, the nature of law school, and the narrow construction of the individual, responsibility, and justice, amongst others.

In a critical book, *Critique of Adjudication (fin de siecle)* (1997), Duncan Kennedy explained that judges were not merely instruments of capitalist elites, but rather made decisions based on the Freudian defense mechanism of denial and Sartrian notion of bad faith. They were neither fully conscious nor fully unconscious of their own decision-making. Rather, they were half-consciously attempting to decide the hard cases by showing that they did abide by the rule of law and did not have personal prejudices intruding on decision-making. They saw themselves as strict constructionists abiding by the rule of law and formal rationality.

The key theorist who has gone beyond trashing (currently called deconstruction) is Roberto Unger. Since the mid-1980s he has argued for a "superliberalism," a more Weberian-inspired analysis for social change. In *False Necessity* (1987), for example, he outlines a blueprint for a nonhierarchical, responsive, and dynamic society. *What Should Legal Analysis Become?* (1996) argues against formal rationality in law and advocates a more pragmatic orientation and experimentalism for positive social change and social justice. Formal rationality, he argues, restricts the development of new ideas, new visions, and alternatives in the pursuit of social justice.

British critical legal studies (Brit Crits) soon followed their U.S. colleagues though with some differences in perspective. Both the U.S. and the Brit Crits grew from the political movements of the 1960s. The first major British critical legal conference was held in 1986 (criticallegalthinking.com). The conference hopes to provide progressive interventions, particularly to assist in liberation from the contradictions in law and late capitalism. Douzinas (2005) describes the Brit Crits as a community yet to come in that it does not remain organized beyond the annual conference. Those who attend are the community. He also describes the Brits as an "intellectual movement with lots of politics" (16) and finds the U.S. Crits focus more on the ideological and less on the political. Lloyd (2017) describes the politics of the Brit Crits as politics of resistance. "Western Marxism, postmodernism and deconstruction were the main theoretical influences of the early conferences but soon the new radicalism of race, gender, queer and post-colonial theory were introduced" (Douzinas, 2005, 17).

Critical Feminist Studies ("Fem-Crits")

Having roots in the critical legal studies movement, critical feminists, most notably during the mid-1980s, were to react against the secondary status rendered to women within critical theory. In 1985 the theme of the Annual Conference of Critical Legal Studies was feminism and law.

Social justice, they argued, was hard-pressed to emerge in law due to internal constraints. First, due to formal rationality's focus on precedents (*stare decisis*), a body of laws was continuously being reinforced with male assumptions. Second, in response to violence in the home, women could only seek such remedies as diminished capacity when defending themselves. This in itself disempowers women defendants even while giving them a voice in law. Third, the court focuses on narrow, single issues, whereas women have had to express a multitude of interrelated issues. In the work-place, for example, which sometimes is a hostile environment, she is often given a choice of taking the job or leaving it. Hence, contractual freedom is continuously reinforced but by effectively reducing dissent and the voices of the disenfranchised.

Several higher court cases in the United States have seemingly increased the rights of women. In *Roe v. Wade* (1973), the right for a limited abortion was established. However, others seemed to reinforce dominant male ideology. In *EEOC v. Sears, Roebuck and Co.* (1988), for example, Sears won its lawsuit by arguing that women were disproportionally underrepresented because they lacked interest in working in commission sales. This was due to the fact, Sears argued, that women historically have been more humanistic and nurturing rather than competitive and self-interested as is the case for men. The court argued that the disparities were of women's own choice. To win, following the logic of the Fourteenth Amendment's equal protection clause, the women had to show equal interest. In *Faragher v. City of Boca Raton* (1998), the U.S. Supreme Court dealt with the notion of a sexually hostile atmosphere. In *Oncale v. Sundowner Offshore Services, Inc.* (1998) the higher court dealt with workplace harassment. In both cases, a hostile work environment was narrowly defined and focused primarily on *individual* actions. Moreover, the subtle forms of harassment sometimes referred to as "petit apartheid" (see Russell and Milovanovic, 2001) were often overlooked. Petit apartheid, or microaggressions, are more hidden, more informal, and more ubiquitous, and they are diminishing and distancing people of color.

Another area for activist struggle is the notion of "comparable worth." In brief, advocates argue that jobs with equal skill should be equally compensated. This responds to a long history of worker classification as either more male or female where by "female jobs" were less compensated. When the first case reached a higher level of Federal Appeal Courts, *AFSCME v. Washington*, 770 F.2d 1401 (1985), the Court rejected the claim absent any particular intent to discriminate. Patterns alone would not justify the Court's intervention. The State of Washington, however, negotiated with AFSCME for better connection between skills and pay. In 2010, the United Kingdom passed the "Equality Act 2010" that defined issues of comparable worth (see "Equality Act 2010"). California, in 2015, passed the "Californian Fair Pay Act," which stipulates equal pay for substantially similar work. In 2019, the "Paycheck Fairness Act" was introduced by the Democrats in the U.S. House of Representatives for the eleventh time (see "H.R.P. 7," https://www .congress.gov/bill/116th-congress/house-bill/7/text?r=2).

In short, fem-crits have recognized the dialectics of struggle. On the one hand, by using law as an instrument they obtain a standing in law and can eventually receive some redress of grievances; on the other hand, this reliance on law supports the legitimacy of law—its form of reasoning, its categories, its notion of a neutral forum to resolve conflicts. Feminists in the United States were reminded in the fall of 2018 that even the Supreme Court includes those hostile to women. The hearings that placed Brett Kavanaugh on the Court were traumatically familiar to those of us old enough to recall the 1991 hearings that confirmed Clarence Thomas. In both cases women came forward to report sexual misconduct, which in the case of Kavanaugh, included physical assault. In both cases, the men accused of these behaviors forcefully and ultimately successfully defended them- selves. Sexual harassment and assault remain a common and often unre- ported in the United States. The confirmation of Thomas in 1991 and Kavanaugh in 2018 indicate that such behaviors are not priorities for the U.S. justice system at even the highest level.

Fem-crits seeking social justice often have made use of three main strat- egies (Bartlett 1991, 2000). First, in a feminist legal method, one should ask the "woman question." Here one should look below the surface of tradi- tional legal reasoning and ask how the voices of women are being denied. Second, fem-crits make use of feminist practical reasoning. Here the unique concrete experiences of women should be central. Third is consciousness- raising. The focus is on collective empowerment. In short, advocates for social justice such as Bartlett are arguing for a deconstruction and a reconstruction.

Feminist postmodernists, such as Drucilla Cornell and Judith Butler, have derived guidance from the theoretical insight of Jacques Lacan, a revi- sionist Freudian who introduced a linguistic component in understanding the unconscious. Feminist postmodernists arguing for social justice have identified the male-dominated discourse, how unique desire is channeled into male categories, how gender identities are constructed in discourse itself and are embedded in the unconscious, and how a dominant phallocentric symbolic order resists constructions that deviate from the male form.

Cornell (1993, 1999) has suggested strategies in the struggle for social justice. First, drawing from Cixous (1999) she argues for retelling the myth. In other words, in telling and retelling mythology the male voice is often privileged. The strategy is to tell it in a way that surfaces denied voices. In other words, we can recreate conventional stories to include otherwise denied voices—the contributions of women in history, the struggles of indigenous peoples, the rediscovery of roots. Second, she advocates utopian thinking and privileging the imaginary domain. We must support thinking otherwise. We can reimagine the myths of the past, articulate otherwise unspeakable desire, and create a different reality where voices are resurrected. It is a call for utopian thinking. It demands "the continual exploration and re-exploration of the possible and yet also the unrepresentable" (Cornell 1999, 169; see also Cornell and Seely, 2016; Cornell and Friedman, 2016). Third, there is an inherent slippage of meaning in discourse itself; discourse itself always says more than it intends, yet always less. Here lies the opportunity to create new meanings, new understandings, a new basis for struggles for social justice. Drawing from Irigaray, Cixous, and Kristeva, Cornell offers the idea of mimesis, by which subordination is turned into affirmation (147–152). In other words, she argues for the creative use of metaphors that offer some latitude in meaning. There is always an excess in these metaphors that provides the potential for something new. A surplus of meaning is generated that points to different understandings of what could be. Consider, for example, the strategic use of the recently self-imposed label of queer theory by scholars interested in issues of sexuality and gender expression. Or consider the many existing sexual metaphors where the male is portrayed as dominant and the female subordinate. The task would be to reload the metaphor so that celebration of differences is the message— without difference being the basis of subordination.

Judith Butler (1990; see also Butler et al, 2000) adds to this list by her advocating "contingent universalities" and for practices that undermine repetition—that is, actively disrupting practices that reinforce subordination. We will continue with Butler's work in the section below regarding queer theory. Gender expression and transgendered identities have become important to the work of feminists and queer theorists. We address those identities within queer theory as this is where the work has progressed toward self-directed identities.

Leppänen (2004; see also Gaard, 2011; Mallory, 2010) indicates that eco-feminism addresses the placement in patriarchal structures of both women and nature into political categories limiting the voice and survival of both. Pilgrim and Davis (2015) explain that while third-wave feminism still focused on the human, eco-feminism encompasses the entire planet. Brianson (2016) offers suggestions for integrating eco-feminism into policy and planning. Eco-feminism is inclusive, integrative, and represents an advance for social justice to a just sustainable future for all.

Critical Race Theory ("CRT")

The civil rights movements of the 1960s were followed by retrench-ment by the courts of the late 1960s and early 1970s whereby many of the new rights won were substantially reduced by interpretation. But there was a resurgence of activism in the 1980s. These developments contributed to critical race theory (CRT) that emerged more formally in the late 1980s and early 1990s. The CRTs were to argue that the fem-crits, even though going beyond the crits, did not do enough to consider people of color. In 1989 the CRTs organized their first annual conference in Madison, Wis-consin. In the mid-1990s to present, a continuing differentiation of those in critical legal studies now includes critical Latinx studies, queer theory, and Asian American crits.

The CRTs challenged the very foundations of the liberal order. Notions of formal equality, neutral principles in law, and forms of legal reasoning were all seen as supportive of an order devoid of voices of people of color. The struggle for social justice within the legal arena was seen as offering both the potential for change as well as the occasion for unintentionally reinforcing the rule of law. Valdes and Cho (2011) argue that as long as the law is central to maintaining the social and racial order, CRT will be neces-sary in the struggle for racial justice.

The core concepts of the CRTs have been well expressed by Matsuda et al. (1993) and Delgado and Stefancic (2017). These concepts include: rac-ism is at the core of American life; race is a category created by dominant groups for instrumental purposes; the legal apparatus is not value neutral and it is not colorblind; the struggle for social justice by people of color is part of a larger struggle by other disenfranchised peoples; struggles for social justice must focus on the experiential knowledge of people of color; and only through a historical analysis connected to specific struggles can new concepts of social justice begin to emerge.

CRTs offer a "jurisprudence of color" as a strategy for attaining social justice. Law is inherently political and should therefore be used pragmatically, as an instrument for social change. "Legalism is a tool of necessity" (Matsuda, 1996, 6). CRTs have an uneasy alliance with postmodernists. "People of color," they often argue, "cannot afford to indulge in deconstruction for its own sake" (24). Others, however, do see the utility of integrating some aspects of postmodern analysis (Cornell and Seely, 2016; Crenshaw, 1991; Lawrence,

1987; see also the case made for a useful integration by Arrigo et al., 2005, 69–82). CRTs also focus on counter-narratives, or counter-storytelling—"words are part of the struggle" (Matsuda, 1996, xiii; Delgado and Stefancic, 2017, 48–56).

Retelling of stories to include people of color as essential actors is also a prominent strategy. Consider, for example, Alice Randall's, *The Wind Done Gone*, a parody of the classic *Gone with the Wind*. In Randall's book, African American slaves are presented as much more active and creative agents, and it is the white plantation owners who are seen in a negative light.

Another strategy is consciousness-raising. Matsuda recommends strategies for "learning to talk"—that is, to create spaces in which people of many ways of life can "talk nonconfrontationally about race, gender, and sexuality" (1996, 125). Within these spaces a different discourse may take form and reach a critical mass for social change toward social justice. Paulo Freire's (1972, 1985) notion of dialogical pedagogy and the pedagogy of the oppressed is an especially useful theoretical framework to understanding this process. In the postmodern version, Lacan's four discourses are useful, particularly the discourse of the analyst (see Arrigo et al., 2005, 69–82). This discourse encourages confronting sedimented signifiers and images, and with the analyst, read cultural revolutionary as in Paulo Freire, developing alternative, more responsive, sensitive, dynamic, and forms of representation reflective of power inequalities. These can emerge as the basis of a new constellation of signifiers and images. In this direction, the movement for a culturally responsive education has emerged (see Hammond, 2015). Hammond advocates the role of equity-focused educators entailing three connected components: multicultural education, focusing on celebrating diversity; social justice education, centering on the exposure of the student experience in social political contexts; and culturally responsive pedagogy, emphasizing support for students who have been educationally marginalized.

CRTs also recognize the contradictions in their struggle. Crenshaw (1993), for example, has critiqued "2 Live Crew" for their depictions in their songs of African American women. Waters (2015) similarly offered a critique of the black male empowerment offered through the lyrics of NWA as presented in the film *Straight Outta Compton*. The misogyny aimed at black women in NWA lyrics and the film play into white supremacy and ultimately damage the producers and consumers of an art form presented as liberating. The question was whether exploding stereotypes, the supposed motivation, does indeed do so, or whether it sustains the very stereotypes it is trying to undermine. CRTs recognize the dialectic nature of the struggle in both using and trying to disavow law in their struggles for social justice.

Fasching-Varner et al. (2014) extend CRT's concept of racial realism to educational and penal realism. They illustrate the need to move beyond idealism for change and to instead focus on the realities facing people of color as they move through racist social institutions that are designed to ensure their continued oppression. The school-to-prison pipeline is carefully analyzed as it has become a central focus of CRT and other anti-racists seeking social justice. See also, Loic Wacquant (2001) who argues we are currently in phase four of prisonization, the linkage of the hyper-ghetto with hyper-incarceration, whereby the prison and ghetto become increasingly indistinguishable, where a revolving door has been institutionalized from one to the other. The first three "peculiar institutions" for "*defining, confining,* and *controlling* African Americans in the United States" being: slavery (1619–1865), Jim Crow (1865–1965, particularly in the South), and Ghetto (1915–1968, particularly in the North). Two examples presented of the convergence of the prison and the ghetto are public housing and public schools.

Alexander (2012) established the link between racism in the United States and the continuing over incarceration of African Americans for crimes that would not result in incarceration of whites. Scheck (2014) laments the lack of impact of racial justice acts passed in some states to counter racial biases in jury selections. As he notes, as some states are still attempting to pass such acts, others, such as North Carolina that have passed such acts, are still finding bias in jury selection, which at times results in wrongful convictions, particularly of African American defendants. Butler (1995) suggests that African Americans avoid and/or disrupt the racist justice system where possible. Nullifying juries by refusing to convict people of color is offered as such a disruption in "Nullifying Inequities in the Criminal Justice System" (2000) and in "Q and A Paul Butler" (2013). Butler argues that this is a just response to the highly biased U.S. justice system. Activists attempting to inform potential jurors of this option, however, have been arrested (Gilens, 2019). Gilens (2019) contends that such activism is protected speech. The long history of racism throughout U.S. institutions, but particularly in the criminal justice system, will require multiple means of justice seeking.

Illustrative of many of the challenges for diversity in education is New York City's attempt to diversify their elite public schools, as well as Harvard University grappling with the question of maintaining a diverse student body. At the outset, since *Grutter v. Bollinger* (2003) it has been established (*stare decisis*) that diversity in higher education is a "compelling state interest" subject to "strict scrutiny." Diversity has been recognized to promote learning and preparing students for an increasingly diverse work world and society. In 2019, of the over 600 high schools in New York City, there were eight "elite" high schools where high admission standards were set. At Stuyvesant High School in 2018, of the 895 spots for the incoming freshman class, only seven were offered to African American students and thirty-three spots to Hispanic students. Previous years saw ten and thirteen, respectively. Seventy-four percent of the students at Stuyvesant were Asian American. At Bronx School of Science, twelve spots were offered to African Americans. Sixty-eight percent of all students going to New York City high schools were either African American or Hispanic. Admissions to the elite high schools included only four percent African Americans and six percent Hispanic. Mayor de Blasio is pushing to diversify by, first, getting rid of the entrance exam. He recommends some kind of percentage rule that would admit the top students of every school in New York City. Estimates suggest that in this plan, Asian American students would drop by half and African American students would go up by five times. And herein is the central issue often polarized as merit versus the compelling interest for a diverse student body. However the outcome of the political process, it will surely wind its way to the U.S. Supreme Court. With the recent addition of conservative Supreme Court Justice Kavanaugh, the Court is decisively conservative leaning and many argue that any program that looks like, feels like, smells like affirmative action would succumb to a merit ruling. Recall the *Fisher v. The University of Texas* decision was a narrow 4-3 decision.

Critical Latinx Studies (LatCrits)

Critical Latinx Studies (LatCrits) have focused their attention on immigration policy, farm workers, land rights in the Southwest, bilingual schooling, and language rights. LatCrits include Mexican Americans, Cuban Americans, and Puerto Ricans. They have opposed the English-only movement of the 1990s, whereby dominant groups insisted on English being the only official language. Language for the LatCrits was seen as an inherent element of their very culture.

The Treaty of Guadalupe Hidalgo (1848), ending the U.S.–Mexican War from 1846 to 1848, specified the Rio Grande as the border between Mexico and Texas, and ceded much territory to the United States (present-day California, Texas, New Mexico, Nevada, and areas of Utah, Arizona, and Colorado). Mexican Americans who remained in these areas were provided specific rights, including all those guaranteed to citizens of the United States In other words, Mexican Americans were now incorporated within the legal framework of U.S. law. However, a long history of discrimination was to follow (see Gonzalez, 2000; Valencia et al. 2004).

During World War II and notably after the attack on Pearl Harbor, racial conflict in Los Angeles was high. Rumors began that some U.S. servicemen were assailed by young Mexican Americans who felt a Mexican

American woman was insulted. Serviceman and others responded by attack-
ing so-called zoot-suiters (identified as so because of their distinct dress,
conduct, and language). Ten days of riots followed and, ultimately, twelve
Mexican Americans were wrongfully convicted of murder (see Valencia
et al., 2004) in the "Sleepy Lagoon" trial (*People v. Zammora*, 1944). Appeals
resulted in the initial murder convictions being overturned. However, the
California Court of Appeals noted that the claim of "racial prejudice" was
"without foundation and . . . [had] no support in the record."

LatCrits have also sought educational justice through the courts. In *San
Antonio Independent School District v. Rodriguez* (1973), the higher court
addressed the issue of whether the financing of schools by property taxes
went against the equal protection clause of the Fourteenth Amendment.
The key contention was that differences in wealth produce differences in
education, which goes against formally equal treatment. The court rejected
this principle. The majority opinion was that "it is not the province of this
Court to create substantive constitutional rights in the name of guaranteeing equal protection of the laws" (reported in Valencia et al., 2004, 33). The
dissent by Marshall and Douglas, however, claimed "the Court today
decides, in effect, that a State may constitutionally vary the quality of education which it offers its children in accordance with the amount of taxable
wealth located in the school districts within which they reside" (35). A
decade and a half later, the Texas Supreme Court in *Edgewood Independent
School District v. Kirby* (1989) found the funding methods unconstitutional.

Another area where the courts have provided both reprieve as well as
support for substantively discriminating practices is in issues of language.
The English-only movement of the 1990s insisted that English should be
the only official language. Mexican Americans have, in opposition, cited
the Treaty of Guadalupe Hidalgo as support for Spanish speaking peoples.
Valencia et al. (2004) documented the long history of multilingual communities in the United States. Indigenous populations, they point out, already
had over one thousand specific languages before the arrival of Europeans.
During colonial times, they also noted large groups of German- and French-
speaking peoples had arrived. Perhaps most noteworthy in justice seekers
via law is the U.S. Court of Appeals Court case *Yniguez v. Arizonans for
Official English* (1995). In 1988 a little over half the voters of the state of Arizona voted to have English as the official language and that all business in
the state should be transacted in English. This was challenged by Maria
Kelly F. Yniguez, a state employee. The federal court agreed with her, and
the court of appeals did also. However, when it was appealed, the U.S.
Supreme Court "vacated" the court of appeal's decision as being moot since
Yniguez had left her job. However, the Arizona Supreme Court subsequently agreed to the basic logic of the Court of Appeals.

Proposition 227 was passed in California (1998) banning bilingual education. A U.S. Court of Appeals, in *Valencia v. Davis* (2002), ruled that Proposition 227 did not violate the equal protection clause of the Fourteenth Amendment. Activists, in search for another strategy, devised the "English Plus" initiative. The primacy of English was not challenged, but additional language acquisition was argued to be desirable and should be encouraged. This, the argument goes, would encourage diversity (Valencia et al., 2004, 86).

Montoya (2013) compiled some of the ongoing legal struggles for Latinx people in the United States. Because this group is highly diverse, we look broadly at these. Home ownership, as for African Americans, is an ongoing struggle with continued housing segregation (i.e., "redlining") preventing communities of color from gaining wealth at the same rate as whites. Land rights are also continuing through the courts. Latinx communities in the Southwest have been dispossessed of lands while Puerto Ricans struggle to maintain access to the entirety of their island as investors vie for private beaches. Identity itself, including language usage, maintaining cultural norms in the face of rising racism, and the ability to move freely with or without documents are also domains of legal struggle. In all of these struggles, attending to the history of Latinx communities as citizens, immigrants, indigenous, and/or colonial subjects within the broader America is necessary to assure justice rather than harm.

Grandin (2019a) documents the weaponization of the U.S. border with Mexico, which is the site of legal struggles for immigrant rights, children's rights, women's rights, and transgender rights. For a more complete history of the border myth, see Grandin (2019b). With the separation of children from families on a mass scale with little to no attention to reunification, the plight of mainly Latinx immigrants attempting asylum or other means of immigration at the southern U.S. border has entered a new phase of injustice and justice seeking. Similarly, in 2017, a "Muslim ban" resulted in legal and grassroots struggles to assure equal immigration access for those arriving from countries banned (see *Trump v. Hawaii*).

LatCrits have been active within and without law in their pursuit of social justice. There have been several occasions where the higher court has effectively stymied legal social change. This has been tempered somewhat by activists making use of new strategies to overcome restrictive legal findings and propositions. In short, struggles for social justice within the legal arena have provided mixed results.

Asian American Crits

Leading Asian American scholars, much like LatCrits, have focused on immigration, education, stereotypes, national origin, and language issues.

The stereotype of the Asian as the "perfect minority group"—"quiet, industrious, with intact families and high educational aspiration and achievement"—is, according to Delgado and Stefancic (2017, 81–82), not only untrue, excluding the many poor and working class, but also is the basis of much resentment when other disenfranchised groups are compared and then categorized as blameworthy for not attaining what the Asian stereotype has gained. Connected to this stereotype is the myth that Asians are overly successful, in fact the cause of periodic economic crises in the United States. This thinking often produces an environment for hostile actions by those suffering the fallout of periodic downturns in the economy seeking convenient scapegoats (see Matsuda, 1996, 161–170). Chang et al. (2017) illustrate in their reflections on the Los Angeles uprising of 1992 that conflicts rather than solidarity between oppressed groups can erupt under these false assumptions.

Asian American crits are quick to point out the support for internment of Japanese Americans by the very highest court of the United States. Following the attack on Pearl Harbor in World War II, over 100,000 Japanese Americans were rounded up and placed in internment camps, surrounded by barbed wire. Statistical data clearly indicate that no espionage or disloyalty existed and that hysteria and fabrications were the basis of the violent dispossession. In *Korematsu v. United States* (1944), the U.S. Supreme Court legitimized these internments—a truly shameful chapter in U.S. history. In 1988, reparations for those dispossessed were established. Delgado and Stefanci (2017, 73) also have pointed out that at the time of being rounded up and subsequent appeals, regrettably, no other major disenfranchised group came in support of the interned Japanese Americans.

Asian Americans, much like other minorities, have centered much of their struggle for social justice on language. "Language can construct understanding, language can assault, and language can exclude." Thus "words have power . . . words are part of the struggle" (Matsuda, 1996, xiii). Racist speech demeans, subordinates, reduces one to false stereotypes. According to Matsuda et al., speech is racist if: (1) "the message is of racial inferiority," (2) the message is directed against a historically oppressed group," and (3) "the message is persecutory, hateful, and degrading" (1993, 36). Racist speech, she tells us, has an uneasy alliance with First Amendment protections. Lawrence (1993) argues that racist speech is tantamount to "fighting words," the latter being recognized as an exception to First Amendment protections (see *Chaplinsky v. New Hampshire*, 1942). According to Lawrence, "the experience of being called 'nigger,' 'spic,' 'jap,' or 'kike' is like receiving a slap in the face. The injury is instantaneous. There is neither an opportunity for intermediary reflection on the idea conveyed nor an opportunity for responsive speech." Thus, racial speech should not have

First Amendment protection: "the perpetrators' intention is not to discover truth or initiate dialogue, but to injure the victim" (68).

This logic, however, fell on deaf ears. In June 21, 1990, a cross was placed on an African American family's front yard and burned. The offender was arrested. He claimed his act was a political act and thus protected by the First Amendment. The Minnesota Supreme Court was to reject this position *In the Matter of the Welfare of R.A.V.* (1991). In their words, "the burning cross is itself an unmistakable symbol of violence and hatred on virulent notions of racial supremacy. It is the responsibility, even the obligation, of diverse communities to confront such notions in whatever form they appear" (cited in Matsuda et al., 1993, 134). As Matsuda et al. conclude, the judges decided based on history and context in understanding what cross burning meant. The case was appealed to the U.S. Supreme Court where the defendant's position was supported (see *R.A.V. v. City of St. Paul*, 1992). None of the context or history of cross burning was addressed in the majority decision—"the Ku Klux Klan, lynching, nightriders, the Reconstruction . . ." In effect, the U.S. Supreme Court repressed a century of historical hatred and violence directed at African Americans.

Nielsen (2002, 2009) establishes the actual harm done by racist and sexist speech. Hate speech causes changes in behavior and damages both the health and self-esteem of those targeted with hate speech. Those seeking social justice will need to continue to struggle against hate speech while at the same time preserving free speech. As John A. Powell (2017) stated: "The whole meaning of the First Amendment has been radically shifted since the 1970s. . . . We are moral beings, we have to think about things in a much deeper way than just [accept] what the Supreme Court says" (https://haasinstitute.berkeley.edu).

An illustrative situation concerning Asian American students has arisen at Harvard University (see Lockhart, 2018), concerning Harvard University's admission policy and their consideration of race in admissions (see *Students for Fair Admissions v. Harvard* [2019]). Harvard's holistic approach was offered to ensure a diverse student body. Students for Fair Admissions (SFFA), while accepting diversity in higher education, sued Harvard University on behalf of Asian Americans for its use of race in admissions and argued it was discriminatory and should not be used as it was. In the mix is a moral crusader. Edward Blum, identified with the Project on Fair Representation that challenges racial and ethnic classifications, has lined up with others where race was employed as a factor in college admissions. SFFA argued that Asian Americans were negatively stereotyped and further that an unconstitutional quota system ("racial balancing") was being employed to maintain diversity. Central to the issue was the use of "personal scores." These were part of a holistic decision-making process along with formal test scores, honors, grade point averages. Personal scores, a qualitative measure, including teacher recommendations, and personal statements, appeared with assessments of such characteristics as likeability and courage. Statistics brought to court showed that on this scale, Asian Americans scored lower than other students (white, African American, Hispanic) and thus were the subject of discrimination contrary to law, be they unconscious biases. Harvard replied that their decisions were holistic and Asian Americans exhibited weaker teacher recommendations. Jaschik (2019) reported the district court's siding with Harvard, noting the mixed legacy that the case will face should it be heard at the Supreme Court.

We are witnessing the complexities here concerning establishing a diverse student body, particularly with various identity groups. Legal arguments, as we have noted throughout, are but narrow renditions of cases brought before it; most often, background factors for discrimination and resource distribution are pushed aside, the accumulative nature of disadvantages predating applying for elite high schools or universities are not considered. Neither are the more subtle forms of micro-aggressions ("Petit Apartheid") recognized. The continuous systematic and institutionalized withdrawal of recognition, support for capabilities, and openness for participation—all produce cascades of disadvantage.

Asian American crits support "outsider jurisprudence." Organizations such as the Asian Law Caucus, the Asian American Bar Association, Conference on Asian Pacific American Leadership, and the Media Action Network of Asian Americans have attempted to work within law and outside of law to counter negative stereotypes of Asian Americans. Another component of struggles for social justice, according to Matsuda (1996), is consciousness-raising. She specifically suggests a strategy whereby spaces are generated for open dialogue, often about misconstrued identities. For example, she asked her students questions such as, "Describe something you remember from childhood about how you learned gender roles" or "Describe a time you heard a racist, sexist, anti-Semitic, or homophobic comment."

Gay/Lesbian Studies

It has been argued that whereas gender is the key category for analysis for feminists, sex and sexuality is the key category for gay and lesbian studies (Abelove et al., 1993). In other words, sex and gender are distinguishable. Feminism is more locked into the binary, male and female. Gay and lesbian studies, along with queer theory, problematize the connection between gender and sexuality (Cossman, 2004). Much debate continues in the literature. Queer theorists are quick to point out that feminists, in their acceptance of depicting gender in its binary form, without asking questions about diverse expressive forms of sexuality, are reinforcing the very categories that should be questioned. Feminists, on the other hand, criticize gay and lesbian theorists for their weak notions of ethicality, their nonexamination of material conditions of disenfranchised women, and of dominant discourses that are gendered. Others (Cossman, 2004; Butler, 1997b) argue that both approaches should be used as each informs the other.

The question of a same-sex marriage has been litigated. In *Baker v. Vermont* (1999), a unanimous decision by the Supreme Court of Vermont found that making same-sex marriages illegal was a violation of rights granted by the Vermont constitution. In response, the legislators of Vermont developed a civil union clause for same-sex couples. The Massachusetts Supreme Court, in two cases, *Goodridge v. Department of Public Health* (2003) and *In re. Opinion of Justices to the Senate* (2004), first struck down heterosexual-only marriage laws, and declared "only full civil marriage, and not civil unions, would suffice under state constitution." However, in Florida, in a Federal Appeals court, *Lofton v. Secretary of the Department of Children and Family Services* (2004) upheld a Florida law banning homosexuals from adopting.

In 2015, the U.S. Supreme Court decided in *Obergefell v. Hodges* that all states are required to issue marriage licenses to persons of the same sex and to recognize such marriages that occurred out of state. Lambdalegal.org indicates a complex set of laws, rules, and policies across states, jurisdictions, and agencies that complicate adoption for same sex couples. Foster parenting can also be difficult to achieve for same sex couples as with adoption agencies, many agencies entrusted with the placement of children refuse to place children in homes of same sex couples. Assuring that all children are offered access to parents who seek to provide homes and families requires continued struggle.

The theoretical examination of the efficacy of same-sex partner–headed families has been forcefully discussed by Martha Fineman (1995) and Drucilla Cornell (1998). Fineman, theorizing from more traditional feminist theory, argued for both abolishing the legal category of marriage and for subsidiaries received by those in these categories. She begins by arguing for a centrality of the mother/child dyad. The father can be so only to the extent that he can show that he is a primary caregiver, in many ways following many of the functions of the traditionally understood mother's role. Contract law is the center of any union between men and women. Each negotiates a contract for their subsequent relationship rather than reducing themselves to the dictates of state law and its definition of appropriate relations. Thus, sexual relations would be consensual and contractual. Parents could be two or three or more in number; sexual relations are not an inherent necessity for the caretaker role.

Cornell's (1998) difference with Fineman is with the kind of intimacy that Fineman privileges. Cornell wants to extend Fineman's notion as to sexual intimacy. Both gays and lesbians as well as straights should be able to be caregivers (see also Kramer, 2004). Fineman, Cornell argues, is still privileging the biological family; Cornell wants to liberate the family from traditional state-supported roles.

Accordingly, Cornell offers three suggestions for a new form of family. Cornell's (1998, 123) first suggestion is that "gays, lesbians, straights, and transgendered" should not be bound by a heterosexually defined notion of marriage, supported and subsidized by the state; rather, each should be able to express their sexuate being in their own ways. What should be protected in civil statutes are lovers. Her second suggestion is that it would be the responsibility of the government to "provide a structure for custodial responsibility for children" (125). In other words, sexual expression and custodial responsibility of caretakers would be split. Thus, "two women friends who were not sexually involved could assume parental responsibility for a child; three gay men could assume parental responsibility for a child; and finally, a traditional heterosexual couple could also assume parental responsibility for a child." Hence, each child will have custodial parents, a family recognized in law. Her third component would be some form of income support for families. Mothering "should no longer be a class privilege" (128). Thus, part of her program includes "publicly funded child care as part of parental entitlement" and maximal sexual freedom of expression for the custodial caretakers ("parents"), as well as stability and support for children (128).

Apart from theoretical work in the areas of families and many other areas, we briefly here indicate as being exemplary gay activists' standing in the military (for a concise summary, see Pruitt, 2018). Until 1993, being identified as gay in U.S. military was grounds for discipline and dismissal. In 1994, President Clinton, who had made the issue part of his campaign, signed the "Don't Ask, Don't Tell" policy. Gay, lesbian, and bisexual troops could stay in the military as long as their identities were not shared. It was a start, but superficial, since prejudice remained, and active discharges from the military still prevailed. Much earlier and highly publicized in 1975, Leonard Matlovich, a sergeant and Vietnam veteran, was discharged from the military after acknowledging his gay identity. He sued in court for reinstatement, and in 1980, Judge Gerhard Gesell ordered him reinstated. Matlovich, however, accepted financial compensation. By 2009, under the "Don't Ask, Don't Tell" policy, some 13,000 gays, lesbians, and bisexuals had been discharged from the military. Barack Obama's presidential campaign included a promise to overturn the "Don't Ask, Don't Tell" policy. In 2010, a new law that repealed this policy was passed and became effective in 2011. In 2015, sexual orientation was added to the Military Equal Opportunity policy, which provided equal protection in law. In-coming President

Donald Trump tried unsuccessfully in 2017 to repeal protection for trans-gendered personnel.

Rights gained by gays, lesbians, and bisexuals were only gained through sustained struggle. There still remains the more invisible discrimination that takes place in the form of "micro-aggressions" or "petit apartheid" (Pruitt, 2018).

Queer Theory (Queer-crits)

Queer theory, sometimes argued as being separate from lesbian and gay studies, sometimes as a subset of gay and lesbian studies, goes beyond fem-crits in arguing against a dualism, either man or woman. Assuming the most extreme form of anti-essentialism, queer theorists argue identity is not fixed, biologically nor psychologically. Rather, it is a social construct. Identities are unstable, changeable; in fact, there should be no attempt to create stable categories for they produce closure (see de Lauretis, 1994a). Being queer is always a becoming; there is no final point of fixed identity (Halperin, 1995; Eldeman, 1995; Jagose, 1996; Sedgwick, 2008). As Butler (1990, 24–25) says, "gender is not a noun . . . [it] is always a doing." What accounts for the fixity of the binary, man/woman, is thus political, ideological, and discursive determinants.

Arguably, its early key groundbreaking theorists were Judith Butler, in her books *Bodies That Matter* (1990), *Gender Trouble* (1993), and *Undoing Gender* (2004), and Teresa de Lauretis, who wrote *Queer Theory: Lesbian and Gay Sexualities* (1991; see also her later book [1994a], where she distances herself from the term). Butler's early work (1990) criticized feminists for trying to essentialize women, which had the effect of creating a binary notion of sexuality. Inadvertently, in its struggles for social justice, feminism sustains and legitimizes two distinct classes—women and men—and thus closed options of being otherwise. For example, in the *Twyman v. Twyman* (1993) case, an ongoing sadomasochistic sexual relationship between husband and wife, which was terminated by the wife, who also pursued a legal claim for the emotional injuries she suffered. Queer theorists would be quick to point out that the claimed harm and the legal discourse employed reinforced dominant categories of man/woman and male/female, the very categories that needed critical analysis, disrupting, and debunking (Butler, 2004; Cossman, 2004; Halley, 2004a).

The U.S. Supreme Court decision *Lawrence v. Texas* (2003) involved two gay men arrested in 1998 for having consensual anal sex in their home. The Court reconsidered and overturned a previous U.S. Supreme Court case, *Bowers v. Hardwick* (1986), which stood as the anti-homosexual legal statement for some seventeen years. The 6-3 decision in *Lawrence* specified

TRUGGLES FOR SOCIAL JUSTICE

that "liberty presumes an autonomy of self that includes freedom of thought, belief, expression, and certain intimate conduct" (1). The majority ruled that "the liberty protected by the Constitution allows homosexual persons the right to make this choice" (6; for a useful summary of some of the key legal decisions related to discrimination, see "Examples of Court Decision"; for the relation between queer phenomenology and the law, see Sciullo, 2019).

Looking to queer theory in relation to anti-sodomy statutes and the *Lawrence* decision, Weinstein and DeMarco (2004) have argued that law dealing with the sex/gender binary is problematized in a radical way. For example: "what would the law prescribe in the case of a woman-identified-female who engaged in the prohibited sexual acts with a female-to-male transgendered partner (a person who identifies as a male but is anatomically female)?" Further, "how, too, might the law treat that same woman-identified-female if she were to practice this prohibited conduct with a male-to-female transsexual (a person who has, for argument's sake, completed the whole battery of surgeries, takes estrogen, and has been completely sex reassigned) or an intersexed person (one of the 1/2000 people who does not, for one reason or another fit in either the male or female categories)?" Not only heterosexual and homosexual but also bisexual dualities will be fundamentally problematized. For example, given the two examples above, "what would constitute a homosexual sexual interaction? What criteria would we use to determine whether the individuals involved were of the same or different sex?" "How would gender figure in determining orientation?" Thus, the terms "mother" and "father" are complicated.

People who identify as neither male nor female, but nonbinary, complicate things further for those wishing to police sexual interactions and gender expressions. On October 8, 2019, the U.S. Supreme Court began hearing oral arguments in three sex discrimination cases. The outcome of these decisions will either solidify employment rights for LGBTQ+ persons and others or set social justice back to the days when employers could fire a person for not expressing their gender or sexuality in a way acceptable to the employer (democracynow.org, 2019b). There has arisen conflict between essentialist feminists and those embracing a less restrictive understanding of self. This conflict has given rise to thoughtful debates regarding not just the social construction of gender but also the social construction of sex. A senior research fellow at the Global Health Justice Partnership at Yale University, Karkazis (2019) contends that there is no "true sex." As she illustrates, one of the basic traits that has been used to identify sex, hormones, are not actually determinate. Other "sex characteristics" are also under debate. The term TERF (trans-exclusionary radical feminist) has been applied to feminists who criticize some gender/sex expressions that do not fit within the binary. Judith Butler continues to be a leading theorist and advocate for sex and gender expressions beyond the binary and offers insights in an interview with theterfs.com (2014). The outcome of these discussions will inform our progress in understanding sex, gender, transgender, and nonbinary expressions. Regardless of the debate, allowing for each individual to express (or not) a gender or sex as is appropriate to themselves is required to doing justice and avoiding harm.

Polk (2001) asserts that it is through an ecologically queer identity that we can best realize the self that we embody as well as the connections that go beyond the physical self. In relationship with other beings, human and otherwise, we can best understand and fulfill ourselves individually and in unity with our ecological realm.

In sum, queer theory radically resituates discussion of identity and asks how they are continuously in flux without boundaries. Addressing these identities in social justice struggles in the days to come will no doubt lead to radically new visions as to personhood, identity, sexual orientation, gender, sex, and ways of being.

Intersections

Intersectionality stands for the idea of multiple affiliations, identities, consciousness, and loyalties, many of which are often in conflict. Delgado and Stefancic (2017, 51) define its study as "the examination of race, sex, class, national origin, and sexual orientation, and how their combination plays out in various settings." Intersectional persons thus often find themselves in complex relations that disadvantage (Crenshaw, 1993), in other words, situations of double, triple, and quadruple jeopardy. How should we consider each identity? Separately? Cumulatively? Proportionally? Consider a working class, gay African American male. Consider the various additive factors that place him in a disadvantaged position in dominant society.

Consider, too, the U.S. Census done every ten years, originally started in 1790 with three categories and in 2010 with 19 categories for "race" (see Vo, 2018) and recent discussion to eliminate race as a category (D'Vera, 2015). Why is this important? "Census data," Vo summarizes, "is used to allocate federal programs and heavily informs how lawmakers craft policies, especially around civil rights. From legislative redistricting to promoting equal employment opportunities to detecting whether some racial groups are exposed to more health risks than others, the more granular our definitions of who we are, the better our analysis of the current state of our country." How people are counted matters. And this must also reflect changing identity patterns. Census Bureau researchers, for example (Vo, 2018), found that between 2000 and 2010 about ten million people had changed their identification of race. The Census Bureau is considering for 2020 eliminating the language of race and "origin" and asking respondents to check off the appropriate categories with which they identify (D'Vera, 2015).

Speaking more theoretically, we noted (chapter 9) that identities are *performed* and *enacted*, according to new materialists/post postmodernists; that is, following Karan Barad's work, identities undergo "mattering," they come to realization in intra-action that can become stabilized as seemingly real identities rather than social constructions. Thus, the census apparatus does not merely register differences, but creates and solidifies identities in performative, enacted, intra-actions. And Leong (2016) reminds us in a critical engagement of both postmodernists and new materialists of the neglect of "mattering of Black Lives" having a long history in the legacy of slavery, distancing, and diminishing.

Delgado and Stefancic ask, "What role do intersectional persons play in social movements like gay liberation or feminism?" (2017, 52) Consider also the conflict between and among the various locations. As the HBO documentary *Leaving Neverland* (Reed, 2019) presents the possible pedophilia and incidents of child sexual abuse of the late and beloved Michael Jackson, and another documentary, *Surviving R. Kelly* (Brandin, 2019) implicates another beloved African American male entertainer, African Americans can be seen as pressured to side with white children (Michael Jackson) and black girls (R. Kelly) against black men. These expectations did not arise for white women during the Kavanaugh hearings in which he was approved for appointment to the Supreme Court. It is women of color who stand at this intersection. White women do not stand on that ground. For an empirical study of intersectionality in judicial decisions concerning equal employment opportunity indicating the effects are greater than the sum of the parts, see Rachel et al. (2011).

Cole (2009), while documenting the importance of racialization, would also ask that we consider class. In the cases of Michael Jackson and R. Kelly that would allow for standing for the declared victims, poor and working-class boys and girls who became enamored of the celebrity of their alleged abusers. Given the notion of intersectionality, how then does one strive for social justice? That is, how does one prove additive, separate, and cumulative effects in a court of law? How does one get "standing" before the law? Does one do so by inadvertently reinforcing an essentialist argument?

McNally (2017) asks us to consider the interwoven nature of identities. He reminds us of the work of Angela Davis (1983) regarding race, class, and gender suggesting a system that is beyond intersections. As a working class, Latina, I (LC) had an early experience that over years of reflection solidified some of these notions. At around the age of seven years a white classmate told me that she had seen me shopping with my maid. Women in my family often were maids, but never had maids. I am often assumed to be white because of both my last name and my appearance. In the context of South Texas, my whiteness in relation to my identifiably Latinx grandmother was assumed by my classmate, whose relation to Latinx women was as employer, not family member. Considering the complexity of identity as it is perceived by others, understood within the self, and marked by history and other contexts, a more sophisticated scheme than intersections may be necessary.

Beyond Intersectionality

McNally (2017, 107) invites us to "stand in the river of life, where multiple creeks and streams have converged into a complex pulsating system." As with Quantum Holographic Theory (Milovanovic, 2014a) we can move away from simplistic labels meeting at intersections and into a fuller understanding of an emerging, becoming, ever-materializing self, nurtured, to use Deleuze and Guattari's notion, by a continuous "becoming other," whereby self and other are mutually co-constituted in dialogical encounters. Through this more holistic understanding of self we can gain insight into nuanced and more complex becoming identities. Not intra-actions based on dichotomies of difference *or* sameness, self, separate from other (often replete with distancing and diminishing the other), but embracing and enriching, sensitive to diversity of needs, cultivating capabilities of each in social practices of intra-action.

Whiteness has gained attention as the identity against which all others are measured. The rejection of whiteness and the behaviors assumed and required of that identity may be necessary for progress toward justice (Liu, 2017). Whiteness holds norms beyond color and is often imposed upon people of color (Matias and Newlove, 2017). Whiteness is also used to uphold a gender binary, heterosexism, ableism, English language usage, and other dominant norms. Overcoming whiteness then is to overcome normative identities and allows for the recognition of more complex identities and for release of those identities from the oppression of whiteness. Jennings (2018) writes that refusing to be or to become white through the assimilation of norms will allow us to live together across the identities that currently divide us. In that sense, moving beyond intersectionality allows for a solidarity among people that encourages the becoming of the people yet to come and social justice yet to be.

REVIEW QUESTIONS

1. Why do some find that they are ambivalent toward legal struggles? Find a recent legal case that might offer an example of this ambivalence.

2. Essentialism and anti-essentialism are competing understandings of our identities. Think of an identity that might be best understood through essentialism and another identity that might be best understood through anti-essentialism. Bring notes on these identities to class for a discussion of these perspectives.

3. The critical legal studies tradition first sought to "trash" or decon-struct the legal process. Why would it be necessary to do this deconstruction? What does this deconstruction offer those looking for a new way of approaching justice?

4. Fem-Crits are concerned with how the law deals with women. Why would women find that they need their own critical analysis? What are the central concerns of the Fem-Crits?

5. Critical race theorists concern themselves with the ways in which the law is oppressive based on race. Find a recent case in which it appears that a person was treated in an unjust manner within the legal process because of their race. Explain how the treatment was not just and how the treatment was related to race. Then think about the context within which this treatment occurred. What was hap-pening outside of the legal process that may have also resulted in the unfair treatment? When you have your example and answers, share them with at least one other person in the class, and read through their answers to this question. Discuss what you found that was sim-ilar and what you found that was different in your respective cases.

6. In chapter 8, you were asked to design a hologram depicting your relationship with people at work, or school, or in your family. Now that you have read about the complications of multiple identities (race, ethnicity, class, gender, which may at times be called inter-sections), design a hologram that depicts your identity and how that identity relates to at least one other person that you interact with regularly. How do you interact on your similarities and how on your differences? Does your entire identity interact with their entire iden-tity at all times? Do you find that one or two of your identities are more important than others? Is it possible to pull all of your identities apart or are they tightly bound? Bring your design to class for discussion.

CHAPTER 11

Justice and Grassroots Struggles

THE DIALECTICS *of Legal Repression*, a classic study by Isaac Balbus (1977), shows how grassroots struggles are channeled into legal categories, discourses, and procedures, often "cooling out the mark." Issues are often framed narrowly, dividing struggles, and redefining their intent (see also Cole and Foster, 2001; Delgado and Stefancic, 1994; Milovanovic, 1988; Unger, 1996; Molyneux, 2014). The goals of dissidents are often depoliticized. Activist lawyers, too, often inadvertently reinforce the ideology of law at the cost of the goals of those in opposition. In addition, public opinion on an issue often finds a ready and willing corporate interest to reformulate emerging grievances into corporate campaigns. Corporate interests often attempt to co-opt grassroots movements and transform emerging insurgent language into the interests of profit and organizational well-being, referred to as "astroturfing" (Cho, 2011; Wear, 2014). Astroturfing—derived from AstroTurf, a brand of artificial grass—contrasts grassroots movements that emerge from people in struggle. These practices and outcomes have been defined in terms of the dialectics of struggle.

Along with external dialectics of struggle are internal ones. Mary Bernstein (2002, 85) has argued "by advocating for rights based on an identity such as 'woman' or 'gay,' identity movements reinforce the identity on which the movements are based and, as a result, sometimes fail to recognize diversity, homogenize and ignore differences within the identity category, and inhibit the creation of a 'politics of commonality'." In other words, terms such as race, class, and gender are ultimately categories without any "real" meaning. They are constructs appropriated in struggle as rallying points for identity politics; but ironically, they may often become hindrances for fuller appreciation of differences (see Klatch, 2002; Robnett, 2002).

Grassroots struggles are necessarily group processes and focus on group-level justice. Consider Poggi's (2019) definition: "Grassroots organizing's power is in the sense of justice about an issue and the power of ordinary folks to influence people in powerful positions, whose power always depends on cooperation from many, many people. Its power is not of money, issue expertise or relationships to decision-makers . . . By engaging ordinary people on its campaigns, it works from the bottom up to make its decisions. It does this by working with its constituency to determine issues, strategies, and tactics, and finding its volunteer leadership from the folks it is organizing" (1).

While these struggles can be and have been supported by legal struggles and/or support legal struggles, they are important and progressive in their own rights and often allow for a broader understanding of justice by those engaged in and witness to these struggles (see, for example, *Grass Roots Global Justice Alliance*; list provided by Poggi, 2019). This chapter, therefore, is more concerned with group struggles and only secondarily with individual struggles. When group struggles are created in the interest of social justice, they have an impact far beyond the individual named in the case and are most often supported by others in the interest of social justice. This is not to say that individual concerns are not important; rather, our focus is more on how social movements take form and what role they play in social change and the development of social justice. Some suggest that it was not in the legal arena that social justice ultimately took place but by collective action and/or the threat of such action. Consider, for example, *Brown v. Board of Education* (1954). Bell (1980) has argued that the U.S. Supreme Court responded as they did not because of enlightened, rational, human concerns. Instead, what had more weight was the potential for mass disturbance as returning black soldiers from the Korean War and the worldwide push by communist ideologies created a potential volatile group exhausted of and less inclined to sitting in the back of the bus.

Social movements are an expression of a desire for justice that has gone unmet. When those concerned for social justice, including equality, need, and/or desert, find that their demands are not considered nor seriously addressed by the political structures in place, they will often turn to social mobilization in an attempt to be heard and/or attain justice (McAdam, 1982). The definition or ideals of justice advocated in social movements are not always consistent between movements or even within movements. Ideas of individuals within movements also changed over time allowing for further variation. Here we will examine movements as ideal types, for the purpose of organizing the chapter. Greater variation appears in the real world than in narratives of them. It should be noted, however, that no movement is a monolith and many of the movements examined had overlapping ideas, interests, and support.

Movements themselves inform our understandings of justice. Those involved in social movements are influenced by their involvement and they influence those witnessing these movements. Shriver, Miller, and Cable (2003) document the development of women's political self-efficacy within the movement to obtain rights and benefits for those experiencing Gulf War illness. As these authors explain, activism develops participants' self-confidence as well as their understanding of social structure and social justice. The activists studied indicated that they had become involved in the movement out of concern for family members' access to health care. During the course of their activist work they became aware of the needs of others for access to health care (within and outside the military) as well as the workings of a Veterans Administration system that they found was not designed to benefit veterans. This resulted in the development of activists engaged in a variety of movement issues—including increasing access to health care in general, improving veterans benefits, and pressuring for access to information regarding Gulf War syndrome. Along with their previous activist experiences they developed a sophisticated level of understanding of and concern for social justice. This finding is similar to the political development of environmental activists described by Cole and Foster (2001). Therefore, as activists engage in the process of demanding justice, they are also developing their own understanding of justice and building their own processes for expression of justice.

Justice understandings also inform the process and success of movements. The democratic or nondemocratic nature of the movements themselves can support or damage movements. The Greek philosophers examined earlier are instructive to our understanding of democracy. While the ancient Greeks were far from inclusive in their debates, their understandings of democracy went beyond our current notions that are often limited to voting rights. Open inclusive debate and discussion are also central to democratic decision-making. As we will see in the following analyses, movements have at times failed in their own democratic practice by limiting their success and impact upon social justice.

BOTTOM-UP/GRASSROOTS JUSTICE

Types of Social Movements

Although there is great variety in the types of social movements toward justice, a useful typology has been offered by Harper and Leicht (2010) (see Table 11-1).

Radical reform seeks fundamental transformation of the system (i.e., Russian revolution, American revolution, decolonization); reform is more issue specific or piecemeal (i.e., labor movements, court decisions); instrumental is more concerned with changing structures (i.e., civil rights movement); expressive is more individual change (i.e., self-improvement movements, care of the self, see Foucault, 1986). We can now locate, as a beginning point of understanding, how various struggles may exist at the intersections of the two dimensions, noting, of course, with Max Weber, that these are only ideal types, conceptually pure categories. They do not include the dimension of the dialectics of struggle. Nevertheless, in studying grassroots struggles for social justice they begin to orient our thoughts. Transformative justice, for example,

TABLE 11-1

Types of Social Movements

	Instrumental	Expressive
Reform	Reformative	Alternative
Radical	Transformative	Redemptive

SOURCE: Adopted from Harper and Leicht (2010, 137)

could be situated in the transformative category. Restorative justice could be situated in the reformative intersection.

Harper and Leicht also conclude with offering an additional dimension, "progressive movements" and "conservative movements." The former are directed to future change, the latter a return to some past or to prevent new changes. "If progressive movements are utopian, conservative movements are usually oriented around the vision of some partly mythical 'golden age' of the past" (137). Latter examples would include the white power movement, white nationalism, and white supremacy movements, some of which have been traced to the aftermath of the post-Vietnam War era (Belew, 2018). A regressive form of conservative movements, loaded with moral hate and hate politics, a view that one's identity category is above all others, that other identity categories are less than and require distancing from, has been identified by some commentators (see Cornell's notion of "reversal of hierarchies," 1998).

Four Stages

Social movements, including grassroots movements for justice, can be conceptualized as progressing through stages. Eitzen and Stewart (2007, 5–6) offer four stages: initially, some social condition attracts the attention of a potential segment of the population due to potential or actual harm, or other social injustices, but still remains unfocused; a second stage whereby grievances now take on a more focused form often precipitated by some spark that turns "moral outrage into political action"; a third stage includes mobilization of resources along with the development of an organization and strategies for social change—this "is a bureaucratization stage in which a once unfocused number of people now have become an organization"; and a fourth possible stage if goals are successfully realized, institutionalization. They also note some dangers. These include: displacement of goals to some other issue, splintering with the organization, and leadership attempting to maintain power (6).

Revolutions

There has been ample debate in the literature as to the use of violence in revolutionary struggles. Some (Huntington, 1972, 282) view revolution as "a rapid, fundamental, and violent domestic change in the dominant values and myths of a society, in its political institutions, social structure, leadership, and government activities and politics"; others (Harper and Leicht, 2010, 186) distance themselves from the use of violence, defining "revolution as rapid and fundamental transformations in socioeconomic, cultural, and political institutions that are accompanied by class upheavals from below." Harper and Leicht (274; see also Vago, 2004, 368–374) do, however, acknowledge that violence may accompany social struggle movements, such as occurrences in the U.S. civil rights movement, ghetto resistance such as in the 1960s, labor movements, abolitionists, antiwar movements, and the environmental justice movements. We have also witnessed violence in social struggles to overthrow repressive regimes. As to terrorism as a tactic, "terrorism has been used by groups on the far right and the far left. Terrorist acts have been committed by groups that have been vindicated by history, as well as by those that have been condemned by it" (Vago, 2004, 372). Whereas some argue for the negative effects in the use of violence (Benjamin, 1978; Oppenheimer, 1969), others, such as Derrida (see chapter 9), argue that the very founding of a new state is often based on violence employed by some segment of the population, which then instills its constitution. The wealthy land and slave-owning all-male "founding fathers" of the U.S. Constitution and Declaration of Independence were responsible for violence against Native Americans, slaves, and women. Further, consider that if the founding figures were a cross section of all people in society, including those against whom violence had been perpetrated, the United States would have a different Declaration of Independence and Constitution. For Derrida, this neglect is further violence done to the disenfranchised. And lest it be forgotten, the U.S. use of armed forces abroad since World War II has resulted, in some estimates, in over 12 million killed (see "Killed," 2019); for others, over 20 million killed (Lucas, 2019; this includes an extensive listing of countries, and supported evidence; this excluded post 2015 deaths in the Middle East; for that figure see, for instance, Crawford, 2018).

"Do Revolutions Always Fail?" asks John Molyneux (2014) as some reactionary sentiment has it, pointing to, for example, "the failure of the squares" (Tiananmen, Tahrir, Puerto del Sol, Taksim, Maidan, etc.). Although some revolutions have degenerated in dictatorships, mostly according to Molyneux, due to transfer of power during the transition was maintained by or established by the bourgeoisie who instituted the rule of law and formal equality as but a hidden dimension of power and control.

But recent developments in the working classes (and we would add, Internet networking), he continues, are producing a concentrated, empowered and mobilized force: "the working class is the first oppressed class in history that has the ability to run society without exploiting or oppressing others." He concludes, however, the necessity of "mass strikes and occupation of work-places," since "it is at the point of production that capital is most vulnerable and working class power is concentrated" (8). Nor are arguments regarding human nature sufficient for dismissing revolutionary change. History pro-vides us with plentiful examples of varieties of humans, even as system-serving ideology continues to spin out the myth of the self-made person, or placing responsibility for change on the individual.

Other progressives have also noted nonviolent strategies such as "slow motion general strike" (see Holland, 2011) whereby gradual withdrawal, a disengagement from capitalism methods, ideologies and a repudiation of wage slavery, toward new forms of social formations and production will produce a qualitative change in the mode of production. Holland acknowl-edges (155–158) the work of Benjamin, "Critique of Violence" (1978) and Deleuze and Guattari's notion of a "minor Marxism" (1987).

Legacy of Mahatma Gandhi: Nonviolent Activism (1869–1946)

Gandhi provided a counter to the use of violence in struggles for social justice. His work has been influential on countless struggles for justice (see, for example, Martin Luther King, Jr., below). His work originated with the background of British colonizers of India. He received a degree from Uni-versity College, London, where he studied law. He was influenced by Hin-duism, Buddhism, Islam, and Christianity and writers such as Leo Tolstoy and Henry Thoreau. He became an activist in South Africa and subse-quently the movement for independence from Britain. Desai and Vahed (2015) and others, however, have indicated the problematic nature of Gan-dhi's various positions, documenting incidences of Gandhi's racism against black South Africans and his support for the British Empire even while supporting the rights of the Indian population of South Africa. As we illus-trated in the "Intersections" portion of chapter 10, such contradictions can arise in the politics of identity where disenfranchised persons/groups may re-establish hierarchies. Gandhi was inspired by his Indian religious heri-tage with the high value placed on nonviolence. He applied this heritage to political action. He provided an iconic image of ethical purist and passive resistance as a way of life and struggle as part of a larger political involve-ment. Discussions in general literature and in activists' tactics have inherited from him the need to assume a position between the continuum, violence and nonviolent change. Tamembaum (2011), however, notes the futility of nonviolence in the face of those willing to kill. Despite his limitations,

Gandhi has had and continues to have a major influence in the academic fields of peace studies, peacemaking criminology, as well as in applications such as restorative justice.

RACE/ETHNICITY, GENDER, SEXUALITY, AND CLASS STRUGGLES FOR JUSTICE

African American Movements for Justice: Historical Developments

We begin with the civil rights era in the United States because it is often raised when considering the impact of social movements upon ideas of justices, concrete changes toward justice, and the development of individuals within movements themselves. The movements for African American justice inspired and informed the many movements that followed. None of these movements was homogeneous in its demands, tactics, or outcomes. We cannot examine each organization or group seeking justice in the short space here. Instead, we will review several and offer a beginning analysis for understanding their impact.

Justice demands vary by social movements. They also vary within the organizations themselves. In a broad sense, these movements attempt to fulfill the demands of justice—equality, needs, and deserts as outlined by Miller (1999). Equality in education, housing, work/wages, health care, and other social needs were often the focus of movements for racial/social justice. Fulfillment of needs in each of these areas fell short because of the racial/ethnic prejudices that pervade society and because of the structural biases that resulted in inadequate schools, housing, employment, health care, and other basic needs.

The civil rights movements of the previous century did not bring the sort of justice required of Miller's (1999) principles of justice. In general, African Americans, Latinxs, and other racial/ethnic minority groups still suffer inequalities. The unequal access to even basic resources for nonwhites compared to whites indicates a failure to meet the distributive principles of justice such as needs, equality, deserts. Former President Barak Obama, Oprah Winfrey, and other successful minorities serve as the exceptions rather than the rule for racial/ethnic minorities in the United States. Oliver and Shapiro (2006) thoroughly document the continuing wealth inequalities between blacks and whites.

The deleterious legacy of slavery remains entrenched in the national consciousness, see, for example, Joy Degruy's (2017) notion of "post traumatic slave syndrome." A study completed in 2018, a 50-year perspective (1968–2018) by Jones et al. (2018), indicates continuous inequalities between white and African American rates on key indicators. African Americans: incarceration rates have increased during the period of study by almost three times and were six times the rate of white incarceration (604 per

100,000 in 1968 compared to 1,730 per 100,000 in 2016); receive college degrees at half the rate of whites; are paid 82.5 percent of white workers' earnings; are two-and-a-half times likely to live in poverty as whites; have 1/10 times the wealth of white families; have unemployment rates about twice the white unemployment rates even as their proportion in the population has increased from 6.7 percent in 1968 to 7.5 percent in 2018; have home ownership rates around 40 percent, the same as 1968, and fully 30 percent lower than white home ownership rates.

Economic inequalities persist and include greater likelihood of impoverishment, unemployment, and lower returns on educational success for blacks than whites. Some have argued that "black genocide" prevails (Johnson and Leighton, 1995; see also Glen, 2019, referring to the 1951 petition by the Civil Rights Congress delivered by William Patterson to the United Nations that argued that the U.S. government was violating the U.N. Genocide Convention). The definition of genocide includes (reported by Glen) "acts committed to destroy, in whole or in part, a national, ethnical, or religious group as such" including "killing members of the group" and "causing serious bodily or mental harm to members of the group." Given the number of recent killings of African American males by police and given legal decisions like *McCleskey v. Kemp* (see chapter 10, African Americans are much more likely to be sentenced to death than white males, based on a highly verifiable empirical study by David Baldus, see Gross, 2012), and with the American Indian genocide (Dunbar-Ortiz, 2015), one has pause to seriously consider the argument concerning genocide.

In the United States, African Americans and other minority groups have not yet won justice (based on distributive principles of equality, needs, and desert). However, the movements of the civil rights era did bring about some progressive social change and improved conditions. These movements resulted in changes to everyday life that had not been forthcoming prior to the movements. As Zinn (1995) reminds us, it is social movements that create progressive social change (see also the organization "Showing Up for Racial Justice"). Politicians often step in front of movements after they have developed broad support. However, as the civil rights era clearly shows, no mainstream political official was pushing for the sorts of changes demanded by these movements. Instead, it was an active minority of people engaged in struggle that was responsible for the progress of the era.

These activists did not appear without a historical understanding, and in many cases, historical experience of struggle and movements. Included among those active in the civil rights struggles of the 1950s and 1960s were persons formerly active in seeking the release of conscientious objectors imprisoned for opposing U.S. involvement in World War II and refusing to fight in that war. Bennett (2003) chronicles the movement while Zinn

(1995) explains the importance and reasoning of conscientious objectors and others who stood against U.S. involvement in World War II.

Of course, African Americans had been in struggle in the United States against injustice for centuries before the modern civil rights era. Frederick Douglass was among those alive to witness the end of slavery in the United States and the beginnings of the deplorable repressive conditions such as Jim Crow laws and other racist/genocidal practices, against which the civil rights movements were to rise. Ture and Hamilton (1992, xviii) quote Frederick Douglass's famous West India Emancipation Speech of August 1857 in the introduction of their text to illustrate the necessity of protest: "Those who profess to favor freedom yet deprecate agitation, are men who want crops without plowing up the ground; they want rain without thunder and lightning . . . . Power concedes nothing without demand. It never did and it never will. Find out just what any people will quietly submit to and you have found out the exact measure of injustice and wrong which will be imposed upon them, and these will continue till they are resisted with either words or blow, or with both. The limits of tyrants are prescribed by the endurance of those whom they oppress."

Others argue that real progress has yet to be made, that genocide continues in more subtle, institutional, and systemic form. Some injustices are pushed back to the realm of micro-aggressions and forms of "petit apartheid." Formerly empowering law and legal decisions of the 1950s and 1960s are being systematically reduced and restricted. Redistribution, equality, recognition, capabilities, and participation remain institutionally limited, and liberal paternalistic and condescending forms of "othering" prevail. Genuine liberation and social justice remain to be won.

William Edward Burghardt Du Bois

More commonly known as W.E.B. Du Bois (1868–1963), he was a pioneering writer, sociologist, civil rights activist, the first African American to receive a PhD from Harvard University (1895), and cofounder of the National Association for the Advancement of Colored People (NAACP) (see Du Bois, 2018). His PhD thesis was "The Suppression of the African Slave Trade to the United States of America, 1638–1870." He was a key groundbreaking voice for African Americans. Among his influential books were *The Philadelphia Negro* (1899) and *The Souls of Black Folk* (1903). A novel was also published, *The Quest of the Silver Fleece*. He was also the editor of the NAACP's monthly magazine, *The Crisis*. He was an effective voice in acquainting white readers with the plight of victims of racism. He also had some internal differences with the more conservative noted African American, Booker T. Washington, which led him to join his opposition in the Niagara Movement. He ran unsuccessfully for the U.S. Senate in 1950 and was to be a victim of investigations of the anti-communist McArthur witch hunt. He developed an interest in Marxist literature and communism and in 1961 joined the American Communist Party and subsequently left to reside in Ghana. An unfinished manuscript, *Encyclopedia Africana*, celebrating the achievements of African Americans, was never completed with his death in 1963. But in 1999, Kwame and Gates were to complete and publish his work in *Africana: The Encyclopedia of the African and African American Experience*. W.E.B. Du Bois continues to be a major influential voice for activists and academics bringing to light the condition of African Americans.

Martin Luther King Jr., Malcolm X, and Ali: The Mighty Trinity

Martin Luther King Jr. was the grandson of two African Americans who may have been influenced by Washington. Reverend A. D. Williams and Jennie C. Parks, King's maternal grandparents, were graduates of Morehouse College and Spelman College. Their daughter, Alberta, would also graduate from Spelman before marrying Mike (who would later change his and his first son's first names to Martin) King. Mike King, born into a rural farm family with little education, became a laborer and a successful preacher. He developed a congregation of middle-class African American families to support the financial needs of his church. He also became politically active within the context of local elections and the few small struggles of that time in Atlanta (Branch, 1988).

Though his grandparents clearly followed the Washington way of educational attainment and his father sought economic security for his church while engaging in some political struggle, the legacy of Martin Luther King Jr. would be far more aligned with the understanding of justice struggle espoused by Frederick Douglass. Booker T. Washington, a contemporary of Douglass, had a very different vision of methods for seeking justice. Washington encouraged African Americans to work within the system in order to develop their educational and economic prospects and become productive and respected citizens (Ture and Hamilton, 1992, 124). Washington was more interested in assimilation and reform than in protest and radical change. Most of the U.S. public became aware of King Jr.'s activism with the much media-covered Montgomery bus boycotts of 1955–1956. Notwithstanding King's and others' places at the forefront of these movements, and these were considerable, social change occurred not because of any one leader, but because of the commitment of a large minority in the country who were willing to maintain oppositional activity and due to the growing numbers of those willing to support those movements. The pressure that these activists and their supporters put on the political structure ultimately led to the progressive changes of the time.

The NAACP was actively supporting mainstream, mostly middle-class ideas of progress of which Booker T. Washington would have approved. Growing impatient with these tactics, King formed the Southern Christian Leadership Conference (SCLC), which later spawned the Student Nonviolent Coordinating Committee (SNCC). SCLC and SNCC were more radical than the NAACP because they were willing to demand acceleration toward justice and to take direct action to attain it. The nonviolence principle of these organizations, however, was problematic for Malcolm X and other black nationalists, some of whom were active within the Nation of Islam (NOI) and other organizations. While Malcolm X and other black nationalists did not espouse violence for the sake of violence, neither did they require passivity in the face of attack (Marable, 2003). Cobb (2014) documents his and others' experiences in movements espousing nonviolence while protected by armed supporters willing to defend the movement if and when such armed defense became necessary. These may seem contradictory stances, yet were necessary, advocates argue, to the survival of the movement, particularly in the face of violence actively practiced by the KKK and other racists.

From the bus boycotts forward, King was known and unknown to mainstream U.S. society. He was known as the persona presented by the mainstream media and often unknown for his constant reconsideration and expansion of his ideas of justice. Branch (1988), Dyson (2000), Garrow (2004), and others have documented the life and impact of King from a variety of perspectives. These texts are important in understanding the complexities of King, the movements he was involved in, and the movements that were going on around him. Within these complexities is a clear and consistent dedication to social justice that developed through King's own struggles and through the movements of the time.

This development is of importance and particular concern for this examination. While other texts have articulated and catalogued the details of the victories of the civil rights movements, here we are attending to the struggles and their impact on our ideas, expectations, and experiences of justice. The life and work of King within social movements is a study in the development of ideas through grassroots struggle. As he worked within a variety of movements, these movements had an impact on his ideas. His work and ideas also had an impact on those around him. King and Malcolm X are often counter-posed as the pacifist versus the nonpacifist leaders of the civil rights era. Their religious beliefs and political methods did differ; however, their goals were not so far apart and their political ideas and ideas of justice were very close on many issues, especially toward the end of each of their lives.

Both of these important leaders expanded beyond their original concerns for justice for African Americans and became concerned with justice
in general. They each became involved in antipoverty and antiwar movements and spoke of the need for greater structural change to include economic justice for all (Breitman, 2002; Haley, 1992; and Zinn, 1995). As
with many involved in social movements of the time, it became clear to
both of these men that only a broader social justice agenda would fully
emancipate African Americans. King and Malcolm X not only shaped
movements and each other, but each developed in such a way that they had
much in common including a personal and political relationship with an
important sports figure: Muhammad Ali. Muhammad Ali could reach
beyond movements into mainstream America with his powerful voice.

Ali was greatly influenced by Malcolm X not only in his joining of the
NOI, but also in the larger political picture (Zirin, 2005). The two were
friends until Ali was pressured to break this tie by the leadership of the
NOI, which had become fearful and suspicious of Malcolm X. Turning his
back on Malcolm X turned out to be of great regret to Ali. In the mean-
time, Ali was influencing a small antiwar movement drawing connections
between oppression of African Americans in the United States and the war
in Vietnam. His outspoken criticisms and refusal to submit to the draft in
1966 were a powerful influence in a period when most Americans were not
yet questioning the war, even as the anti-war movement was beginning.
The combination of Ali's incredible talent as a boxer, popularity, especially
among African Americans, and ability to speak clearly to the injustices of
the time were exactly what the movements needed to build in size and confidence. He also greatly influenced others within the sports world, inspiring
the Olympic Project for Human Rights (OPHR) and the public defiance of
Tommie Smith and John Carlos on the medal stand during the 1968 Olym-
pics displaying their support for the Black Power movement and the OPHR
(Zirin, 2005).

Referencing Ali's antiwar stance, King also made his antiwar stance
clear in 1967. By this time King and Ali had worked together in the housing
movement in Chicago and the two were committed to antipoverty struggles around the country. Although Malcolm X had been assassinated in
1965, his legacy continued as the Black Panther Party organized movements
committed to self-defense in response to increasing police brutality in African American neighborhoods. While the political methods espoused by
King and Malcolm X were often in opposition to one another, they were
often pushed to defend one another to a media determined to draw one into
denouncing the other (Haley, 1992; Zinn, 1995). While the differences and
divisions within the civil rights movement were even more complex and

numerous than can be attended to here, this examination of three famous leaders allows for an understanding of how difference need not be a barrier to success. Rather than denounce each other for their differences, these three were able to respectfully disagree, work toward common goals, and continue the work within their own politics and methods to the benefit of greater progress. The legacy of each continues within various struggles today and continues to benefit those committed to progress.

The limitations faced by the Black Power movements and those surrounding King were not so severe as to preclude real change. However, with the perspective of history, we can examine these effective movements to inform an understanding of the needs of future movements. The ability of the leadership and membership of the civil rights movements to struggle together despite their differences was powerful, progressive, and successful. However, as Marable (2003) shows, the cult of leadership and personality that surrounded King and Malcolm X resulted in a great setback for the movement when these men were assassinated. Also of concern to Marable (2003) was the inability of some organizations, specifically the NAACP, to tolerate political differences and to bow to outside pressures to purge communists and other radicals from their membership. This intolerance not only limited the movements but expelled some of the best anti-racist activists of the period from the larger mainstream organizations.

Ella Baker: A Collective Work

Ella Baker was involved in social justice movements for over fifty years and worked within the NAACP, SCLC, and SNCC, among other organizations. Her experience within these movements is both a testament to her own commitment and points the way forward. She was often frustrated by the overreliance upon a few leaders within the movement and instead argued for broader inclusion. She was also very aware of the ageism, sexism, and elitism within the movement and the impact that these had on her ability to sway the opinions of others, especially when she disagreed with King (Ransby, 2003).

Rather than be silenced or thwarted, however, she continued her work as she saw best and developed a layer of activists who would continue in struggle beyond the lives of King or Malcolm X. Because she was committed to a radical democracy, she insisted that authentic leadership could only come from those most affected by injustice. Rank-and-file activism by and for those seeking justice was Baker's view of progress. As biographer Ransby (2003) expresses: "For Baker, revolution was above all about a protracted and layered democratic process" (372).

Baker's work toward and vision of a radical democratic process inclusive of the voices of the most oppressed strengthened the movements of her time.

One can only imagine the impact she might have had if these movements had not contained the injustices of sexism, ageism, and elitism. It is important to look critically at these and other social movements in order to learn from their mistakes and limits and to move beyond them. Baker's critiques and work illustrate how one can work within, without, and around imperfect movements while insisting on a better way.

Black Lives Matter

Perhaps initiated by much publicized police killings of African Americans, the movement Black Lives Matter took off in 2013. The acquittal of George Zimmerman after his extrajudicial killing of Trayvon Martin and the police killings of Michael Brown (in Ferguson) and Eric Garner (in New York City) were of particular concern. Protests expanded in 2014 through 2016. Alicia Garza, Patrisse Cullors, and Opal Tometi galvanized the movement with their "hashtag" BlackLivesMatter. The movement has now extended internationally (see the Black Lives Matter Global Network, 2019; Wikipedia.org, 2019c). Some who may misunderstand or misinterpret the movement or who do not believe that black lives should matter have called this movement racist. Some developed a counter slogan, "All Lives Matter" (see response by President Obama, explaining Black Lives Matter, Townes, 2016); yet, others counter argue "Blue Lives Matter" (supporters of police). Supporters of the latter in Louisiana, with much controversy, were instrumental in passing a "hate crime" law directed at those targeting police, firefighters, and medical emergency crews.

Another more informal movement that brought attention to police killings of African Americans was started by a now-former National Football League (NFL) player, Colin Kaepernick, who took a knee during the playing of the national anthem in protest. The resulting controversy inspired another NFL player, Michael Bennett, to write a book about his experiences with racism within the college football system, the NFL, and from police. Bennett's work is both political and personal and explains why he became active in the Black Lives Matter movement after a young mother was killed by police in Seattle. He also examines what that activism has meant to him as an African American, to his career as an NFL player, and for his family relationships (Bennett and Zirin, 2018).

This highly emotive discussion can polarize, or, more constructively, engage those pursuing social justice to genuinely actualize distributive principles of justice—need, equality, desert, recognition, redistribution, participation, capabilities. With robust discussion comes the necessity of truly realizing the historical origins, the legacy of racism that permeates all facets in society, and the continued injustices suffered by African Americans.

Struggles for Latino(a)/Latinx Justice

The Black Power movement had a great influence on other movements for racial/ethnic justice. There has been quite intense discussion of the identity categories Latino(s), Hispanic, Chicano, but increasingly, perhaps with the insightful early work by Latina feminists such as Gloria Anzaldua (1987; see also Ortega, 2016), the notion of Latinx has become a more general category responding to ethnic and racial emphases (for discussion of the use of Latinx, see Vargas, 2018). An early groundbreaking work tracing the historical development of legal practices, "gringo justice," was authored by Alfredo Mirandé (1994). Below, we highlight some early developments in struggles for justice.

The La Raza Unida Party (LRUP) was a small political party that developed in the U.S. Southwest as a response to the racist practices against Latinx people of the region who were mainly Mexican Americans and Mexicans. The Mexican American Youth Organization (MAYO) was developed through LRUP and organized among students on various college campuses. The demands of these organizations were more radical than those of the League of United Latin American Citizens (LULAC), which aligned with the Democratic Party and middle-class Latinx interests. LRUP was explicitly nationalistic, calling for the return of lands of the Southwest as well as equal education, health care, and employment opportunities (Meier and Ribera, 1998).

While middle-class Latinxs and Anglos were fearful of LRUP and MAYO, these organizations were successful in attracting a large number of activists. Their efforts resulted in school boycotts and threats to the conservative Democrats who failed to address issues of injustice against Latinxs in the southwestern part of the United States. Latinxs, Mexican Americans specifically, were and remain a clear majority in southwest Texas where LRUP originated, yet they were rarely allowed to engage in the political process in a meaningful way. The activism of the late 1960s and early 1970s changed much of this. Latinxs organized and printed a Spanish-language newspaper that addressed the concerns of the community. The paper also presented an alternative to the Anglo paper and its nonpolitical or reactionary coverage of the area. These activists won greater rights in local elections and representation on local school boards. While these gains were real and necessary, the weaknesses of LRUP and MAYO led to early erosion of these gains.

Melendez (2003) describes similar weaknesses in the Young Lords organization following some successes for Puerto Rican justice (see also Enck-Wanzer, 2010). While the Young Lords were active mainly in urban areas and LRUP was more rurally focused, their nationalistic demands and radical politics were not so different. These demands were more readily received in urban centers and among a population with a homeland, which was and is perceived as colonized by the United States. The Young Lords and their co-activists were successful in attaining better health services, greater educational supports, and attention to the plight of Puerto Rico as a colony. Their tactics were far more radical than those of LRUP and MAYO and included activities that necessitated the move of several members into an underground system for protection from arrest. They were the target of the FBI's notorious COINTELPRO program. While many of these activists have now been cleared of numerous charges levied against them, there was a systematic attempt to remove them from their activism through illegal surveillance and trumped-up criminal charges. Some Puerto Rican activists are still serving prison terms and are considered political prisoners by many who were involved in these movements. Their activities, arguably, were no more dangerous than those of white activists of the time (the Weather Underground, for example) most of whom were never imprisoned, but have often been celebrated for their activities.

The demise of the Young Lords was precipitated by a top-down organizational structure that would not tolerate the independence or voices of a broader group of activists. As Melendez (2003) explains, he was directed away from activities that had proved successful to the goals of the organization by a leadership that had lost interest in his input. While some, including Melendez, were suspicious, rightfully so in some cases, of the infiltration of government agents into the movement, it was the structural problem that led to the decline of Puerto Rican activism just as it did with Mexican American activism. A strong democratic organization, history has shown, can overcome repressive tendencies whether that tendency comes from the membership, from an outside agitator, or even from governmental pressures and clandestine activities directed toward their division. This lack of democratic organizing also allowed for the interests of the minority of middle-class Latinxs to move the organizations into more conservative work. Ultimately, radical politics declined and those remaining were either isolated or co-opted into the Democratic Party.

In 1999, after much international pressure and grassroots organizations in support, President Clinton granted a provisional clemency to twelve Puerto Rican political prisoners, eleven of whom accepted and were released. None were convicted of an actual violent act, but "seditious conspiracy," conspiracy to transport explosives and transportation of firearms with the purpose to attack government property. They were said to be connected with the "terrorist" organization, Fuerzas Armadas de Liberación Nacional (FALN). Oscar Lopez Rivera, who was initially sentenced to fifty-five years and subsequently fifteen more years for conspiring to escape prison, refused the conditions of clemency and remained a prisoner until 2017 when President Obama commuted his sentence. This commutation came after Lopez Rivera served thirty-six years and thirty eight years after President Carter provided amnesty to four other Puerto Rican political prisoners. (For the continued struggle for the independence of Puerto Rico and for other political prisoners, see the websites: http://prolibertadweb .com; http://prisonactivist.org; as well as Prison Activist Resource Center, https://www.prisonactivist.org/.)

The question of the status of the "undocumented" (Federal Government officials continue to call them "illegal aliens," others, pejoratively, "illegals") concerns some estimated 10–12 million migrants entering the United States predominantly from Central America and Mexico, many of whom subsist in hidden economies, seasonal farming, and secondary markets where they are subject to fewer protections and more outright exploitation (the numbers since 2010 have been decreasing notably, see Warren, 2019). Another about half a million people (not from Mexico or Central America) overstay their visas every year in the United States. However, an article in the *New York Times* (Dickerson, 2019) reports those migrants crossing the border increased in February 2019, totaling 76,000.

In response to much human tragedy, including concern for young children who immigrated with their parents, the Dream Act has been introduced several times by Congress, the most recent in 2017, all unsuccessful. The Dream Act would provide protection from deportation to immigrant children living in the United States for four years. This was the basis for the "Dreamers." President Obama, by Executive Order in 2017, issued orders to stop deportation of those falling under the Deferred Action for Childhood Arrivals (DACA) rules. Incoming President Trump rescinded this limited protection and began to push building a wall between the U.S. southwest border and Mexico. In 2018 a sizeable caravan, the Central American Migrant Caravan, worked its way to the U.S. border bringing much attention to the plight of immigrants and refugees. The Trump administration responded with a brutal and traumatizing practice of separating refugee and immigrant children from their parents. Thousands of these children have been lost through the lack of policies and practices to assure their tracking, safety, or ultimate return to their families (Thrush, 2019). Calls for justice for these immigrants and children have increased substantially within the United States and internationally.

Undocumented and Unafraid (Burciaga, 2019) is a movement of DACA recipients who seek not only to normalize their own status but to also protect other immigrants. #NotOneMoreDeportation (http://www .notonemoredeportation.com/about/) is a campaign seeking to assist immigrants and others through the reformation of immigrant laws and practices.

A tangible justice strategy is the establishment of "safe zones." One move-ment has been the "Sanctuary School and Safe Zone Movement," even though the federal government has threatened penalties. This has a histori-cal legacy traced to the Sanctuary Movement in the 1980s that protected those fleeing from Central American strife.

Struggles for Gender Justice

Issues of democratic organizing would also plague those in the women's movements, which often did not represent all women. Women involved in these movements were often silenced by a top-down organizing structure that looked to its own interests rather than those of the women it claimed to represent. Women's and feminists' movements were inspired by the civil rights successes of the 1950s and 1960s, and they were diverse in their tac-tics, expectations, and membership. Many goals overlapped, yet the differ-ences in demands were important during the active movement period and continue to be important today.

The demands of middle-class, mainly white women during the early to late twentieth century often centered on the right to work in professional careers with wages equal to men. Working-class women and poor and minor-ity women had been working for generations. While they were interested in higher wages, they had a different set of demands, such as quality day care, equal treatment in the jobs that they already had, and access to health care, including reproductive choices and paid maternity leave. Johnnie Tillmon illustrated the class differences apparent in the women's movement: "For a lot of middle-class women in this country, Women's Liberation is a matter of concern. For women on welfare it's a matter of survival" (Zinn, 1995, 503).

Perhaps the justice demand that most clearly exemplifies the historic and current divides within the women's and feminist movements is access to abortion. The U.S. Supreme Court decision *Roe v. Wade* (1973) set the legal right to access abortion, but did little to assure actual access. While this legal victory did much to prevent the back-alley abortions that took so many women's lives before the decision, it in itself did little to guarantee access to women without funds for medical care. Instead, it set the stage for a social movement made of women and men demanding free abortion with-out apology. This, however, continues to undergo re-articulation into safer demands. This backward slide in demands has less to do with the changing legal notions of reproductive justice than it has to do with the limits on expectations imposed from within a movement that is currently dominated by middle-class interests.

Much of the current debate within the mainstream feminist move-ment is centered on power feminism and climbing the corporate ladder rather than questioning corporate power. Most women are left out of this power-feminist model. The politics of the women's and feminists' move-ment is mostly limited to the Democratic Party. This extends to supporting liberal candidates even when they themselves are accused of sexual harass-ment (as President Clinton was accused by Paula Jones) or decline to support abortion rights (as in the case of the John Kerry campaign).

The careerist notions of feminism and women's rights extend to aca-demia as well as to corporate women. Coates and Dodds (1998) documented the problems inherent in academic settings where feminist research and pedagogy often take precedence over activism. While there is nothing unworthy with feminist research or pedagogy, the privileging of these tenure-related tasks at the expense of activism is understandable within a system that is entrenched in the status quo. As Coates and Dodds point out, students and faculty who choose to engage in political struggle do so at the expense of a second shift or time-out of what might otherwise be personal time. However, it is also quite apparent that most activists must earn a living and/or attend school while engaging in political activism. This reality seems to escape the authors whose concern was exclusively the academic world. The authors did note a need for academics to engage with the community and with activists outside of academia. They did not address, however, the importance of understanding the realities of the lives of those in that com-munity and that this community is already doing double duty.

Ryan (2004) offered insight into the academic community divide sug-gesting that by working in imperfect unions, each can come to understand and respect the work of the other. Through this process there is no doubt that the lives and interests of activists and academics would be exposed to each other and perhaps influence each other. Ella Baker would have much to offer on this topic (see, for example, Ransby, 2003). She would undoubt-edly suggest that women most oppressed by the current system, not neces-sarily exclusively corporate women or academics, take the leading roles in the movement and engage others through a radical democracy that would ensure decisions and actions based on the needs of those whom the move-ment claims to serve.

Feminist activism in academia often can be conceptualized in various perspectives, each of which makes common assumptions that differ from each of the other perspectives, of the etiology of women's subjugation and possible emancipation. Feminist activism, not necessarily located in aca-demia, is still driven by common assumptions about the wherewithal of women's subjugation (see, for example, Snyder, 2008). Accordingly, per-spectives identified in the literature are: liberal feminism, includes struggles for formal equality, often based on the "equal protection clause" of the Fourteenth Amendment to the U.S. Constitution; radical feminism, traced to patriarchy, the historical domination of women by men; Marxist feminism, class nature of subjugation in capitalism, women as "slaves of men"; social feminism, combines Marxist with radical approach; postmodern/post-structuralist, notes how language structure itself defines identities and their attributes; decolonial feminism, how racialization takes place stemming from colonial periods and continues (see Lugones, 2010; Spivak, 2010); performative feminism, arguably an outgrowth of postmodern and constitutive theory, argues identities are created in everyday performative acts that do not necessarily begin with binaries in gender (see Cornell, 2007; Krause, 2008); and intersectionality, identities are multiple, situated in the intersections of gender, race, ethnicity, sexual orientation, age, class, etc. (see, for example, Crenshaw, 1989; Whisnant, 2016).

Another form of feminist activism, not necessarily situated in academia, is the "Me Too Movement" (see https://metoomvmt.org/). Traced to about 2006 (articulated by Tarana Burk) and perhaps given more formal momentum in hashtags on the Internet in 2007 (among others, by Alyssa Milano), it highlights often more-hidden societal abuses particularly at the workplace, but more recently extended to other areas. The allegations beginning in 2017 against powerful Hollywood producer Harvey Weinstein and popular comedian and television producer Louis CK, as well as the much-publicized trial and conviction of Bill Cosby in 2018, brought the issue to center stage in the public mind. Me-too stories began to be more forcefully articulated and redress began to be a central issue. The movement is empowering those subject to sexual exploitation and harassment, providing recognition, participation, and relief.

Struggles for LGBTQ+ Justice

Sexuality is sometimes approached as a divisive or controversial topic. Here we will accept that sexuality varies. The following descriptions are by no means complete but offer an accessible understanding of these differences in thought. There are at least four broad schools of thought with intricate and developed sets of understanding regarding sexuality: biological, psychological, sociological, and postmodernist. Biological theories contend that sexuality is determined and expressed based upon chemical, hormonal, and/or brain structures. Psychological theories assert that expressions of sexuality are shaped by the interaction between biological characteristics and experiences during developmental stages. Sociological theories assert that as modern societies provided the opportunity for people to reject the normative family structures that had been in place since feudal times, non-heterosexual forms of organizing and expressing sexuality would develop and become more accepted. Postmodernists argue that making distinctions between biological sex and gender are illusory, and rather they are socially constructed, particularly in constitutive performances (Butler, 1996). This position does not insist on real material differences, but rather what is socially constructed on these differences.

Additionally, we have witnessed and are witnessing a growing diversity in the original term, LGB (lesbian, gay, bisexual) to, among others: LGBT with the "T" including transgender; LGTQ, with the "Q" indicating queer or questioning; LGBTIQ, with the "I" indicating intersex (see, for example, University of California at Davis, LGBTQIA Resource Center); and LGBTQQIA+, standing for lesbian, gay, bisexual, transgender, queer, questioning, intersex, asexual people with the plus (+) standing for inclusion. Some have argued that this listing of letters needs to be replaced perhaps by an all-encompassing term. The outcome of this debate remains open. A number of demonstrations and organizations have evolved around all or parts of these identities. We have also seen internal divisions, recently most notably by a much-publicized statement by legendary tennis star, and self-identified gay, Martina Navratilova (Zirin, 2019) who said that "transgender athletes wanting to complete in women's sports are cheats." She was immediately branded by many critics as "transphobic." She subsequently apologized and revised her statement to say, "I know that my use of the word 'cheat' caused particular offence among the transgender community. I'm sorry for that because I attached the label to a notional case in which someone cynically changes gender, perhaps temporarily, to gain a competitive advantage."

Some critiques of the continued proliferation of identity categories include: that it splinters social movements and reduces their effectiveness in the political arena; that the very identity categories socially constructed are continuously re-invested with energy and clear boundaries and components supporting a fundamental essentialism; that the intersectional nature of identities is not fully acknowledged; and that rather than producing creative cross-difference experiences, solid boundaries are emerging reducing the interaction between and among disenfranchised groups, and hence potential compassionate understanding, recognition, and support.

Let us offer a brief historical summary of the social movements that developed in response to the oppression of those with other than heterosexual identities. The gay rights movement emerged at the time of the Black Power and antiwar movements of the time (1960s). The Stonewall Riots of 1969 were the beginning of the modern gay and lesbian rights movement. The riots were a response to a police raid of a bar frequented by homosexuals in New York City. While this was not the first police raid on a gay bar, it would seem to be the last straw for many in the New York gay community. The Gay Liberation Front formed to demand "public respect and an end to antigay legislation and police harassment" (Wolf, 2004, 56). This movement clearly indicated its understanding of gay oppression as a social problem in need of social structural change, specifically the abolition of some social institutions and for genuine forums for redress.

Divisions within the movement and differing ideas of liberation took their toll on the movement. Like the women's rights and feminist movements, some within the gay rights movement began to look to and promote personal liberation as the way forward. This individualistic notion of liberation necessarily demobilized the social movements and relied upon individual consciousness and action rather than social change. While coming out and claiming one's sexuality are clearly positive moves for those who are able to do so and maintain their social and economic well-being, these actions are not aimed at social structures, but at individuals. Not all within the movements went down this individualistic path, but those remaining within the movements were isolated into direct action groups, including ACT-UP, Queer Nation, and Lesbian Avengers with powerful, yet limited, voices for justice (Wolf, 2004).

These splits between those looking to individual change and those looking to small radical groups for social change continue today. Many within the gay rights community have placed their hope for social justice in the mainstream Democratic Party. The 2004 presidential election is instructive in terms of limits placed on electoral politics as a way forward for possible realization of social justice. As the 2004 presidential election approached, states and cities were making decisions regarding gay marriage and at times deciding to allow same-sex partners to gain access to marriage. While civil unions had been allowed in some cities and states previously, the demands for marriage rights are broader, including tax benefits, retirement benefits, and health care coverage, and desired by some of those to whom they had been previously denied. Some cities and states began to react to the liberalization of marriage rights by passing bans on gay marriage.

The issue of gay marriage had been raised and expectations for equal marriage were raised along with it. Rather than embrace the issue as a campaign platform, Democratic candidate John Kerry instead avoided the issue calling for each states' right to decide the issue for itself. Fearing the reelection of the Republican candidate, George W. Bush, as president of the U.S., many supportive of gay marriage rights backed off of their demands in hopes that a postelection President Kerry would support equal marriage. Fourteen states took Kerry's advice and decided per referendums to ban gay marriage on the same ballot that Bush was re-elected to the presidency. It is unclear just how far the gay marriage movement would have progressed had it not collapsed under the hopes of electing a Democratic candidate. It is clear that this strategy actually set back the struggle for equal marriage in at least the fourteen states that passed bans on gay marriage. It would take eleven more years to gain equal marriage in the United States.

Despite the original resistance by general public opinion and the courts in the early 1970s to equal marriage, activist movements turned public opinion increasingly to favor equality. This culminated in 2015 in the U.S. Supreme Court decision relying on the Fourteenth Amendment to the U.S. Constitution, *Obergefell v. Hodges*, which guaranteed equality between same-sex marriages and opposite-sex partners.

Struggles for Class Justice

The labor movement is central to class-based social movements because labor unions clearly represent those engaged in wage labor as opposed to those representing the class that gains profit from workers. Unionization in the United States peaked in the 1950s with over 35 percent of workers in unions (Sustar, 2004). According to the U.S. Bureau of Labor, by 1983 the percentage of U.S. workers in unions was down to 20 percent and declined to 10.5 percent in 2018 (see U.S. Bureau of Labor, 2019). Movements for class justice have been in decline for some time. And recurring statistics cite a correlation between a decline of unionization and rising income inequality. Statistics have shown a sharp and continuous increase in income inequality between the rich and poor in the last 30 years (Inequality.org, 2019c). "America's top 10% now average more than nine times as much income as the bottom 90% . . . the top 1% . . . average over 40 time more income than the bottom 90% . . . the top .1% . . . over 198 times the income of the bottom 90%," and real wage increases (after calculating for inflation) over the last twenty years have not witnessed significant increases in purchasing power. There are many reasons for the decline of unionization that range from more effective strategies by corporations, more conservative courts, globalization, an increase in "right to work laws" (against compulsory payment of union dues), and the changing nature of the workforce. In 2018, by way of a conservative bloc of justices ruling 5-4, the U.S. Supreme Court in *Janus v. American Federation of State, County and Municipal Employees, Council 31* stated that public sector workers are no longer required to pay union dues. The impact on unionization remains to be seen. The bureaucratic structure of labor unions and their reliance on the Democratic Party for progress are also central to this decline.

The U.S. labor movement was born in the late 1800s in response to the draconian working conditions and poverty wages of workers that accompanied the vast profits for the industrialists of that time. The eight-hour day, the weekend, safety improvements, and limits on child labor were among the demands and wins of that era. Montgomery (1987), however, documented the fall of the labor movement. This decline was in great part due to the alignment of labor bureaucrats (those working exclusively for the union and removed from the working conditions of the dues payers) with industrial managers to control wages and labor actions during World War I. This coalition continued through the Great Depression and was only reversed during new labor uprisings during the 1930s.

Dobbs (2002) documented the struggle of teamsters in Minneapolis, Minnesota, to gain decent contracts. As his text makes clear, this struggle was not merely against the employers, but was also against the union itself. "The AFL officialdom grew into a complacent bureaucracy enjoying high salaries and lavish expense accounts" (Dobbs, 2002, 35). Because of this distance from the workers they were presumed to represent, the union officials accepted wage cuts on behalf of the workers in 1930. By 1933 the union members were ready to fight back regardless of the desires of the officials. The result was city-wide strikes with cooperation between unions against the wishes of the union bureaucracy and the coalition of employers known as the Citizens Alliance. The success of the teamsters in rebuilding their unions in a democratic fashion, with union members representing union members, gave new strength to the movement, which reached its peak in the 1950s.

Because of the low level of unionization and the return of bureaucratic control within the existing unions, labor struggles are currently relatively rare. However, a few struggles have broken out that exemplify the problems in this movement. Chicago is a stronghold of the Democratic Party with a Democratic mayor. Given the continued support of unions for Democratic politicians, one might expect that Chicago would be home to a strong and successful labor movement. This is not the case.

Both of the authors of this text were on strike in the fall of 2004 responding to many of the problems facing the union movement. To illustrate these in an immediate fashion, we will offer an overview of this struggle. The university, at which we both worked, Northeastern Illinois University (NEIU), is located in the city of Chicago. City workers in Chicago had been without a contract for over a year when faculty and staff at the city colleges went out on strike in October 2004. While this strike did not directly affect the strike at our university, it offered insight into things to come.

The members of the faculty/staff union at NEIU had been disappointed by raises that had failed to keep up with the cost of living, increasing workloads, and concerns for health care costs. Most of the faculty had never participated in a faculty strike. This certainly led to various degrees of anxiety and to escalation of conflicts, particularly within the membership. Like the teamsters of 1933, the first battle in this struggle was against segments of the union bureaucracy that were uninterested in and unprepared for a real fight back. Perhaps it was partly due to the fact that most had not themselves participated in a faculty strike. The membership actively organized itself beginning with democratically run meetings and requests for feedback from the membership. Once the broader membership realized that they were having an impact on the direction of the union, more people became involved and the movement for a decent contract strengthened.

Apart from the challenge directed toward the university, there were also internal differences. There were questions raised about the relationship between union members and the executive board and the relationship of the campus union chapter and its statewide union local, umbrella organization that collects dues and is intended to represent campus unions in statewide matters and to support organizing on campuses. Allowing members to communicate back to the bureaucracy proved more difficult because segments of the union bureaucracy and the statewide local were not always attentive to the voices of the membership or misconstrued their intent.

There were internal issues concerning delays in beginning the strike, even though the membership had overwhelmingly voted for the strike— necessary procedural issues notwithstanding. There were also allegations of divisive tactics along political lines, and allegations of race and gender bias. The local for our campus union had no provision for a strike or any meaningful strike fund. This left the membership in the position of surviving without paychecks, outside of provisions for no-interest loans, for the three and a half weeks we were on strike.

Several months later, the local regrettably did not exert their influence in the then-Democratic governor's proposal to use state university retirement money to bail out the state budget. Only after the fact did they argue that they were outmaneuvered. This has put the retirement funds in some jeopardy.

Overcoming these internal obstacles was a distraction from the struggle against an administration that attempted to cut off health care benefits and illegally threatened to deport faculty without U.S. citizenship who honored the strike. The organization of our strike lines with strike captains enabled us to continuously communicate information to members on the lines.

The university administration seemed caught off guard with the strike and resorted to bringing in a high-powered outside attorney for negotiations. This, however, escalated the conflict. Ultimately, Alderman Ed Meese was asked to act as mediator and was able to broker a settlement. However, the favorable settlement was due to the perseverance of the union members on the strike lines. We ultimately prevailed in the strike. In retrospect, given our annual dues money ($500 to $1,000), some members raised voices as to the need of better preparation and more sensitivity to voices from below. The union received no support from the Democratic mayor or then governor, both of whom had received generous support from various unions funded by member dues.

There were a number of noteworthy efforts to reconcile internal differences. These initiatives arose spontaneously from the membership. On a theoretical level, this brings out the internal dialectics of struggle. This experience has been an important lesson for our campus membership and should ultimately serve to inform future struggles. The faculty has grown in confidence in its voice and willingness to express it.

In 2012, the Chicago Teacher's Union (CTU), American Federation of Teachers Local One went out on strike led by Karen Lewis who had been elected president of the union on a platform to break from bureaucratic unionism. She was supported by a group of teachers known as CORE (Caucus of Rank and file Educators) a grassroots group of young educators seeking to gain social justice within their union and schools. The strike was for teacher pay and control over curriculum to counter high-stakes testing. CTU won gains in the strike, but many were concerned about the announcement of a settlement prior to a vote on the agreement by teachers. After contentious meetings, the teachers did approve the settlement (conversations between LC and CTU activists).

In 2018 and 2019 teacher strikes broke out across the United States. Even in right- to-work states (West Virginia and Oklahoma) teachers risked their careers and took to picket lines to support their colleagues and their students. The West Virginia teachers are credited with starting a wave of teacher strikes, and have shown the necessary tenacity for assuring that the gains they won in their nine-day strike were not undone (Strauss, 2019). When the West Virginia legislature attempted to violate some of the gains won in the strike through authorizing charter schools, the teachers closed the schools again and went back on strike to demand a withdrawal of the legislation (Fernández Campbell, 2019). They won that battle in only hours. The West Virginia teachers' struggle grew from a grassroots organizing effort with no pushback from the Democratic Party, as is often the case in cities/states with a strong Democratic Party presence. For example, the Oakland teachers, while making some gains in their 2019 strike, like the CTU heard that they had a tentative agreement from a public statement from the union leadership rather than in a rank-and-file meeting to review the offer. Harrington (2019) covered the Oakland school board's decision to cut millions of dollars and 100 jobs and even the district's restorative justice program only one day after the teachers voted to end the strike. Unlike West Virginia where the union is not beholden to any political party, the Oakland teachers did not walk out to defend their schools in the face of these cuts. While there are likely other factors, it is notable that where one would expect strong support for labor and education, in Democratic Party–controlled cities/states, this is not often the case.

Beyond direct actions by union members, some have attempted coalitions with consumers in the form of boycotts. Barger and Reza (1994) illustrate one of the problems of this strategy, failure to participate. As they report, a survey in California indicated that 74 percent of respondents had a favorable view of the United Farm Workers and 85 percent supported the goals of improving the working conditions of farm laborers. However, over 57 percent supported the idea of a boycott and only 22 percent had participated in a boycott (50). Unlike a direct labor action where the workers themselves are responsible to and for the action, consumers are not directly affected by their participation or lack thereof.

Frank (2003) offers a review of the history of consumer-labor campaigns, suggesting that transitioning the core of activism out of the hands of labor and into the hands of consumers is problematic for many reasons. Among these is the demobilization and disempowerment of workers in deference to the consumer market. This does not suggest that support by outsiders is not important and welcomed. While on strike at NEIU, we (the membership, not the bureaucrats) welcomed students onto our strike lines and welcomed their solidarity in not crossing our picket lines. The difference here is that we the union were acting on our own behalf and welcoming support from the outside. To turn that around and expect supporters on the outside to take the actions necessary to win your struggle is doubly problematic. As Barger and Reza (1994) report, even those supportive of the issues will not necessarily act and more importantly, as Frank (2003) shows, leaving one's interests in the hands of an unknown shopper disempowers the movement. It is only through direct action that labor activists, like other activists, can develop their own way forward. Democratic decisions made by the workers themselves, not by bureaucrats who have little understanding of and even less investment in the struggle, will inform the correct direction of the struggle.

Two examples of worker's mobilization of struggle for more genuine justice are the Living Wage Movement and Occupy Wall Street (OWS). The Living Wage Movement, initiated in 1994, seeks changes in wage scales for a living wage that assures economic well-being (see ACORN Living Wage Resource Center; Eitzen and Stewart, 2007). Social justice movements, often broadly constituted, push for pay increases that assure workers at least a minimum living wage. Public education campaigns, research, and action in high-poverty areas are central.

Occupy Wall Street is a movement that began in 2011 in Zuccotti Park in the Wall Street area of New York City and was opposed to the immense, unjust wealth accumulated by the top one percent of the population (see their Website, Occupy Wall Street). Their home webpage spells out their focus: "Occupy Wall Street is a leaderless resistance movement with people of many colors, genders and political persuasions. The one thing we all have in common is that We Are The 99% that will no longer tolerate the greed and corruption of the 1%. We are using the revolutionary Arab Spring tactic to achieve our ends and encourage the use of nonviolence to maximize the safety of all participants." OWS quickly spread across the United States and many countries of the world. They stressed a unique leaderless form of organization that formed the basis of uprisings for social justice. However, some, including one of its cofounders, Micah White, are now questioning its efficacy given its many disappointments including the election of Donald Trump as president of the United States. White identified four problems with OWS: lack of a vetting procedure for new adherents, limited abilities to counter reactionary forces, difficulty for members to come to an agreement on establishing demands, and using old tactics. White (2016, 183–206) argues that regardless of the many frustrations, new forms of social movements are on the horizon, including rural revolts, digital populist, computer-assisted revolutions, and world parties utilizing guidance by the justice principle of mutual aid.

New Struggles, the "Fourth Model": Affirmative Nomadology, Innocence Projects, and Intentional Communities as Nonlinear Social Movements

Dynamic systems theory has been the basis of a possible alternative social justice movement. Holland (2011), for example, building on the more implicit chaos theory of Deleuze and Guattari, has presented an affirmative nomadology model and advocates a new identity category, nomad citizenship (see also chapter 9). Nomadology rejects the linear Cartesian model highly prevalent in conventional thought, and argues that we are ever in search of higher forms brought about by continuous differentiation. These new forms are dissipative structures, more open to even the very smallest of inputs that will produce disproportional effects, transforming a previous structure to an entirely different dissipative structure. These are emergent and cannot be predicted in advance. So, vigilance must always exist for both the progressive and regressive possibilities of social change. His model follows the metaphor of radical jazz as opposed to classical music. Accordingly, organizations are leaderless, such as in Occupy Wall Street and in many interactive websites such as Wikipedia, Kuro5hin, and the open-source operating system Linux. Mary Parker Follet's (1998) organizational model, which argues for multiple citizenship, provides a prototype for Holland. Instead of capitalist marketplaces, he advocates the development of nomad markets: "self-organizing systems of distributed intelligence and collective decision making" (103), building further on the metaphor of improvisational jazz music and cultivating the ethos of "personal desires and price information but information regarding products circumstances of production, condition of distribution, environmental impact, and so on" (109). For Holland, "the result of the aggregation mechanism of the market would then be more than mere efficiency: it would be an aggregated version of the Common Good" (109) similar to the leaderless organizations cited above. This would be a further cultivation of a "slow motion general strike" and further the emergent of a new identity category, "global citizenship" (154). Let's provide one early model, the "fourth model" of social movements," that follows the logic of affirmative nomadology developed by Robert Schehr and Bruce Arrigo.

Schehr has developed a fourth model of social movements that relies on dynamic systems theory (chaos theory) and builds on its predecessor, the new social movement paradigm (NSM, and sometimes referred to as the identity paradigm). It has been applied to innocence projects and intentional communities (Schehr, 1997, 1999b; Arrigo and Schehr, 1998; Arrigo, et al. 2005, chap. 8). Schehr places priority on subaltern modes of resistance, explaining how otherwise silenced voices redefine oppressive practices, be they seemingly small. These inputs, consistent with chaos theory, have disproportional effects on social systems (the butterfly effect). His conceptual framework, distinguishable from earlier models of social movements, borrows heavily from the concepts of dynamic systems theory (for an introduction, see Milovanovic, 1997, 2003). In late capitalism we cannot have long-term homogeneous opposition groupings but instead require a "plurality of antagonisms' (Laclau and Mouffe, 1985). That is, conflicts cut across class, gender, race, and other issues. There are, at best, provisional organizations and alliances, organized around particular issues.

Among other concepts assimilated from chaos theory, Schehr uses the idea of nonlinearity, disproportional effects, attractors, and dissipative structures (see Young 1997a, 1997b, 1999; Milovanovic, 1997a). This framework has been applied to innocence projects—organizations that sprouted in the late 1990s that advocate for inmates, mostly minority, convicted of capital offenses by evidence that was questionable or by procedures that minimized a full day in court. This framework has also been applied to intentional communities.

Innocence projects are concerned with wrongful convictions and strive toward obtaining exonerations. Schehr (1999b; see also Arrigo et al., 2005) argues that these projects do not necessarily follow spelled-out formal law and look elsewhere for counter evidence (nonlinearity). They seek to show

how particular evidence may have disproportional effects in rendering guilt when connected with racist stereotypes (disproportionality); how new outcome basins (possible solutions) emerge for the basis of alternative theorizing of what happened (attractors); and how emerging implications and conclusions in law follow spontaneously in these alternatively created frameworks (dissipative structures).

Schehr has applied this fourth way to intentional communities, identified as communities in struggle for social change, that are pluralistically oriented, nonhierarchical in organization, innovative in strategies, sensitive to differences rather than sameness, and that take on a more holistic orientation to problem-solving (Schehr, 1997, 1999a; Arrigo and Schehr, 1998, 126; see also the Wikipedia page "List of Intentional Communities" [Wikipedia.org, 2019b]). Arrigo (1997) has applied the fourth way to how residents of a single-room occupancy facility organized around principles of nonlinear logic as an alternative strategy to house the homeless. For example, according to Arrigo's field research, resolution of conflict situations often entailed attractors (a more fuzzy logic was employed in determining what happened that did not follow rigid bureaucratic lines) and dissipative structures (new ideas were constantly emerging in response to changing demands of the housing facility). In short, "nonconventional social arrangements materialized: persons with psychiatric disorders were elected floor representatives; drug-use was situationally accepted and legitimized to the extent that one's routine interactions and ongoing responsibilities did not result in total disintegration; and a loose, evolving, and flexible confederation of rules and procedures informed resident decision making in the community" (Arrigo et al., 2005, 128).

The affirmative nomadology approach and derivatives such as the fourth way in social movement research suggests the development of more spontaneous notions of justice in context. It is a call for "nonlinear justice systems" (Young 1999, 278). Concepts of justice are emergents arising in far-from-equilibrium conditions. They recognize flux, uncertainty, change, becoming, multiplicity, indeterminacy, instabilities, irony, discovery, and surprise. These emerging principles of justice have compatibilities with what Judith Butler (1996) theorized as contingent universalities as a basis of generating political agendas for social change and for social justice. These emergents provide a temporary basis of order (i.e., political agendas). They are not universals. They are neither essentialist nor anti-essentialist conceptualizations. Notions of social justice—reflecting various articulations of need, desert, and equality—will always be in flux, always subject to reflection, augmentation, qualification, specification, deletion, and even replacement with a more responsive concept of social justice in context. They are ever contingent. There is no grand narrative that can encompass all of their nuances. There is no one justice that will incorporate all the dimensions of struggle, becoming, and the development of a good society. A notion of ethics sustaining the developed concepts of social justice in context is needed.

LESSONS FROM JUSTICE STRUGGLES

The history of social movements in the United States provides many lessons for the current state of justice and for improving this state should it be found lacking. While we were unable to provide an extensive history here, we encourage further exploration into this history with attention to the organization, goals, and contradictions of the various struggles. Those who have organized themselves in keeping with the goals of justice have succeeded if not in every one of their goals then at least in the development of activists that will carry on the next struggle.

Equality in the form of democratic debate and decision-making within movements is primary for the continued success of that movement just as equality is primary to justice. When people engage directly in social movements they do so because they have come to realize that the legal and political structure that espouses justice without delivering it must be confronted. In this confrontation, organized movements can deliver their own justice. Resisting the temptation to await a savior is essential to this confrontation. Ella Baker warned in 1947: "The negro must quit looking for a savior, and work to save himself" (Ransby, 2003, 170). Then she offered the way forward in 1967: "One of the major emphases of SNCC, from the beginning, was that of working with indigenous people, not working for them, but trying to develop their capacity for leadership" (Ransby, 2004, 273). The development of those suffering injustice through our struggles for self-emancipation has and will continue to bring greater fulfillment of more genuine principles of equality, needs, and deserts.

REVIEW QUESTIONS

1. "Astroturfing" is sometimes used to usurp grassroots movements. How do we know if a particular movement's goals are indigenously developed or have been co-opted because of corporate media interests?

2. We described four general types of social movements. Provide two examples for each type. Be prepared to defend why they belong in the type chosen to a small group or to your class.

3. Entrenched powers, it has been said, often spin out the ideology of "you cannot change human nature." How effective has it been? Consider a time when you used this phrase. Why did you use it? Did it answer the issue at hand?

4. The thesis of black genocide has been developed in the literature with statistical support (a case too could be made with the American

Indians). What does this tell you about the American sociopolitical economy? Race relations? Institutional beliefs?

5. "Dreamers," it has been argued, suffer a full range of injustices. Many schools have offered "safe zones." What other strategies could be mobilized by concerned people?

6. Does the proliferation of sexual preference identities produce more recognition or does it produce counter results (dialectics of struggle)?

7. Describe a situation where you were the subject of regressive "political correctness." How did you feel? How did you respond?

8. Affirmative nomadology is presented as an alternative basis for movement politics and organization. Research the Web and identify a grassroots organization that is struggling for social justice and appears to be using affirmative nomadology. (Do not use any examples from the chapter.) Explain how the affirmative nomadology is being employed.

9. Research the Web for an activist group seeking social justice. Outline and bring to class a summary of its purpose, target group, composition, and the advocated principle(s) of justice (need? equality? recognition? merit? redistribution? capabilities?).

CHAPTER 12

Emerging Conceptions of Justice
in a Global Arena

THE CIVIL RIGHTS and other movements within the United States are examples of progressive moves toward social justice. Other nations have experienced even broader movements, which brought greater justice in some ways and problematic outcomes in others. We will focus on a few in diverse locations to offer insight into the justice motives and varied outcomes of these actions worldwide. It is intended that these examples will offer insight into the process of these historical times, the progress attained, and the lessons offered. Many books have been written and are available to offer more complete descriptions of these points in history, and we encourage the reader to consult these works.

SOUTH AFRICA: TRUTH AND JUSTICE?

The history of South Africa is very much the history of countries throughout the continent of Africa. While it is now one country, it is a large geographical area of diverse terrain and inhabitants. As Ross (1999) describes, the people of the region, not yet one country, were divided by space, economic interests, political interests, and other realities as European colonization of the region began. The economic interests of Europe through this colonization quickly set the pattern for what would become the country of South Africa. Local politics were contained through the interests of local political elites in the economic success of European colonial enterprises (Ross, 1999; see also Norval, 1996).

While resistance to slavery and other European savageries continued among the population, the complicity of local power holders assured the continued influence of European ideas and norms, including Christianity, educational structures, rigid sexual divisions of labor and domesticity, and the social, political, and economic dominance of Europeans. This dominance was attained within the four colonies unified in 1911 to form what is the current nation of South Africa. Soon after unification, laws for segregation (apartheid) were devised and implemented to maintain the dominance of the white minority over the majority nonwhites of the country (Ross, 1999).

Resistance was immediate with women struggling against apartheid directly in the rural areas, demonstrating in the streets of the towns in warrior dress, and more placidly within the confines of the co-opted churches through prayer. These struggles were limited in success partly due to the power of the opposing state and partly due to the divided demands of the women. The men went on strike in the mines and were quickly smashed, directly by state intervention and indirectly by new legal constraints imposed to protect mine owners' profits (Ross, 1999; Moodie, 2002).

By the 1940s, the white nationalist government was becoming more reactionary, taking on many of the characteristics of the defeated German ideology. At the same time, the people of South Africa were also radicalizing in their ideas about the possibilities for change. These developments were largely untapped by the African National Congress (ANC) and other organized parties and resulted in uprisings in the absence (though at times claimed presence) of the ANC. These movements were mostly independent and localized throughout the 1950s. In the 1960s, the ANC and Pan African Congress (PAC) clashed in their attempts to gain power and reforms from the white-run government. Meanwhile, oppression and injustice for the black majority escalated as the elite became emboldened to increase state control on the daily lives of black South Africans (and whites who opposed apartheid). Among these oppressions was the establishment of homelands for the seven ethnic identities imposed onto the nonwhite population. These homelands were highly fragmented, of little recorded historic significance, and without basic services. By the end of the 1960s the ANC and PAC were defeated, ending organized resistance on any large scale for some time. In the early 1970s, however, students and workers began their own form of resistance. Student movements mainly focused on black consciousness, and workers' movements resulting in large strikes put forward complementary struggles that ultimately would become the beginning of the end of apartheid (Ross, 1999; see also Norval, 1996).

Also driving the end of apartheid were the economic changes that were becoming more evident within South African society. Although famine and unpredictable food supplies had been all but eliminated by the commercialization of agriculture, so too had the ability of the rural population to sustain themselves on the land. Immigration (illegal in most cases under apartheid) into the cities set the stage for the exposure of the contradictions of capitalism in one of its most racist expressions. Because there was now plenty to eat did not mean that there was no hunger. Poverty and need were clearly tied to economic status and in the case of South Africa almost directly with race. The crowding of the rural poor into the highly stratified cities only intensified these contradictions and their productions of violence both within and against poor black areas of the cities (Ross, 1999).

The United States and other nations had recently experienced civil rights movements and were less able to accept the conditions of blacks in South Africa as they had done in the past. Pressures were mounting within and without South Africa for change. The political instabilities within the country lead to divestment by larger banking interests and to greater economic instability. This translated to greater political instability as the misery of those at the bottom of the economic structure intensified. In the late 1980s, trade unionism increased as the unemployed were organized and coordinated gold mine strikes called. Although these strikes did not win, they did build the solidarity and assert the power of unionized labor. Further, Angola defeated the South African army and forced compliance with the U.N. resolution for Namibian independence. These developments greatly improved the strength of the ANC, which was supported by unions and the governments of Angola and Namibia. Under intense pressures, newly elected President F. W. de Klerk lifted the ban on dissident political parties, including the ANC, the South African Communist Party, and the PAC, and released many prisoners being held for their political activities (Ross, 1999).

Negotiations took place in an agitated context. Those representing the white elite desired a pace to be measured in geologic time of little if any real change. Nelson Mandela, representing the ANC, but not necessarily all of anti-apartheid South Africa, desired timely change. Conflicts existed between pro- and anti-apartheid groups and between various factions of each. Within the pro-apartheid end of the spectrum were over twenty groups of various ideological stances; some saw no need to justify their racism while others couched their racism in terms of Christian ideology and/or a desire to protect their birthrights as whites. Sometimes violent in nature, protests and strikes continued throughout the country as talks between de Klerk's representatives and Mandela protracted. Violence was by no means one sided in this conflict. It was, however, most severe when supported by the National Party and their well-armed and well-funded military force (Sparks, 1996).

Activists were essential to keeping the negotiations moving forward. It was in the interest of the white elite to drag the process out as long as possible and within the norm for Mandela to acquiesce to that process. Street protests, strikes, and other activities supported Mandela in the negotiations and the demands of the people beyond those of Mandela. Without these protests, negotiations would have no doubt gone on much longer and produced fewer progressive reforms. Extended negotiations would have doubtless resulted in even further bloodshed as the National Party and its various pro-apartheid supporters attempted to maintain dominance by all means at their disposal. Great gains were made when negotiations ended and the old government was put down. Blacks had won full citizenship in their country, which allowed for equal voting rights and the ultimate election of Mandela as president (Sparks, 1996).

Truth and Reconciliation Commission

As progressive as these changes were, social justice has still not attained an ideal level in South Africa. The Truth and Reconciliation Commission (TRC) and ongoing inequalities illustrate justice limits. Newman (2005) reviews three rationales that have been provided in the literature for TRCs. First, it provides an opportunity for forgiveness and reconciliation, whereas pursuing criminal prosecution would undermine the movement toward peace. Second, it is a necessary transitional step toward peace, since otherwise entrenched offenders would resist change. Third, it might be impossible to pursue prosecution, given the sheer magnitude of offenders, and thus it would be hugely costly and time and resource consuming. "There are undoubtedly times when countries may have to sacrifice legal principles in the name of political pragmatism, in order to end war or achieve peace" (Simpson cited in Newman, 2005, 309).

The most noted spokesperson for the TRC, its first chairperson, Desmond Tutu (2000), was to argue for a third way, a journey toward healing and peace, restorative justice rather than retributive justice (see also commentary by Bassiouni, 2002; Hayner, 2002; Newman, 2005; and Teitel, 2002). Teitel (2002; see also Elster, 2004) explores the possibility of "transitional justice" (referred to as "post-conflict justice" by Bassiouni, 2002) during regime changes as offering a moment for balancing various short- and long-range interests toward peace and justice. According to Elster (2004, 1), "transitional justice is made up of the process of trials, purges and reparations that take place after the transition from one political regime to another." There has been much commentary on truth and reconciliation commissions. Many have noted the relatively peaceful nature of the transition in South Africa benefited by the TRC. More recent literature has been more critical, indicating the more difficult balance between establishing peace *and* justice (the conflict between finding historical truth, procuring healing, and establishing peace versus prosecuting offenders and establishing justice for the victims, see Simpson, 2002; Newman, 2005).

Van Zyl (1999) concludes that the pact to keep the final report on the agreement between apartheid and post-apartheid rulers from public view was evidence of the success of the TRC. One could just as easily argue that keeping the public in the dark was evidence of the failure of the TRC. Nagy (2002) illustrates the limits of the TRC project in her analysis of the relationship between apology and forgiveness. She points out the weak nature of much apology that is performed with the expectation of nonprosecution of war crimes. This itself is highly problematic and points to a lack of real acceptance for responsibility, allowing further diminishing of the oppressed population. At the same time, great pressures from new leaders informed by Christian tradition persuade many to forgive while true apology, understanding, and remedy were lacking. While the direct perpetrators seek release through apology and the violated forgive without true recognition of the wrongs done, many throughout South Africa have become impatient with the process to such an extent as to vocalize impatience with the complaints of those seeking redress (Nagy, 2002).

This characterization by onlookers exposes the lack of progress made through the TRC. Telling real and complete truths of the atrocities would inform those interested in social justice of the harms inflicted and the requirements of redress. Because the truths, in many cases, were not told, support for justice has eroded and attaining reconciliation is dubious. Without knowledge of the intensity and depth of harms done, justice attainment is severely curtailed.

Wilson (2000) acknowledges the flexible nature of the TRC and the promise of such an exercise in justice to reflect local understandings of and desires for justice. This promise is not a small one and should be seriously considered and analyzed in light of the realities of the situations to which it is applied. These situations are always held within contexts wider than the individuals involved. Wilson further elaborates that because of the entrenched history of apartheid, the interests of elite blacks with bureaucratic positions and property to defend, and the advanced capitalist economic structure in place in South Africa, the TRC is necessarily limited in its ability to bring justice. James (2000) notes the commonalities in apartheid era black-and-white structures that further limit successes based on local norms and customs. As she notes, capitalistic ideas did not only inform the structure of apartheid and the ideas of the elite in that system but also affected the structures and ideas of the oppressed. Those oppressed under apartheid would find it hard to escape the racist, sexist, or elitist ideas and structures imposed on them. These ideas were useful to the elite in controlling those oppressed but were not always analyzed or understood in this way and therefore uncritically permeated the lives of the oppressed. Overthrowing the oppression of racism, sexism, and elite dominance of the economy will require more than the end of apartheid.

Nagy (2012) reported that white settlers in South Africa as well as Canada are only interested in reconciliation that maintains the status quo. This is an impossible barrier for entering into reconciliation toward justice. Further, as South Africa emerged from apartheid, the world economy was entering an intense phase of neoliberalism. The focus of nations was on increasing investments and privatizing public goods. This context is important in understanding the continual failure of reparations schemes. Attempts to require that corporate and other moneyed interests pay restitution to South Africa's black population have failed as the TRC has instead focused on symbolic and spiritual reparations. Instead of including communities in discussions of their needs, post-apartheid discussions of reparations have taken place behind closed doors including only business interests (Norris, 2017).

Nagy (2002) contends that the biggest barrier to reconciliation is the continuing inequalities that require economic reparation and redistribution for redress. As she notes, truth and apology are hollow and do little to address justice without substantial material indemnification. A more genuine justice and democracy require an end to racism, inequalities, and poverty. Aiken (2016) found that the failure of the TRC to focus on broad social justice issues and instead focus on individual cases, the lack of reparations, and the stark socioeconomic inequalities between black and white South Africans have prevented reconciliation. The South African legislature approved a report that calls for a constitutional amendment to allow for land expropriation. Land is one of the many resources held mainly by the white minority in South Africa. It is hoped that through a redistribution of this land, some equity will be achieved. However, the white minority will fight any expropriation of land that they currently own (Aljazeera.com, 2018). Justice will require further progress. In South Africa, as elsewhere, this progress has historically come in the form of collective social action.

Restorative Justice?

Truth and reconciliation commissions have some similarities to restorative justice programs. In both, notions of social justice move away from retributive to restorative principles. However, restorative justice that is practiced with individuals is more likely to consider the victim's side in deliberations than in truth and reconciliation, and there is more concern with recompense—some tangible step toward making things right beyond apology. We have seen practices of reparations. This form of restorative justice would also be a distributive principle—retroactively correcting for unfair distributions of burdens and rewards. We have also witnessed the notion of sustainable economies and forms of justices compatible with environmental justice that is connected with it. Bassiouni (2002, 3) has called for a "post-conflict justice," a "sustainable justice," which is characterized as "a level of domestic justice compatible with the building and maintenance of a viable state legal system." These forms of transitional justice are nonstatic conceptualizations, historically specific, and subject to constant reflection and change. In addition, we have come across indigenous forms of justice that are highly nuanced, historically and culturally specific, and often unwritten.

What we are witnessing are novel articulations of principles of social justice that go beyond traditional retributive principles. An examination of truth and reconciliation commissions in practice offers opportunities for more sensitive understanding of the often conflictual relationship between punishment and forgiveness, and universal standards of social justice versus culturally and historically contextually specific developments and applications. Future uses of these commissions will require that reparations not be individual, but social and encompassing of all harm and violence perpetrated, not only the immediate. In this case, reparation may allow for a genuine reconciliation honoring all.

STRUGGLES IN THE MIDDLE EAST

We have chosen to look at struggles within the region of the Middle East because this is an area of intense ongoing conflict and debate. Historical and ongoing struggles in the Middle East are not necessarily centered on or inspired by Islamic tendencies. Islam, like Christianity, Judaism, and other religions, is a faith with a long and noble history. As with other religious tendencies, when the most conservative and retrogressive elements take the forefront against more progressive tendencies within the same tradition, struggles can become distorted and move away from justice. Therefore, when we examine the imposition of religious faiths upon social movements, it is with attention to justice. Religious initiatives can and have fought for justice, and they can and have fought for or condoned injustice. Here we do not, because it would be incorrect to do so, favor or disfavor any religious belief or tradition. We do critically examine movements containing various levels of religious identity or character for their impact on justice.

Iran: Islamic Revolution and National Independence

The Iranian Revolution of 1979 was greatly affected by a conservative Islamic reaction that came to power in the vacuum of a well-organized alternative. The revolution itself was not entirely Islamic in character but resulted in an Islamic state. Understanding just how this could happen requires a brief look at recent Iranian history.

The need for a revolution in Iran can be directly connected to the U.S.-backed and British-born coup in 1953, which installed Mohammed Reza Shah to rule Iran in place of the democratically elected Prime Minister Mohammad Mossadegh. The British had commercial interests in Iran dating back to the 1890s when Nasir al-Din Shah privatized much of Iran's wealth and resources into the hands of British corporations at a pace that would make current transnational companies blush green with envy. The deals were especially profitable to Baron Julius de Reuter, of newspaper fame, but German, French, and Austrian companies were quick to make their own deals (Kinzer, 2003).

The people of Iran campaigned for reform of their government and independence from foreign investors. While some reforms were won, the British and Russians divided their interests and the nation of Iran north and south and declared their supremacy in each section. The Russian Revolution of 1917 led the Bolsheviks to renounce Russian interests in Iran and forgive all debts outstanding to the czar. When the Bolsheviks lost control to Stalin, the Soviet Union reoccupied northern Iran. The British intensified their control of the Iranian economy by imposing the Anglo-Persian Agreement on the ineffective Ahmed Shah to protect their vast and highly profitable oil interests. The British stronghold in Iran continued through the 1940s, when Mohammed Reza Shah hardened his own brutal control with political oppression and corruption in an attempt to maintain power in the face of increasing pressures from workers and activists. British oil interests and the Shah were profiting handsomely from their arrangements. However, most Iranians were suffering declines in their standard of living, and oil workers were laboring under harsh conditions and receiving very low wages (Kinzer, 2003).

After the assassination of Prime Minister Razmara in March 1951, the Majlis, elected representatives of the people, voted for the principle of nationalization of oil. Mohammad Reza Shah did this reluctantly by establishing the National Iranian Oil Company on May 1, 1951. Five days later, the Majlis approved Mossadegh as Prime Minister of Iran. Mossadegh's leadership was a turn toward justice as the people of Iran were almost immediately able to freely speak their frustrations with the past. A radio broadcaster referring here to the oil company when controlled by the British stated, "All of Iran's misery wretchedness, lawlessness and corruption during the last fifty years, has been caused by oil and the extortions of the oil company" (Kinzer, 2003, 91).

The British oil interests, of course were looking to force Mossadegh back into their one-sided agreement. The British press denounced Mossadegh as a fanatic and supported the British oil interests. In Iran, documents verifying the oil company's interference with the Iranian government were made public. The United Nations International Court of Justice recommended that Iran allow the British oil company to resume operations, and the threat of military intervention from the British was constant. Also constant was the economic devastation caused by the embargo placed on oil technicians into Iran to help run the now nationalized oil company. Because the British had always held these jobs, keeping Iranians in less-skilled jobs, few Iranians had the expertise necessary to fully run the oil apparatus. Fearing reaction from the United Kingdom, other nations with available technicians refused their exit to Iran (Kinzer, 2003).

Mossadegh proved a popular and persuasive speaker, keeping the British oil company at bay in the world courts and winning the support of people around the globe. No significant movement occurred in this battle for Iranian independence until Prime Minister Churchill of the United Kingdom and President Eisenhower of the United States agreed to use the newly minted U.S. Central Intelligence Agency (CIA) to overthrow Mossadegh (Kinzer, 2003).

Mossadegh, who was not only a democratically elected leader but also very popular, served the interests of the citizens of Iran in the face of growing pressure. His overthrow orchestrated by U.S. and British interests was a great injustice. This injustice was against the will of the people of Iran in their election and support of Mossadegh. It was also an injustice against the will of the people to control their natural resource, oil, and use it in their own interests rather than to enrich foreign elites. Further, it was an injustice in the re-establishment of Mohammed Reza Shah's rule over Iran. The Shah, unlike Mossadegh, had long ruled against the interests of the majority of Iranians and against justice. New movements would be required to reassert the rule of the people.

While Kinzer (2003) argues that the coup of 1953 was the precipitator of Middle East terrorism, there are other ways to interpret this history. Many current U.S. politicians claim a wish to bring democracy to the Middle East as their motive for ongoing military operations. This seems unlikely given the history of U.S. interventions and interests in the region. We prefer to present some of the movements on the ground in Iran so that the struggles for democracy by Iranians might be understood. It is certain that the people of any nation must develop democracy in their own interests. Democracy cannot be imposed or imported.

Mottahedeh (1986, 384) describes the vision of leftist intellectuals of the revolution as "a riddle wrapped in a mystery inside an enigma." Poya (1987) refers to the confusion of the left following the ouster of the Shah. She describes the many progressive projustice slogans used during this period. These included slogans against imperialism and the United States and for workers' rights, equal pay for men and women, education for children, an end to child labor, for the rights of peasants and the unemployed, and for free speech and presses. These activists apparently made some critical tactical errors following the revolution. Among these was a failure to confront the fundamentalists calling for an Islamic regime. Also problematic was the lack of organization and cohesion between the various progressive groups. Rather than joining around their common demands, splits were allowed to widen, limiting any joint efforts. For example, the Mujahedin, who espoused both Islam and socialist ideology, did not join the worker's rally on the May Day following the victory against the Shah for fear of appearing in opposition to the conservative Islamicists (Poya, 1987). The Mojahedin (MEK or PMOI, Mojahedin-e Khalq), however, remained opposed to the Khomeini Islamic State (Abrahamian, 1989; Cohen, 2009).

While Mottahedeh (1986) argues that religion offered more inspiration to the Iranian people than did progressive politics, the outcome of the Iranian revolution is more and less complex. Khomeini did not explicitly argue for an Islamic state until after the Shah was defeated. This promise of an Islamic state gained acceptance after the mass revolutionary movements had completed their task of removing the leader imposed by U.S. and British interests. Before and after the overthrow of the Shah, Khomeini presented a strong pro-nationalist anti-imperialist front. This front was quickly exposed when Khomeini colluded with the United States in Iran-gate (Poya, 1987).

National independence was an important goal of the Iranian people. The calls for equality and women's rights and subsequent resistance to women's oppression would indicate more progressive desires among the population than Khomeini ultimately delivered. Shahidian (1997) points to the limits within the left of the revolutionary movement. These limits include an unwillingness to defend women's rights on principle instead allowing these important concerns to be subsumed under abstract arguments.

Since the 1980s, many struggles in Iran have dealt with issues of identity. However, more recent struggles, particularly beginning in 2009, have brought concerns of precarious existence to the forefront of struggles. Obućina (2015) reports on the commitments of the Islamic regime in Iran to attain social and economic equality binding the people to the regime. However, many young people in Iran, as in much of the rest of the world, are facing falling standards of living, even when they are able to attain higher education. Falling wages and inflation combine to cause precarity rather than security in their lives. OpenDemocracy (2018) finds that this precarity is a reality that unites Iranians of various identities and draws struggles to class concerns for economic security. When the Trump administration re-imposed sanctions against Iran, economic struggles intensified for many (BBC.com, 2018).

The Iranian people, like many around the world, continue in their struggle to establish a government that represents the wishes of the majority.

Looking forward, Vahabzadeh (2017) provides a variety of ideas for assuring social justice in Iran as neoliberalism intensifies around the globe. Looking back, Shahidian (1997, 37) offers an optimistic quote from an Iranian woman: "I'm glad that I participated in the movement, I'm so proud of myself. Although our effort was not entirely successful, I'm sure that better days are ahead." This woman's hopes are echoed in the ongoing struggles within Iran for more inclusive democratic engagement as the people attempt to move beyond theocratic control and toward social justice.

Palestine: Freedom Fighters or Terrorists?

The Israeli-Palestinian conflict is between the state of Israel and the people of Palestine. It is not a conflict predominantly between religions. Persons looking for justice outcomes must be clear and keep sight of these realities to avoid the often-misleading rhetoric surrounding the issues. As Said (1994) suggests, principles are of utmost importance especially when in struggle. Therefore, these strivings will be considered in light of justice principles. As mentioned earlier, it would be neither appropriate nor useful to privilege one religious tradition over the other. While many of the people involved in these conflicts have religious identities, it is their ethnic/political/state identities that are at the forefront of these conflicts. "Israel is a state. It is not a religion or a people" (Mamdani, 2005, 247).

Terrorism has been elevated to an archetypal threat through a variety of policies and schemes, such as the color-coded terror threat alerts, employed by the U.S. Department of Homeland Security and other official governmental agencies after September 11, 2001. While that day will be remembered for the terror inflicted, it has also come to represent the beginning of a new understanding of people, places, and politics, especially in the region of the Middle East. The battle for territory in the Middle East between Israel and Palestine has been active for decades but has come to the forefront of concern for a variety of reasons. Mamdani (2005) explains the parallels between the U.S. invasion of Iraq and the increased violence against Palestinians. This violence is arguably a form of terrorism just as are the suicide bombers who react to it. The sources and causes of terrorism are issues of great debate.

Osama bin Laden was the best-known "terrorist" in the world and was arguably created by the CIA of the United States. There is a long tradition of U.S. intervention throughout the Middle East, including the CIA's economic and military support of bin Laden during the cold war. At that time, it was in the interests of the United States to keep Afghanistan out of the Soviet Union. Bin Laden was essentially the same person with the same political motives utilizing similar techniques when the United States armed and supported him. The common enemy of the Soviet Union made for this alliance, which would come back to haunt the United States in the form of the trade tower bombing (Mamdani, 2005).

The longstanding strife between Israel and Palestine has been especially fierce since the United Nations in 1947 imposed itself and its plan upon the struggle (Collins and Lapierre, 1988). U.S. relations with Israel have also influenced the conflict. The institutionalization of the Israeli agenda within the U.S. media, the U.S. Department of Defense, and CIA has given legitimacy to the Israeli side of the conflict. Further, the vilification of Arabs and Muslims has delegitimized the Palestinian plight (Ahmad, 2000).

Returning to the basic justice principles of need, equality, and desert, we can locate injustices on both sides of this conflict. The individual Palestinians who bomb civilians do violate the need for safety of these persons. Some may find these bombings understandable given the limited alternatives available. These bombings are not just in a scheme of justice that includes the meeting of human need including life itself. The actions of the state of Israel are also unjust and are so in their violation of the justice principles of need, equality, and desert. Further, the resources of Israel are far greater than are those of the Palestinians, thus allowing the perpetration of greater injustices from the Israeli side of the conflict.

The state of Israel imposes third-class citizenship on the few remaining Palestinians within its borders (Ahmad, 2000, 107). This third-class citizenship requiring Palestinians to submit to numerous security checks, limiting employment possibilities, and denying access to many areas of Israel and the occupied territories exemplifies the inequalities suffered by Palestinians from the Israeli state. Ongoing bombings and shootings by Israeli soldiers, and long-term detentions of suspects, signify a barring of Palestinians from their need for life and equal citizenship. Desert is impossible without life and equality.

The horrors of the occupation are not typically exposed in mainstream Western media. However, according to Mamdani (2005), the *New York Times* gave a glimpse of the extremes of this state-sponsored terrorism when it ran an interview on February 2, 2002. The paper quoted an Israeli reservist explaining his and hundreds of other Israelis' opposition to the policies of his state as "dominating, expelling, starving and humiliating an entire people" (212). When considering the injustice of the occupation, it must be considered in light of its state sponsorship and agenda. Israelis, like Palestinians, are not of one mind. It should not be assumed that all Israelis are in agreement with the agenda or the expression of the occupation.

Lesser citizenship within the borders of Israel, the ongoing occupation of Palestinian lands, and destruction of Palestinian homes recalls the history of apartheid South Africa. While policies in South Africa were more direct in their racism against blacks, policies in Israel were directed against

Palestinians through language of security against a terrorist threat. However, Prime Minister Benjamin Netanyahu brought a more explicitly racist character to the Zionism expressed by the Israeli government (Greenstein, 2019). A collective punishment against all Palestinians is justified through a blanket assumption of terroristic motives and/or racial inferiority. When this group is vilified through culture talk equating Muslim and/or Arab politics and identity with barbarism and terrorism, few outside the Arab world are willing to defend Palestine. Those that do defend Palestine are often called anti-Semitic and sometimes punished with threats to funding and job loss (Alexander, 2019). Further, the sympathies for Israel as a homeland for a long-oppressed group pull many into alliance with or defense of Israel as an idea. This is often done without consideration for Palestinians or an understanding of the character of the Israeli state (Mamdani, 2005).

Mamdani (2005) draws parallels between the practice of "necklacing" by the South African resistance and bombings by Palestinians. As he points out, both practices are horrifying on their face but must be examined for their short- and long-term effect to understand why they continue/d. Necklacing (the practice of tying a cloth or tie around the neck of a suspected informant, soaking it with a propellant such as gasoline, and lighting it in order to gruesomely kill the suspect) in the short term had a deterring affect. The suspect killed could no longer inform on the group and any thinking lightly of becoming an informant might reconsider. This saved the lives of those within the resistance. The long-term impact made it easy for condemnation of the resistance and may have alienated potential allies. Bombings rid the occupied territory of a few occupiers. They also damage the credibility of the resistance for many.

"Give us your bombs and you can have our women's baskets" (Said, 1994, 344). The scene from the movie *The Battle for Algiers* from which the above quote was taken depicts a verbal engagement between an Algerian resister and a French military commander. As the scene and Said suggest, a well-armed state military complaining about the possibilities of bombs in women's baskets or tied to the bodies of resisters is hypocritical when that military not only has, but regularly uses, its incredible military might against this resistance.

The Israeli state utilized its army extensively against the Great March of Return that began on March 30, 2018 (Wikipedia.org, 2019d). As of this writing, the Friday protests continue as does the killing by Israeli soldiers of Palestinians in that struggle. The United Nations Human Rights Council (2019) found that these killings were not warranted. One member of the council stated: "There can be no justification for killing and injuring journalists, medics, and persons who pose no imminent threat of death or serious injury to those around them. Particularly alarming is the targeting of children and persons with disabilities. . . . Many young persons' lives have been altered forever. 122 people have had a limb amputated since 30 March last year. Twenty of these amputees are children." These deaths and injuries are a high price to pay for justice. Erakat (2019) reminds us of the political nature of the law and that international law can provide justice when it is responsive to social movements.

When considering the justice struggles of the Palestinian people, religious differences must be set aside and racist notions of Arab and/or Palestinian propensities toward terrorism must be rejected. Instead, we must look at the situation in a clear historical light, analyzing the actions of the state and the people applying justice principles.

The history of this region is quite complex and contested. We encourage further reading on this topic as it cannot be fully explored here. As with other regions, entire texts are available for further study. We ask that the reader consider the possibilities of justice for any in the region when there is ongoing state-sponsored oppression of an entire people. We can look to U.S. history and the treatment of Native Americans to understand that the occupation of the lands of one group by another imposing labels of barbarism and savagery to justify state atrocities does not serve justice. If we fail to learn from these histories and to rectify ongoing injustices, we cannot progress toward a society that attends to need, equality, and desert.

Because the United States provides billions of dollars in aid to the Israeli government and military, it is necessary that those living in the United States be especially clear regarding our ideas and understandings of this area. We may not all agree about what is and is not just in the region, but having an understanding of the realities of the conflict and the injustices perpetrated will draw us closer to agreement. We can then influence decisions regarding U.S. policy that match our own justice principles.

Other Middle Eastern Struggles

Thompson (2013) offers an analysis of a variety of justice struggles in the Middle East. We do not have the space to go over all of those here, but will briefly cover a few. We invite readers to engage in other texts on this topic. The Arab Spring was heavily dependent on the Internet for communication and organization. Karagiannopoulos (2012) looks specifically at the Green revolution in Iran of 2009 and the Egyptian Spring of 2011 and these movements' use of the Internet. While the Internet facilitated communications, it was the actual numbers of people in the streets and in the squares that resulted in progress. Oppressive leaders were overthrown in Tunisia, Yemen, Saudi Arabia, Libya, and Egypt, while Moroccans won constitutional changes to limit the power of their monarchy.

Tahrir Square was the center of the Egyptian uprising. Activists and others around the world were able to witness the activists as they risked their lives and livelihoods on a daily basis in a call for justice. This uprising and the broadcasting of the daily occupation of Tahrir Square on alternative media as well as the Internet inspired other movements. When teachers, firefighters, and other unionized workers in Madison, Wisconsin, occupied the state capital building, signs reading "Walk Like an Egyptian" were common. These offered thanks to the people of Egypt for their leadership and example from only a few days earlier. Later in 2011, in the United States, the Occupy Wall Street movement also followed the Egyptian lead.

Globalization and the impact of social media has allowed for an interconnection between struggles and a space in which different activists can learn from each other's experiences. The countries of the Arab Spring improved justice in their respective countries and taught people across the world the power of mass struggle. Those struggles continue as justice has yet to fully arrive in the Middle East or elsewhere.

EUROPEAN STRUGGLES

Struggles throughout Europe continue even though we often consider its countries advanced democracies. We offer only a few struggles here as examples of the variety of movements across the region.

Poland: Solidarity without Independence

In August 1980, shipyard workers went on strike in Gdansk, Poland, inspiring strikes elsewhere to support workers' demands. Despite winning the right to organize an independent union, Solidarity was declared illegal by the Polish government and forced underground. This illegal status continued until 1989, but did not deter continued organizing and union activities including mass strikes (Senser, 1989).

The demands of those on strike went beyond wages to include greater family supports, the closure of shops that priced most working-class people out of the ability to buy scarce goods, and a free press among other progressive reforms. This movement was a broad justice movement looking to improve the material circumstances of Polish citizens isolated from political power. Activists were also working toward a more open society that would allow a wider range of voices and ideas in their unions and in the press (Barker, 1987).

As Solidarity continued in its efforts to win greater social justice for the Polish people, difficulties did arise. Biezenski (1996) describes two waves within Solidarity, with the first wave led by blue collar workers and the second by white collar workers. These waves were in conflict with each other and isolated from the rank and file within the unions. The representation of union members and their desires were thus limited within the union structure. While winning many of their demands and allowing more voice to workers, greater justice for the Polish people, and ultimately playing a role in the fall of the Berlin wall, the structure of Solidarity was flawed.

These flaws may have resulted in the subsequent decline in support for Solidarity leaders. Sikorski (1996) contends that the rejection of Solidarity candidates in elections in the 1990s indicated a break from strident anti-communist politics and a move to a more pragmatic and flexible style of politics represented by the Communist Party in Poland. This analysis may appear contradictory on its face given the Western view of communism and the former Soviet states. While many might view communism as strident and anti-communists as more flexible, it is important to consider the character of the communism practiced within the former Soviet Union and the movements necessary to combat the oppression exercised by its member states.

The union movements that brought power to Solidarity developed during a period of economic crisis and growing inequalities among the population. While many in the West assumed that Poland as part of the Soviet Union was an equal society giving power to the workers, the reality of the Soviet Republics was to the contrary. Harman's (2003) analysis of the Soviet Union after the rise of Stalin is one that accounts for the position of workers. He argues that because workers were not in control of production under Stalin, socialism had ceased to exist, preventing the development of communism. The term *state capitalism* is applied recognizing the position of the Soviet state as the new oppressor of the working class (Harman, 2003). This analysis holds for Poland and the workers there who were not in control of their workplaces but required to fight for the right to organize into unions.

Whether one views Poland in the last century as a communist nation or a state capitalist regime, the Polish workers were not in control of the means of production (factories, etc.) as required by a Marxist view of socialism and/or communism. In Poland at this point in history, the state regime, rather than a corporate boss (as is more typical elsewhere and since), was the adversary of organized workers. Barker (1987) argues that the failure of Solidarity and others to organize for removal of the state limited the progress of the movement for greater justice. Senser (1989) argues that moving toward a removal of the oppressive Polish government would have been unwarranted.

Following the electoral success of the conservative Law and Justice Party (LJP) in Poland in the fall of 2015, demonstrations filled many Polish streets. In particular, women and young people were present in these demonstrations. The LJP called for restrictions on abortion and other human rights, weakening the judiciary, and control of media critical to the party. Having joined the European Union in 2004, Poland now finds itself under pressures for possible violations of Article 7 of the Lisbon Treaty, which requires respect for the rule of law (Bagenal, 2018). These legal protections are important in the face of human rights violations. The Polish people have a history of movements toward social justice that will very likely continue. The future of justice for Poland will depend on the ability of the Polish people to insist on democratic structures that allow for the free association of workers in unions, the voice of all in state decisions, and respect for the freedom of various expressions of all people.

Other European Struggles

On November 9, 1989, the people of the Soviet Union forced down the Berlin wall. Since then, ongoing change continues throughout the former Soviet states. Three Baltic States—Latvia, Estonia, and Lithuania—had already developed democracies. Change has been slow as suggested by Senser (1989) and moving toward free market capitalism. Popular nonviolent revolutions in Georgia in 2003, in Ukraine in 2004, in Kyrgyzstan in 2005, and in Belarus in 2005 have signaled a yearning of people in struggle for social justice. The former three were successful in setting up new governments. Belarus is still in process. Of the twelve former Soviet Republics, only Belarus and Turkmenistan are still considered oppressive regimes. Both countries restrict human rights and individual liberties (Human Rights Watch, 2018, 2019a). Belarus is the only country in Europe to continue to use the death penalty. All of the former Soviet States as all other nations will need to continue to attend to the voices of the people to assure continued progress toward social justice.

Ferry (2003) delineates the reforms taking place in response to demands/recommendations of the European Union (EU). In 2005, both French and Danish voters rejected the EU constitution. Activists organizing for "no" votes on the constitution argue that this constitution is nondemocratic and removes decision-making from national citizens and places those decisions in the hands of representatives at the EU (European No Campaign). As of 2013 with the entry of Croatia, the EU has twenty eight member nations. The people of the United Kingdom (U.K.) voted to exit the EU in 2016 (Europa.eu, 2019). The U.K. has been a member of the EU since 1973 and difficulties with an exit abound. A million people demonstrated in London on March 23, 2019, to demand a second vote on Brexit (BBC.com 2019). Some at the protest spoke of concerns for losing the sexual equalities and travel and family unity freedoms currently in place within the EU. Throughout Europe the future of the EU will move toward justice if the people are allowed a voice in the structure and policies of this political-economic agreement.

Yellow vest protests broke out across France, an EU member, when a fuel tax was imposed by President Macron, whose approval ratings have fallen dramatically since his election. The imposition of the fuel tax and other austerity measures hit the working class of France particularly hard. The fuel tax was promoted by the French government as a way to curb fossil fuel use. While most of France's working class and poor support curbing fossil fuels, they do not believe that they should be the ones to pay for such changes. Instead, they want corporations and the wealthy that have benefited from Macron's policy decisions to carry that financial burden (Wikipedia.org, 2019e). The people of France will continue in their struggle as their government continues to impose the costs of global economic growth upon workers and the poor.

Piño (2019) reports on the struggle for the independence of Catalonia from Spain, another EU member. While the people of Catalonia passed an independence referendum in 2017, the government of Spain has rejected that call and instead placed the leaders of the Catalonian independence movement on trial. This repressive response has led to more demonstrations by those supportive of Catalonian independence. A leader at a demonstration against the arrests of independence leaders stated: "Spain cannot be governed without listening to Catalonia" (Piño, 2019). As protesters stated, self-determination is not a crime. Social justice requires self-determination, and a voice that is heard and responded to, not repressed, allowing for just responses to need, equality, and desert.

LATIN AMERICA

Social movements throughout Latin America have a long and inspiring history. In the current historical period of increasing imperialist aggression, a neoliberal agenda is going largely unquestioned throughout much of the north. This agenda includes unrestrained privatization and has sparked new movements throughout Latin America. While the countries in this region are greatly varied in histories, economies, and people, the movements here often aim toward similar notions of justice: greater worker control in workplaces, an end to imperialist oppression from the United States (and/or other countries) and international corporations, and democratic decision-making over the use of natural resources (Katz, 2005). These demands are sometimes relegated to electoral processes as was the case on January 16, 2006, when the people of Chile elected their first female president, Michelle Bachelet, who ran on the Socialist ticket. But, at other times and/or places, these demands break out into mass movements.

Bolivia: Water, Oil, and Democracy

Bolivia is a country of interest because of the success of the popular movement in Cochabamba in 2000 to reclaim local control of water resources and the 2005 battles for control of water and oil that led to the ouster of President Mesa. These movements were dynamic and show the need for developing ideas and drawing lessons within struggle. Tom Lewis characterizes the water war in Cochabamba as "the first great victory against corporate globalization in Latin America" (Olivera, 2004, xiii). As the Bolivian people have proved since, it will not be the last. This battle for access to and control of water began in response to the privatization of this necessary resource in the city of Cochabamba. The New Economic Policy (NEP) that began in 1985 in Bolivia allowed for the expansion of neoliberal policies through the privatization of public resources (Olivera, 2004).

The privatization of water is particularly problematic because it is a necessity of life. The World Bank and the International Development Bank recommended this privatization as a condition for loans to the Bolivian government. In further support of privatization, the Bolivian government imposed Law 2029 in October 1999 to prevent the collection of water through traditional practices, including the collection of rainwater. This limitation meant water could only be legally acquired from the expensive private company.

When the international water consortium known as Aguas del Tunari took control of the water in November 1999, it quickly became clear why the government had been supportive of this plan. Government officials were to profit from privatization through their partial ownership in the four Bolivian companies included in the consortium. International Water, based in Spain, and owned by U.S.-based Bechtel, was also to profit greatly from this scheme. The vast majority of people in Bolivia, however, had much to lose. Just as they had suffered declining wages and increased unemployment since the beginning of the NEP, they would now suffer a loss of their water (Olivera, 2004).

For the half of the population who were linked to the approved private system, water bills bloated from about five dollars to over twenty five dollars a month. Teachers, whose salaries are about eighty dollars per month, had difficulty paying, and those with less income were unable to pay. Many refused to pay at all, while others resisted by continuing to use their alternative sources, in violation of Law 2029. The nondemocratic nature and apparent profit motives for this privatization scheme exposed the need to demand a voice in the process of decisions affecting public resources (Olivera, 2004).

In the mid-1990s, workers and others in Bolivia had begun to organize themselves to address a variety of problems. This organizing proved valuable when in 1999 the Coordinadoras de Defensa del Agua y de la Vida (Coalition in Defense of Water and Life, often referred to simply as the Coordinadoras) was formed. Coordinadoras were workers, peasants, environmentalists, teachers, and others forming a broad-based public group to demand a return of public water (Olivera, 2004).

Beginning in early November 1999, roadblocks, demonstrations, and strikes were coordinated and drew large and growing crowds. By February the government began to respond to these mass demonstrations and roadblocks with repressive violence using state police, teargas, and clubs on the peaceful demonstrations. This repression was met with even larger demonstrations that entirely closed the city. Even the smallest streets were blockaded by small bicycles and barricades clearly assembled by the children of the neighborhoods (Olivera, 2004).

By April the government had failed to meet a promised deadline for restructuring the water arrangement. Organized crowds took over the Aguas del Tunari offices, refusing to move until the company left the city. The Civic Committee (made up of political and business elite) began to meet with city officials to find a solution in the absence of representatives from the Coordinadoras. When Olivera and others went into the meeting and demanded a voice, they were arrested. These arrests resulted in even larger demonstrations. Blockades continued as city officials refused to negotiate. The youth in the movement took control of the plaza from the military. Everyone involved feared that Olivera, the leader of the movement, would be assassinated, including Olivera himself. In mid-April, city officials became convinced that they must negotiate with the people. Although there were rumors that the movement was a drug dealers' movement, city officials recognized their own neighbors and friends, many of them elderly, within the demonstrations and realized this could not be the case. The contention that the movement was merely a few radicals was also proved false by the hundreds of thousands of a variety of political views filling the streets, plaza, and occupying offices (Olivera, 2004).

Olivera was finally called to negotiate with officials. The settlement included the reclaiming of the water from corporate hands and a board of directors to make decisions about the water, which included members of the Coordinadoras, two representatives from the mayor's office, and two unionized workers from the water plant. This settlement was a victory over privatization. However, as Olivera himself points out, the negotiation was not entirely to the liking of those in the movement. He found in later discussions with people on the streets that they preferred complete control by the Coordinadoras (Olivera, 2004).

This recognition that his own ideas about a proper settlement were not the same as those outside the negotiations was an awakening for Olivera and indicates the dangers of isolated leadership. Negotiations such as those that Olivera was engaged in can be intense and distort the desires of the majority. Clearly, city officials would be arguing that a settlement should include the desires of the elite. In a negotiating room with these representatives, the elite can appear a large force. In relation to the masses on the street, their real size and proportion is better judged. Under different circumstances, a vote by all affected by the decision would have produced greater justice than the negotiations in which city officials held disproportionate power and were able to obtain one-third of the board seats when they are not one-third of the citizens. This critique is not offered to diminish the incredible advances made by the people of Cochabamba, but as a point to consider as a counter to the sorts of negotiations that typically result from behind-closed-doors meetings with representatives of the powerful.

Friedsky (2005) describes how the lessons from the water war of 2003 were applied to the struggle for the nationalization of gas resources and for a constituent assembly. With the election of Evo Morales as president of Bolivia in 2005, the stage was set for such progress. President Morales ascended to his office in 2006 and became the longest-serving president in Bolivian history as well as the first of indigenous identity. The constituent assembly was formed and developed a new constitution that was passed in 2009. The gas industry was nationalized on May 1, 2006, without expropriation (Kaup, 2008). This kept the multinational petroleum companies in place while requiring a sharing of profits with the Bolivian government. The context of this nationalization was one including neoliberal global pressures, financial, and material constraints. As in postrevolutionary Iran, there was also a history of external forces controlling the petroleum industry and little development of internal expertise. These realities prevented full expropriation setting up multiple difficulties and contradictions (Kaup, 2008).

Iamamoto (2017) offers an analysis of the neighborhood movements during the Bolivian gas wars noting that these movements were concerned with equality and modernization rather than group superiority. These movements are important in the understanding of how Bolivia turned toward national self-determination. This turn, however, was unable to free the people of Bolivia from powerful outside corporations and nations. Haarstad (2009) offers the view from labor unions also noting that Bolivian petroleum labor unions supported the nationalization of the gas industry. Labor unions across the globe, including in Bolivia, were weakened by impositions such as the International Monetary Fund seeking to take more profits from petroleum out of Bolivia and put it into the hands of international investors. This left unions marginalized when nationalization occurred, resulting in less capacity for negotiating in their interests. Schilling-Vacaflor and Eichler (2017) illuminate the divide and rule tactics utilized in practices meant to include the voices of indigenous people affected by gas extraction in Bolivia. As they show, without protection for collective rights, there can be no emancipation. Powerful petroleum interests with primary profit motivations will assure the continuation of marginalization of peoples and nature.

While the future of Bolivia is still uncertain, prior years prove that within a reflective mass movement toward the will of the people, great strides toward social justice can be made. Rather than rely upon political leaders, the people of Bolivia took to the streets and won a basic necessity of life, water. Future actions may win the rights of actual control of the rich gas resources of their nation rather than merely sharing in the profits extracted by multinational corporations. These actions may also develop the structures and consciousness needed to support a democracy equally inclusive of all voices and responsible to the will of the people.

Venezuela: Twenty-First Century Socialism

In 2002, the people of Venezuela were roused to defend their democratically elected president, Hugo Chávez, against a coup attempt by local elites supported by the U.S. government. In 2019, history repeats. The success of the 2002 defense allowed for continued organizing around progressive justice demands. Chavez, understanding the ideological war before him, espousing "twenty-first century socialism," furthered media laws specifying that at least half of the music should be of Venezuelan origins. Local radio provided alternatives to CNN reportage. Other media messages announce "Unstoppable Revolution" (Marx, 2005). Chavez also pressed for a new distributive justice model, more based on the needs principle. In an interview (Woods, 2005a, 3), he said, ". . . it is necessary to transcend capitalism. But capitalism can't be transcended from within capitalism itself, but through socialism, true socialism, with equality and justice. But I'm also convinced that it is possible to do it under democracy, but not in the type of democracy being imposed from Washington."

The core of Chavez's economic model was two-pronged. First, the foreign policy entailing the production and sale of huge oil reserves reoriented toward other Latin American countries. Venezuela signed a trade pact for discounted oil to thirteen Caribbean neighbors (Marx, 2005). The second prong dealt with fostering endogenous development, whereby monies from the oil sales would support the development of thousands of small cooperatives. The government also encouraged and supported workers to buy interests in their companies so they would have a greater voice in the companies (Marx, 2005). The larger goal is "to lift millions out of poverty by reducing Venezuela's reliance on oil, which has left the country with a weak manufacturing and agricultural base and over-dependent on imports of food and almost everything else" (5).

Chavez continually had an approval rating of over 70 percent. He won two elections by a considerable majority, offered a new constitution "that gives the people the right to hold a referendum to dismiss an unpopular government," and had numerous of his programs ratified (Woods, 2005b). He was, however, not without critics (see Osorio, 2003). Former U.S. Secretary of State Condoleezza Rice referred to him as a destabilizing influence.

The United States failed in its attempts to isolate Chavez from other leaders in Latin America and from political relevance. Chavez's successor, Maduro, was elected to a second six-year term in 2018 with 67.8 percent of the vote (Wikipedia.org, 2019f). While Maduro's presidency has had its difficulties, particularly with continued trade embargoes from the United States and its allies, he was elected president of Venezuela by Venezuelans. The United States intervened in the sovereign nation of Venezuela in 2019 to secure its imperial interests in oil as it did in Iraq (Sharma et al., 2004). With backing from the United States, an unknown member of the minority party in the Venezuelan parliament declared himself president of Venezuela on January 23, 2019, and has been recognized by the United States and its allies (Wikipedia.org, 2019g). On January 28, 2019, U.S. National Security Advisor John Bolton said: "It will make a big difference to the United States economically if we could have American oil companies invest in and produce the oil capabilities in Venezuela" (Bodine, 2019a). However, Maduro has been able to maintain his presidency within Venezuela.

While Maduro, like most political leaders, has not delivered all that was promised, or promised by Chavez or the turn toward twenty-first century socialism, he has withstood incredible outside pressures. Among those is the stoppage of oil exports, which are needed to fund internal projects and have been essential to other nations. Haiti in particular has suffered from the lack of access to Venezuelan oil during the 2019 U.S. intervention (Ives, 2019).

Given all of this, and the continual rhetoric accusing Maduro of everything from ineptitude to corruption, how is he still president? "Venezuela continues to rank high on the Human Development Index (HDI). Based on 2017 data, the 2018 HDI reports that Venezuela has a 'high human development,' putting the country 78th of 189 countries. It means Venezuela has a higher HDI than both Brazil and Colombia which are key right-wing allies in the U.S. war drive" (Bodine, 2019b). Weisbrot, Sandoval, and Rosnick (2006) utilize extensive data to explain why claims of widespread poverty in Venezuela are incorrect. Instead, they show that poverty declined over their years of study while access to medical care and education increased. Those outside of Venezuela are exposed to information that is often divergent to the lived realities of Venezuelans. Therefore, it is only Venezuelans who can decide the best path forward for themselves.

While many in Venezuela do not support Maduro, so far, the majority have not been willing to allow the United States to select their next president. As Venezuela progresses and has setbacks in its movement toward social justice, imperialist interventions from the United States do great harm internally and to Venezuela's allies. If the United States decides to use military force as has been threatened, great harm will likely be visited upon all of us. Venezuela illuminates the importance of a global understanding of justice. Imperialist nations have influence over others. This influence is not used for democratization or for justice. Instead, it is used to impose the needs and desires of the imperialist nation upon those it is able to subjugate. As they resist such subjugation, Venezuelans will continue to be a study in popular movements toward justice.

Zapatistas and Informational-Based Struggles

Early in 1994 the Zapatistas emerged from the Chiapas province of Mexico to challenge years of neglect, repression, and indifference to the local population. They placed a high value on civil society and grassroots struggle. Political and economic democracy could only be accomplished by ground-up reorganization (Burbach, 2001; Lippens 2002, 2003). What distinguished their movement from earlier ones, however, was the extensive use of the Internet and media as an organizing tool (see, for example, www .ezln.org). In fact, the noted theorist of the current information age, Manuel Castells (2004, 75), has referred to this as the "first informational guerrilla movement." Hardt and Negri (2004, 79) have referred to this as a form of "network struggles." Burbach (2001, 116) has referred to it as the "first postmodern revolutionary movement."

From the beginning, the Zapatista National Liberation Army, claimed that its goal was not to seize power, that they did not have a "blueprint" of the society to come, that their leaders were not the articulators of the political agenda, but rather that it was indigenous struggles and emerging platforms that would be the motor of social change. It was civil society—defined as a complex, interconnected configuration of cultural, economic, social, and political relationships (Burbach, 2001, 133)—that needed to be rearticulated especially by those with traditionally excluded voices.

The Zapatistas saw themselves as presenting a mirror for all to reflect on their own social being. Contrary to the conventional connection with the criminal justice system, "*justice*," according to Nash, "means not to punish, but to give back to each what he or she deserves, and that is what the mirror gives back [more a distributive notion of justice]." And "*liberty* is 'not that each one does what he or she wants, but to choose whatever road that the mirror wants in order to arrive at the true world' . . . and *democracy* requires 'not that all think the same, but that all thoughts or the majority of the thoughts seek and arrive at a good agreement'" (Nash, 1997, 261).

The Zapatistas' revolution was not vertically defined; it extended horizontally to the global arena, taking advantage of the movement of globalization and the contemporary revolution in information technology (136; see also Castells, 2004; Hardt and Negri, 2004). The Internet was vital to the emerging reorganization of civil society, providing the maximum circulation, sharing, and discussion of materials of those in struggle that could democratically take place. It is an image of oppositional forces in the jungles of Chiapas logging onto the Internet to engage in further struggles. The information age is now being used by indigenous activists in their regional *and* global struggles. Klein (2019) wrote that the Zapatistas "succeeded in communicating a vision of a just society so universal that people all over the world living in very different contexts from them felt included in their struggle." The ability of the Zapatistas to articulate such an inclusive vision has allowed for expanded understandings of the justice to come.

Hardt and Negri's much discussed book, *Multitude: War and Democracy in the Age of Empire* (2004), which followed their monumental work, *Empire* (2000), defined the Zapatista movement as the emerging modal form of struggle against the power of empire and globalization. It is borderless, in flux, with emerging concepts of social justice that are regionally specific, yet informed by the global economy and its consequences. It is a network struggle that privileges the multitude over any one party. It promises to "produce new subjectivities and new forms of life . . . . Creativity, communication, and self-organized cooperation are its primary values" (Hardt and Negri 2004, 83).

Notions of social justice, to respond to David Miller's query about the definition of justice in an age of globalism and multiculturalism, is responded to by arguing that conceptions of justice based on need, merit, and equality will appear in multi-articulated formats that will be regionally defined and practiced. It is to put a premium on civil society, the power of social change by human beings in struggle, and the capacity for transcendence. It is a practice of social justice that emphasizes "localism, autonomy and horizontal relationships among all the participating groups and organizations" (Burbach, 2001, 136). As Zapatista Subcommandant Marcos says, "the result will not be the triumph of a party, organization, or alliance of organizations with their particular social programs, but rather the creation of a democratic space for resolving the confrontations between different political proposals" (Burbach, 2001, 135).

The Zapatistas continue to build a new culture and a new world in the face of opposition (Innes, 2018). They have carried out their struggle informed by European theory, but adapting and appropriating that theory to serve their vision. At the same time, they inform those theories and us with the legacies of colonial resistance hundreds of years in the making (de Oca Valadez, 2018.). "A quarter-century after their uprising, perhaps the most meaningful, lasting lesson from the Zapatista movement is a spark of hope, a sense of what is possible, even in dark and uncertain times" (Klein, 2019). Beyond hope, continued struggle and vigilance are needed to assure that the Zapatistas and others are able to continue to progress toward social justice.

Other Latin American Struggles

Led by women, youth, and LGBTQ+ activists, the people of Puerto Rico forced the resignation of Governor Ricardo Rosello after disclosure of homophobic, misogynistic, and callous conversations with his top staff and advisors (Morales, 2019). Brazilians may need to hold their leadership accountable in a similar fashion. Atencio (2014) laments the inability of Brazil to hold those responsible for the horrific human rights abuses during the military dictatorship (1964–1985) accountable. The Truth Commission of Brazil had no ability to bring charges. The transition from dictatorship to democracy was therefore without any serious reckoning with the past or accountability on the part of those in power. Pagliarini (2018) bemoans the election of one of those guilty of brutality during the dictatorship, retired army captain (serving between 1977 and 1988) Jair Bolsonaro. President Bolsonaro has alarmed many within Brazil and around the world with his openly expressed desires to return Brazil to a military style dictatorship. According to Human Rights Watch (2019b), he reinstated the celebration commemorating the 1964 military coup. He has openly regretted the mistakes of the dictatorship in torturing rather than killing dissidents.

Telesurenglish.net (2018) reported on the demonstrations against Bolsonaro beginning on the day of his election. Those in Brazil concerned with indigenous rights, women's rights, LGBTQ+ rights, and human rights will need to continue in struggle as this new/old regime continues in its efforts to bring back the dictatorship. Those of us outside of Brazil will need to be vigilant in our understanding of the relationship between our own countries and Bolsonaro. Those of us in the United States will need to understand why President Trump was so quick to embrace Bolsonaro. The relationship between these United States and Brazil was not warm while left-leaning presidents were in Brazil; with this new leader the relationship is strengthening (France24.com 2019).

INITIATIVES IN THE EVALUATION OF TRANSITIONAL JUSTICE

A growing body of literature is beginning to accumulate on "transitional justice," a field that queries how to deal with a past evil regime and how to move on toward a just society (see, for example, Teitel, 2002; Murphy, 2017; Simic, 2016). Various strategies have been offered: reparations, truth and reconciliation, lustration, legalistic/trials, retribution, restorative, amnesty, pardons, etc. Realists often argue that political change must precede legal change, whereas idealists argue that legal change precedes political change (Teitel, 2002, 3). Alternatively, it is phrased as a liberal/critical dichotomy where the former argue that some idealist legal conceptions of justice precede change, and the latter more aligned with the realists who argue that even though law and social change are often connected, it is political change that comes first (4). Counteracting these dichotomies, Teitel (2002) suggests a constitutive role of both the political and law: conceptions of justice developed during political change are inherently connected with legal *and* justice principles and are more inductive—each co-constitutes the other in practice, in struggle (we have previously presented the constitutive approach more generally). Along with this, active research is taking place to measure the effectiveness of different responses to prior repressive regimes (see, for example, Olsen, Payne, and Reiter, 2010), including developing some measure of effectiveness (see, for example, the Historical Peace Index, the Global Peace Index, and the Transitional Justice Database Project). And the *International Journal of Transitional Justice* was developed in 2007. We briefly address the question of evaluation.

A useful beginning has been offered by Olsen, Payne, and Reiter (2010), *Transitional Justice in Balance*. We use this book as illustrative of quantitative evaluations. There has been lively engagement with this book (see book review by Moyo, 2012, as well as more substantive critiques of quantitative measures, suggesting qualitative forms, see Salehi and Williams, 2016; Stewart and Wiebelhaus-Brahm, 2017). Olsen, Payne, and Reiter's questions are: "what works in transitional justice?", "does transitional justice work?" (xv, 6). They draw from the Transitional Justice Database Project (tjdbproject.com). Their definition of transitional justice is "a set of mechanisms and approaches to address past violence" (9). They separate literature as "maximalists," which argue for prosecution of past evils and strict accountability; and the "minimalists" that argue for some form of amnesty rather than combative trials in hopes of future peace. They (21) suggest two other models: the "moderate" approach, advocating both accountability and the use of truth commissions and amnesty; and a holistic approach (24) supported by the International Center for Transitional Justice, which argues against singular attempts or mechanisms. Relying on the Transitional Justice Data Base and their five models of transitional justice (trials, truth commissions, amnesties, reparation, and lustration), they summarize the frequency of use of each, test several hypotheses, and conclude from their statistical analysis that "those countries with the highest level of violence in the past, and where the violence occurred long ago, prove more likely to grant amnesties and not trials" (58). They also develop several hypotheses concerning economic constraints during transitions. They conclude from their empirical investigation that "the health of the economy corresponds to transitional justice choices" (77) and "as the economies of transitional countries improve, they are more likely to adopt expensive mechanisms of accountability," the latter conclusion lending credence to the dynamic nature of transitions.

A further set of hypotheses concerns to what extent has promotion of justice come from the "outside in." Their statistical analysis leads to the conclusion, "justice often occurs from the outside-in" (95). Their outside factors include for example, the U.N. promoting ad hoc tribunals, the International Criminal Court, the International Center for Transitional Justice. The next set of hypotheses test the "justice cascade," which asserts that countries undergoing transitions tend toward accountability rather than amnesty. Their data suggests that the justice cascade thesis has been overstated, "the rate of accountability" has not changed (108), and the accountability insistence is more place specific, more European, and from Latin America. They then look at the "peace dividend." They find "there is no strong evidence that amnesties to rebels encourage them to lay down their arms in the midst of conflict" (128), but "while not effective in ending violence, may be the key to preventing renewed violence" (129).

Well, does transitional justice work? The authors conclude that "transitional justice" is effective, but that it takes some time for realization (146); that "encouraging the truth about the past may catalyze spoilers to reemerge and threaten human rights and democracy"; "that trials or amnesties alone simply do not prove to have a statistically significant effect in improving human rights or democracy"; and that a holistic approach seems suggested (153), that includes a combination of mechanisms, which they refer to as a "justice balance approach." The latter have been most effectively advanced, for the research team, by international nongovernment organizations (160).

There has been some critique of the book as well as purely quantitative measures. See, for example, Moyo (2012) who argues the researchers' notion of human rights and democracy may be "derived from Western liberal tradition of privileging procedural democracy and civil and political rights" and that other measures could be pursued. The measurement problem and the question of causality reappear in Stewart and Wiebelhaus-Brahm (2017).

They (120), too, suggest that the measurements often employed in quantitative studies, although not useless, are more "Western notions of rights and justice . . . that neglects deeper structural, socioeconomic issues." Qualitative studies, they argue, can provide the specific case details. They advocate both quantitative and qualitative measures (121) and specifically point to the "second wave" quantitative research employed in Transitional Justice Research Collaborative and the Justice Data Project. Salehi and Williams (2016), on the other hand, advocate a "qualitative comparative analysis" (QCA), particularly making use of the Justice Data website and their Post-conflict Justice Dataset. Their focus is on qualitative analysis of case studies along with cross-national comparisons suggesting not all generalizations can be applied in specific cases. They suggest their QCA can culminate in directions for sustained peace.

Moving beyond, it remains to be seen how quantum-based ontologies as well as quantum holographically based ontologies will be employed. At the present, the Newtonian ontology provides the deep structure of core assumptions on which Western science builds (see chapter 9). How, in other words, can we measure human well-being along with nonhuman well-being? How do we operationalize our concepts and measures? Can we make use of such measures as heart-brain coherence (Bradley and Tomasino, 2011) as an operationalization of well-being in a comparative, cross-national approach? How would a quantum logic or quantum probability provide an alternative to classic logic and probability? Measures of well-being, for example, embraced by new materialists, suggest that a person's well-being is intimately intraconnected with the constellation of forces within which they live; each co-constitutes the other in performative enactments. From a quantum holographic approach, the work of Raymond Bradley focusing on quantum nonlocality (Bradley and Tomasino, 2011) as well as the Heart-Math Institute and their electrophysiological tests of brain-wave coherence or noncoherence (McCraty et al., 2012) are useful in gaining insights as to social cohesion, the wherewithal of intuitive practices, and individual well-being (Bradley and Tomasino 2011, 212). Can these measures become useful or insights for qualitative measures for case studies as well as cross-national comparisons? Could they aid in the development of a more just society based on measures of well-being? Can a prolegomenon be developed on transitional justice based on a transformative justice that is based on a quantum holographical ontology (Milovanovic, 2011)?

THE WORLD SOCIAL FORUM AND THE ROADS TO GLOBAL JUSTICE

Teaching justice studies to undergraduates is to witness students' awakening to new understandings of justice in the world. This awakening can be at once rewarding and frightening. It is rewarding because without an understanding of the world based on principles of justice, injustice is bound to continue. It is frightening because experiencing the light bulb moment for students exposes the disregard of these principles in earlier education, the mainstream media, and mainstream politics. As noted before, information and debate are essential to democracy, and democracy is essential to justice. Exposing even in this brief form a few of the justice struggles ongoing in the world is only a beginning toward fully informed debate. It is our hope that the reader will continue to gather information from a variety of sources and to debate ideas openly with peers, professors, and colleagues.

This process of information sharing and debate developed into a new international forum in 2001. This is an important step toward international justice. The World Social Forum is the culmination of years of organizing and resistance and was particularly inspired by the Seattle protests of 1999 against the World Trade Organization, which disrupted those meetings while the whole world watched. The World Social Forum also allows greater exchange of information and ideas between activists around the world. This peer-to-peer event allows those engaged in the pursuit of social justice to converse directly rather than rely upon often unreliable media interpretations of other struggles (Corrêa Leite, 2005).

The World Social Forum continues in its tradition of bringing together activists engaged in a variety of social justice struggles. These activists come from all five continents to engage in issues of concern to all. The title for 2020 is: World Social Forum of Transformative Economies (Ripess.org, 2019). Bringing a transformative justice model to the global economy is essential to social justice. Globalization and the neoliberal project have necessitated a common struggle by all of those interested in the pursuit of justice. As we have shown in the examples above, the injustices that occur in one nation are often directly or indirectly linked to the policies of another. For those of us living in the Western world and especially the United States, it is important to include in the analysis of any international injustice the impact of the policies of the United States and other imperial powers. It is important to remember that neoliberalism has a price in our own lives, in the form of defunding public programs, job losses, and other injustices.

Engaging with others, especially those directly affected by U.S. policies abroad and in our own neighborhoods, whether at an international conference, over the Internet, or in the street, will assure a broader understanding. These understandings are the precursor to fully informed debate and democratic decision-making. It will be up to those armed with this knowledge and tradition to act on their collective motives for justice and to develop the means and opportunity to execute global social justice.

There is no simple linear path, nor is there likely only one path, nor are there unidimensional persons to make and walk those paths. We have come to a place in human development where we must recognize and respect our infinite differences as well as our similarities. And, we need to account for the dialectical relationships that develop between individuals, groups, and nations. In doing this, we can better work toward engaging the complexities that will move us forward. Often, we have relied on mechanical calculations of fixed orbital relationships. This form of Newtonian physics is not dialectical and does not work well in the complex realities of social systems, least in systems seeking profound change.

Instead, quantum theory, aspects of which have been incorporated by new materialists through the work of Karan Barad, and Quantum Holographic theory applied to the social sciences (see chapter 9), much of which has been pioneered by Raymond Bradley, is useful to our imagining of the roads ahead (Wendt, 2015; Milovanovic, 2011, 2014a, 2014b, 2018). This body of literature is re-orienting our core assumption away from a Newtonian ontology toward a quantum and/or quantum holography ontology. We have in prior chapters considered the complexity of relationships through this theory, then considered relationship to self and others through various claimed and assumed identities. In a global perspective we can further apply this theory. Recognizing that relationships change, our identities are both self and other referential, that much of our identities and relationship norms are place/nation/culture specific, and that we are all interconnected with the plight of others, we can consider opening our understandings to include those whose own experiences are very different from our own and who have much to teach us. Courage is contagious and there are many courageous justice seekers in the world today. When we engage with those who have been in struggle, we not only learn, but we may be infected with their courage and their commitment. We can also provide our understandings within the framework of common desires for meeting the needs of all, doing so equally, and offering desert. If we are able to remain open to possibilities without preordained equations, we may become the multitude and we may find justice.

It is in our immediate common global interest to seek roads toward social justice. "We are running out of time. Even as we speak, the circle of violence is closing in. Either way, change will come. It could be bloody, or it could be beautiful. It depends on you" (Roy, 2004, 118). It is okay to not have all of the answers, in fact, it would be wrong to assume that one could have. We may be uncertain. If we are committed to justice, we must "go forth and try anyway" (Said, 2004, 144).

REVIEW QUESTIONS

1. South Africa's Truth and Reconciliation Commission has not been successful in reaching justice related to need, equality, or desert. If you were to design a post-apartheid agreement, what would you be sure to include as required for the oppressors and what would you include as required for the oppressed? Don't worry about costs, focus on the living beings and how justice would best be served. Bring your ideas to class to share and discuss with at least one other person.

2. The Middle East and Latin America have seen many struggles in their histories. Chose a country in each of these regions and describe a recent or ongoing struggle that was not extensively covered in the chapter. What are/were the demands of the struggle? How were these demands answered? Are/were there interests outside the country attempting to influence the outcome of that struggle? If so, what are/were those interests?

3. What is the benefit of membership in the European Union? What are some of the costs? Have any nations who have joined the union left the EU? If so, what were their stated reasons for doing so? Were there any unstated reasons? If none have left, what were the stated reasons that the United Kingdom gave for possibly leaving in 2019? Were there other reasons that were not stated by those representing the nation, but were stated by persons within the United Kingdom or elsewhere?

4. Thinking about the various struggles reviewed in this chapter, pick a struggle that might be best served by a restorative justice process. Then pick a struggle in which a transformative justice might serve best. Be sure to explain what the process might entail and why the chosen process is best.

5. Find a popular press presentation of a current justice struggle in a country not your own. What are the justice demands of those in struggle? How are those demands currently being answered? Does the presentation seem complete to you? Is it possible that the struggle is different from or more complex than it is presented in the press presentation? What more would you want to know about this struggle? Bring your press article and answers to these questions to class for a discussion.

6. Select one of the struggles presented in the chapter. Imagine that you are meeting one of the people involved on the justice side of this struggle for coffee. How could you best attend to that discussion assuring that you are respecting the complexity of the person,

their struggle, and their perspective, as well as present yourself and your perspective? Utilize quantum holographic theory and your prior models of relationships from prior chapters to build yet another, even more complex model. Again, utilize a method that works for you. This is an exercise in creative thinking as related to social justice within social interactions. No artistic skill is required, nor will such be judged. Bring your model to class for small group sharing and discussion.

CHAPTER 13

Conclusion

JUSTICE IS NOT STATIC, nor does it exist outside of human construction. Pets may appear to act justly (or in the case of some crankier sorts, unjustly) toward each other, but our judgement of this is based on our own understandings of justice and not theirs. Justice is defined, sought, and attained through our social understandings and expressions.

As illustrated in the first part of the text, definitions of justice have historically been devised by and/or for the elite. Plato, Socrates, and other philosophers of old were beholden to elite rulers and their own interests. Women and slaves were not engaged in the process of justice defining nor were they invited to seek or attain justice by those espousing classical definitions. However, the ideas and the democratic process of debate have held sway over time and continue to inform our current notions of justice.

By the time that classical social theories of justice developed, the world had changed significantly and voices beyond the elite were emerging. These voices were not always welcomed or heeded, but nonetheless have had a great impact on our understandings of justice. Our first approximation of justice includes the following elements: distributive principles (fair allocation of rewards and burdens) and retributive principles (appropriate responses to harm); how they relate to political economy and historical conditions; their local and global manifestations; the struggle for their institutionalization; how human well-being and development at the social and individual levels is enhanced by their institutionalization; and developing evaluative criteria or processes by which their enhancement or denial is actualized.

We have addressed these elements throughout the text with specific chapters dealing with distributive (chapter 3) and retributive justice (chapter 4). As we illustrated, the classical thinkers are especially important to our understandings of distributive justice. The theorists concerned with distributive justice looked to the organization of society to inform justice and just relationships within that structure.

Retributive justice is also important to our current justice understandings. Defining crime, deciding upon punishment, and invoking just procedures persist within the concerns of contemporary justice. While restorative justice has been long important to other nations/societies, it is only recently beginning to gain acceptance within the United States. This model, however, is problematic in its acceptance of a former condition as just without critique of the social conditions that create and/or sustain that condition. Transformative justice allows progress from the restorative model and toward a more just condition of the individual and society. Distributive, retributive, restorative, and transformative models of justice allow for an analysis of justice as understood within each and for the continued progress toward ever more just models.

The text provided an understanding of the conceptions of justice that form the basis of our current notions; it also allowed us to critically examine these and to understand the historical placement and motivations of each. It should be clear that defining justice is a political and not merely a legal matter. Because this is so, any development and institutionalization of a definition of justice must include an open and democratic dialogue (more inclusive than Plato would like) and encourage critique of previous understandings. Progress toward this end has occurred, but we have yet to devise a definition of justice informed by an inclusive engaging debate.

The second part of the text illustrated the need for an inclusive well-informed definition of justice and exemplified the relationship between the political economy and justice and the local and global manifestations. As was shown, the globe has shrunk, not literally, but in reality for our social lives. This has created exciting prospects and challenges for justice. Globalism and its pulling together of our diverse multicultural world has extended our base of information and our reach. Because we are now in contact with each other and our social worlds overlap so extensively we must necessarily engage in a global defining of justice. The development of the World Wide Web has certainly enhanced this process.

Environmental, ecological, and species justice are at once a small part of and an inclusive example of our need to seek justice on a global scale and within our local settings. As we have shown, environmental and ecological damage are ubiquitous in their scope and local in their effect. Only more recently have we turned an active eye toward species justice, addressing the injustice against nonhuman forms. While we seek environmental and ecological justice within our communities, we necessarily seek the same for the planet.

Indigenous forms of justice are essential to the discussion and debate for social justice. Because these forms of justice do not recognize property in the same way that modern capitalist states choose to do, these justice models are especially important to developing critical ideas on intellectual property and cyberspace. Indigenous justice is also informative to understanding cultural relativism and human rights. It will be our challenge in justice seeking to respect the maintenance of the best indigenous justice practices while informing these with useful nonindigenous practices, and informing nonindigenous practices with those of indigenous peoples. So too with post-colonial and counter-colonial studies, which indicate the continuous nature of struggle, well after "liberation" has been attained. This dialogue and exchange of ideas will allow for the emergence of newly informed justice.

Similarly, postmodern forms of justice allow for a broader understanding of what justice may and may not entail. These ideas grow specifically from a rejection of previous assumptions derived from Renaissance thought and ask that new understandings be allowed to emerge and develop. The major thinkers within this tradition were reviewed to offer a view of how these ideas emerged and where they have yet to proceed. Postmodern ideas continue to develop, to question our understandings of justice, and to provide a challenge for further progress in ideas. As with indigenous ideas, postmodern thought informs a further understanding of justice. Even as postmodernists have opened up a new dialogue, since the early 2000s a post-postmodernism has emerged with varieties such as post-humanism, new materialism, digimodernism, and a turn to quantum and even quantum holography ontology as alternatives to the traditional Newtonian ontology than informs dominant discourse. These new perspectives are beginning to create a stir in traditional thought on social justice.

The challenges toward justice offered in the part II of the text were followed by examples of historical and ongoing justice struggles. Part III of the text continued the examination of local and global manifestations of justice and allowed an examination of struggles for institutionalization as well as the understanding of how justice at both the individual and social levels is enhanced by institutionalization. We began with a look at struggles within the legal arena. These struggles were engaged by individuals and groups excluded from legal justice. As the legal struggles evolved, notions of justice also developed. The dialectics of this relationship of struggle within the legal arena informing ideas are important to understanding the development of justice.

Grassroots struggles within the United States were also presented, and, like the legal struggles, often witness a dialectical development of justice ideas. Ideas of people and groups engaged in struggles shifted through those struggles. These struggles and shifts have an impact on our collective understanding of justice. Most important in U.S. history were the civil rights struggles, which literally shaped our current notions of racial justice and expanded our visions of social justice.

National justice struggles outside the United States were presented in part III for the purpose of showing that large-scale movements continue around the world and have resulted in a variety of justice outcomes. These struggles have a direct impact on the persons in the affected nation but also have an impact on the world as we watch and learn from these movements. Gatherings such as the World Social Forum will continue to be powerful modes of democratic debate and discussion for those engaged in movements toward justice. Further illustrated was how we might develop evaluative criteria by which justice enhancement or denial result.

Justice is contained within our social possibilities and will arrive when we demand it. It always concerns theory *and* practice, and particularly informed by ground-up struggles and movements. As we have shown, a variety of justice ideas and ideals currently exist, which if implemented, would vastly improve the lives and justice conditions of the majority of people on the planet, as well as eco- and species conditions. If the basic needs of all on the planet were met, if more genuine substantive equality were attained, and if all desiring and deserving of desert had access to such, the world would be a far different and more just place in which to exist. Certainly, more complex notions of justice will continue to compete. We have, for example, included just sustainabilities as well as other principles of justice in addition to equality, merit, and need to include redistribution, recognition, participation, capabilities, and justification. Allowing a full discussion and debate of these notions within conditions of fulfilled basic needs and genuine equality within a developing world of differences and sameness would allow for the best ideas to fully emerge.

It is certain that continuing to allow justice to be defined by the few and to silence the many will not serve justice. History and this text document the possibilities of the silenced majority to take back their collective voice and demand justice. The Coordinadoras in Bolivia, as well as the Zapatista movement and organizational structure, are only two of the examples for this possibility. The first step toward justice is the serious consideration of justice and the ideas that inform it. An equally important step toward the attainment of justice is participation in struggles informed by these ideas. Theory *and* practice!

These struggles may be large (national revolutionary movements) or "small" (anti-death penalty movements), but all movements toward justice are important. This engagement will necessarily allow for a dialectical relationship between the ideas brought into the struggle and the lessons learned within it. This dialectic in turn has and will advance ideas and struggle. If democratic values are respected within these struggles, they will allow for the emergence of a new and advanced form of justice. We can look at history and witness these advances. In the years between the first edition of this text and this edition, we have seen reason for despair and reason for great hope. It is the people rising against injustice that continue to inform us and offer hope. If we take the lessons of history seriously, we will look to our future and find justice.

References

Abelove, Henry, Michele Ama Barale, and David M. Halperin, eds. 1993. *The Lesbian and Gay Studies Reader*. New York: Routledge.

Abrahamian, Ervand. 1989. *Radical Islam: The Iranian Mojahedin*. New York: I. B. Tauris.

Abu El-Haj, Thea R. 2002. "Contesting the Politics of Culture, Rewriting the Boundaries of Inclusion: Working for Social Justice with Muslim and Arab Communities." *Anthropology and Education Quarterly* 33(3): 308–316.

Acorn, Annalise. 2004. *Compulsory Compassion: A Critique of Restorative Justice*. Vancouver: UBC Press.

ACORN Living Wage Resources Center. American Institute for Social Justice. Retrieved on March 5, 2019, from: https://www.mott.org/grants/american-institute -for-social-justice-acorn-living-wage-resource-center-200000347-01/

Adams, Carol, and Josephine Donovan, eds. 1995. *Animals and Women*. Raleigh, NC: Duke University Press.

Adeola. F. O. 2000. "Cross-National Environmental Justice and Human Rights Issues—A Review of Evidence in the Developing World." *American Behavioral Scientist* 43(4): 686–706.

Agamban, Giorgio. 1993. *The Coming Community*. Minneapolis: University of Minnesota Press.

Agnew, Robert. 2012. "Dire Forecast: A Theoretical Model of the Impact of Climate Change on Crime." *Theoretical Criminology* 16(1): 21–42.

Agozino, Biko. 2003. *Counter-Colonial Criminology: A Critique of Imperialist Reason*. Sterling, VA: Pluto Press.

———. 2004. "Reparative Justice." In *Pan- African Issues in Crime and Justice*, eds. A. Kalunta-Crumpton and B. Agozino, 228–248. Aldershot, UK: Ashgate Publishing Company.

———. 2014. "Indigenous European Justice and Other Indigenous Justices." *African Journal of Criminology & Justice Studies* 8(1): 1–19.

Agyeman, Julian, Robert Bullard, and Bob Evans. 2003. *Just Sustainabilities: Development in an Unequal World*. Cambridge, MA.: MIT Press.

Agyeman, Julian, and Bob Evans. 2004. "'Just Sustainability': The Emerging Discourse of Environmental Justice in Britain?" *The Geographical Journal* 170(2): 155–164.

Ahmad, Eqbal. 2000. *Confronting Empire*. Cambridge, MA: South End Press.

Ahmad, Maryam, and James Deshaw Rae. 2015. "Women, Islam, and Peacemaking in the Arab Spring." *Peace Review: A Journal of Social Justice* 27: 312–319.

Aiken, Nevin T. 2016. "The Distributive Dimension in Transitional Justice: Reassessing the South African Truth and Reconciliation Commission's Ability to Advance Interracial Reconciliation in South Africa." *Journal of Contemporary African Studies* 34(2): 190–202.

Aiyer, Ananthakrishnan. 2001. "Hemispheric Solutions? Neoliberal Crisis, Criminality, and 'Democracy' in the Americas." *Urban Anthropology* 30(2–3): 239–268.

Alexander, John. 2008. *Capabilities and Social Justice*. Farnham, UK: Ashgate Publishing, Ltd.

Alexander, Michelle. 2012. *The New Jim Crow: Mass Incarceration in the Age of Colorblindness*. New York: The New Press.

———. 2019. "Time to Break the Silence on Palestine." *New York Times*. January 20.

Alexander, Peter. 1987. *Racism Resistance and Revolution*. London: Bookmarks Publishing Co-operative.

Aljazeera.com. 2018. "South African parliament backs land reform report: Opposition Democratic Alliance says it could go to court to stop proposed land reforms." Retrieved on March 20, 2019, from: https://www.aljazeera.com/news/2018/12/south-africa-parliament-backs-land-reform-report-181205075732856.html

Alkire, Sabina. 2005. *Valuing Freedom*. Oxford: Oxford University Press.

Allen, Walter R., Channel McLewis, Chantal Jones, and Daniel Harris. 2018. "From Bakke to Fisher: African American Students in U.S. Higher Education over Forty Years." *RSF: The Russell Sage Foundation Journal of the Social Sciences* 4(6): 41–72.

Almeida, Shana. 2013. (Re)cognition: A Move to Explicate Race in Axel Honneth's Critical Theory of Social Justice." *Critical Social Work* 14(2): 83–97.

Amnesty International. 2018. "Six Months On: Gaza's Great March of Return." Retrieved on January 31, 2019, from: https://www.amnesty.org/en/latest/campaigns/2018/10/gaza-great-march-of-return/

Anantharaman, M. 2018. "Critical Sustainable Consumption." *Journal of Environmental Studies and Science* 8(4): 553–561.

Andrews, Kenneth. 2002. "Creating Social Change: Lessons from the Civil Rights Movement." In *Social Movements: Identity, Culture and the State*, eds. David Meyer, Nancy Whittier, and Belinda Robnett, 105–117. Oxford: Oxford University Press.

Annas, Catherine. 1999. "Irreversible Error: The Power and Prejudice of Female Mutilation." In *Health and Human Rights*, eds. Jonathan Mann, Sofia Gruskin, Michael Grodin, and George Annas, 336–362. New York: Routledge.

Anzaldua, Gloria. 1987. *Borderlands/La Frontera*. San Francisco, CA: Aunt Lute Books.

Appelbaum, Richard, and William Robinson. 2005. *Critical Globalization Studies*. London: Routledge.

Aquinas, St. Thomas. 2018. *Summa Theologica*. Retrieved on November 21, 2018, from: http://www.ccel.org/ccel/aquinas/summa

Arena, Richard. 2015. "On the Intellectual Foundations of Hayk's and Schumpeter's Economics: An Appraisal." *Journal of Evolutionary Economics* 25: 77–90.

Aristotle. 2000. *Nicomachean Ethics*. Cambridge: Cambridge University Press.

Armstrong, Jac. 2014. "Rethinking the Restorative-Retributive Dichotomy: Is Reconciliation Possible?" *Contemporary Justice Review* 17(3): 362–374.

Aronowitz, Stanley. 2003. "Global Capital and Its Opponents. In *Implicating Empire: Globalization and Resistance in the 21st Century World-Order*, eds. Stanley Aronowitz and Heather Gautney, 179–195. New York: Basic Books.

Aronowitz, Stanley, and Heather Gautney, eds. 2003. *Implicating Empire: Globalization and Resistance in the 21st Century World-Order*. New York: Basic Books.

Arrigo, Bruce. 1997. "Dimensions of Social Justice in an SRO (Single Room Occupancy): Contributions for Chaos Theory, Policy, and Practice." In *Chaos, Criminology, and Social Justice: The New Orderly (Dis)Order*, ed. Dragan Milovanovic, 179–194. Westport, CT: Praeger.

———. 1999. "Constitutive Theory and the Homeless Identity: The Discourse of a Community Deviant." In *Constitutive Criminology at Work*, eds. Stuart Henry and Dragan Milovanovic. Albany, NY: State University of New York Press.

Arrigo, Bruce, and Dragan Milovanovic. 2009. *Revolution in Penology*. NY: Rowman and Littlefield.

———, eds. 2010. *Postmodernist and Post-Structuralist Theories of Crime*. Farnham Surrey, England: Ashgate Publishing.

Arrigo, Bruce, Dragan Milovanovic, and Robert Schehr. 2005. *The French Connection in Criminology*. New York: SUNY Press.

Arrigo, Bruce, and Robert Schehr. 1998. "Restoring Justice for Juveniles." *Justice Quarterly* 15: 629–666.

Asad, Talal. 1997. *Anthropology and the Colonial Encounter*. New York: Prometheus Books.

Asch, Michael. 1999. "From Calder to Van der Peet." In *Indigenous Peoples' Rights in Australia, Canada and New Zealand*, ed. Paul Havemann, 428–446. Oxford: Oxford University Press.

Associated Press, 2014. *A Look at the Dual Justice System in the West Bank, AP English Worldstream—English*. Retrieved on January 30, 2019, from: https://uprm.idm .oclc.org/login?url=http://search.ebscohost.com/login.aspx?direct=true&db=n5h &AN=AP82dd9652929140389b482d6ada287aab&site=ehost- live&scope=site

Astor, Hilary. 1994. "Swimming Against the Tide: Keeping Violent Men Out of Mediation." In *Women, Male Violence and the Law*, ed. Julie Stubbs. Annandale, NSW: Federation Press.

Atencio, Rebecca J. 2014. *Memory's Turn: Reckoning with Dictatorship in Brazil*. Madison: University of Wisconsin Press.

Augustine, St. 1964. *On Free Choice of the Will*, trans. Anna Benjamin and L. H. Hackstaff. Indianapolis, IN: Bobbs-Merrill.

Aurora Project. Retrieved on February 15, 2019, from: https://auroraproject.com.au /what-native-title

Austin, Beatrix, ed. 2012. *Berghof Glossary on Conflict Transformation*. Berlin: Berghof Foundation.

Ayala, Cèsar J. 2018. "Behind Puerto Rico's Debt, Corporations That Drain Profit from the Island. *Committee for the Abolition of Illegitimate Debt*. Retrieved on February 5, 2019, from: http://www.cadtm.org/Behind-Puerto-Rico-s-Debt-Corpo rations-That-Drain-Profits-from-the-Island

Baca, Herman. 2012. "La Raza Unida Party's Convention 40 Years Later." *San Diego Free Press*, September 4.

Baerwaldt, Neske. 2018. "The European Refugee Crisis: Crisis for Whom? Retrieved on January 7, 2019, from: http://www.law.ox.ac.uk/research-subject-groups/centre -criminology/centreborders-criminologies/blog/2018/03/european-refugee

Bagenal, Flora. 2018. "Unrest Continues as Poland's Government Moves Further to the Right." *Pacific Standard*. Retrieved on March 26, 2019, from: https://psmag .com/social-justice/unrest-on-the-rise-in-poland

Balbus, Issac. 1977. *The Dialectics of Legal Repression*. New York: Russell Sage.

Baldus, David, George Woodworth, and Charles Pulaski. 1994. "Reflections on the 'Inevitability' of Racial Discrimination in Capital Sentencing and the 'Impossibility' of its Prevention, Detection, and Correction." *Washington and Lee Law Review* 51: 359.

Balkin, J. M. 1987. "Deconstructive Practice and Legal Theory." *Yale Law Journal* 96(4): 743–786.

———. 1998. "Deconstructive Practice and Legal Theory." Retrieved on February, 21, 2019, from: www.yale.edu/lawweb/jbalkin/articles/decpracl.htm

Banda, Maria. 2018. "Why Should Trees Have Legal Rights? It's Second Nature." *Globe and Mail*. Retrieved on December 18, 2018, from: https://www.the globeandmail.com/opinion/article-why-should-trees-have-legal- rights-its-second -nature/

Bannerji, Himani. 2000. *The Dark Side of the Nation*. Toronto: Canadian Scholars Press.

Barad, Karan. 2007. *Meeting the Universe Halfway*. Durham, NC: Duke University Press.

———. 2010. "Quantum Entanglement and Hauntological Relations of Inheritance: Dis/continuities, SpaceTime Enfoldings, and Justice-to-Come." *Derrida Today* 3(2): 240–268.

———. 2015. "On Touching—The Human That Therefore I Am." In *Power of Materiality/Politics of Materiality*, eds. Kristen Stakemeier and Susanne Witzgall. Zurich: Diaphanes.

Barger, Lillian. 2018. *A World Come of Age*. Oxford: Oxford University Press.

Barger, W. K., and Ernesto M. Reza. 1994. *The Farm Labor Movement in the Midwest: Social Change and Adaptation among Migrant Farmworkers*. Austin: University of Texas Press.

Barker, Colin. 1987. "Poland 1980–91: The Self Limiting Revolution." In *Revolutionary Rehearsals*, ed. Colin Barker, 169–216. Chicago, IL: Bookmarks.

Barlow, Jeffrey. 2002. "Globalism and Changes to the Internet." Retrieved on February 15, 2019, from: http://mce1.pacificu.edu/jahc/jahcv1/editorial/jahcedit.html

Barmaki, Reza. 2014. "Emile Durkheim's Concepts of Justice and Freedom." *International Journal of Criminology and Sociology* 7(2): 69–79.

Barry, Brian M.1989.*Theories of Justice*. Berkeley: University of California Press.

Bartlett, K. 1991. "Feminist Legal Methods." In *Feminist Legal Theory*, eds. K. Bartlett and R. Kennedy, 370–403. Oxford: Westview Press.

———. 2000. "Cracking Foundations as Feminist Method." *American University Journal of Gender, Society and Policy and Law* 8: 31–48.

Bassiouni, M. Cherif, ed. 2002. *Post-Conflict Justice*. Ardsley, NY: Transnational Publications.

Batiz, Zoltan, and Dragan Milovanovic. 2017. "Quantum Holography and Agency." *Neuroquantology* 15(1): 45–59.

Bator, Paul. 1963. "Finality in Criminal Law and Federal Habeas Corpus for State Prisoners," *Harvard Law Review* 76: 441–442.

Bauman, Z. 2004. *Europe: An Unfinished Adventure*. London: Polity Press.

Baxi, Upendra. 2012. *The Future of Human Rights*. New Delhi; Oxford: Oxford University Press.

BBC.com. 2018. "Iran Sanctions: How Iranians Are Feeling the Impact." *BBC News*. Retrieved on March 23, 2019, from: https://www.bbc.com/news/world-middle -east-46102017

BBC.com. 2019. "Brexit March: Million Joined Brexit Protest, Organisers Say." *BBC News*. Retrieved on March 26, 2019, from: https://www.bbc.com/news/uk -politics-47678763

Beccaria, Cesare. 1986. *On Crimes and Punishment*. Indianapolis, IN: Hackett Publishing Company.

Beck, Ulrich. 1992. *Risk Society: Towards a New Modernity*. London: Sage Publications.

———. 1999. *World Risk-Society*. Cambridge: Polity Press.

———. 2000. *What is Globalism?* Cambridge: Polity Press.

Becker, Howard. 1963. *Outsiders*. New York: The Free Press.

Beckford, Robert. 2000. *Dread and Pentecostal: A Political Theology for the Black Church in Britain*. Eugene, OR: WIPF and Stock Pub.

Been, Vicki. 1995. "Analyzing Evidence of Environmental Justice." *Journal of Land Use and Environmental Law* 11: 1–13.

———. 1997. "Coming to the Nuisance or Going to the Barrios? A Longitudinal Analysis of Environmental Justice Claims." *Ecology Law Quarterly* 24: 1–24.

Beirne, Pierce. 2009. *Confronting Animal Abuse*. New York: Rowman and Littlefield.

Bell, Derrick. 1980. "Brown v. Board of Education and the Interest-Convergence Dilemma." *Harvard Law Review* 93: 518–548.

Belew, Kathleen. 2018. *Bring the War Home: The White Power Movement and Paramilitarism in America*. Cambridge, MA: Harvard University Press.

Benatar, Solomon R. 2001. "South Africa's Transition in a Globalizing World: HIV/AIDS as a Window and a Mirror." *International Affairs* 77(2): 347–375.

Benjam, Medea. 2004. "Why Hugo Chavez Won a Landslide Victory." Retrieved on January 20, 2019, from: http://www.commondreams.org/cgi-bin/print.cgi?file=/views 04/0817-01.htm

Benjamin, Walter. 1978. "Critique of Violence." In *Reflections: Essays, Aphorisms, Autobiographical Writings*, ed. Peter Demetz, 277–300. New York: Harcourt Brace Jovanovich.

Bennett, Michael, and Dave Zirin. 2018. *Things That Make White People Uncomfortable*. Chicago: Haymarket Books.

Bennett, Scott H. 2003. "'Free American Political Prisoners': Pacifist Activism and Civil Liberties, 1945–48." *Peace Research* 40(4): 413–433.

Berk, Richard. 2012. *Criminal Justice Forecasts of Risk*. NY: Springer.

Berlin, I. 1969. "Two Concepts of Liberty." In *Four Essays on Liberty*, ed. I. Berlin. Oxford: Oxford University Press.

Berman, Harold. 1983. *Law and Revolution*. Cambridge, MA: Harvard University Press.

Bernstein, Mary. 2002. "The Contradictions of Gay Ethnicity: Forging Identities." In *Social Movements: Identity, Culture and the State*, eds. David Meyer, Nancy Whittier, and Belinda Robnett, 85–104. Oxford: Oxford University Press.

Bhabha, Homi I. 1990. *Nation and Narration*. London: Routledge.

———. 1994. *The Location of Culture*. New York: Routledge.

Biezenski, Robert. 1996. "The Struggle for Solidarity 1980–81: Two Waves of Leadership in Conflict." *Europe-Asia Studies* 48(2): 261–284.

Black, Donald. 1976. *The Behavior of Law*. New York: Academic Press.

Black Lives Matter. Retrieved on March 1, 2019, from: https://blacklivesmatter.com/

Blake, Michael. 2000. "Rights for People, Not for Cultures." *Civilization* August-September: 50–52.

Blauner, Ro. 1969. "Internal Colonialism and Ghetto Revolt." *Social Problems* 16: 393–408.

Bluhdorn, Ingolfur. 2016. "Sustainability—Post-Sustainability—Unsustainability." In *The Oxford Handbook of Environmental Political Theory*, eds. Teena Gabrielson, Cheryl Hall, John Meyer, and David Schlosberg. E-Publication. Oxford: Oxford University Press. Retrieved on January 2, 2019, from: http://oxfordindex.oup.com/view/10.1093/oxfordhb/9780199685271.013.39

Blum, L. 1998. "Recognition, Value, and Equality." *Constellations* 5(1): 51–68.

Blum, William. 2004. *Killing Hope: U.S. and C.I.A. Interventions since World War II*. Monroe, ME: Common Courage Press.

Blyth, Carolyn, Emily Colgan, and Katie B. Edwards, eds. 2018. *Rape Culture, Gender Violence, and Religion: Christian Perspectives*. New York: Palgrave Macmillan.

Bodine, Alison. 2019a. "Imperialist Aggression and What We Can Learn from the Attempted Coup Against Venezuela." *GlobalResearch.ca*. Retrieved on March 27, 2019, from: https://www.globalresearch.ca/imperialist-aggression-learn-attempted-coup-venezuela/5668496?utm_campaign=magnet&utm_source=article_page&utm_medium=related_articles

Bodine, Alison. 2019b. "Huge Defeat for Imperialists: The U.S. Broke Its Teeth in Venezuela." *GlobalResearch.ca*. Retrieved on March 27, 2019, from: https://www.globalresearch.ca/huge-defeat-for-imperialists-the-u-s-broke-its-teeth-in-venezuela/5672236

Boekmann, H. J, H. J. Smith, and Y. J. Huo. 1997. *Social Justice in a Diverse Society*. Boulder, CO: Westview Press.

Bonilla-Silva, Eduardo. 2017. *Racism Without Racists: Color-Blind Racism and the Persistence of Racial Inequality in America*, 5th ed. Lanham, MD: Rowan and Littlefield.

Bova, Gus. 2019. *Texas Observer*. "Indigenous Activists Set up Protest Camp at South Texas Cemetery to Stop Trump's Wall." Retrieved on February 1, 2019, from: https://www.texasobserver.org/indigenous-activists-set-up-protest-camp-at -south- texas-cemetery-to-stop-trumps-wall/?fbclid=IwAR3uizCcE_udIbWhu0S - ig3MmZ2sd_qmAfGUEXVXtR—28I4qAGHSoChqDU

Boyett, Jason. 2016. *12 Major World Religions*. Berkeley, CA: Zephyros Press.

Bracher, March. 1993. *Lacan, Discourse, and Social Change*. Ithaca, NY: Oxford University Press.

Bradley, Raymond. 2006. "The Psychophysiology of Entrepreneurial Intuition." Proceedings of the Third AGSE International Entrepreneurship Research Exchange, February 8–10, 2006, Auckland, New Zealand.

———. 2012. "Nonlocality, Consciousness and the Eye of Love." *Consciousness and Development* 2: 193–295.

———. 2016. "Bonds and Quanta." *Journal of Theoretical and Philosophical Criminology* 2: 95–136.

Bradley, Raymond, and Dana Tomasino. 2011. "A Quantum-Holographic Approach to the Psychophysiology of Intuitive Action." In *World Encyclopedia of Entrepreneurship*, ed. Leo-Paul Dana, 318–347. Northampton, MA: Edward Elgar Publishing.

Braidotti, Rosi. 2013. *The Posthuman*. Cambridge: Polity Press.

Braithwaite, John. 1989. *Crime, Shame and Reintegration*. Cambridge: Cambridge University Press.

———. 2002. *Restorative Justice and Responsive Regulation*. Boston: Oxford University Press.

Braithwaite, John, and Philip Pettit. 1990. *Not Just Deserts*. Oxford: Oxford University Press.

Branch, Taylor. 1988. *Parting the Waters: America in the King Years 1954–1963*. New York: Simon and Schuster.

Brandin, Allison. 2019. *Surviving R. Kelly*. Lifetime Television. Documentary Film.

Brara, Rita. 2017. "Nurturing Nature: Advances in Indian Jurisprudence." In *RCC Perspectives* 6: 31–36. Retrieved on December 20, 2019, from: http://www .environmentandsociety.org/sites/default/files/brara_2017_i6_0.pdf

Breitman, George. 2002. *The Last Year of Malcolm X: The Evolution of a Revolutionary*. New York: Pathfinder Press.

Brianson, Alex. 2016. "Europa and Gaia: Towards an Ecofeminist Perspective in Integration Theory." *Journal of Common Market Studies* 54(1): 121–135.

Brisman, Avi. 2014. "Of Theory and Meaning in Green Criminology." *International Journal for Crime, Justice and Social Democracy* 3(2): 21–24.

———. 2017. "On Narrative and Green Cultural Criminology." *International Journal for Crime, Justice and Social Democracy* 6(2): 64–77.

Britannica.com. "Neoliberalism." Retrieved on January 7, 2019, from: https://www .britannica.com/topic/neoliberalism

Brosius, J. Peter. 1999. "On the Practice of Transnational Cultural Critique." *Identities* 6(2–3): 179–200.

Brouwer, Jeimer, Maartje van der Woude, and Joanne van der Leun. 2017. "Framing Migration and the Process of Crimmingration." *European Journal of Criminology* 14(1): 100–119.

Brown, Nicholas, and Imra Szeman. 2006. "What Is the Multitude?" *Cultural Studies* 3: 372–387.

Buckingham, Susan. 2004. "Ecofeminism in the Twenty-First Century." *The Geographical Journal* 170(2): 146–154.

Bullard, Robert, ed. 1997. *Unequal Protection: Environmental Justice and Communities of Color.* Oakland, CA: Sierra Club Books for Children.

Burbach, Roger. 2001. *Globalization and Postmodern Politics: From Zapatistas to High-Tech Robber Barons.* London, UK: Pluto Press.

Burciaga, Edelina M. 2019. "Still Undocumented and Still Unafraid: Undocumented Immigrant Activism in Hostile Times." Retrieved on March 12, 2019, from: https://mobilizingideas.wordpress.com/2019/01/02/still-undocumented-and-still-unafraid-undocumented-immigrant-activism-in-hostile-times/

Burger, Joanna, and Michael Gochfeld. 2011. "Conceptual Environmental Justice." *American Journal of Public Health* 101(51): S64–S73.

Burnside, Jonathan, and Nicola Baker, eds. 1994. *Relational Justice.* Winchester, UK: Waterside Press.

Burton, J. W. 1979. *Deviance, Terrorism and War.* New York: St. Martin's Press.

———. 1987. *Resolving Deep-Rooted Conflict.* Lanham, MD.: University Press of America.

———. 1989. *Conflict and Prevention.* London: Macmillan.

———. 1990. "The Need for Human Needs Theory." In *Human Needs and Conflict Resolution.* ed. J. W. Burton. London: Macmillan.

Buschman, John. 2016. "Citizenship and Agency under Neoliberal Global Consumerism: A Search for Informed Democratic Practices." *Journal of Information Ethics* 25(1): 38–53.

Busemeyer, Jerome, and Peter Bruza. 2014. *Quantum Models of Cognition and Decision.* Cambridge: Cambridge University Press.

Bush, Robert, and Joseph Folger. 2004. *The Promise of Mediation: The Transformative Approach to Conflict.* San Francisco: Jossey-Bass.

Butler, Judith. 1988. "Performative Acts and Gender Constitution: An Essay in Phenomenology and Feminist Theory." *Theatre Journal* 40(4): 519–531.

———. 1990. *Bodies That Matter.* New York: Routledge.

———. 1993. *Gender Trouble: Feminism and the Subversion of Identity.* New York: Routledge.

———. 1996. *Gender Trouble.* London: Routledge.

———. 1997a. "Against Proper Objects." In *Feminism Meets Queer Theory*, eds. Elizabeth Weed and Naomi Schor, 1–30. Bloomington: Indiana University Press.

———. 1997b. "Merely Cultural." *Social Text* 52/53: 265–277.

———. 2004. *Undoing Gender.* Boca Raton, FL: Routledge.

———. 2015. *Undoing Gender.* New York: Routledge.

Butler, J., E. Laclau, and S. Žižek. 2000. *Contingency, Hegemony, Universality: Contemporary Dialogues o the Left.* London and New York: Verso.

Butler, Paul. 1995. "Racially Based Jury Nullification: Black Power in the Criminal Justice System." *Yale Law Journal* 105(3): 677.

Byrd, Jodi A. 2011. *The Transit of Empire.* Minneapolis: University of Minnesota Press.

Cachelin, Adrienne, and Jeff Rose. 2018. "Guiding Questions for Critical Sustainability." *Journal of Environmental Studies* 8(4): 518–525.

Cahill, Lisa Sowle. 2003. "Biotech and Justice: Catching up with the Real World Order." *Hastings Center Report* 33(4): 34–44.

Cain, Maureen, and Alan Hunt. 1979. *Marx and Engels on Law.* New York: Academic Press.

Callahan, Manuel. 2004. "Zapatismo Beyond Chiapas." *Globalize Liberation: How to Uproot the System and Build a Better World*, ed. David Solnit, 217–228. San Francisco: City Lights Books.

Callicott, J. Baird. 1997. *A Multicultural Survey of Ecological Ethics from the Mediterranean Basin to the Australian Outback.* Berkeley: University of California Press.

Cameron, Angela. 2006. "Stopping the Violence: Canadian Feminist Debates on Restorative Justice and Intimate Violence." *Theoretical Criminology* 10(1): 49–66.

———. 2005. "Restorative Justice and Intimate Violence: A Critical Review of the Literature." Vancouver: British Columbia Institute Against Family Violence.

———. 2004. "A Sphere of Discipline: The Gendered Subject and Judicially Convened Sentencing Circles." MS.

Campbell, Elaine. 2019. "Witnessing Riot: A Political Ecology of Digital Things." *Journal of Theoretical and Philosophical Criminology* 11: 18–37.

Caputo, John. 1997. "Justice, If Such a Thing Exists." *Deconstruction in a Nutshell*, ed. Jacques Derrida, 125–155. New York: Fordham University Press.

Caraballo-Cueto, Jose, and Juan Lara. 2017. "Deindustrialization and Unsustainable Debt in Middle-Income Countries: The Case of Puerto Rico." *Journal of Globalization and Development* 8(2): 1–11.

Carneiro, Robert, ed. 1967. *The Evolution of Society: Selections from Herbert Spencer's Principles of Sociology*. Chicago: University of Chicago Press.

Carrington, Kerry, and Russell Hogg. 2012. "History of Critical Criminology in Australia." In *Routledge Handbook of Critical Criminology*, eds. Molly Dragiewicz and Walter DeKeseredy, 46–60. London: Routledge.

Carver, T. N. 1915. *Essays in Social Justice*. Cambridge, MA: Harvard University Press.

Castells. Manuel. 2000. *The Rise of the Network Society, vol 1*. Oxford: Blackwell.

———. 2001. *The Internet Galaxy*. New York: Oxford University Press.

———. 2004. *The Power of Identity*. Oxford: Blackwell.

Celello, Peter. 2018. "Desert." The Internet Encyclopedia of Philosophy. Retrieved on November 1, 2018, from: www.iep.utm.edu

Chang, Jeff, Daniel M. HoSang, Soya Jung, Chandan Reddy, and Alex Tom. 2017. "Twenty-Five Years after Sa-I-Gu: Multiracial Politics in Times of Crisis." *Kalfou* 4(2): 252–278.

Charlesworth, Hilary. 2000. "Martha Nussbaum's Feminist Internationalism." *Ethics* October: 64–78.

Charusheeta, S. 2001. "The Promise and Limits of Martha Nussbaum's Universalist Ethics" (Unpublished paper).

Chase, Steve. 2003. "Professional Ethics in the Age of Globalization: How Can Academics Contribute to Sustainability and Democracy Now?" *Ethics, Place and Environment* 6(1): 52–56.

Checker, Melissa. 2001. "'Like Nixon Coming to China': Finding Common Ground in a Multi-Ethnic Coalition for Environmental Justice." *Anthropological Quarterly* 74(3): 135–147.

Cherokee.org. Retrieved on March 3, 2019, from: https://cherokee.org/News /Stories/Archive_2018/20181015_Cherokee-Nation-responds-to-Senator-Warrens -DNA-test

Cho, Charles. 2011. "Astroturfing Global Warming." *Journal of Business Ethics* 104(4): 571–587.

Chowdhury, Kanishka. 2018. "Rosa Luxemburg's the Accumulation of Capital, Postcolonial Theory, and the Problem of Present Day Imperialisms." *New Formations* 94(1): 142–160.

Christie, Isham. 1988. "A Marxist Critique of John Rawls' Theory of Justice." Retrieved on November 1, 2018, from: https://www.ndsu.edu/fileadmin/history /Marxist_Critique_of_Rawls.pdf

Cixous, Helene. 1999. *The Third Body*, trans. Keith Cohen. Evanston, IL: Hydra Books/Northwestern University.

Clark, B, D. Auerbach, and S. Longo. "The Bottom Line: Capital's Production of Social Inequalities and Environmental Degradation." *Journal of Environmental Studies and Science* 8(4): 562–569.

Clement, Grace. 1998. *Care, Autonomy, and Justice: Feminism and the Ethic of Care.* Boulder, CO: Westview Press.

Coates, Jacky, and Michelle Dodds. 1998. "'Isn't Just Being Here Political Enough?' Feminist Action-Oriented Research as Challenges to . . . ." *Feminist Studies* 24(2): 333–347.

Cobb, Charles E., Jr. 2014. *This Nonviolent Stuff'll Get You Killed: How Guns Made the Civil Rights Movement Possible.* New York: Basic Books.

Cobb, Sara. 1997. "The Domestication of Violence in Mediation." *Law and Society Review* 31: 397–440.

Cock, J. 2011. "Green Capitalism or Environmental Justice: A Critique of Sustainabilities Discourse." *Focus* 63(November): 45–51.

Cohen, Roger. 2009. "Iran's Inner America." *New York Times.* Retrieved on October 5, 2019, from: https://www.nytimes.com/2009/02/12/opinion/12Cohen.html

Coker, Donna. 1999. "Enhancing Autonomy for Battered Women: Lessons from Navaho Peacemaking." *UCLA Law Review* 47: 1–111.

Cole, David. 1999. *No Equal Justice: Race and Class in the American Criminal Justice System.* New York: New Press.

Cole, Luke W., and Sheila R. Foster. 2001. *From the Ground Up: Environmental Racism and the Rise of the Environmental Justice Movement.* New York: New York University Press.

Cole, Mike. 2009. "The Color-Line and the Class Struggle: A Marxist Response to Critical Race Theory in Education as It Arrives in the United Kingdom." *Power and Education* 1(1): 111.

———. 2017. "'A Bright Future' for 'Something New and Highly Significant' or a Bit of a Damp Squib?: (Neo-) Marxist Reflections on Recent Theoretical Developments in 'BritCrit' in the Journal 'Race, Ethnicity and Education'." *Journal for Critical Education Policy Studies* 15(3): 57–104.

Colebrook, Claire. 2002. *Gilles Deleuze.* London: Routledge.

Collins, John. 2006. "Copyright, Folklore and Music Piracy in Ghana." *Critical Arts: A South-North Journal of Cultural & Media Studies* 20(1): 158–170.

Collins, Larry, and Dominique Lapierre. 1988. O Jerusalem! New York: Simon and Schuster.

Collins, Patricia Hill. 2000. *Black Feminist Thought: Knowledge, Consciousness, and the Politics of Empowerment,* 2nd ed. New York: Routledge.

Colón Morera, Jose Javier. 2016. "Puerto Rico: A Case of American Imperial Doubts?" *Revista Jurídica University of Puerto Rico* 85(4): 883–896.

Community Environmental Legal Defense Fund. Retrieved on January 2, 2019, from: https://celdf.org/rights/rights-of-nature/

Cone, James. 1969. *Black Theology and Black Power.* New York: Orbis Books.

———. 2010. *Black Theology of Liberation.* New York: Orbis Books.

Conen, Ronen. 2009. *The Rise and Fall of the Mojahedin Khalq, 1987–1997* Sussex, UK: Academic Press.

Conty, Arianne. 2018. "The Politics of Nature." *Theory, Culture, Society* 35(7–8): 73–96.

Conway-Long, Don. 2016. "Indigenous Peoples and Human Rights." *Human Rights Review* 17: 115–120.

Cornell, Drucilla. 1998. *At the Heart of Freedom: Feminism, Sex, and Equality.* Princeton, NJ: Princeton University Press.

———. 1988. *At the Heart of Freedom.* Princeton, NJ: Princeton University Press.

———. 1993. *Transformations.* New York: Routledge.

———. 1999. *Beyond Accommodation.* Boston Way, MD: Rowman and Littlefield.

———. 2007. *Moral Images of Freedom.* Lanham, MD: Rowman and Littlefield.

Cornell, Drucilla, and Nick Friedman. 2016. *The Mandate of Dignity.* NY: Fordham University Press.

Cornell, Drucilla, and Stephen Seely. 2016. *The Spirit of Revolution*. London: Polity Press.

Corrêa Leite, José. 2005. *The World Social Forum: Strategies of Resistance*. Chicago, IL: Haymarket Books.

Cossman, Brenda. 2002. "Family Feuds." In *Privatization, Law, and the Challenge to Feminism*, eds. Brenda Cossman and Judy Fudge. Toronto: University of Toronto Press.

———. 2004. "Sexuality, Queer Theory, and 'Feminism After.'" *McGill Law Journal* 49: 847–868.

Crasnow, Sharon. 2009. "Is Standpoint Theory a Resource for Feminist Epistemology? An Introduction" *Hypatia* 24(4): 189–192.

Crawford, Neta. 2018. "Costs of War." Brown University: Watson Institute. Retrieved on March 1, 2019, from: https://www.globalresearch.ca/us-has-killed-more-than-20-million-people-in-37-victim-nations-since-world-war-ii/5492051

Crenshaw, Kimberle. 1989. "Demarginalizing the Intersection of Race and Sex." *University of Chicago Legal Forum* 1(8): 139–167.

———. 1991. "Mapping the Margins: Intersectionality, Identity Politics, and Violence against Women of Color." *Stanford Law Review* 43(6): 1241–1299.

Cunneen, Chris, and Juan Tauri. 2016. *Indigenous Criminology*. Chicago, IL: University of Chicago Press.

Curle, A. 1971. *Making Peace*. London: Tavistock Publications.

Dalsheim, Joyce. 2013. "Theory for Praxis Peacemaking, Cunning Recognition, and the Constitution of Enmity." *Social Analysis* 57(2): 59–80.

Daly, Kathleen. 2003a. "Mind the Gap: Restorative Justice in Theory and Practice." In *Restorative Justice and Criminal Justice*, eds. Andrew von Hirsch, Julian Roberts, and Anthony Bottoms, 219–236. Oxford: Hart Publishers.

———. 2003b. "Restorative Justice: The Real Story." In *A Restorative Justice Reader*, ed. Gerry Johnstone, 361–372. Cullompton, UK: Willan Publishing.

———. 2016. "What Is Restorative Justice? Fresh Answers to a Vexed Question." *Victims and Offenders* 11: 9–29.

Dansie, Elizabeth. 2011. "A Multigroup Analysis of Reintegrative Shaming Theory: An Application to Drunk Driving Offenses." PhD Dissertation, Utah University. Retrieved on December 12, 2018, from: https://pqdtopen.proquest.com/doc/854464331.html?FMT=ABS

Davis, Angela Y. 1983. *Women, Race, and Class*. New York: Vintage Books.

Dawson, Jane I. 2000. "The Two Faces of Environmental Justice: Lessons from the Eco-Nationalist Phenomenon." *Environmental Politics* 9(2): 22–60.

De Genova, Nicholas. 2013. "Spectacles of Migrants' Illegality." *Ethnic and Racial Studies* 36(7): 1180–1198.

Degruy, Joy. 2017. *Post Traumatic Slave Syndrome*. Milwaukee, OR: Uptone Press.

———. *Post Traumatic Slave Syndrome*. Retrieved on March 1, 2019, from: https://www.youtube.com/watch?v=BGjSday7f_8   https://www.youtube.com/watch?v=MH7tpAK8APY

De Haan, Peter. 2016. *From Keynes to Piketty: The Century That Shook Up Economics*. London: Palgrave Macmillan.

Delanda, Manuel. 2002. *Intensive Science and Virtual Philosophy*. New York: Continuum.

De Lauretis, Teresa. 1991. *Queer Theory: Lesbian and Gay Sexualities*. Bloomington, IN: Indiana University Press.

———. 1994a. *The Practice of Love: Lesbian Sexuality and Perverse Desire*. Indianapolis: Indiana University Press.

———. 1994b. "Habit Changes." *Differences: A Journal of Feminist Culture Studies* 6: 296–313.

———. 1994c. "Fellini's 9 ½." In *Gender: Literary and Cinematic Representation*, ed. Jeanne Ruppert, 51–65. Miami: University Press of Florida.

"Delayed Choice Quantum Eraser Experiment Explained." Retrieved on February 4, 2019, from: https://www.youtube.com/watch?v=H6HLjpj4Nt4

Deleuze. Gilles. 1983. *Nietzsche and Philosophy*. New York: Columbia University Press.

———. 1986. *Foucault*, trans. Sean Hand. Minneapolis: University of Minnesota Press.

———. 1988. *Spinoza*, trans. Robert Hurley. San Francisco: City Lights Books.

———. 1990. *The Logic of Sense*, trans. M. Lester with C. Stivale. New York: Columbia University Press.

———. 1993. *Critique et Clinique*. Paris: Minuit.

———. 1994. *Difference and Repetition*, trans. P. Patton. New York: Columbia University Press.

———. 1996. "L'Abécédaire de Gilles Deleuze." Directed by Pierre-André Boutang. Paris: Editions Montparnasse. Retrieved on March 1, 2019, from: https://www.youtube.com/watch?v=L_GZ_LZvpZc

Deleuze, Gilles, and Felix Guattari. 1983. *Anti-Oedipus: Capitalism and Schizophrenia*. Minneapolis: Minnesota University Press.

———.1987. *A Thousand Plateaus*. Minneapolis: Minnesota University Press.

Delgado, Richard. 2001. "Two Ways to Think about Race: Reflections on the Id, the Ego, and Other Reformist Theories of Equal Protection." *Georgia Law Journal* 89: 2279–2291.

———. 2003. "Crossroads and Blind Alleys: A Critical Examination of Recent Writing about Race. *Texas Law Review* 82: 121–166.

Delgado, Richard, and Jean Stefancic. 1994. *Failed Revolutions: Social Reform and the Limits of Legal Imagination*. San Francisco: Westview Press.

———. eds. 1998. The Latino/a Condition: A Critical Reader. New York: New York University Press.

———. 2001. *Critical Race Theory: An Introduction*, 2nd ed. New York: New York University Press.

———. 2017. *Critical Race Theory: An Introduction*, 3rd ed. New York: New York University Press.

DeMartino, George. 2003. "Realizing Class Justice." *Rethinking Marxism* 15(1): 1–31.

Democracynow.org. 2019a. "Puerto Rico: Vulture Funds to Make a Killing as Judge Approves Deal to Restructure Island's Debt." Retrieved on February 6, 2019, from: https://www.democracynow.org/2019/2/6/puerto_rico_vulture_funds_to_make

Democracynow.org. 2019b. "'We Have to Mass Mobilize': Laverne Cox & Chase Strangio Sound the Alarm on Major LGBTQ SCOTUS Cases." Retrieved on October 9, 2019, from: https://www.democracynow.org/2019/10/7/trans_rights_us_supreme_court_hearings

de Oca Valadez, Gerardo Montes. 2018. "Zapatistas - Between Us and Them." *Krisis* 2: 178–183.

Derrida, Jacques. 1967. *Of Grammatology*. Baltimore, MD: Johns Hopkins University Press.

———. 1986. "Declarations of Independence," trans. Tom Keenam and Tom Pepper. *New Political Science* 15: 7–17.

———. 1989. "Force of Law: The Mystical Foundations of Authority." In *Deconstruction and the Possibility of Justice*, eds. D. Cornell, M. Rosenfeld, and D. Carlson. New York: Routledge.

———. 1992. "Before the Law." In *Jacques Derrida: Acts of Literature*, ed. Derek Attridge. New York: Routledge.

———. 1995. *The Gift of Death*, trans. David Wills. Chicago: University of Chicago Press.

———. 1997a. *Deconstruction in a Nutshell*, ed. John Caputo. New York: Fordham University Press.

———. 1997b. *The Politics of Friendship*. London: Verso.

Desai, Ashwin and Goolam Vahed. 2015. *The South African Gandhi: Stretcher Bearer of Empire*. Redwood City, CA: Stanford University Press.

De Vitoria, Francisco. 1934. "De Indis." In *The Spanish Origin of International Law*, ed. James Brown Scott, Appendix A. Oxford: Clarendon Press.

Dhaliwal, Sukhwant, and Kirsten Forkert. 2015. "Deserving and Undeserving Migrants." *Soundings* 61(13): 49–61.

DiChiro, G. 2018. "Canaries in the Anthropocene." *Journal of Environmental Studies and Science* 8(4): 526–538.

Dickerson, Caitlin. 2019. "Border at 'Breaking Point' as More Than 76,000 Migrants Cross in a Month. *New York Times*, March 6, 2019.

Dicochea, Perlita. 2012. "Discourses of Race and Racism Within Environmental Justice Studies: An Eco-Racial Intervention." *Ethnicity and Race in a Changing World: A Review Journal* 3(2): 17–38.

Dietz, Adolf. 1993. "The Moral Right of the Author: Moral Rights and the Civil Law Countries." *Columbia-VLA Journal of Law and the Arts* 19: 199.

Dobbs, Farrell. 2002. *Teamster Rebellion: The 1930s Strikes and Organizing Drive That Transformed the Labor Movement in the Midwest*. New York: Pathfinder Press.

Dobson, Andrew. 1998. *Justice and the Environment: Conceptions of Sustainability and Dimensions of Social Justice*. Oxford: Oxford University Press.

———. 2003. "Social Justice and Environmental Sustainability: Ne'er the Twain Shall Meet?" In *Sustainabilities: Development in an Unequal World*, eds. Julian Agyeman, Robert Bullard, and Bob Evans, 83–95. Cambridge, MA: MIT Press.

Dolan, M., and M. Doyle. 2000. "Violence Risk Prediction." *British Journal of Psychiatry* 177: 303–311.

Donohoe, Martin. 2003. "Causes and Health Consequences of Environmental Degradation and Social Injustice." *Social Science and Medicine* 56: 573–587.

"Double-Slit Experiment," YouTube. Retrieved on February 3, 2019, from: https://www.youtube.com/watch?v=uva6gBEpfDY

Douzinas, Costas. 2005. "Oubliez Critique." *Law and Critique* 16: 47–69.

Dual Citizen. Retrieved on January 20, 2019, from: http://dualcitizeninc.com/global-green-economy-index/

Du Bois, W.E.B. 2018. History: A+E Televisions Network. Retrieved on January 3, 2019, from: https://www.history.com/topics/black-history/w-e-b-du-bois

Dudas, Jeffrey R. 2005. "In the Name of Equal Rights: "Special" Rights and the Politics of Resentment in Post-Civil Rights America." *Law & Society Review* 39(4): 723–757.

Dudouet, Veronique. 2006. "Transitions from Violence to Peace." In Berghoff Research Center for Constructive Conflict Management, Berghoff Report Nr. 15. Berlin.

Dudziak, Mary. 1988. "Desegration as a Cold War Imperative." *Stanford Law Review* 41: 61–89.

Dugan, M. 1996. "A Nested Theory of Conflict." *A Leadership Journal: Women in Leadership—Sharing the Vision* 1(1): 9–30.

Dunbar-Ortiz, Roxanne, 2015. *An Indigenous Peoples' History of the United States*. Boston: Beacon Press.

Du Rees, H. 2001. "Can Criminal Law Protect the Environment?" *Journal of Scandinavian Studies in Criminology and Crime Prevention* 2(2): 109–126.

Durkheim, Emile. 1958. *Professional Ethics and Civic Morals*. Glencoe, IL: The Free Press.

———. 1964a. *The Rules of Sociological Method*. New York: The Free Press.

————. 1964b. *The Division of Labor in Society*. New York: The Free Press.

————. 1984. *On Morality and Society*. Chicago: University of Chicago Press.

D'Vera, Cohn. 2015. "Census Considers new Approach to Asking about Race—By Not Using the Term at All." Pew Research Institute. Retrieved on March 15, 2019, from: http://www.pewresearch.org/fact-tank/2015/06/18/census-considers-new-approach-to-asking-about-race-by-not-using-the-term-at-all/

Dworkin, Ronald. 1973. "The Original Position." *University of Chicago Law Review* 40: 500–533.

————. 1978. *Taking Rights Seriously*. London: Duckworth.

————. 2000. *Sovereign Virtue*. Cambridge, MA: Harvard University Press.

Dyck, David. 2000. "Reaching Toward a Structurally Responsive Training and Practice of Restorative Justice." *Contemporary Crises Review* 3(3): 239–265.

————. 2006. "Reaching Toward a Structurally Responsive Training and Practice of Restorative Justice." In *Handbook of Restorative Justice*, eds. Dennis Sullivan and Larry Tifft, 527–545. New York: Routledge.

Dyer-Witheford, Nick. 1999. *Cyber-Marx: Cycles and Circuits of Struggle in High-Technology Capitalism*. Chicago: University of Illinois Press.

Dyson, Michael Eric. 2000. *I May Not Get There with You: The True Martin Luther King, Jr*. New York: The Free Press.

Eglash, Albert. 1977. "Beyond Restitution: Creative Restitution." In *Restitution in Criminal Justice*, eds. Joe Hudson and Burt Gataway. Lexington, MA: D. C. Heath.

Eitzen, Stanley, and Kenneth Stewart. 2007. *Solutions to Social Problems*. Boston: Allyn and Bacon.

Eldeman, Lee. 1995. "Queer Theory: Unstating Desire." *GLQ: A Journal of Lesbian and Gay Studies* 2(4): 343–346.

Elder-Vass, Dave. 2008. "Searching for Realism, Structure and Agency in Actor Network Theory." *British Journal of Sociology* 59(3): 455–473.

Elster, John. 2004. *Closing the Books: Transitional Justice in Historical Perspective*. Cambridge, MA: Cambridge University Press.

Enck-Wanzer, Darrel, ed. 2010. *The Young Lords*. New York: NYU Press.

Engels, Frederick. 1972. *The Origin of the Family, Private Property and the State*. New York: International Publishers.

"Equality Act 2010." Equality and Human Rights Commission. Retrieved on March 12, 2019, from: https://www.equalityhumanrights.com/en/equality-act-2010/what-equality-act

Erakat, Noura. 2019. *Justice for Some: Law and the Question of Palestine*. Stanford, CA: Stanford University Press.

Ericson, Richard, and Kevin Haggerty. 1997. *Policing the Risk Society*. Toronto: University of Toronto Press.

Erikson, Kai. 1966. *Wayward Puritans*. New York: John Wiley and Sons.

Europa.eu. 2019. European Union. Retrieved on March 26, 2019, from: https://europa.eu/european-union/index_en

European No Campaign. N.D.. Retrieved on July 24, 2005, from: www.europeannocampaign.com

Evans, Brian. 2004. "Principles of Kyoto and Emissions Trading Systems: A Primer for Energy Lawyers." *Alberta Law Review* 42: 1–30.

Evans, Gary W., and Lyscha A. Marcynyszyn. 2004. "Environmental Justice, Cumulative Environmental Risk, and Health among Low- and Middle-Income Children in Upstate New York." *Research and Practice* 94(11): 1942–1944.

Ewick, Patricia, and Susan Silbey. 1998. *The Common Place of Law*. Chicago: University of Chicago Press.

"Examples of Court Decisions," U.S. Equal Employment Opportunity Commission. Retrieved on March 12, 2019, from: https://www.eeoc.gov/eeoc/newsroom/wysk/lgbt_examples_decisions.cfm

Fanon, Franz. 1967. *The Wretched of the Earth*. London: Penguin.

————. 1986. *Black Skins, White Masks*. London: Pluto Press.

Farber, Daniel, and Suzanna Sherry. 1997. *Beyond All Reason: The Radical Assault on Truth in American Law*. New York: Oxford University Press.

Farley, Christine. 1997. "Protecting Folklore of Indigenous Peoples: Is Intellectual Property the Answer?" *Connecticut Law Review* 1: 31.

Farmer, Paul. 2006. *AIDS and Accusation: Haiti and the Geography of Blame*. Berkeley: University of California Press.

————. 2013. *To Repair the World: Paul Farmer Speaks to the Next Generation*, ed. Jonathan Weigel. Berkeley: University of California Press.

Fasching-Varner, Kenneth J., Roland W. Mitchell, Lori L. Martin, and Karen P. Bennett- Haron. 2014. "Beyond School-to-Prison Pipeline and Toward an Educational and Penal Realism." *Equity & Excellence in Education* 47(4): 410–429.

Feeley, Malcolm M., and Jonathan Simon. 1994. "Actuarial Justice: The Emerging New Criminal Law." In *The Futures of Criminology*, ed. David Nelken, 173–201. London: Sage.

————.2004. "The New Penology." In *Theorizing Criminal Justice*, ed. Peter Kraska, 302–322. Long Grove, IL: Waveland Press.

Feingold, Jonathan P., and Evelyn R. Carter. 2018. "Eyes Wide Open: What Social Science Can Tell Us about the Supreme Court's Use of Social Science." *Northwestern University Law Review* 112(6): 1689–1711.

Fergusen, Andrew. 2017a. "Policing Predictive Policing." *Washington University Law Review* 94(5): 1111–1188.

————. 2017b. *The Rise of Big Data Policing: Surveillance, Race and the Future of Law Enforcement*. NY: NYU Press.

Fernández Campbell, Alexia. 2019. "West Virginia Teachers Are on Strike Again. Here's Why. This Time, It's Not about Pay Raises." *Vox*. Retrieved on March 13, 2019, from: https://www.vox.com/2019/2/19/18231486/west-virginia-teacher-strike-2019

Fernando, Jude L. 2003. "The Power of Unsustainable Development: What Is to Be Done?" *The Annals of the American Academy of Political and Social Sciences* 590: 6–34.

Ferrara, Alessandro. 2003. "Two Notions of Humanity and the Judgment Argument for Human Rights." *Political Theory* 31(3): 392–420.

Ferreira, Felipe. 2017. "Critical Sustainability Studies: A Holistic and Visionary Conception of Socio-Ecological Conscientization." *Journal of Sustainability Education* E-Journal. Retrieved on January 2, 2019, from: http://www.susted.com/wordpress/content/critical-sustainability-studies-a-holistic-and-visionary-conception-of-socio-ecological-conscientization_2017_04/

Ferry, Martin. 2003. "The EU and Recent Regional Reform in Poland." *Europe-Asia Studies* 55(7): 1097–1116.

Fieguth, Paul. 2016. *An Introduction to Complex Systems: Society, Ecology, and Non- Linear Dynamics*. Cham, Switzerland: Springer Publishers.

Figueroa, Robert. 2003. "Bivalent Environmental Justice and the Culture of Poverty." *Rutgers University Journal of Law and Urban Policy* 1(1): 27–42.

Fineman, Martha. 1995. *The Neutered Mother, the Sexual Family, and Other Twentieth-Century Tragedies*. New York: Routledge.

Fitzpatrick, Peter. 2001. *Modernism and the Grounds of Law*. Cambridge: Cambridge University Press.

Fleras, Augie. 1999. "Politicizing Indignity." In *Indigenous Peoples' Rights in Australia, Canada and New Zealand*, ed. Paul Havemann, 187–235. Oxford: Oxford University Press.

Flew, Antony. 1979. "Definition of Punishment." In *Contemporary Punishment: Views, Explanations, and Justifications*, eds. Rudolph Gerber and Patrick McAnany, 31–35. Notre Dame, IN: University of Notre Dame Press.

Foley, Duncan K. 2010. "Lineages of Crisis Economics from the 1930s: Keynes, Hayek, and Schumpeter." *Eastern Economic Journal* 36: 413–422.

Folger, Joseph, and Robert Baruch Bush. 2014. "Transformative Mediation." *International Journal of Conflict Engagement and Resolution* 2(62). Retrieved on November 30, 2018, from: scholarlycommons.law.hofstra.edu/faculty_scholarship/441

———. 2015. "Reclaiming Mediation's Future: Getting over the Intoxication of Expertise, Re-Focusing on Party Self-Determination." Mediate Online. Retrieved on November 18, 2018, from: mediate.com/pfriendly.cfm?id=11094

Follet, Mary Parker. 1998. *The New State: Group Organization the Solution of Popular Government*. University Park, PA: Pennsylvania State University Press.

Foreman, Christopher H. 1998. *The Promise and the Peril of Environmental Justice*. Washington D.C.: Brookings Institute Press.

Forst, Reiner. 2007. "First Things First: Redistribution, Recognition and Justification." *European Journal of Political Theory* 6: 291–304.

———. 2014. *The Right to Justification*. New York: Columbia University Press.

Foucault, Michel. 1977a. *Discipline and Punish*. New York: Pantheon Books.

———. 1977b. *Language, Counter-Memory, Practice*. Ithaca, NY: Cornell University Press.

———. 1986. *The Care of the Self*. NY: Random House.

Fox, Nick, and Pam Alldred. 2018. *Sociology and the New Materialism*. London: Sage.

———. 2018. "New Materialism." In *The Sage Encyclopedia of Research Methods*, eds. P. Ankinson, D. Delamont, S. Hardy, and M. Williams. London: Sage.

France24.com. 2019. "Trump Bonds with Brazil's Bolsonaro in White House Visit." Retrieved on March 27, 2019, from: https://www.france24.com/en/20190319 -usa-brazil-trump-bolsonaro-white-house

Francis, Diane. 2010. *From Pacification to Peace Building*. London: Pluto Press.

Frank, Dana. 2003. "Where are the Workers in Consumer-Worker Alliances? Class Dynamics and the History of Consumer-Labor Campaigns." *Politics and Society* 31(3): 363–379.

Fraser, Nancy. 1997. "Heterosexism, Misrecognition and Capitalism: A Response to Judith Butler." *Social Text* 52/53: 279–289.

———. 2000. "Rethinking Recognition." *New Left Review* 3: 107–120.

———. 2007. "Re-Framing Justice in a Globalizing Order." In *(Mis)recognition, Social Inequality and Social Justice*, eds. Nancy Fraser and Pierre Bourdieu, 17–35. NY: Routledge.

Fraser, Nancy, and Alex Honneth. 2003. *Redistribution or Recognition?* London: Verso.

Freire, Paulo. 1972. *Pedagogy of the Oppressed*. New York: Herder and Herder.

———. 1985. *The Politics of Education*. South Hadley, MA: Bergin and Garvey.

Friedsky, Jean. 2005. "Bolivia's Gas War Moves Inside." *ZNet*. Retrieved on June 16, 2005, from: http://www.zmag.org/content/showarticle.cfm

Fuchs, Christian. 2017. "Reflections on Michael Hardt and Antonia Negri's book, 'Assembly.'" *tripleC* 15(2): 851–865.

Fuchs, Josef. 1965. *Natural Law*. New York: Sheed and Ward.

Fuller, Steve. 2004. "The Future of Scientific Justice: The Case of *The Sceptical Environmentalist*." *Futures* 36: 631–636.

Gaard, G. 2011. "Ecofeminism Revisited." *Feminist Formations* 23(2): 26–53.

Gaarder, Emily, and Lois Presser. 2006. "A Feminist Vision of Justice?" In *Handbook of Restorative Justice*, eds. Dennis Sullivan and Larry Tifft, 483–495. New York: Routledge.

Gabbidon, Shawn. 2015. *Criminological Perspectives on Race and Crime*. London: Routledge.

Gannon, Megan. 2016. "Race is a Social Construct, Scientists Argue." *Scientific American*. Retrieved on March 21, 2019, from: https://www.scientificamerican .com/article/race-is-a-social-construct-scientists-argue/

Garcon, Francisco. 2007. "The Quest for Cognition in Plant Neurobiology." *Plant Signaling and Behavior* 2(2): 208–211.

Garrow, David J. 2004. *Bearing the Cross: Martin Luther King, Jr. and the Southern Leadership Conference.* New York: Harper Perennial.

Gaus, Gerald F. 2000. *Political Concepts and Political Theories.* Boulder, CO: Westview Press.

Gbadegesin, Segun. 2001. "Multinational Corporations, Developed Nations, and Environmental Racism: Toxic Waste, Exploration, and Eco-Catastrophe." In *Faces of Environmental Racism: Confronting Issues of Global Justice,* eds. Laura Westra and Bill E. Lawson, 187–202. New York: Rowman and Littlefield.

Gerber, Rudolph, and Patrick McAnany. 1979. *Contemporary Punishment: Views, Explanations, and Justifications.* Notre Dame, IN: University of Notre Dame Press.

Gibson, James. 2014. *The Ecological Approach to Visual Perception.* London: Routledge.

Giddens, Anthony. 1986. *Durkheim on Politics and the State.* Cambridge: Polity Press.

Gilens, Naomi. 2019. "It's Perfectly Constitutional to Talk about Jury Nullification." *ACLU.org.* Retrieved on March 7, 2019, from: https://www.aclu.org/blog/free - speech/its-perfectly-constitutional-talk-about-jury-nullification

Gill, Aisha K., and Karen Harrison. 2013. "Sentencing Sex Offenders in India: Retributive Justice versus Sex-Offender Treatment Programmes and Restorative Justice Approaches." *International Journal of Criminal Justice Sciences* 8(2): 166–181.

Gilley, Bruce. 2017. "The case for colonialism." *Third World Quarterly.* Reprinted in *Academic Questions,* Summer 2018: 167–185.

Gilligan, Carol. 1982. *In a Different Voice.* Cambridge, MA: Harvard University Press.

Gledhill, John. 2001. "'Disappearing the Poor?': A Critique of the New Wisdoms of Social Democracy in an Age of Globalization." *Urban Anthropology* 30(2–3): 123–156.

Glen, Susan. 2019. "'We Charge Genocide': The 1951 Black Lives Matter Campaign." Retrieved on March 1, 2019, from: http://depts.washington.edu/moves /CRC_genocide.shtml

Gochfeld, Michael, and Joanna Burger. 2011. "Disproportionate Exposure in Environmental Justice and Other Populations." *American Journal of Public Health* 101(51): S53–S63.

Goldberg, D. T. 1993. *Racist Culture.* Boston, MA: Blackwell Publishers, Ltd.

Gonzalez, Juan. 2000. *Harvest of Empire: The History of Latinos in America.* New York: Viking Press.

Goodchild, Philip. 1996. *Deleuze and Guattari: An Introduction to the Politics of Desire.* London: Sage Publications.

Grad, Rachael. 2003. "Indigenous Rights and Intellectual Property Law: A Comparison of the United States and Australia." *Duke Journal of Comparative and International Law* 13: 203–227.

Graeber, David. 2003. "The Globalization Movement and the New Left." In *Implicating Empire: Globalization and Resistance in the 21st Century World-Order,* eds. Stanley Aronowtiz and Heather Gautney, 325–338. New York: Basic Books.

Gramsci, Antonio. 1971. *Selections from the Prison Notebooks.* New York: International Publishers.

Grandin, Greg. 2019a. "How the U.S. Weaponized the Border Wall." *The Intercept.* Retrieved on March 7, 2019, from: https://theintercept.com/2019/02/10/us-mexico -border-fence-history/

———. 2019b. *The End of the Myth: From the Frontier to the Border Wall in the Mind of America.* New York: Metropolitan Books.

Graves, Benjamin. 1998a. "Homi K. Bhabha: The Liminal Negotiation of Cultural Differences." Retrieved on March 1, 2019, from: http://postcolonialweb.org /poldiscourse/bhabha/bhabha2.html

———. 1998b. "Homi K. Bhabha: An Overview." Retrieved on March 2, 2019, from: http://postcolonialweb.org/poldiscourse/bhabha/bhabha1.html

———. 1998c. "'Signs Taken for Wonders'—Hybridity and Resistance." Retrieved on March 2, 2019, from: http://postcolonialweb.org/poldiscourse/bhabha/bha bha4.html

Green, Ross. 1998. *Justice in Aboriginal Communities: Sentencing Alternatives.* Saskatchewan: Purish Publishers.

Greenberg, David, and Agozino, B. 2012. "Execution, Imprisonment, and Crime in Trinidad and Tobago. *British Journal of Criminology* 52: 113–140.

Greenspan, Alan. 2001. "Globalization: Remarks." Retrieved on March 18, 2019, from: http://www.federalreserve.gov/boarddocs/speeches/2001/20011024/default .htm

Greenstein, Tony. 2019. "How Netanyahu's Embrace of the Israeli Far Right Unmasked Zionism." Aljazeera.com. Retrieved on March 23, 2019, from: https:// www.aljazeera.com/indepth/opinion/netanyahu-embrace-israel-190228090 750630.html

Griffiths, John. 1970. "Ideology in Criminal Procedure *Or* a Third 'Model' of the Criminal Process." *Yale Law Journal* 79(3): 359–417.

Gross, Samuel. 2012. "David Baldus and the Legacy of *McCleskey v. Kemp.*" *Iowa Law Review* 97: 1905–1924.

Grosz, Elizabeth. 1994. *Volatile Bodies.* Bloomington: Indiana University Press.

Guattari, Felix. 1984. *Molecular Revolution: Psychiatry and Politics.* Harmondsworth, UK: Penguin.

Guattari, Felix, and Toni Negri. 1990. *Communists Like Us.* New York: Autonomdeia.

Gubrium, Jaber, and James Holstein. 1997. *The New Language of Qualitative Method.* Oxford: Oxford University Press.

Gutierrez, Gustavo.1971. *A Theology of Liberation.* New York: Orbis Books.

Gutierrez, Gustavo, and Ludwig Muller. 2015. *On the Side of the Poor.* New York: Orbis Books.

Haarstad, Håvard. 2009. "Globalization and the New Spaces for Social Movement Politics: The Marginalization of Labor Unions in Bolivian Gas Nationalization." *Globalizations* 6 (2): 169–185.

Haber, Honi Fern. 1994. *Beyond Postmodern Politics: Lyotard, Rorty, Foucault.* New York: Routledge.

Habermas, Jurgen. 1975. *Legitimation Crisis*, trans. Thomas McCarthy. Boston: Beacon Press.

———. 1976. "Some Distinctions in Universal Pragmatics." *Theory and Society* 3: 161.

———. 1979. *Communication and the Evolution of Society*, trans. Thomas McCarthy. Boston: Beacon Press.

Haggerty, Kevin, and Richard Ericson. 2006. *The New Politics of Surveillance and Visibility.* Toronto: University of Toronto Press.

Hagopian, Amy, Abraham D. Flaxman, Tim K. Takaro, Sahar A. Esa Al Shatari, Julie Rajaratnam, Stan Becker, et al. 2013. "Mortality in Iraq Associated with the 2003–2011 War and Occupation: Findings from a National Cluster Sample Survey by the University Collaborative Iraq Mortality Study." *PLOS Medicine.* Retrieved on January 15, 2019, from: https://doi.org/10.1371/journal.pmed.1001533

Haley, Alex. 1992. *The Autobiography of Malcolm X as Told to Alex Haley.* New York: Ballantine Books.

Hall, Matthew. 2017. "Exploring the Cultural Dimensions of Environmental Victimization." *Palgrave Communications* 3: 17076, doi: 10.1057/palcomms.2017.76.

Hallas, Duncan. 2003. *Trotsky's Marxism.* Chicago: Haymarket Books.

Halley, Ian. 2004a. "Feminism and the Law." *Duke Journal of Gender Law and Policy* 11: 7–45.

————. 2004b. "Queer Theory by Men." *Duke Journal of Gender Law and Policy* 11: 7.

Halley, Janet. 2002. "Sexuality Harassment." In *Left Legalism/Left Critique*, eds. Janet Halley and Wendy Brown. Durham, NC: Duke University Press.

————. 2004. "Take a Break from Feminism?" In *Gender and Human Rights*, ed. Karen Knop. Oxford: Oxford University Press.

Halloway, John. 2002. *Change the World Without Taking Power*. London: Pluto.

Halperin, David. 1995. *Saint Foucault. Towards a Gay Hagiography*. New York: Oxford University Press.

Halsey, Mark. 2004. "Against 'Green' Criminology." *British Journal of Criminology* 44(6): 833–853.

Hamilton, Melissa. 2012. "Risk-Needs Assessment—Constitutional and Ethical Challenges." *American Law Review* 52: 231.

————. 2019. "The Biased Algorithm: Disparate Impact on Hispanics." *American Criminal Law Review*, forthcoming.

Hammond, Zaretta. 2015. *Culturally Responsive Teaching and the Brain*. Thousand Oaks, CA: Sage Publications.

Haraway, Donna. 2018. *A Cyborg Manifesto*. London: Routledge.

Harding, Sandra, ed. 2004. *The Feminist Standpoint Reader*. New York: Routledge.

Harding, Sandra. 2009. "Standpoint Theories: Productively Controversial." *Hypatia*. 24(4): 192–200.

Hardt, Michael. 1993. *Gilles Deleuze: An Apprenticeship in Philosophy*. Minneapolis: Minnesota University Press.

————. 2018. "Interview, Empire and Multitude: Shaping Our Century." *Great Transition Initiatives: Toward a Transformative Vision and Praxis*. Retrieved on March 12, 2019, from: https://www.greattransition.org/publication/empire-and-multitude

Hardt, Michael, and Antonio Negri. 1994. *Labor of Dionysus*. Minneapolis: University of Minnesota Press.

————. 2000. *Empire*. Cambridge, MA: Harvard University Press.

————. 2004. *Multitude: War and Democracy in the Age of Empire*. New York: Penguin Books.

————. 2009. *Commonwealth*. Cambridge, MA: Harvard University Press.

————. 2017. *Assembly*. London: Oxford University Press.

Harman, Chris. 2003. "How the Revolution Was Lost." In *Russia: From Workers' State to State*, ed. Anthony Arnove, 13–36. Chicago: Haymarket Books.

Harper, Charles, and Kevin Leicht. 2010. *Exploring Social Change*. New York: Prentice Hall.

Harrington, Theresa. 2019. "Oakland School Board Cuts $20.2 Million from Budget, Including 100 jobs." Edsource.org. Retrieved on March 13, 2019, from: https://edsource.org/2019/oakland-school-board-cuts-20-2-million-from -budget-including-100-jobs/609483

Harris, Kay. 1989. "Alternative Visions in the Context of Contemporary Realities." In *New Perspectives on Crime and Justice: Occasional Papers of the MCC Canada Victim Offender Ministries Program and MCC U.S. Office of Criminal Justice*, Issue 7. Elkhart, IN: Mennonite Central, Committee.

————. 2003. "Globalization and Democracy." In *Implicating Empire: Globalization and Resistance in the 21st Century World-Order*, eds. Stanley Aronowtiz and Heather Gautney, 109–121. New York: Basic Books.

————. 2004. *Multitude: War and Democracy in the Age of Empire*. New York: Penguin Books.

————. 2006. "Transformative Justice: The Transformation of Restorative Justice." In *Handbook of Restorative Justice*, eds. Dennis Sullivan and Larry Tifft, 555–565. New York: Routledge.

Harrison, James. 2018. "Significant International Environmental Law Cases." *Journal of Environmental Law* 30(3): 527–541.

Harsanyi, John. 1975. "Can the Maximin Principle Serve as a Basis of Morality?" *American Political Science Review* 69(2): 594–606.

Hart, Nicole. 2004. "The Progress and Pitfalls of *Lawrence v. Texas.*" *Buffalo Law Review* 52: 1417–1449.

Hart, S. D. 1998a. "Psychopathy and Risk for Violence." In *Psychopathy: Theory, Research and Implications for Society*, eds. D. Cooke, A. E. Forth, and R. D. Hare, 355–375. Dordrecht, Netherlands: Kluwer.

———. 1998b. "The Role of Psychopathy in Assessing Risk for Violence: Conceptual and Methodological Issues." *Legal and Criminological Psychology* 3: 121–137.

Harvey, David, Michael Hardt, and Antonio Negri. 2009. "Commonwealth: An Exchange." *Art-forum* 48(3): 210–221.

Haskell, David. 2017. "10 Ways to Listen to Trees." Retrieved on January 20, 2019, from: https://blogs.scientificamerican.com/observations/10-ways-to-listen-to-trees

———. 2018. *The Songs of Trees*. New York: Penguin Books.

Haughton, G. 1999. "Environmental Justice and the Sustainable City." *Journal of Planning, Education and Research* 18(3): 233–243.

Hausheer, Justine. 2015. "Eavesdropping on the Sounds of the Rainforest." Retrieved on January 20, 2019, from: https://blog.nature.org/science/2015/09/14/eavesdropping-on-the-sounds-of-the-rainforest

Havermann, Paul. 1999. "Indigenous Rights in the Political Jurisprudence of Australia, Canada, and New Zealand." In *Indigenous Peoples' Rights in Australia, Canada and New Zealand*, ed. Paul Havemann, 22–64. Oxford: Oxford University Press.

Hawkins, Gordon. 1979. "Punishment as a Moral Educator." In *Contemporary Punishment: Views, Explanations, and Justifications*, eds. Rudolph Gerber and Patrick McAnany, 120–128. Notre Dame, IN: University of Notre Dame Press.

Hawthoren, Michael. 2005. "Smelter in Pilsen over Lead." *Chicago Tribune*, July 7.

Hayner, Priscilla. 2002. *Unspeakable Truths: Facing the Challenge of Truth Commissions.* New York: Taylor and Francis.

Hegel, G.W.F. 1977. *Phenomenology of Spirit*, trans. A. V. Miller. New York: Oxford University Press.

Held, Virginia, ed. 1995. *Justice and Care: Essential Readings in Feminist Ethics*. Boulder, CO: Westview Press.

Held, V. 2006. *The Ethics of Care*. Oxford: Oxford University Press.

Hendrix, Burke. 2012. *Ownership, Authority, and Self Determination: Moral Principles and Indigenous Rights Claims*. University Park, PA: Pennsylvania University Press.

Henry, Stuart, and Dragan Milovanovic. 1996. *Constitutive Criminology: Beyond Postmodernism*. London: Sage.

———. 2019. "Constitutive Criminology." In *The Sage Dictionary of Crime*, 2nd ed., eds. Eugene McLaughlin and John Muncie, 86–90. London: Sage Publications.

Henry, Stuart, and Mark Lanier, eds. 2001a. *What Is Crime?* New York: Rowman and Littlefield.

———. 2001b. "The Prism of Crime." In *What Is Crime?* eds. Stuart Henry and Mark Lanier, 227–243. New York: Rowman and Littlefield.

———. 2006. *The Essential Criminology Reader*. Boulder, CO: Westview Press.

Hertsgaard, Mark. 2019. "On March 15, the Climate Kids Are Coming." *The Nation.* Retrieved on March 31, 2019, from: https://www.thenation.com/article/greta-thunberg-climate-change-strike/

Herzog, Lisa. 2018. "Durkheim on Social Justice." *American Political Science Review* 112(1): 112–124.

Hill, Sarah. 2001. "The Environmental Divide: Neoliberal Incommensurability at the U.S.-Mexico Border." *Urban Anthropology* 30(2): 157–187.

Hillebrecht, Anna, and Maria Berds, eds. 2017. "Can Nature Have Rights?" *RCC Perspectives*, Retrieved on January 2, 2019, from: http://www.environmentandsociety.org/perspectives

Hippchen, L. J. 1981. "Social Justice Model for a World Criminology." *International Journal of Comparative and Applied Criminal Justice* 5(1): 107–117.

Hirst, Paul, and Grahame Thompson. 1999. *Globalization in Question.* Cambridge: Polity Press.

Hobbes, Thomas. 1958. *Leviathan.* Indianapolis, IN: Bobbs-Merrill.

Hoberman, John. 2012. *Black and Blue: The Origins and Consequences of Medical Racism.* Berkeley: University of California Press.

Hobson, Kersty. 2004. "Environmental Justice: An Anthropocentric Social Justice Critique of How, Where and Why Environmental Good and Bads Are Distributed." *Environmental Politics* 13(2): 474–481.

Holland, Eugene. 1999. *Deleuze and Guattari's Anti-Oedipus.* London: Routledge.

———. 2004. "Studies in Applied Nomadology: Jazz Improvisation and Postcapitalist Markets." In *Deleuze and Music*, eds. Ian Buchanan and Marcel Swiboda, 20–35. Edinburgh: Edinburgh University Press.

———. 2006. "Nonlinear Historical Materialism and Postmodern Marxism." *Culture, Theory, Critique* 47(2): 181–196.

———. 2011. *Nomad Citizenship.* Minneapolis: University of Minnesota Press.

———. 2013. *Deleuze and Guattari's a Thousand Plateau.* New York: Bloomsbury Academic.

"The Holographic Universe." YouTube. Retrieved on January 20, 2019, from: https://www.youtube.com/watch?v=SXmETZpwhYQ

Homer. 1961. *The Iliad of Homer.* Chicago: Phoenix Books and University of Chicago Press.

Honneth, Axel. *The Struggle for Recognition.* Cambridge, MA: MIT Press.

Hooks, Bell. 2000. *Feminist Theory: From Margin to Center*, 2nd ed. Boston: South End Press.

Houston, Barbara. 1987. "Rescuing Womanly Virtues." In *Science, Morality and Feminist Theory*, eds. Marsha Hanen and Kai Nielsen, 237–262. Calgary: University of Calgary Press.

"How the Quantum Eraser Rewrites the Past," YouTube. Retrieved on February 3, 2019, from: https://www.youtube.com/watch?v=8ORLN_KwAgs

Hudson, Barbara. 2002. "Restorative Justice and Gendered Violence: Diversion or Effective Justice?" *British Journal of Criminology* 42(3): 616–634.

Human Rights Watch. 2018. "Turkmenistan Events of 2017." Retrieved on March 26, 2019, from: https://www.hrw.org/world-report/2018/country-chapters/turkmenistan

Human Rights Watch. 2019a. "Belarus Events of 2018." Retrieved on March 26, 2019, from: https://www.hrw.org/world-report/2019/country-chapters/belarus

Human Rights Watch. 2019b. "Brazil: Bolsonaro Celebrates Brutal Dictatorship Reinstates Commemorations of 1964 Military Coup." Retrieved on March 27, 2019, from: https://www.hrw.org/news/2019/03/27/brazil-bolsonaro-celebrates-brutal-dictatorship

Humes, David. 1983. *An Enquiry Concerning the Principles of Morals.* Indianapolis, IN: Hackett.

Hunt, Alan. 1978. *The Sociological Movement in Law.* Philadelphia, PA: Temple University Press.

Huntington, Samuel. 1972. "Reform and Political Change." In *Creating Social Change*, eds. Gerald Zaltman, Philip Kotler, and Ira Kaufman, New York: Holt, Rinehart and Winston.

Hutchinson, Darren Lenard. 2004. "Critical Race Theory: History, Evolution, and New Frontiers." *American University Law Review* 53: 1187–1215.

Iamamoto, Sue A. S. 2017. "Home-Made Development in Bolivia." *Civitas - Revista de Ciências Sociais* 17 (2): 233–250.

Igbinovia, P. 1989. "Criminology in Africa." *International Journal of Offender Therapy and Comparative Criminology* 33: v–x.

Inequality.org. 2019a. "Global Inequality." Retrieved on March 5, 2019, from: https://inequality.org/facts/global-inequality/

Inequality.org. 2019b. "Have the Rich Always Laughed Stiff Tax Rates Away?" Retrieved on March 30, 2019, from: https://inequality.org/great-divide/have-the-rich-a lways-laughed-stiff-tax-rates-away/

Inequality.org. 2019c. "Income Inequality." Retrieved on March 30, 2019, from: https://inequality.org/facts/income-inequality/

Innes, Erin. 2018. "We Don't Need Permission to be Free." *Briarpatch* 47(4): 14.

Innocence Networks. Retrieved on March 1, 2019, from: https://innocencenetwork.org/

Innocence Projects. Retrieved on March 1, 2019, from: https://www.innocenceproject .org/about/

"Instances of Use of United States Armed Forces Abroad, 1798–2018." Congressional Research Services. Retrieved on January 3, 2019, from: https://fas.org/sgp/crs /natsec/R42738.pdf

Iser, Mattias. 2013. "Recognition." *Stanford Encyclopedia of Philosophy*. Retrieved on January 20, 2019, from: https://plato.stanford.edu/entries/recognition/

Ismail, Suzi Fadhilah, and Ida Madieha Abdul Ghani Azmi. 2015. "Criminalisation of Misappropriation of Traditional Cultural Expression (TCE)." *Pertanika Journal of Social Sciences & Humanities* 23 (October): 183–196.

Ives, Kim. 2019. "How Trump's Attacks on Venezuela Sparked a Revolution in Haiti." *Counterpunch*. Retrieved on March 27, 2019, from: https://www.counterpunch .org/2019/02/22/how-trumps-attacks-on-venezuela-sparked-a-revolution-in -haiti/

Jagose, Annamarie. 1996. *Queer Theory*. Melbourne, AU: University of Melbourne Press.

———. 1997. "Queer Theory." *Australian Humanities Review*. Retrieved on March 15, 2019, from: www.lib.latrobe.edu.au/AHR/archive/Issue-Dec-1996/jagose.html

James, Deborah A. 2000. "Comments on Wilson's Reconciliation and Revenge in Post- Apartheid South Africa." *Current Anthropology* 41(1): 75–98.

Jamison, Andrew, and Ronald Eyerman. 1991. *Social Movements*. University Park, PA: Penn State University Press.

Jaschik, Scott. 2019. "Judge Upholds Harvard's Admissions Policy." *Inside Higher Ed*. Retrieved on October 5, 2019, from: https://www.insidehighered.com/admissions /article/2019/10/01/federal-judge-finds-harvards-policies-do-not-discriminate -against

Jaszi, Peter. 1991. "Toward a Theory of Copyright: The Metamorphosis of 'Authority'." *Duke Law Journal* 40(2): 455–502.

Jenkins, Simon. 2014. "Maidan, Ukraine . . . Tahrir, Egypt . . . the Square Symbolises Failure, Not Hope." Opinion Piece, February 26, in *The Guardian*. Retrieved on March 1, 2019, from: https://www.theguardian.com/commentisfree/2014/feb /26/ukraine-maidan-square-symbolises-failure

Jennings, Willie James. 2018. "Whiteness Isn't Progress." *Christian Century* 135(23): 28.

Jersey, Nicholas. 2014. "Occupy Dame Street as Slow Motion General Strike. *Global Discourse* 4(2–3): 1–18.

Johnson, Robert, and Paul Leighton. 1995. "Black Genocide? Preliminary Thoughts on the Plight of America's Poor Black Men." *Journal of African American Men* 1(2): 3–22.

Johnston, E. Lea. 2013. "Vulnerability and Just Desert: A Theory of Sentencing and Mental Illness." *Journal of Criminal Law and Criminology* 103(1): 147–229.

Jones, Janelle, John Schmitt, and Valerie Wilson. 2018. "50 Years after the Kerner Commission." Economic Policy Institute. Retrieved on March 1, 2019, from: https://www.epi.org/publication/50-years-after-the-kerner-commission/

Jordan, David. 2001. "Square Pegs and Round Holes: Domestic Intellectual Property Law and Native American Economic and Culture Policy: Can It Fit?" *American Indian Law Review* 25: 93.

Jordan, Glenn, and Chris Weedan. 1995. *Cultural Politics: Class, Gender, Race, and the Postmodern World*. Oxford: Blackwell.

Kagan, Donald. 1965. *The Great Dialogue: History of Greek Political Thought from Homer to Polybius*. New York: MacMillan.

Kalas, Peggy. 2001. "International Environmental Dispute Resolution and the Need for Access by Non-State Entities." *Colorado Journal of International Environmental Law and Policy* 12: 1–40.

Kamminga, Menno. 1996. "The Precautionary Approach in International Human Rights Law: How It Can Benefit the Environment." In *The Precautionary Principle and International Law*, ed. David Freestone, 171–173. Amsterdam: Springer Publishers.

Kanatli, Mehmet. 2015. "Rawlsian Theory of Justice as Fairness: A Marxist Critique." Retrieved on November 1, 2018, from: http://dergipark.gov.tr/download /article- file/86110

Kant, Immanuel. 1965. *Critique of Pure Reason*, trans. Norman Kemp Smith. New York: St. Martin's Press.

———. 1969. *Foundations of the Metaphysics of Morals*. Ed. Robert P. Wolf. Indianapolis, IN: Bobbs-Merrill.

———. 1983. *Perpetual Peace and Other Essays*, trans. Ted Humphries. Indianapolis, IN: Hackett.

Karagiannopoulos, Vasileios. 2012. "The Role of the Internet in Political Struggles: Some Conclusions from Iran and Egypt." *New Political Science* 34(2): 151–171.

Karpinksi, Stanislaw, and Magdaelna Szechynska-Herbda. 2012. *Journal of Biotechnology, Computational Biology and Bionanotechnology* 93(1): 27–29.

Karkazis, Katrina. 2019. "Stop Talking about Testosterone–There's No Such Thing as a 'True Sex'." *The Guardian*. Retrieved on March 7, 2019, from: https://www .theguardian.com/commentisfree/2019/mar/06/testosterone-biological-sex -sports-bodies

Kashwan, Prakash. 2017. *Democracy in the Woods*. Oxford: Oxford University Press.

Katz, Claudio. 2005. "A New Center-Left Bloc in Latin America?" *International Socialist Review* 41: 58–64.

Kaup. 2008. "Negotiating through Nature: The Resistant Materialities and Materialities of Resistance in Bolivia's Natural Gas Sector." *Conference Papers—American Sociological Association*. Retrieved on March 27, 2019, from: https://uprm.idm.oclc .org/login?url=http://search.ebscohost.com/login.aspx?direct=true&db=sxi&AN =36954228&site=ehost-live&scope=site

Kelsey, Arthur. 2013. "The Law of Physics and the Physics of Law." *Regent University Law Review* 33: 89–102.

Kendi, Ibram X. 2016. *Stamped from the Beginning: The Definitive History of Racist Ideas in America*. New York: Nation Books.

Kennedy, Duncan. 1997. *A Critique of Adjudication*. Cambridge, MA: Harvard University Press.

Kennedy, Randall. 1989. "Racial Critique of Legal Academia." *Harvard Law Review* 102: 1745–1798.

Kerr, Philip G. 2010. "Bioprospecting in Australia—Sound Biopractice or Biopiracy?" *Social Alternatives* 29(3): 44.

Kheel, Marti. 1995. "License to Kill: An Ecofeminist Critique of Hunter's Discourse." In *Animals and Women*, eds. Carol Adams and Josephine Donovan, 85–125. Raleigh, NC: Duke University Press.

Kieresy, Nicholas. 2014. "Occupy Dame Street as Slow-Motion Strike?" *Global Discourse* 4(2–3): 141–158.

"Killed in the Name of 'Freedom': Over 12 Million Dead in America's Wars since World War Two." World Future Fund. Retrieved on March 1, 2019, from: http://www.worldfuturefund.org/Reports/Imperialism/usmurder.html

Killingray, D. 1986. "The Maintenance of Law and Order in British Colonial Africa." *African Affairs* 85: 411–437.

Kim, Hee Jo, and Jorg Gerber. 2011. "The Effectiveness of Reintegrative Shaming and Restorative Justice Conferencing." *International Journal of Offender Therapy and Comparative Criminology* 56(7): 63–79.

Kinzer, Stephen. 2003. *All the Shah's Men: An American Coup and the Roots of Middle East Terror.* Hoboken, NJ: John Wiley and Sons, Inc.

Kirby, Alan. 2009. *Digimodernism.* London: Bloomsbury.

Kitossa, Tamari. 2012. "Criminology and Colonialism: Counter Colonial Criminology and the Canadian Context." *Journal of Pan African Studies* 4(10): 204–226.

Kittay, E. F. 1999. *Love's Labor.* New York: Routledge.

Klatch, Rebecca. 2002. "The Development of Individual and Consciousness among Movements of the Left and Right." In *Social Movements: Identity, Culture and the State,* eds. David Meyer, Nancy Whittier, and Belinda Robnett, 185–201. Oxford: Oxford University Press.

Klein, Hilary. 2019. "A Spark of Hope: The Ongoing Lessons of the Zapatista Revolution 25 Years On." *NACLA.org.* Retrieved on March 27, 2019, from: https://nacla.org/news/2019/01/18/spark-hope-ongoing-lessons-zapatista-revolution-25-years

Klein, Naomi. 2018. *The Battle for Paradise.* Chicago: Haymarket Books.

Kohlberg, Lawrence. 1969. "Stage and Sequence: The Cognitive Development Approach to Socialization." In *Handbook of Socialization Theory and Research,* ed. D. A. Goslin, 347–480. Chicago: Rand McNally.

Kohn, Eduardo. 2013. *How Forests Think.* Berkeley: University of California Press.

Korzeniewicz, Roberto Patricio, and William C. Smith. 2000. "Poverty, Inequality, and Growth in Latin America: Searching for the High Road to Globalization." *Latin American Research Review* 35(3): 7–55.

Kosoy, Nicolas, and Esteve Corbera. 2010. "Payments for EcoSystems Services as Commodity Fetishistic." *Ecological Economics* 69(1): 1228–1236.

Kourany, Janet. 2009. "The Place of Standpoint Theory in Feminist Science Studies." *Hypatia* 24(4): 209–218.

Kozol, Jonathan. 2005. *The Shame of the Nation: The Restoration of Apartheid Schooling in America.* New York: Crown Publishing.

Kramer, Zachary. 2004. "Same-Sexed Marriage." *Seattle Journal of Social Justice* 2: 505–524.

Kraska, Peter. 2004. *Theorizing Criminal Justice.* Long Grove, IL: Waveland Press.

Krause, Sharon. 2008. "Contested Questions, Current Trajectories." *Politics and Gender* 7(1): 105–111.

Kropotkin, Peter. 1902. *Mutual Aid: A Factor of Evolution.* New York: McClure Phillips.

———. 1924. *Ethics: Origins and Development.* London: Piroshnikoff.

———. 1926. *The Conquest of Bread.* New York: Benjamin Blom.

Kumar, Deepa. 2017. "National Security Culture: Gender, Race, and Class in the Production of Imperial Citizenship." *International Journal of Communication* 11: 2154–2177.

Kuttner, Ran. 2011. "The Wave/Particle Tension in Negotiation." *Harvard Negotiation Law Review* 16: 331–355.

Kwame, Appiah, and Henry Gates, Jr., eds. 1999. *Africana: The Encyclopedia of the African and African American Experience.* Oxford: Oxford University Press.

Kymlicka, Will. 1995. *Multicultural Citizenship.* Oxford: Oxford University Press.

Lacan, Jacques. 1977. *Ecrits.* New York: Norton.

Laclau, Ernesto, and Chantal Mouffe. 1985. *Hegemony and Socialist Strategy*. New York: Verso.

Laidler, Pawel. 2013. "Separate, Equal, or Separate-But-Equal? The Changing Image of Race in the U.S. Supreme Court's Decisions." *Politeja* (23): 249–273.

Lake, Robert W. 2002. "Bring Back Big Government." *International Journal of Urban and Regional Research* 26(4): 815–822.

Lamanna, Mary. 2002. *Emile Durkheim on the Family*. Thousand Oaks, CA: Sage.

Lambdalegal.org. Retrieved on March 7, 2019, from: https://lambdalegal.org

Lamont, Julian, and Christie Favor. 2017. "Distributive Justice." In *The Stanford Encyclopedia of Philosophy*, ed. Edward Zalta. Retrieved on March 18, 2019, from: https://plato.stanford.edu/entries/justice-distributive/

Lamont, Julian. 1994. "The Concept of Desert in Distributive Justice." *The Philosophical Quarterly* 44(174): 45–64.

Landry, Donna, and Gerald MacLean, eds. 1996. *The Spivak Reader: Selected Works of Gyatri Chakravorty Spivak*. New York: Routledge.

Lanier, Mark, and Stuart Henry, 2006. *Essential Criminology*,3rd ed. Boulder, CO: Westview Press.

Lanier, Mark, Stuart Henry, and Desire Anastasia. 2015. *Essential Criminology*, 4th ed. Boulder, CO: Westview Press.

Laszlo, Irvin. 2007. *Science and the Akashic Field*. Rochester, VT: Inner Traditions.

Latour, Bruno. 2005. *Reassembling the Social*. Oxford: Oxford University Press.

———. 2014. "Agency at the Time of the Anthropocene." *New Literary History* 45: 1–18.

Lautner, Fromm. 2007. "Electrical Signals and Their Physiological Significance in Plants." *Plant, Cell and Environment* 30(3): 249–257.

Law Commission of Canada. 1999. "From Restorative Justice to Transformative Justice: Discussion Paper." Retrieved on February 3, 2019, from: lcc.gc.ca/en/themes/sr/rj/2000/paper.asp

Law, John. 2007. "Actor Network Theory and Materials Semiotics." Version of 25th April 2007. Retrieved on May 18, 2019, from: http://www. heterogeneities. net/publications/Law2007ANTandMaterialSemiotics.pdf

Lawrence, Charles R. III. 1987. "The Id, the Edo, and Equal Protection: Reckoning with Unconscious Racism." *Stanford Law Review* 39: 317–388.

———. 1993. "If He Hollers Let Him Go: Regulating Racist Speech on Campus." In *Words that Wound: Critical Race Theory, Assaultive Speech, and the First Amendment*, eds. M. J. Matsuda, C. R. Lawrence, R. Delgado, and K. W. Crenshaw, 53–86. San Francisco: Westview Press.

Lederach, John Paul. 1995. *Preparing for Peace. Conflict Transformation across Cultures*. New York: Syracuse University Press.

———. 1997. "Building Peace: Sustainable Reconciliation in Divided Societies. Washington, DC: United States Institute of Peace Press.

———. 2003. *The Little Book of Conflict Transformation*. New York: Good Books.

Lederer, Katrina. ed. 1980. *Human Needs*. Cambridge, MA: Oelgeschlager, Gunn and Hain.

Ledwon, Lenora. 1996. "Native American Life Stories and 'Authorship': Legal and Ethical Issues." *St. Thomas Law Review* 9: 69.

Lee, Amanda. 2019. "U.S. Poverty Thresholds and Poverty Guidelines: What's the Difference?" Retrieved on October 3, 2019, from: https://www.prb.org/insight/u-s-poverty-thresholds-and-poverty-guidelines-whats-the-difference

Lee, Christopher. 2019. "Only 7 Black Students Got into New York's Most Selective High School." Retrieved on March 20, 2019, from: https://www.nytimes.com/2019/03/18/nyregion/black-students-nyc-high-schools.html

Lee, John. 2000. "The Underlying Legal Theory to Support a Well-Defined Human Rights to a Healthy Environment as a Principle of Customary International Law." *Columbia Journal of Environmental Law* 25: 1–38.

Lee, Spike. 2006. *When the Levees Broke.* New York: 40 Acres and a Mule Filmworks.

Lefebvre, Alexander. 2008. *The Image of Law.* Stanford, CA: Stanford University Press.

———. 2018. *Human Rights and the Care of the Self.* Durham, NC: Duke University Press.

Lehmann, Jennifer. 1994. *Durkheim and Women.* Lincoln: University of Nebraska.

Lemert, Edwin. 1951. *Social Pathology.* New York: McGraw Hill.

Lemke, Thomas. 2001. "Foucault, Governmentality, and Critique." Paper delivered at Rethinking Marxism Conference. Amherst, MA, September 21–24.

Lenin, Vladimir Ilich. 1975. *Imperialism, the Highest Stage of Capitalism.* Moscow: Progress Publishers.

———. 1989. *"Left-Wing" Communism, an Infantile Disorder.* International Publishers: New York.

Leong, Diana. 2016. "The Mattering of Black Lives: Octavia Butler's Hyperempathy and the Promise of the New Materialisms." *Catalyst: Feminism, Theory, Technoscience* 2(2): 1–35.

Leppänen, Katarina. 2004. "At Peace with Earth-Connecting Ecological Destruction and Patriarchal Civilisation." *Journal of Gender Studies* 13(1): 37–47.

Levinas, Emmanuel. 1969. *Totality and Infinity.* Pittsburgh, PA: Duquesne Press.

———. 1987. *Time and the Other.* Pittsburgh, PA: Duquesne Press.

Lewis, Hannah, Peter Dwyer, Stuart Hodkinson, and Louise Waite. 2015. "Hyperprecarious Lives: Migrants, Work, and Forced Labour in the Global North." *Progress in Human Geography* 39(5): 580–600.

Lewis, Reina, and Sara Mills, eds. 2003. *Feminist Postcolonial Theory: A Reader.* New York: Routledge.

Lichterman, Paul. 1995. "Piecing Together Multicultural Community: Cultural Differences in Community Building among Grass-Roots Environmentalists." *Social Problems* 42(4): 513–533.

Liebesman, Yvette Joy. 2015. "When Does Copyright Law Require Technology Blindness? Aiken Meets Aereo." *Berkeley Technology Law Journal* 30(2): 1383–1449.

Lipietz, A. 1996. "Geography, Ecology, Democracy." *Antipode* (28(3): 219–228.

Lippens, Ronnie. 2000. *Chaohybrids: Five Uneasy Pieces.* New York: University Press of America, Inc.

———. 2002. "Negotiating Humanity: Subcommanding the Tender Fury of Justice." *Alternatives* 27: 513–531.

———. 2003. "The Imaginary of Zapatista Punishment: Speculations on the 'First Postmodern Revolution'." *Punishment and Society* 5(2): 179–195.

———. 2005a. "Tracing the Legal Boundary Between Empire and Multitude: Wavering with Hardt and Negri." *Leiden Journal of International Law* 3: 389–402.

———. 2005b (forthcoming). "Deep Structures of Empire: A Note on Imperial Machines and Bodies." *Social Justice.*

Lipton, Douglas, Robert Martinson, and Judith Wilks. 1975. *The Effectiveness of Correctional Treatment.* New York: Praeger.

Litowitz, Douglas. 1997. *Postmodern Philosophy and Law.* Lawrence: University Press of Kansas.

Liu, Helena. 2017. "Undoing Whiteness: The Dao of Anti-Racist Diversity Practice." *Gender, Work & Organization* 24(5): 457–471.

Lloyd, Anthony, and Philip Whitehead. 2018. "Kicked to the Curb: The Triangular Trade of Neoliberal Polity, Social Insecurity, and Penal Expulsion." *International Journal of Law, Crime, and Justice* 55: 60–69.

Lloyd, Chris. 2017. "The 'politics' of British Critical Legal Studies." Retrieved on March 5, 2019, from: https://socialandlegalstudies.wordpress.com/2017/07/14/the-politics-of-british-critical-legal-studies/

Locke, John. 1924. *An Essay Concerning the True Original, Extent and End of Civil Government. In Two Treatises of Government*. London: Dent and Sons.

Lockhart, P. R. 2018. "The Lawsuit Against Harvard that Could Change Affirmative Action in College Admissions, Explained." *Vox News*. Retrieved on March 20, 2019, from: https://www.vox.com/2018/10/18/17984108/harvard-asian-americans -affirmative-action-racial-discrimination

Logan, Wayne. 2000. "A Study in 'Actuarial Justice': Sex Offender Classification Practice and Procedure." *Buffalo Law Review* 3: 592–637.

Lomborg, Bjørn. 2001. *The Skeptical Environmentalist: Measuring the Real State of the World*. New York: Cambridge University Press.

Londono, Oscar. 2013. "A Retributive Critique of Racial Bias and Arbitrariness in Capital Punishment." *Journal of Social Philosophy* 44(1): 95–105.

Lorraine, Tamsin. 1999. *Irigary and Deleuze*. Ithaca, NY: Cornell University Press.

Low, Nicholas, and Brendan Gleeson. 1998. *Justice, Society and Nature: An Exploration of Political Ecology*. Routledge: New York.

Lucas, James. 2019. "US Has Killed More than 20 Million People in 37 'Victim Nations' since World War II." Reproduced in *Global Research*, January 2019 (originally, November, 2015). Retrieved on March 1, 2019, from: https://www.global research.ca/us-has-killed-more-than-20-million-people-in-37-victim-nations -since-world-war-ii/5492051

Lugones, Maria. 2010. "Toward a Decolonized Feminism." *Hypatia* 25(4): 742–759.

Luke, T. W. 1999. "Environmentality as Green Governmentality." In *Discourses of the Environment*, ed. E. Darier, 121–151. Oxford: Blackwell.

Lukes, Steven. 1985. *Emile Durkheim*. Stanford: Stanford University Press.

Lycos, Kimon. 1987. *Plato on Justice and Power: Reading Book I of Plato's Republic*. Albany: State University of New York Press.

Lynch, Michael. 1990. "The Greening of Criminology." *The Critical Criminologist* 2(3): 1–4, 11–12.

———. 2015. "Green Criminology and Social Justice." *Critical Sociology* 43(3): 449–464.

Lynch, Michael, Michael Long, Paul Stretesky, and Kimberly Barrett. 2017. *Green Criminology*. Berkeley: University of California Press.

Lynch, Michael, and Paul Stretesky. 2010. "Global Warning, Global Crime." In *Global Environmental Harm*, ed. Rob White, 62–84. Cullompton, UK: Willan Publishing.

Lyon, Travis W. 2016. *Global Citizen*. "An Oil Pipeline, Ancient Native American Burial Grounds, and the Story Nobody is Talking About." Retrieved on January 30, 2019, from: https://www.globalcitizen.org/en/content/an-oil-pipeline -ancient-indian-burial-grounds-and/

Lyotard, Jean-Francois. 1984. *The Postmodern Condition*. Minneapolis: Minnesota University Press.

———. 1988. *The Differend*. Minneapolis: Minnesota University Press.

———. 1999. *Just Gaming*. Minneapolis: Minnesota University Press.

MacArthur, John R. 2008. *You Can't Be President: The Outrageous Barriers to Democracy in America*. New York: Melville House Publishing.

MacDonald, Kelly. 2001. "Literature Review: Implications of Restorative Justice in Cases of Violence Against Aboriginal Women and Children." Vancouver: Aboriginal Women's Action Network.

MacIntyre, Alasdair. 1984. *After Virtue*. Notre Dame, Indiana: University of Notre Dame Press.

MacKinnon, Catharine. 1987. *Feminism Unmodified*. Cambridge, MA: Harvard University Press.

———. 1989. *Toward a Feminist Theory of the State*. Cambridge, MA: Harvard University Press.

MacLean, Brian, and Dragan Milovanovic. 1997. *Thinking Critically About Crime.* Vancouver, Canada: Vancouver Press.

Mallory, C. 2010. "What is Ecofeminist Political Philosophy?" *Environmental Ethics* 32(3): 306–322.

Mamdani, Mahmood. 2005. *Good Muslim, Bad Muslim: America, the Cold War, and the Roots of Terror.* New York: Doubleday.

Manning, Rita. 1996. "Caring for Animals." In *Beyond Animal Rights*, eds. C. Adams and J. Donovan. New York: Continuum.

Marable, Manning. 2003. *Race, Reform, and Rebellion: The Second Reconstruction in Black America, 1945–1990.* Jackson: University Press of Mississippi.

Marcos, Subcomandante. 2002. *Our Word Is Our Weapon: Selected Writings*, ed. Juana Ponce de Leon. New York: Seven Stories Press.

Marcuse, Peter. 2002. "Urban from and Globalization after September 11th: The View from New York." *International Journal of Urban and Regional Research* 26(3): 596–606.

Marder, Michael. 2012. "Plant Intentionality and the Phenomenological Framework of Plant Intelligence." *Plant Signaling and Behavior* 7(11): 1365–1372.

Margil, Mari. 2018. "Our Law Make Slave of Nature: It's Not Just Humans Who Need Rights." *The Guardian.* Retrieved on December, 24 2018, from: https://www.theguardian.com/commentisfree/2018/may/23/laws-slaves-nature-humans-rights-environment-amazon

Martin, Edward J. 2003. "Liberation Theology, Sustainable Development, and Postmodern Public Administration." *Latin American Perspectives* 30(4): 69–91.

Martinez, Elizabeth, and Arnoldo Garcia. 2004. "What is Zapatismo? A Brief Definition for Activists." In *Globalize Liberation: How to Uproot the System and Build a Better World*, ed. David Solnit, 213–216. San Francisco, CA: City Lights Books.

Martinez, Gabriela. 2019. *PBS News Hour.* "How a Cockfighting Ban Could Affect Puerto Rico's Struggling Economy." Retrieved on January 30, 2019, from: https://www.pbs.org/newshour/economy/making-sense/how-a-cockfighting-ban-could-affect-puerto-ricos-struggling-economy

Martinson, Robert. 1974. "What Works?" *The Public Interest* 35: 25–44.

Marx, Gary. 2005. "Chavez Touts' 21st Century Socialism." *Chicago Tribune*, July 15.

Marx, Karl. 1967. *Capital.* New York: International Publishing House.

———. 1977. "Critique of the Gotha Programme." In *Karl Marx: Selected Writings*, ed.

———. 2005. *The Communist Manifesto.* Chicago: Haymarket Books.

Marx, Karl, and Frederick Engels. 1973a. *Selected Work, Volume One.* Moscow: Progress Publishers.

———. 1973b. *Selected Work, Volume Three.* Moscow: Progress Publishers.

Maskovsky, Jeff. 2001. "The Other War at Home: The Geopolitics of U.S. Poverty." *Urban Anthropology* 30(2–3): 215–238.

Maslow, Abraham. 1954. *Motivation and Personality.* New York: Harper.

Matias, Cheryl E., and Peter M. Newlove. 2017. "The Illusion of Freedom: Tyranny, Whiteness, and the State of US Society." *Equity & Excellence in Education* 50(3): 316–330.

Matsuda, Mari. 1996. *Where Is Your Body?* Boston: Beacon Press.

Matsuda, Mari, Charles Lawrence, Richard Delgado, and Kimberlè Crenshaw, eds. 1993. *Words that Wound: Critical Race Theory, Assaultive Speech, and the First Amendment*, Boulder, CO: Westview.

Matza, David. 1964. *Delinquency and Drift.* New York: John Wiley and Sons.

McAdam, Doug. 1982. *Political Process and the Development of Black Insurgency.* Chicago: University of Chicago Press.

McAlevey, Jane. 2018. "The West Virginia Teachers' Strike Shows That Winning Big Requires Creating a Crisis." *The Nation.* Retrieved on February 12, 2019,

from: https://www.thenation.com/article/the-west-virginia-teachers-strike-shows
-that-winning-big-requires-creating-a-crisis/

McArthur, Jan. N.D. "Conceptions of Difference Within Theories of Social Justice." Retrieved on December 15, 2018, from: https://www.lancaster.ac.uk/fass/events /hecu7/papers/mcarthur.pdf

McCraty, Rollin, Mike Atkinson, Dana Tomasino, and Raymond Bradley. 2012. "The Coherent Heart." *Integral Review* 5(2): 1–106.

McCrea, Aisling. 2018. "Self-Care Won't Save Us." *Current Affairs*. Retrieved on February 12, 2019, from: https://www.currentaffairs.org/2018/11/self-care-wont -save-us

McDonald, J. and D. Moore. 2001. "Community Conferencing as a Special Case of Conflict Transformation." In *Restorative Justice and Civil Society*, eds. John Braithwaite and H. Strang. Cambridge: Cambridge University Press.

McLaren, Duncan. 2003. "Environmental Space, Equity and the Ecological Debt." In *Just Sustainabilities: Development in an Unequal World*, eds. Julian Agyeman, Robert Bullard, and Bob Evans, 19–37. Cambridge, MA: MIT Press.

McLaughlin, E., ed. 2002. *Restorative Justice: Critical Issues*. Thousand Oaks, CA: Sage Publications.

McNally, David. 2017. "Intersections and Dialectics: Critical Reconstructions in Social Reproduction Theory." In *Social Reproduction Theory: Remapping Class, Recentering Oppression*, ed. Tithi Bhattacharya, 94–111. London: Pluto Press.

Meier, Matt S., and Feliciano Ribera. 1998. *Mexican Americans/American Mexicans: From Conquistadors to Chicanos*. New York: Hill and Wang.

Melendez, Miguel "Mickey." 2003. *We Took the Streets: Fighting for Latino Rights with the Young Lords*. New York: St. Martin's Press.

Melton, Ada Pecos. 2005. "Indigenous Justice Systems and Tribal Society." In *Justice as Healing: Indigenous Ways. Writings on Community Peacemaking and Restorative Justice from the Native Law Centre*, ed. Wanda D. McCaslin, 108–120. St. Paul, MN: Living Justice Press.

Menon, Nivedita. 2002. "Universalism Without Foundation?" *Economy and Society* 31(1): 152–169.

Miall, Hugh. 2004. "Conflict Transformation: A Multidimensional Task." In *Berghoff Handbook of Conflict Transformation*, eds. Austin Beatrix, Veronique Dudouet, and Hans Giessmann, 1–20. Berghoff Foundation: https://www.berghof-foundation .org/en/publications/handbook/berghof-handbook-for-conflict-transformation/

Michalowski, Raymond. 2012. "The History of Critical Criminology in the United States." In *Routledge Handbook of Critical Criminology*, eds. W. DeKeseredy and M. Dragiewicz, 32–45. London: Routledge.

Middleton, N., and P. O'Keefe. 2001. *Redefining Sustainable Development*. London: Pluto Press.

Mies, Maria, and Vandana Shiva. 1993, *Ecofeminism*. New Jersey: Zed Books.

Mihaylov and Perkins. 2015. "Local Environmental Grassroots Activism." *Behavioral Science* 5: 121–153.

Mill, John Stuart. 1961. *Essential Works of John Stuart Mill*. Ed. Max Lerner. New York: Bantam Books.

———. 1970. "The Subjection of Women." In *Essays on Sex Equality*. Ed. A. S. Rossie. Chicago: University of Chicago Press.

Miller, David L. 1976. *Social Justice*. Oxford: Clarendon Press.

———. 1999. *Principles of Social Justice*. London: Harvard University Press.

———. 2001. *Principles of Social Justice*. Cambridge, MA: Harvard University Press.

———. 2017. "Justice." *Stanford Encyclopedia of Philosophy*. Retrieved on November 1, 2018, from: https://plato.stanford.edu/entries/justice/

———. 2000. "Social Justice and Environmental Goods." In *Fairness and Futurity*, ed. Andrew Dobson, 151–172. Oxford: Oxford University Press.

Mills, Charles W. 2001. "Black Trash." In *Faces of Environmental Racism: Confronting Issues of Global Justice*, eds. Laura Westra and Bill E. Lawson, 73–91. New York: Rowman and Littlefield.

Milovanovic, Dragan. 1985. "Anarchism, Liberation Theology, and the Decommodification of the Linguistic and Juridic Form." *Humanity and Society* 9: 182–196.

———. 1988. "Jailhouse Lawyers and Jailhouse Lawyering." *International Journal of the Sociology of Law* 16(3): 455–475.

———. 1995. "Dueling Paradigms: Modernist versus Postmodernists." *Humanity and Society* 19(1): 1–22.

———. 1996. "'Rebellious Lawyering'" *Legal Studies Forum* (20)3): 295–321.

———. ed. 1997a. *Chaos, Criminology and Social Justice: The New Orderly (Dis)Order*. Westport, CT: Praeger.

———. 1997b. *Postmodern Criminology*. New York: Garland.

———. 2003. *An Introduction to the Sociology of Law*. New York: Criminal Justice Press.

———. 2004. "Psychoanalytic Semiotics, Chaos, and Rebellious Lawyering." In *Lacan: Topologically Speaking*, eds. Ellie Ragland and Dragan Milovanovic, 174–204. New York: Other Press.

———. 2011. "Justice Rendering Schemas." *Journal of Theoretical and Philosophical Criminology* 3(1): 1–55.

———. 2014a. *Quantum Holographic Criminology*. Durham, NC: Carolina Academic Press.

———. 2014b. "Revisiting Societal Reaction (Labeling) by Way of Quantum Holographic Theory." *Crime: Journal for Criminal Justice* 5(2): 123–135.

———. 2018. "Touching You, Touching Me in Law and Justice: Toward a Quantum Holographic Process-Informational Paradigm." In *Routledge Research Handbook on Law and Theory*, ed. Andreas Philippopoulos-Mihalopoulos, 203–222. London: Routledge.

Milovanovic, Dragan, and Stuart Henry. 2001. "Constitutive Definition of Crime." In *What Is Crime?*, eds. Stuart Henry and Mark Lanier, 165–178. New York: Rowman and Littlefield.

Milovanovic, Dragan, and Jim Thomas. 1989. "Overcoming the Absurd." *Social Problems* 36(1): 48–60.

Minelli Perez, Sharon. 2019. "Cofina Plan Sets a 'Dangerous Precedent'." *El Nuevo Dia. English Version*. Retrieved on February 6, 2019, from: https://www.elnuevodia.com/english/english/nota/cofinaplansetsadangerousprecedent-2470925/

Mirandé, Alfredo. 1994. *Gringo Justice*. Notre Dame, IN: University of Notre Dame Press.

Molina, Eduardo. 2016. "Puerto Rico: Debt, Crisis, and Colonialism." *Left Voice*. September 6. Retrieved on January 7, 2019, from: http://www.leftvoice.org/Puerto-Rico-Debt-Crisis-and-Colonialism

Molyneux, John. 2014. "Do Revolutions Always Fail? *Socialist Review* (April). Retrieved on March 1, 2019, from: http://socialistreview.org.uk/390/do-revolutions-always-fail

Monahan, J. 1984. "The Prediction of Violent Behavior: Toward a Second Generation of Theory and Policy." *American Journal of Psychiatry* 141: 10–15.

Montana, Omar. 2016. "The Effect of Trump: Resentment, Marginalization, and the Policing of Surplus Migrant Life." Conference Paper. New Orleans: American Society of Criminology.

Montgomery, David. 1987. *The Fall of the House of Labor: The Workplace, the State, and American Labor Activism, 1865–1925*. New York: Cambridge University Press.

Montoya, Margaret E. 2013. "Latinos and the Law: American Latinos and the Making of the United States: A Theme Study." Retrieved on March 6, 2019, from: http://digitalrepository.unm.edu/law_facbookdisplay/113

Moodie, Dunbar. 2002. "Mobilization on the South African Gold Mines." In *Social Movements: Identity, Culture, and the State*, eds. David Meyer, Nancy Whittier, and Belinda Robnett, 47–65. New York: Oxford University Press.

Moore, Basil. 1974. *The Challenge of Black Theology in South Africa.* John Knox Press.

Morales, Ed. 2019. "Why Half a Million Puerto Ricans Are Protesting in the Streets." *The Nation.* Retrieved on October 5, 2019, from: https://www.thenation.com/article/puerto-rico-protests-scandal-rossello

Moreton-Robinson, Aileen. 2001. "Witnessing Whiteness in the Wake of Wik." *Social Alternatives* 17: 11–25.

Morris, Ruth. 1994. *A Practical Path to Transformative Justice.* Toronto, Canada: Rittenhouse.

———. 1996. *Restored to What?* Baltimore, MD: Maryland Justice Policy Institute, Inc.

———. 1999. "Why Transformative Justice?" Paper presented at Reconciling and Restoring Relationships—A Responsibility for all Christians. ICCPPC World Congress. Mexico City. September 13.

———. 2000. *Stories of Transformation.* Toronto: Canadian Scholar's Press.

Moss, Andrew. 2013. "Responding to Retributivists: A Restorative Justice Rejoinder to the Big Three Desert Theories." *Contemporary Justice Review* 16(2): 214–227.

Most, Michael T., Raja Sengupta, and Michael A. Burgener. 2004. "Spatial Scale and Population Assignment Choices in Environmental Justice Analyses." *The Professional Geographer* 56(4): 574–586.

Mottahedeh, Roy. 1986. *The Mantle of the Prophet: Religion and Politics in Iran.* New York: Pantheon Books.

Moyo, Khanyisela. 2012. "Review of Transitional Justice in Balance." *The Cambridge Law Journal* 71: 239–241.

Mun, Seung-Hwan. 2010. "A Different Fate of the Print Revolution: Why Imperial China Had No Copyright?" *Conference Papers—International Communication Association*, 1. Retrieved on January 30, 2019, from: https://uprm.idm.oclc.org/login?url=http://search.ebscohost.com/login.aspx?direct=true&db=ufh&AN=59227482&site=ehost-live&scope=site

Murakami Wood, D. 2017. "Editorial: The Global Turn to Authoritarianism and After." *Surveillance & Society* 15(3/4): 357–370.

Murphy, Colleen. 2017. *The Conceptual Foundations of Transitional Justice.* Boston, MA: Cambridge University Press.

Murphy, John. 1984. "Paul Tillich and Western Marxism." *American Journal of Theology and Philosophy* 5(1): 13–24.

Murphy, Kristine, and Nathan Harris. 2007. "Shame, Shame and Recidivism: A Test of Reintegrative Shaming in the White Collar Context." *British Journal of Criminology* 47(6): 900–917.

Myers, G. D., and S. Raine. 2001. "Australian Aboriginal Land Rights in Transition (Part II)." *Tulsa Journal of Comparative and International Law.* 9: 95–157.

Nagel, Thomas. 1973. "Internal Difficulties with Justice as Fairness." In *What Is Justice? Classic and Contemporary Readings*, eds. Robert C. Solomon and Mark C. Murphy, 295–300. New York: Oxford University Press.

Nagy, Rosemary. 2002. "Reconciliation in Post-Commission South Africa: Thick and Thin Accounts of Solidarity." *Canadian Journal of Political Science* 35(2): 323–346.

———. 2012. "Truth, Reconciliation and Settler Denial: Specifying the Canada-South Africa Analogy." *Human Rights Review* 13(3): 349–367.

Najam, Adil, and Nick Robins. 2001. "Seizing the Future: The South, Sustainable Development and International Trade." *International Affairs* 77(1): 49–68.

Nash, June. 1997. "The Fiesta of the Word: The Zapatista Uprising and Radical Democracy in Mexico." *American Anthropologist* 99(2): 261.

Naude, P. J. (N.D.). "In Defense of Partisan Justice—An Ethical Reflection on 'the Preferential Option for the Poor.'" Forthcoming, *African Journal of Business Ethics.*

Neckel, Sighard. 2017. "The Sustainability Society." *Culture, Practice and Europeanization* 2(2): 46–52.

Newman, Dwight. 2005. "The Rome Statute, Some Reservations Concerning Amnesties, and a Distributive Problem." *American University International Law Review* 20: 293–325.

Newman, Graeme. 2017. *The Punishment Response.* London: Routledge.

Nielsen, Laura Beth. 2002. "Subtle, Pervasive, Harmful: Racist and Sexist Remarks in Public as Hate Speech." *Journal of Social Issues* 58(2): 265–280.

———. 2009. *License to Harass: Law, Hierarchy, and Offensive Public Speech.* Princeton, NJ: Princeton University Press.

Nietzsche, Friedrich. 1967. *On the Genealogy of Morals*, trans. Walter Kaufman. New York: Vintage.

———. 1974. *The Gay Science*, trans. Walter Kaufman. New York: Vintage.

———. 1986. *Human, All Too Human*, trans. R. J. Hollingdale. Cambridge: Cambridge University Press.

Niezen, Ronald. 2003. *The Origins of Indigenous Human Rights and the Politics of Identity.* Berkeley: University of California Press.

Niță, O. A. 2018. "The Morality of Law in the Era of Globalization." *Challenges of the Knowledge Society* 12: 572–582.

Nodding, N. 1984. *Caring: A Feminist Approach to Ethics and Moral Education.* Berkeley: University of California Press.

Noël, Alain and Jean-Philippe Thérien. 2002. "Public Opinion and Global Justice." *Comparative Political Studies* 35(6): 631–656.

Norval, Aletta. 1996. *Deconstructing Apartheid Discourse.* New York: Verso.

Norris, Zachary. 2017. "Repairing Harm from Racial Injustice: An Analysis of the Justice Reinvestment Initiative and the Truth and Reconciliation Commission." *Denver Law Review* 94 (3): 515–535.

Norval, Aletta. 1996. *Deconstructing Apartheid Discourse.* New York: Verso.

#NotOneMoreDeportation. Retrieved on March 12, 2019, from: http://www.notonemoredeportation.com/about/

Nozick, Robert. 1974. *Anarchy, State and Utopia.* New York: Basic Books.

"Nullifying Inequities in the Criminal Justice System." 2000. *Black Issues in Higher Education* 17(2): 18–24.

Nurse, Angus. 2017. "Green Criminology." *Palgrave Communications*, doi: 10.1057/s41599-017-0007-2.

Nussbaum, Martha. 2004. *Hiding from Humanity: Disgust, Shame, and the Law.* Princeton, NJ: Princeton University Press.

———. 2006a. *Frontiers of Justice: Disability, Nationality, Species Membership.* Cambridge, MA: Harvard University Press.

———. 2006b. "The Moral Status of Animals." *The Chronicles of Higher Education* 52(22): B6–B8.

———. 2011. *Creating Capabilities.* Cambridge, MA: Harvard University Press.

Obućina, Vedran. 2015. "Social Populism and the Future of the Islamic Republic of Iran." Politicka Misao: *Croatian Political Science Review.* 52(4/5): 163–186.

Occupy Wall Street. Retrieved on March 1, 2019, from: http://occupywallst.org/

O'Donnell, Erin. 2017. "At the Intersection of the Sacred and the Legal: Rights for Nature in Uttarakhand, India." *Journal of Environmental Law* 30(1): 135–144.

———. 2018. "Creating Legal Rights for Rivers: Lessons from Australia, New Zealand, and India. *Ecology and Society* 23(1): 7–23.

Okin, Susan Moller. 1989. "Justice, Gender, and Equity in the Family." In *What Is Justice? Classic and Contemporary Readings*, eds. Robert C. Solomon and Mark C. Murphy, 332–339. New York: Oxford University Press.

————. 2003. "Poverty, Well-Being and Gender." *Philosophy and Public Affairs* 31(3): 280–316.

Oliver, K. 2001. *Witnessing: Beyond Recognition*. Minneapolis: University of Minnesota Press.

Oliver, Melvin L., and Thomas M. Shapiro. 2006. *Black Wealth/White Wealth: A New Perspective on Racial Inequality.* New York: Routledge.

Olivera, Oscar. 2004. ¡*Cochabamba! Water War in Bolivia.* Cambridge, MA: South End Press.

Olsaretti, Serena. 2018. "Introduction: The Idea of Distributive Justice." In *The Oxford Handbook of Distributive Justice*, ed. Serena Olsaretti. Retrieved on November 1, 2018, from: http://www.oxfordhandbooks.com/view/10.1093/oxfordhb/9780199645121.001.0001/oxfordhb-9780199645121-e-38

Olsen, Tricia D., Leigh A. Payne, and Andrew G. Reiter. 2010. *Transitional Justice in Balance: Comparing Processes, Weighing Efficacy.* Washington, DC: United States Institute of Peace Press.

O'Malley, Pat. 1992. "Risk, Power and Crime Prevention." *Economy and Society* 21: 252–275.

————. 1996. "Risk and Responsibility." In *Foucault and Political Reason*, eds. A. Barry, T. Osborne, and N. Rose, 189–207. London: UCL Press.

————. 1999. "Reconfiguring Risk: Crime Control and Risk Societies." Paper presented at the British Criminology Conference, Liverpool, UK, July 14.

————. 2004. "The Uncertainty of Risk: Actuarial Forecasting of Criminal Justice." *Australian and New Zealand Journal of Criminology* 37(3): 323–344.

Onuf, N. G. 1991. "Sovereignty: Outline of a Conceptual History." *Alternatives* 16(1): 425–445.

Onwuachi-Willig, Angela. 2013. *According to Our Hearts.* New Haven, CT: Yale University Press.

OpenDemocracy. 2018. "The Return of 'Class and Social Justice' in Iran and Tunisia." Retrieved on March 20, 2019, from: https://uprm.idm.oclc.org/docview/1993801852?accountid=28498

Oppenheimer, Martin. 1969. *The Urban Guerilla.* Chicago: Quadrangle Press.

Orlikowski, W. 2007. "Sociomaterial Practices." *Organizational Studies* 28(9): 1435–1448.

Ortega, Mariana. 2016. *In-Between: Latina Feminist Phenomenology, Multiplicity, and the Self.* Albany, NY: SUNY Press.

Osorio, Ivan. 2003. "Venezuela's Tyrant Hugo Chavez Must Go." Retrieved on March 3, 2019, from: http://www.CapMag.com/article.asp?ID=2312

Packer, Herbert. 1998 (originally in 1968). "Two Models of the Criminal Process." In *The Criminal Justice System*, eds. George Cole and Marc Gertz, 9–23. Boston: West/Wadsworth.

Pagliarini, Andre. 2018. "Drifting Toward Dictatorship." *New Republic* 249(12): 10–11.

Pangle, Thomas L. 1980. *The Laws of Plato.* New York: Basic Books.

Parenti, Christian. 2005. "Hugo Chavez and Petro Populism." Retrieved on January 20, 2019, from: http://www.thenation.com/doc/mhtml?i=20050411&s=parenti

Paris Climate Agreement, 2015. Retrieved on January 2, 2019, from: https://unfccc.int/process-and-meetings/the-paris-agreement/what-is-the-paris-agreement

Parker, Christine. 1999. *Just Lawyers.* Oxford: Oxford University Press.

Pashukanis, E. 1980. "The General Theory of Law and Marxism." In *Pashukanis: Selected Writings in Marxism and Law*, eds. P. Beirne and R. Sharlet, 302–345. New York: Academic Press.

Passavant, Paul, and Jodi Dean, eds. 2003. '*Empire's' New Clothes: Reading Hardt and Negri.* London: Routledge.

Patton, Paul. 2001. *Deleuze and the Political.* London: Routledge.

Pavlich, George. 1996. "The Power of Community Mediation." *Law and Society Review* 30: 707–733.

———. 2001. "The Force of Community." In *Restorative Justice and Civil Society*, eds. H. Strang and J. Braithwaite, 56–68. Cambridge, UK: Cambridge University Press.

———. 2005. *Paradoxes of Restorative Justice*. London: Glasshouse Press.

Pecharroman, Lidia. 2018. "Rights of Nature: Rivers That Can Stand in Court." *Resources* 7: 13–27.

Peetors, Rik. 2019. "Manufacturing Responsibility: Governmentality of Behavioral Power." *Social Policy and Society* 18(1): 51–65.

Peirce, C. Sanders. 1931. The Collected Papers of Charles Sanders Peirce. Eds. C. Hartshorne and P. Weiss. Cambridge, MA: Harvard University Press.

People's Summit at Rio+20 for Social and Environmental Justice. 2012. Retrieved on January 21, 2019, from: https://www.internationalrivers.org/sites/default/files/attached-files/rio20_peoplessummit_eng.pdf

Pepinsky, Hal. 2013. "Peacemaking Criminology." *Critical Criminology* 21: 319–339.

Pepinsky, H. E., and Quinney, R., eds. 1991. *Criminology as Peacemaking*. Bloomington: Indiana University Press.

Perez, Beverly. 2003. "Woman Warrior + Meets Mail-Order Bride." *Berkeley Women's Law Journal* 18: 211–240.

PETA. N.D. "Give Roosters Something to Crow About." Retrieved on January 30, 2019, from: https://www.peta.org/issues/animals-in-entertainment/animals-used-entertainment-factsheets/give-roosters-something-crow-end-cockfighting/

Phillimore, Jenny. 2018. "In Aid of World Day of Social Justice." Retrieved on January 2, 2019, from: https://blog.bham.ac.uk/socialsciencesbirmingham/2018/02/20/forced-migrants-and-social-justice-no-justice-for-asylum-seekers-in-the-uk/

Phillips, Derek. 1986. *Toward a Just Social Order*. Princeton, NJ: Princeton University Press.

Phillips, Jake. 2009. "Australia's Heritage Protection Act: An Alternative to Copyright in the Struggle to Protect Communal Interests in Authored Works of Folklore." *Pacific Rim Law & Policy Journal* 18(3): 547–573.

Piaget, Jean. 1965. *The Moral Judgment of the Child*. New York: Free Press.

Piketty, Thomas. 2014. *Capital in the Twenty-First Century*. Cambridge, MA: Harvard University Press.

Pilgrim, Karyn, and H. Louise Davis. 2015. "'More Crucial' Matters: Reclaiming 'Sustainability' and Transcending the Rhetoric of 'Choice' through Ecofeminist Pedagogy." *Ethics and the Environment (Project Muse)* 20(1): 123–139.

Pinderhughes, Charles. 2008. "African Americans and Internal Colonial Theory." *Conference Papers: American Sociological Association*. Retrieved on January 31, 2019, from: https://uprm.idm.oclc.org/login?url=http://search.ebscohost.com/login.aspx?direct=true&db=sxi&AN=36953679&site=ehost-live&scope=site

Piño, Angels. 2019. "Thousands Protest in Barcelona Against Trial of Catalan Separatist Leaders." *El País*. Retrieved on March 26, 2019, from: https://elpais.com/elpais/2019/02/18/inenglish/1550477932_980984.html

Plato. 1951. *The Republic*. New York: E. P. Hutton and Company.

Pockock, J.G.A. 1992. "Tangata Whenua and Enlightenment Anthropology." *New Zealand Journal of History* 25(1): 28–53.

Pogge, Thomas. 2002. "Can the Capability Approach Be Justified?" *Philosophical Topics* 30(2): 167–228.

Poggi, Sara. 2019. "Grassroots Movements." Retrieved on March 11, 2019, from: http://my.ilstu.edu/~skhunt2/pep/Downloads/poggi.pdf

Polk, Danne. 2001. "Ecologically Queer: Preliminaries for a Queer Ecofeminist Identity Theory." *Journal of Women & Religion* 19: 72–89.

Popp, Trey. 2017. "Black Box Justice." *Pennsylvania Gazette.* August 28.

Posel, Deborah, and Graeme Simpson, eds. 2003. *Commissioning the Past: Understanding South Africa's Truth and Reconciliation Commission.* Witwatersrand: University Press Publications.

Posner, Richard. 1997. "The Skin Trade." *New Republic,* October 13, p. 40.

Poster, Mark. 1984. *Foucault, Marxism and History: Mode of Production versus Mode of Information.* Cambridge: Polity Press.

Powell, John A. 2017. "Right Wing Speakers Coming to Berkeley for Conflict, Not Dialog." Retrieved on March 6, 2019, from: https://haasinstitute.berkeley.edu /right-wing-speakers-coming-berkeley-conflict-not-dialogue

Powell, Kathy. 2017. "Brexit Positions: Neoliberalism, Austerity, and Immigration—the (im)Possibilities? of Political Revolution." *Dialectical Anthropology* 41: 225–240.

Poya, Maryam. 1987. "Iran 1979: Long Live Revolution . . . Long Live Islam?" In *Revolutionary Rehearsals,* ed. Colin Barker, 123–168. Chicago: Bookmarks.

Pratt, John. 1999. "Assimilation, Equality, Sovereignty. The Maori and the Criminal Justice and Welfare Systems." In *Indigenous Peoples' Rights in Australia, Canada and New Zealand,* ed. Paul Havemann, 316–328. Oxford: Oxford University Press.

Presser, L., and E. Gaarder. 2000. "Can Restorative Justice Reduce Battering? Some Preliminary Considerations." *Social Justice* 27(3): 175–200.

Presser, Lois, and Sveinung Sandberg. 2015. "Introduction: What Is the Story?" In *Narrative Criminology,* eds. L. Presser and S. Sandberg, 1–20. New York: New York University Press.

Preston, Brian. 2011. "The Use of Restorative Justice for Environmental Crime." *Criminal Law Journal* 35: 136–145.

———. 2014. "Characteristics of Successful Environmental Courts and Tribunals." *Journal of Environmental Law* 26: 365–393.

Preston, Ted. 2004. "Environmental Values, Pluralism, and Stability." *Ethics, Place and Environment* 7(1): 73–83.

Pring, George, and Catherine Pring. 2010. "Specialized Environmental Courts and Tribunals." Paper presented at the Yale University and U.N. Institute for Training and Research's 2nd Global Conference on Environmental Governance and Democracy.

———. 2016. "Environmental Courts and Tribunals: A Guide for Policy Makers." U.N. Environmental Programme. Retrieved on December 15, 2018, from: https://www.eufje.org/images/DocDivers/Rapport%20Pring.pdf

Print, Murray, and Caroline Ugarte. 2008. "Moral and Human Rights Education." *Journal of Moral Education* 37(1): 115–132.

Prudham, Scott. 2016. "Commodification." In *Companion to Environmental Geography,* eds. Noel Castee, David Demeritt, Diana Liverman, and Bruce Roads, 123–142. Oxford: Wiley-Blackwell.

Pruitt, Sarah. 2018. "Was 'Don't Ask, Don't Tell' a Step Forward for LGBT in the Military?" History.com. Retrieved on March 12, 2019, from: https://www.history .com/news/dont-ask-dont-tell-repeal-compromise

Public Citizen and Friends of the Earth. 2001. "NAFTA Chapter 11 Investor-to-State Cases: Bankrupting Democracy." Washington, DC: Public Citizen and Friends of the Earth.

Puwar, N. 2004. *Space Invaders: Race, Gender and Bodies Out of Place.* New York: Berg Publishers.

Pycroft, Aaron, and Clemens Barollas. 2014. *Applying Complexity Theory: Whole Systems Approaches to Criminal Justice and Social Work.* New York: Policy Press.

"Q & A Paul Butler." 2013. *Nation* 297(20): 5.

Quantum Entanglement Documentary. 2019. YouTube. Retrieved on February 3, 2019, from: https://www.youtube.com/watch?v=BFvJOZ51tmc

Quinney, Richard. 1974. *Critique of Legal Order*. Boston: Little Brown.

———. 1978. "The Theology of Culture: Marx, Tillich, and the Prophetic Tradition in the Reconstruction of Social and Moral Order." *Union Seminary Quarterly Review* 34: 203–214.

———. 1980a. *Providence: The Reconstruction of Social and Moral Order*. Cincinnati, OH: Anderson Publishing Co.

———. 1980b. *Class, State and Crime*, 2nd ed. New York: Longman.

———. 1982. *Social Existence*. London: Sage.

Rachel, Best, Linda Krieger, Lauren Edelman, and Scott Eliason. 2011. "An Empirical Test of Intersectionality Theory in EEO Litigation." *Law and Society* 45(4): 991–1025.

Randeria, Shalini. 2003. "Glocalization of Law: Environmental Justice, World Bank, NGOs and the Cunning State in India." *Current Sociology* 51(3): 305–326.

Ransby, Barbara. 2003. *Ella Baker & the Black Freedom Movement: A Radical Democratic Vision*. Chapel Hill: University of North Carolina Press.

Rao, J. Mohan. 1999. "The Social Basis of International Cooperation." *International Social Science Journal* 162: 585–592.

Ranker. N.D. "Crime and Law Entertainment." Retrieved on December 11, 2018, from: https://www.ranker.com/list/legal-drama-tv-shows-and-series/reference

Ransley, Janet, and Elena Marchetti. 2001."The Hidden Whiteness of Australian Law: A Case Study." *Griffith Law Review* 10(1): 139–150.

Ravallion, Martin. 2003. "The Debate on Globalization, Poverty, and Inequality: Why Measurement Matters." *International Affairs* 79(4): 739–753.

Rawls, John. 1963. "Constitutional Liberty and the Concept of Justice." In *John Rawls: Collected Papers*, ed. Samuel Freeman, 73–96. Cambridge, MA: Harvard University Press.

———. 1971. *A Theory of Justice*. Cambridge, MA: Harvard University Press.

———. 1999. *The Law of Peoples*. Cambridge, MA: Harvard University Press.

Razack, Sherene. 1999. *Looking White People in the Eye: Gender, Race and Culture in the Courtrooms and Classrooms*. Toronto: University of Toronto Press.

Reed, Dan. 2019. *Leaving Neverland*. Home Box Office. Documentary Film.

Rees, William, and Laura Westra. 2003. "When Consumption does Violence? Can There Be Sustainability and Environmental Justice in a Resource-Limited World?" In *Just Sustainabilities: Development in an Unequal World*, eds. Julian Agyeman, Robert Bullard, and Bob Evans, 99–124. Cambridge, MA: MIT Press.

Regret, Paul. 2018. "The Head, the Hand, and Matter." *Theory, Culture and Society* 35(7–8): 49–72.

Reiman, Jeffrey. 1990. *Justice and Modern Moral Philosophy*. New Haven: Yale University Press.

Religious Literacy Project: Christianity. 2018. *Harvard Divinity School*. Retrieved on October 31, 2018, from: https://rlp.hds.harvard.edu/religions/christianity/life-and-teachings-jesus

Religious Literacy Project: Hinduism. 2018. *Harvard Divinity School*. Retrieved on October 31, 2018, from: https://rlp.hds.harvard.edu/religions/hinduism/karma-way-action and https://rlp.hds.harvard.edu/religions/hinduism/dharma-social-order

Religious Literacy Project: Islam. 2018. *Harvard Divinity School*. Retrieved on October 31, 2018, from: https://rlp.hds.harvard.edu/religions/islam/quran-word-god

Religious Literacy Project: Judaism. 2018. *Harvard Divinity School*. Retrieved on October 31, 2018, from: https://rlp.hds.harvard.edu/religions/judaism/torah-covenant-and-constitution and https://rlp.hds.harvard.edu/religions/judaism/kabbalah-and-hasidism

Renteria, Melissa. 2003. "Ideas and Insights." Retrieved on March 25, 2019, from: https://www8.gsb.columbia.edu/articles/authors/melissa-renteria

Renton, James. 2017. "The British Empire's Jewish Question and the Post-Ottoman Future." In *The Jew as Legitimation: Jewish-Gentile Relations beyond Antisemitism and Philosemitism*, ed. David J. Wertheim, 135–151. London: Palgrave Macmillan.

Reyes, Hèctor. 2017. "A New Dangerous Stage of the Colonial Plunder of Puerto Rico." *Left Voice*. May 25. Retrieved on January 7, 2019, from: http://www.left-voice.org/A-New-Dangerous-Stage-of-the-Colonial Plunder-of-Puerto-Rico

Ridgeway, G. 2013. "Linking Prediction to Prevention." *Criminology and Public Policy* 12(3): 545–550.

Rieland, Randy. 2018. "Artificial Intelligence Is Now Used to Predict Crime: But Is It Biased?" Retrieved on December, 11, 2018, at Smithsonian.com: https://www.smithsonianmag.com/innovation/artificial-intelligence-is-now-used-predict-crime-is-it-biased-180968337/

Rigakos, G. 1999. "Risk Society and Actuarial Criminology." *Canadian Journal of Criminology* 41(2): 137–51.

Rigakos, George, and Richard Hadden. 2001. "Crime, Capitalism and the 'Risk Society.'" *Theoretical Criminology* 5(1): 61–84.

Rights of Indigenous Peoples, University of Minnesota Human Rights Library. Minneapolis, MN. Retrieved on February 15, 2019, from: http://hrlibrary.umn.edu/edumat/studyguides/indigenous.html

Riley, Angela. 2000. "Recovering Collectivity: Group Rights to Intellectual Property in Indigenous Communities." *Cardoza Arts and Entertainment Law Journal* 18: 175–211.

Ripess.org. 2019. "World Social Forum of Convergence of Transformative Economies." Retrieved on March 27, 2019, from: http://www.ripess.org/forum-social-mondial-economies-transformatrices/?lang=en

Robeyns, Ingrid. 2016. "The Capability Approach." In *The Stanford Encyclopedia of Philosophy*, ed. Edward Zalta. Retrieved on January 21, 2019, from: https://plato.stanford.edu/entries/capability-approach/

Robnett, Belinda. 2002. "External Political Change, Collective Identities, and Participation in Social Movement Organizations." In *Social Movements: Identity, Culture and the State*, eds. David Meyer, Nancy Whittier, and Belinda Robnett, 266–285. Oxford: Oxford University Press.

Rorty, Richard. 1989. *Contingency, Irony, and Solidarity*. Cambridge: Cambridge University Press.

Ross, Alf. 1974. *On Law and Justice*. Berkeley: University of California Press.

Ross, Robert. 1999. *A Concise History of South Africa*. New York: Cambridge University Press.

Rothbaum, Noah. 2016. "Is a Restaurant Serving 'British Colonial' Food Racist?" *Daily Beast*. Retrieved on January 30, 2019, from: https://www.thedailybeast.com/is-a- restaurant-serving-british-colonial-food-racist?ref=scroll

Rouse, Joseph. 2009. "Standpoint Theories Reconsidered." *Hypatia* 24(4): 200–209.

Rousseau, Jean-Jacques. 1973. *The Social Contract and Discourses*. London: Dent and Sons.

Roy, Arundhati. 2004. *An Ordinary Person's Guide to Empire*. Cambridge, MA: South End Press.

Ruddick, S. 1989. *Maternal Thinking*. NY: Ballantine Books.

Rudrum, David, and Nicholas Stavris, eds. 2015. *Supplanting the Postmodern*. London: Bloomsbury Academic.

Ruggiero, Vincenzo, and Nigel South. 2013. "Green Criminology and Crime of the Economy." *Critical Criminology* 21: 359–373.

Russell, Katheryn, and Dragan Milovanovic. 2001. *Petit Apartheid in the U.S. Criminal Justice System: The Dark Figure of Racism*. Durham, NC: Carolina Academic Press.

Rutherford, Stephanie. 2017. "Environmentality and Green Governmentality." In *International Encyclopedia of Geography*, ed. Douglas Richardson. Hoboken, NJ: John Wiley and Sons.

———. 2007. "Green Governmentality." *Progress in Human Geography* 31(3): 291–307.

Ryan, Charlotte. 2004. "Can We Be Compañeros?" *Social Problems*. 51(1): 110–113.

Sachs, Andrea. 2018. "'Better than Before' Puerto Rico's Recovery Is Nearly Complete." *Chicago Tribune*. Retrieved on December 11, 2018, from: https://www .chicagotribune.com/lifestyles/travel/ct-trav-puerto-rico-recovery-travel-2018 1210-story.html

Said, Edward. 1978. *Orientalism*. New York: Pantheon.

———. 1983. *The World, the Text, and the Critic*. Boston: Harvard University Press.

———. 1993. *Culture and Imperialism*. London: Chatto and Windus.

———. 1994. *Representations of the Intellectual*. New York: Vintage Books.

———. 1995. *The Politics of Dispossession: The Struggle for Palestinian Self- Determination, 1969–1994*. New York: Vintage Books.

———. 2004. *Humanism and Democratic Criticism*. New York: Columbia University Press.

Salazar, Debra J., and Donald K. Alper. 2002. "Reconciling Environmentalism and the Left: Perspectives on Democracy and Social Justice in British Columbia's Environmental Movement." *Canadian Journal of Political Science* 35(3): 527–566.

Saleh-Hanna, V., and C. Ume. 2008. "An Evolution of the Penal System: Criminal Justice in Nigeria." In *Colonial Systems of Control*, ed. V. Saleh-Hanna, 55–68. Ottawa: University of Ottawa Press.

Salehi, Mariam, and Timothy Williams. 2016. "Transitional Justice Review Beyond Peace and Justice." *Transitional Justice Review* 1(4), 96–123.

Samuel, Sigal. 2019. "Lake Erie Just Won the Same Legal Rights as People." *Vox*. Retrieved on March 31, 2019, from: https://www.vox.com/future-perfect/2019 /2/26/18241904/lake-erie-legal-rights-personhood-nature-environment-toledo -ohio

Sandel, Michael. 1982. *Liberalism and the Limits of Justice*. Cambridge, U.K.: Cambridge University Press.

Sander-Staudt, Maureen. 2018. "Care Ethics." *Internet Encyclopedia of Philosophy*. Retrieved on January 2, 2019, from: https://www.iep.utm.edu/care-eth/

Sanders, Katherine. 2018. "Beyond Human Ownership? Property, Power and Legal Personality for Nature in Aotearoa New Zealand." *Journal of Environmental Law* 30(1): 207–234.

Saunders, Harold. 2003. *A Public Peace Process—Sustained Dialogue to Transform Racial and Ethnic Conflicts*. New York: Palgrave.

Schaap, A. 2004. "Political Reconciliation Through a Struggle for Recognition?" *Social and Legal Studies* 13(4): 523–540.

Schaible, Lonnie, and Lorine Hughes. 2011. "Crime, Shame, Reintegration and Cross- National Homicide: A Partial Test of Reintegrative Shaming Theory." *The Sociological Quarterly* 52(1): 104–131.

Scheck, Barry. 2014. "Barry Scheck: Stunning New Case Highlights How Race Bias Corrupts Juries." *Salon*. Retrieved on March 7, 2019, from: https://www.salon .com/2014/04/15/barry_scheck_stunning_new_case_highlights_how_race_bias _corrupts_juries/

Schehr, Robert. 1996. *Dynamic Utopia*. Westport, CT: Praeger.

———. 1997. "Surfing the Chaotic: A Non-Linear Articulation of Social Movement Theory." In *Chaos, Criminology and Social Justice: The New Orderly (Dis)Order*, ed. Dragan Milovanovic, 157–178. Westport, CT: Praeger.

———. 1999a. "Conflict Mediation and the Postmodern." *Social Justice* 25: 208–232.

———. 1999b. "Intentional Communities, the Fourth Way: A Constitutive Integration." In *Constitutive Criminology at Work*, eds. Stuart Henry and Dragan Milovanovic, 249–274. New York: State University of New York Press.

———. 2000. "From Restoration to Transformation." *Mediation Quarterly* 18: 151–169.

Scheper-Hughes, Nancy. 1992. *Death Without Weeping: The Violence of Everyday Life. in Brazil*. Berkeley: University of California Press.

Schilling-Vacaflor, Almut, and Jessika Eichler. 2017. "The Shady Side of Consultation and Compensation: 'Divide-and-Rule' Tactics in Bolivia's Extraction Sector." *Development & Change* 48 (6): 1439–1463.

Schlosberg, David. 2004. "Reconceiving Environmental Justice: Global Movements and Political Theories." *Environmental Politics* 13(3): 517–547.

———. 2007. *Defining Environmental Justice*. New York: Oxford University Press.

Schoenfeld, Eugen. 1989. "Durkheim's Concept of Justice and Its Relationship to Social Solidarity." *Sociological Analysis* 50(2): 111–127.

Schroeder, Jeanne. 2008. *The Four Lacanian Discourse*. New York: Routledge Press.

Schroeder, Theodore. 1998. "Fables of the Deconstruction: The Practical Failures of Gay and Lesbian Theory in the Realm of Employment Discrimination. *American University Journal of Gender, Society, Policy and Law* 6: 333–354.

Schum, D. 1994. *The Evidential Foundations of Probabilistic Reasoning*. New York: John Wiley and Sons, Inc.

Schweigert, F. J. 2002. "Moral and Philosophical Foundations of Restorative Justice." In *Restorative Justice*, ed. J. Perry. Alexandria, VA: American Correctional Association.

Schwendinger, Herman, and Julia Schwendinger. 1985. *Adolescent Subcultures and Delinquency*. New York: Praeger.

———. 2001. "Defenders of Order or Guardians of Human Rights?" In *What Is Crime?* eds. Stuart Henry and Mark Lanier, 65–98. New York: Rowman and Littlefield.

———. 2014. *Who Killed the Berkeley School?* Brooklyn, NY: Punctum Books.

Scimecca, Joseph. 1991. "Conflict Resolution and a Critique of Alternative Dispute Resolution." In *Criminology as Peacemaking*, eds. Harold Pepinsky and Richard Quinney. Bloomington. Indiana University Press.

Sciullo, Nick J., 2019. "Queer Phenomenology in Law: A Critical Theory of Orientation." *Pace Law Review* 39. Retrieved on March 16, 2019, from: http://dx.doi.org/10.2139/ssrn.3312372

Sedgwick, Eve Kosofsky. 2008. *Epistemology of the Closet*. Berkeley: University of California Press.

Seis, Mark. 2001. "Confronting the Contradiction: Global Capitalism and Environmental Health." *International Journal of Comparative Sociology* 42(1): 123–144.

Sen, Amartya. 1992. *Inequality Reexamined*. Cambridge: Harvard University Press.

———. 2002. "How to Judge Globalism." Retrieved on March 1, 2019, from: http://www.prospect.org/print/v13/1/sen-a.html

———. 2006. "What Do We Want from a Theory of Justice?" *Journal of Philosophy* 103(5): 215–238.

———. 2011. *The Idea of Justice*. Cambridge, MA: Harvard University Press.

Senate Bill 358, Chapter 566, California. Retrieved on March 12, 2019, from: http://www.vtzlawblog.com/uploads/file/California%20Equal%20Pay%20Act%20(SB358).pdf

Senser, Robert A. 1989. "How Poland's Solidarity Won Freedom of Association." *Monthly Labor Review* 112(9): 34–39.

"Settlers in West Bank Fight Eviction." 2003. *Chicago Tribune*. June, 20.

Shahidian, Hammed. 1997. "Women and Clandestine Politics in Iran, 1970–1985." *Feminist Studies* 23(1): 7–43.

Sharma, Sohan, Sue Tracy, and Surinder Kumar. 2004. "Venezuela-ripe for U.S. Intervention?" *Race and Class* 45(4): 61–74.

Sherman, L. W. 2000. "Domestic Violence and Restorative Justice: Answering Key Questions." *Virginia Journal of Social Policy and Law* 8(4): 263–298.

Showing Up for Racial Justice. Retrieved on March 1, 2019, from: http://www. showingupforracialjustice.org/

Shriver, Thomas E., Amy Chasteen Miller, and Sherry Cable. 2003. "Women's Work: Women's Involvement in the Gulf War Illness Movement." *Sociological Quarterly* 44(4): 639–658.

Sikorski, Radek. 1996. "How We Lost Poland." *Foreign Affairs* 75(5): 15–22.

Simic, Olivera. 2016. *An Introduction to Transitional Justice.* New York: Routledge.

Simmons, John. 2010. "Ideal and Nonideal Theory." *Philosophy and Public Affairs* 38(1): 5–36.

Simon, Jonathan. 1987. "The Emergence of Risk Society: Insurance Law and the State." *Socialist Review* 95: 61–89.

———. 1988. "The Ideological Effects of Actuarial Justice." *Law and Society Review* 22: 771–800.

Simpson, Graeme. 2002. "Tell No Lies, Claim No Easy Victories: A Brief Evaluation of South African Truth and Reconciliation Commission. In *Commissioning the Past: Understanding South Africa's Truth and Reconciliation Commission*, eds. Deborah Posel and Graeme Simpson, 220–247. Witwatersrand: University Press Publications.

Sirianni, Carmen. 1984. "Justice and the Division of Labour. *Sociological Review* 32(3): 449–470.

Sites, P. 1973. *Control, the Basis of Social Order.* New York: Dunellen.

Skousen, Mark. 2005. *Vienna & Chicago, Friends or Foes?: A Tale of Two Schools of Free-Market Economics.* Washington, DC: Capital Press.

Smith, Adam. 1976. *Theory of Moral Sentiments.* Indianapolis, IN: Liberty Classics.

———. 2000. *Theory of Moral Sentiments.* Amherst, NY: Prometheus Books.

———. 2003. *Wealth of Nations.* New York: Bantam Books.

Smith, Don. 2018. "Environmental Courts and Tribunals." *Journal of Energy and Natural Resources Law* 36(2): 137–140.

Smith, Huston. 2009. *The World's Religions.* New York: Harper One.

Smith, Jackie. 2017. "Local Responses to Right-Wing Populism: Building Human Rights Cities." *Studies in Social Justice* 11(2): 347–368.

Smith, Linda Tuhiwai. 1999. *Decolonizing Methodologies: Research and Indigenous Peoples.* New York: Zed Books Ltd.

Snyder, Claire. 2008. "What is Third-wave Feminism?" *Signs* 34(1): 175–196.

Solland, B. 2008. "Causes of Speciesism." In *Global Harms: Ecological Crime and Speciesism*, ed. R. Solland. New York: Nova Science Publishers.

Solnit, David, ed. 2004. *Globalize Liberation: How to Uproot the System and Build a Better World.* San Francisco, CA: City Lights Books.

Solomon, Robert C., and Mark C. Murphy. 2000. *What is Justice? Classic and Contemporary Readings.* New York: Oxford University Press.

Sorrenson, M.P.K. 1999. "The Settlement of New Zealand from 1835." In *Indigenous People's Rights*, ed. Paul Havermann, 162–179. Oxford: Oxford University Press.

South, Nigel. 2014. "Green Criminology." *International Journal for Crime, Justice and Social Democracy* 3(2): 5–20.

Sovacool, Benjamin K., May Tan-Mullins, and Wokje Abrahamse. 2018. "Bloated Bodies and Broken Bricks: Power, Ecology, and Inequality in the Political Economy of Natural Disaster Recover." *World Development* 110: 243–255.

Sparks, Allister. 1996. *Tomorrow Is Another Country: The Inside Story of South Africa's Road to Change.* Chicago: University of Chicago Press.

Spelman, Elizabeth V. 1982. "Woman as Body: Ancient and Contemporary Views." *Feminist Studies* 8(1): 109–131.

———. 1988. *Inessential Woman: Problems of Exclusion in Feminist Thought.* Boston: Beacon Press.

Spencer, Herbert. 1897. *The Principles of Sociology.* New York: D. Appleton and Co.

———. 1978. *The Principles of Ethics.* Indianapolis, IN: Liberty Classics.

———. 1969. *The Study of Sociology.* Ann Arbor: University of Michigan Press.

Spitzer, Aaron J. 2018. "Reconciling Shared Rule: Liberal Theory, Electoral-Districting Law and "National Group" Representation in Canada." *Canadian Journal of Political Science* 51(2): 447–466.

Spivak, Gayatri Chakravorty. 1988. "Can the Subaltern Speak?" In *Marxism and the Interpretation of Culture*, eds. Cary Nelson and Larry Grossberg, 271–313. Chicago: University of Chicago Press.

———. 1998. *Don't Call Me Postcolonial.* Cambridge, MA: Harvard University Press.

———. 1999. *A Critique of Post-Colonial Reason.* Cambridge, MA: Harvard University Press.

———. 2003. *Death of a Discipline.* New York: Columbia University Press.

———. 2010. *Can the Subaltern Speak?* New York: Columbia University Press.

Staretz, Robert, and Edgar Mitchell. 2011. "The Quantum Hologram and the Nature of Consciousness." *Journal of Cosmology* 14: 1–19.

Starr, Sonja. 2014. "Evidence-based Sentencing and the Scientific Rationalization of Discrimination." *Stanford Law Review* 66: 803–872.

Steadman, H. J., and J. J. Cocozza. 1974. *Careers of the Criminal Insane.* Lexington, MA: Lexington Books.

Stedman, Susan. 2001. *Durkheim Reconsidered.* Cambridge: Polity Press.

Steinberg, Marc. 2002. "Toward a More Dialogic Analysis of Social Movement Culture." In *Social Movements: Identity, Culture and the State*, eds. David Meyer, Nancy Whittier, and Belinda Robnett, 208–225. Oxford: Oxford University Press.

Stewart, Brandon, and Eric Wiebelhaus-Brahm. 2017. "The Quantitative Turn in Transitional Justice Research." *Transitional Justice Review* 1(5): 97–133.

Stewart, Frances. 1995. "Basic Needs, Capabilities and Human Development." *Greek Economic Review* 17(20): 83–96.

Stone, Christopher. 1972. "Should Trees Have Standing?" *Southern California Law Review* 45: 450–487.

Strauss, Valerie. 2019. "West Virginia Teachers Who Started a Wave of Strikes Last Year Just Authorized a New Labor Action, Here's Why from an Educator." *Washington Post.* Retrieved on March 13, 2019, from: https://www.washingtonpost.com/education/2019/02/15/west-virginia-teachers-who-started-wave-strikes-last-year-just-authorized-new-labor-action-heres-why-an-educator/?utm_term=.5e21d87b5a3f

Street, Paul. 2016. "Miranda, Obama, and Hamilton: An Orwellian Ménage à Trois for the Neoliberal Age." *Counterpunch.* Retrieved on January 8, 2019, from: https://www.counterpunch.org/2016/06/24/miranda-obama-and-hamilton-an-orwellian-menage-a-trois-for-the-neoliberal-age/

Stretesky, P. 2006. "Corporate Self-Policing and the Environment." *Criminology* 44(3): 671–708.

Stretesky, Paul, Michael Long, and Michael Lynch. 2013. *The Treadmill of Crime: Political Economy and Green Criminology.* London: Routledge.

Stubbs, J. 2002. "Domestic Violence and Women's Safety: Feminist Challenges to Restorative Justice." In *Restorative Justice and Family Violence*, eds. H. Strang and J. Braithwaite, 42–61. Oxford: Cambridge University Press.

Sullivan, Dennis, and Larry Tifft. 1980. *The Mask of Love.* Port Washington, NY: Kennikat Press Corp.

———. 2005. *Restorative Justice: Healing the Foundations of Our Everyday Lives.* Monsey, NY: Willow Tree Press.

Sullivan, Dennis, and Larry Tifft, eds. 2006. *Handbook of Restorative Justice.* New York: Routledge.

Sustar, Lee. 2004. "The U.S. Labor Movement: State of Emergency, Signs of Renewal." *International Socialist Review* 34: 31–40.

Swanson, Jacinda. 2005. "Recognition and Redistribution." *Theory, Culture and Society* 22(4): 87–118.

Switala, Kristin. 1999. "Feminism and Postcolonialism: Bibliography." Retrieved on March 1, 2019, from: www.cddc.vt.edu/feminism/poc.html

Sylvain, Renée. 2002. "'Land, Water, and Truth': San Identity and Global Indigenism." *American Anthropologist* 104(4): 1074–1085.

Taguchi, H. 2012. "A Diffractive and Deleuzian Approach to Analyzing Interview Data." *Feminist Theory* 13(3): 265–281.

Tamembaum, Yoav. 2011. "The Success and Failure of Non-Violence." *Philosophy Now.* Retrieved on March 11, 2019, from: https://philosophynow.org/issues/85/The_Success_and_Failure_of_Non-Violence

Tampio, Nicholas. 2009. "Assemblages and the Multitude." *European Journal of Political Theory* 8(3): 383–400.

Tappan, Paul. 2001. "Who Is the Criminal?" In *What Is Crime?* eds. Stuart Henry and Mark Lanier, 27–36.New York: Rowman and Littlefield.

Tatum, B. 1994. "The Colonial Model as a Theoretical Explanation of Crime and Delinquency." In *African American Perspectives on Crime Causation, Criminal Justice Administration and Prevention*, ed. A. Sulton, 33–52. Englewood, CO: Sulton Books.

Taylor, Charles. 1985. "What's Wrong with Negative Liberty?" In *Collected Papers, Volume 2*, ed. Charles Taylor. Cambridge: Cambridge University Press.

———. 1994. "The Politics of Recognition." In *Multiculturalism*, ed. Amy Gutmann, 25–74. Princeton, NJ: Princeton University Press.

Taylor, D. E. 2000. "The Rise of the Environmental Justice Paradigm: Injustice, Framing and the Social Construction of Environmental Discourses." *American Behavioral Scientist* 43(4): 508–580.

Taylor, Kenneth Bruce. 2016. "Sunset for the American Dream." *International Journal of Social Economics* 44(12): 1639–1653.

Taylor, Ralph. 2008. "Student Guide to Accompany Donald Black's Behavior of Law." Temple University, Department of Criminal Justice, unpublished manuscript. Retrieved November 15, 2018, from: http://www.rbtaylor.net/resource_guide_black_20080225.pdf on 11/15/2018

Teitel, Ruti. 2002. *Transitional Justice.* Oxford: Oxford University Press.

Telesurenglish.net. 2018. "Brazil's Social Movements Rally Against Bolsonaro." Retrieved on March 27, 2019, from: https://www.telesurenglish.net/multimedia/Brazils-Social-Movements-Rally-Against-Bolsonaro-20181031-0016.html

Terfs.com. 2014. Retrieved on March 8, 2019, from: http://theterfs.com/2014/05/01/judith-butler-addresses-terfs-and-the-work-of-sheila-jeffreys-and-janice-raymond/

Tew, Yvonne. 2011. Georgetown University Law Center. "The Malaysian Legal System: A Tale of Two Courts." Retrieved on January 30, 2019, from: https://scholarship.law.georgetown.edu/cgi/viewcontent.cgi?article=2944&context=facpub

Thakur, Shivesh. 1996. *Religion and Social Justice.* London: Macmillan.

Tharoor, Ishaan. 2015. "The Dark Side of Winston Churchill's Legacy No One Should Forget." *Washington Post.* Retrieved on January 31, 2019, from: https://www.washingtonpost.com/news/worldviews/wp/2015/02/03/the-dark-side-of-winston-churchills-legacy-no-one-should-forget/?utm_term=.29241c018527

Thomas, Kimberly, and Paul Reingold. 2017. "From Grace to Grids: Rethinking Due Process Protection for Parole." *Journal of Criminal Law and Criminology* 107(2): 213–251.

Thomassen, Lasse. 2010. "Unstable Universalities." *Contemporary Political Theory* 9(1): 137–139.

Thompson, Elizabeth F. 2013. *Justice Interrupted: The Struggle for Constitutional Government in the Middle East*. Cambridge, MA: Harvard University Press.

Thompson, Simon. 2005. *Critical Review of International Social and Political Philosophy* 8(1): 85–102.

Thrush, Glenn. 2019. "Family Separation May Have Hit Thousands More Migrant Children Than Reported." *New York Times*. Retrieved on March 12, 2019, from: https://www.nytimes.com/2019/01/17/us/family-separation-trump-administration-migrants.html

Tiersma, Peter. 2000. *Legal Language*. Chicago: University of Chicago Press.

Tifft, Larry. 1979. "The Coming Redefinition of Crime: An Anarchist Perspective." *Social Problems* 26(4): 392–402.

Tifft, Larry, and Dennis Sullivan. 1981. *Restorative Justice: Healing the Foundations of Our Everyday Lives*. Monsey, NY: Willow Tree Press.

Tillich, Paul. 1957. *Systematic Theology and Dynamics of Faith*. New York: Harper and Row.

———. 1983. *The Socialist Decision*. Eugene, OR: Wipf and Stock Publishers.

Tong, Rosemarie. 1993. *Feminine and Feminist Ethics*. Belmont, CA: Wadsworth Publishing Company.

Tong, Rosemarie, and Nancy Williams. 2009. "Feminist Ethics." In *The Stanford Encyclopedia of Philosophy*, ed. Edward Zalta. Retrieved on March 18, 2019, from: https://plato.stanford.edu/entries/feminism-ethics/

Toomey, Diane. 2017. "How Listening to Trees Can Help Reveal Nature's Connections." Retrieved on January 20, 2019, from: https://e360.yale.edu/features/how-listening-to-trees-can-help-reveal-natures-connections

Torres, Maria Idall. 2005. "Organizing, Educating, and Advocating for Health and Human Rights in Vieques, Puerto Rico." *American Journal of Public Health* 95(1): 9–12.

Touval, Saadia, and I. William Zartman. 1985. *International Mediation in Theory and Practice*. Boulder, CO: Westview Press.

———. 1989. "Mediation in International Conflicts." In *Mediation Research*, eds. Kenneth Kressel and Dean G. Pruitt. San Francisco: Jossey-Bass.

Townes, Carimah. 2016. "Obama Explains the Problem with 'All Lives Matter'." Retrieved on March 1, 2019, from: https://thinkprogress.org/obama-explains-the-problem-with-all-lives-matter-780912d54888/

Transitional Justice Database Project. Retrieved on October 15, 2019, from: http://www.tjdbproject.com

Treanor, Tim 2018. "Review: Why Hamilton is the Greatest Musical Yet Written." *DC Theatre Scene*. Retrieved on January 8, 2019, from: https://dctheatrescene.com/2018/06/15/review-why-hamilton-is-the-greatest-musical-yet-written/

Tronto, Joan. 2005. "An Ethics of Care." In *Feminist Theory*, eds. Anne Cudd and Robin Andreasen, 251–263. Oxford: Blackwell Publishing.

Tucker, Robert C. 1972. *The Marx Engels Reader*, 2nd ed. New York: W. W. Norton and Company.

Tulloch, J. 1999. "Fear of Crime and the Media: Sociocultural Theories of Risk." In *Risk and Socio-Cultural Theory*, ed. D. Lupton, 34–58. New York: Cambridge University Press.

Tully, J. 1995. *Strange Multiplicity*. Cambridge: Cambridge University Press.

Ture, Kwame, and Charles V. Hamilton. 1992. *Black Power*. New York: Vintage Books.

———. 2003. "The Struggle of Indigenous Peoples for and of Freedom." In *Box of Treasures or Empty Box?* eds. A. Walem and H. Bruce, 272–307. Vancouver: Theytus Books.

Turner, D. 2004. "Perceiving the World Differently." In *Intercultural Dispute Resolution in Aboriginal Contexts*, eds. C. Bell and D. Kahane, 57–69. Vancouver: UBC Press.

Turner, Michael. 2010. "The Place of Desert in Theological Concepts of Distributive Justice." *Journal of Society of Christian Ethics* 31(2): 131–149.

Turner, Terence. 1997. "Human Rights, Human Difference: Anthropology's Contribution to an Emancipatory Cultural Politics." *Journal of Anthropological Research* 53: 273–291.

Tutu, Desmond. 1999. *No Future Without Forgiveness*. London: Rider.

Unger, Roberto. 1987. *False Necessity*. Cambridge: Cambridge University Press.

———. 1996. *What Should Legal Analysis Become?* New York: Verso.

UNICEF. 2016. "UNICEF's Data Work on FGM/C." Retrieved January 30, 2019, from: https://www.unicef.org/media/files/FGMC_2016_brochure_final_UNICEF _SPREAD(2).pdf

United Nations. N.D. Department of Economic and Social Affairs, Indigenous Peoples. Retrieved on January 30, 2019, from: https://www.un.org/development /desa/indigenouspeoples/declaration-on-the-rights-of-indigenous-peoples.html

United Nations General Assembly. 2017. "Special Committee Approves Text Calling on United States to Expedite Puerto Rico's Self-Determination Process, Welcomes Release of Long-Time Independence Activist." Retrieved January 31, 2019, from: https://www.un.org/press/en/2017/gacol3312.doc.htm

United Nations High Commissioner for Refugees. 2017. Retrieved on January 22, 2019, from: http://reporting.unhcr.org/sites/default/files/gr2017/pdf/GR2017_English _Full_lowres.pdf

———. 2017. "Global Focus." Retrieved on January 22, 2019, from: http://reporting .unhcr.org/population

United Nations Human Rights Council. 2019. "No Justification for Israel to Shoot Protesters with Live Ammunition." Retrieved on March 25, 2019, from: https:// www.ohchr.org/EN/HRBodies/HRC/Pages/NewsDetail.aspx?NewsID=24226 &LangID=E

United States Bureau of Labor Statistics. 2019. U.S. Department of Labor. Retrieved on March 4, 2019, from: https://www.bls.gov/news.release/union2.nr0.htm

Vago, Steven. 2004. *Social Change*. New York: Prentice Hall.

Vahabzadeh, Payman, ed. 2017. *Iran's Struggles for Social Justice Economics, Agency, Justice, Activism*. New York: Palgrave Macmillan.

Valdes, Francisco, and Sumi Cho. 2011. "Critical Race Materialism: Theorizing Justice in the Wake of Global Neoliberalism." *Connecticut Law Review* 43(5): 1513–1572.

Valencia, Reynaldo Analya, Sonia R. Garcia, Henry Flores, and Jose Roberto Juarez Jr. 2004. *Mexican Americans and the Law*. Tucson, AR: University of Arizona Press.

Van, Jon. 2005. "Cybercrime Being Fought in New Ways." *Chicago Tribune*. October, 2005.

Van den Brink, Bert. 2008. "The Right to Justification." *Krisis* 3: 56–61.

Van Ness, Daniel. 1990. "Restorative Justice." In *Criminal Justice, Restitution, and Reconciliation*, eds. Burt Galaway and Joe Hudson. Newbury Park, CA: Sage.

———. 1995. "Anchoring Just Deserts." *Criminal Law Forum* 6: 507–517.

———. 1999. "Legal Issues Related to Restorative Justice." In *Restorative Juvenile Justice*. eds. Gordon Bazemore and Lode Walgrave, 263–284. Monsey, NJ: Willow Tree Press.

Van Ness, Daniel W., and Karen Heetderks Strong. 2002. *Restoring Justice*. Cincinnati, OH: Anderson Publishing.

———. 2014. *Restoring Justice*, 5th ed. New York: Routledge.

van Zyl, Paul. 1999. "Dilemmas of Transitional Justice: The Case of South Africa's Truth and Reconciliation Commission." *Journal of International Affairs* 52(2): 647–667.

Vargas, Manuel. 2018. "Latinx Philosophy." In *The Stanford Encyclopedia of Philosophy*, ed. Edward Zalta. Retrieved on March 13, 2019, from: https://plato.stanford.edu/archives/win2018/entries/latinx/

Vattel, Emer de. 1971. "Emer de Vattel on the Occupation of Territory." In *Imperialism*, ed. R. Curtin, 41–71. London: Macmillan.

Vo, Lam Thuy. 2018. "220 Years of Census Data Proves Race Is a Social Construct." Von Hirsch, Andrew. 1993. *Censure and Sanctions*. Oxford: Clarendon Press.

Vox. Retrieved on March 16, 2019, from: https://www.vox.com/2016/8/18/12404688/census-race-history-intersectionality

Wacquant, Loic. 2001. "Deadly Symbiosis: When Ghetto and Prison Meet." *Punishment and Society* 3(1): 85–134.

———. 2009. *Punishing the Poor: The Neoliberal Government of Social Insecurity*. Durham, NC: Duke University Press.

———. 2015. *The Two Faces of the Ghetto*. New York: Oxford University Press.

Wagner, Peter, and Wendy Sawyer. 2018. "Mass Incarceration: The Whole Pie." *Prison Policy Initiative*. Retrieved on January 10, 2019, from: https://www.prisonpolicy.org/reports/pie2018.html

Walgrave, Lode, and H. Geudens. 1996. "The Restorative Proportionality of Community Service for Juveniles." *European Journal of Crime, Criminal Law and Criminal Justice* 4: 361–380.

Wallace, Maurice. 2004. "Feminism and the Law." *Duke Journal of Gender Law and Policy* 11: 1–7.

Walsh, Mary Williams. 2015. "The Bonds That Broke Puerto Rico." *New York Times*. Retrieved on December 12, 2018, from: https://www.nytimes.com/2015/07/01/business/dealbook/the-bonds-that-broke-puerto-rico.html

Walters, Reece, and Dianne Westerhuis. 2013. "Green Crime and the Role of Environmental Courts." *Crime, Law and Social Change* 59: 279–290.

Walzer, M. 1983. *Spheres of Justice: A Defense of Pluralism and Equality*. Oxford: Martin Robertson.

Warren, Karen, and Nisvan Erkal, eds. 1997. *Ecofeminism: Women, Culture, Nature*. Bloomington: Indiana University Press.

Warren, Robert. 2019. "U.S. Undocumented Population Continued to Fall, 2016–2017." *Journal on Migration and Human Security* February 14, 1–4. Originally published online, http://doi.org/10.14240/cmsesy011619

Waters, Billye Sankofa. 2015. "Straight Outta Intersectionality: A Review of 'Straight Outta Compton' from My Six Selves." *Praxis Center, Arcus Center for Social Justice Leadership*. Retrieved on March 6, 2019, from: http://www.kzoo.edu/praxis/straight-outta-intersectionality/#billye

Watson, Hilbourne A. 2002. "Globalization as Capitalism in the Age of Electronics." *Latin American Perspectives* 29(6): 32–43.

Wear, Rae. 2014. "Astroturf and Populism in Australia." *Australian Journal of Political Science* 49(1): 54–67.

Weber, Max. 1958. *The Protestant Ethic and the Spirit of Capitalism*. New York: Charles Scribner's Books.

———. 1978. *Economy and Society* Vols. 1–2. Eds. G. Roth and C. Wittich. Los Angeles: University of California Press.

Wei, Xiaoping. 2008. "From Principle to Context: Marx Versus Nozick and Rawls on Distributive Justice." *Rethinking Marxism* 20(3): 472–512.

———. 2015. "Did Marx Have a Principle of Distributive Justice?" Paper delivered at the 8th International Marx and Engels Colloquium Marxist Studies Centre,

Brazil, July 2015, Retrieved on October 28, 2018, from: https://www.ifch .unicamp.br/formulario_cemarx/selecao/2015/trabalhos2015/Xiaoping_Wei.pdf

Weinstein, Jami, and Tobyn DeMarco. 2004. "Challenging Dissent: The Ontology and Logic of *Lawrence v. Texas.*" *Cardozo Women's Law Journal* 10: 423–456.

Weisbrot, Mark, Luis Sandoval, and David Rosnick. 2006. "Poverty Rates in Venezuela: Getting the Numbers Right." *International Journal of Health Services.* 36: 813–823.

Wells, Thomas. 2018. "Sen's Capability Approach." *Internet Encyclopedia of Philosophy.* Retrieved on October 28, 2018, from: https://www.iep.utm.edu/sen-cap/

Wendt, Alexander. 2015. *Quantum Mind and Social Science.* Cambridge: Cambridge University Press.

Whisnant, Rebecca. 2016. "Our Blood: Andrea Dworkin on Race, Privilege, and Women's Common Condition." *Women's Studies International Forum* 58: 568–576.

White, Jeremiah. 2004. "Is Iowa's Sexual Predator Statute 'Civil.'"? *Iowa Law Review* 89: 339–373.

White, Micah. 2016. *The End of Protest.* Toronto: Alfred Knopf Canada.

White, Rob. 2011. *Transnational Environmental Crime.* London: Routledge.

———. 2013a. "Environmental Crime and Problem-Solving Courts." *Crime, Law, and Social Change* 59: 267–278.

———. 2013b. "Eco-Global Criminology and the Political Economy of Environmental Harm." In *Routledge International Handbook of Green Criminology,* eds. N. South and A. Brisman. London: Routledge.

———. 2013c. *Environmental Harm.* Bristol, U.K.: Policy Press.

White, Rob, and Diane Heckenberg. 2014. *Green Criminology.* New York: Routledge.

White, Stephen. 1991. *Political Theory and Postmodernism.* Cambridge: Cambridge University Press.

Whorf, Benjamin. 1964. *Language, Thought and Reality.* Boston: MIT Press.

Wiegman, Robyn. 2004. "Dear Ian." *Duke Journal of Gender Law and Policy* 11: 90–96.

Wierder, Lawrence. 1988. *Language and Social Reality.* Landham, MD: University Press of America.

Wiessner, Siegfried. 2001. "Introduction for the Sixth Annual Tribe Sovereignty Symposium: Defending Indigenous Peoples' Heritage." *St. Thomas Law Review* 14: 270–293.

Wikipedia.org. 2019a. "Institute for Conflict Transformation and Peacebuilding." Retrieved on January 20, 2019, from: https://en.wikipedia.org/wiki/Institute_for _Conflict_Transformation_and_Peacebuilding

Wikipedia.org. 2019b. "List of Intentional Communities." Retrieved on February 28, 2019, from: https://en.wikipedia.org/wiki/List_of_intentional_commu nities

Wikipedia.org. 2019c. "Black Lives Matter." Retrieved on March 1, 2019, from: https://en.wikipedia.org/w/index.php?title=Black_Lives_Matter&oldid =883099650

Wikipedia.org. 2019d. "2018 Gaza Border Protests." Retrieved on March 25, 2019, from: https://en.wikipedia.org/wiki/2018_Gaza_border_protests

Wikipedia.org. 2019e. "Yellow Vests Movement." Retrieved on March 26, 2019, from: https://en.wikipedia.org/wiki/Yellow_vests_movement

Wikipedia.org. 2019f. "2018 Venezuelan Presidential Election." Retrieved on March 27, 2019, from: https://en.wikipedia.org/wiki/2018_Venezuelan_presi dential_election

Wikipedia.org. 2019g. "Juan Guaidó." Retrieved on March 27, 2019, from: https://en .wikipedia.org/wiki/Juan_Guaid%C3%B3#2015_parliamentary_vote

Wikipedia.org. 2019h. "GNU." Retrieved on October 6, 2019, from: https://en .wikipedia.org/wiki/GNU

Wikiquote. 2018. Retrieved on December 6, 2018, from: https://en.wikiquote.org
/wiki/Law_%26_Order

Wilkie, Christina. 2018. "Trump Claims Feds Did 'A Fantastic Job' in Puerto Rico
One Day After Death Toll Estimate Soars to Nearly 3,000." *CNBC Politics.*
Retrieved on February 5, 2019, from: https://www.cnbc.com/2018/08/29/trump
-we-did-a-fantastic-job-in-puerto-rico.html

Wilkins, David. 1997. *American Indian Sovereignty and the U.S. Supreme Court: The
Masking of Justice.* Austin: University of Texas Press.

Williams, Chris, and Bruce Arrigo. 2001. "Anarchaos and Order: On the Emergence
of Social Justice. *Theoretical Criminology* 5(2): 223–252.

Williams, Kaya Naomi. 2017. "Public, Safety, Risk." *Social Justice* 44(1): 36–61.

Williams, Robert A., Jr. 1990. "The Rights and Status of Indigenous Peoples under
International Law during the Classical Era Treaty Period (1600–1840)." *Law and
Anthropology* 5: 237–257.

Willoughby, W. W. 1900. *Social Justice.* New York: Macmillan.

Wills, Jenny Heijun. 2016. "Paradoxical Essentialism: Reading Race and Origins in
Jane Jeong Trenka's Asian Adoption Memoirs." *Canadian Review of American Studies* 46(2): 202.

Wilson, E. O. 1975. *Sociobiology.* Cambridge: Harvard University Press.

Wilson, Richard A. 2000. "Reconciliation and Revenge in Post-Apartheid South
Africa." *Current Anthropology* 41(1): 75–98.

Wing, Katherine, ed. 1996. *Critical Race Feminism: A Reader.* New York: New York
University Press.

Wittgenstein, Ludwig. 1953. *Philosophical Investigations*, trans. G.E.M. Anscombe.
New York: Macmillan.

Wolf, Sherry. 2004. "The Roots of Gay Oppression." *International Socialist Review* 37:
48–58.

Wolff, Robert. 1977. *Understanding Rawls.* Princeton, NJ: Princeton University Press.

Wolford, Wendy. 2010. *This Land Is Ours Now: Social Mobilization and the Meanings of
Land in Brazil.* Durham, NC: Duke University Press.

Wollstonecraft, Mary. 1988. *A Vindication of the Rights of Women.* London: Penguin.

Woods, Alan. 2005a. "Chavez: 'Capitalism Must Be Transcended.'" Retrieved on
March 30, 2019, from: http://www.marxist.com/Latinam/chavez_speech_wsf
.htm

———. 2005b. "Encounter with Hugo Chavez." Retrieved on January 21, 2019,
from: http://www.marxist.com/Latinam/enounters_with_hugo_chavez.html

Woodmansee, Martha. 1992. "On the Author Effect: Recovering Collectivity." *Cardoza Arts and Entertainment Law Journal* 10: 279.

Woolford, Andrew. 2010. *The Politics of Restorative Justice.* Winnipeg, Canada: Fern-
wood Press.

Wooton, Barbara. 1979. "Crime, Responsibility, and Prevention." In *Contemporary
Punishment: Views, Explanations, and Justifications*, eds. Rudolph Gerber and Patrick
McAnany, 164–174. Notre Dame: University of Notre Dame Press.

Worldatlas.com. 2018. Retrieved on February 5, 2019, from: https://www.worldatlas
.com/articles/20-biggest-cities-in-china.html

World Future Fund. "Killed in the Name of 'Freedom': Over 12 Million Dead in
America's Wars since World War Two." Retrieved on March 1, 2019, from: http://
www.worldfuturefund.org/Reports/Imperialism/usmurder.html

World Justice Project. Retrieved on December 30, 2018, from: https://worldjustice
project.org/

Wozniak, John. 2000. "The Voices of Peacemaking Criminology." *Contemporary Justice Review* 3(3): 267–289.

Wright, Martin. 1982. *Making Good: Prisons, Punishment, and Beyond.* London: Bur-
nett Books.

Xu, Deqiang, and Hong Xianonan. 2015. "Critical Reflection on Nancy Fraser's Theory of Justice." *Cross-Cultural Communication* 11(9): 43–47.

Yardley, Jim. 2005. "Rural Chinese Riot as Police Try to Halt Pollution Protest." *New York Times*. Retrieved on February 1, 2019, from: http://www.nytimes.com/2005/04/14international/asia/14riot.html

Yosso, Tara. 2005. *Critical Race Counterstories along the Chicana/Chicano Educational Pipeline*. New York: Routledge.

Young, Iris. 1997. "Unruly Categories: A Critique of Nancy Fraser's Dual Systems Theory." *New Left Review* 222: 147–160.

———. 2000. *Justice and the Politics of Difference*. Princeton, NJ: Princeton University Press.

———. 2001. "Activist Challenges to Deliberate Democracy." *Political Theory* 29(5): 670–690.

Young, Jock. 2007. *The Vertigo of Late Modernity*. London: Sage Publications.

———. 2011. *The Criminological Imagination*. Malden, MA: Polity Press.

Young, Marlene. 1995. *Restorative Community Justice*. Washington, DC: National Organization for Victim Assistance.

Young, T. R. 1997a. "Challenges: For a Postmodern Criminology." In *Chaos, Criminology and Social Justice: The New Orderly (Dis)Order*, ed. Dragan Milovanovic, 29–51. Westport, CT: Praeger.

———. 1997b. "The ABCs for Crime: Attractors, Bifurcations, and Chaotic Dynamics." In *Chaos, Criminology and Social Justice: The New Orderly (Dis)Order*, ed. Dragan Milovanovic, 77–96. Westport, CT: Praeger.

———. 1999. "A Constitutive of Justice." In *Constitutive Criminology at Work*, eds. Stuart Henry and Dragan Milovanovic, 275–285. Albany, NY: State University of Albany Press.

Zehr, Howard. 1995. *Changing Lenses: A New Focus for Crime and Justice*. Scottdale, PA: Herald Press.

———. 2011. "Restorative Justice or Transformative Justice?" Retrieved on January 12, 2019, from: http://zehr-institute.org/resources/restorative-or-transformative-justice

Zinger, Ivan. 2004. "Actuarial Risk Assessment and Human Rights." *Canadian Journal of Criminology and Criminal Justice* 46(5): 607–621.

Zinn, Howard. 1995. *A People's History of The United States*. New York: Harper Perennial.

Zirin, Dave. 2005. *What's My Name Fool? Sports and Resistance in the United States*. Chicago: Haymarket Books.

———. 2019. "Martina Navratilova Is Expelled from an LGBTQ Advocacy Group over Transphobia Accusations." *The Nation*. Retrieved on March 12, 2019 from: https://www.thenation.com/article/martina-navratilova-athlete-ally-transphobia/

Zizek, S. 2001. "Have Michael Hardt and Antonio Negri Rewritten the Communist Manifesto for the Twenty-First Century?" *Rethinking Marxism* 9: 3–4.

CASES CITED

18 U.S. Code 4248. Civil commitment of a sexually dangerous person. Retrieved on December 11, 2018, from: https://www.law.cornell.edu/uscode/text/18/4248

Baker, et al. v. Vermont 170 Vt. 194 (1999)

Baxstrom v. Herald 383. U.S. 107 (1966)

Bowers v. Hardwick 478 U.S. 186 (1986)

Brown v. Board of Education 347 U.S. (1954)

Burrow-Giles Lithographic Co. v. Sarony 111 U.S. 53 (1884)

Calder et al. v. British Columbia (Attorney General) SCR 313 (1973)

Chaplinsky v. N. Hampshire 315 U.S. 568 (1942)

Delgamuukw v. British Columbia 3 SCR 1010 (1997)

Dred Scott v. Sanford 60 U.S. 393 (1857)

Edgewood Independent School District v. Kirby 777 S.W. 2d 391 (Tex. 1989)

EEOC v. Sears Roebuck and Co. (1988)

Faragher v. City of Baca Raton (1989)

Fisher v. University of Texas at Austin 579 U.S. 136 (2016)

Goodridge v. Department of Public Health 798 N.E. 2d 941 (Mass. 2003)

Gratz v. Bollinger 539 U.S. (2003)

Grutter v. Bollinger 123 S. Ct. 2325 (2003)

Griswold v. Connecticut 381 U.S. 479 (1965)

In Ex parte Crow Dog 109 U.S. 556 (1883)

In Re Opinion of Justices to the Senate 802 N.E. 2d 565 (Mass. 2004)

In the High Court of Uttarakhand at Ninital. 2017. Retrieved on December 18, 2018, from: https://hindi.indiawaterportal.org/sites/default/files/library/WPPIL-126 -14_HC-UTTARAKHAND_ORDER_ON_GANGA_AND_YAMUNA _RIVER_RIGHTS-1.pdf

In the Kansas Indians 72 U.S. 737 (1867)

In the Matter of the Welfare of R.A.V. 464 N.W. 2d 507 (Minnesota, 1991)

Janus v. American Federation of State, County and Municipal Employees, Council 31 585 U.S. (2018)

Johnson v. McIntosh 21 U.S. 543 (1823)

Kansas v. Crane 534 U.S. (2002)

Kansas v. Hendricks 521 U.S. 346 (1997)

Korematsu v. United States 324 U.S. 885 (1945)

Lawrence v. Texas 539 U.S. 558 (2003)

Lofton v. Secretary of Department of Children and Family Services No. 01-16723, 2004 WL 161275 (11th Cir. Jan. 28, 2004)

Mabo v. Queensland (No. 2) 175 CLR 1 (1992)

McCleskey v. Kemp 481 U.S. 279 (1987)

Merrion v. Jicarilla Apache Tribe 455 U.S. 130 (1982)

Mohd Salim v. State of Uttarakhand and Others (2017) http://lobis.nic.in/ddir/uhc /RS/orders/22-03-2017/RS20032017WPPIL1262014.pdf Access on 1/18/19.

Narayan Dutt Bhatt vs Union of India and Others (2018). Retrieved on December 18, 2019, from: http://www.indiaenvironmentportal.org.in/files/horse%20cart%20 Nepal%20India%20Uttarakhand%20High%20Court%20Judgement%20Nara yan_Dutt_Bhatt.pdf

Obergefell v. Hodges 576 U.S. 135 (2015)

Oncale v. Sundowner Offshore Services, Inc. (1998)

People v. Burns 209 Ill. 2d. 551 (2004)

People v. McDougle 303 Ill. App. 3d 509 (1999)

People v. Zammora 152 P. 2d 180 (Calif. 1944)

Plessy v. Ferguson 163 U.S. 537 (1896)

R.A.V. v. City of St. Paul 505 U.S. 377 (1992)

Regents of University of California v. Bakke 438 U.S. 265 (1978)

R.I.S.E., Inc. v. Kay 768 F. Supp. 1144, 1149 (E.D. Va. 1991), aff'd, 977 F. 2d 573 (4th Cir. 1992)

Roe v. Wade 410 U.S. 113 (1973)

San Antonia Independent School District v. Rodriguez 411 U.S. 1 (1973)

Talton v. Mayes 163 U.S. 376 (1896)

Students for Fair Admissions v. Harvard ED-MA-0002 1:14-cv-14176-DJC (Mass. 2019)

Trump v. Hawaii No. 17–965, 585 U.S. 377 (2018)
Twyman v. Twyman 855 S.W. 2d 619 (Texas, 1993)
United States v. Salerno 481 U.S. 739 (1987)
United States v. Winans 198 U.S. 371 (1905)
Valencia v. Davis 307 F. 3d 1036 (2002)
Washington v. Davis 426 U.S. 229 (1976)
Worcester v. Georgia 31 U.S. 515 (1832)
Yniguez v. Arizonans for Official English 69 F. 3d 920 (1995)

Index

Index

About the Authors

LORETTA CAPEHEART is a retired associate professor of justice studies at Northeastern Illinois University. She was the community engagement analyst for a Department of Justice settlement agreement and a college equity officer. She has published on inequities in education and criminal justice. Her activism focuses on immigrant rights, worker rights, and antiracism.

DRAGAN MILOVANOVIC is professor emeritus and Bernard J. Brommel Distinguished Research Professor at Northeastern Illinois University. In addition he has been a college instructor in a jail, a dormitory counselor of incarcerated juveniles, a member of a prison inspection team, and an activist in post-revolutionary Nicaragua (1983–1985). He is author or coauthor of more than twenty-five books.

Available titles in the Critical Issues in Crime and Society series:

Anthony M. Platt, *The Child Savers: The Invention of Delinquency*, 40th anniversary edition with an introduction and critical commentaries compiled by Miroslava Chávez-García

Lois Presser, *Why We Harm*

Joshua M. Price, *Prison and Social Death*

Diana Rickard, *Sex Offenders, Stigma, and Social Control*

Jeffrey Ian Ross, ed., *The Globalization of Supermax Prisons*

Dawn L. Rothe and Christopher W. Mullins, eds., *State Crime, Current Perspectives*

Jodi Schorb, *Reading Prisoners: Literature, Literacy, and the Transformation of American Punishment, 1700–1845*

Susan F. Sharp, *Hidden Victims: The Effects of the Death Penalty on Families of the Accused*

Susan F. Sharp, *Mean Lives, Mean Laws: Oklahoma's Women Prisoners*

Robert H. Tillman and Michael L. Indergaard, *Pump and Dump: The Rancid Rules of the New Economy*

Mariana Valverde, *Law and Order: Images, Meanings, Myths*

Michael Welch, *Crimes of Power and States of Impunity: The U.S. Response to Terror*

Michael Welch, *Scapegoats of September 11th: Hate Crimes and State Crimes in the War on Terror*

Saundra D. Westervelt and Kimberly J. Cook, *Life after Death Row: Exonerees' Search for Community and Identity*

Printed in the United States
By Bookmasters